lonely planet

Mongolia

Bradley Mayhew

L ONELY PLA███████████ NS
Melbourne • Oakland • London ~ ʳaris

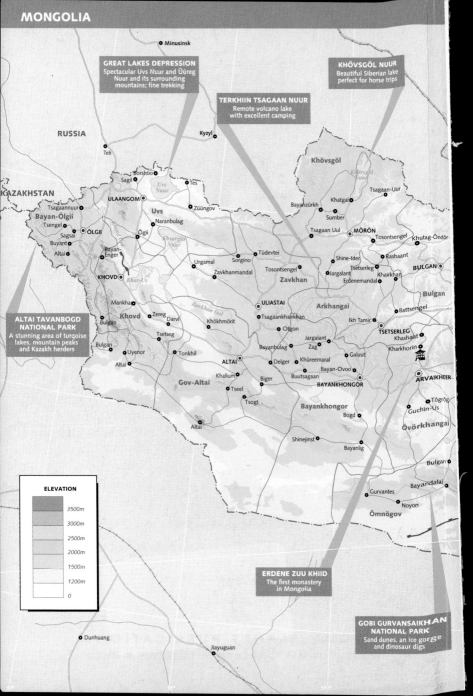

MONGOLIA

RUSSIA

KAZAKHSTAN

GREAT LAKES DEPRESSION
Spectacular Uvs Nuur and Üüreg
Nuur and its surrounding
mountains; fine trekking

TERKHIIN TSAGAAN NUUR
Remote volcano lake
with excellent camping

KHÖVSGÖL NUUR
Beautiful Siberian lake
perfect for horse trips

**ALTAI TAVANBOGD
NATIONAL PARK**
A stunning area of turqoise
lakes, mountain peaks
and Kazakh herders

ERDENE ZUU KHIID
The first monastery
in Mongolia

**GOBI GURVANSAIKHAN
NATIONAL PARK**
Sand dunes, an ice gorge
and dinosaur digs

ELEVATION

- 3500m
- 3000m
- 2500m
- 2000m
- 1500m
- 1200m
- 0

Minusinsk

Kyzyl

Teli

Borshoo
Sagil
Tes
Uvs
Nuur
ULAANGOM
Uvs
Naranbulag
Zűüngov

Khövsgöl
Khövsgöl
Nuur
Tsagaan-Uur
Bayanzürkh
Khatgal
Sumber
Tsagaan Uul
MÖRÖN
Tosontsengel
Khutag-Öndör
BULGAN

Tsagaannuur
Bayan-Ölgii
Tsengel
Sagsai
ÖLGII
Buyant
Altai
Bayan-
Enger
KHOVD
Khar-Us

Ögii
Khyargas
Nuur
Urgamal
Sorgino
Tüdevtei
Shine-Ider
Rashaant
Tsetserleg
Jargalant
Khairkhan
Erdenemandal
Bulgan

Zavkhanmandal
Tosontsengel
Zavkhan

Mankha
Zavkhan Gol
ULIASTAI
Arkhangai
Battsengel

Khovd
Zereg
Darvi
Bulgan
Tsetseg
Khökhmörit
Tsagaankhairkhan
Otgon
Ikh Tamir
TSETSERLEG
Khashaat
Kharkhorin

Bulgan
Uyenor
Tonkhil
ALTAI
Bayanbulag
Jargalant
Zag
Khalium
Biger
Delger
Khüreemaral
Galuut
Bayan-Ovoo
ARVAIKHEER

Altai
Gov-Altai
Tseel
Buutsagaan
BAYANKHONGOR
Tögrög
Guchin-Us
Övörkhangai

Tsogt
Bayankhongor
Bogd

Altai
Shinejinst
Bayanlig
Bulgan
Bayandalai

Gurvantes
Noyon
Ömnögov

Dunhuang
Jiayuguan

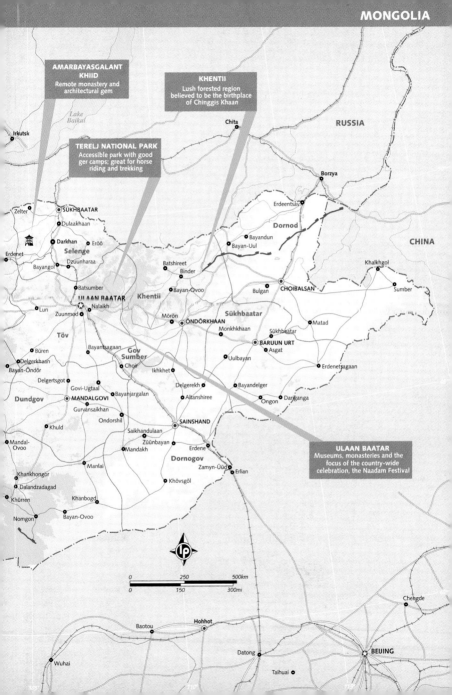

AMARBAYASGALANT KHIID
Remote monastery and architectural gem

KHENTII
Lush forested region believed to be the birthplace of Chinggis Khaan

TERELJ NATIONAL PARK
Accessible park with good ger camps; great for horse riding and trekking

ULAAN BAATAR
Museums, monasteries and the focus of the country-wide celebration, the Naadam Festival

RUSSIA

CHINA

Lake Baikal

Irkutsk

Chita

Borzya

Zelter
SÜKHBAATAR
Dulaakhaan
Darkhan
Eröö
Selenge
Erdenet
Bayangol
Dzüünharaa
Batsumber
ULAAN BAATAR
Nalaikh
Zuunmod
Lun

Erdeentsav
Dornod
Bayandun
Bayan-Uul
Khalkhgol

Batshireet
Binder
Bayan-Ovoo
Bulgan
CHOIBALSAN
Sumber

Khentii
Mörön
ÖNDÖRKHAAN
Sükhbaatar
Monkhkhaan
Sükhbaatar
BARUUN URT
Asgat
Matad

Erdenetsagaan

Töv
Büren
Bayantsagaan
Gov Sumber
Choir
Ikhkhet
Uulbayan

Delgerkhaan
Bayan-Öndör
Delgertsgot
Govi-Ugtaal
MANDALGOVI
Bayanjargalan
Gurvansaikhan
Ondorshil
Saikhandulaan
Züünbayan
Mandakh
SAINSHAND
Erdene
Zamyn-Üüd
Erlian
Khövsgöl

Delgerekh
Altanshiree
Bayandelger
Ongon
Dariganga

Dundgov
Khuld
Mandal-Ovoo
Manlai
Khankhongor
Dalandzadgad
Khürren
Khanbogd
Nomgon
Bayan-Ovoo
Dornogov

Chengde

Baotou
Hohhot
Datong
Erlian

BEIJING

Wuhai
Taihuai

0   250   500km
0   150   300mi

Mongolia
3rd edition – May 2001
First published – May 1993

Published by
Lonely Planet Publications Pty Ltd ABN 36 005 607 983
90 Maribyrnong St, Footscray, Victoria 3011, Australia

Lonely Planet Offices
Australia Locked Bag 1, Footscray, Victoria 3011
USA 150 Linden St, Oakland, CA 94607
UK 10a Spring Place, London NW5 3BH
France 1 rue du Dahomey, 75011 Paris

Photographs
All of the images in this guide are available for licensing from
Lonely Planet Images.
Web site: www.lonelyplanetimages.com

Front cover photograph
A wild camel in the subrange of the Mongol Altai Nuruu mountains in
Uvs, western Mongolia (Scott Darsney)

ISBN 1 86450 064 6

Printed by Craft Print International Ltd, Singapore

Although the authors and Lonely Planet try to make the information as accurate as possible, we accept no responsibility for any loss, injury or inconvenience sustained by anyone using this book.

Contents – Text

Contents – Maps

FACTS ABOUT THE COUNTRY

GETTING AROUND

ULAAN BAATAR

CENTRAL MONGOLIA

NORTHERN MONGOLIA

EASTERN MONGOLIA

WESTERN MONGOLIA

THE GOBI

MAP INDEX

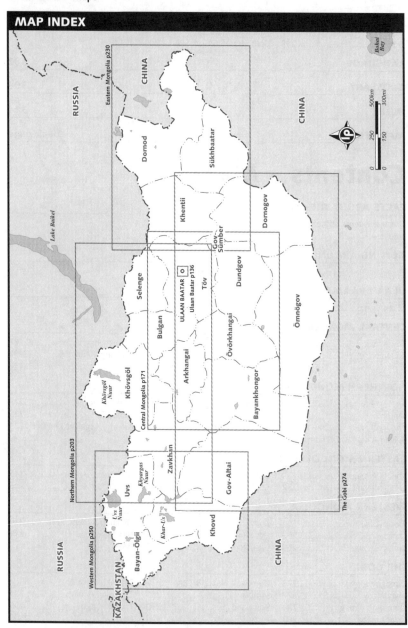

CHINA

RUSSIA

CHINA

CHINA

RUSSIA

KAZAKHSTAN

Lake Baikal

Bohai Bay

Dornod

Sükhbaatar

Khentii

Dornogov

Gov-Sümber

Selenge

ULAAN BAATAR

Töv

Dundgov

Ömnögov

Bulgan

Övörkhangai

Arkhangai

Bayankhongor

Khövsgöl

Khövsgöl Nuur

Zavkhan

Gov-Altai

Uvs

Khyargas Nuur

Uvs Nuur

Khar-Us

Khovd

Bayan-Ölgii

0   250   500km

0   150   300mi

The Author

Bradley Mayhew

Bradley started travelling in South-West China, Tibet and northern Pakistan while studying Chinese at Oxford University. Upon graduation he fled to Central America for six months to forget his Chinese and now regularly travels to China's borderlands in a futile attempt to get it back. He is also the co-author of Lonely Planet's *Pakistan*, *Karakorum Highway*, *Tibet*, *South-West China* and *Central Asia*, as well as the author of the first edition of the *Shanghai* city guide.

Bradley is also the co-author and photographer of the Odyssey Guide to *Uzbekistan*, and has lectured on Central Asia at the Royal Geographical Society. He splits his time between Sevenoaks in south-east England and obscure parts of Montana, USA.

Thanks

Special thanks to Andre Ticheler for yet more fine travels and for helping out everywhere, in particular Bayankhongor and Altai, and for generating good karma in monasteries across Mongolia, and to Michael Kohn, formerly of the *Mongol Messenger*, without whom much of eastern Mongolia would remain a blank.

For their professional help and advice, thanks to Graham Taylor of Karakorum Expeditions, Monkhtuya and Helge at Nomads, as well as Galbaatar Jav and Attai in Bayan-Ölgii. Thanks to Baya and Ben for saving us several times in Khövsgol Nuur. Lea Mclennan helped out with cultural information. Cheers to Andy Smith for the lowdown on nightlife and bars in Ulaan Baatar. Thanks to Rene Henkens for information on Hustai Nuruu and to Ben Dineen for information on Dadal. KC Dedinas offered invaluable help with customs and responsible tourism once again.

Happy travels to the Gobi crew – Omar Gorali, Christian Flanagan and Patrick (sorry John) Williamson. Cheers to Jenya and to my drivers Ganbat and Davakhuu for finding roads throughout Mongolia.

Many Peace Corps volunteers sent in information. Thanks to the following: Carra Davies, Chris Schweiger, David Amidon, Hope Rokosz, Jane Baldwin, Jaspar Ip, Jeff Cook, Karen Jumisko, Lita Anglin, Peg Green, Phillip Riersgard, Shawn Decarlo, Tally Briggs. Thanks in particular to Jennifer Jerret for information on Chandiman-Öndör, Seung-Jin So in Khovd and Josh Evans in Ulaangom. Best wishes to Eric Smith and his wife.

Finally, thanks and love as ever to Kelli, who puts up with my absences, keeps me in good humour and offers the love and support a weary, homeless, muttoned-out traveller so dearly needs. Thank you.

This Book

This Book

The first edition of Mongolia was researched and written by Robert Storey. Paul Greenway researched and thoroughly updated the second edition, with the assistance of Gabriel Lafitte on the introductory chapters. This edition, the third, was researched and updated by Bradley Mayhew. The historical illustrations in this edition are taken from the travel narrative *From the Arctic Ocean to the Yellow Sea* by Julius M. Price, published by Sampson Low, Marston & Company Limited, London (1893).

From the Publisher

This third edition of Mongolia was edited in the Melbourne office by Kate Daly and Nicole Buckler, with proofing assistance from Michael Day. Corinne Waddell co-ordinated the mapping and design, with mapping assistance from Sophie Reed, Kusnandar, and Chris Tsismetzis. Illustrations were co-ordinated by Matt King, and drawn by Kelli Hamblett, Sarah Jolly and Adam McCrow. Suzanne Waddell illustrated the chapter-ends. Glenn Beanland, of Lonely Planet Images, sourced photographs far and wide for the colour wraps (thank you, thank you), and Jenny Joy Jones designed the gorgeous cover. A big thank you to the crew of Babylon, namely Emma Koch and Quentin Frayne for taking charge of the Language chapter, which was then checked by Dr Mingan Choct, Dr Baatar Shirchin and Nyamsuren Jargal. Thanks also to Kusnandar for the climate chart, Shahara Ahmed for fact checking the Health section, Leonie Mugavin for fact checking and input on the Getting There & Away chapter, and to Jocelyn Harewood, Jack Gavran and Chris Love for final layout checks. Thanks also to the author, Bradley Mayhew, for providing a good read.

Acknowledgments

Thanks

Many thanks to the travellers who used the last edition and wrote to us with helpful hints, useful advice and interesting anecdotes:

Val Afualo, Arnold Ahlback, Olivier Arifon, Stuart Attwood, James Baker, Tony Bantts, Iain Barclay, Ofer Becker, Carol Billings, Alex Black, James Blogg, Al Boelter, Juergen Braunbach, Julie Brittain, Shane Bryans, T Buyannemeh, Romano Cassar, Jy Chan, Melissa Cheung, Tina Chong, Juan Christobal, Adyagiin Chuluunbat, Joe Claven, Ken Coghill, Iris Coomans, Roel Cosijn, Alan Craghill, Francis De Beir, Tycho De Feijter, Rita Di Pietro, Steve Dushan, Irja Katrine Einholm, Pierre Elias, Hilary Anne Exon, Hanneke Fialka, Jonathan Forster, John Liermie Goodman, Rogier Gruys, Karan Haruatak, Andrea Hampton, Tom Harrimon, Alex Hartley, Pierre Herbert, Andrew Holten, Simon Huang, Chris Jackson, G D Jarvis, Claudie Kibler, Simon Kidd, Jan King, John Kupiec, Garett Kutcher, Andreas Kyprianou, Richard Leavitt, Teng Lee, Niels Van Linder, Albert Rosieiro-Llorente, Gillain Long, Jen Makin, Eugene Marschall, Todd McWhirter, Ron Miller, Lauri Narinen, Lars Christer Nillson, Byron Nordstrom, Norjmaa Ojunbileg, Pascal Oupinie, Patrik Parkes, Don Parris, Matt Perrement, Brian Phillips, Kurt Piemonte, Massimo Pratelli, Francesco Randisi, Chris Rintoul, Guy Rozanes, Laura Salasco, Jennifer Sandblom, Susan Schwartz, John Simms, Nick Stephen, Nathalie Stirnimann, Chris Taheny, Rao Talasila, Bjorn Tingstadengen, Nancy Tsai, Erwin & Diana van Engelen, Llja Van Roon, Dominique Vanthier, Frank Varsangi, John Verdult, Braum Verweij, Ian Vincent, John Weidman, Danny Williams, Monica Wojtaszewski, Evgeny Wolter, Adam Zenko, David Zetland

Foreword

ABOUT LONELY PLANET GUIDEBOOKS

The story begins with a classic travel adventure: Tony and Maureen Wheeler's 1972 journey across Europe and Asia to Australia. Useful information about the overland trail did not exist at that time, so Tony and Maureen published the first Lonely Planet guidebook to meet a growing need.

From a kitchen table, then from a tiny office in Melbourne (Australia), Lonely Planet has become the largest independent travel publisher in the world, an international company with offices in Melbourne, Oakland (USA), London (UK) and Paris (France).

Today Lonely Planet guidebooks cover the globe. There is an ever-growing list of books and there's information in a variety of forms and media. Some things haven't changed. The main aim is still to help make it possible for adventurous travellers to get out there – to explore and better understand the world.

At Lonely Planet we believe travellers can make a positive contribution to the countries they visit – if they respect their host communities and spend their money wisely. Since 1986 a percentage of the income from each book has been donated to aid projects and human rights campaigns.

Updates Lonely Planet thoroughly updates each guidebook as often as possible. This usually means there are around two years between editions, although for more unusual or more stable destinations the gap can be longer. Check the imprint page (following the colour map at the beginning of the book) for publication dates.

Between editions up-to-date information is available in two free newsletters – the paper *Planet Talk* and email *Comet* (to subscribe, contact any Lonely Planet office) – and on our Web site at www.lonelyplanet.com. The *Upgrades* section of the Web site covers a number of important and volatile destinations and is regularly updated by Lonely Planet authors. *Scoop* covers news and current affairs relevant to travellers. And, lastly, the *Thorn Tree* bulletin board and *Postcards* section of the site carry unverified, but fascinating, reports from travellers.

Correspondence The process of creating new editions begins with the letters, postcards and emails received from travellers. This correspondence often includes suggestions, criticisms and comments about the current editions. Interesting excerpts are immediately passed on via newsletters and the Web site, and everything goes to our authors to be verified when they're researching on the road. We're keen to get more feedback from organisations or individuals who represent communities visited by travellers.

Lonely Planet gathers information for everyone who's curious about the planet – and especially for those who explore it first-hand. Through guidebooks, phrasebooks, activity guides, maps, literature, newsletters, image library, TV series and Web site we act as an information exchange for a worldwide community of travellers.

Research Authors aim to gather sufficient practical information to enable travellers to make informed choices and to make the mechanics of a journey run smoothly. They also research historical and cultural background to help enrich the travel experience and allow travellers to understand and respond appropriately to cultural and environmental issues.

Authors don't stay in every hotel because that would mean spending a couple of months in each medium-sized city and, no, they don't eat at every restaurant because that would mean stretching belts beyond capacity. They do visit hotels and restaurants to check standards and prices, but feedback based on readers' direct experiences can be very helpful.

Many of our authors work undercover, others aren't so secretive. None of them accept freebies in exchange for positive write-ups. And none of our guidebooks contain any advertising.

Production Authors submit their raw manuscripts and maps to offices in Australia, USA, UK or France. Editors and cartographers – all experienced travellers themselves – then begin the process of assembling the pieces. When the book finally hits the shops, some things are already out of date, we start getting feedback from readers and the process begins again ...

WARNING & REQUEST

Things change – prices go up, schedules change, good places go bad and bad places go bankrupt – nothing stays the same. So, if you find things better or worse, recently opened or long since closed, please tell us and help make the next edition even more accurate and useful. We genuinely value all the feedback we receive. A well travelled team reads and acknowledges every letter, postcard and email and ensures that every morsel of information finds its way to the appropriate authors, editors and cartographers for verification.

Everyone who writes to us will find their name in the next edition of the appropriate guidebook. They will also receive the latest issue of *Planet Talk*, our quarterly printed newsletter, or *Comet*, our monthly email newsletter. Subscriptions to both newsletters are free. The very best contributions will be rewarded with a free guidebook.

Excerpts from your correspondence may appear in new editions of Lonely Planet guidebooks, the Lonely Planet Web site, *Planet Talk* or *Comet*, so please let us know if you *don't* want your letter published or your name acknowledged.

Send all correspondence to the Lonely Planet office closest to you:

Australia: Locked Bag 1, Footscray, Victoria 3011
USA: 150 Linden St, Oakland, CA 94607
UK: 10A Spring Place, London NW5 3BH
France: 1 rue du Dahomey, 75011 Paris

Or email us at: talk2us@lonelyplanet.com.au

For news, views and updates see our Web site: www.lonelyplanet.com

HOW TO USE A LONELY PLANET GUIDEBOOK

The best way to use a Lonely Planet guidebook is any way you choose. At Lonely Planet we believe the most memorable travel experiences are often those that are unexpected, and the finest discoveries are those you make yourself. Guidebooks are not intended to be used as if they provide a detailed set of infallible instructions!

Contents All Lonely Planet guidebooks follow roughly the same format. The Facts about the Destination chapters or sections give background information ranging from history to weather. Facts for the Visitor gives practical information on issues like visas and health. Getting There & Away gives a brief starting point for researching travel to and from the destination. Getting Around gives an overview of the transport options when you arrive.

The peculiar demands of each destination determine how subsequent chapters are broken up, but some things remain constant. We always start with background, then proceed to sights, places to stay, places to eat, entertainment, getting there and away, and getting around information – in that order.

Heading Hierarchy Lonely Planet headings are used in a strict hierarchical structure that can be visualised as a set of Russian dolls. Each heading (and its following text) is encompassed by any preceding heading that is higher on the hierarchical ladder.

Entry Points We do not assume guidebooks will be read from beginning to end, but that people will dip into them. The traditional entry points are the list of contents and the index. In addition, however, some books have a complete list of maps and an index map illustrating map coverage.

There may also be a colour map that shows highlights. These highlights are dealt with in greater detail in the Facts for the Visitor chapter, along with planning questions and suggested itineraries. Each chapter covering a geographical region usually begins with a locator map and another list of highlights. Once you find something of interest in a list of highlights, turn to the index.

Maps Maps play a crucial role in Lonely Planet guidebooks and include a huge amount of information. A legend is printed on the back page. We seek to have complete consistency between maps and text, and to have every important place in the text captured on a map. Map key numbers usually start in the top left corner.

Although inclusion in a guidebook usually implies a recommendation we cannot list every good place. Exclusion does not necessarily imply criticism. In fact there are a number of reasons why we might exclude a place – sometimes it is simply inappropriate to encourage an influx of travellers.

Introduction

Mongolia has always stirred up visions of the exotic – Chinggis Khaan (also known by the Persianised spelling of his name, Genghis Khan), camels wandering in the Gobi Desert and wild horses galloping across the steppes. Even today, Mongolia seems like the end of the earth – outside the few major cities you begin to wonder if you haven't stepped into another century, rather than another country.

Mongolia's survival as an independent nation is miraculous. For the first time in centuries the Mongolians, once rulers of the vast Eurasian Steppes, are no longer colonial subjects of the Russian and Chinese empires. Only a century ago, so few Mongolians were left it seemed that their ancient, nomadic civilisation might disappear altogether.

Today Mongolia is free, democratic and energetically rediscovering its many pasts – but it's spectacularly broke. In the postwar years, Soviet Big Brother transformed Mongolia from a nomadic society into an industrialised and urbanised country, with its own astronauts, physicists and nation-wide health and education systems. By the 1980s, even nomadic camel herders in the Gobi Desert knew the state would supply them with a pension in their old age. All that stopped suddenly and dramatically when the Soviet Union fell apart in the early 1990s.

Survival of the nomadic people and the country still depends enormously on domestic animals – camels, yaks, horses, sheep and goats. An intimate knowledge of animals, both wild and domestic, and of

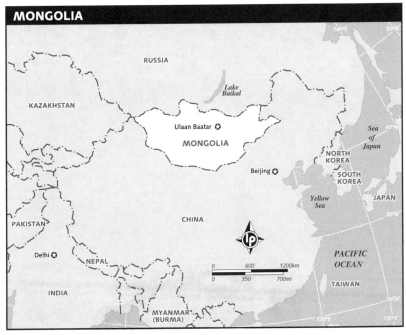

MONGOLIA

11

the environment is a major feature of Mongolian life.

The capital, Ulaan Baatar, is full of surprises and offers excellent places to stay and eat. It's home to the Naadam Festival, Mongolia's famous three-day sporting event. The capital also has fascinating monasteries, museums and art galleries, and it's also the best place to see a performance of traditional music and dance – something not to be missed.

Out in the countryside Mongolia is a boy scout's dream (male tourists outnumber women three to one...) and very much a hands-on destination – a place of camping in the wilds, washing in rivers and repairing broken jeeps. Although travel in the countryside can be hard and facilities poor, a warm welcome awaits the adventurous traveller at every traditional *ger*, the collapsible, white felt tent of the Mongols.

The emptiness of a land with no fences and no privately owned land is awesome and at times it feels like you can see the curvature of the earth. And just when you think you are completely alone, herders on horseback will appear, equipped with bowls of yoghurt and Soviet spyglasses, looking like the lost foot soldiers of Chinggis Khaan.

Mongolia, the 'Land of Blue Sky', is a remarkable country where dense Siberian forests, rolling Central Asian Steppes, vast Gobi Desert, glacier-wrapped mountains and crystal pure lakes meet. It is an invigorating and exhilarating place to visit, and remains one of the last unspoiled travel destinations in Asia.

Facts about Mongolia

HISTORY

The Mongolians, or Mongols as they were previously known, recorded their history for centuries in oral epics, sung by bards, until writing was introduced nearly 800 years ago. Because of their substantial – and mostly unhappy – contacts with neighbouring countries, much has also been written about them. Chinese dynastic histories, stretching back 5000 years, tell of the Mongols and their predecessors, describing them as ravenous barbarians greedy for Chinese produce and likening them to wolves. However, much of the history has now been rewritten from a more objective point of view.

In the Beginning

Little is known about Mongolia's earliest inhabitants, but archaeological digs have uncovered human remains in the Gobi and other regions dating back nearly 500,000 years. It is thought that the earliest inhabitants of the region were among America's first settlers, crossing Siberia and the Bering Strait in search of pasture. Certainly superficial similarities such as facial features, the teepees of the Tsataan and the spirit worship of shamanism point to a link with Native Americans.

Agriculture preceded nomadic herding, and despite Mongolia's short summers, wheat growing has coexisted with nomadic life for thousands of years. It was only after climate change around 1500 BC that the Mongols tamed horses, yaks and camels and took to a nomadic herding lifestyle.

Early Chinese manuscripts refer to 'Turkic-speaking peoples' living in what we now call Mongolia as early as the 4th or 5th century BC. The Chinese – who had numerous military clashes with these nomadic tribes – referred to them as the Xiongnu or 'The State Holding the Bows Beyond the Great Wall'.

The Chinese fought their first major war with the Xiongnu – a forerunner of things to come – in the 3rd century BC. Xiongnu military tactics were fierce and effective – warriors charged on horseback firing arrows and wielding lances and swords. The Xiongnu advanced far into China before being repelled.

In about 200 BC the Xiongnu launched a major invasion and again reached the Yellow River. It wasn't until the middle of the 1st century AD that the Chinese succeeded in expelling them. Although some Xiongnu continued to harass the Chinese, it wasn't long before the Chinese found themselves fighting other nomadic tribes from the north. Among these northern enemies were the Xianbei, Toba, Ruruan and Turkic.

Some remnants of the Xiongnu moved west, and their descendants, the Huns, united under Attila and terrorised central Europe in the last days of the Roman empire. Ruins of Xiongnu cities have been excavated in several Mongolian provinces, with one site close to Ulaan Baatar at Gua Dob.

The Mongols

The name 'Mongol' was first recorded by the Chinese during the Tang dynasty (AD 618–907). At that time, Mongolia was dominated by the Uighurs, a Turkic people who built several cities. The Uighurs followed the teachings of a Persian saint, Mani, who was much influenced by Christianity. An inscription found in the ruins of their city, Kharbalgasun, tells how Manicheism transformed 'this country of barbarous customs, full of the fumes of blood, into a land where people live on vegetables; from a land of killing to a land where good deeds are fostered'. The Uighurs, after taking control of Mongolia, went on to help out the ailing Tang rulers of China, saving them from an internal revolt.

The Uighurs continued to control most of Mongolia until AD 840, when they were defeated by the Kyrgyz, who now live in Xinjiang, a Chinese province. The Uighur's lasting legacy in Mongolia is the downward flowing script – *The Secret History of the*

Mongols epic and all subsequent Mongolian texts were written in this script until Stalin intervened in the 1940s.

The defeat of the Uighurs created a vacuum, which was filled by the Kitans, a Mongol tribe from what is now north-east China. By the 10th century, the Kitans had control of most of Manchuria, eastern Mongolia and much of China north of the Yellow River. The Kitans continued warring with other Mongol tribes, most significantly the Western Xia during the 11th and 12th centuries. The Kitan empire was finally defeated in AD 1122 by the Chinese and their allies, the Jurchen (predecessors of the Manchus).

A Chronology of Mongolian History

200 BC	Xiongnu Mongolian empire reaches the Yellow River
AD 1–100	Xiongnu expelled from China
840	The Kyrghz defeat ruling Uighurs
1122	The ruling Kitan defeated by the Chinese
1162	The child Temujin, later to become Chinggis Khaan, is born
1189	Temujin takes the title of Chinggis Khaan (Universal King)
1206	Chinggis Khaan proclaims himself ruler of the Mongol empire
1211	Chinggis Khaan launches attacks on China
1215	Khanbalik (Beijing) falls to the Mongols
1227	Chinggis Khaan dies
1229	Ögedei Khaan, Chinggis' third and favourite son, proclaimed the second khaan
1235	Karakorum built by Ögedei Khaan
1237	Start of campaigns to Russia and Europe
1241	Death of Ögedei
1246	Güyük, son of Ögedei, becomes khaan; he dies that year
1251	Möngke, from another wing of the family becomes khaan
1259	Death of Möngke; his brother, Kublai becomes khaan
1264	Capital moved from Karakorum (Kharkhorin) to Khanbalik (Beijing)
1275	Marco Polo arrives in China
1276	Hangzhou, capital of Song China falls to the Mongols
1279	Kublai Khaan, Genghis Khaan's grandson, completes the conquest of China
1294	Kublai Khaan dies
1299	Mongol invasion of Syria
1368	Mongols driven out of China
1400–1454	Civil war in Mongolia
1578	Altan Khaan converts to Buddhism and gives the title Dalai Lama to Sonam Gyatso
1586	Erdene Zuu, Mongolia's first monastery, is started
1641	Zanabazar proclaimed leader of Buddhists in Mongolia
1911	Independence from China
1915	Russia, China and Mongolia sign agreement to grant independence to Mongolia
1919	Chinese invade Mongolia again
1921	Chinese defeated; Mongolia's independence proclaimed by Sükhbaatar
1924	Bogd Khaan (Holy King) dies; the Mongolian People's Republic declared by the communists
1939	Russian and Mongolian troops fight Japan in eastern Mongolia
1990	Pro-democracy protests held; communists win multi-party elections
1992	New constitution announced; communists win another election
1996	Democratic Coalition unexpectedly thrashes communists in an election
2000	Communists unexpectedly thrash the Democrats in the election

The Mongols and other nomadic peoples of northern Asia seldom united and had little inclination to do so, preferring instead to be nomadic, widely scattered over great areas and frequently on the move with their animals in search of pasture. They wanted to live as separate clans, united only in the face of a common threat. Chinese penetration of the pastures of the Xiongnu (1300 years before Chinggis Khaan) prompted the nomads to eventually regroup and create a federation of nomadic tribes strong enough to challenge China.

Chinggis Khaan Until the end of the 12th century, the Mongols were little more than a loose confederation of rival clans. A Mongol named Temujin was born in 1162. At the age of 20, he emerged from a power struggle to become the leader of the Borjigin Mongol clan, and later managed to unite most of the Mongol tribes. In 1189 he was given the honorary name of Chinggis Khaan, meaning 'universal (or oceanic) king' and in 1206 he declared the formation of the Mongol empire, with himself as supreme leader.

Chinggis Khaan set up his capital in Karakorum, in present-day Kharkhorin, and

launched his cavalry against China and Russia. In 1209 he headed south to beat the Tangut (Western Xia) empire on the Yellow River and then harassed the Jin dynasty of China, themselves 'barbarian' nomads known as the Jurchen. He then turned westwards to conquer his last rivals, the Karakhitai, an offshoot of the Naiman tribe.

He was about to return to finish off China when news arrived that a group of Mongol merchants in Central Asia had been killed and several ambassadors had been roughed up by the forces of the Khorezmshah. It was a strategic mistake and Chinggis turned his fury towards the west. In 1219 the Mongols took Otrar in modern day Kazakhstan and poured molten silver into the eyes of the Khorezmshah commander Inalchuk. The Mongol forces swept through Gurganj (Uzbekistan) and Nishapur as far as the Indus River and the Caspian Sea, where they finally hunted down the Khorezmshah on a remote island in the Caspian Sea. The great Central Asian cities of Samarkand, Bukhara, Merv, Balkh, Herat and Ghazni were all destroyed. After six years of bloody campaigning Chinggis Khaan finally returned to Mongolia in 1225.

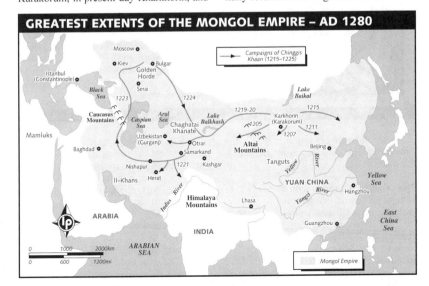

GREATEST EXTENTS OF THE MONGOL EMPIRE – AD 1280

Chinggis Khaan

Chinggis was born in 1162 (some say 1155 or, more likely, 1167) and named Temujin (Ironsmith), after a Tatar chief his father had just killed. His father, Yesügei, was a leader of the Kiyat-Borjigin tribe, whose ancestral lands were centred around the source of the Onon River, and before that in southern Siberia. Legend says that Temujin was born with a clot of blood the size of a knucklebone in his fist, auguring great bloodshed. His ruthlessness became obvious when, as a teenager, he killed his half-brother Bekter in cold blood for stealing one of his fish.

When his father was poisoned by the Tatars in 1171, the nine-year-old outcast was plunged into years of struggle as he strove to keep himself and his family alive. Gradually a band of followers, including his *anda* (sworn brothers), Jamukha and Borchi, grew up around him. Revenge became Chinggis' obsession.

Temujin eventually married his long-betrothed wife, Bortei of the Konggirait tribe. Shortly afterwards Bortei was abducted by the Merkit tribe and the legitimacy of his first son Jochi, born nine months later, was always open to question. Eventually Temujin allied himself with Toghril, the khaan of the Kerait tribe, and his father's sworn brother. In 1189 he was proclaimed Chinggis Khaan, or 'Oceanic King', and the khaan of the Borijan Mongols, when eight princes swore allegiance to him.

Within 15 years he had destroyed the Tatar, Taichuut and Naiman tribes and at a *khurilati* (tribal meeting) in 1206 he was proclaimed leader of 'all the people who live in felt tents'. Within a few years, he managed to create a confederation of Mongol tribes, assemble a loyal army of up to

200,000 men and, with the help of his brilliant generals Subedai and Jebe, created the largest empire that the world had ever seen.

Little is known about the man himself. We know that he was afraid of dogs and a great believer in spirits and shamans. One of most influential people in Mongol empire was Chinggis' shaman Kököchu, also known as Töv Tengri, who eventually tried to install a rival to Chinggis, until the khaan ordered the shaman's back broken during a staged wrestling bout.

Towards the end of his life Chinggis summoned the 71-year-old Chinese Taoist and alchemist Chang Chun to his camp in the Hindu Kush to demand the elixir of immortality. On August 1227, the 66-year-old Chinggis died near Yinchuan, in modern China's Gansu province, from injuries sustained after, of all things, falling off his horse. Much to the chagrin of historians, the site of Chinggis' grave has still not been found, although it is most probably somewhere in the Khentii mountains.

By the time of his death in 1227, the Mongol empire extended from Beijing to the Caspian Sea.

The Great Khaans With the death of Chinggis Khaan the empire was divided between his sons. Chaghatai (Tsagaadai) inherited the lands of Central Asia, Hülegü formed the Il-Khanate in Persia and Tolui took Central Mongolia. Jochi died a few months before Chinggis, and his son Batu went on to establish the Golden Horde in

central Eurasia, with its capital at Serai. Tolui administered the empire for an interim two years, before he finally died of alcoholism.

Power passed into the hands of Chinggis' favourite son, Ögedei, in 1229, who continued the military conquest. His generals swept through the Volga region and the Russian cities of Rostov, Yaroslavyl and Novgorod, sacking Kiev in 1240. The Mongols pushed into Poland and Lithuania, burned Krakow and swung south into Hungary and Bohemia, poised to inflict more

The Tartar Tribe

The Tatars were one of the Mongol tribes in the 12th century, who Chinggis Khaan quashed in his efforts to unite the country. The name is derived from Dada or Tata, although rather ironically the West adopted the name Tatar, as it closely resembled the Greek word *tataros*, transforming the Mongols into a tribe 'from Hell'. Today the Tatars remain a Turkic ethnic group in the Russian Volga and Crimea.

carnage as the rest of Europe prayed in their cathedrals for a miracle.

Then in 1241 the Mongols suddenly stopped, turned around and headed back to Mongolia. Both Chaghatai and Ögedei Khaan had died and Mongol custom dictated that all noble descendants of Chinggis had to return to Mongolia to democratically elect a new leader. Europe was saved.

Ögedei's Christian widow Toregene Khatan ruled for five years. She set her unpopular son Güyük on the throne in 1246 but he was poisoned within the year. In 1251 another wing of the family represented by Möngke (or Monkh) Khaan was elected king and the remarkable Toregene was put to death.

The Mongol conquest continued as Hülegü, son of Chinggis, swept through Iran and destroyed Baghdad, killing the caliph in traditional Mongol fashion by wrapping him in a carpet and trampling him to death with horses, thus avoiding the spillage of any royal blood.

In 1259 the Mongols were poised to take Egypt when they suddenly stopped, turned around and headed back to Mongolia, yet again – Möngke Khaan had died (of dysentery). His brother Kublai was elected khaan mid-campaign in southern China.

Kublai Khaan After overcoming an initial challenge from his brother Arik-Böke, Chinggis' grandson, Kublai Khaan (circa 1216–94), completed the subjugation of China, effectively ending the Song dynasty (960–1279). He became the emperor of China's Yuan dynasty (1271–1368). Arik-

Böke had led a faction of Mongols who wanted to preserve the Mongol way of life, simply plundering neighbouring countries without intermingling with other races but Kublai wanted to establish a more lasting system of government. Kublai established his winter capital in Khanbalik (City of the Khan), known then in Chinese as Dadu (Great Capital) – today's Beijing. It was here in 1274 that he met, and subsequently hired, a young Marco Polo. Kublai's summer camp was further north at Shangdu, later immortalised as Xanadu by the opium-inspired poet Samuel Coleridge.

Kublai soon realised that the Mongol empire had reached the limits of its expansion. In 1260 the Mongols lost a major battle to the Egyptian Mamluks. An attack on Java briefly succeeded, but the Mongol troops were finally expelled in 1293. Two attempts to invade Japan (in 1274 and 1281) ended in failure; the second was thwarted when a typhoon claimed the lives of 140,000 Mongol troops, the largest fleet of its time ever assembled. The Japanese claimed this was divine intervention, or *kamikaze* – the Mongols put it down to bad weather, and retreated.

Instead of looking for more wars to fight, Kublai concentrated his efforts on keeping the vast empire together. This was the height of the Mongols' glory: the empire stretched from Korea to Hungary and as far south as Vietnam, making it the largest empire the world has ever known. The Mongols improved the road system linking China with Russia and promoted trade throughout the empire and with Europe. Tens of thousands of horses were on stand by to enable pony express riders to cross the empire with important messages at great speed.

In China, the Mongol Yuan dynasty instituted a famine relief scheme and expanded the canal system, which brought food from the countryside to the cities. It was the first empire to enforce paper money as the sole form of currency. Over 60 million Chinese were ruled by a few hundred thousand Mongols. This was the China that Marco Polo and other travellers visited and described in their journals to an amazed Europe.

THE GREAT KHAANS

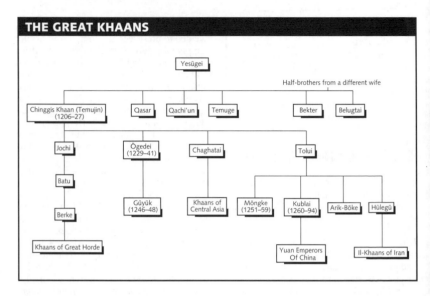

The grandeur of the Mongol empire in China lasted over a century. After Kublai Khaan died in 1294, the Mongols became increasingly dependent on and influenced by the people they ruled. They were deeply resented as an elite, privileged class exempt from taxation, and the empire became ridden with factions vying for power. By the mid 14th century, Mongol rule began to disintegrate, until they were expelled from Beijing by the first emperor of the Ming dynasty (1368–1644), Zhu Yuanzhang.

The Mongol Legacy

The Mongols left a mixed legacy. Though demonised by foreign historians, Chinggis Khaan nonetheless managed to introduce a written script for the Mongolian language, and instituted a tradition of religious tolerance and initiated the first major direct contact between East and West, in what later became known as the Pax Mongolica. He is attributed with the introduction of the Yasaq, or Mongolian legal code, which influenced Mongol government for centuries. Mongolian rule was an artistic high point for many of the khaans' domains, and Chinggis brought back craftsmen into Mongolia to create Mongolian artistic renaissance.

There was, however, a darker legacy. The Mongols introduced the Black Death to Europe in 1347, and its war machine destroyed great cultures of the Middle East and Central Asia, many of which were never to recover.

The Decline

The collapse of the Yuan dynasty caused over 60,000 Mongols to return to Mongolia. Their unity dissolved and they resumed their traditional lifestyle of frequent clan warfare. A major civil war was fought from 1400 to 1454 between two main groups, the Khalkh in the east and the Oyrat (Oirad) in the west. A long period of stagnation and decline followed.

A revival of sorts occurred under Altan Khaan (1507–83), who united the Khalkh, defeated the Oirad and brought most of Mongolia under his control. The war with the Ming dynasty of China was renewed in an attempt to recapture the lost empire of the Yuan dynasty, but this proved fruitless. Altan signed a peace treaty with China in 1571 and turned his troops south-west against Tibet.

East meets West

Giovanni de Piano Carpine (1180–1252)

Carpine was sent to the Mongols in 1245 by Pope Innocent IV. He travelled via the ruins of Kiev to the Mongol's summer camp at Sira Ordu and then covered 3000 miles in 106 days to Karakorum, following the Mongol post system. He had an audience with Güyük Khaan and became friends with Cosmos, a Russian goldsmith being held by the Mongols. He was told by the khaan that if Europe wanted peace then the pope, all the kings and emperors of Europe and 'anyone else important' would have to come and see him to earn his good will. He took the less than cheering message back to Europe in mid-winter, arriving two years after he first set out.

William of Rubruck (1215–1295)

The missionary William of Rubruck (also known as Willem van Ruysbroeck), from French Flanders, travelled to Karakorum in 1253 to search for a group of German Catholics who had been abducted by the Mongols. Rubruck travelled first to Sarai and visited the court of Batu at Saratov, before crossing the Altai to reach the court of Möngke Khaan at Karakorum.

Rubruck debated religion with Nestorians and shamans at the court and made friends with a resident Englishman named Basil and a French jeweller, Guillaume Bouchier. In the course of his religious debates he gave the West its first description of Tibetan Buddhism. His first interview with the khaan apparently ended inauspiciously when the great khaan and his interpreter became too drunk to speak.

On his return to Europe he became friends with Roger Bacon, a fellow Franciscan, and it is thought that he passed on the secret of gunpowder. He was still alive when Marco Polo arrived home.

At the height of his power, Altan was seduced by Buddhism – strangely enough, the religion of Tibet (with whom they were at war). Altan became a devout believer and Buddhism – the religion of the Mongol nobility for 200 years – became the state religion. The monks tried desperately to reunite the quarrelling clans, but Mongolia's tendency to fragment persisted and the nation sunk into medieval stagnation.

After the death of Altan Khaan, Mongolia reverted to a collection of tiny tribal domains. Meanwhile, the Manchus (whose predecessors were the Jurchen), ancient enemies of the Mongols, established the Qing dynasty (1644–1911). Despite their military prowess, the Manchus at first made no aggressive moves against Mongolia; they did not need to – the Mongols were doing a great job of defeating themselves. The Zungar Mongols of the west (who ruled Bukhara, Kashgar and Turfan) were locked into a fierce military struggle with the Khalkh Mongols of the east.

The Zungar seemed to be gaining the upper hand, and it was at this time that the Khalkh made what was probably a fatal mistake – they invited the Manchu Qing emperor, Kangxi, to send troops to fight their Zungar enemy. Like most Mongols, the Zungar warriors were highly skilled horseback archers. However, the Manchus possessed new technology in the form of muskets and cannons, which the Mongols couldn't combat. In 1691 Khalkh Mongolia submitted to Manchu rule and by 1732 the Zungar had been roundly defeated.

The Manchus encouraged Buddhism in Mongolia and built temples throughout the country. Manchu rule over China was competent and reasonably benign up until around 1800; thereafter, the Qing emperors became increasingly corrupt and despotic. In both China and Mongolia, peasants suffered ruthless exploitation, ruinous taxes and brutal punishment (including torture) for the slightest offence or resistance to authority. The Manchus ruled Mongolia from Urga (Ulaan Baatar), Uliastai and Khovd. The brutality of the Manchu era has never been forgiven or forgotten, and to this day Mongolians despise the Chinese. Mongolia was ripe for rebellion, and so was China.

The Mongol War Machine

Thanks to the Mongols, the 13th century was to be exceeded in cruelty and bloodshed only by the 20th century. Chroniclers reported horrific massacres of 1.6 million people at Herat, 1.7 million at Nishapur and 800,000 at Baghdad. In the words of Ata-Malik Juvaini, a contemporary historian who was in the service of the Mongol governors of Northern Persia 'in retribution for every hair on their heads it seemed that a hundred thousand heads rolled in the dust'. (*Genghis Khan: The History of the World Conqueror*, written in 1260). Up to 30% of the population of Central Asia was massacred in an unprecedented catastrophe that decimated irrigation and agriculture for generations.

When word reached Europe of the Mongol atrocities they were described as the 'Scourge of God', the 'Devil's Horsemen' and the 'Storm from the East', let loose from 'beyond the borders of civilisation' to herald the end of the world. They were in fact merely the finest fighting force the world had ever seen.

Mongol military technique was honed in epic hunting expeditions. Forces were organised decimally into *tümen* (10,000 soldiers), *zuun* (100 soldiers) and *arvan* (10 soldiers). Members of hostile tribes were separated and spread throughout different tümen. Chinggis Khaan was protected by a *keshig*, or imperial guard of 10,000 soldiers. There simply was no such thing as a civilian population in Mongolia.

One of the earliest terrorist groups, the Mongols were the masters of psychological warfare. Cities that surrendered to the Mongols without a fight were spared, while those that resisted were utterly obliterated, so as to induce the surrender of the next city. Yet rarely was torture used; killing was business-like, with soldiers given strict quotas on the number of civilians to kill. Chinggis perfected the techniques of feigned flight, mobility, hostage taking, surprise attack and human shields, at times lighting bonfires and tying man-sized dolls onto horses to give the impression of more troops. He also developed a large intelligence network of spies and traders who sent information along an efficient communications system. Contrary to popular misconceptions, diplomacy was chosen over warfare whenever possible.

At the root of their dominance was the Mongol's horsemanship. Each Mongol soldier took five horses on campaign and could ride for weeks, allegedly surviving only on mare's milk and horse's blood. Technology was also on their side. They had the best stirrups in the world. Their compound bows of bone, sinew and wood had a range of 250m, twice as long as the European longbow, and they could shoot riding forward or backwards. Archers could choose from an array of different arrows, including some dipped in naptha and set on fire. They completed their arsenal with mangonels (giant catapults used to hurl stones), and explosives given to them by the Chinese. Ironically, it was firearm technology that later kept the nomads at a continual disadvantage.

Ultimately it was easier for the Mongols to conquer than hold on to power. For as a Chinese general once told Kublai Khan, the empire that is conquered on horseback can not be governed on horseback.

Revolutions

In 1911 China's last dynasty, the Qing, crumbled. The Mongol princes quickly saw their opportunity: Mongolian independence from China was declared on 1 December 1911, with a theocratic government under the leadership of the eighth Jebtzun Damba (Living Buddha), who was declared the Bogd Khaan (Holy King). The Chinese government did not recognise Mongolian independence, but it was fully preoccupied with its own domestic chaos. On 25 May 1915, the Treaty of Kyakhta – which granted Mongolia limited autonomy – was signed by Mongolia, China and Russia.

The Russian Revolution of October 1917 came as a great shock to Mongolia's aristocracy. Taking advantage of Russia's weakness, a Chinese warlord sent his troops into Mongolia in 1919 and occupied the capital. In February 1921, retreating White Russian (anticommunist) troops entered Mongolia and expelled the Chinese. At first the Bogd Khaan seemed to welcome the

Russians as saviours of his regime, but it soon became apparent that the Russians were just a ruthless army of occupation. The brutality of both the Chinese and Russian forces inflamed the Mongolians' desire for independence.

As the Russian Bolsheviks were steadily advancing against the White Russian forces in Siberia, Mongolian nationalists believed their best hope for military assistance was to ask the Bolsheviks for help. In July 1921, Mongolian and Bolshevik fighters recaptured Ulaan Baatar and, on 11 July of that year, the People's Government of Mongolia was declared. The Bogd Khaan was retained as a ceremonial figurehead with no real power. The newly formed Mongolian People's Party (the first political party in the country's history, and the only one for the next 69 years) took over government. Mongolia's first leader was Damdin Sükhbaatar, the former commander of Mongolia's troops.

The military campaign continued for a few more months. Thousands of Bolshevik forces poured into Mongolia from Russia. The White Russian forces were finally defeated in January 1922. Almost from the first moment of victory, there was rivalry between the Bogd Khaan and the communists – the latter clearly intended to eliminate the monarchy entirely and seemed to be moving in on the newly 'independent' Mongolia.

Soviet Control

On 26 November 1924, the Mongolian People's Republic (MPR) was declared and Mongolia became the world's second communist country. The Mongolian People's Party was renamed the Mongolian People's Revolutionary Party (MPRP). Soviet and Mongolian communists worked secretly to eliminate all noncommunist contenders for power.

After Lenin's death in Russia in 1924, Mongolian communism remained independent of Moscow until Lenin's successor, Stalin, gained absolute power in the late 1920s. Then the purges began in Mongolia. Once former MPRP leaders Lana Bodoo, Danzan Khorloo and Sükhbaatar were dead

(one or two in suspicious circumstances), and Party Chairman Tseren-Ochiryn Dambadorj was exiled to Moscow in 1928, Stalin's stooge, Khorloogiyn Choibalsan, was selected as leader of the standing legislature, the Little Khural.

Following Stalin's lead, Choibalsan ordered the seizure of land and herds which were then redistributed to peasants. In 1932 more than 700 people – mostly monks – were imprisoned or murdered, their property seized and collectivised. Farmers were forced to join cooperatives and private business was banned, Chinese and other foreign traders were expelled and all transport was nationalised. The destruction of private enterprise without sufficient time to build up a working state sector had the same result in Mongolia as it did in the Soviet Union – famine.

While the government moderated its economic policy during the 1930s, its campaign against religion was ruthless. In 1937 Choibalsan launched a reign of terror against the monasteries in which thousands of monks were arrested and executed (see The Purge entry under Religion later in this chapter). The anti-religion campaign coincided with a bloody purge to eliminate 'rightist elements'. It is believed that by 1939 some 27,000 people had been executed (3% of Mongolia's population at that time), of whom 17,000 were monks.

The Wars

By 1931 the Japanese had seized north-east China (Manchuria), renamed it Manchukuo and returned the last Manchu (Qing) emperor to the throne to serve as a Japanese puppet. Japan planned a similar takeover of Mongolia, creating a state called Mengukuo – the kingdom of the Mongols. Stalin correctly feared Japanese military moves against both the USSR and Mongolia, so the Soviet army started moving back into Mongolia during the early 1930s and built up the Mongolian military as well; eventually, nearly 10% of Mongolia's population was in the military.

In 1939 the Japanese decided to invade eastern Mongolia in a pre-WWII showdown,

The Mad Baron

One of Mongolian history's most unusual characters was Baron Roman Nikolaus Fyodirovich von Ungern-Sternberg, a renegade White Russian officer who believed he was the reincarnation of Chinggis Khaan, destined to restore the Mongol warlord's previous empire. Contemporaries paint a fine picture of Baron von Ungern-Sternberg, later known as the Mad Baron, describing him as haunted-looking, with a psychotic stare, that fixed on people 'like those of an animal in a cave'. He spoke with a high-pitched voice and his bulging forehead bore a huge sword scar, which pulsed with red veins whenever he grew agitated. As a finishing touch, one of his eyes was slightly higher than the other.

The Bolshevik victory in Russia forced the Baron east and he slowly accumulated a desperate army of renegade mercenaries. Amongst his closest advisers was a thug known as the Teapot, who was trained to strangle whoever the Baron was talking to whenever a 'teapot' was called for. Another close adviser was the obviously insane Colonel Sepailov, who witnesses recall was 'always nervously jerking and wriggling his body and talking ceaselessly, making most unattractive sounds in his throat and spluttering with saliva all over his lips'.

The Baron enforced discipline with a reign of terror, roasting deserters alive, baking defiant prisoners in ovens and throwing his rivals in locomotive boilers. He slew many of his own troops in drunken stupors. Believing himself to also be the reincarnated god of war and a descendent of Atilla the Hun, he was a deep believer in soothsayers and also a fervent Buddhist, convinced that he was doing his victims a favour by packing them off to the next life sooner rather than later.

With an army of 6000 troops (and the tacit backing of the Japanese) the Baron crossed the Mongolian border in the summer of 1920 with the aim of establishing a Pan-Mongol empire. By October his forces attacked Urga (as Ulaan Baatar was then called) but were driven back four times, once regrouping on nearby Bogd Uul, before finally taking the city. He freed the Bogd Khaan who had been imprisoned by the Chinese, to general joy but this turned to horror as the next three days saw an orgy of looting, burning and killing. Witnesses recall how his followers were allowed to thrust one hand in the Mongolian treasury and keep whatever they pulled out. In May 1921 the Baron declared himself the Emperor of Russia.

After only a few months the Bolsheviks retook Urga and the Baron fled the city. Out in the desert, his own followers tried to kill him, shooting him in his tent, but he managed to escape. One can only imagine their horror when, only minutes after riding off, he slowly reappeared on horseback out of the darkness. A group of Mongolian herders later found him bleeding in the desert. He was eventually taken by the Bolsheviks, deported to Novosibirsk and shot on September 15, 1921, presumed mad. He was defiant to the end.

but were resoundingly defeated by a joint Mongolian-Soviet force. Largely as a result of this battle, Japan signed a neutrality pact with the USSR in 1941 and the Japanese turned their war machine south instead.

The Soviet Union and Mongolia declared war on Japan in 1945 during the very last days of WWII. After the war, Stalin extracted grudging recognition of the independence of Outer Mongolia from Chinese National Party leader Chiang Kaishek, when the two signed an anti-Japanese Sino-Soviet alliance.

Progress & Conflict

Choibalsan died in January 1952 and was replaced by Yumjaagiyn Tsedenbal – no liberal, but not a mass murderer. Stalin died the following year. From that time until the mid-1960s, Mongolia enjoyed, in relative terms, a period of peace. Relations between the Soviet and Chinese governments warmed during the 1950s and this had beneficial effects on Mongolia. The Soviets felt confident enough about Chinese intentions to withdraw all Soviet troops from Mongolia in 1956. Taiwan and the USA continued to oppose Mongolia's membership in the

United Nations, but this was finally achieved in 1961.

With the Sino-Soviet split in the early 1960s, the Mongolians chose the lesser of evils and sided with the Soviet Union. Chinese aid to Mongolia ceased; the Mongolian government expelled thousands of ethnic Chinese and all trade with China came to a halt. More than 100,000 Soviet troops poured in and Mongolia was once again a potential battlefield.

Throughout the 1970s, Soviet influence gathered strength. Young Mongolians were sent to the USSR for technical training and brought back Russian habits (including the overconsumption of vodka). Many aspects of Russian culture – food, music, opera, dance – were adopted by the Mongolians and Russian became the country's second language. Mongolia swarmed with Polish archaeologists, Czech tractor-makers, Hungarian technicians and East German propaganda film makers.

Reform

As the Soviet regime stagnated and faltered, Party Secretary-General Tsedenbal was forcibly retired in 1984 and moved to Moscow. He was replaced by Jambyn Batmöngke, a reformer heartened by the Soviet reforms under Mikhail Gorbachev. In 1986 Gorbachev announced that the withdrawal of Soviet troops from Mongolia was being considered.

Batmöngke instigated a cautious attempt at perestroika (economic, political and social restructuring) and glasnost (political transparency) in 1986. Decentralisation was the key word in the economic reform package – enterprises were given more freedom to operate without central officials making all the decisions. Government departments were reorganised and high-ranking officials were reshuffled.

By the late 1980s relations with China gradually thawed. Air services between Beijing and Ulaan Baatar – suspended since the 1960s – were resumed in 1986. In 1989 full diplomatic relations with China were established, though many Mongolians still fear Chinese designs on their country.

The unravelling of the Soviet Union resulted in decolonisation by default. Few in Mongolia were ready for the speed of the collapse, or the possibilities of seizing the moment. In March 1990, in sub-zero temperatures, large pro-democracy protests erupted in the square in front of the parliament building in Ulaan Baatar and hunger strikes were held. It was only a few months after the Tiananmen Square massacre in Beijing, and many in the MPRP wanted to deal with the protests with tanks and troops. Batmöngke, however, would not sign the order, and a young man by the name of Zorig exposed the plan to the Mongolian press.

Things then happened quickly: Batmöngke lost power; new political parties with a bewildering variety of names sprang up; and hunger strikes and protests continued. In March the Politburo resigned, and in May the constitution was amended to permit multiparty elections in July 1990.

The Path to Democracy

Ironically, the communists won the elections, taking 85% of the seats in the Great Khural and 62% of the seats in the Little Khural (see Government & Politics). Although Ulaan Baatar residents gave much support to the opposition parties, rural areas voted overwhelmingly for the communists. The MPRP, now calling itself 'ex-communist', announced it would share power with several young democrats – some were even given ministries. Freedom of speech, religion and assembly were all granted. The era of totalitarianism had ended.

The Mongolian constitution was revised again and elections were held in June 1992. The MPRP again came out on top, winning 57% of the popular vote and an astounding 71 parliamentary seats out of 76. The 'ex-communists' ran on a platform promising ill-defined reforms and blaming the country's economic problems on the democratic opposition. The government was soon under pressure from big lenders, including Japan and the World Bank, to privatise ownership of the big state enterprises.

Four years later, on 30 June 1996, the Mongolian Democratic Coalition trounced the ruling MPRP, unexpectedly ending 75 years of unbroken communist rule. M Enkhsaikhan, the 41-year-old leader of the Coalition, was named prime minister.

The inexperienced Democrats did not have an easy time of government. Between 1996 and 2000 the country had had five prime ministers, three of whom resigned.

Corruption reared its ugly head several times. The plug was pulled on the Mon-Macau Casino, one month before its planned opening in the basement of the Chinggis Hotel, and three democratic members of parliament were jailed in 1999 for accepting bribes in return for the casino tender.

A Democratic State

By the turn of the millennium, Mongolia had achieved one of the world's most free economies and had made the peaceful transition from a Soviet satellite to a flourishing democracy – the only former communist state in Asia to do so.

Yet while living standards have risen in Ulaan Baatar, the majority of Mongolians have experienced a sharp decline in living standards, education and health care since independence. In a recent poll, 50% of Mongolians said that their life was much the same since independence, only 10% said it was better and over a third said it was significantly worse.

In the July 2000 general election the democrats paid the price for political squabbling and economic hardships. The ex-communist MPRP won 72 out of 76 seats and their leader N Enkhbayar was sworn in as prime minister. But there is no going back to communism for Mongolia. In the words of one MPRP minister, 'you can't mend a broken egg.'

GEOGRAPHY

Mongolia is a huge, landlocked country: 1,566,500 sq km in area – about three times the size of France; over twice the size of Texas; and almost as large as the Australian state, Queensland. Apart from the period of Mongol conquest under Chinggis Khaan and Kublai Khaan, Mongolia was until the 20th century about twice its present size. A

Mongolia at a Glance

Official name *Mongghol Ulus* – the Republic of Mongolia
Size 17th largest country in the world
Human development indicator Mongolia ranks 118th in world (China ranks 98th, Russia 71st)

Economy
Unemployment 44.5%
GNP US$400 per capita
Inflation 9.5%
Economic (GDP) Growth 3.5%
Average monthly wage Equivalent of US$50

Population
Population growth 1.4%
Life expectancy Males 64 years; females 69 years
Population density (national) 1.52 people/sq km
Population density (Ulaan Baatar) 164,500 people/sq km
Nomadic population 45.7% (2000), 54.1% (1979)

large chunk of Siberia was once part of Mongolia, but it is now securely controlled by Russia, and Inner Mongolia is now firmly part of China.

The southern third of Mongolia is dominated by the Gobi Desert, which stretches into China. Only the southern sliver of the Gobi is true desert. The rest is desert steppe and has sufficient grass to support scattered herds of sheep, goats and camels. There are also areas of desert steppe in low-lying parts of western Mongolia.

Much of the rest of Mongolia is covered by grasslands. Stretching over about 20% of the country, these steppes are home to vast numbers of gazelles, bird life and livestock. The central, northern and western provinces, amounting to about 25% of Mongolia, is classed as mountain forest steppe. It is home to gazelles and antelopes, and has a relatively high number of people and livestock.

Mongolia is also one of the highest countries in the world, with an average elevation of 1580m. In the far west are Mongolia's highest mountains, the Mongol Altai Nuruu, which are permanently snowcapped. The highest peak, Tavanbogd Uul (4374m), has a magnificent glacier towering over Mongolia, Russia and China. Between the peaks are stark but beautiful deserts where rain almost never falls.

The far northern areas of Khövsgöl and Khentii provinces are essentially the southern reaches of Siberia and are covered by larch and pine forests known by the Russian word *taiga*.

Near the centre of Mongolia is the Khangai Nuruu range, with its highest peak, Otgon Tenger Uul, reaching 3905m. On the north slope of these mountains is the source of the Selenge Gol, Mongolia's largest river, which flows northward into Lake Baikal in Siberia. While the river Selenge Gol is the largest in terms of water volume, the longest river is the Kherlen Gol in eastern Mongolia.

Just to the north-east of Ulaan Baatar is the Khentii Nuruu, the highest mountain range in eastern Mongolia and by far the most accessible to hikers. It's a heavily forested region with raging rivers and impressive peaks, the highest being Asralt Khairkhan Uul (2800m). The range provides a major watershed between the Arctic and Pacific oceans.

Mongolia has numerous saltwater and freshwater lakes which are great for camping, watching bird life, hiking, swimming and fishing. The most popular is the magnificent Khövsgöl Nuur, the second-oldest lake in the world, which contains 65% of Mongolia's (and 2% of the world's) fresh water. The largest is the low-lying, saltwater lake Uvs Nuur.

Other geological and geographical features include underwater and above-ground caves, some with ancient rock paintings; dormant volcanoes; hot and cold mineral springs; the Great Lakes Depression in western Mongolia and the Darkhadyn Khotgor depression west of Khövsgöl Nuur; and the Orkhon Khürkhree waterfall.

Mongolia is divided into 18 *aimag*, or provinces – plus four independent munici-

palities, which are also sometimes called aimag. These are Ulaan Baatar, Darkhan-Uul (which contains Darkhan city), Orkhon (with Erdenet city) and Gov-Sumber (with the Free Trade Zone town of Choir). The aimags are further divided into a total of 310 *sum*, or districts.

GEOLOGY

Mongolia was once covered by a shallow sea. Modern Mongolia is the result of a collision between the Cathaysian continental block from the south and the Siberian block to the north. The country is crisscrossed by tectonic fault lines, many of which can actually be seen on the surface, as well as many dormant volcanoes, such as Uran Uul (Bulgan aimag), and Khorgo Uul, whose lava flow created the beautiful lake Terkhiin Tsaggan Nuur in Arkhangai aimag.

CLIMATE

Mongolia has an extreme continental climate, meaning that it is so far inland that no sea moderates its climate. Only in summer does cloud cover shield the sky. Humidity is zilch and sunshine is intense. With over 260 sunny days a year, Mongolia is justifiably known as the 'Land of Blue Sky'.

Long subarctic winters are the norm, however, and you can see snow in the Gobi Desert as late as April, and some lakes remain frozen until June. There is a short rainy season from mid-July to September, but the showers tend to be brief and gentle. Evenings are cool even in summer due to the relatively high altitude. Mongolia is a windy place, especially in spring.

When the wind blows from the north, temperatures drop sharply, but when the

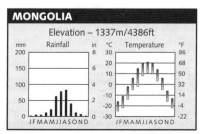

The Great Zud

The Mongolian winter of 1999–2000 was one of the coldest and longest in living memory. It was classed as a *zud*, a Mongolian word which can mean any condition that stops livestock getting to grass; in this case heavy snowfall and an impenetrable ice cover. Unusually early snowfalls in September 1999 compounded an earlier summer drought and rodent infestation, which left animals emaciated and pastures degraded before winter even hit. By summer 2000 over 2.4 million head of livestock had perished, with another three million expected to die in the ensuing months.

In the worst hit areas of Dundgov, Bayankhongor, Arkhangai and Övörkhangai herders lost between a quarter and half of their livestock – their only form of income, food, fuel, security – almost everything in fact. The disaster was not as severe as the great zud of 1944, when 7.5 million livestock were lost, but at that time herders had the safety net of the communist collective. During the recent freeze only a handful of international agencies came to the aid of the herders.

Some analysts have suggested that the disaster was exacerbated by the inexperience of numerous new herders, who chose not to embark on the traditional month-long trek (*otor*), which takes herders to other pastures in autumn. Tragically it was the poorest herders who were the most affected, just when they least needed it.

wind drops, the weather warms up just as rapidly. One minute you're walking around in a T-shirt and sandals, the next you need an overcoat and boots, then it's back to T-shirts. Temperature differences have been known to range over 37.5°C in one day. This is especially the case during the brief autumn and spring.

In the Gobi, summer temperatures hit 40°C but winter winds often send the mercury plummeting to -30°C or lower. Even in summer, the evenings can be astoundingly cold. The steppes are always chilly – the July average is only 10°C and even spring and autumn are frosty.

Ulaan Baatar is the coldest capital city in the world. Temperatures generally start to drop below 0°C in October, sink to -30°C in January and February and remain below freezing until April. You can expect some horrific dust storms during the short spring (May to June). The summer (July to September) is pleasant without being too hot. It can still suddenly turn cold and, unfortunately, most of the city's rain falls in this period. Summer daylight lasts until 10 pm.

ECOLOGY & ENVIRONMENT

Mongolia's natural environment remains in good shape compared with that of many Western countries. The country's small population and nomadic subsistence economy

have been its environmental salvation. The great open pastures of its northern half remain ideal for grazing by retaining just enough forest, usually on the upper northern slopes, to shelter the abundant wildlife.

However, it does have its share of problems. Communist production quotas put pressure on grasslands to yield more than was sustainable. The recent rise in the number of herders, from 134,000 in 1990 to 414,000 in 2000, and livestock numbers is seriously degrading many pastures. The number of wells has halved in the last decade due to neglect and the health of herds has started to decline.

Forest fires are common during the windy spring season. In early 1996 an unusually dry winter fuelled over 400 fires in fourteen of Mongolia's eighteen aimags. An estimated one-quarter (about 80,000 sq km) of the country's forests and up to 600,000 livestock (and unknown numbers of wildlife) were destroyed. Damage to the Mongolian local economy was officially estimated at a staggering US$1.9 billion. Serious fires hit again in 1999 and 2000.

Other threats to the land include mining (there are some 300 mines) and deforestation. Urban sprawl, coupled with a demand for wood to build homes and to use as heating and cooking fuel, is slowly reducing the forests.

Pollution is becoming a serious problem, particularly in Ulaan Baatar. At the top of Zaisan Memorial in the capital, a depressing layer of dust and smoke from the city's three thermal power stations regularly hovers over the city – this is often appalling in winter, when all homes are continuously burning fuel and the power stations are working overtime. Ulaan Baatar has also suffered from acid rain, and pollution is killing fish in the nearby river Tuul Gol in Central Mongolia.

Oil leaks from trucks crossing the frozen bodies of water in winter continue to pollute the pristine lakes of Khövsgöl Nuur and Uvs Nuur, despite an official ban on these crossings.

FLORA & FAUNA
Flora
Mongolia can be roughly divided into three zones: grassland and shrubs (52% of the country), forests (15%) and desert vegetation (32%). Less than 1% of the country is used for human settlements and crop cultivation. Grasslands are used extensively for grazing and, despite the vast expanses, overgrazing is not uncommon.

Forests of Siberian larch (sometimes up to 45m high), Siberian and Scotch pine, and white and ground birch, cover parts of northern Mongolia.

In the Gobi the *saxaul* shrub covers millions of hectares and is essential in anchoring the desert sands and preventing degradation and erosion. Saxual takes a century to grow to around 4m in height, creating wood so dense that it sinks in water.

Khentii aimag and some other parts of central Mongolia are famous for the effusion of red, yellow and purple wildflowers, mainly rhododendrons and edelweiss. Extensive grazing is the major threat to Mongolia's flowers, trees and shrubs: over 200 species are endangered.

Fauna
In Mongolia, the distinction between the domestic and wild, or untamed, animal is often blurry. Wild and domesticated horses and camels mingle on the steppes with wild asses and herds of wild gazelles. In the mountains there are enormous, horned wild argali sheep and domesticated yaks along with wild moose, musk deer and roe deer. Reindeer herds are basically untamed, but strangely enough, they can be ridden and are known to return to the same tent each night for a salt-lick.

Wildlife The wildlife flourishes in Mongolia despite an extreme climate, the nomadic fondness for hunting, the communist persecution of Buddhists who had set aside areas as animal sanctuaries, and a penniless government, which lacks resources to police nature protection laws. Your chances of seeing some form of wildlife are good, though the closest you will get to a snow leopard, argali sheep or moose is musuem.

Despite the lack of water in the Gobi, some species (many of which are endangered) somehow survive. These include (in Mongolian) the wild camel *(khavtgai)*, wild ass *(khulan)*, Gobi argali sheep *(argal)*, Gobi bear *(mazalai)*, ibex *(yangir)* and black-tailed gazelle *(khar suult zeer)*. In the wide open steppe, you may see the rare saiga antelope, Mongolian gazelle, the jerboa rodent (endemic to Central Asia) and millions of furry marmots *(tarvag)* busy waking up after the last hibernation, or preparing for their next.

Further north in the forests live the wild boar, brown bear *(khuren baavgai)*, antelope, wolf *(chono)*, reindeer *(tsaa buga)*, elk *(khaliun buga)*, musk deer and moose, as well as plenty of sable *(bulga)* and lynx *(shiluus)* whose furs, unfortunately, are in high demand. Most of the mountains are extremely remote, thus providing an ideal habitat for argali sheep, very rare snow leopards *(irbis)* and smaller mammals such as the fox, ermine and hare.

Birds Mongolia is home to over 400 species of birds. In the desert you may see the desert warbler, houbara bustard and saxaul sparrow, as well as sandgrouse, finch and the cinereous vulture *(tas)*.

On the steppes, you will certainly see the most common bird in Mongolia – the grey

The Five Snouts

Mongolians define themselves as the 'people of five animals' *(tavun kosighu mal)*: horses, cattle (including yaks), sheep, goats and Bactrian camels. The odd one out is the reindeer, which is herded by the Tsaatan people *(tsaa* means 'reindeer') in small numbers near the Siberian border. Chickens and pigs are not kept in Mongolia. A rough ratio exists for the relative values of the five animals: a horse is worth five to seven sheep or seven to ten goats. A camel is worth 1.5 horses.

The horse *(mor)* is the pride of Mongolia and there are few nomads, if any, who haven't learned to ride as soon as they can walk. Mongolian horses are shorter than those in other countries (don't call them ponies – Mongolians will be offended). They provide perfect transport, can endure harsh winters and, importantly, produce that much-loved Mongolian beverage: fermented mare's milk, or *airag*. Mongolians have over 300 different words to describe the country's 3.1 million horses, mostly relating to colouring.

Together, cows *(ükher)* and yaks *(sarlag)* number around 3.8 million, and are used for milk and meat (especially *borts*, which is dried and salted meat) and for their hides. Most yaks are actually a cross between a yak and cow, known as a *hainag* in Mongolian, as these supply more milk than thoroughbred yaks.

Fat-tailed sheep *(khon)* are easy to herd and provide wool for housing, felt, clothes, carpets and meat (the ubiquitous mutton) – every nomadic family wants to own at least a few sheep. Goats *(yamaa)* are often difficult to please, but they are still popular for their meat and, especially, for cashmere wool. There are around 15 million sheep and 11 million goats in Mongolia.

Camels *(temee)* are used for long-distance (though slow) transport, and once crossed Mongolia in large caravans. They're valuable for their adaptability and their hair. White camels are particularly auspicious.

demoiselle cranes *(övögt togoruu)* – as well as varieties of hoopoes *(övöölj)*, the odd eagle *(shonkhor)* and vulture *(yol)*. Other steppe species include the upland buzzard, steppe eagle, saker falcon, black kite and some assorted owls and hawks *(sar)*. Some of these will even swoop down and catch pieces of bread in mid-air if your throw it up high enough.

These magnificent creatures, perched majestically on a rock by the side of the road, will rarely be disturbed by your jeep or the screams of your guide ('Look. Eagle!! Bird!! We stop?') but following the almost inaudible click of your lens cap, these birds will move and almost be in China before you have even thought about apertures.

In the mountains, you may be lucky to spot species of ptarmigan, finch, woodpecker, owl and the endemic Altai snowcock *(khoilog)*. The lakes of the west and north are visited by Dalmatian pelicans, hooded cranes, relict gulls, and bar-headed geese.

Eastern Mongolia has the largest breeding population of cranes, including the hooded and Siberian varieties and the critically endangered white-naped crane, of which only 4500 remain in the wild.

Fish Rivers such as the Selenge, Orkhon, Zavkhan, Balj, Onon and Egiin, as well as dozens of lakes, including Khövsgöl Nuur, hold about 380 species of fish. They include trout, grayling *(khadran)*, roach, lenok *(eebge)*, Siberian sturgeon *(khilem)*, pike *(tsurkhai)*, perch *(algana)*, the endemic Altai osman and the enormous taimen, a Siberian relative of the salmon, which can grow up to 1.5m long and weigh 50kg.

Endangered Species

According to conservationists, 28 species of mammals are endangered. The more commonly known species are the wild ass, wild camel, Gobi argali sheep, Gobi bear, ibex and the black-tailed gazelle; others include otters, wolves, antelopes and jerboas.

There are 59 species of endangered birds, including many species of hawk, falcon, buzzard, crane and owl. Despite Mongolian belief that it's bad luck to kill a crane, the white-naped crane is threatened with extinction. Serious numbers of falcons continue to be smuggled from Mongolia to the Gulf states, where they are used for sport.

One good news story is the resurrection of the *takhi* wild horse. The takhi – also known as Przewalski's horse – was actually extinct in the 1960s. It was successfully reintroduced into two national parks after an extensive breeding program overseas. For more on the takhi see the boxed text 'Takhi – The Reintroduction of a Species' in the Central Mongolia chapter.

In preserved areas of the mountains, about 1000 snow leopards remain. They are hunted for their pelts (which are also part of some shamanist and Buddhist traditional practises), as are the snow leopards' major source of food, the marmot. See the boxed text 'Saving the Snow Leopards' in The Gobi chapter.

Every year the government sells licenses to hunt 300 ibex and 40 argali sheep, both endangered species, netting the government over US$500,000.

Protected Areas

For centuries, Mongolians have been aware of the need for conservation. The area around Bogdkhan Uul mountain, near Ulaan Baatar, was protected from hunting and logging as early as the 12th century, and was officially designated as a national park over 200 years ago.

Today the Ministry of Nature & Environment (MNE) and its Protected Areas Bureau (PAB) control the national park system with a tiny annual budget of around US$100,000 per annum. This is clearly not enough, but through substantial financial assistance and guidance from international governments and non-governmental organisations, the animals, flora and environment in some parts of the country are being preserved. Unfortunately, in many protected areas the implementation of park regulations are weak, if not non-existent.

The MNE classifies protected areas into four categories which, in order of importance, are:

Strictly Protected Areas Very fragile areas of great importance; hunting, logging and development is strictly prohibited and there is no established human influence.

National Parks Places of historical and educational interest; fishing and grazing by nomadic people is allowed and parts of the park are developed for ecotourism.

Natural Reserves Less important regions protecting rare species of flora and fauna and archaeological sites; some development is allowed within certain guidelines.

Natural & Historical Monuments Important places of historical and cultural interest; development is allowed within guidelines.

In 2000 the government created five new national parks and one new natural reserve. The 48 protected areas now constitute an impressive 13.2% of the total land. The government is aiming for 30% coverage, which will create the largest park system in the world. At the time of independence in 1990, some put forth the proposal that the *entire country* be turned into a national park!

The Bogdkhan Uul, Great Gobi and Uvs Nuur Basin strictly protected areas are biosphere reserves included in Unesco's Man and Biosphere Project.

Permits To visit these parks – especially a strictly protected area or national park – you will need a permit, either from the local Protected Areas bureau office, or from rangers at the entrances to the parks. The permits are little more than an entrance fee, but they are an important source of revenue for the maintenance of the parks.

Entrance fees are set at T1000 per foreigner per day, plus an extra T300 to T3000 for a vehicle, depending on whether it is driven by a Mongolian or a foreigner (though just having a foreigner in the car is enough to qualify for the T3000 fee).

If you are not able to get a permit and are found in a park without one, the worst penalty you're likely to suffer is being asked to leave or pay a fine to the park ranger.

If you want to stay in a park for more than a week or two or if you are carrying out research etc, it is possible to pay your entrance fee in advance at the Protected Areas Bureau (☎ 326 617, fax 328 620), Ministry of Nature & the Environment, Baga Toiruu 44. The bureau is just behind the Ulaan Baatar Hotel.

GOVERNMENT & POLITICS

In 1992, after much debate, a radically new constitution was enacted. The new parliament is known as the Great Khural (Ikh Khural) and has a total of 76 seats (down from 430 seats after the constitution was amended). Representatives are elected for four-year terms. The smaller standing legislature, the Little Khural (Baga Khural), was abolished in 1992. The president serves a four-year term, is elected by direct popular vote and can be re-elected only once. The president must be at least 45 years of age (a rule which would have excluded the national hero, Damdin Sükhbaatar, among others).

Local governments are not directly elected. Rather, the voters in every sum elect a number of deputies who meet in the aimag capital to select the governor and local mayors. The municipalities of Ulaan Baatar, Darkhan, Choir (in Gov-Sumber district) and Erdenet are autonomous: they don't officially belong to any province and have mayors with as much power as aimag governors.

For over 65 years, power was monopolised by the Mongolian People's Revolutionary Party (MPRP). The elections of 1990 and 1992 still left the MPRP in control but the June 1996 elections swept the new Democratic Coalition into power.

The Democrats lacked the necessary majority to pass legislation and were effectively hamstrung by MPRP. The first democratically elected president, P Ochirbat, a democrat, lost the 1997 presidential election to the MPRP candidate N Bagabandi, further weakening their position.

In April 1998, Prime Minister Enkhsaikhan and his cabinet were ousted by fellow democrats. His successor Elbegdorj was engulfed by a banking scandal and lost a parliamentary vote of confidence and resigned in July 1998. In October 1998 the democratic candidate for prime minister, S Zorig, was murdered. The mayor of Ulaan Baatar, J Narantsatsralt took over but was brought down after a share scandal concerning Erdenet copper mine in July 1999. R Amarjargal then replaced him.

The 2000 election was a fiesta of rock music, Mongolian rappers and performances by the Lipsticks – the 'Spice Girls of the Steppe'. Officials set up temporary ballot-box gers, and herdsmen rode as far as 30km to cast their votes for one of 15 political parties and three coalitions. Herdsmen deliberated over the Mongolian Socialist Democratic Party, the Mongolian Democratic New Socialist party or the Mongolian New Social Democratic Party in a range of names that would have had any Monty Python fan in stitches. The MPRP chose not to rename itself, because 'there were no good names left'.

In the end, the July 2000 election saw the MPRP swept back to power. The MPRP leader Nambaryn Enkhbayar became prime minister (apparently he models himself after Tony Blair). The MPRP says it is no longer a communist party, describing itself as a centre-left party, similar to New Labour in the UK or the Social Democrats in Germany.

ECONOMY

Long before the days of Chinggis Khaan, Mongolia's economy rode on the backs of sheep, goats, cattle, horses, yaks and camels. Nowadays, sheep are the most important stock, constituting half of all animals raised. For each Mongolian, there is almost exactly one horse, 1.4 head of cattle (including yaks), nearly four goats and six sheep; there's also one camel for every six Mongolians. In 1998 there were 31 million head of livestock in Mongolia, the largest herd in Mongolian history. Agriculture, including livestock, makes up more than a third of the country's Gross Domestic Product (GDP).

Livestock raising is practical because of the extensive grasslands – the harsh, dry climate makes most forms of agriculture impossible. Less than 1% of the land is under cultivation, and this is mostly used to grow wheat. Potatoes, vegetables, hay and other fodder crops are also grown. Small-scale timber production along the Russian border provides wood for building material.

The country has over 300 mines producing coal (with reserves of 100 billion tonnes), copper and molybdenum (the mine in Erdenet earns the country US$900 million per year), gold (75 mines, many of them now private, produced 4500kg in 1995), fluorspar (15% of the world's output), uranium, tungsten and zinc. These minerals make up nearly one-third of Mongolia's GDP and earn half of all foreign currency but are vulnerable to shifts in world commodity prices.

Mongolia is the world's second largest producer of cashmere wool, and the industry makes up 15% of the national GDP. The hair is combed off goats in spring using small rakes. Aggressive Chinese merchants dominate the cashmere industry much to Mongolia's vexation, buying up Mongolia's cashmere cheap (the price of cashmere fell by 65% in the 1990s) and processing it in China.

Mongolia has no active oil fields, but recent explorations show that Mongolia may hold reserves of up to five billion barrels of oil. One source of energy revenue may come from transit fees as gas and oil is piped across Mongolia from Russia to China.

Central Planning & Subsidies

The model of economic development adopted earlier this century by both the USSR and Mongolia became known as the 'planned economy'. Mongolia became so integrated with the Soviet economy that it was dubbed the '16th republic'. The communist Mongolian government instituted a series of five-year plans to decide how much should be invested and where, what the production quotas should be, and so on. The state owned all means of production and private enterprise was forbidden. When profits were made, they were given to the government. To keep the massive plan on course, the state created an enormous bureaucracy of economists, planners and supervisors. This required widespread literacy, and statistics on everything were collected. To this day, massive data on everything from herd size to cloud cover to geology is available.

Herders and urban workers weren't taxed, but they were paid very little for their labour. However, the state heavily subsidised all goods and services. Thus, medical care and education were free, though basic. Even herders in remote nomadic camps had access to boarding schools in nearby towns, pensions for the old, veterinary services for their flocks, maternity leave and paid vacations at state-run mineral spring spas.

In the countryside the government organised farmers and herders into collectives, known as *negdel*. The state owned every single sheep, cow and camel in the country. In the cities factory workers were assigned to jobs in which they had little interest, and there were no financial rewards for working hard. Wages were low, but no-one starved. The state provided all that was needed to survive, and though the standard of living was basic, there were no great differences between rich and poor.

Economic Collapse

The Mongolians paid a heavy price for their dependency on the USSR. The bubble burst in 1991 when subsidies from the Soviet Union ended. Barter trade was halted and the Russians started demanding hard currency – not wool and mutton – for their petrol and machinery.

With petrol supplies drying up and spare parts for Soviet-built machinery not arriving, the Mongolians watched in dismay as trucks, buses, power stations and agricultural equipment ground to a halt. During the early 1990s, inflation reached a high of 300%, shop shelves were bare, people lost their jobs, and a severe lack of building materials brought the construction industry to a halt. People reverted to traditional herding practices and traditional means of transport like yak carts and horses in an effort to cope with the collapse, which was estimated as equal to the sudden loss of 50% of the entire national expenditure.

The country's urban areas suffered the most as industry closed and unemployment, a relatively new phenomenon in Mongolia, shot up. Dornod aimag in the east has an unemployment rate of around 60%. Today up to 45% of the urban population outside the capital are below the poverty line of US$18 per person per month. The situation is better in the countryside but it is estimated that 887,000 Mongolians live below the poverty line.

Privatisation & Reform

In the 1990s Mongolia chose a unique path to privatisation. All state-owned enterprises, with a few notable exceptions, were nominally given away. Blue vouchers (inscribed with the bust of Chinggis Khaan) worth T10,000 were issued to every Mongolian citizen. In reality no-one had money to buy up the vouchers, so enterprises issued shares in exchange for vouchers, and suddenly former managers became owners. The same communist bureaucrats continue to run these 'privatised' companies with the same inefficiency as before. For a while no-one was fired and workers continued to get paid even though they didn't work, but eventually the biggest enterprises collapsed.

The government has retained at least 50% ownership of crucial industries, such as the telephone company, railways, MIAT (Mongolian Airlines), the travel company Juulchin, mines, a carpet factory in Erdenet, power stations, the Gobi Cashmere company and so on, though the newly elected MPRP has pledged to privatise many of these companies.

The government has overcome its reluctance to approve joint ventures. Mongolia's law on foreign investment, starting from 1993, explicitly encourages foreign investment and protects the right of investors to repatriate their profits, set up joint ventures, buy shares in Mongolian enterprises or create a wholly foreign-owned business. The law awards tax holidays to mining companies for five years, with halved tax payments for a further five years. China (33%) and Russia (20%) remain the largest investors, followed by the US and Japan.

Switzerland is a surprisingly important market, comprising over 15% of Mongolia's total exports.

From 1991 to 1997, Mongolia was granted more than US$1.5 billion in aid, which managed to avert the country's economic collapse. Another US$320 million was pledged in 1999, much of it coming from Japan, making Mongolia proportionately one of the biggest recipients of multinational aid in the world. Aid currently makes up about one third of Mongolia's GDP, which is almost exactly the same as the subsidies from the Soviet Union during communist years.

Tax collection remains a problem. The Erdenet copper mine which was once Mongolia's largest tax payer is badly behind payments due to falling copper prices in the wake of the Asian economic crisis (copper accounted for 60% of Mongolia's export revenues in 1997). Zamyn-Uud, 'Mongolia's Tijuana' on the border with China, is the only town in the whole of the country that sends any revenue back to the capital.

Tourism

The collapse of the Soviet-subsidised economy and the need for hard currency has forced the Mongolian government to take a second look at tourism.

Mongolia managed to attract 23,000 foreign tourists (excluding Chinese and Russians) in 1999. Most were on organised tours, from Japan (40%), the USA (12%), South Korea (11%), Germany (7%), the UK (4%), France (3%), Australia (2.5%) and the Netherlands (1.5%).

Mongolian tourist authorities favour group tourists. They have yet to work out the financial importance of independent travellers and in fact consider them more environmentally and culturally damaging than economically beneficial. Most people on organised tours stay a short time and buy an all-inclusive tour in their home country; they contribute very little to the Mongolian economy but plenty to the coffers of a handful of influential Mongolian travel companies. Independent travellers, who invariably stay longer than those on organised tours, may

The lush meadows and pure alpine water of Khövsgöl Nuur are great for hiking and swimming.

Terkhiin Tsagaan Nuur

Sunset at Erdene Zuu Khiid

Mongolia's highways...

Sand-sliding at Mongol Els sand dunes

Heading across Uvs into the Altai Nuruu

Detail, Gandan Janraisig

Monks perform a ceremony at Gesar Süm, Ulaan Baatar.

Migjid Janraisig Süm at Gandan Khiid survived the Stalinist purges.

Prayer wheel, Gandan Khiid

Amarbayasgalant Khiid

Sunset at the Museum-Monastery of Choijin Lama, Ulaan Baatar

spend less per day, but *everything* they spend gets diffused through the local economy.

POPULATION

In 1918 Mongolia's population stood at a fraction of what it had been in the 13th century, mainly due to the monastic influence of Tibetan Buddhism, and the nation faced a precarious future. The latest census of January 2000 shows a population of 2,382,500, but this still only represents 1.4 persons per sq km. Many aimags have a population density of less than 0.5 people per sq km.

Inspired by classic Mongolian nationalism, the government actively promoted population growth. Until recently, Mongolians were offered all sorts of incentives and subsidies to reproduce. Women who produced five children were awarded the 'Order of Glorious Motherhood Second Class', and those with eight got the 'Order of Glorious Motherhood First Class'. Under the communists a woman with ten children earned as much as a full-time factory worker.

The pastoral economy could not sustain a large population increase without greater competition for grazing land and damage to the environment. Some of Mongolia's rapidly growing workforce was exported to Siberia, where labourers were badly needed, but the majority wound up in the cities. The government actively encouraged migration to urban areas in the belief that this would increase industrialisation and productivity.

With the economic downturn in the 1990s, urban migration continues and the populations of Dornod, Zavkhan, Töv, Khentii, Gov-Altai and Bayan-Ölgii have all fallen in recent years. Today over half the population lives in the three main cities and one third of the country lives in the capital.

In the early 1990s the government was unable to meet the needs of urban Mongolians, and many returned to relatives in the countryside. Nutrition dropped to bare survival level, even for soldiers, and child deaths rose sharply. In the last ten years population growth has dropped from 2.4% to 1.4%.

Families are now being encouraged to take up farming again. The punitive taxes for remaining childless have been removed, and there are no longer any prizes for prolific reproduction. The international aid agencies promote family planning, but Mongolians, aware of how outnumbered they are on all sides, are reluctant to curb family size. Couples can now have as many or as few children as they wish. The only means of

Buryats

Around 48,000 Buryats live in northern Mongolia, while another 210,000 Russian Buryats live in Buryatia (around Lake Baikal) and another 210,000 are spread around other areas of Russia. Many Buryats joined Chinggis' hordes that invaded Europe and some believe that Chinggis Khaan's mother was a Buryat from the eastern shore of Lake Baikal.

Buryats have a separate language, which is not widely spoken, and there are attempts to revive Buryat script (written, like Mongolia, from top to bottom). Buryats have been Buddhists since the 17th century (except during the communist reign), but have never fully given up their shamanist beliefs.

You can recognise a Buryat by their traditional dress. The male *del* (traditional garment) bears a large patch across the chest with three coloured stripes. The female del consists of a dress and vest. The Buryats are known as hard workers – and unlike other ethnic groups in Mongolia they store hay for the winter.

The Buryat creation myth describes a beautiful creature that was a swan by day and a woman by night. One evening a man met the woman and fell in love. He stole her wings so that she could no longer transform into a swan. The two married and had 11 children. Years later the woman asked for her wings back, saying she just wanted to fly one more time. The man agreed and unlocked the chest that held his wife's wings. The woman flew away, never to return and her sons became the leaders of the 11 Buryat clans.

birth control available to some Mongolians today (but very rarely in the countryside) are condoms and abortion, both of which were prohibited under communism.

PEOPLE

More Mongolians live outside of Mongolia than in it – about 3½ million in China and nearly a million in Russia. Even along the Caspian Sea, in Central Afghanistan and in deepest Yunnan (China), thousands of kilometres from Mongolia, there are descendants of Mongolian armies. Those armies impressed Europe with Mongol unity, but throughout history nomads have usually preferred to go their own way, scattered across a huge land, with their primary loyalty being to their tribe or family. Mythology traces the Mongols back to the pairing of a blue wolf and a deer (the blue wolf was a standard of Chinggis Khaan's armies).

The great majority (about 86%) of Mongolians are Khalkh Mongols (*khalkh* means 'shield'). Clan or tribal divisions are not a significant social or political issue in modern Mongolia. The other major ethnic group, the Kazakhs, make up about 6% (130,000) of the population and live in western Mongolia, mainly in Bayan-Ölgii aimag. Many Kazakhs emigrated to Kazakhstan in the early 1990s, but many have since returned, disillusioned with life in the 'mother republic'.

The other major ethnic groups are:

Barga Originally from the Lake Baikal region of Siberia, they number about 2000 and live in remote pockets of Dornod and Töv.

Bayad Descendants of Oyrad Mongols; about 40,000 live in Malchin, Khyargas and Züüngov districts in Uvs aimag.

Buryat Also found in Siberia, they number about 47,500 and congregate in the northern aimag of Bulgan, Dornod, Khentii and Selenge.

Dariganga About 32,300 live in southern Sükhbaatar.

Darkhad Descended from Turkic people; there are about 15,000 in Khövsgöl.

Dorvod About 55,000 live in Uvs and Khovd.

Khoton Of Turkic descent; about 6000 live in Uvs.

Myangad Also of Turkic descent; about 5000 live in Khovd.

Oold About 11,400 live in Khovd and Arkhangai.

Torguud About 10,500 live in Khovd.

Tsaatan Also known as the 'reindeer people', they are perhaps the smallest ethic group; only about 200 live in northern Khövsgöl.

Uriankhai Also known as Tuvans; about 21,000 live in the Mongol Altai Nuruu mountains in Khovd and Bayan-Ölgii.

Uzemchin Only about 2000 live in Dornod and Sükhbaatar, sharing similarities to the ethnic Mongolians of Inner Mongolia.

Zakhchin About 24,700 live in Khovd.

Before 1990 Russians constituted about 1.5% of Mongolia's population, though very few remain. The Russians were more tolerated than liked but most Mongolians still have better things to say about the Russians than the Chinese, who are generally regarded with suspicion.

EDUCATION

Until the start of communism, education was solely provided by the hundreds of monasteries which once dotted the landscape. Since 1921, modern Mongolian education has been a reflection of its dependence on the USSR.

On the one hand, elementary education is universal and free, with the result that Mongolia boasts a literacy rate of between 80% and 90%. Mongolians receive 11 years of education, from ages seven to 17. In remote rural areas where there are no schools, children are often brought to the aimag capitals to stay in boarding schools, returning home only for a two-week rest during winter and a three-month holiday in summer.

The Mongolian State University (originally named Choibalsan University in honour of Mongolia's most bloodstained ruler) was opened in 1942. In the last 10 years private universities, teaching everything from computing to traditional medicine, have sprung up: the country currently has 29 state and 40 private universities, mostly in Ulaan Baatar.

Unfortunately, education standards have plummeted since independence and literacy rates are starting to fall. Economic pressures have forced increasing numbers of students to drop out of school; the percentage of students completing compulsory

Nomads

Ethnographers divide Mongolia's population according to their ethnicity, but all Mongolians have one thing in common: they are nomads, or nomads at heart. Even urbanised Mongolians love to go to the countryside during their holidays, and often dream of retiring to a ger on the steppes.

About half of the 2.3 million people in Mongolia live in *ger*; and 390,000 herdsmen look after nearly 30 million livestock. They are semi-nomadic, moving their ger and animals several times a year, normally in May and October, in the search for better grazing, water and weather. Most families band together in family groups called *ail* of between five and eight ger. Family groups normally relocate to a winter camp from November to April, which has some stone shelters for the animals. During the summer, camels are left unattended for months at a time, at a distance of up to 50km away.

The life of a nomad, and therefore Mongolia, is inextricably linked with the environment and the animals. Nomads learn to ride as soon as they can walk to a horse; they spend about half their time looking for stray animals (there are almost no fences in Mongolia) carrying a type of lasso pole called an *uurga*.

Days are spent making felt, spinning wool, making dairy products, milking animals, collecting firewood, brushing cashmere, and shearing sheep, amongst other chores. Care of the horses is normally the male prerogative; tending to, and milking the sheep is the women's. Boys and young men normally herd the goats and sheep. Women normally lead the caravan during the spring and autumn migrations. One common sight is women and girls collecting dried dung *(arghal)* with a pitchfork and putting it into a large basket on their back. It is truly a hard life. Most nomads have no electricity, though a surprising number have battery powered radios, through which they receive news and educational programs.

The communists failed to conquer the nomads with collectivism, but, ironically, capitalism may threaten the nomadic lifestyle through development, urbanisation and unequal distribution of wealth between the countryside and the cities. Currently, 26,000 nomadic families own motorbikes, and 16,000 have televisions, while 60% of nomads own less than 100 livestock, the smallest size of a sustainable herd.

---

education fell from 87% in 1990 to 57% in 1995. Tertiary students realise they will have to study abroad to gain a worthwhile, internationally accepted qualification. Corruption among low-paid teachers is reportedly rife; students can virtually 'buy' good marks at some universities.

An interesting gender imbalance is opening up in higher education (although if the reverse were the case it wouldn't warrant reporting); in 1999 over 70% of university students were female. Around 77% of doctors and 60% of lawyers in Mongolia are women.

Distance education has always been important in Mongolia, as so many herders live in remote areas, but economic hardship and higher tuition fees force students to stay at home. A nationwide radio education program, supported by Unesco, teaches no-

mads everything from marketing skills to how to best care for Bactrian camels.

ARTS

From prehistoric oral epics to the latest movie from MongolKino film studios in Ulaan Baatar, the many arts of Mongolia convey the flavour of nomadic life and the spirit of the land. Influenced by Tibet, China and Russia, Mongolia has nonetheless developed unique forms of music, dance, costume, painting, sculpture, drama, film, handicrafts, carpets and textiles.

Most Mongolians may be unable to afford to see their own circus or dance and opera troupes, but a major cultural renaissance is under way, as Mongolians rediscover what the Soviets once repressed.

Recent exhibitions such as the *Legacy of Chinggis Khaan* exhibition in San Francisco

Tsam Dances

Like other Buddhist countries, religion dominates Mongolian arts, including traditional dance. The most common dance, the *tsam*, is a mask dance. Tsam dances were suppressed during the communist reign and are now very rarely held. Performed to exorcise evil spirits, tsam dances are ritualised and theatrical, and are influenced by unique Mongolian nomadic folklore, as well as shamanism.

Tsam was introduced into Mongolia in the 8th century from India, via Tibet. It was first performed at the monastery Erdene Zuu Khiid. A few hundred years ago, an estimated 500 of the 700 monasteries in the country had their own distinct masks and dances. The biggest tsam dances, the Mil Bogdo and Geser, were usually held on the ninth day of the last month of summer.

The masks are usually made from papier-mâché; and often implanted with precious stones. Some of the more common masks are of the terrifying Begze Darmapala (a defender of Buddhism) and the round and jolly Lash-Khan (the patron of art). Possibly the most famous tsam figure is Tserendug, the White Old Man, a former shamanic figure whose image you will see outside the Zanabazar Museum of Fine Arts in Ulaan Baatar. Tserendug wears the white robes of the shamans of Chinggis Khaan. He is revered as the guardian of the fertility of the Mongolian people and their flocks.

You can see some of the tsam masks that survived the Stalinist purges at the Monastery-Museum of Choijin Lama and Erdene Zuu Khiid, both in Ulaan Baatar.

in 1995 and New York's Festival of Mongolia in 2000 have began to raise awareness of Mongolia abroad. Mongolia itself has seen the Roaring Hoofs Music Festival in summer 2000 and is due to host the Mongolian International Arts and Technology Festival in 2001.

If you want more information on the arts in Mongolia contact the Cultural Information Resource Center (☎ 01-316 022, fax 315 358, ℮ circ@mol.mn) in Ulaan Baatar or check out the Web site at www.mongolart.mn.

Music
Modern Young Mongolians in Ulaan Baatar can now watch videos of Western music on satellite TV, but they also enjoy listening to local groups, which sing in the Mongolian language but have definite Western influences. These include heavy metal rockers Kharanga and Niciton ('Mongolia's Nirvana'); pop bands like Chinggis Khaan; the sweet sounds of the popular female vocalists, Ariunna and Saraa; and the band Hurd, who mix rock and ballads

with local instruments. In summer, especially around Naadam, they often perform at the Palace of Culture. Most souvenir stores sell cassettes and compact discs of these and other Mongolian musicians.

Traditional
Get an urbanised Mongolian into the countryside, and they will probably sing and tell you it is the beauty of the countryside that created the song on their lips. Mongolians sing to their animals: there are lullabies to coax sheep to suckle their lambs; songs to order a horse forward, make it stop or come closer; croons to control a goat, to make a cow or imitate a camel's cry. There are far more Mongolian songs about the love of a good horse than the love of a good woman.

Traditional music involves a wide range of instruments and uses for the human voice found almost nowhere else. Voices often sing solo, but are also combined with fiddles, lutes, zithers *(yattak)*, Jew's harp, drums and other instruments. In some traditional Mongolian music, the small drum *(zo)* and large drum *(damar)* are used;

percussion and brass instruments are rarely used. The main instruments, played alone or accompanying singers, are the horse-head violin or fiddle *(morin khuur)*, a two-string vertical violin *(khuuchir)* similar to a Chinese erhu, and the lute *(tovshuur)*.

Another unique traditional singing style, apart from throat singing, is *urtyn-duu*. Sometimes referred to as 'long songs' because of the long trills, not because they are long songs (though some epics are up to 20,000 verses long), they are also called 'drawling songs'. With possible ancient Chinese influences, urtyn-duu involves extraordinarily complicated, drawn-out vocal sounds, which relate traditional stories about love and the countryside. As the legend goes, urtyn-duu sounds best while galloping on a horse along the steppe. Norovbanzad is Mongolia's most famous long-song diva.

Music is often played at weddings and other traditional and religious gatherings. If you cannot attend any traditional ceremonies, make sure not to miss a performance of Mongolia's traditional music while in Ulaan Baatar. The Tumen Ekh Ensemble, Temurjin and the Altai Hangai Ensemble are all well worth a listen. The traditional ensemble Egschiglen (Beautiful Melody) has toured abroad, performing at the 2000 WOMAD festival in the UK.

Several souvenir shops Ulaan Baatar, including the State Department Store, sell recordings of traditional music. Anyone who takes a long-distance trip on public transport will hear impromptu Mongolian folk songs – normally when the transport breaks down.

Literature

The heroic epics of the Mongols were all first committed to writing over 750 years ago – historic texts of war and feuding, myths of origin, administrative manuals of empire, diplomatic histories of hordes and dynasties and biographies of great khaans. Later, Mongolia developed an enormous Buddhist literature, with thousands of subtle treatises on meditation, philosophy and the meaning of life, including the 108 volume *Kanjur*, and *Sandui Djud*, a 10 volume

Deep Throat

Khoomi or throat singing is one of the most enigmatic arts of Mongolia, redolent of the vast steppes of Central Asia and the remote mountain forests of Siberia. The style of singing produces a whole harmonic range from deep in the larynx, throat, stomach and palate, and has the remarkable effect of producing two notes and melodies simultaneously – one a low growl, the other an ethereal whistling. Throat singing is traditionally centred in Western Mongolia (particularly Khovd) and the neighbouring republic of Tuva.

Several recordings of throat singing are available abroad, though most are from Tuva, and there have even been some bizarre throat-singing fusions, with artists like Frank Zappa, the Chieftains and Afro Celt Sound System incorporating samples. To check out some throat singing try the CDs *Spirit of the Steppes: Throat Singing From Tuva & Mongolia*, or *Voices from the Distant Steppes* by Shu-De (Real World).

collection of sutras (Buddhist dialogues and discourses) decorated with an estimated 50kg of gold and 400kg of silver. Surprisingly, the State Central Library in Ulaan Baatar holds the world's largest single collection of Buddhist sutras.

Only recently have scholars translated into English the most important text of all – *Mongol-un Nigucha Tobchiyan* (The Secret History of the Mongols). The text was lost for centuries until a Chinese copy was discovered in 1866 by the implausibly named Archimandrite Palladius, a Russian scholar-diplomat then resident in Beijing. An original Mongolian copy has never been found. The date of the work is known as AD 1240, but so far the author remains a mystery. Intriguing structural comparisons have been made between *The Secret History of the Mongols* and the Bible, prompting theories that the Mongolian author was strongly influenced by the teachings of Nestorian Christianity.

Dashdorjiin Natsagdorj (1906–37) is Mongolia's best known modern poet and playwright, and is regarded as the founder of Mongolian literature. His own writing included the dramatic nationalist poems *My Native Land* and *Star*, and the famous play, *Three Fateful Hills*, which is still performed in Ulaan Baatar.

Natsagdorj also worked for the Mongolian Communist Government and was secretary for the Stalinist puppet, Choibalsan. Natsagdorj was arrested in 1936 for reasons unknown, and died a year later in mysterious circumstances; his body and grave have never been found.

Painting & Sculpture

Much of Mongolian traditional art is religious in nature and is closely linked to Tibetan art. Traditional sculpture and scroll painting follows strict rules of subject, colour and proportion, leaving little room for personal expression.

Tragically, most early examples of Mongolian art were destroyed during the communist regime. More recently, statues have been the target of theft from museums and monasteries throughout Mongolia. In 1999, two teenage monks were charged with stealing several dozen statues from the monastery Gandantegchinlen Khiid in Ulaan Baatar.

Mongolian painting in the 20th century has been dominated by socialist realism but has recently spread to embrace abstract styles. There is a vibrant modern art scene in Ulaan Baatar (see the Art Galleries section in the Ulaan Baatar chapter for more information).

Traditional Mongolia's most renowned painter was Balduugiyn Sharav (1869–1939). He spent his childhood in a monastery and later travelled all around the country. His most famous painting is *One Day in Mongolia*, which you can see in the Zanabazar Museum of Fine Arts. It is classic *zurag* (landscape storytelling), crowded with intricate sketches depicting just about every aspect of the Mongolian life, from felt-making to dung-collecting. Mongolians can stand in front of it and spin yarns for hours.

Zanabazar was a revered sculptor, politician, religious teacher, diplomat and living Buddha. Many Mongolians refer to the time of Zanabazar's life as Mongolia's Renaissance period. His most enduring legacy is the sensuous statues of the incarnation of compassion, the deity Tara. For more on the man, see the boxed text 'Zanabazar' in the Northern Mongolia chapter. Some of his bronze sculptures and paintings can be seen today in Ulaan Baatar's Gandan Khiid, the Zanabazar Museum of Fine Arts and the Winter Palace of Bogd Khaan.

Another of Mongolia's most famous artists is the sculptor Süren, who worked in the early 20th century.

Scroll Painting Religious scroll paintings *(thangka)* once graced the inner sanctuaries and chanting halls of monasteries all over the country. Some survived communist confiscation and have been recovered from the Gobi and other hiding places. They are tools of meditation, used by practitioners to visualise themselves developing the enlightened qualities of the deities depicted.

Thangka cloth is traditionally made by stretching cotton on a frame and covering it with chalk, glue and *arkhi* (milk vodka). Colours are made from minerals mixed with yak skin glue. Mongolian scroll paintings generally mirror the Tibetan variety but you can notice distinctive regional features like the introduction of camels, sheep and yaks in the background. Soviet-style scroll paintings were even produced at one stage, portraying the glorious working classes in thangka-style, as if they were religious figures. Many of Mongolia's scroll paintings are miniatures, and thus easier to carry on horseback.

Scroll paintings can be found once again in many homes, now that there are no more bans on family altars. The most popular deity is White Tara, the female incarnation of compassion.

Appliqué scroll paintings, made from Chinese silks, were popular at the turn of the century. There are some fine examples in the Zanabazar Museum of Fine Arts.

Jewellery & Folk Art

Nomads have traditionally valued jewellery, both as a means of storing and transporting their wealth, and of conveying marital status and clan affiliation. Amulets performed the added function of protection against spirits. Jewellery was traditionally passed down to daughters as part of their dowry. The traditional *ugalz*, or sheep horn headdress, of Mongolian noble women was an amazing sculpture of hair, stiffened with congealed mutton fat and held in place with silver, turquoise and coral clips, amulets and tassels.

19th-century Mongolian noble woman

Nomadic art has generally been utilitarian, as there simply isn't enough space to carry art from pasture to pasture. Traditional Mongolian saddles are particularly beautiful, made with dyed and appliquéd leather, embossed with silver and decorated with eight leather straps. Mongol, Kazakh and Buriyat saddles are quite distinct. Even noblemen rode horses.

Wealthy Mongolians traditionally wore a silver flint, knife and chopstick set on their belts, and carried an ornate snuff bottle, silver bowl and often an amulet under their *del* (traditional garment). Back at the ger you could find a carved ceremonial milk spoon (*satzal*) and a leather airag-holder (*kokuur airag*). Other items include painted chests (*khairtzing*) and felt goods. You can see many of these crafts in local museums.

Man Stones

Littered around Mongolia are enigmatic stone figures known as *balbals*, or in Mongolian as *khunni chuluu* (man stones). The Turkic stones mostly date from the 6th to 8th centuries and are thought to be grave markers, erected to commemorate either fallen warriors or their slain enemies. Balbals are found in most Turkic areas of Central Asia, including Kyrgyzstan, Kazakhstan, the Altai region of China, Russia and Mongolia, and Tuva and Xinjiang.

Most of the figures hold a sword and bowl and wear a distinctive belt and earring. The orientation of the stones seems to have a ritual significance as almost all face east, towards the rising sun. They are often accompanied by stone slabs and/or processional pathways of stones. Archaeologists believe that these represent either the number of clans that could have attended the funeral, or the number of men killed by the deceased. Many balbal are now in pieces, with their heads lying on ground or balancing on the stone body.

Balbals are not to be confused with **deer stones** (*bugan chuluu*), upright grave markers from the Bronze and Iron ages on which are carved stylised images of deer, and sometimes the sun, moon or various ancient weapons. There are around 450 deer stones in Mongolia, most in Bulgan, Khovd and Ulaangom provinces. They are between 3m to 5m in height and, like balbals, almost all face east.

If you drive around Arkhangai, Zavkhan or Övörkhangai you may also come across **burial stones** set in circles or squares. Some of these burial mounds (*herigsuur* in Mongolian or *kurgan* in Turkic) are up to 4000 years old, which conceal slab-lined tombs. Other ancient stone patterns may also have marked crossroads on Mongol trade routes.

SOCIETY & CONDUCT

The Mongolian way of life is laid-back, patient, tolerant of hardship and intimately connected with the ways of animals. Despite urbanisation, the traditions of the steppes live on. In the cities, many Mongolians continue to live, by preference, in a ger, snug against the bitter winds from

Siberia inside their canvas and felt tent. In summer, city folk head for the hills to gather wild berries and pine cones, enjoying the open spaces. Whenever possible, apartment dwellers arrange with relatives in the country to get a big churn of airag sent to town. Mongolians can drink a dozen or more litres of the sour, fizzy, mildly alcoholic liquid in a day.

On the steppes, the population is scattered more or less evenly over the available pasture, depending on the season, so neighbours are few but always present in the distance. There's always a rider on the horizon, and in the event of trouble, such as a bogged jeep, there's usually someone who can get a tractor to tow you out; though it may take some time.

Traditional Dress

Many young Mongolians in Ulaan Baatar wear Western-style clothes, however, at traditional gatherings and for just about anyone who lives in the countryside, there is a distinct, simple and common type of traditional clothing. The main garment is the del, a long one-piece gown made from wool. Most Mongolians have several different del, suitable for the different seasons, as well as a more decorative del for special occasions. The del has a high collar, is often brightly coloured, comes with a multipurpose sash, and is worn by men and women all year. Many Mongolians can differentiate ethnic groups from the colour and shape of their del.

The *khantaaz* is a shorter traditional jacket, often made of silk, which is also buttoned to the side. It is not very common these days.

The *gutul* is the high boot made from thick leather. They are easy to fit on – both the left and right boot are the same shape. The reasons for the curled, upturned toe are varied, but are more likely to be religious – the upturned end touches less earth and therefore theoretically kills fewer bugs, in accordance with Buddhist teachings about the non-taking of life. Many Mongolian men prefer, however, to wear the almost-indestructible Russian army boots.

To top this off, men often wear the Mongolian hat known as a *loovuz*. Usually made from wolf or fox skins, they are particularly useful for protection against the howling winter winds. Other traditional hats such as the decorative *toortsog* and the *khilen malgai* are rarely worn.

Most museums in Ulaan Baatar and the aimag capitals have displays of traditional clothing. The best collection is on the 2nd floor of the National Museum of Mongolian History in Ulaan Baatar.

Traditional Medicine

Based on Indian, Tibetan and Chinese teachings, and heavily influenced by Buddhism, traditional medicine was first introduced into Mongolia by the revered (and unpronounceable) Luvsandanzanjantsan in the late 17th century – but was suppressed during communist domination from 1921 to 1990.

Diagnosis and treatment are based on the five vital elements of earth, water, fire, wind and wood. Medicines are often made from herbs, plants, mineral water and organs from unfortunate animals, and administered according to the weather, the season and the individual's metabolism. Acupuncture, massage and blood-letting, as well as prayers, are also important factors.

With the lifting of prohibitions against religion, and several highly publicised and successful treatments of Mongolians whose illnesses could not be cured by Western medicine, traditional practices are popular once more. Forty-five hospitals and monasteries, including the Manba Datsan clinic at the monastery Otochmaaramba Khiid in Ulaan Baatar, contain trained, registered doctors of traditional medicine.

Traditions & Symbols

Zolgokh This is a traditional greeting, rather like shaking hands in the West, usually reserved for Tsagaan Sar (White Month, or lunar new year). The younger person places his or her forearms under those of the elder to gently support the arms of the elder person. It is always important to show respect to anyone who is elderly and if you're under 20 years old, to anyone older.

Soyombo

The national symbol of Mongolia, dating back to at least the 14th century is the *soyombo*, signifying freedom and independence. It is found on the covers of Mongolian passports and on the national flag. Legend attributes its creation to Zanabazar, the Living Buddha.

Explanations of its complicated symbolism have changed and become lost over time. From top to bottom, the shapes are most likely to represent the following: the three-tongued flame symbolises the past, present and future prosperity of the country; the sun and moon are what they seem, but can also represent the father and mother of the nation; the inverted triangles are arrowheads indicating victory; the two small horizontal rectangles symbolise honesty and integrity; the interlocking symbols in the middle represent fire, water, earth and sky, or alternatively the duality of yin and yang; and the two large, vertical rectangles stand for friendship. A five-pointed communist star was introduced on the top of the soyombo in 1924 but has since disappeared.

Family Book Traditionally, every Mongolian family kept a book – a record of births, deaths and important events. For early historians, these family books must have been a gold mine of information. After the 1921 revolution, the communists denounced this practice in an effort to break up clan ties. Mongolians were told to use their first name, in conjunction with their paternal name. Most of the family books were destroyed or hidden.

In April 2000 the government reintroduced clan names and Mongolians have been trying to rediscover and reinvent names (though most Mongolians still use only one name when addressing each other). As many as 20% of the country immediately staked a claim to the name Borjigan – the clan of Chinggis Khaan. Mongolia's first (and only) cosmonaut, Guragchaa, chose the unique surname of Cosmos.

One of the reasons for the family books and new law is to prevent inbreeding – relatives traditionally have to be separated by at least seven generations before it is possible to marry within the same family.

Time Like the Chinese, the Mongolians use a lunar calendar to celebrate traditional holidays, such as the lunar new year. Years are traditionally grouped into five blocks of 12 years. Each block is named after one of the elements (earth, fire, water etc) and each year is named after the 12 animals of the zodiac.

Nomads divide winter into periods of time in multiples of nine – the lucky number for Buddhists. The winter is 81 days long (nine lots of nine). At the start of winter, the first nine days are named the 'Lambs Must be Covered'; the weather starts to improve when it is 'Not Cold Enough to Freeze Soup'; and the oncoming spring 'Brings Back Life to Normal'.

At the end of the 81 days, Tsagaan Sar (White Month), is widely celebrated at the start of the lunar new year. Names of some of the upcoming seasons are 'Dairy Goods are Plentiful' and 'The Animals Cast off Their Hair'.

Do's & Don'ts

Besides the complicated set of do's and don'ts to observe when entering a ger and interacting with a nomadic family (see 'The Mongolian Ger' special section), there are several others to remember.

Hats are crucial for survival, but it's rude to wear them indoors, especially in a temple, a ger or in an office. Never step on, sit on, or move another person's hat. When visiting people, you should also take off your coat and gloves, particularly when sitting, eating or drinking tea, unless it's really freezing. Also, try not to let a post or fence come between you and a Mongolian.

Mongolians are normally disturbed by any talk or suggestion of death, divorce, accidents and the like. Any such talk is considered an ill omen and will be taken seriously, even if it was meant as a joke. For example, when flying MIAT, don't say something like 'I hope the wings don't fall off'. Even if the aircraft does have bald tyres and an overloaded cargo hold, Mongolian passengers will not appreciate the suggestion. As the Mongolians say: 'If you are afraid, don't do it. If you do it, don't be afraid'.

There are no special hand signals, though an extended little finger infers that something is bad (much like a thumbs up in the West means good). As in the rest of Russian-influenced Central Asia, a flick to your throat with your index finger signifies that someone is drunk.

Treatment of Animals

Poaching and hunting are common practice in the countryside, despite efforts by conservationists and some government officials. As long as there is demand in countries like China for 'delicacies' such as powdered argali sheep horns, boiled Gobi bear gall bladders, musk deer glands and snow leopard bones, precious and often highly endangered wildlife will be killed.

The very occasional fence or vehicle, as well as mining, overgrazing, deforestation and pollution, are responsible for the deaths of many domesticated and wild animals. An estimated three million are killed every year by nomadic people for food and skins, plus many more by poachers.

RELIGION
Buddhism

Mongolians have always taken Buddhism of the Tibetan, or Lamaist, variety wholeheartedly. Their warrior spirits were tamed by Tibetan lamas when the Mongolian empire was at its height and the khaans were coming to grips with the complexities of controlling a multicultural empire.

Kublai Khaan found himself with a court in which all philosophies of his empire were represented. Teachers of Islam, Taoism, Nestorian Christianity, Manicheism (a system of religious doctrines, including elements of Gnosticism, Zoroastrianism, Christianity, Buddhism etc, taught by the Persian prophet Mani), Confucianism and Buddhism all congregated at court, offering advice in managing state affairs, and offering the Mongols a very comforting form of divine insurance.

It was a Tibetan Buddhist, Phagpa, who influenced the mind of the great khaan (probably because it was the religion that most closely resembled shamanism). Only two generations after Chinggis Khaan, the imperial court took to Buddhism and was persuaded that the energies at the command of the lamas were greater than those of the warriors and their gods.

It took centuries before Buddhism really took hold. In 1578 Altan Khaan, a descendant of Chinggis Khaan, met the Tibetan leader Sonam Gyatso, was converted, and bestowed on Sonam Gyatso the title Dalai Lama (*dalai* means 'ocean' in Mongolian). Sonam Gyatso was named as the third Dalai Lama and his two predecessors were named posthumously. The Dalai Lama issued new laws forbidding the sacrificial slaughter of women, slaves and animals as funeral offerings. He ordered that an image of Gonggor (Sanskrit: Mahakala) be worshipped in every ger.

Reincarnate lamas *(khutuktu)* were also (re)born in Mongolia, the most prominent being the Jebtzun Damba, or Living Buddha, of the Khalkh Mongols, who ranks as Tibetan Buddhism's third highest incarnation, after the Dalai and Panchen lamas. The first Jebtzun Damba reincarnation was the great Zanabazar, sculptor and energetic diplomat. He had to yield ultimate secular authority to the emperor of China in 1691 as the power of the Manchu Qing dynasty reached its zenith. Many of the Manchu emperors were themselves devout Tibetan Buddhists, and their patronage ensured Buddhism flourished throughout Mongolia, with many Mongolian reincarnate lamas regularly visiting Beijing to bless the emperor. The Chinese were particularly grateful for the calming effect Buddhism seemed to have on the Mongols!

The Jebtzun Damba reincarnations never lost their dream of Mongolian independence, and as soon as Qing China collapsed in 1911, the eighth Jebtzun Damba, or Bogd Khaan, declared Mongolia's independence. He wielded sacred and secular power, as did the Dalai Lama in Tibet.

The Purge When the revolution of 1921 brought the communists to power, an uneasy peace existed between Mongolia's monasteries and the government. The communists realised that they were not strong enough to take on the religious establishment. In 1921 this amounted to 110,000 lamas (including young boys), or one-third of the male population, who lived in about 700 monasteries and controlled about 20% of the nation's wealth. (Currently, there are about 1000 lamas in 150 monasteries.)

In 1924, when the eighth Jebtzun Damba (or Bogd Khaan) died, the communist government prevented a successor from being found. (Mongolians believe that a ninth Jebtzun Damba, reincarnated at a later date, is today a middle-aged lama living among other exiled Tibetans in Dharamsala, India. (See the boxed text 'Ninth Jebtzun Damba' in the Ulaan Baatar chapter.) In 1929 some of the property and herds belonging to the monasteries were seized and redistributed. Arrests and executions came in 1932, but the government quickly backed off as rebellions broke out. However, harassment continued – young lamas were 'reclassified' and conscripted into the army and it was forbidden to build new monasteries.

Arrests of high-ranking lamas resumed in 1935. In 1937 the bloody purge began in earnest. Choibalsan's secret police descended on the monasteries. Young students were spared, but it is estimated that over 17,000 monks of middle and high rank were arrested,

Mongolia and Tibet

The links between Mongolia and Tibet run old and deep. Once in a lifetime, every devout Buddhist Mongolian tries to reach the holy city of Lhasa on a pilgrimage, despite the hardship and distance. Mongolian Buddhists have translated hundreds of texts into Mongolian and most of the Jebtzun Damba, or Living Buddhas, were born in Tibet. The 4th Dalai Lama was Mongolian. The Tibetans in turn relied on various Mongolian tribes to sustain their power and vanquish rival sects. When the British invaded Tibet in 1903, the Dalai Lama fled to Mongolia for safety and stayed there for a few years.

and virtually none were ever heard from again. Presumably they were either executed or died in Siberian labour camps. The monasteries were closed, ransacked and burned. Only four monasteries (out of more than 700) were preserved as museums of the 'feudal period' – but even these were damaged.

Besides ideology, the government had other reasons for wanting to eliminate the lamas. First of all, they didn't work, and the Russians were anxious to send Mongolian labourers to Siberia. Secondly, lamas were celibate and Mongolia's population was either stable or declining, which ran counter to the Marxist goals of 'more people, more production'. Thirdly, the communists believed – with some justification – that the monasteries were backward and opposed to modernisation. Finally, the monasteries were the centre of political and economic power in the country, and the government didn't appreciate the competition.

Except at the monastery Gandan Khiid in Ulaan Baatar – which was kept as a showcase temple to impress foreigners – all religious worship and ceremonies remained outlawed until 1990. It was then that the democracy movement took hold and freedom of religion was restored. In the past few years, there has been a phenomenal revival of Buddhism (and other religions). This is most evident during the Dalai Lama's visits, when hundreds of thousands of people flock to be blessed. Up

Important Figures of Tibetan Buddhism

Sakyamuni

This is a brief guide to some of the deities of the Tibetan Buddhist pantheon. It is neither exhaustive nor scholarly, but it may help you to recognise a few of the statues you encounter in Mongolia. Sanskrit names are given as these are most recognisable in the West; Mongolian names are in brackets.

Sakyamuni – The Historical Buddha Born in Lumbini in the 5th century BC in what is now southern Nepal, Sakyamuni attained enlightenment under a *bo* (pipal) tree and his teachings set in motion the Buddhist faith. In Tibetan-style representations he is always pictured sitting cross-legged on a lotus-flower throne. Buddha is recognised by 32 marks on his body, including a dot between the eyes and a bump on the top of his blue hair. His right hand touches the earth in the witness mudra, or hand movement, and the left hand holds a begging bowl. He is often flanked by his two disciples.

Maitreya (Maidar) – The Future Buddha Maitreya is passing the life of a bodhisattva and will return to earth in human form 4000 years after the disappearance of Sakyamuni Buddha to take his place as the next earthly Buddha. He is normally seated with his hands by his chest in the mudra of 'turning the Wheel of Law'.

Dhyani Buddha Also known as Contemplation Buddhas, they are comprised of Akhshobya (white), Amithaba (red), Amoghasiddhi (green), Ratnasambhava (yellow) and Vairochana. They form a set of famous sculptures by Zanabazar.

Amitayus (Ayush) – Buddha of Longevity This Buddha is often red and holds a vase in his hands.

Medicine Buddha (Otoch Manal) He is worshipped for his healing properties.

Avalokitesvara (Janraisig) – Glorious Gentle One He is the Bodhisattva of Compassion and is either pictured with 11 heads and 1000 pairs of arms (*chogdanjandan janraisig*), or in a white, four-armed manifestation (*chagsh janraisig*). The Dalai Lama is considered an incarnation of Avalokitesvara.

A standing Maitreya

to 150 monasteries have reopened, although some of them are little more than a part-time altar in a ger, and even some ex-Communist Party officials have become lamas.

An entire generation of Mongolians have grown up without Buddhism. Most people no longer understand the Tibetan texts and the monasteries suffer from a chronic lack of trained Buddhists lamas, a problem that is currently being addressed by visiting theological teachers from Tibet, India and the West.

Important Figures of Tibetan Buddhism

Manjushri (Zöölön Egshigt) – Princely Lord of Wisdom Regarded as the first divine teacher of Buddhist doctrine. His right hand holds the flaming sword of awareness, which cuts through ignorance, his left arm cradles a Scripture in a half-opened lotus blossom and his left hand is in the teaching mudra. Manjushri is often yellow.

Vajrapani (Ochir Vaany or Ochir Barigch) – Thunderbolt in Hand Vajrapani is the wrathful Bodhisattva of Energy. The thunderbolt (*dorje* in Tibetan; *vajra* in Sanskrit) represents indestructibility and is a fundamental symbol of Tantric faith. Vajrapani is worshipped as a previous incarnation of Chinggis Khaan.

Tara – The Saviour Tara has 21 different manifestations. She symbolises purity and fertility and is believed to be able to fulfil wishes. Tara was born from a tear of compassion that fell from Chenresig's eyes. Statues of Tara usually represent Green Tara (Nogoon Dar Ekh), who is associated with night, or White Tara (Tsagaan Dar Ekh), who is associated with day. White Tara is the female companion of Janraisig, holds a lotus bud in her left hand and has eyes of wisdom in the palms of her hands and soles of her feet.

Begze (Jamsaran) The protector of Mongolia.

Yamantaka (Yamandag) A wrathful form of Manjushri. Known as the conqueror of Yama – god of death (Choijil). Yamantaka has the head of a buffalo, 16 legs and 34 arms.

Mahakala (Gonggor or Gombo) Represented as either a six-armed white manifestation worshipped as the god of wealth, or 'the great black one' (ikh khar). As in Tibet, Mahakala is believed by nomads to be the guardian of the tent.

Palden Lhamo (Bandal Lham) An angry manifestation of Tara.

Four Guardian Kings Comprised of Virupaksa (red, holding a snake), Dhitarastra (white, holding a lute), Virudhaka (blue, holding a sword) and Vaishrovana (yellow, sitting on a snow lion). The kings are mostly seen guarding monastery entrances.

Tara – symbol of purity and fertility

Monasteries Every visitor must try to visit at least one of the 'big three' monasteries, or *khiid*: the busy and popular Gandantegchinlen Khiid (popularly shortened to Gandan Khiid) in Ulaan Baatar, which also contains a Buddhist university; the magnificent Erdene Zuu Khiid, built on the ruins of the ancient capital of Karakorum at Kharkhorin in Övörkhangai aimag; and the remote Amarbayasgalant Khiid, near Darkhan, which has been extensively renovated.

The best time to visit a monastery is in the morning (from about 9 to 11 am), when chanting and prayers are usually in progress. You may enter a temple during chanting but must not step in front of the monks. Instead, go clockwise around the back. You can even go up to the altar, make a small cash offering, and then bow before the altar. You can also bow before the monks, and they will touch your head with their prayer books.

You should never take photos of anything or anyone inside a temple – see Photography & Video in the Facts for the Visitor chapter. Most temples open at about 9 am and close around 3 pm, although Gandan Khiid is open during daylight hours.

Monasteries and temples *(süm)* always have Tibetan names. After the communist purges, many religious artefacts were returned to the monasteries from their hiding places – though over time, many hiding places have been forgotten and artefacts lost forever. Scroll paintings, statues, butter lamp candles, altar cloths and prayer wheels (which must be spun in a clockwise direction) decorate the monasteries and temples, but they are rarely as old as the ones in India or Tibet.

Buddhist Symbols

Some common Buddhist symbols include:

Prayer Wheel These are filled with up to a mile of prayers and are turned manually by pilgrims to gain merit. Wheels can be the size of a fist or the size of a small building, and are powered by hand, water, wind and even hot air (a cylinder made of paper and suspended over a hot flame). Prayers are pasted to the outside of the wheels.

Dharma Wheel The eight-spoked Wheel of Law symbolises the Eightfold Path of Buddhism. It is often flanked by two deer, which symbolise the Buddha's first sermon at Sarnath, and seen on monastery roofs.

Wheel of Life Symbolises the earthly cycle of death and rebirth, held by Yama, the god of the Dead. The six sections of the circle are the six realms of rebirth ruled over by gods, titans, hungry ghosts, hell, animals and humans. Around this are the 12 experiences of earthly existence.

Rosary Beads These are formed by a string of beads (traditionally 108) made from dried seeds. Prayers are marked off by each bead, with a second string to mark off higher multiples.

Balin Known as *torma* in Tibetan, balin are wheat dough cakes, decorated with coloured medallions of goat or mutton fat, held in place with tiny nails.

Om Mani Padme Hum Is the most common mantra carved on prayer wheels and ovoo (a shamanistic offering to the gods). Its six syllables mean 'Hail to the Jewel in the Lotus' and form the mantra of Janraisig (Sanskrit: Avalokitesvara), the bodhisattva of compassion.

Stupas Known as *suburgan* in Mongolian, were originally built to house the cremated relics of the historical Sakyamuni Buddha and as such have become a powerful symbol of Buddhism. Later stupas also became reliquaries for lamas and holy men.

The Eight Auspicious Symbols

Known as naimin takhel in Mongolian, these symbols are associated with gifts made to Sakyamuni Buddha upon his enlightenment and appear as protective motifs and good luck charms.

Precious Parasol Placed over Buddha images as a protection against evil influences; it is a common Buddhist motif and can be seen as far away as Thailand and Japan.

Banner of Victory Heralds the triumph of Buddhist wisdom over ignorance.

White Conch Shell Blown in celebration of Sakyamuni's enlightenment.

Two Golden Fishes Shown leaping from the waters of their captivity; thus they represent liberation from the Wheel of Life. They are sometimes depicted as complementary forces of yin and yang.

Vase of Great Treasures A repository of the jewels of enlightenment.

Knot of Eternity (Ulzii Hey) A commonly seen Tibetan motif, representing the entwined, never-ending passage of harmony and love.

Eight-Spoked Golden Wheel Represents the Noble Eightfold Path, and is also referred to as the Wheel of Dharma. In Mongolia it is connected to the similarly shaped circular roof of a ger.

Lotus Flower Represents Sakyamuni's purity and compassion, and symbolises the blossoming of good deeds.

Islam

In Mongolia today, there is a significant minority of Sunni Muslims, constituting as much as 6% of the total population. Most of them are ethnic Kazakhs, who live primarily in the far western aimag of Bayan-Ölgii.

Christianity

Nestorian Christianity was part of the Mongolian empire long before Western missionaries arrived. These days, with poverty, unemployment, alcoholism, domestic violence and confusion in abundance, Christian and Mormon missionaries, often from obscure fundamentalist sects, have been keenly seeking converts.

Mongolian authorities are wary of these missionaries, who sometimes come to the country under the pretext of teaching English. In Ulaan Baatar, there are now more than 30 non-Buddhist places of worship, including a new US$1 million Catholic Mission Centre.

Shamanism

Whether shamanism is actually a religion is open to debate (there is no divine being or book of teachings), but it is a form of mys-

ticism practiced by some Mongolians in the north, including the Tsaatan, Darkhad, Uriankhai and Buryats. It was the dominant belief system of Chinggis Khaan and the Mongols but has now been pushed to the cultural fringes.

The most obvious manifestation of shamanism in Mongolia is the *ovoo*, made of stones, wood and other matter. The ovoo is a shamanistic pyramid-shaped offering to the gods, which you see all over the countryside. The blue *khatag*, or scarf offering, has its roots in the blue of the sky spirit Tengger, or Tengri. Shamanism has deep connections to the earth; digging the

Ovoo

A few minutes in the countryside is all that it takes to see your first *ovoo*. An ovoo is a pyramid-shaped collection of stones, wood and other offerings, like vodka bottles and silk scarves, placed on top of a hill or mountain pass in a shamanistic traditional offering to the gods. They are often just a handful of rocks, but sometimes they are spectacular arrangements with a head of a moose or yak, wooden poles and even the odd pair of crutches. Ovoos are sacred, and all digging, hunting and logging nearby is strictly prohibited. Mongolians believe that people who disrespect ovoo will fall sick and even die.

If travelling in a jeep, the driver will probably drive to the left of the ovoo and often stop at important ones. Mongolians argue about what to do exactly when you come to an ovoo, but it normally involves walking around it three times in a clockwise direction, making an offering of anything (a rock, vodka, small amounts of money), and making a wish.

If you have Mongolian friends and get lucky you may see an ovoo worship ceremony. Monks say prayers, people give offerings and afterwards there is feasting and some traditional sports like horse racing and wrestling. The rituals are held to celebrate the end of winter and pray for good rainfall, plentiful grass for the livestock and abundant fish and animals for hunting.

soil and cutting the grass is seen as profane, and one of the reasons why agriculture has traditionally been looked down on by Mongolians.

Shamanism is based around the shaman – called a *boo* if a male, or *udgan* if a female – who has special medical and religious powers. If a shaman's powers are inherited, it is known as *udmyn*, or if they become apparent after a sudden period of sickness and apparitions it is known as *zlain*.

Shamans live alone and in isolation, but are available at any time to protect the clan and livestock from disease and evil spirits, known as *lus*. One of a shaman's main functions is to cure any sickness caused by the soul straying, and to accompany the soul of a dead person to the other world. Shamans act as intermediaries between the human and spirit worlds and communicate with spirits during trances, which can last up to six hours. During the main ceremony, called the Great Sacrifice, often held on the third day of the new lunar year, many animals are sacrificed to the gods. Shamans have traditionally prophesied by interpreting cracks found in the heated shoulder blades of dead sheep.

Shamanism, which flourished during the communist days because no books or buildings could be destroyed, has coexisted with Buddhism for centuries. In fact, Mongolian Buddhism has incorporated shamanic beliefs in a similar way to Tibetan Buddhists adopting the animist Bön religion of pre-Buddhist Tibet. Pockets of shamanism survive, particularly in the Khövsgöl and Dornod aimags, and among the Khoton people of Uvs. Several museums in the aimags, and in Ulaan Baatar, contain shaman clothes and implements, like the drums used to place shamans into a trance.

LANGUAGE

The official national language is Mongolian, though other dialects such as Dariganga, Dorbet, Dzakchin, Western Oirod and Buryat are spoken. The language spoken in China's Inner Mongolia province constitutes another dialect. Many older Mongolians also speak Russian well.

See the Language chapter for more information on Mongolian and a list of useful words and phrases. For a more comprehensive look at the language, get a copy of Lonely Planet's *Mongolian phrasebook*.

THE MONGOLIAN GER

The large, white felt tent, known as a *ger* and seen all over Mongolia, is probably the most identifiable symbol of the country. (The word 'yurt' is a Turkic word introduced to the west by the Russians. If you don't want to offend the nationalistic sensibilities of the Mongolians, use the word 'ger'.) Most Mongolians still live in gers, even in the suburbs of Ulaan Baatar. And it's not hard to understand why: wood and bricks are scarce and expensive, especially out on the steppes and animal hides are cheap and readily available. Nomadic people obviously have to be flexible and mobile and gers can be moved easily – depending on the size, a ger can be assembled in one to three hours. If the opportunity arises, an invitation to visit or stay in a ger is one that should not be missed.

Gers can be surprisingly comfortable. In urban areas, they may have electricity but in rural regions, candles or lamps supply the only artificial light. There is normally a stove in the centre of the ger, which provides both heat and cooking facilities. In forested areas, firewood can be burned in the stove, but out on the steppes the main fuel is dried dung. Without exception, the toilet will be outside, though there normally aren't any toilets. If showers exist at all, they will normally be in a bathhouse *(khaluun us – 'hot water')*, serving a whole group of gers. Lakes and rivers are the normal place to bathe, though in summer only.

Ger Design

The outer and innermost material of the ger is usually canvas, with an insulating layer of felt sandwiched in between (with more felt layers added in winter and fewer in summer), all supported by a collapsible wooden frame. They may appear flimsy, but gers hold up amazingly well to Mongolia's fierce winds. During hot weather the sides can be rolled up and mosquito netting is introduced to stop bugs. The felt *(esgi)* is made in the autumn by sprinkling several layers of sheep's wool with water, layering it with grass and rolling it up tight, wetting

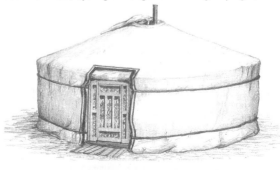

Icon: The door *(khaalag)* of a ger is always brightly painted. (Photograph by Cathleen Naundorf)

Right: The exterior view of a ger.

KH

it again and then rolling the whole thing back and forth over the steppe.

The gers of the great Mongol khaans were more solidly built: when it was necessary to move them, they had to be placed on carts and pulled by oxen. You'll see images of this on some Mongolian banknotes, and a few replicas have been set up around Ulaan Baatar to aid efforts in flogging tourist souvenirs.

The internal layout of a ger is universal throughout Mongolia. The door always faces south. Once across the threshold, men move left (to the west, under the protection of the great sky god, Tengger); women to the right (east, under the protection of the sun). Towards the back, and a little to the west, is the place of honour set aside for guests.

The back of the ger is the *khoimor*, the place for the elders, where the most honoured people are seated and where treasured possessions are kept. On the back wall is the family altar, decorated with Buddhist images and family photos (mostly taken during very occasional visits to Ulaan Baatar). Near the door, on the male side are saddles, ropes and a big leather milk bag and churn, used to stir the brews of milky tea and *airag*. On the female side of the door are the cooking implements and water buckets. Around the walls there are two or three low beds and cabinets. In the centre sits a small table with several tiny chairs. Hanging in any vacant spot, or hung on the latticed walls, are toothbrushes, clothes, children's toys and plenty of tasty slabs of uncooked mutton.

Making a Ger

The small cartwheel-shaped opening at the top, called a *toon*, allows smoke to exit and air to enter. It is covered with an *örkh*, which can be adjusted from the ground using ropes. The wooden roof poles, *uni*, are orange (the colour of the sun); the concertina-like latticed walls are known as *khan*. Each ger has four to 12 latticed-walls, each with about 10 to 15 roof poles.

Depending on the mobility and wealth of the family, the ger is placed on a wooden, felt or bare earth floor. In western Mongolia, gers

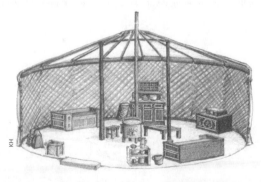

Left: Interior layout of a ger.

owned by Kazakhs are darker, larger and almost always decorated inside with bright carpets and rugs. The first part of the ger to be assembled is the floor (if there is one). Next, the stove *(zuukh)* is placed in the centre of the ger. The walls and door *(khaalag)* – always brightly painted, and facing south – are erected; two columns, called a *bagana*, are connected; and then the ger is covered with felt and weighed down against strong winds.

The average weight of a ger is about 250kg, without furniture. In early summer, you may see many nomadic families taking their gers and all their worldly goods and animals for several hundred kilometres in search of better water, fodder or weather. Transport has traditionally been by camel or yak, but trucks are more common these days.

Ger Etiquette

It is considered poor form to knock on the brightly decorated or painted doors of the ger. Instead, you should call out *'Nokhoi khor'*, which roughly translates to 'Can I come in?', but literally means 'Hold the dog!'. To avoid being eaten alive by a vicious and highly protective (and possibly rabid) mongrel, learn how to say this properly.

As you enter the ger take care not to smash your head on the low door frame or step on the hearth. As a guest, move to the left of the ger and take a seat to the left at the back. One of the most important things to remember when you enter a ger is to be confident: feel at home, relax and don't worry if people come and go. Your driver may even take a short nap, which is in no way impolite.

Most gers will have a hospitality plate, usually an aluminium bowl, piled with offerings, ready for any passer-by who drops in. You will almost certainly be offered some dairy products *(tsagaan idee*, literally 'white food'), especially in summer, such as dried cheese, as well as a bowl of milky, salty Mongolian tea, or sometimes a vodka. You should always take what is offered – try not to refuse anything. If you don't like what you have been given, take a small sip or bite (or pretend to) and leave the rest on the table. An empty plate is a sign to the host that the guest is still hungry and the plate or bowl will be refilled. In a Kazakh ger, placing a hand over a plate or bowl simply indicates that you do not want a refill.

An older man may offer his snuffbox to a male visitor, even if you don't have one to exchange. If you want some snuff, empty a tiny portion on your hand, between your (downward-facing) index finger and thumb. Raise your hand to a nostril, take a long, deep inhalation and smile widely. If you don't want any, just go through the motions or just sniff appreciatively at the half-opened lid. If the snuffbox is empty, don't make any comment (it will mean that your host has run out of snuff, or can't afford any) – pretend there is some. Pass back the snuff box in the upturned palm of the right hand.

Conversation always starts with inquiries about your trip and the state of the animals, grazing conditions, the weather etc. After an hour of warming-up you can progress to more personal questions. This is where good guides really comes into their own. Try to keep ger visits to less than two hours to avoid interrupting the family's work.

Do's and Don'ts

Whenever you approach a nomadic family, or enter a ger, you will, without knowing, break one or several of the many traditional, religious and superstitious customs. If you do become confused, don't panic, minor indiscretions will be tolerated and forgiven. The following do's and don'ts will help minimise cultural differences.

Do
- Say hello *(sain bainuul)* when you arrive (but repeating it again when you see the same person is considered strange to Mongolians)
- Take at least a sip, or a nibble, of the delicacies offered
- Keep your sleeves rolled down, if you have any (or pretend to, if you have short sleeves); try not to expose your wrists
- Accept food and drink with your right hand (or with both if the dish or cup is heavy), with the left hand supporting the right elbow
- Pick up everything with an open hand, with your palm facing upwards
- Hold a cup by the bottom, and not by the top rim
- Sleep with your feet pointing towards the door
- Leave weapons outside

Don't
- Lean against a support column
- Whistle inside a ger
- Stand on, or lean over, the threshold
- Stamp out a fire, or put water or any rubbish on it (fire is sacred to Mongolians)
- Walk in front of an older person; or turn your back to the altar, or religious objects (except when leaving)
- Take food from a communal plate with your left hand
- Touch other people's hats
- Have a long conversation in your own language in front of your hosts

Rituals & Superstitions
- Don't write anything in red pen
- Don't point a knife in any way at anyone; pass a knife handle first; use the knife to cut towards you, not away
- Don't spill any milk
- When offered some vodka, dip your ring finger of your right hand into the glass, and lightly flick a drop (not too much – vodka is also sacred!) once towards the sky, once in the air 'to the wind', and once to ground. If you don't want any vodka, go through the customs anyway, put the same finger to your forehead, say thanks, and return the glass to the table.
- Don't point your feet at the hearth, the altar or at another person
- Don't walk over an *uurga*, a lasso on a pole. If you have stepped on anyone, or kicked their feet, immediately shake their hand.

Facts for the Visitor

HIGHLIGHTS

Mongolia has few 'sights' as such, apart from a couple of monasteries and the capital. The country's real attraction lies in the untouched beauty of the countryside, in the exhilarating sense of space and the rich nomadic culture of the Mongolian people.

It is often experiences rather than places that you will remember. Riding with Mongolians on horseback, visiting a ger, the light between 6 and 8 pm when the land shines, camping in the Gobi underneath a star-filled sky and watching the sun set over one of western Mongolia's stunning lakes are all memories that will be hard to shake.

For regional highlights see the 'Highlights' boxed text at the beginning of each chapter.

SUGGESTED ITINERARIES

Mongolia's lack of basic infrastructure like roads and buses means that travel in Mongolia is different from most other countries. Unless you have lots of time (and the visa to back it up) you will only be able to see limited areas on public transport.

The best advice for anyone coming to Mongolia is not to try and pack in every part of Mongolia, otherwise you'll spend most of your time bumping over dirt tracks with your face squished against the window of your jeep. Choose one area, such as Khövsgöl (northern Mongolia), western Mongolia or central Mongolia and spend some time exploring, preferably on horseback, not just by jeep. You'll have a better time this way and you'll discover more about Mongolia.

Most travellers will want at least four days in the pleasant capital, Ulaan Baatar, or longer if arranging a jeep trip.

Hitching & Public Transport

To travel truly independently in the countryside you will probably have to hitch, which is generally safe and a recognised form of transport. It's not all that difficult to get to any *aimag* (province) capital, the problem is that many sites and experiences are away from these dreary places and it's hard to get there by hitching.

From Ulaan Baatar, it is relatively easy to get to Kharkhorin (for the Erdene Zuu monastery) and Khujirt, to Delgerkhaan, to Mörön and Khatgal (but not around the lake Khövsgöl Nuur), to Dalanzadgad (but you will need a jeep to get around the south Gobi), and to the big cities of Erdenet and Darkhan.

Jeep

If you have a private jeep or minivan, and a good driver (driving a jeep yourself around the countryside is not a good idea), four or five trips are recommended:

Central Loop From Ulaan Baatar go to Darkhan, Amarbayasgalant monastery, Erdenet (via Bugant) and then to Mörön, and around the area of the lake Khövsgöl Nuur. From the lake, head south to Terkhiin Tsagaan lake and back to Ulaan Baatar via Tsetserleg, Kharkhorin and the mountain, Khogno Khan Uul. The total distance is about 2000km, and will take a minimum of eight days, but 12 is more realistic, especially if you want to see anything of Khövsgöl Nuur.

The West If you fly to Khovd (or to Ulaangom, and do it in reverse), you can visit Khovd town, Tasmbagarav Uul, Ölgii, Tavanbogd Altai National Park, the lakes of Achit Nuur and Üüreg Nuur, Ulaangom, Uvs Nuur, Kharkhiraa Valley and Khar Us Nuur. This is about 1200km; allow at least a week to see it all.

The East From Ulaan Baatar or Öndörkhaan, travel around the Dariganga district via Baruun Urt, and visit Shiliin Bogd, with its lakes, volcanoes and sand dunes. This will take a week, or add on three or four days and visit the forested birthplace of Chinggis Khaan in Dadal (Khentii).

The Gobi From Ulaan Baatar, head south via Erdenedalai and Ongiin Khiid to Dalanzadgad, and visit Yolyn Am, the sand dunes of Khongoryn Els and the surrounds of the south Gobi. You can then return via Kharkhorin, Khogno Khan Uul and Hustai National Park. Allow at least 10 days. Alternatively, fly straight to and from Dalanzadgad and hire a jeep there for a three- or four-day trip.

To Karakorum From Ulaan Baatar head to Kharkhorin, stopping in Hustai National Park, Khogno Khan Uul, and Mongol Els sand dunes en route (with the option to visit the waterfall Orkhon Khürkhree and Naiman Nuur region) and then back via Ogii Nuur. This can take anywhere from four to seven days.

For an exhausting trip of a month's solid travel, add on the Central Loop to western Mongolia, or join the Gobi with the Central Loop. If you want to go exploring then try the lesser visited Gobi sites of Bayankhongor or Zavkhan or explore Khentii.

Around Ulaan Baatar

If you have limited time and want to base yourself in Ulaan Baatar, you can go on day trips (preferably overnight) by private jeep, or possibly public transport, to such wonderful places as Gachuurt, Khustai National Park, Khogno Khan Uul, Terelj, the monasteries of Manzshir Khiid and Amarbayasgalant Khiid, and Bogdkhan Uul.

Greater Mongolia

One interesting idea is to combine Mongolia with other culturally Mongolian regions in neighbouring China or Russia. Travel from inner Mongolia to outer Mongolia, making a pilgrimage to the Genghis Khan Mausoleum in Dongsheng.

Alternatively head north to Buryatia (Russia), centred around Lake Baikal and the capital Ulan-Ude, or visit the very remote Tuvan Republic further west, which has strong cultural links to Mongolia. For information on these places see Lonely Planet's *Russia, Ukraine & Belarus* guide.

PLANNING
When to Go

The travel season is from May to early October, though Ulaan Baatar can be visited any time of year if you can tolerate the cold. From mid-October to mid-May, sudden snowstorms and extreme cold can ground flights, block roads and cause the transport system to break down completely.

June and September are both very pleasant times to visit. Early July gives you the best weather for the northern part of the country. July and August are the rainiest months, which can make jeep travel on dirt roads difficult. July is also the time to see the Naadam Festival. Unfortunately, this is the peak tourist season, when Ulaan Baatar's inadequate accommodation and creaky transport is stretched to breaking point.

The best time to see the Gobi is September and October. May isn't a bad time though there can be wind storms during this time and weather can be unpredictable.

What Kind of Trip?

This depends on your flexibility and intrepidity, available time and money. An organised tour gives you more comfort and less hassle, but it is inflexible, expensive and you may not see what you really want. That said there are some things and places, such as eagle hunting or camel riding that you cannot see or do any other way. Travelling by public transport will limit your travel unless you are prepared to do some hitching also – but you will still need to hire a jeep to see most attractions.

Easily the best way is to arrive independently, in a group of three or more (to share costs), and stay for at least one month. Bring a tent, sleeping bag and petrol stove from home, hire a jeep or a minivan, with a driver and/or guide in a major city, and bring food from Ulaan Baatar. With this combination, you'll make the most of your trip.

Maps

In 1978 President Tsedenbal decided to double the number of Mongolian place names overnight by giving the district *(sum)* capitals different names to the districts themselves. Slowly, the capitals and districts are reverting to the same name, which is what we use in this guide.

If you are on an organised tour (especially if it's combined with a trip to China), the following maps provide some detail but are not good enough for independent travel: *China & Far East* (1:6,000,000) by Hallway, *China* (1:5,000,000) by Kümmerly &

Frey and *China* (1:6,000,000) by Carto-graphia – the latter is probably the best of the lot.

If you are travelling independently, the best country maps are available in Ulaan Baatar only. The best map for jeep travel is the 1:2.5 million *Road Map of Mongolia* (1999, T4000), with a blue cover. It has the most accurate road layout and town names and usefully marks the kilometres between all towns, so you can work out the distance and approximate cost of jeep hire before you head out.

Another useful tourist map is *Welcome to Mongolia/ Ulaanbaatar City Map* (1999, T5000), which marks a host of obscure his-torical, archaeological and natural sights and has a 1:500,000 insert of Around Ulaan Baatar. The back side has the best available map of Ulaan Baatar, though one version, entitled *Tourist Map of Mongolia* (with a blue cover) lacks the city map so make sure you get the right one.

Explorers will want to check out the 1:500,000 series of topographic maps, which cover Mongolia in eight maps. There is also a 1:250,000 series but these are essentially the same maps blown up. The topographic maps are particularly useful if you are travelling by horse or foot, or using a GPS (global positioning system), but at T11,300 a pop, or T90,500 for the set, they are too expensive for long-distance touring (plus the roads are not as accurately marked as the *Road Map of Mongolia*).

All these maps are available from the Map Shop in Ulaan Baatar (see Maps & Guides under Orientation in the Ulaan Baatar chapter). They also stock a detailed 1:500,000 topographic (Cyrillic) map of the Khövsgöl Nuur region (T4000), a useful 1:100,000 *Guide Map to Harhorum* (T1500) and a 1:200,000 topographic map (1997) of the Ulaan Baatar region, which includes Terelj and Bogd Khan Uul. The other aimag maps are generally not as useful.

Chinggis Khaan junkies will want to check out the *Chinggis Khaan Atlas*, avail-able around Ulaan Baatar for around T8000, which maps his every presumed movement in obsessive detail.

In many Western countries, you can buy the ONC and TPC series of topographical maps published by the Defense Mapping Agency Aerospace Center in the USA. The maps are topographically detailed but dated and are not reliable for place names or road layout. Mongolia is covered by ONC (1: 1 million) and TPC (1:500,000) map Nos E-7, E-8, F-7 and F-8.

For these and other maps of Mongolia try the following map shops abroad:

Edward Stanford Ltd (☎ 020-7836 1321, fax 7836 0189) 12-14 Long Acre, Convent Garden, London WC2E 9LP, UK
Galaxy of Maps (☎ 1-800-388 6588, fax 954 267 9007, **e** sales@galaxymaps.com) Fort Lauderdale, Florida, USA
GeoCenter ILH (☎ 0711-788 93 40, fax 788 93 54, **e** geocenterilh@t-online.de) Schocken-riedstrasse 44, D-70565 Stuttgart, Germany
Map Link (☎ 805-965 4402, fax 962 0884 **e** custserv@maplink.com) 30 S La Patera Lane, Unit 5, Santa Barbara, CA 93117, USA

What to Bring

As with most travel, bring as little as you can, though if you intend to hire a jeep you won't have much difficulty hauling your stuff around. Remember that you have a 15kg weight limit for domestic flights. Camping equipment is more useful to have in Mongolia than in most other countries and it's worth considering even if you are not a gung-ho survivalist.

Backpacks Before deciding what to bring, think about what you are going to carry it in. If you decide to base yourself in Ulaan Baatar and use buses or planes to get to the provinces, then you can leave a lot of gear securely in the luggage room of your hotel or guest house and take only what you need.

A backpack is still the most convenient bag and is the only choice if you have to do any walking. However, a backpack is awk-ward to load on and off buses and trains, and doesn't offer much protection against theft. Rather than the 'open top' design, a backpack with zipped and lockable com-partments is best. Backpacks get really trashed in Mongolia so bring a couple of heavy duty plastic bags to protect your gear against dust, oil and rain etc.

Clothes There are no special dress codes, though you should avoid wearing revealing clothes in the countryside, even on hot summer days. In Ulaan Baatar on the other hand, Mongolian women dress in contemporary Western-style fashions, so you may dress quite freely whilst there.

Warm clothes will be needed for any time of the year: even summer evenings can be chilly. If you are only travelling in the height of summer you don't need a down jacket – a rain shell will do. A long-sleeved shirt is useful against the sun and bugs. A good wide-brimmed hat to protect you from the sun is essential. Women travellers have suggested bringing sports bras for bumpy jeep rides.

From September to June (inclusive) you'll also need a down coat and a fleece or jumper (sweater) – it's surprising how cold it gets when the sun goes down and the wind picks up. A woollen or fleece hat takes up little space and makes a considerable difference, as most heat loss occurs through your head.

In winter bring the warmest clothes you have, including thermal underwear, ski mask, mittens, scarf and thermal boots.

Camping Gear An important decision, whether you are camping or not, is whether to bring a sleeping bag. If you are on an organised tour during the summer and staying in *ger* (traditional circular felt yurt) camps, it is not necessary. A sleeping bag is vital, however, if you are travelling independently in the countryside on any form of transport (breakdowns are inevitable) or if you are in Mongolia between October and May (when heating in hotels often fails).

A tent offers you far more flexibility and is a worthy alternative to the lousy choice of hotels in the provinces. Tents are available cheaply in Beijing and Ulaan Baatar but the quality is not great. A few tents are available for rent in Ulaan Baatar but, again, the quality is poor. An inflatable or foam mat is important as it provides an important layer

between you and the ground – without one a down sleeping bag is far less effective.

A portable stove to cook your own food, rather than rely on the bland and tasteless stuff served in restaurants in the countryside, is definitely worth considering. Take a petrol stove because petrol is the only fuel widely available. For any other type of stove, you will have to bring your own fuel, which is often dangerous and illegal to carry on planes. Gas canisters are only available in Beijing and can be used if you are travelling to Mongolia by train.

Fishing equipment is always useful, even if it's just a handline and some lures.

Other camping necessities include:

- cup, bowl (most camping meals will be thick soups or stews so a deep bowl or mess kit is more useful than a plate), cutlery, knife, water bottle (a metal one can hold boiling water and double as a hot water bottle)
- abrasive sponge for cleaning, cloth (for cleaning and as a picnic table cloth), torch, tape to fix broken tent poles or fabric tears, mosquito net, mosquito repellent

Miscellaneous Basic toiletries are available in Ulaan Baatar and at most markets in provincial capitals, but the quality and choice will be inferior to what you may be used to. There's no need to bring bottles of shampoo – use the individual sachets available in the markets. Resealable bags are useful for transporting opened packets or jars, washing powder or coffee.

If you are taking a long-distance jeep trip or camping, consider clever little luxuries like Wet Wipes, anti-bacterial gel and dry leaves of soap, as there won't be much washing en route. A bandanna or headscarf is useful to keep off the Gobi dust.

You don't have to bring basic foodstuffs these days but a few luxuries like instant sauces and, especially, spices can be a lifesaver. Empty film canisters serve as good salt and pepper containers if the lids are tight. Multivitamins are a good idea as is high factor sun screen, which is very hard to find in Mongolia or China. Bring some

Responsible Tourism

To ensure that independent travellers are encouraged by Mongolian authorities and accepted by the nomadic people, two vital factors should be taken into account.

Firstly, hospitality is an old custom on the steppes, where distances are great; visitors are always invited in without question on arrival at a distant ger. While you should enjoy Mongolia's unique hospitality, please do not take advantage of it. We continue to hear disturbing reports about travellers staying for weeks or months in gers around the country without contributing to their upkeep, or paying (in money or kind) for their accommodation or food.

Secondly, Mongolia's environment, flora and fauna are precious. Decades of Soviet exploitation, urban sprawl and development have greatly affected the ecology; Mongolia does not need the detriment of tourism to exacerbate the problems. If you are travelling independently in the countryside, please bear in mind the considerable impact that the thoughtless deeds of one person can have on a forest, grassland, water supply, fossils site, mountain or desert. Please bear the following pointers in mind as you travel around Mongolia:

• In protected areas or areas of natural beauty try to keep to existing jeep tracks rather than pioneering new trails, which quickly degenerate into an eroded mess and take decades to disappear.
• Patronise travel companies and ger camps which you feel advance sustainable development, safe waste management, water conservation and fair employment practices.
• Don't buy goods made from endangered species.
• Observe any rules and regulations particular to the national or state reserve that you are visiting. Acquaint yourself with local customs and dress appropriately.
• Don't disturb animals that you come across and definitely don't chase them.
• Don't pay to take a photo of someone, nor photograph someone if they don't want you to. If you agree to send someone a photograph, please follow through on this.
• Don't spend all your money with one company (easily done on a tour) but spread your money through the economy. Support local services and guides and initiatives.
• Acquaint yourself with local customs and dress appropriately.

iodine or water purification tablets to treat water in the countryside.

See the boxed text 'Ger Welcome Gifts' later in this chapter for ideas about gifts to give to families who open their homes up to you. Photos of your family (but not including displays of wealth, such as expensive homes, cars or furniture) go down well. Drivers often like stickers or air fresheners for their jeep or van. In the cities, some Mongolians are trying to learn English and appreciate foreign magazines, books or newspapers, especially if written simply.

Song books, any kind of musical instrument, or just the lyrics to some favourite songs are useful because you'll often be asked to sing or play something. Birders and animal lovers should bring a pair of binoculars. A short wave radio is useful to find out what is happening in the rest of the world.

Other essential items include candles for blackouts in the countryside, a torch for museums without electricity, a one or two litre leak-proof water bottle, mosquito repellent with as much DEET as can be squeezed in the bottle, and sticky tape to hold your maps together (and even to repair your jeep!). Insect repellent is almost impossible to get in Mongolia and is hard to find in Beijing.

The following is a comprehensive checklist of other things to consider packing when travelling, especially if you intend to go hiking:

US dollars cash, money belt, emergency space blanket, writing paper and envelopes, pens, sticky tape, spare passport photos, Swiss army knife, coffee, tea, sweetener, padlock, chain (to padlock your pack to buses, hotel rooms etc), spare camera batteries, film, torch (flashlight) with extra bulbs and batteries, lighter, compass, razor, razor blades, shaving cream, sewing kit, sun hat, sunscreen (UV) lotion, sunglasses, chap stick, Vaseline, tampons, dental floss, deodorant, ear plugs, multivitamins, painkillers, laxatives, medical kit (see the Health section later in this chapter), contact lens solution, plastic bags and twist ties.

TOURIST OFFICES
Local Tourist Offices
Juulchin, once the sole agency responsible for the entire tourist industry, has now been privatised. It is just another travel agency, but still the biggest (see Travel Agencies in the Ulaan Baatar chapter). For a list of overseas offices see the Getting There & Away chapter. Despite a recent change of government and shake-up of ministries, there is still no dedicated government tourist department.

The Mongolian National Tourism Center (see Tourist Offices under Information in the Ulaan Baatar chapter) is a government agency and is not available for advice and information, but it does plan to open some kind of tourism information centre in Ulaan Baatar in the near future. Until then, you will have to rely on local travel agencies, guesthouse owners, guides and not very knowledgeable hotel staff.

Tourist Offices Abroad
Mongolia also has no official tourist offices abroad. For information about the country, contact a local embassy, consulate or honorary consulate; write to one of the various friendship organisations (see Useful Organisations later in this chapter); get on the Internet (see Internet Resources); or ring one of the specialised travel agents abroad listed in the Getting There & Away chapter.

VISAS & DOCUMENTS
Passport
A passport is essential, and it must have more than six months of validity left. Also, be sure that it has at least a few blank pages for visas and entry and exit stamps. Losing your passport in Mongolia is very bad news indeed, so try not to do it. If your country has an embassy in Ulaan Baatar, it's a good idea to register there in case of an accident or lost passport.

Visas
Currently, a 30-day tourist visa is easily obtained at any Mongolian consulate, consulate-general or honorary consulate.

To get a visa for longer than 30 days, you must be invited or sponsored by a Mongolian, a foreign resident or a Mongolian company, or be part of an organised tour from a Mongolian or foreign travel agency.

If you absolutely cannot get to a Mongolian consulate, it is theoretically possible to get a 30-day tourist visa on arrival at Ulaan Baatar airport. To do this you will need an invitation from a Mongolian travel company. It's best that a representative from this company meets you at the airport on arrival to liaise with visa officials.

It is also theoretically possible to get a visa at the land entry points at Zamyn-Uud and Sükhbaatar train stations, though until this becomes common practice you are better off using this as a last resort only. For both land border visas and on-arrival airport visas you will need US$50 and two passport photos.

Polish citizens do not require visas for a stay of up to 90 days, Israeli and Malaysian citizens can stay visa-free for up to 30 days and Hong Kong and Singaporean citizens can stay visa-free for up to 14 days.

Several sources and even embassies claim that foreigners who stay in Mongolia for longer than 90 days need to take a HIV test, but this rule seems widely ignored and no expat we talked to had to take such a test.

To check current regulations, try the Web site of the Ministry of External Relations at www.extmin.mn.

Tourist Visas Standard tourist visas generally last 30 days from the date of entry and you must enter Mongolia within three months of issue. Tourist visas cost US$25 for a single entry/exit (US$50 for a double), though there is often a service fee which jacks up the price to US$45 in the US and £25 in the UK. Visas normally take several days, or even up to two weeks, to issue. If you want your visas quicker, possibly within 24 hours, you will have to pay an 'express fee', which is double the normal cost.

If you want a tourist visa for longer than 30 days you will need to arrange for a travel agency to invite you. Your sponsor will need to know your full name; date and place of birth; country of citizenship; passport number, date and place of issue and expiry date; your date of arrival and departure; and a general itinerary. They must send your invitation to the Ministry of External Relations in Ulaan Baatar. If accepted, a copy will be sent from the ministry to your designated embassy or consulate, where you fill out a visa application form and hand over your cash. Try to get a copy of your invitation if possible.

If this seems too much hassle, remember that 30-day tourist visas are easily extendible by 30 days in Ulaan Baatar. The only snag is that you'll probably have to return to the capital to do this.

Multiple entry/exit tourist visas (which cost US$65 and are valid for six months after the date of issue) are usually only issued to foreign residents who do a lot of travel.

Mongolian honorary consulates (see www.extmin.mn for a list) can issue transit visas and non-extendable tourist visas but only for 14 days from the date of entry. Importantly, they often issue visas without requiring a sponsor or invitation. However, these visas are for entry only; they cannot issue normal entry/exit visas, so you will have to spend some of your precious time in Ulaan Baatar arranging an exit visa from the ministry.

Transit Visas These visas last 48 hours (sometimes 72 hours) from the date of entry. This will only allow you to get off the Trans-Mongolian train for a very short time before catching another train to Russia or China. A single entry/exit transit visa costs US$15 (US$30 for double), but cannot be extended. You will need to show the train or plane ticket and a visa for the next country (Russia or China).

Visa Extensions If you have a 30-day tourist visa you can extend it by another 30 days. If you are lucky and can rustle up an invitation letter you can theoretically extend it by a second 30 days, but this can be difficult.

For extensions, go to the Ministry of External Relations, on Enkh Taivny Örgön Chölöö; it is the grey building just south of Sükhbaatar Square. The consular department, where you will have to wrestle with the visa people, is at the back (enter from the southern door). The office is open weekdays from 9.30 am to noon.

You should apply for an extension about a week before your visa expires. It officially costs US$15 for the first seven days and a further US$2 per day for a maximum of 30 days (which therefore costs a total of US$61). You will need a passport-sized photo. It should take two or three days to process. Several guesthouses in Ulaan Baatar will take care of visa extensions (and registration) for a small fee.

Exit Visas Transit and tourist visas are good for one entry and one exit (unless you have a double or multiple entry/exit visa). If you are working in Mongolia, or if you obtained your visa at an honorary consulate, you are usually issued a single-entry visa (valid for one entry only). In this case, another visa is required to leave the country. These visas are available from the Ministry of External Relations, involve the same procedures as an extension and cost US$20.

Registration If you intend to stay in Mongolia for more than 30 days you must register with the police in Ulaan Baatar within 10 days of arriving in the country.

Registration is not difficult, but it can be a confusing process. You must go to the last room on the right on the 3rd floor of the Police Registration Office (☎ 327 182), officially known as the Citizens Registration and Information Bureau, about 1km north of the corner of Ikh Toiruu and Erkhuugiin Gudamj, on the right-hand side of the road. Outside the building is a small sign that reads 'Government Council for Foreign

Citizens Issui' in English (*'Zasgiin gazryn gadaadyn irgediin asuudal erkhlekh zövlöl'* in Mongolian).

The registration form is in Mongolian, but some of the staff speak enough English to help you. In theory European and American citizens are served at the window to the right; all others to the left. After you get the form you need to go downstairs to pay the T500 fee at the Golomt Bank, get a receipt and go back to the third floor. Bring a copy of your invitation (if possible), one passport-size photo and your passport. The whole process takes about 30 minutes if it's not too busy. Your Mongolian visa is marked with a registration stamp. Most guesthouses can rustle up an invitation for you if you require one.

If you only have a 30-day tourist visa the office will not register you until you have extended your visa.

Before you leave Mongolia you need to 'close' your registration, which means going back to the registration office to get a second stamp on your visa. If you don't register, or close your registration you are liable for a fine (theoretically from US$40 to US$75) when you leave the country.

Travel Permits

Several border areas require permits, either from the police in the aimag capital or from the local border guards. These include Dariganga and Shiliin Bogd in Sükhbaatar aimag; Khalkhiin Gol and Nomrog Strictly Protected Area in Dornod; Altai Tavanbogd National Park in Bayan-Ölgii; north of Dadal in Khentii; and parts of the Darkhat Depression in Kövsgöl. See the relevant chapters for more details. The general rule is that you should check with border police whenever you head within 30km of the border.

Once you have registered with the Ulaan Baatar police, they will tell you that you need to pay T1000 for a permit that allows you to travel in the countryside. This is easily done and probably worth getting but the permit is fairly useless. No-one will check it and most permits are only valid for Töv and Arkhangai aimag anyway.

National Parks Foreigners need permits to visit the various 'strictly protected areas' and national parks around the country, though these are little more than entrance fees and can be bought on the spot. Details are under Protected Areas in the Flora & Fauna section of Facts about Mongolia.

Mountain Climbing Despite what some agencies may tell you, permits are not required to climb any mountain unless it is in a designated national park. See the Activities section later in this chapter for more details.

Travel Insurance

If ever there was a country where you needed travel insurance, Mongolia is it. With the outdoor lifestyle, unpredictable weather and bad roads, accidents are not uncommon. Virtually no travel agency, hotel or ger camp in the whole country has any insurance, including public liability, so you will be liable for all costs incurred from any accident. If that is not enough, Air China or MIAT (Mongolian Airlines) may lose your luggage.

Some policies offer lower and higher medical-expense options; the higher ones are chiefly for countries such as the USA, which have extremely high medical costs. If you're a frequent traveller it's possible to get year-round insurance at reasonable rates. Agencies like Council Travel, Trailfinders, Flight Centre and Campus Travel sell insurance along with tickets. There is a wide variety of policies available, so check the small print.

Some policies specifically exclude 'dangerous activities', which can include mountaineering, horse riding and even trekking. If these are on your agenda, ask about an amendment to permit some of them (at a higher premium).

Few, if any, medical services in Mongolia will accept your foreign insurance documents for payment; you'll have to pay on the spot, get receipts for everything, save all the paperwork, and claim later.

For Mongolia, a 'medivac' clause or policy, covering the costs of being flown to

Beijing, Hong Kong or home for treatment, is essential: staying in a Mongolian hospital will probably only make you get worse.

Student Cards & Other Documents

Student cards are of little or no help in Mongolia, though some travellers have reported using them to get discounts on fines.

It's a good idea to carry a driver's licence or any ID card with your photo on it – some embassies want this before issuing a replacement passport. Any document with your photo on it is a very useful alternative to handing over your passport to the hotel receptionist when you check in. If you are game enough to drive your own vehicle in the country, an international driving licence is required.

If you're thinking about working in Mongolia, or anywhere else along the way, photocopies of university diplomas, transcripts and letters of recommendation could prove helpful – especially if translated into Mongolian. Also useful, though not essential, is an International Health Certificate to record your vaccinations.

Copies

All important documents (passport data page and visa page, credit cards, travel insurance policy, air/train tickets, driving licence etc) should be photocopied before you leave home. Leave one copy with someone at home and keep another with you, separate from the originals.

It's also a good idea to store details of your vital travel documents in Lonely Planet's free online Travel Vault in case you lose the photocopies or can't be bothered with them. Your password-protected Travel Vault is accessible online anywhere in the world – create it at www.ekno.lonely planet.com.

EMBASSIES & CONSULATES
Mongolian Embassies & Consulates

Mongolia has a few embassies which can issue entry/exit visas and provide some limited tourist information.

Australia
Honorary Consulate: (☎/fax 02-9966 1922, or ☎ 02-9966 1916, e monconoz@yahoo.com) Level 10, 80 Mount St, North Sydney NSW 2060, PO Box 1731, North Sydney NSW 2060. The Web site at www.acay.com.au/~sckscp /moncon has downloadable visa forms.
Belgium
Embassy: (☎ 2-344 6974, fax 344 3215, e embassy.mongolia@skynet.be) 18 Ave Besme, 1190 Forset, Brussels
Canada
Consulate-General: (☎ 416-865 7779, fax 863 1515, e consulgen@mongolia.org) BCE Place, Suite 1800, PO Box 754, 181 Bay St, Toronto, Ontario M5J 2T9
China
Embassy: (☎ 10-6532 1203, fax 6532 5045, e monembbj@public3.bta.net.cn) 2 Xiushui Beilu, Jianguomenwai Dajie, Beijing (See the boxed text 'Beijing Stopover Survival Information' in the Getting There & Away chapter for more information.)
Consulate: (☎ 471-430 3254, fax 430 3250) Xincheng Gu Wulanxiagu, Bldg No 5, Hohhot, Inner Mongolia
Czech Republic
Embassy: (☎ 2-2431 1198, fax 2431 4287, monemb@bohem-net.cz) Na Marne 5, Prague-6, 160000
France
Embassy: (☎ 01 46 05 23 18, fax 01 46 05 30 16, e 106513.2672@compuserve.com) 5 Ave Robert Schumann, 92100 Boulogne, Billancourt
Germany
Consulate: (☎ 30-446 9320, fax 446 9321, e mongolbot@aol.com) Gotlandstrasse 12, 10439, Berlin
Japan
Embassy: (☎ 33-469 2088, fax 469 2216, e embmong@gol.com) 21-4 Kamiya-cho Shibuya-ku, Tokyo 150
Kazakhstan
Embassy: (☎ 3272-200 865, fax 293 259, e monkazel@kazmail.asdc.kz) Ul Aubakerova 1/1
Netherlands
Honorary Consulate (fax 020-644 9638) Notarissen De Cuserstraat 5, 1081 CK Amsterdam-Buitenveldert, Postbus 791094, 1008 88 Amsterdam
Poland
Embassy: (☎ 22-849 9391, fax 849 9391, e mongamb@ikp.atm.com.pl) 00478 Warsawa, ul Rejtana, 15 m 16

Russia
Embassy: (☎ 95-290 6792, fax 291 6171, ✉ mongolia@glasnet.ru) Borisoglebskaya pereulok 11, Moscow. The embassy is close to the Smolenskaya metro station. The consular section (☎ 244 7867) for visas is on Spasopeskovsky pereoluk 7, and is open weekdays from 9 am to 1 pm. Single entry/exit transit visas cost US$15, and can be collected the same day (between 4.30 and 5.30 pm) if you pay double. Single entry/exit tourist visas cost US$25, or US$50 for the 'express' service.
Consulate: (☎ 3952-342 145, fax 342 143, ✉ irconsul@angara.ru) ulitsa Lapina 11, Irkutsk
Consulate: (☎ 3012-220 499, fax 214 188, ✉ mnc@bss.ru) Hotel Baikal, ulitsa Erbanova-12, Ulan-Ude

South Korea
Embassy: (☎ 2-794 1350, fax 794 7605, ✉ monemb@uriel.net)
33-5 Hannam-Dong Yongsan-gu, Seoul

Sweden
Honorary Consulate: (☎/fax 31-160 770)
Gotabergsgatan 34, S-411 34, Goteborg

Switzerland
Consulate & UN Representative: (☎ 22-774 1974, fax 774 3201, ✉ mongolia@ties.itu.int)
4 chemin des Mollies, 1293 Bellevue, Geneva

UK
Embassy: (☎ 020-7937 0150, fax 7937 1117, ✉ embmong@aol.com) 7 Kensington Court, London W8 5DL

USA
Embassy: (☎ 202-333 7117, fax 298 9227, ✉ monconsul@aol.com) 2833 Main St NW, Washington, DC 20007. The Web site at www.mongolnet.com has downloadable visa forms.
Consulate & UN Representative: (☎ 212-472 6517, fax 861 9464, ✉ mngun@un.int) 6 East 77th St, New York, NY 10021

For details of other embassies and consulates, see the Web site of the Ministry of External Relations at www.extmin.mn.

Embassies in Mongolia

A few countries operate embassies in Ulaan Baatar, though for most nationalities, the nearest embassies are in Beijing and/or Moscow. If your country has an embassy in Ulaan Baatar, it's a good idea to register with it if you're travelling into the remote countryside, or in case you lose your passport.

Canada (☎ 328 281, fax 328 289) Suite 56, Diplomatic Services Corps Bldg, Bldg 95

China (☎ 320 955, fax 311 943) 5 Zaluuchuudyn Örgön Chölöö. The consular section, to the left of the embassy's front gate, is a good place to get a visa for China. It is open from 9.30 am to noon Monday, Wednesday and Friday. Transit visas (single or double entry) last up to seven days from each entry; single and double tourist visas are valid for 30 days from the date of each entry and you must enter China within 90 days of issuing the visa. Single/double entry tourist visas cost US$30/60 and take a week to issue. For three-day or same-day service, you'll have to fork out an extra US$50 or US$60. You must pay in US dollars.

Czech Republic (☎ 321 886) Gate 5, Diplomatic Services Corps Bldg

France (☎ 324 519, fax 329 633) Apartment 48, Diplomatic Services Corps Bldg

Germany (☎ 323 325, fax 323 905) 7 Negdsen Undestnii Gudamj. This embassy also looks after the interests of Spanish, Dutch, Belgian Austrian, Greek and Portuguese citizens.

Japan (☎ 320 777, 313 332) Olympiin Gudamj 6

Kazakhstan (☎ 312 240) Diplomatic Services Corps Bldg

Russia (☎ 326 037, fax 324 425) A6, Enkh Taivny Örgön Chölöö. If at all possible get your Russian visa somewhere else; getting it here will give you severe headaches. The consular section is open for visas daily from 2 to 3 pm; pick up time is from 11.15 am to 12.30 pm. At the time of research a Russian visa costs approximately US$15 for a transit visa and US$25 for a tourist visa. You will need three photos and an invitation or sponsor. A visa normally takes two days to issue or, if 'urgent', it can be issued on the spot for double the normal cost. The embassy will also issue visas for former Soviet Central Asian republics which are not represented individually.

South Korea (☎ 321 548, fax 311 157) Olympiin Gudamj 10

UK (☎ 458 133, fax 358 036, ✉ britemb@magic net.mn) 30 Enkh Taivny Örgön Chölöö. Handles normal consular duties for all Commonwealth countries (except India).

USA (☎ 329 095, fax 320 776, ✉ cons@us embassy.mn) Ikh Toiruu 59/1.
Web site: www.us-mongolia.com.

Other countries with embassies in Ulaan Baatar include Bulgaria (☎ 322 841), Cuba (☎ 323 778), Hungary (☎ 323 973), India

(☎ 329 522), Laos (☎ 320 972), Turkey (☎ 311 200), Vietnam (☎ 358 917) and Yugoslavia (☎ 322 380).

Your Own Embassy

It's important to realise what your own embassy – the embassy of the country of which you are a citizen – can and can't do to help you if you get into trouble. Generally speaking, it won't be much help in emergencies if the trouble you're in is remotely your own fault. Remember that you are bound by the laws of the country you are in. Your embassy will not be sympathetic if you end up in jail after committing a crime locally, even if such actions are legal in your own country.

In genuine emergencies you might get some assistance, but only if other channels have been exhausted. For example, if you need to get home urgently, a free ticket home is exceedingly unlikely – the embassy would expect you to have insurance. If you have all your money and documents stolen, it might assist with getting a new passport, but a loan for onward travel is out of the question.

CUSTOMS

Customs officials want to keep out pornography, drugs and expensive imports that might be sold to Mongolians; and want to keep in old paintings, statues, fossils, works of art and mineral samples. Baggage searches of foreigners exiting Mongolia by air are sometimes rigorous, but rarely so at border crossings by train to China or Russia, when most passengers are asleep.

If you are legally exporting any antiques, you must have a receipt and customs certificate from the place you bought them. Most reliable shops in Ulaan Baatar can provide this. If you don't get one of these you'll need to get one from the Department of Culture (☎ 320 024) at the Ministry of Enlightenment in Ulaan Baatar (behind the Ulaan Baatar Hotel). You'll need to fill in a form giving your passport number, where the antique was purchased and two photos of the antique itself.

If you have anything which even *looks* old, it is a good idea to get a document to indicate that it is not an antique. That goes for Buddha images and statues as well.

During your trip you will probably be offered furs of rare animals, antique items like snuffboxes, bits and pieces from the Erdene Zuu monastery, and even fossilised dinosaur bones and eggs. Locals will only sell these things as long as foreigners buy them, so please do not buy anything rare, old or precious to Mongolia's history. The fine for illegally exporting fossils is from US$100 to US$150, or five years in jail.

When you enter Mongolia, you must fill out an English-language Customs Declaration form to declare any prohibited items, all precious stones and all 'dutiable goods'. You are also asked to list all 'money instruments' – ie currencies – which you bring into the country. There is no need to be too accurate; this form is not checked on your way out. You should, nevertheless, keep all receipts when you change money at banks, though changing money with licensed moneychangers (who will not issue receipts) is legal.

The Customs Declaration is checked by the customs official and then returned to you. When you leave Mongolia, you will be asked to hand in the form – so keep it safe during your trip.

You can bring one litre of spirits, two litres of wine, three litres of beer and 200 cigarettes into Mongolia duty-free.

MONEY

In a nutshell, take US dollar travellers cheques for security; have some US dollars (or major Asian and European currencies) to change for better rates in Ulaan Baatar; use Mongolian currency in the country almost exclusively; and take a credit card for emergency cash advances in Ulaan Baatar, or for top-end hotels and any flights *from* Ulaan Baatar.

Currency

The currency of Mongolia is called the *tögrög* (it is normally written as T, but is sometimes written as Tg). There used to be 100 *mongo* to the tögrög, but years of hyper-inflation put the mongo out of circulation. Banknotes are issued in denominations of 1, 3, 5, 10, 20, 50, 100, 500, 1000, 5000 and 10,000 – all marked with the faces of either the ubiquitous Chinggis Khaan or Damdin Sükhbaatar. The smallest bills can be lacking in some shops, especially the countryside, so you may find you get your change in the form of sweets or sticks of chewing gum.

Mongolian law states that all transactions must be made in tögrög and not in US dollars. Excepted are companies and individuals with special permits, such as airlines and major travel agencies. All hotels have to accept tögrög, but most tourist ger camps continue to accept US dollars, albeit illegally.

Prices in this guide are generally quoted in tögrög; at the time of research the rate was around T1000 to the US dollar. US dollars are quoted when payment is required in that currency.

Exchange Rates

The following currencies (cash only, except for US dollar travellers cheques) are convertible in Ulaan Baatar. The exchange rates in July 2000 were:

country	unit		tögrög
Canada	C$1	=	T708
China	Y1	=	T126
France	FF10	=	T1500
Germany	DM1	=	T505
Italy	10 Lira	=	T51
Japan	¥100	=	T970
Russia	R1	=	T37
Switzerland	SFr1	=	T628
UK	UK£1	=	T1582
USA	US$1	=	T1050

Exchanging Money

Cash At several banks and countless licensed moneychangers in Ulaan Baatar, you can change most major European and Asian currencies. The US greenback is still the easiest to change in Ulaan Baatar, and is the only currency you might be able to change in the countryside.

Note that moneychangers (see the entry in this section later) will give you slightly

better rates for new (ie, post-1996) US dollar bills and for higher denominations (US$50 and US$100). US dollar bills dated pre-1988 are difficult to exchange anywhere. In the countryside however anything larger than a US$20 will be hard to change. You can change US dollar travellers cheques into US cash in Ulaan Baatar for 2% commission.

American dollars can sometimes be changed for tögrög at banks in aimag capitals but it is bound to take forever as officials try to find out the exchange rate, which is likely to be considerably lower than in the capital.

Watch out for counterfeit American dollar bills in Mongolia. In June 2000 the sum of US$1,000,000 was confiscated at Darkhan, and bills were subsequently confiscated in Ulaan Baatar. The fake notes are so far all US$100 bills.

Travellers Cheques Most major banks and top-end hotels in Ulaan Baatar will change travellers cheques – but only those in US dollars and from major companies – into tögrög, usually with no commission and with the minimum of fuss. Travellers cheques are useless for any transactions in Mongolia and cannot be changed anywhere outside the capital city.

If you lose your American Express travellers cheques or credit card, or Thomas

Mongolia's Currencies

Mongolia's various rulers have ensured a constant change of currencies. During Chinggis Khaan's time, coins in use, *sükh*, made from gold and silver, were used as currency. During the Manchurian rule, Chinese currency was used, but Mongolian traders preferred to use Russian gold, British notes and goods such as tea, silk and furs.

In 1925, four years after independence from China, the tögrög was first introduced. At that time, one tögrög was worth US$0.88 cents; by 1928, one tögrög was worth up to US$52! Currently, about 1000 tögrög are worth just US$1.

Do not lean against a support pole when inside a *ger*!

Lollipop overload!

A family dressed in *del*, Uvs

The motorbike has replaced the horse for many Mongolians.

A view of Gandantegchinlen Khiid, Ulaan Baatar

A monk at Gandan Khiid

A theatre performer prepares for the stage, Ulaan Baatar.

Airag sales from a truck

Loovuuz (hats) up for grabs

'Welcome to Mongolia', downtown Ulaan Baatar

Chess matches on a street corner in Ulaan Baatar

Sükhbaatar, the people's hero

Cook travellers cheques, contact the Trade & Development Bank in Ulaan Baatar. Although it's not the representative of these companies (the nearest office for both is in Beijing), it will start the ball rolling for replacements.

Credit Cards You can use Visa, MasterCard, American Express and sometimes Diners' Club cards in Ulaan Baatar at top-end hotels, expensive souvenir shops, all airline offices and most travel agencies. With the exception of the souvenir shop at Erdene Zuu, you won't be able to buy anything on credit anywhere outside the capital.

The Trade & Development Bank in Ulaan Baatar can arrange US dollar cash advances on your Visa, MasterCard and American Express cards for a 4% commission (no commission for American Express). The process takes only around 15 minutes. You cannot buy tögrög with a credit card – you'll have to get US dollars, then convert them into tögrög (no commission).

International Transfers These days Mongolia is awash with aid workers, missionaries, traders, consultants and big corporations, all sending money in and out, so currency transactions are no longer a mystery to bank clerks. But don't be too surprised if things go awry. Whatever you do, have the money sent in US dollars.

The Trade & Development Bank in Ulaan Baatar (3rd floor) can efficiently arrange transfers of money to/from Mongolia. Transfers take three to five days and cost US$40, plus 0.01% of the amount transferred. The bank can give you a list of their correspondent banks abroad, which include Midland Bank, NatWest Bank, Bank of Tokyo, Bank of China, Credit Lyonnais, Deutsche Bank and Chase Manhattan Bank.

Moneychangers Licensed moneychangers have made the black market obsolete; and in Ulaan Baatar moneychangers will often give you about a 2% better exchange rate than banks for cash and also change a wider range of currencies. The chances of being ripped off by licensed moneychangers are slim.

At some shops and most markets in aimag capitals, and at Darkhan and Erdenet (and possibly at tourist ger camps), you can normally find someone to change US dollars, as well as Chinese yuan and Russian roubles in areas close to the respective borders. However, take all the tögrög you need from Ulaan Baatar as you cannot rely on always finding moneychangers in the countryside (and the rates are always lower).

Security

At some point in a trip through Mongolia most travellers end up carrying a fair amount of US dollars or tögrög; all you can do is bury it deeply in a money belt and in several different places, with only small sums in wallets and outside pockets. At exchange kiosks have your US dollars in hand and don't go fumbling in your money belt in full view.

Costs

If you are travelling on an organised tour you will probably pay around US$100 per day (more for extra luxuries), plus transport fare to Mongolia. You can travel independently and see the same sights and stay in the same places as an organised tour for about US$80 per day. If you share the cost of a private jeep or minivan and camp rather than stay in expensive ger camps you can

The Relative Value of Money

The tögrög was fairly stable at the time of research and so tögrög prices are generally quoted in this book, except for ger camps and flight tickets, which are priced in US dollars (and converted into tögrög at the rate of the day). You can expect the tögrög to fall over time and so prices in this book are an indication more of *relative* than absolute values, based on an exchange rate of around T1000 to the US dollar. Jeeps rates, for example, are bound to rise from T300 per km, but should remain around US$0.30.

bring this down to around US$30 to US$40 per day.

Accommodation and food will cost at least US$10 per day in Ulaan Baatar, but allow up to US$20 per day for half-decent accommodation, some tastier, Western meals and trips to the theatre and museums. If you are hitching and using public transport around the countryside, allow about US$10 to US$15 per day. If you take a tent and camp, and especially if you have a portable petrol stove, you will be hard-pressed to spend more than about US$7 per day.

Dual-Pricing Thirty per cent of Mongolians earn less than US$20 a month and many services are subsidised to take this into account, so try to understand why westerners are expected to pay more than Mongolians for some things. In any case, travelling independently around Mongolia is still far cheaper than doing it in your own country, and in most other countries in the region.

In general tourists pay around double the Mongolian rate for theatre tickets and hotels and five to seven times more for (subsidised) internal airline tickets. National parks charge foreigners 10 times the local price but at least this goes to some form of conservation. During the Naadam Festival, hotels and guesthouses will often hike room rates as high as they can get away with.

Tipping & Bargaining

In top-end restaurants and hotels in Ulaan Baatar, there is often a mandatory 13% value-added tax, but most cheaper places don't bother with it. Tipping is often expected in top-end places, but is still definitely optional – just round up the bill. Give the tip at the time you pay the bill, because if you leave money lying on the table someone besides the staff may take it. It is not customary to tip taxi drivers.

Nobody bargains in government shops, but in the budding private sector bargaining is definitely catching on. In the markets, a fair price is very much a matter of negotiation, whether it's a carpet, a Mongolian *del*

(traditional garment) or a pair of jeans. Don't start bargaining if you're not prepared to buy the item and always keep it light-hearted. You can negotiate everything from your hotel room to the price of a jeep ride but don't get carried away – a few hundred tögrög means nothing to you but can be important to locals.

POST & COMMUNICATIONS
Postal Rates

Postal rates are often relatively expensive, especially for parcels, for which there is only an 'air mail' rate – yet they often arrive months later (probably by sea). Normal-sized letters cost T550 and postcards cost T400 to all countries. A 1kg airmail parcel costs anywhere from T13,000 to T17,000 to most countries.

The Old Postal System

Mongolia can pride itself on developing one of the world's first long-distance internal postal systems. During the time of Chinggis Khaan, a 'pony express' postal service, known as *urton*, would cover over 100km per day. Bells were attached to the saddle to warn locals of an approaching rider. The rider was quickly fed and the horses changed, before both went on their way. At a pinch riders could change mounts without touching the ground or even slowing down. All male herdsmen were required to work for several weeks a year to ensure the continuing success of urton. The postal system was steadily improved over the centuries, and continued until 1949.

Sending Mail

The postal service is reliable but can often be *very* slow. Allow *at least* a couple of weeks for letters and postcards to arrive from Mongolia. Foreign residents of Ulaan Baatar find it much faster to give letters (and cash to buy stamps) to other foreigners who are departing.

You won't find letter boxes on the streets. In most cases, you will have to post your letters from the post office. You can buy stamps in post offices (and top-end hotels) in Ulaan Baatar and aimag capitals; elsewhere, stamps are in short supply.

Receiving Mail

The poste restante at the Central Post Office in Ulaan Baatar seems to work quite well; bring along your passport as proof of identification. Don't even think about using a poste restante anywhere else in the country. Most locals receive mail at post office boxes because residential deliveries are uncertain in a city without clear addresses.

Couriers

DHL and TNT have offices in Ulaan Baatar. Packages of 500g cost around US$40 to the UK and Australia and US$50 to the US and take up to a week to arrive.

Telephone

Mongolia's telecommunications system is being upgraded by the French company Alcatel and the quality is improving rapidly. In Ulaan Baatar it is easy to make international or domestic calls. Outside of Ulaan Baatar, making calls is difficult: no-one will understand you unless you speak reasonable Mongolian or Russian, and the telephones may not work anyway. In the countryside, the telltale satellite dish indicates a telephone office.

Ulaan Baatar now has a few card-phones; cards are available in post and telecom offices in units of 150, 300 and 3000, the latter costing around T20,000, for use with international calls.

Mobile Phone The two main companies are Mobicom (☎ 312 222) and Skytalk

(☎ 318 488). The mobile phone network is GSM. If you bring a GSM you can get a new SIM card installed in Mongolia. Mobicom mobile phone numbers begin with ☎ 9911. To dial these numbers from abroad, just dial the country code of ☎ 976; there is no area code.

Domestic Calls In Ulaan Baatar, most telephone numbers have six digits (older ones have five); Erdenet has six digits; and elsewhere in the country, where there are very few telephones, numbers often have just three or four digits. If you are given a five-digit number in Ulaan Baatar, and it doesn't work, try adding a 3 or 4 in front of it.

For domestic calls, try to use your hotel telephone, rather than battle with the local post or telephone office. Domestic calls can also be made by dialling the domestic

Telephone Area Codes

If telephoning from within Mongolia add a '0' to the initial digit of the area code.

Arkhangai	☎ 73
Baganuur	☎ 31
Bayankhongor	☎ 69
Bayan-Ölgii	☎ 71
Bulgan	☎ 67
Choir	☎ 64
Darkhan	☎ 37
Dornod	☎ 61
Dornogov	☎ 63
Dundgov	☎ 59
Erdenet	☎ 35
Gov-Altai	☎ 65
Khentii	☎ 39
Khovd	☎ 43
Khövsgöl	☎ 41
Nalaikh	☎ 33
Ömnögov	☎ 53
Övökhangai	☎ 55
Selenge	☎ 49
Sükhbaatar	☎ 51
Töv	☎ 47
Ulaan Baatar	☎ 11
Uvs	☎ 45
Zavkhan	☎ 57

operator (☎ 107), but only if you are able to speak Mongolian or have a friend who can help.

In Ulaan Baatar there are an increasing number of public telephones – often just someone's telephone stuck out their apartment window on a long extension cable. These cost a flat T100 per call.

International Calls If you have access to an IDD telephone, just dial ☎ 00 and then your international country code. On non-IDD telephones you can make direct long-distance calls by dialling the international operator (☎ 106), who may know enough English to make the right connection (but don't count on it).

Otherwise, you will have to book a call from your local post office. You pay a deposit in advance (a minimum equivalent of three minutes) and the final total is subtracted from that. To Australia/New Zealand, Europe and North America, it costs between T2000 and T3000 per minute; less to Russia and China.

If you want to save the hassle, but not the money, you can easily make international calls from any of the business centres or reception desks at the top-range hotels, though these can be very pricey.

A couple of the top-end hotels have Home Country Direct dialling, where the push of a button gets you through to international operators in America, Japan and Singapore. You can then make a credit card, charge card or collect (reverse charges) call.

Making a call *to* Mongolia is a lot easier. Dial the international access code in your country (normally ☎ 00), the Mongolian country code (☎ 976), the local code (Ulaan Baatar is ☎ 1) and then the number.

Fax

Business centres in major hotels in Ulaan Baatar charge about T5000 to T6000 to send a one-page fax abroad and around T800 per page to receive one. The Central Post Office is less convenient but cheaper at T3000 per page. Outside Ulaan Baatar, forget it.

Email & Internet Access

Email, the Internet and mobile phones have now reached Mongolia and indeed the country is putting much stock on this technology to leapfrog it into the 21st century.

For travellers, email is easily the most reliable, cheapest and quickest way of communicating with the outside world. You may want to open a free Web-based email account such as Lonely Planet's eKno (www.ekno.lonelyplanet.com), Hotmail (www.hotmail.com) or Yahoo! Mail (mail.yahoo.com). You can then access your mail from anywhere in the world using any Internet-connected computer.

There are dozens of Internet cafes in Ulaan Baatar that charge around T1500 to T2000 per hour but this rate is always fluctuating (and generally falling). The better ones will even scan photos and help you send these to friends and folks back home.

Outside of the capital, Internet access is rare, though larger towns have email facilities at the post/telecom office (so you can send an email but not access Internet-based accounts like Hotmail). The non-profit Soros Foundation has installed public access Internet in post offices at Choibalsan, Dalanzadgad and others.

If you want to open an account in Ulaan Baatar there are three Internet service providers (ISPs) in the country; Datacom (with its domain name Magicnet), Mongolnet and Mongolia Online. They charge around USS$50 a month.

INTERNET RESOURCES

The World Wide Web is a rich resource for travellers. You can research your trip, hunt down bargain air fares, book hotels, check on weather conditions or chat with locals and other travellers about the best places to visit (or avoid).

There's no better place to start your Web explorations than the Lonely Planet Web site (www.lonelyplanet.com). You'll find a succinct summary on Mongolia, postcards from other travellers and the Thorn Tree bulletin board, where you can ask questions before you go or dispense advice when you get back. You can also find travel news and updates to this guidebook in the Upgrades section, and the subWWWay section links you to the most useful travel resources elsewhere on the Web.

Most travel agencies have good Web sites (see the Travel Agencies entry under Information in the Ulaan Baatar chapter, and the Organised Tours section in the Getting There & Away chapter). Some of the best general Mongolia-related Web sites are:

Cyber Mongolia Has lots of useful links to get you started.
www.mng.net/
Eurasia Insight A useful resource for news on the wider region.
www.eurasianet.org/
Mongolei Online A German-language site.
www.mongolei.de/
Mongolia Online Covers news, currency rates, arts calendar and weather in Ulaan Baatar.
www.mol.mn
Mongolia National Tourism Centre Includes lists of hotels, ger camps and travel agencies.
www.mongoliatourism.gov.mn
Mongolia This Week A subscription-only online English-language newspaper
www.mongoliathisweek.mn
Mongolia Today A colourful online magazine covering all aspects of Mongolian culture.
www.mongoliatoday.com
Mongolia WWW Virtual Library Excellent resource with lots of links.
www.indiana.edu/~mongsoc
United Nations in Mongolia This Web site has lots of information, especially on its Eastern Steppe Diversity project; check out the cultural magazine 'Ger'.
www.un-mongolia.mn

A daily email news service from Ulaan Baatar in English provides useful information about Mongolian issues and entertainment, and costs US$10 per month (☎/fax 1-372 925, **e** ganbold@magicnet.mn).

BOOKS

Most books are published in different editions by different publishers in different countries. As a result, a book might be a hardcover rarity in one country while it's readily available in paperback in another. Fortunately, bookshops and libraries search by title

or author, so your local bookshop or library is best placed to advise you on the availability of the following recommendations.

Web sites such as Adventurous Traveller Bookstore (www.gorp.com/atbook.htm), Amazon (www.amazon.com), Barnes & Noble (www.bn.com) and Waterstones (www.waterstones.co.uk) can also be a useful resource for tracking down books.

You can pick up a few dictionaries and souvenir-type books in Ulaan Baatar, but in general you are better off buying your books before you leave home.

Lonely Planet

Lonely Planet publishes the pocket-size *Mongolian phrasebook*, which is indispensable for travelling around Mongolia, especially in the countryside. If you are travelling to other nearby countries, Lonely Planet publishes books on *Central Asia, Russia, Ukraine & Belarus, Moscow, China* and *Beijing*.

Guidebooks

There are a couple of locally produced guidebooks available in Ulaan Baatar.

Fifty Routes Through Mongolia by Professor Sh Shagdar is a mildly useful guide that covers some wonderfully obscure sites. It's good if you are covering a small area in detail.
Gobi Gurvansaikhan National Park by Bernd Steinhauer-Burkhart. Useful background information on the park.
Mongolia by Kh Oyungerel. A trilingual guide, with details on Ulaan Baatar and a language section.

Travel

Edge of Blue Heaven by Benedict Allen. The latest book by intrepid explorer Allen chronicles a horse trek to western Mongolia, followed by a solo camel trek across the Gobi.
In the Empire of Genghis Khan (2000) by Stanley Stewart. Traces the author's 1000 mile horseback journey through Central Asia and Mongolia.
In Search of Genghis Khan (1997) by Tim Severin. Well written and with great photos, this book provides an in-depth and fascinating look at nomadic lifestyles. Recommended.
In Secret Mongolia and *Men & Gods* by Haslund Henning. Turn of the century travelogue recently reprinted.

The Last Disco in Outer Mongolia by Nick Middleton. An easy-to-read, but dated journal of his limited travels in the late 1980s.

The Lost Country: Mongolia Revealed (1993) by Jasper Becker is insightful and recommended reading for anyone going to Mongolia. It is available in Mongolia in a special printing for around T5000.

Nomads and Commissars: Mongolia Revisited (1962) by Owen Lattimore. Arguably the greatest scholar on Mongolia this century; Lattimore's many books are analytical and warm.

Riding Windhorses: A Journey into the Heart of Mongolian Shamanism by Julie Ann Stewart and Sarangerel Odigan.

Wild East: The New Mongolia by Jill Lawless. Portrait of contemporary Mongolia by a Canadian journalist who lived in Mongolia for two years.

History & Politics

China under Mongolian Rule (1981) by John D Langlois. Details the impact of the Mongols during their century of rule over all of China.

Encyclopaedia of Asian History by Alan Sanders. This 19-volume opus includes a separate book by renowned Mongolist, Alan Sanders (author of the Lonely Planet *Mongolian phrasebook*). It details ancient and recent history and politics, and includes a vital bibliography.

Khublai Khan (1988) by Morris Rossabi. A biography of the man who bridged Mongolia and China.

The Modern History of Mongolia by Charles R Bawden. Excellent overview, with special emphasis on post-Mongol Mongolia.

The Mongol Warlords by David Nicolle. Well-illustrated look at the personalities and campaigns of Genghis, Kublai and Hülegü, as well as the later Central Asian warlord Tamerlane.

The Mongols (1986) by David Morgan. A comprehensive account of Mongolia's history.

The Secret History of the Mongols Mongolia's most famous book has no known author. This epic history of the life and deeds of Chinggis Khaan has been translated into English by Igor de Rachewiltz (1996), Francis Cleaves (1982) and Urgunge Onon (1990).

The Secret History of the Mongols: the Origin of Chingis Khan (1984) by Paul Kahn. This is regarded as the best study of the *Secret History*.

Storm from the East by Robert Marshall. Excellent overview of the Mongol conquests; the small paperback format makes it easy to travel with.

Twentieth Century Mongolia by Baabar. New views on modern history by Mongolian historian and politician.

Culture

Mongolia: The Legacy of Chinggis Khan by Patricia Ann Berger & Terese Tse Bartholomew. Available in Ulaan Baatar (US$40), it contains beautiful examples of Mongolian art. Several chapters and illustrations can be viewed at www.asianart.com/mongolia.

This Is Mongolia (1991). Available in Ulaan Baatar, this colourful and easy-to-read booklet provides interesting explanations of culture, history and traditions – recommended reading, and a good souvenir.

Women of Mongolia (1996) by Martha Avery. This book contains a string of interviews that enable local women to speak about the changes and challenges affecting both nomadic and urban women.

Religion

The Jebtsundampa Khutukhtus of Urga (1961) by Charles Bawden. This is a renowned Buddhist history of the greatest Mongolian lamas.

A Mongolian Living Buddha (1983) by Paul Hyer & Sechin Jagchid. One of Mongolia's great lamas Kanjurwa Khutukhtu collaborated with these scholars to produce a biography before he died in 1980.

Religions of Mongolia (1980) by Walther Heissig. This is one of Heissig's best works about religion.

Shamanism: Archaic Techniques of Ecstasy (1972) by Mircea Eliade. A lyrical study of shamanism worldwide, including Mongolia.

Nature & Environment

Dinosaurs of the Flaming Cliffs by Michael Novacek. Fascinating account of dinosaur expeditions in the south Gobi in the early 1990s with scholarly, but always accessible, discussions of dinosaur evolution.

Les Oiseaux de Chine, de Mongolie at de Corée (1978) by RD Etchecopar. This French work is the most thorough work about birdlife in Mongolia and the region.

Mongolia's Wild Heritage (1999) by Christopher Finch. Written in collaboration with the Mongolian Ministry of Nature & Environment, this is an outstanding book about Mongolia's fragile ecology and contains excellent photos.

On the Trail of Ancient Man (1926) by Roy Chapman Andrews. An autobiography about his exploits seeking dinosaur fossils in the Gobi and around the world.

Today's Mongolia

The Changing World of Mongolia's Nomads (1994) by Melvyn Goldstein & Cynthia Beall.

An interesting account of the changes affecting the country's nomads.

Mongolia: Country of Contrasts by R Enkhbat. On sale in Ulaan Baatar for about US$20, this is a startling collection of contemporary photos by one of the country's top photographers.

Language

Besides the Lonely Planet *Mongolian phrasebook*, which includes a concise vocabulary list, a few dictionaries have been published:

A Concise English-Mongolian Dictionary (1970) and *A Modern Mongolian-English Dictionary* (1986) by John G Hangin.

A Concise Mongol-English and English-Mongol Dictionary (1996) by William Rozycki. A handy, pocket-sized book which translates both ways, but hard to justify its price tag.

Mongolian-English Dictionary (1997) by D Altangerel. Excellent value; available in Ulaan Baatar.

Worterbuch Mongolisch-Deutsch (1988) by Hans-Peter Vietze. German-Mongolian dictionary.

Magazine Articles

National Geographic has some great articles on the Mongols. The December 1996 issue has an article on Chinggis Khaan's conquests. Excerpts can be viewed at www.nationalgeographic.com. The May 1993 edition has an article on Mongolia's nomads and the September 1999 issue has a photo-essay on the eagle hunters of Bayan-Ölgii. If you have access to National Geographic archives or their CD Rom set there are several more interesting articles, including a couple by Roy Chapman Andrews and Owen Lattimore written in the late 1920s and early 1930s.

FILMS

Lonely Planet produces a video, Mongolia, featuring Ian Wright hunting marmots, digging up dinosaurs, and committing social gaffes across Mongolia in indomitable style.

Movies made in Mongolia bring to life the steppes and nomadic way. Mongolian directors seldom get a screening outside Mongolia, but video stores may well have the 1991 art house hit, *Close to Eden*, also released as *Urga*, by the Russian director Mikhalkov.

Epic documentaries and feminist fantasies of the German director Ulrike Ottinger are the most intimate immersion in the life of Mongolian reindeer herders. And, of course, Hollywood did its fantasies too, with Richard Widmark in the war epic *Destination Gobi* (1953) and Orson Welles, Tyrone Power and Herbert Lom in *The Black Rose* (1950) as Saxon warriors off to meet the great Mongolian leaders.

Film maker Roland Blum's documentary *The Riders of the Mongolian Steppe* is available for rent from Boojum Expeditions for US$20, which includes postage both ways within the US. Contact Boojum (☎ 1-800-287 0125, 406-587 0125, fax 585 3474, e boojum@mcn.net), 14543 Kelly Canyon Rd, Bozeman, MT 59715.

One gem to look out for is the documentary *Chinggis Blues* by Roko and Adrian Belic, which traces the journey of a blind American blues singer through Mongolia and Tuva to learn the secrets of *khoomi* (throat singing).

State of Dogs is a Mongolian documentary that has been translated into English.

For something a tad more mainstream track down the documentary by Tigress Productions, UK, which follows the American actress Julia Roberts as she travels through Mongolia.

NEWSPAPERS & MAGAZINES

The media used to be little more than state-controlled propaganda vehicles, but liberalisation has certainly changed the atmosphere. Literally hundreds of newspaper have sprung up, with controversies and scandals forming popular topics; but some are little more than soft porn rags.

Major private dailies in Mongolian include *Ardiin Erkh* (People's Right), *Zunny Medee* (Century News), *Odriin Sonin* (Daily News) and *Önöödör* (Today).

Mongolia has two English-language weekly newspapers, *The Mongol Messenger* (www.mongolnet.mn/mglmsg/index.html) and *The UB Post* (www.ulaanbaatar.net/ubpost). Both are well worth picking up for local news and entertainment information. In Ulaan Baatar you can pick up current copies of *Time*, *Newsweek*, the *Economist* and the Russian edition of *Cosmopolitan*.

RADIO & TV

Mongolian state-run radio is strong on rhetoric, keeps alive traditional folk music and oral epics, and often contains good-quality classical music, as well as weird Russian disco. If you have a radio in Ulaan Baatar try Jag (107 FM), Blue Sky Radio (100.9 FM) and Radio Ulaanbaatar (102.5 FM).

The BBC World Service is also available in Ulaan Baatar at 103.1 FM, so you don't necessarily need a short-wave radio to stay in touch in the capital. Out in the steppe the reception of short-wave services, such as Voice of America (www.voa.gov/), the BBC (www.bbc.co.uk/worldservice/tuning/) and Radio Australia (www.abc.net.au/ra/), are usually good. For current frequencies and times check the Web sites.

Except where satellite TV is available, Mongolian TV is nothing to get excited about. Ulaanbaatar TV and Mongol TB (not a disease), and stations beamed from Russia, provide a poor diet of viciously dubbed Russian films (with one male actor providing the voice of all the characters, even the women!) and Mongolian news and sports (including hours and hours of wrestling), as well as interesting documentaries about nomads (even if you don't understand them, the scenery is great).

The new missionary-owned station, Eagle (Burged) TV, regularly shows NBA basketball, CNN news and scary evangelical shows on most days. Sansar TV and Himer Cable serve better-off locals and foreigners with Western music, sports and movies.

VIDEO SYSTEMS

The predominant video format in Mongolia and the countries of the former Soviet Union is SECAM, a system incompatible with that used in most of Europe (France and Greece excepted), Australia, China and the USA.

PHOTOGRAPHY & VIDEO
Film & Equipment

Mongolia is a very photogenic country so take loads of film with you, especially if you are there during the Nadaam Festival period. Major brands of print and even Polaroid film are available in upmarket hotels and souvenir shops in Ulaan Baatar (but nowhere in the countryside), though prices tend to be high, and you should always check the expiry date. Several places around Sükhbaatar Square will process print film cheaply, but the quality may not be great; it's best to wait until you get home.

Slide film is rare, so bring what you need and get it developed elsewhere. Mongolia is definitely *not* the place to buy camera accessories, though you never know what sort of ancient relic you might find in the department stores.

Technical Tips

In summer, days are long, so the best time to take photos is before 10 am and between 6 and 8 pm, when Mongolia basks in gorgeous light. As bright, glaring sunshine is the norm, a polarising filter is essential. If you do a jeep trip on an unsurfaced road, you can expect plenty of dust, so keep the camera well sealed in a plastic bag.

Don't put your film through Mongolian X-ray machines (Western machines are generally OK). Most inspectors are happy to inspect film by hand, especially if you take the film out of the canisters and put them in a clear plastic bag.

Keep your film out of the Gobi's summer sun and Mongolia's winter freeze, when your automatic cameras and batteries may not work properly. Bring a spare camera battery, as these can stop working because of the cold, even in summer.

Restrictions

Photography is prohibited inside monasteries and temples, although you may photograph the exterior building and the monastery grounds. Also you can sometimes obtain special permission to take photographs in exchange for an extra fee. Remember that monks and nomads are not photographic models, so if they do not want to be photographed, their wishes should be respected. Always ask before taking a photograph.

In most museums throughout the country you need to pay an (often outrageously high) extra fee to use your still or video camera. It is best to have a look around first before you decide whether to fork out the extra tögrög for photographs.

Be careful about photographing potentially sensitive areas, especially border crossings and military establishments.

Photographing People

Mongolians are not especially enthusiastic about having their photos taken. The days of state surveillance are a recent memory, and some Mongolians are ashamed of the shabbiness they and the whole country have been reduced to. Many westerners don't seem to care what the locals think, and poke camera lenses into the face of whoever looks interesting. This has led to arguments and even fist fights. Markets are often a place where snap-happy foreigners are not welcome. Some visitors have even been stoned after taking photos at the Central (Black) Market in Ulaan Baatar.

On the other hand, people in the countryside are often happy to pose for photographs if you ask first. If you have promised to send them a copy, *please* do it, but explain that it may take several months to reach them – some nomads believe that all cameras are (instant) Polaroids. Several nomads also told us how devastated they were because they had not received photos as promised by foreigners. Ask them to write their address in Mongolian on a piece of paper. You can then glue the address on an envelope, and add the word 'Mongolia' in the roman alphabet to ensure that it gets to the right place.

When Mongolians pose for a portrait they instantly put on a face that looks like they are in mourning at Brezhnev's funeral. You may need to take this Soviet-style portrait in order to get a more natural shot later.

'Can I take your photograph?' in Mongolian is *'Bi tany zurgiig avch bolokh uu?'* (Би таны зургийг авч болох уу).

TIME

Mongolia is divided into two time zones: the three western aimags of Bayan-Ölgii, Uvs and Khovd are one hour behind Ulaan Baatar, while the rest of the country follows Ulaan Baatar's time.

The standard time in Ulaan Baatar is UTC/GMT plus eight hours. When it is noon in Ulaan Baatar, it is also noon in Beijing, Hong Kong, Singapore and Perth; 2 pm in Sydney; 8 pm the previous day in Los Angeles; 11 pm the previous day in New York; and 4 am in London. Mongolia no longer observes daylight-saving time.

There is another form of 'Mongolian time' – add two hours to any appointments you make. Mongolians are notorious for being late, and this includes nearly everyone likely to be important to you, such as jeep drivers, your guide or the staff at a museum you want to visit. You could almost adjust your watch to compensate for the difference. The Mongolian version of 'manana' (tomorrow) is *margash*.

It is interesting to note that dates are usually written with the years first, followed by the month in roman numerals, and then the day in normal numbers. For example, 16 August 2000 is often written as 2000-VIII-16.

ELECTRICITY

Lenin defined communism as socialism plus electricity. Mongolia's abundant coal has meant widespread electrification; however, the power stations are in the middle of the towns, belch black smoke, and use technology on the brink of breakdown. In western Mongolia, power (electricity and hot water) supplies are connected to the Russian grid and get turned off whenever Mongolia forgets to pay its bills.

Power surges, blackouts and hot water shortages are common in the countryside. Expats will tell you horrendous stories about electricity and hot water 'blackouts' lasting weeks during winters of -20°C. The surges can also damage sensitive electrical equipment. Electrical wiring in old hotels can be dangerous. Where water meets electricity, be doubly careful. Hot water always seems to get turned off in Ulaan Baatar in May as the pipes are cleaned.

Voltages & Cycles

Electric power is 220V, 50Hz. Thanks to Russian influence, the sockets are designed to accommodate two round prongs in the European style. Unfortunately the Russian socket holes are slightly smaller than some European plugs so you may have to play around with it a bit.

WEIGHTS & MEASURES

Mongolia follows the international metric system. As in the USA, the ground floor is called the 1st floor – as opposed to the UK system, where the next floor above ground level is the 1st floor.

LAUNDRY

Most hotels in Mongolia, especially the guest houses in Ulaan Baatar, will do your laundry for a negotiable price. There are a couple of dry-cleaners in the capital. Brand-name detergent, and even bleach, is available in Ulaan Baatar, and in most larger aimag capitals, so with the (normally available) hot water and very dry climate, you'll probably end up washing your own clothes.

PUBLIC BATH HOUSES

Almost all aimag capitals have a public bathhouse that provides hot showers for locals for around T300 to T500. The opening hours are often erratic but in general the most reliable time is on the weekends. Look for the sign that reads 'Халуун Ус' (*khaluun us*, or hot water). Better bath houses will have a hairdresser *(uschin)* and even a sauna *(saun)*.

TOILETS

In most hotels in Ulaan Baatar and aimag capitals and in most ger camps, toilets are the sit-down European variety. Strangely, there are only about three intact toilet seats in the entire country. In other hotels, and some more remote ger camps, you will have to use pit toilets and hold your breath. Squat toilets are the norm in the Muslim-influenced Bayan-Ölgii province and sit-down toilets

here will often have blocks placed on either side so that it becomes a squat toilet.

In the countryside, where there may not be a bush or tree for hundreds of kilometres, modesty is not something to worry about – just do it where you want to, but away from gers. Also, try to avoid such places as an *ovoo* (a sacred cairn of stones), rivers and lakes (water sources for nomads) and marmot holes.

The plumbing is decrepit in many of the older hotels, and toilet paper can easily jam up the works. If there is a rubbish basket next to the toilet, this is where the paper should go. The hotel management will get quite upset if you plug things up. Toilet paper and tissues are available in most markets.

HEALTH

Travel health depends on your predeparture preparations, your daily health care while travelling and how you handle any medical problem that does develop. While the potential dangers can seem quite frightening, in reality few travellers to Mongolia experience anything more than an upset stomach.

Summary of Risks

Except for getting frostbite in winter, Mongolia is generally a healthy country to travel in. The dry, cold climate and sparse human habitation means few of the infectious diseases that plague tropical countries. Mongolian food may not taste too good but it's usually safe to eat.

Mongolia, however, is a terrible place to get ill. The number of doctors is chronically low and the standard of medical training is patchy at best, and often very bad. There are now about 850 poorly trained and under-equipped Mongolian medical graduates struggling to maintain the health of a country gone broke.

If you do become seriously ill in Mongolia, your local embassy can provide details of Western doctors. Otherwise ask a foreign resident, your hotel (or any top-end hotel) for current advice about which hospital or doctor to visit. A couple of hospitals and at

Medical Kit Check List

Following is a list of items you should consider including in your medical kit – consult your pharmacist for brands available in your country.

☐ **Aspirin or paracetamol (acetaminophen in the USA)** – for pain or fever
☐ **Antihistamine** – for allergies, eg, hay fever; to ease the itch from insect bites or stings; and to prevent motion sickness
☐ **Cold and flu tablets, throat lozenges and nasal decongestant**
☐ **Multivitamins** – consider for long trips, when dietary vitamin intake may be inadequate
☐ **Antibiotics** – consider including these if you're travelling well off the beaten track; see your doctor, as they must be prescribed, and carry the prescription with you
☐ **Loperamide or diphenoxylate** –'blockers' for diarrhoea
☐ **Prochlorperazine or metaclopramide** – for nausea and vomiting
☐ **Rehydration mixture** – to prevent dehydration, which may occur, for example, during bouts of diarrhoea; particularly important when travelling with children
☐ **Insect repellent, sunscreen, lip balm and eye drops**
☐ **Calamine lotion, sting relief spray or aloe vera** – to ease irritation from sunburn and insect bites or stings
☐ **Antifungal cream or powder** – for fungal skin infections and thrush
☐ **Antiseptic (such as povidone-iodine)** – for cuts and grazes
☐ **Bandages, Band-Aids (plasters) and other wound dressings**
☐ **Water purification tablets or iodine**
☐ **Scissors, tweezers and a thermometer** – note that mercury thermometers are prohibited by airlines

Blood-letting is part of traditional practices, and Mongolian doctors just love to inject things like vitamins. Except in dire emergencies, avoid injections like the plague – the syringe may not be clean (so bring your own), and you will have little idea about what is being pumped into you.

If you are unlucky enough to stay for a while in a Mongolian hospital, you will definitely need a good friend to look after you – the nurses won't have the time, resources or motivation to do it themselves. This means bring your own food and get someone to change your sheets, find medicines and things like syringes, and cheer you up. Blackouts are common in Ulaan Baatar (more so in the countryside), and hospital generators don't exist, or, if they do, they often fail. Each year, several Mongolians die in the middle of simple operations after power failures.

If you are suffering from any illness or injury that you feel could be very serious, but not immediately life-threatening, make a beeline for Beijing. In a real life-threatening emergency, international medical evacuation services claim they can send a private plane from Beijing to fly you out of Mongolia, but we haven't heard of it happening. This service does not come cheaply, unless you know your travel insurance company will bear the cost, which can be tens of thousands of dollars.

Most hospitals and clinics in Mongolia are critically short of medical supplies, especially antibiotics, and it's a good idea to take all your medical supplies with you, especially if you require regular medication. This does *not* mean that you should dose yourself with antibiotics without medical supervision.

There are numerous kinds of antibiotics and you can hardly be expected to carry your own travelling pharmacy, but tetracycline in 250mg capsules taken four times daily for seven days (a total of 28 capsules) is a fairly standard course for most general infections. However, tetracycline is contraindicated in women who are pregnant or breastfeeding and must not be given to children.

least one private clinic in Ulaan Baatar cater for foreigners (see Medical Services under Information in the Ulaan Baatar chapter).

In the countryside, head for the nearest aimag capital or, if you can, rush back to Ulaan Baatar. A translator is essential for any visit to, or stay in, a Mongolian hospital.

Predeparture planning

Immunisations Plan ahead for getting your vaccinations: some of them require more than one injection, while some vaccinations should not be given together. Note that some vaccinations should not be given during pregnancy or in people with allergies – discuss with your doctor. It is recommended you seek medical advice at least six weeks before travel. Be aware that there is often a greater risk of disease with children and during pregnancy. If you bring children to Mongolia, it's especially important to make sure that their vaccinations are up to date.

Discuss your requirements with your doctor, but vaccinations you should consider for this trip include the following (for more details about the diseases themselves, see the individual disease entries later in this section). Whatever vaccinations you get should be recorded in an International Health Certificate. No specific vaccinations are legally required to enter Mongolia.

Hepatitis A Hepatitis A vaccine (eg Avaxim, Havrix 1440 or VAQTA) provides long-term immunity (possibly more than 10 years) after an initial injection and a booster at six to 12 months. Alternatively, an injection of gamma globulin can provide short-term protection against hepatitis A – two to six months, depending on the dose given. It is not a vaccine, but is ready-made antibody collected from blood donations. It is reasonably effective and, unlike the vaccine, it is protective immediately, but because it is a blood product, there are current concerns about its long-term safety. Hepatitis A vaccine is also available in a combined form, Twinrix, with hepatitis B vaccine. Three injections over a six-month period are required, the first two providing substantial protection against hepatitis A.

Cholera The current injectable vaccine against cholera is poorly protective and has many side effects, so it is not generally recommended for travellers.

Meningococcal Meningitis A single injection gives good protection against the major epidemic forms of the disease for three years. Protection may be less effective in children under two years.

Hepatitis B Travellers who should consider vaccination against hepatitis B include those on a long trip, as well as those visiting countries where there are high levels of hepatitis B infection, where blood transfusions may not be adequately screened or where sexual contact or needle sharing is a possibility. Vaccination involves three injections, with a booster at 12 months. More rapid courses are available if necessary.

Rabies Vaccination should be considered by those who will spend a month or longer in the countryside, especially if they are cycling, handling animals, caving or travelling to remote areas. Pretravel rabies vaccination involves having three injections over 21 to 28 days. If someone who has been vaccinated is bitten or scratched by an animal, they will require two booster injections of vaccine; those not vaccinated require more and within a shorter period of time.

Tuberculosis The risk of TB to travellers is usually very low. Vaccination against TB (BCG) is recommended for children and young adults living in these areas for three months or more.

Health Insurance Make sure that you have adequate health insurance. See Travel Insurance under the Visas & Documents section for details. Even with insurance, hospitals may require payment *before* they treat you. Make sure that your health insurance covers repatriation, as least as far as Beijing.

Travel Health Guides Lonely Planet's handy, pocket-sized *Healthy Travel Asia & India* is packed with useful information, including pretrip planning, emergency first aid, immunisation and disease information, and what to do if you get sick on the road. *Travel with Children* by Maureen Wheeler, also from Lonely Planet, includes advice on travel health for younger children.

Other detailed health guides include:

CDC's Complete Guide to Healthy Travel, Open Road Publishing, 1997. The US Centers for Disease Control & Prevention recommendations for international travel.

Staying Healthy in Asia, Africa & Latin America by Dirk Schroeder, Moon Publications, 1994. Detailed and well organised.

Travellers' Health by Dr Richard Dawood, Oxford University Press, 1995. Comprehensive, easy to read, authoritative and highly recommended, although it's rather large to lug around.

Where There Is No Doctor by David Werner, Macmillan, 1994. A very detailed guide intended for someone, such as a Peace Corps worker, going to work in an underdeveloped country.

There are also a number of excellent travel health sites set up on the Internet. There are useful links from the Lonely Planet home page at www.lonelyplanet.com/weblinks /wlheal.htm to the World Health Organization and the US Centers for Disease Control & Prevention.

Other Preparations Make sure you're healthy before you start travelling. If you are going on a long trip make sure your teeth are OK. If you wear glasses take a spare pair, your prescription and an ample supply of lens-cleaning solution.

If you require a particular medication take an adequate supply, as it may not be available locally. Take part of the packaging showing the generic name rather than the brand, which will make getting replacements easier. It's a good idea to have a legible prescription or letter from your doctor to show that you legally use the medication to avoid any problems.

Basic Rules

Food There is an old saying that says: 'If you can cook it, boil it or peel it you can eat it...otherwise forget it'. Vegetables and fruit should be washed with purified water or peeled where possible. Beware of ice cream which is sold in the street or anywhere it might have been melted and refrozen; if there's any doubt (such as a power cut in the last day or two), steer well clear.

Water Mongolians insist that the tap water is safe to drink in Ulaan Baatar and most other places – indeed, we never had any problems drinking tap water in the larger cities. However, there can be occasions in late summer when the water table in the city rises as a result of heavy storms and the water becomes unsafe to drink – in this case, public health alerts are issued. The number one rule is *be careful of the water*.

If you don't know for certain that the water is safe, assume the worst.

Before filling your cup with water from the tap, let it run for about 30 seconds to get the rust out of the pipes. Bottles of mineral water are available in Ulaan Baatar (not in the countryside), but try alternatives because the plastic bottles are not biodegradable. Only use water from containers with a serrated seal – not tops or corks. Take care with fruit juice, particularly if water may have been added.

Underground well water is almost always safe to drink, though in the Gobi it's high in mineral content and not too good for the liver if you drink it continuously for several years. However, surface water from rivers and lakes may well have been contaminated by livestock faeces and should be purified. If you do any camping and hiking, you may occasionally find it necessary to drink unboiled surface water. It's always better to drink moving rather than stagnant water, and select a stream away from livestock.

It's essential to carry a water bottle with you, regardless of where you are going or how you are travelling. Even in cold weather, the bone-dry climate demands that you increase your water intake. If you find you are urinating infrequently or if your urine turns a deep yellow or orange, you may be dehydrating – you may also find yourself getting headaches.

Dairy products in the countryside are always unpasteurised and should, in theory, be treated with suspicion, though boiled milk is fine if it is kept hygienically. Mongolian tea should also be OK, since the water should have been boiled.

Water Purification The simplest way of purifying water is to boil it thoroughly. Vigorous boiling should be satisfactory; however, at high altitude water boils at a lower temperature, so germs are less likely to be killed. Boil it for longer in these environments.

Consider purchasing a water filter for a long trip. There are two main kinds of filter. Total filters take out all parasites, bacteria and viruses and make water safe to drink.

They are often expensive, but they can be more cost effective than buying bottled water. Simple filters (which can even be a nylon mesh bag) take out dirt and larger foreign bodies from the water so that chemical solutions work much more effectively; if water is dirty, chemical solutions may not work at all. It's very important when buying a filter to read the specifications, so that you know exactly what it removes from the water and what it doesn't. Simple filtering will not remove all dangerous organisms, so if you cannot boil water it should be treated chemically. Chlorine tablets will kill many pathogens, but not some parasites like giardia and amoebic cysts. Iodine is more effective in purifying water and is available in tablet form. Follow the directions carefully and remember that too much iodine can be harmful.

Medical Problems & Treatment

Self-diagnosis and treatment can be risky, so you should always seek medical help. Although we do give drug dosages in this section, they are for emergency use only. Correct diagnosis is vital. In this section we have used the generic names for medications – check with a pharmacist for brands available locally.

Note that antibiotics should ideally be administered only under medical supervision. Take only the recommended dose at the prescribed intervals and use the whole course, even if the illness seems to be cured earlier. Stop immediately if there are any serious reactions and don't use the antibiotic at all if you are unsure that you have the correct one. Some people are allergic to commonly prescribed antibiotics such as penicillin; carry this information (eg, on a bracelet) when travelling.

Environmental Hazards

Altitude Sickness Except in rare cases, only mountaineers will experience altitude sickness in Mongolia. Mild symptoms include headache, lethargy, dizziness, difficulty sleeping and loss of appetite. Treat mild symptoms by resting at the same altitude until recovery, usually a day or two.

Paracetamol or aspirin can be taken for headaches. If symptoms persist or become worse, however, *immediate descent is necessary*; even 500m can help. Drug treatments should never be used to avoid descent or to enable further ascent.

Constipation Most travellers worry about diarrhoea, but Mongolia's standard diet of mutton, fat and flour lacks fibre and can cause the opposite problem, constipation. Eating fruit and vegetables is the best solution, but these are not readily available. Although constipation is usually nothing to get worried about, it is uncomfortable. Some travellers throw a bottle of laxatives into their first-aid kit. Laxatives are OK for occasional use, but their overuse is harmful and can even lead to illnesses like irritable bowel syndrome. The best solution for constipation might be to bring some bran flakes or chewable high-fibre pills or fibre bars.

Heat Exhaustion Dehydration and salt deficiency can cause heat exhaustion. Take time to acclimatise to high temperatures, drink sufficient liquids and do not do anything too physically demanding.

Salt deficiency is characterised by fatigue, lethargy, headaches, giddiness and muscle cramps; salt tablets may help, but adding extra salt to your food is better.

Heatstroke This serious, occasionally fatal, condition can occur if the body's heat-regulating mechanism breaks down and the body temperature rises to dangerous levels. Long, continuous periods of exposure to high temperatures and insufficient fluids can leave you vulnerable to heatstroke.

The symptoms are feeling unwell, not sweating very much (or at all) and a high body temperature (39° to 41°C or 102° to 106°F). Where sweating has ceased, the skin becomes flushed and red. Severe, throbbing headaches and lack of coordination will also occur, and the sufferer may be confused or aggressive. Eventually the victim will become delirious or convulse. Hospitalisation is essential, but in the interim get victims out of the sun, remove their clothing, cover them with a wet sheet or towel and then fan continually. Give fluids if they are conscious.

Hypothermia In a country where temperatures can plummet to -40°C, cold is something you should take seriously. If you are trekking at high altitudes or simply taking a long bus trip cross country, particularly at night, be prepared. In Mongolia you should always be prepared for cold, wet or windy conditions even if you're just out walking or hitching. Even in the lowlands, sudden winds from the north can send the temperature plummeting, and people have indeed frozen to death during 'balmy' May weather.

Hypothermia occurs when the body loses heat faster than it can produce it and the core temperature of the body falls. It is surprisingly easy to progress from very cold to dangerously cold due to a combination of wind, wet clothing, fatigue and hunger, even if the air temperature is above freezing. It is best to dress in layers; silk, wool and some of the new artificial fibres are all good insulating materials. A hat is important, as a lot of heat is lost through the head. A strong, waterproof outer layer (and a 'space' blanket for emergencies) is essential. Carry basic supplies, including food containing simple sugars to generate heat quickly and fluid to drink.

Symptoms of hypothermia are exhaustion, numb skin (particularly toes and fingers), shivering, slurred speech, irrational or violent behaviour, lethargy, stumbling, dizzy spells, muscle cramps and violent bursts of energy. Irrationality may take the form of sufferers claiming they are warm and trying to take off their clothes.

To treat mild hypothermia, first get the person out of the wind and/or rain, remove their clothing if it's wet and replace it with dry, warm clothing. Give them hot liquids – not alcohol – and some high-kilojoule, easily digestible food. Do not rub victims: instead, allow them to slowly warm themselves.

This should be enough for the early stages of hypothermia, but if it has gone further it may be necessary to place the victim in a warm sleeping bag and get in with them since their body will not be able to generate enough heat by itself. A warm bath is best of all, but make sure it's not too hot.

The early recognition and treatment of mild hypothermia is the only way to prevent severe hypothermia, which is a critical condition.

Frostbite is a cold injury of the limbs, most commonly occurring on the toes, fingers and sometimes the nose and ears. Like hypothermia, frostbite is insidious; the victim feels nothing but a little numbness during the time the injury occurs, but severe pain follows when the tissue is thawed out. Ironically, the result looks and feels much like a severe burn, and can be just as traumatic. Prevention is the best medicine, but if you do get frostbitten, don't delay in seeking medical attention. It is possible that the dead tissue will need to be removed surgically and antibiotics given to prevent infection. Scarring and permanent injury are possible.

Motion Sickness Eating lightly before and during a trip will reduce the chances of motion sickness. If you are prone to motion sickness try to find a place that minimises movement – near the wing on aircraft, near the centre on minivans. Fresh air usually helps; reading and cigarette smoke don't. Commercial motion-sickness preparations, which can cause drowsiness, have to be taken before the trip commences. Ginger (available in capsule form) and peppermint (including mint-flavoured sweets) are natural preventatives.

Sunburn In Mongolia you can get sunburnt surprisingly quickly, even through cloud. Use a sunscreen, a hat, and a barrier cream for your nose and lips. Calamine lotion or a commercial after sun preparation are good for mild sunburn. Protect your eyes with good quality sunglasses, particularly if you will be near water, sand or snow.

Infectious Diseases
Brucellosis The United Nations Food & Agricultural Organization (FAO) reports that Mongolia is a high-risk area for brucellosis. This is a disease of cattle, yaks, camels

and sheep, but it can also infect humans. The most likely way for humans to contract this disease is by drinking unboiled milk or eating homemade cheese. Another way is for humans with open cuts on their hands to handle freshly killed meat. Cow dung (which the Mongolians use for building fires) is another possible source of infection.

In humans, brucellosis causes severe headaches, joint and muscle pains, fever and fatigue. There may be diarrhoea and, later, constipation. The onset of the symptoms may be rapid or slow, and can occur from five days to several months after exposure, with the average time being two weeks.

One of the sinister aspects of this disease is that the fever may come and go. Most patients recover in two or three weeks, but some people get chronic brucellosis which recurs sporadically for months and years and can cause long-term health problems. Fatalities are rare but possible.

Brucellosis is a serious disease which requires blood tests to make the diagnosis. If you think you may have contracted the disease, you need medical attention, preferably outside Mongolia. The disease often presents as an intermittent fever and the many other causes of such a fever should be excluded. Returning travellers should mention the possibility of the disease to their doctor if they remain unwell after their return from Mongolia.

Bubonic Plague For the past 10 years this disease (which wiped out one-third of Europe's population during the Middle Ages) has made an appearance in remote parts of Mongolia in late summer (from August to October), when the ban on hunting marmots stops, and their meat is eaten.

The disease (also known as the Black Plague) is normally carried by marmots, squirrels and rats and can be transmitted to humans by bites from fleas which make their home on the infected animals. It can also be passed from human to human by coughing. The symptoms are fever and enlarged lymph nodes. The untreated disease has a 60% death rate, but if you get a doctor it can be quickly treated. The best drug is the antibiotic streptomycin, which must be injected intramuscularly, but it is not available in Mongolia. Tetracycline is another drug which may be used.

During an outbreak, travel to affected areas is prohibited, which can greatly affect overland travel. All trains, buses and cars travelling into Ulaan Baatar from infected areas are also thoroughly checked when an outbreak of the plague has been reported.

Diarrhoea Simple things like a change of water, food or climate can all cause a mild bout of diarrhoea. In some parts of Mongolia, the high mineral content of the water can trigger diarrhoea, but your body should soon adjust. A few rushed toilet trips with no other symptoms is not indicative of a major problem.

Dehydration is the main danger with any diarrhoea, particularly in children or the elderly as dehydration can occur quite quickly. Under all circumstances *fluid replacement* (at least equal to the volume being lost) is the most important thing to remember. Mongolian salty tea, weak black tea with a little sugar, soda water, or soft drinks allowed to go flat and diluted by 50% with clean water are all good.

With severe diarrhoea a rehydrating solution is preferable to replace minerals and salts lost. Commercially available (but not in Mongolia) oral rehydration salts (ORS) are very useful; add them to boiled or bottled water. In an emergency you can make up a solution of six teaspoons of sugar and a half teaspoon of salt to a litre of boiled or bottled water. You need to drink at least the same volume of fluid that you are losing in bowel movements and vomiting. Urine is the best guide to the adequacy of replacement – if you have small amounts of concentrated urine, you need to drink more. Keep drinking small amounts often. Stick to a bland diet as you recover.

Gut-paralysing drugs such as loperamide or diphenoxylate can be used to bring relief from the symptoms, although they do not actually cure the problem. Only use these drugs if you do not have access to toilets, eg, if you *must* travel. Note that these drugs are not recommended for children under 12 years.

In certain situations antibiotics may be required: diarrhoea with blood or mucus (dysentery), any diarrhoea with fever, profuse watery diarrhoea, persistent diarrhoea not improving after 48 hours and severe diarrhoea. These suggest a more serious cause of diarrhoea and in these situations gut-paralysing drugs should be avoided.

In these situations, a stool test may be necessary to diagnose what bug is causing your diarrhoea, so you should seek medical help urgently. Where this is not possible the recommended drugs for bacterial diarrhoea (the most likely cause of severe diarrhoea in travellers) are norfloxacin 400mg twice daily for three days or ciprofloxacin 500mg twice daily for five days. These are not recommended for children or pregnant women. The drug of choice for children would be co-trimoxazole with dosage dependent on weight. A five day course is given. Ampicillin or amoxycillin may be given in pregnancy, but medical care is necessary.

Two other causes of persistent diarrhoea in travellers are giardiasis and amoebic dysentery.

Giardiasis is caused by a common parasite, *Giardia lamblia*. Symptoms include stomach cramps, nausea, a bloated stomach, watery, foul-smelling diarrhoea and frequent gas. Giardiasis can appear several weeks after you have been exposed to the parasite. The symptoms may disappear for a few days and then return; this can go on for several weeks.

Amoebic dysentery, caused by the protozoan *Entamoeba histolytica*, is characterised by a gradual onset of low-grade diarrhoea, often with blood and mucus. Cramping abdominal pain and vomiting are less likely than in other types of diarrhoea, and fever may not be present. It will persist until treated and can recur and cause other health problems.

You should seek medical advice if you think you have giardiasis or amoebic dysentery, but where this is not possible, Fasigyn (tinidazole) or Flagyl (metronidazole) are the recommended drugs. Treatment is a 2g single dose of tinidazole or 250mg of metronidazole three times daily for five to 10 days. Never drink alcohol with these tablets.

Hepatitis This is a general term for inflammation of the liver. It is a common disease worldwide. There are several different viruses that cause hepatitis, and they differ in the way that they are transmitted. The symptoms are similar in all forms of the illness, and include fever, chills, headache, fatigue, feelings of weakness and aches and pains, followed by loss of appetite, nausea, vomiting, abdominal pain, dark urine, light-coloured faeces, jaundiced (yellow) skin and yellowing of the whites of the eyes. People who have had hepatitis should avoid alcohol for some time after the illness, as the liver needs time to recover.

Hepatitis A is transmitted by contaminated food and drinking water. You should seek medical advice, but there is not much you can do apart from resting, drinking lots of fluids, eating lightly and avoiding fatty foods. Hepatitis E is transmitted in the same way as hepatitis A; it can be particularly serious in pregnant women.

There are almost 300 million chronic carriers of **hepatitis B** in the world and the disease is endemic in Mongolia. It is spread through contact with infected blood, blood products or body fluids, for example through sexual contact, unsterilised needles and blood transfusions, or contact with blood via small breaks in the skin. Other risk situations include having a shave, or getting a tattoo or body piercing with contaminated equipment. The symptoms of hepatitis B may be more severe than type A and the disease can lead to long term problems such as chronic liver damage, liver cancer or a long term carrier state. Hepatitis C and D are spread in the same way as hepatitis B and can also lead to long term complications.

There are vaccines against hepatitis A and B, but there are currently no vaccines against the other types of hepatitis. Following the basic rules about food and water (hepatitis A and E) and avoiding risk situations (hepatitis B, C and D) are important preventative measures.

HIV & AIDS The Mongolian government announced its discovery of the first known case of AIDS in 1993, but given the low standard of medical care and medical testing facilities, it's likely many other cases will remain undetected for some time.

Infection with the human immunodeficiency virus (HIV) may lead to acquired immune deficiency syndrome (AIDS), which is a fatal disease. Any exposure to blood, blood products or body fluids may put the individual at risk. The disease is often transmitted through sexual contact or dirty needles – vaccinations, acupuncture, tattooing and body piercing can be potentially as dangerous as intravenous drug use. HIV/AIDS can also be spread through infected blood transfusions; Mongolia cannot afford to screen blood used for transfusions.

If you do need an injection, ask to see the syringe unwrapped in front of you, or take a needle and syringe pack with you. In this case, it can be useful to bring a letter from your GP to wave at customs, in case they start jumping to the wrong conclusions.

It should be noted that fear of HIV infection should never preclude treatment for serious medical conditions.

Meningococcal Meningitis This serious disease can be fatal and there are recurring epidemics in Mongolia.

A fever, severe headache, sensitivity to light and neck stiffness which prevents forward bending of the head are the first symptoms. There may also be purple patches on the skin. Death can occur within a few hours, so urgent medical treatment is required.

Treatment is large doses of penicillin given intravenously, or chloramphenicol injections.

Sexually Transmitted Infections HIV/ AIDS and hepatitis B can be transmitted through sexual contact – see the relevant sections earlier for more details. Other STIs include gonorrhoea, herpes and syphilis; sores, blisters or rashes around the genitals and discharges or pain when urinating are common symptoms. In some STIs, such as wart virus or chlamydia, symptoms may be less marked or not observed at all, especially in women. Chlamydia infection can cause infertility in men and women before any symptoms have been noticed. Syphilis symptoms eventually disappear completely but the disease continues and can cause severe problems in later years. While abstinence from sexual contact is the only 100% effective prevention, using condoms is also effective. The treatment of gonorrhoea and syphilis is with antibiotics. The different sexually transmitted diseases each require specific antibiotics.

Cuts, Bites & Stings

See Less Common Diseases for details of rabies, which is passed through animal bites.

Cuts & Scratches Wash well and treat any cut with an antiseptic such as povidone-iodine. Where possible avoid bandages and Band-Aids, which can keep wounds wet. Coral cuts are notoriously slow to heal and if they are not adequately cleaned, small pieces of coral can become embedded in the wound.

Bedbugs & Lice Bedbugs live in various places, but particularly in dirty mattresses and bedding, evidenced by spots of blood on bedclothes or on the wall. Bedbugs leave itchy bites in neat rows. Calamine lotion or a sting relief spray may help.

All lice cause itching and discomfort. They make themselves at home in your hair, your clothing, or in your pubic hair. You catch lice through direct contact with infected people or by sharing combs, clothing and the like. Powder or shampoo treatment will kill the lice and infected clothing should then be washed in very hot, soapy water and left in the sun to dry.

Bites & Stings Bee and wasp stings are usually painful rather than dangerous. However, in people who are allergic to them severe breathing difficulties may occur and victims may require urgent medical care.

Calamine lotion or a sting relief spray will give relief and ice packs will reduce the pain and swelling.

Tarantulas are found in Mongolia. However, their venom is not very strong, and unless you pick one up and play with it, you aren't likely to be bitten.

Ticks You should always check all over your body if you have been walking through a potentially tick-infested area as ticks can cause skin infections and other more serious diseases. If a tick is found attached, press down around the tick's head with tweezers, grab the head and gently pull upwards. Avoid pulling the rear of the body as this may squeeze the tick's gut contents through the attached mouth parts into the skin, increasing the risk of infection and disease. Smearing chemicals on the tick will not make it let go and is not recommended.

Snakes Mongolia has four species of poisonous snakes: Halys viper *(agkistrodon halys)*, common European viper or adder *(vipera berus)*, Orsini's viper *(vipera ursini)* and the small *taphrometaphon lineolatum*.

To minimise your chances of being bitten always wear boots, socks and long trousers when walking through undergrowth where snakes may be present. Don't put your hands into holes and crevices, and be careful when collecting firewood.

Snake bites do not cause instantaneous death but the chances of finding antivenin in Mongolia are fairly remote. Immediately wrap the bitten limb tightly, as you would for a sprained ankle, and then attach a splint to immobilise it. Keep the victim still and seek medical help, if possible with the dead snake for identification. Don't attempt to catch the snake if there is a possibility of being bitten again. Tourniquets and sucking out the poison are now comprehensively discredited.

Women's Health
Gynaecological Problems Antibiotic use, synthetic underwear, sweating and contraceptive pills can lead to fungal vaginal infections, especially when travelling in hot climates. Fungal infections are characterised by a rash, itch and discharge and can be treated with a vinegar or lemon-juice douche, or with yoghurt. Nystatin, miconazole or clotrimazole pessaries or vaginal cream are the usual treatment. Maintaining good personal hygiene and wearing loose-fitting clothes and cotton underwear may help prevent these infections.

Sexually transmitted diseases are a major cause of vaginal problems. Symptoms include an odorous discharge, painful intercourse and sometimes a burning sensation when urinating. Medical attention should be sought and male sexual partners must also be treated. For more details see the entry Sexually Transmitted Diseases earlier. Besides abstinence, the best thing is to practise safer sex using condoms.

Less Common Diseases
Cholera In the summer of 1996, Mongolia reported its first outbreak of cholera. This is the worst of the watery diarrhoeas and medical help should be sought. *Fluid replacement is the most vital treatment* – the risk of dehydration is severe as you may lose up to 20L a day. If there is a delay in getting to hospital, then begin taking tetracycline. The adult dose is 250mg four times daily. It is not recommended for children under nine years nor for pregnant women. Tetracycline may help shorten the illness, but adequate fluids are required to save lives.

Rabies In the Mongolian countryside, family dogs are often vicious and can be rabid; it is their saliva which is infectious. Any bite, scratch or even lick from an animal should be cleaned immediately and thoroughly. Scrub with soap and running water, and then apply alcohol or iodine solution. Medical help should be sought promptly to receive a course of injections to prevent the onset of symptoms and death. The incubation period for rabies depends on where you're bitten. If on the head, face or neck then it's as little as 10 days, whereas on the arms it's 40 days and on the legs it's 60 days.

Tetanus This disease is caused by a germ which lives in soil and in the faeces of horses and other animals. It enters the body via breaks in the skin. The first symptom may be discomfort in swallowing, or stiffening of the jaw and neck; this is followed by painful convulsions of the jaw and whole body. The disease can be fatal. It can be prevented by vaccination.

Tuberculosis (TB) TB is a bacterial infection usually transmitted from person to person by coughing but which may be transmitted through consumption of unpasteurised milk. Milk that has been boiled is safe to drink, and the souring of milk to make yoghurt or cheese also kills the bacilli. Travellers are usually not at great risk as close household contact with the infected person is usually required before the disease is passed on. You may need to have a TB test before you travel as this can help diagnose the disease later if you become ill.

WOMEN TRAVELLERS
Mongolia doesn't present too many problems for foreign women travelling independently. The majority of Mongolian men behave in a friendly and respectful manner, without ulterior motives. However, you may come across an annoying drunk or the occasional macho idiot. You should also be more conservative in the mostly Muslim Bayan-Ölgii aimag. Those who have travelled in Central Asia can breathe easier while in Mongolia.

GAY & LESBIAN TRAVELLERS
There is little, if any, gay and lesbian culture in Mongolia. Straight or gay, it's best to avoid public displays of affection.

We have received information on Mongolia's first gay & lesbian rights group, Tavilan (Destiny), formed in April 2000. Members intend to create a social network, link with gay rights groups overseas and encourage better understanding amongst the general public. It can be contacted at PO Box 405, Ulaanbaatar 210644.

DISABLED TRAVELLERS
Mongolia is a difficult place for wheelchair travellers as most buildings and buses are not wheelchair accessible, and in addition there are rough roads and general poor standards of accommodation. Still, travel to Ulaan Baatar, and jeep trips to places such as Kharkhorin shouldn't cause insurmountable problems.

If any specialised travel agency might be interested in arranging trips to Mongolia, the best bet is Accessible Journeys (☎ 800-tingles, ☎ 610-521 0339, fax 521 6959, e sales@disabilitytravel.com) in Pennsylvania, USA. At the very least, hire your own transport and guide through one of the agencies listed under Travel Agencies in the Information section of the Ulaan Baatar chapter.

Also, try any of the agencies under Organised Tours in the Getting There & Away chapter. If you explain your disability, these organisations may be able to accommodate you.

The following organisations offer general travel advice for the disabled but provide no specific information on Mongolia.

Australia
NICAN (☎ 02-6285 3713, fax 6285 3714) PO Box 407, Curtin, ACT 2605. Provides information on recreation, tourism, sports and the arts for disabled people.

UK
Holiday Care Service (☎ 01293-774535, fax 784647) Imperial Buildings, Victoria Rd, Horley, Surrey RH6 7PZ
Travelcare (☎ 0120-8295 1797, fax 8467 2467) 35A High St, Chislehurst, Kent BR7 QAE. Specialises in travel insurance for the disabled.

USA
Access (The Foundation for Accessibility for the Disabled; ☎ 516-887 5798) PO Box 356, Malverne, NY 11565
Mobility International USA (☎ 541-343 1284 V/TTY, fax 343 6812, e info@miusa.org) PO Box 10767, Eugene, OR 97440. Organises international exchanges.
Web site: www.miusa.org.
SATH (Society for the Advancement of Travel for the Handicapped; ☎ 212-447 0027, fax 725 8253) 347 Fifth Ave No 610, New York, NY

10016. Its Web site contains tips on how to travel with diabetes, arthritis, visual and hearing impairments, and wheelchairs. Web site: www.sath.org

For general advice, bulletin boards and searchable databases on the Internet try the following Web sites.

Access-able Travel Source Provides access information for mature and disabled travellers. Web site: www.access-able.com

New Mobility Magazine An excellent online resource for disability culture and lifestyle. Web site: www.newmobility.com

Disabled Peoples' International (DPI) A cross-disability network dedicated to promoting the human rights of people with disabilities. Web site: www.dpi.org

SENIOR TRAVELLERS

There seems no reason why senior travellers can't enjoy Mongolia. The extremes of temperatures in deserts and mountains, however, and the lack of decent medical care may pose a risk. Consult your doctor before travelling and if you travel in a tour group, let the organisation know of any existing medical condition. Two companies worth contacting (although neither has much, if any, experience) in Mongolia are:

Seniors Travel (☎ 02-6285 2644, fax 6285 2430, e tbriton_justtravel@atlasmail.com) This Australian company arranges group tours for clients aged fifty and over Web site: www.seniorstravel.com.au

Travel Aides International (☎ 530-873 2977, e travel@c-zone.net), 14885 Snowberry Cir, Magalla USA. If you wish to travel more independently but still require some health care. The travel agency that also provides health care companions. Web site: www.members.tripod.com/~Travel_us

TRAVEL WITH CHILDREN

Children can be a great icebreaker and are a good avenue for cultural exchange with the local people; however, travelling in Mongolia is difficult for even a healthy adult. Long jeep rides over non-existent roads are a sure route to motion sickness. Mongolian food is difficult to stomach no matter what your age and the endless steppe landscape may leave your children comatose with boredom. That said children often like the thrill of camping, for a night or two at least. The only truly child friendly places in Mongolia are the Nairamdal Zuslan International Children's Centre outside Ulaan Baatar and the very tame rides at Nairamdal Park in Ulaan Baatar.

When travelling in the countryside, deluxe hotel rooms normally come with an extra connecting room, which can be ideal for children.

USEFUL ORGANISATIONS

If you need some information about Mongolia before you come, or want to meet some people once you arrive, there are several Mongolian friendship societies and organisations to contact.

Australia
Australia-Mongolia Society (☎/fax 02-9966 1922, or ☎ 02-9966 1916, e monconoz @yahoo.com) PO Box 1731, North Sydney NSW 2060

France
Association Culturelle Franco-Mongolie 94 rue Broca, F-75013, Paris

Germany
Mongolische Notizen (☎ 2244-6081) Waldfriedenstr 31, D-53639, Königswinter

Italy
Associazone Italia-Mongolia (☎ 40-362 241, fax 363 494) PO Box 979, Viale XX, Settembre 37, Trieste

UK
Anglo-Mongolian Society (☎ 0113-233 3460, fax 233 6741) Dept of Far Eastern Studies, University of Great Britain, Leeds LS2 9JT

Tibet Foundation (☎ 020-7404 2889, fax 7404 2366, e getza@gn.apc.org) 10 Bloomsbury Way, London WC1A 25H. The foundation has a program 'Buddhism in Mongolia' helping the Mongolian revival of Buddhist culture. Web site: www.tibet-foundation.org

USA
Mongolia Society (☎ 812-855 4078, fax 855 7500, e monsoc@indiana.edu) 322 Goodbody

Hall, Indiana University, Bloomington, IN 47405.
Web site: www.indiana.edu/~mongsoc/index.html

Mongol-American Cultural Association
(☎/fax 908-297 1140) 50 Louis St, New Brunswick, NJ 08901

The Mongolian Business Development Agency (☎ 311 694, **e** mbda@magicnet.mn) in Ulaan Baatar is an independent nongovernment organisation, which assists business throughout Mongolia and can provide information on Mongolian businesses.

DANGERS & ANNOYANCES

Before you get angry and complain about why things just don't work as well as they could or should, take a second to think about what Mongolia has experienced and is still enduring: years of Chinese domination and Soviet communism; a perverse climate; a terrible road and transport system; a lifestyle based on nomadism, which rarely complements Western thinking and economics; a young, sparse population which suffers from poverty and poor health; and unrestrained capitalism and development since 1990.

Theft

Mongolia is a very safe country and Mongolian people are some of the friendliest and most helpful in Asia. Most Mongolians are very poor and foreign goodies are a real temptation. Theft is seldom violent against foreigners, just opportunistic. Pickpocketing and bag slitting with razor blades are increasingly common on buses and in the Central Market (Black Market) in Ulaan Baatar, but is not nearly as rife as in China. At the monastery Gandantegchinlen Khiid, unsuspecting tourists, mesmerised by enchanting ceremonies, have been relieved of their money and passports. If you camp at Yarmag near Ulaan Baatar during the Naadam Festival, be especially careful.

Valuables should be kept in a money belt and buried under your clothes. Some people find this arrangement uncomfortable, so another alternative is to keep these valuables in pockets sewn on the *inside* of a vest (waistcoat). On public transport in Ulaan Baatar, carry your bag in front of you.

After Dark

It is not a good idea to walk around ger suburbs in Ulaan Baatar, and in the countryside, after dark, especially if you are travelling alone and don't speak Mongolian. In Ulaan Baatar, street lights often cease at 2 am, so be home by then, or take a taxi. Foreigners should use an official taxi – as opposed to a private vehicle – for lifts around town late at night.

Be careful when leaving nightclubs alone in Ulaan Baatar, where alcohol and comparatively rich foreigners are a potentially vulnerable mixture. Try to leave in a group rather than alone.

Virtually no stairways in the whole country have lights, so a torch (flashlight) is a good idea. In Ulaan Baatar it will save you from crashing down the stairways of apartments, which are always pitch-black, even during the day. It's also handy when street lights go out during a blackout.

Dogs

Stray dogs in the cities and domestic dogs around gers in the countryside can be vicious, and possibly rabid. In the countryside, some dogs are so damn lazy that you are unlikely to get a whimper if a hundred lame cats hobbled past; others may almost headbutt your vehicle and chase it for 2 or 3km while drooling heavily. Before approaching any ger, especially in the countryside, make sure the dogs are friendly or under control and shout the phrase '*Nokhoi khor*', which roughly translates as 'Can I come in?', but literally means 'Hold the dog!'.

If you need to walk in the dark in the countryside, perhaps for a midnight trip to the toilet, locals have suggested that if you swing a torch in front of you it will stop any possible dog attack.

Alcoholism

Alcoholism is a real problem and is far worse in the cities than in the countryside. Drinking often starts early in the morning,

Some Handy Advice

In Ulaan Baatar, you should never walk around the ger suburbs and away from street lighting after dark; if the drunks don't get you, the stray dogs probably will.

and the problem becomes progressively worse in the evenings. Drunks are more annoying than dangerous, except when they are driving your bus or taxi – so avoid any vehicle which you know or suspect is driven by a drunk.

Be sensible in bars: don't get into arguments about the virtues or otherwise of Chinggis Khaan, or flash around a lot of money. One Voluntary Service Overseas (VSO) worker was hospitalised a couple of years ago when he moved a Mongolian's hat while in a bar.

If camping, always make sure that you have pitched your tent somewhere secluded, and that no drunks have seen you set up camp – otherwise, they will invariably visit you during the night.

Queues

It could be the warrior-like bloodlines from Chinggis Khaan, a penchant for wrestling or habits from the communist days where demand always exceeded supply, but Mongolians rarely queue – they bustle, huddle and scramble. You will often need to sharpen your elbows, learn some appropriately argumentative phrases in Mongolian, and plough head first through the throng. Being polite won't really help, nor will getting angry.

Corruption & Greed

Mongolians complain loudly because they suffer the consequences of corruption daily – aid money doesn't reach its intended beneficiaries, the old elite still controls everything and no-one believes the prime minister survives just on his official salary. Anyone trying to do business in Mongolia will soon discover that corruption is rampant and growing.

At the lake Terkhiin Tsagaan Nuur, we have heard reports of locals demanding 'fines' for fishing or 'fees' for camping, among other such things. Problems like this are often due to frustration about the lack of income reaching locals, in spite of increasing tourism. If someone says that they are a ranger or government official ask to see identification and get a receipt for all monies paid. The main problem in protected areas is that park rules, such as the system of fishing permits, are often vague and hard to implement. Rangers can be devilishly hard to find until you commit the smallest infraction and then five jump on you at once.

Other Annoyances

Electricity, heating and hot water shortages and blackouts are common all year, and permanent restrictions are endemic in the countryside. Although official policies have relaxed considerably since the arrival of democracy, some of the old KGB-inspired thinking still occurs among the police, especially in rural backwaters and border areas.

Most offices have security guards in the lobby checking the ID cards of everyone who enters and leaves the buildings – it can sometimes be a nightmare getting past them. Street children in Ulaan Baatar are an increasing annoyance, though they are nothing compared to India or even China.

Quarantine sometimes affects travel in Mongolia; in mid-2000 there were several cases of foot and mouth disease and plague. Areas are often quarantined for a month or more.

EMERGENCIES

If you are in an emergency, try to find a Mongolian who speaks English (or your native language) because almost all of the people you will need to speak to understand only Mongolian or Russian. It can be useful to carry the contact details of your embassy with you. Emergency numbers in Ulaan Baatar are as follows:

Fire	☎ 101
Emergency aid/Ambulance	☎ 103
Police emergency	☎ 102

LEGAL MATTERS

Arrest is unlikely unless there are supportable charges against you. If you are arrested, however, the Mongolian authorities are obliged to inform your embassy immediately and allow you to communicate with embassy staff without delay. The Mongolian for 'I wish to contact my embassy' is *'Bi elchin yamtaigaa yarimaar baina'*. If you are polite and respectful to officials, things will go far more smoothly for you. Most embassies can provide a list of recommended local lawyers.

BUSINESS HOURS

Government offices are usually open from 9 am to 5 pm on weekdays. Banks are supposed to open from 10 am to 3 pm weekdays. Mongolia introduced a five-day working week in 1998. Most private and state-run businesses open at about 10 am and close sometime between 5 and 8 pm. In the countryside most *guanz* (canteens) seem to close for dinner (and often lunch as well). In reality, opening hours are often at the whim of staff.

Most shops and businesses will close for an hour at lunch, sometime between noon and 2 pm. In Ulaan Baatar, many restaurants – especially the good ones – will be busy and often full between about 1 and 2 pm. It pays to get a table before 12.30 pm to beat the rush.

Museums have contracted hours in winter and are normally closed an extra couple of days a week.

PUBLIC HOLIDAYS & SPECIAL EVENTS

The following public holidays are celebrated in Mongolia, but not necessarily with a day off work:

Shin Jil (New Year's Day) 1 January
Constitution Day 13 January, the adoption of the 1992 constitution (generally a normal working day)
Tsagaan Sar (Lunar New Year) A three-day holiday in January/February, held at the same time as Chinese New Year
Women's Day 8 March (generally a normal working day)
Mother & Children's Day 1 June, a great time to visit parks
National Day Celebrations 11 to 13 July, are more famously celebrated as the Naadam Festival
Mongolian Republic Day 26 November (generally a normal working day)

You can expect Mongolia to go mad in the summer of 2006, when it celebrates the 800th anniversary of the founding of the nation by Chinggis Khaan in 1206.

Tsagaan Sar

After months of enduring a bitter winter, Mongolians love to celebrate Tsagaan Sar (White Month), the start of the lunar new year. The festivities are held over three days in January or February. Most travellers are unlikely to be in Mongolia at this time, but if you are, be prepared to eat a lot of food. The holiday was outlawed during the communist era but continued in the countryside, where it was renamed The Herder's Holiday.

During the first day, the fattest sheep (ie, the one with the most fat) is killed and hundreds and hundreds of steamed dumplings called *buuz* are made. The tail, which is the most prized part of the sheep is kept until the end of the celebrations.

The days are filled with traditional songs, greetings called *zolgokh*, where younger people give their respect to the older generations, and visits to other gers and, these days, to monasteries. A cast-iron liver is required to cope with the amount of airag and vodka which is traditionally consumed.

Buddhist Festivals

Ikh Duichin, or Buddha's Birthday, is held on May 18 and marked by *tsam* (lama) dancing in the monastery Gandantegchinlen Khiid in Ulaan Baatar and by special services in most other monasteries. Monasteries also hold special services during the full moon and mid-moon of the lunar calendar.

ACTIVITIES
Skiing

If you can bear the cold, Mongolia is a great place for cross-country skiing. Snow

The Cult of the Great Khaan

Contrary to popular belief, Chinggis Khaan is alive and well. His ubiquitous face adorns bottles of Chinggis Khaan vodka, as well as money and postage stamps. Ulaan Baatar's best hotel, rock band and brewery is named after him. Despite his reputation abroad, an understandable, renewed nationalism has resulted in a reverence for the Great Khaan, history's best known Mongolian.

'Genghis Khan' has suffered from over 800 years of bad press in the West. The Muslim historian Rashid-al-din summed up the Western perception of the man when he 'quoted' Chinggis, saying that the single greatest pleasure in his life was 'to cut my enemy to pieces, drive them before me, seize their possessions, witness the tears of those who are dear to them and to embrace their wives and daughters.'

To the Mongolians, Chinggis Khaan embodies strength, unity, law and order. He is the young king who united the warring clans and gave Mongolians a sense of direction. This is what post-communist Mongolia looks for today, and Chinggis Khaan epitomises the historic ability to rise above confusion and uncertainty.

is often thin, but it's blanketed throughout the long winter, sometimes for seven months a year. The Juulchin travel agency runs skiing tours near Ulaan Baatar, or if you have your own gear go to Terelj or Nairamdal Zuslan in central Mongolia, the best and most accessible places, and ask about some safe trails. In winter you can hire Russian-made cross-country (but not downhill) skis and sleds in Khandgait (central Mongolia).

The best months for skiing are in January and February, although be warned: the average temperature in these months hovers around a very chilly -25°C.

Ice Skating

In winter, you won't have to worry about falling through the ice, as many lakes and rivers freeze right down to the bottom. Many Mongolians are keen ice skaters – at least those who live near water, or in big cities with rinks. Nadaam Stadium in Ulaan Baatar is normally flooded and frozen in winter and provides a good area to skate. Although it is possible to buy ice skates in Mongolia, don't count on it – if you're serious about this sport, bring your own equipment.

Horse & Camel Riding

Riding on horses and camels (and even yaks) is part of many organised tours and great fun – if only for a few minutes. (Mongolians watching you will probably enjoy it even more.) Most ger camps can arrange horse riding – the prettiest (but not cheapest) places to try are the camps at Terelj and Khövsgöl Nuur, where you can normally hire a horse and guide for less than US$20 a day.

If you are a serious rider, horses are everywhere; with some luck, guidance and experience, you should be able to find a horse suited to your needs. Mongolians swap horses readily, so there's no need to be stuck with a horse you don't like, or which doesn't like you. The only exception is in April and May, when all animals are weak after the long winter and before fresh spring plants have made their way through the melting snows. The best time for riding is in the summer (June to September), though it is usually wetter then.

See Horse Riding in the Getting Around Chapter, as well as Travel Agencies in the Information section of Ulaan Baatar. Of the dozens of possible horse treks, several are popular and not difficult to arrange:

Tsetserleg to Khujirt Via Kharkhorin.
Khövsgöl Nuur Circuiting the lake or the region around it.
Khentii aimag Possibly as far as Dadal, near the Siberian border.
From Ulaan Baatar A shorter trek between Terelj, Gachuurt, Manzshir Khiid and the mountain Bogdkhan Uul.
Bayankhongor to Tsetserleg You'll need a good guide for this wilderness trip.
Circuit of Tsast Uul and Tsambagarav Starting in the Namarjin or Bayangol valleys, taking in Mongol and Kazakh encampments.

At touristy places like the ger camps at Terelj and in the south Gobi you can ride a camel, though these are more like photo sessions rather than serious sport.

Hiking

Mongolia has many outstanding opportunities for hiking, though very few locals do it and think foreigners are crazy for even thinking about it. The biggest obstacle faced by hikers is finding transport to the mountains once they get far afield from Ulaan Baatar. However, in the regions around Bogdkhan Uul and Terelj, which are not far from Ulaan Baatar, there are enough mountains to keep hikers busy for months.

Way out west, you can break out the expedition gear and scale dozens of mountains with glaciers. Warm-weather hikers can head for the Gobi Desert, which despite its vast flatness also harbours a few rugged mountain ranges.

Essential survival gear includes a leakproof water bottle (take a minimum of two litres a day, preferably more during summer) and emergency food rations. Don't forget about Mongolia's notoriously changeable weather – a sudden wind from the north will make you think you're in the Arctic rather than the Gobi. Only from June to August can you usually expect balmy temperatures, but this is also when it rains most.

Some good trekking areas include Gorkhi-Terelj National Park (central Mongolia) and Khan Khentii Strictly Protected Area (eastern Mongolia), the Kharkhiraa Valley in Uvs (western Mongolia), around Tavanbogd Uul in Bayan-Ölgii, Khoton Nuur and the Sagsai Valley in Bayan-Ölgii (western Mongolia) and around Khövsgöl Nuur.

Decent maps are hard to come by. The ONC/TPC series or the 1:1 million topographic maps available in Ulaan Baatar are your best bet. It will also be handy to have a working knowledge of appropriate phrases such as: 'Where am I?' and 'Is that dog dangerous?'

Mosquitoes and midges are a curse. The situation is at its worst during spring and early summer.

It's best to hike with at least one companion, always tell someone where you're going and refer to your compass frequently so you can find the way back. Unless you're planning a camping trip, start out early in the day so that you can easily make it back before dark.

Mountaineering

Mongolia also offers spectacular opportunities for mountain climbing. In the western provinces, there are over 100 glaciers, and 30 to 40 permanently snowcapped mountains. You must have the necessary experience, be fully equipped and hire local guides. The best time to climb is from the start of July until the end of August.

While you don't need permits from the Ministry of Nature & Environment unless the mountain is in a national park, you should consult the undisputed experts in mountain climbing, the Mongol Altai Club (☎/fax 455 246, 343 500), PO Box 36-146, Ulaan Baatar. The club runs specially designed mountain climbing trips. The office is often closed, so get a Mongolian speaker to ring first.

Mongolia's highest peaks in ascending order are:

Otgon Tenger Uul (3905m) In Zavkhan.

Türgen Uul (3965m) In Uvs; one of the most accessible and spectacular.

Kharkhiraa Uul (4032m) In Uvs; a great trekking area.

Sutai Uul (4090m) On the border of Gov-Altai and Khovd aimags. This awesome mountain is accessible and dominates the road between Altai and Khovd city.

Tsast Uul (4193m) On the border of Bayan-Ölgii and Khovd aimags; it is accessible and the camping in the area is gorgeous.

Tsambagarav Uul (4202m) In Khovd; it is relatively easy to climb with crampons and an ice axe. In 1996 a Japanese man skied down this mountain in 24 minutes.

Mönkh Khairkhan Uul (4362m) On the border between Bayan-Ölgii and Khovd aimags. You will need crampons, ice axe and ropes.

Tavanbogd Uul (4374m) In Bayan-Ölgii, on the border of Mongolia, China and Russia. It is full of permanent and crevassed glaciers.

Kayaking & Rafting

Mongolia's numerous lakes and rivers are often ideal for kayaking and rafting. Rafting is organised along the Tuul and Khovd rivers by the Juulchin travel agency. Boojum Expeditions has started kayaking trips on the Khövsgöl Nuur. Both agencies are based in Ulaan Baatar.

The best time for kayaking is in the summer (June to September); for rafting, the best time is July and August after some decent rain.

Mountain Bike

Mongolian roads are made for strong mountain bikes and masochist riders, villages and people are few and far between, and Mongolian dogs just *hate* bikes but it's still a great way to travel. See the Car & Motorcycle section in the Getting Around chapter for more information. The best places to try are:

Around Ulaan Baatar To Terelj, Khandgait and/or Manzshir Khiid.
From Mörön or Khatgal Along either side of the lake Khövsgöl Nuur.
Darkhan to Amarbayasgalant Khiid On to Erdenet via Bugant.
Kharkhorin to Khujirt On to Orkhon waterfall.

Fishing

With Mongolia's large number of lakes and rivers, and a sparse population that generally prefers red meat, the fish are just waiting to be caught. The best places to dangle your lines at are Khövsgöl Nuur (northern Mongolia) in summer (June to September) and the nearby Five Rivers area in September and October. The Shishugt Gol in the Tsagaannuur region west of Khövsgöl Nuur, the river Orkhon Gol in Övörkhangai, and the Chuluut Gol in Arkhangai aimag (both in central Mongolia) are also excellent. You'll need a fishing permit in many areas, which are either available from the national park rangers or local government office. Catch and release is standard practice.

Equipment is hard to rent anywhere in the country, so bring your own gear. In many places, all you need is a strong handline and a lure. Fishing is officially only allowed after June 15.

Helifishing is becoming popular, especially with diplomats from Beijing. Several companies can arrange for you to be dropped in remote and pristine areas an hour after leaving Ulaan Baatar.

If you are an enthusiast, one book to look out for is *Fishing in Mongolia* published by the US-based Avery Press.

Golf

Despite perfect terrain, there is currently no formal place in the country to play golf. The Japanese tried to build a golf course in southern Ulaan Baatar but they were ordered to stop after a dispute over the types of chemical fertiliser to be used. Expats sometimes knock some balls around at Gachuurt, about 20km from Ulaan Baatar.

Birding

The best places to get out your binoculars and telephoto lens are the following lakes:

Sangiin Dalai Nuur Mongolian lark, eagles, geese and swans
Khar Us Nuur Geese, wood grouse and relict gull
Khar Nuur and Airag Nuur Migratory pelicans
Uvs Nuur Spoonbills, cranes and gulls
Ganga Nuur Migratory swans

Other Activities

The Mongolian Air Sports Federation is trying to arrange a series of aerial sports such as paragliding (behind the Zaisan Memorial), parachuting and ballooning. If this is your thing you'll just have to ask around travel companies to see if they know if anything is happening.

COURSES
Language Courses

Several language schools in Ulaan Baatar organise long and short term language courses. They can also hook you up with a private tutor for around US$5 per hour. You can also learn Mongolian from someone who wants to learn or practise your language. (English, French, German and Japanese are particularly popular.) Two recommended schools in Ulaan Baatar include:

Bridge Mongolian Language Center (☎ 367 149, e bridgeinst@magicnet.mn), Room 205, Sunrise Center, Jalhanz Hutagt Damdinbazer St. Located in the suburbs of the 4th district, it's a cheaper option than Santis, and offers an intensive two-week survival course, as well as longer courses and individual tuition.

Santis (☎ 318 313, fax 326 373, e santis@ magicnet.mn), 5th floor, Unen Newspaper Bldg, just east of the Tuvshin Hotel. It can arrange private Mongolian language tuition for US$5 per hour, and also offers 50 hour, six-week group courses for around US$4 per hour, though most of these start in September.

The best places to ask around for 'exchange lessons' are the National University of Mongolia and the Institute of Foreign Languages in Ulaan Baatar, as well as the embassies and development agencies. Also check out the English-language newspapers for any advertisements about language courses.

Buddhism & Scroll Painting

The Federation for the Preservation of Mahayana Tradition (FPMT; ☎ 9911 9765, e fpmt-mongolia@magicnet.mn) is involved in the regeneration of Buddhist culture in Mongolia. The centre offers free lectures and courses on various aspects of Buddhist tradition and meditation. Lectures are given in English and held in the pink-tiled building, next to the Center Hotel, on Khudaldaany Gudamj.

The Mongol-Korean Buddhist Institute of Culture at Gandan Khiid in Ulaan Baatar sometimes runs long-term *thangka* (scroll painting) classes for the serious student. However, they may also be able to offer private tuition to interested foreigners.

WORK

Mongolia is certainly not somewhere you can just turn up and expect to get paid employment – even for teaching English the demand is not high, and working regulations are fairly stringent for foreigners. Also, you will receive poor pay (possibly the same as locals), unless you can score a job with a development agency, but these agencies usually recruit their non-Mongolian

staff in their home country, not from within Mongolia.

If you are keen to work in Mongolia and are qualified in teaching or health, contact the organisations listed in the Useful Organisations section earlier, or in the Volunteer Work section later. They will appreciate it if you contact them *before* you come to Mongolia.

Language Teaching

Some Mongolians want to forget Russian and learn a useful European language, particularly English, so there is a demand (albeit low) for teachers. Colleges and volunteer agencies are, however, on the lookout for qualified teachers who are willing to stay for a few terms (if not a few years), and not just for a week or two. Contact the voluntary service agencies in your home country or the ones listed below.

Informal, short-term work may be possible through smaller organisations, such as the many private universities which have sprung up, or you may be able to do freelance tutoring for a while, but don't expect to make much money. Try the Mongolian Knowledge University (☎ 327 165, fax 358 354), the Institute of Foreign Languages, or the International School (☎ 452 959).

Volunteer Work

Some organisations are anxious to receive help from qualified people, particularly in education and health. Unless you are particularly well qualified, or your expertise is in desperately short supply, you are asked to contact these agencies *before* you come to Mongolia.

They are more interested in committed people who are willing to stay two years or more. In most instances, you will be paid in local wages (or possibly a little more).

Australian Volunteers Abroad (AVA; ☎ 03-9279 1788, fax 9419 4280, e osb@osb.org.au) PO Box 350, Fitzroy Vic 3065. AVA has a handful of Australian volunteers in Mongolia.

Peace Corps (Enkh Tavnii Korpus in Mongolian; ☎ 311 520) The organisation is well represented throughout the country. Alternatively, contact your local Peace Corps office in the

USA (☎ 1-800-424 858, 202-606 3970, fax 606 3110)
Web site: www.peacecorps.gov.

United Nations Development Program (UNDP; ☎ 327 585, fax 326 221) PO Box 49/207, Ulaan Baatar, 7 Erkhuugiin St. The UNDP is always on the lookout for committed and hard-working volunteers but it normally recruits abroad.

Voluntary Service Overseas (VSO; ☎/fax 320 460, [e] vsomongolia@magicnet.mn) PO Box 678, Ulaan Baatar. This British-run organisation is set up mainly for Brits. They prefer you to contact them through their head office in the UK (☎ 020-8780 2266, fax 8780 1326) 317 Putney Bridge Rd, London SW15 2PN.

ACCOMMODATION

Like most things about Mongolia, the accommodation situation in Ulaan Baatar is vastly different to what you will find anywhere outside of the capital city. In Ulaan Baatar, there is a wide range of accommodation, from dormitory-style places for US$3 a night to suites in the Chinggis Khaan Hotel, which cost almost as much as Mongolia's Gross Domestic Product. Yet only 30 minutes by bus from the capital city, the hotels are decrepit, closed or offer very little comfort or service.

One unique option, particularly popular with organised tours, is to stay in tourist gers, like the ones used by nomads (except, of course, for the hot water, toilets, sheets and karaoke bars). The best type of accommodation is to bring your own tent and camp – it is free, and you really experience what Mongolia has to offer.

Except for top-end hotels, which have caught on to the single/double room concept, all prices are per person – not per bed or per room. Always check for taxes and hidden extras. Remember that most hotels in the countryside will charge you a 'foreigners' price' (see Dual-Pricing under Money earlier in this chapter).

If you negotiate a reasonable price with the management, try to pay immediately and get a receipt. Asking for a receipt sometimes drops the price dramatically; in some cases the staff will officially register you as a Mongolian, charge you the 'Mongolian

price' on paper, charge you the 'foreigners' price' in reality, and pocket the difference themselves.

Hotel staff may ask to keep your passport as 'security'. This is not a good idea, for three reasons: the common tendency for staff not to show up for work (the person with your passport cannot be found when you want to depart); once they have your passport, it leaves you open to extortion; or you may simply forget to pick it up and be 300km away before you realise it. An expired passport, student card or some other ID with your photo is a great alternative to leaving your real passport.

Security should be a consideration. Always keep your windows and door locked (where possible). Since the hotel staff may enter your room while you're not around, take any valuables with you or at least keep them locked inside your luggage and don't leave cameras and money lying around your room. Most hotels have a safe where valuables can be kept. When you retrieve things from it, they are often as anxious as you that you check everything on the spot, lest they be accused of sticky fingers.

Camping

Mongolia is probably the greatest country in the world for camping. With 1.5 million sq km of unfenced and unowned land, spectacular scenery and freshwater lakes and rivers, it is just about perfect. The main problem is a lack of public transport to great camping sites, though there are some near Ulaan Baatar, such as Gachuurt, Khandgait and Terelj. Camping is also worth considering given the dire lack of hotels in the countryside and the expense of ger camps.

Local people (and even a few curious cows or horses) may come to investigate your camping spot, but you are very unlikely to encounter any hostility. Your jeep driver will have ideas about good places to stay, otherwise look for somewhere near water, or in a pretty valley. If you're hitching, it is not hard to find somewhere to pitch your tent within walking distance of most aimag capitals and towns. You will need to bring your own tent, as well as cooking

Minimum Impact Camping

If you are camping, please be aware of the fragile ecology of Mongolia and take notice of a few guidelines.

- Carry out all non-biodegradable items and deposit them at rubbish bins in the nearest town. Don't overlook easily forgotten items, such as silver paper, orange peel, cigarette butts and plastic wrappers.
- When on a jeep trip have a designated rubbish bag. Make an effort to carry out rubbish left by others.
- Where there is no toilet, choose a spot at least 100m from any water source, bury your waste at least 15cm (6 inches) deep, and bury or burn toilet paper, if possible. In snow, dig down to the soil; otherwise, your waste will be exposed when the snow melts.
- For personal washing, use biodegradable soap and a water container (or even a lightweight, portable basin) at least 50m (160 feet) away from the watercourse. Disperse the waste water widely to allow the soil to filter it fully before it finally makes it back to the watercourse.
- Camp at least 300 or 400m from the nearest ger.
- Don't rely on open fires for cooking and use a petrol stove whenever possible. If building a fire, use existing fire rings wherever possible, only use dead, fallen wood and remember that it is sacred to Mongolians.
- Ensure that you fully extinguish a fire after use. Spread the embers and douse them with water. A fire is only truly safe to leave when you can comfortably place your hand in it.
- Don't rely on bought water in plastic bottles. Disposal of these bottles can be a major problem, particularly in developing countries. Use iodine drops or purification tablets instead.

equipment, if you are not camping near main towns or want to avoid the local guanz.

You can often get boiled water, cooked food, uncooked meat and dairy products from nearby gers in exchange for other goods, but don't rely on nomads, who may have limited supplies of food, water and fuel. It is best to bring a portable, petrol stove – petrol is the only widely available fuel in Mongolia – rather than use open fires, which are potentially dangerous, use precious wood and are useless in a country where wood is scarce.

Be mindful of your security. If drunks spot your tent, you could have a problem. If the owners (and their dog) give you permission, camping near a ger is a good idea for extra security; otherwise camp at least 300m from other gers. Mongolians have little or no idea of the Western concept of privacy, so be prepared for the locals to open your tent and look inside at any time – no invitation is needed.

Here are a few extra tips:

- Burn dried dung if you are being eaten alive by mosquitoes (you may then have to decide which is worse: mossies or burning cow shit) and bring strong repellent with as much DEET as possible. Other anti-mosquito advice includes: wear light-coloured clothing, avoid perfumes or aftershave, impregnate clothes and mosquito nets with permethrin (nontoxic insect repellent), make sure your tent has an insect screen and camp away from still water or marshes.
- Make sure that your tent is waterproof before you leave home and always pitch it in anticipation of strong winds and rain.
- Store your food carefully if you don't want a midnight visit from a bunch of ravenous marmots (or worse).
- Don't pitch your tent under trees (because of lightning), or on or near riverbeds (flash floods are not uncommon).

Traditional Gers

If you are particularly fortunate, you may be invited to spend a night or two out on the steppes in a genuine ger, rather than a tourist ger camp. This is a wonderful experience, offering a chance to see the 'real' Mongolia.

If you are invited to stay in a family ger, in very rare cases only, you may be expected to pay for this accommodation, but in most cases no payment is wanted if you stay for one or two nights. See The Mongolian Ger special section for information on ger etiquette. If you stay longer (unless you have been specifically asked to extend your visit), you will outstay your welcome and abuse Mongolian hospitality, making it less likely that others will be welcome in the future. (Never rely on families to take you in; always carry a tent as a back up.)

Tourist Ger Camps

Tourist ger camps are springing up everywhere. It may seem touristy, and they are never good value, but if you are going into the countryside, a night in a tourist ger is a great way to experience some Western-oriented, 'traditional Mongolian nomadic lifestyle' without the discomforts or awkwardness of staying in a private ger. If on an organised tour, you will certainly stay in one for a few nights; if travelling independently, one or two nights in a tourist ger is often worth a splurge, particularly at somewhere as remote as the south Gobi or as beautiful as Terelj in central Mongolia.

A tourist ger camp is a patch of ground with up to two dozen traditional gers, with separate buildings for toilets, hot showers (!) and a ger-shaped restaurant/bar. Inside each ger, there are usually two to three beds, an ornate table, four tiny chairs and a wood

Ger Welcome Gifts

If it's late, you may be invited to stay the night at someone's ger. Some travellers feel they should pay for this, but unless money is asked for, it would be insulting and culturally damaging to offer your host a cash payment. Hospitality is the rule of the steppes.

However, travellers should never freeload off locals, who are often very poor, and you should never leave without offering something. Small practical gifts are always appreciated, especially items in short supply, in return for food and accommodation. It's far better to provide worthwhile gifts for the whole family, including the women (who look after the guests), rather than just for the men. Cigarettes and vodka are appreciated by men, but are rarely enjoyed by women. Similarly, sweets for young children aren't going to do their teeth any good. Constructive presents include children's text books written in the Mongolian language. Postcards from home are a nice thought but they won't mean much to your hosts; you are better off choosing a picture of horses, cowboys or some such from your own country.

Some useful gifts include: small packets of soap and shampoo; razors; needles (with large eyes) and thread for women; matches; lighters; toothbrushes; toothpaste; strong string; candles; cloth or ribbons; Sellotape; notebooks; stickers; colouring books, pens, pencils and paper for children; puzzles; recent editions of Mongolian newspapers; glue; first aid items; aspirin; hand mirrors; snuff; pictures of the Dalai Lama; AA batteries.

Make sure the gifts are small, otherwise there are greater expectations from future visitors. Pick three or four items and put them in a resealable bag (itself a useful gift). Sweets and tobacco, should you decide to give these, should be presented separately. To show respect, and to avoid any arguments, give practical gifts with both hands to the oldest woman and the tobacco, snuff, matches etc to the oldest man.

If your host is cooking for you, offer to supply some food, such as biscuits, fruit, salt, rice, pasta and noodles. Don't offer any tinned goods, because they may not have a tin opener, and they certainly won't have any suitable means of disposing of the can.

If you've got nothing to spare, at least offer to photograph your host's family and send the photos to them later. Be sure to get their address and, please, keep your promise.

Even if your host is dirt poor, you may be offered a small sum of cash when you get ready to leave. Rather than refuse, which would be insulting, accept the money. Then a few minutes later, offer a gift of money to the children. Hand this directly to the children, not to the adults. This saves face, since you are not acknowledging that the adults need the money.

stove which can be used for heating during the night – ask the staff to make it for you (though it may be with dried dung). The beds are really just smallish cots – if you are built like an NBA basketball player or a sumo wrestler, you'll need to make special arrangements.

Toilets are usually the sit-down types, though they may be (clean) pit toilets.

Expect to pay from US$35 to US$40 per person per night, including meals, which is a lot of money for an elaborate tent. Occasionally this price may include a trip to a nearby attraction, but normal activities, such as horse or camel riding, will cost extra. A surprising amount of the charge goes to the food bill, so you shave off from 50% to 65% of the cost by bringing your own food. If business is slack many ger camps will negotiate a price, which can often be as low as US$10 per person, which is pretty reasonable for a clean bed and a hot shower.

Meals are taken in a separate restaurant, often in a ger and often quite opulent (some gers even have chandeliers!). Although the food is Western, and definitely better than in any restaurant anywhere in the countryside, it is rarely a culinary delight! Most camps have a bar (and, sometimes, even satellite TV and a blasted karaoke machine), but drinks will never be cold and they will always be expensive. There's often little to differentiate ger camps; it's normally the location that adds charm and makes your stay special.

If you plan to stay in a ger camp you may want to bring a torch for nocturnal visits to the outside toilets; candles to create more ambience than stark electric lights (not all have electricity); towels (the ones provided are invariably smaller than a handkerchief); and toilet paper (they usually run out).

If travelling around the countryside independently and you want to stay in a ger camp, it is best to book ahead to ensure that the camp is open and has decent food. This is fine for camps owned by big companies such as Nature Tours, Tsolmon or MAT Tours in Ulaan Baatar, but private ger camps rarely have a telephone. Except for a

handful of ger camps in Terelj catering to expat skiers, most ger camps are only open from 1 June to mid-September; while in the Gobi, they open a month earlier and close a little later.

In a few touristed places, like Terelj or Khövsgöl Nuur, private families often have a guest ger and take in paying guests. In this case the advice on non-payment and offering gifts does not apply – this is a commercial transaction. These families are rarely registered with local authorities so they don't advertise – you'll have to ask around (any ger set up next to a road is a good bet).

Guesthouses

Ulaan Baatar now has around seven guesthouses firmly aimed at foreign backpackers. Most are in apartment blocks and have dorm rooms for US$3 or US$4 a bed, cheap meals, a laundry service, Internet connection and travel services. They are a great place to meet other travellers to share transportation costs but can get pretty crowded during Nadaam.

Outside Ulaan Baatar only Dalanzadgad in the Gobi and Khövsgöl Nuur have accommodation aimed at backpackers.

Apartments

If you are staying in Ulaan Baatar for a week or more, it is cheaper and more convenient to rent an apartment – the hard part is finding one and arranging a short-term lease. Several of the guesthouses can arrange an apartment for between US$10 and US$20 per day, which is generally a bargain and much better value than the hotels. You must pay for the electricity and telephone. Water and heating is free thanks to the unmetered centralised hot-water system installed by the Russians.

Hotels

Hotels in Ulaan Baatar are generally pretty good, though they are all chronically overpriced. Most places not in the budget range cost at least US$40 per single room. This is very poor value – rooms with far better facilities cost less in most Western countries. These rooms will be comfortable and clean, but have very little extra to justify the expense, except English-speaking staff and, perhaps, satellite TV – hot water and heating is standard for most buildings and hotels in Ulaan Baatar, and air-conditioning is never needed.

Staff at budget places in Ulaan Baatar and anywhere in the countryside (except for ger camps) will speak no English. The 'foreigners' price may be quoted in US dollars in an attempt to get the green stuff, but you should pay in tögrög because it is now the law.

A sleeping bag is generally not needed if you are staying in mid-range or top-end places or ger camps, though it's an added luxury (and useful if the heating breaks down outside of summer, which is not uncommon). If you are not camping but staying in budget hotels in the countryside you should bring a sleeping bag. An inner sheet (the sort used inside sleeping bags) is also handy if the sheets are dirty; blankets are always available, but are generally dirty or musty.

Most hotels (zochid budal) have three types of rooms: a 'deluxe' (büten lyuks) room, which includes a separate sitting room, usually with TV, and a private bathroom; a half-deluxe (khagas lyuks), which is much the same only a little smaller but often much cheaper; and a 'simple' (engiin) room, usually with a shared bathroom. Sometimes, dormitory-style (niitiin bair) beds are also available. Invariably, hotel staff will initially show you their deluxe room, which usually costs a ridiculous foreigners' price of up to T15,000 per person per night. Simple rooms are cheaper but generally still overpriced at about T5000 per person per night. Unless the hotel offers satellite TV, don't bother paying extra for a TV – it will only show distorted and incomprehensible Mongolian and Russian programs.

In the countryside, the hotels are generally empty and falling apart, though a few aimag capitals such as Tsetserleg, Arvaikheer and Uliastai have new private hotels which are quite good. They will normally be very cheap if you can get the Mongolian price (about T1000 per person per night), but they have few facilities. The newer private hotels are normally owned by a local business and may not be advertised. You may have to find out where the manager lives to get the hotel opened; the hotel may have no food; the toilets may be unbearable pit toilets or may be locked; and the electricity will probably be turned off by midnight or may not work at all. The quality of hotels in the countryside is reason enough to take a tent and camp.

As for service, it is generally poor, except for top-end places in Ulaan Baatar. You'll gain little by getting angry – just be businesslike and eventually you'll get what you want. If they haven't seen guests for a long time (very possible in the countryside), staff might have to search for some sheets, blankets, even a bed, washstand and water, and then rouse a cook to light a fire to get some food ready a few hours later.

If the hotel has no hot water (most likely), or no water at all it's worth knowing that most aimag capitals have a public bathhouse. See the Public Bathhouse section earlier in this chapter.

FOOD

Again, the quality and choice of food in Ulaan Baatar is vastly different from what you will find in the countryside. In the capital city, restaurants serve everything from Indian to Tex-Mex and the markets are well stocked. Less than 30 minutes by road from Ulaan Baatar, be prepared for a gastronomical purgatory.

In restaurants in the countryside and the cheaper places in Ulaan Baatar, the one and only item on the menu (not that there is usually a menu) is mutton; either mutton with noodles, mutton with rice, or mutton disguised as something else, like goulash. If that doesn't excite you, add liberal doses of chilli or tomato sauce and pickled vegetables (both available in most markets in the country). In reality, the food you'll get in restaurants and in a guanz (cheap restaurant or canteen) isn't really as bad as everyone makes out – it's just bland and monotonous.

Mongolians rarely eat horsemeat, though the Kazakhs of western Mongolia make horse sausages. Dairy products are the staple for herdsmen in the summer; in fact, the only animals killed during this time are for guests. During winter, the vast majority of Mongolians eat little more than greasy boiled mutton, with lots of fat (a highly valued commodity), and flour. Revealingly, there is no word in Mongolian for 'cholesterol'.

If you are doing some extensive travelling in the countryside, you may wish to bring supplies from Ulaan Baatar, especially if you are hiring your own jeep or minivan.

There are very few foodstuffs that you need to bring with you to Mongolia, now that packaged foods are imported in bulk from Germany, Russia and China, but you might want to consider your own tea bags, sachets of hot chocolate, curry powder and spices, vitamin tablets, and packets of just-add-boiling-water pastas, noodles, rice and soups. A few of these will definitely add nutrition and taste to your diet; not to mention lift your morale. If you don't have a portable (petrol) stove, hot water is usually easy to get from hotels and restaurants.

In the Mongolian language, bon appetit is *saikhan khool loorai*.

Guanz

A guanz is an all-purpose word to describe a canteen. Guanz are usually found in buildings, gers or even in train wagons, and can be found in most aimag towns, all over Ulaan Baatar and along major roads where there is some traffic. In the countryside, the ger guanz are a great way to see the interior of a ger and meet a family, without the lengthy stops and traditions expected with normal visits.

If a ger is within 50m of a main road, it is probably a guanz. A table and chairs outside, a picture of a knife and fork, or even a sign with the words 'ГУАНЗ', will make them easier to spot. Not surprisingly, they offer virtually nothing but mutton and noodles (about T800), either fried and on a plate, or boiled and in a soup. If you are lucky or prepared to wait, some steamed mutton dumplings *(buuz)* or fried mutton pancakes *(khuurshuur)* may be available. A bottle of sauce, and a jar of pickled vegetables are very handy at these places. The supplies of salty tea are endless, or staff will usually boil some hot water if you ask, so bring your own tea or coffee.

Restaurants

Rarely in English, menus are normally hand-scrawled in undecipherable Cyrillic. Don't be surprised to find 80% of the menu made up of varieties of beer, wine, vodka, cigarettes and even chewing gum. You can expect to hear the response *'baikhgui'* ('we don't have any') frequently as most of the items on any large restaurant menu have been unavailable since the fall of the Soviet Union.

Three words which are often understood by Mongolian waiters and cooks are 'beefsteak' (a large mutton mince patty, often topped with a fried egg), 'schnitzel' and 'goulash'. These are generally served with squishy mashed potato, gluggy rice or pickled vegetables. There is often a long list of salads, of which the cabbage and (if you are lucky) potato salads will be available. Bread or *mantuu*, a doughy steamed bread roll, similar to the Chinese *mantou*, are normally available.

In some places, it can take ages to find anyone interested in cooking you anything. It's often good practice to give a hotel restaurant a couple of hours warning that you want to eat there. At least that way they'll stay open; many places are closed by about 9 pm and sometimes earlier at around 7 pm. Always check your bill as overcharging is not uncommon.

Dairy Products

Known as white foods *(tsagaan idee)*, yoghurt, milk, fresh cream, cheese and fermented milk drinks are normally delicious and available throughout Mongolia in the summer.

Milk *(süü)* may be cow, sheep or goat milk. Yoghurt *(tarag)* is always delicious, as is Mongolian cream *(tsotgii)*. When you visit a ger you will be offered some dairy snacks, such as dried milk curds *(aaruul)*, which are as hard as a rock and often about as tasty. You may also be served a very sharp soft fermented cheese called *aarts*, which will clear your sinuses, and *öröm*, a type of thick cream which, if fresh, is delicious with bread and jam for breakfast. *Khoormog* is yoghurt made from camel's milk and *tsötsgiin tos* is butter.

If you camp at respectful distance to gers, herders and their families will normally come over, bringing yoghurt, cream and other delights. It's polite to refill and return the empty containers with food from your own supplies, like biscuits or noodles. To buy yoghurt and other dairy products in a market you'll probably need to bring your own bottle or container.

Traditional Food

Forget everything you ever learned about Mongolian hot pot, or the last time you ate in a 'Mongolian' barbecue restaurant back home. In cities all over the western world, Chinese restaurants try to differentiate themselves from their competitors by calling themselves 'Mongolian', but very little is Mongolian about them.

The most common dishes are *buuz* (steamed dumplings), with mutton filling, plenty of fat and flour. Smaller boiled dumplings are called *bansh* and are often served in soup or even in salty tea. In a guanz, you will probably be offered a mutton noodle soup *(guriltai shol)*, or if you are lucky vegetable soup *(nogotoi shöl)*. Another common dish is a greasy pancake

The Smell of the Steppe

Most Mongolians prefer their mutton boiled, so in the countryside the smell permeates everything – even Mongolian biscuits and butter smell like boiled mutton. Since there is no vegetable oil, mutton lard is used. When you try to wash the smell off, you may find the soap and towels smell like mutton too. Even old paper money and telephone receivers soon develop that distinctive mutton fragrance. Foreigners who have spent a lot of time in Mongolia claim that even after they land home, it takes weeks to get rid of the mutton smell from their skin.

made with flour and mutton called a *khuushuur*. They can be large and fried, and they sit in your stomach like a lead brick. The small, deep-fried variety are much crispier and tastier.

If you visit Mongolians in their homes, you will invariably be served a snack from the hospitality bowl, along with salty, milky tea. Some snacks are rather exotic, like camel meat sausages. Another stand-by for the Mongolian hostess with unexpected visitors is twists of deep fried bread. If you're offered a snack, it's most impolite to refuse (but it is not necessary to consume it all).

If you are lucky you may be able to try *boodog*, when an entire goat, or preferably marmot, is slowly roasted from the inside out by placing hot rocks inside the skinned carcass, sealing it and then placing the carcass on the fire. The preparation is not a pretty sight. These days boodog is normally cooked with a blowtorch, making Mongolia the only place in the world where you can mend your jeep and cook using the same utensil! One boodog normally feeds 20 foreigners (or 10 Mongolians). Marmots are only eaten from mid-August to mid-October, when there is less chance of bubonic plague (see Infectious Diseases under the Health section earlier).

The other main highlight of Mongolian cuisine is *khorkhog*, which is made by placing hot stones from the fire into a pot or milk urn with chopped sheep, some water and sometimes vodka and then sealing the pot and putting it on the fire. When eating both boodog and khorkhog, it is customary to pass the hot greasy rocks from hand to hand, as this is thought to be good for your health.

Dried meat, or *borts*, is very popular among Mongolians and jeep drivers like to take it on long-distance trips to add to soups.

Vegetarian

Mongolia is difficult, but not impossible, for vegetarians. Indeed, up until recently the Mongolian language only had one word to describe both grass and vegetables. Many vegetarian travellers suspend their principles merely to survive.

If you don't eat meat, you can survive in Ulaan Baatar, but in the countryside you will need to take your own supplements and preferably a petrol stove. Vegetables other than potatoes, carrots and onions are rare, relatively expensive and usually pickled in jars, so the best way for vegetarians to get protein is from the wide range of dairy products. In general, it is difficult to get food which doesn't have some kind of meat in it.

Self-Catering

Given the state of Mongolian restaurants, self-catering isn't a bad idea. In Ulaan Baatar, you won't save much money but it will provide some variety and nutrition and is ideal for vegetarians – especially if you have a portable (petrol) stove.

The markets (zakh) and shops (delguur) in Ulaan Baatar now sell most things you need like jam, salami, noodles, bread, chocolate spread, tinned fish, pickled vegetables, tea, coffee, rice, flour and fruit and vegetables in season. You can get apples, bananas, melons, and oranges in season but they are more expensive than in the West. There are plenty of luxury foods around and you should be able to track down things like smoked cheese, cans of Pringles, paté, Coffee Mate, muesli and corn flakes. Some of this stuff comes overland from Germany so always check the expiry date.

Self-catering is almost essential when travelling in the countryside. The markets in major aimag capitals are really quite good and you can get almost all staples like bread, noodles, potatoes, onions and chocolate bars. You'll be lucky, however, to find bottled water or Western soft drinks. In sum, or district, capitals you'll be lucky to find much at all.

If you are travelling by hired jeep or van take all your luxury goods and most supplies from Ulaan Baatar and stock up with staples as you pass through aimag capitals. For a list of possible foodstuffs to take on a long-distance jeep trip see the entry Hiring a Jeep or Minivan under Jeep in the Getting Around chapter.

Some markets and shops in Ulaan Baatar are still based on the old-fashioned Russian system: you chose what you want, pay for it at the cashier's desk, produce your itemised receipt at the counter, and only then are you given what you ordered. These days most shops in Mongolia, however, do let you browse, inspect the goods, and then pay.

DRINKS
Nonalcoholic Drinks

The Mongolians are big tea drinkers and they will almost never start to eat a meal until they've had a cup of tea first, as it aids digestion. However, Mongolian tea (tsai) tends to be of the lowest quality. In fact, it's mostly 'tea waste', which is made up of stems and rejected leaves that are processed into a 'brick'.

A classic Mongolian drink is salty tea, called süütei tsai, with or without milk and sugar. Some foreigners find it revolting but many learn to tolerate it. The taste varies by region, but tends to be best in western Mongolia. Many foreigners complain that drinking too much of this salty tea just makes them thirstier.

If you can't get used to the salty tea, try asking for black tea (khar tsai), which is like European tea, with sugar and no milk. (The word 'Lipton' is often understood and used in restaurants as an alternative to black tea.) Your best bet is to bring tea bags or coffee from Ulaan Baatar (or home) and ask for hot water (which may have a mutton tang to it).

Coffee is a popular drink. It is available in markets, shops and restaurants in Ulaan Baatar, and is invariably the 'three-in-one' packet of coffee, powdered milk and sugar. If you prefer it black and without sugar, bring your own and ask for hot water.

There are some nice fruit drinks, supposedly vitamin enriched, which go by the name of Vitsamo, Vitafit and Monvit. If you want to take away the bottle you'll have to leave a deposit of a couple of hundred tögrög.

The Mongolians also produce a variety of bottled fizzy soft drinks, some better than others, commonly called undaa. Children sell these drinks on the streets and around the markets of most towns for about T100 a bottle – they are a cheap and safe way to quench your thirst. You must drink them on site and return the bottle when you finish. In general it's not a good idea to drink the tap water in Mongolia. Even in the countryside it's a good idea to purify stream water as you never know what (or who) has been in it. Bottles of mineral water are available from shops and kiosks *(tuuts)* in Ulaan Bataar but not in the countryside.

Alcoholic Drinks

Mongolias can drink you under the table if you challenge them. There is much social pressure to drink, especially on males – those who refuse to drink vodka *(arkhi)* are considered wimps. The Russians can be thanked for this obnoxious custom, which started in the 1970s. The Mongolians have over 200 distilleries, and used to export vodka to Russia, but now they drink it themselves, and in increasingly large quantities.

Cans and bottles of imported Western beers are expensive and usually only available in larger towns, but most aimag capitals stock decent Russian beer like Orkonchi (in plastic bottles) or Baltika (glass bottles), or the occasional green bottle of Chinese beer. Except for decent restaurants in Ulaan Baatar, beer will always be served at room temperature. Two pubs in Ulaan Baatar brew their own light and dark beers. Even a few bars in the countryside have some kind of beer on tap.

Herders make their own unique home brew, *airag*, which is fermented mare's milk, with an alcohol content of about 3%. Although you aren't likely to get drunk from airag alone, many Mongolians distil it further to produce *shimiin arkhi* (known to medieval travellers as *kara cosmos* – or black airag), which boosts the alcohol content to around 12%.

Many Mongolians will conveniently insist that airag and shimiin arkhi are good for your health because both are milk products, which is rather like claiming that wine is good for you because it's made from grapes!

ENTERTAINMENT

Except for the occasional Russian film at a cinema in Erdenet or Darkhan, entertainment in Mongolia can only be found in Ulaan Baatar. Many aimag capitals have a Soviet-inspired drama theatre but most lie derelict.

Nightlife

Ulaan Baatar has a dozen or so discos and clubs to cater for students and the nouveaux riches. To make money – but more to put off the poorer Mongolians – there is often a hefty entrance fee of between T3000 and T5000, equivalent to a week's wage for some Mongolians.

Don't expect any nightlife in the countryside. Some of the larger aimag capitals have a 'sports palace' in which occasional dances

Airag

'At the taste of it I broke out in a sweat with horror and surprise…It makes the inner man most joyful, intoxicates weak heads and greatly provokes urine.'

So wrote William of Rubrick in the 13th century about fermented mare's milk *(airag)*, or *cosmos* as it was then known to medieval travellers. First drunk in Mongolia over 1000 years ago, airag is still revered and enjoyed throughout the country, so you'll have every opportunity to have a glass or two before you head home.

Since the days when Mongolian warriors lived on very little else, the method of collecting milk in huge leather bags, and churning it, have not changed. Marco Polo, wide of the mark as always, compared airag to a good white wine.

Experts claim they can almost tell which region or valley the airag comes from by the taste. The aimag of Arkhangai, Bulgan, Övörkhangai and even Dundgov in the Gobi, are renowned for the quality of airag, because of the special grasses eaten by the horses there.

Before drinking airag, a Mongolian will dip their ring finger in the bowl, smear some on their forehead and flick some airag to the four directions, as a mark of respect.

are held, usually to the accompaniment of badly recorded pirated tapes played on an equally precarious Russian cassette player. Nevertheless, they do help you meet the locals.

Ulaan Baatar has a few bars catering to trendy locals and rich foreigners, as well as thirsty and drunk Mongolians. The bars in the countryside are generally awful and should be avoided.

Opera & Theatre

Opera and drama are still thriving in Mongolia, the various theatres being one worthwhile legacy of Russian domination. In Ulaan Baatar (but almost never in the countryside), local and foreign plays and operas are staged in the Mongolian language. This generally takes place in summer for the tourists and more regularly in winter for bored locals. These energetic shows are often worth seeing, even if you don't understand anything.

Traditional & Cultural Shows

One highlight of your trip should be a performance of traditional music and dance in Ulaan Baatar. These are regularly held during summer and should not be missed. Around the time of the Naadam Festival, there are also occasional puppet shows. The State Circus in Ulaan Baatar is reasonably impressive, if a little amateurish, but probably not for animal lovers.

Cinemas

Several cinemas operate in Ulaan Baatar, but in each aimag capital the cinemas *(kino)*, which dominate most town centres, are mostly closed. In the past, most foreign films were Russian, but these days a few more flicks are coming from the USA, India, North and South Korea and Japan. Unfortunately, they are generally bad action or soft porn films, often not dubbed (or badly dubbed) and virtually beyond watching.

SPECTATOR SPORTS

Mongolia is generally not passionate about sport, but the 'three manly sports' of wrestling, archery and horse racing are very popular (see the Nadaam Festival special section).

Recently a new form of wrestling called *hasu* has been introduced to liven up the wrestling scene. Hasu bouts have a time limit of five minutes and are played on a mat, similar to sumo. Wrestling purists have already turned their nose up at the sport, but its popularity was ensured when the government allowed bets to be placed of up to T5000.

A football (soccer) league is held in Ulaan Baatar, Erdenet and Darkhan but the game is still not as popular as in most countries. Boxing tournaments are held in major cities, and basketball is increasingly popular – it is not unusual to see a ring and backboard in the most remote places. Stadiums in Ulaan Baatar and various sports palaces around Mongolia sometimes hold various sporting events. The Mongolian judo, wrestling, shooting and boxing teams qualified for the Sydney 2000 Olympics.

Khövsgöl Nuur is the venue for the 100km long ultramarathon, held along the west side of the lake in July.

SHOPPING

Except for a couple of shops in the south Gobi, and the Erdene Zuu monastery, almost all souvenir and antique shops are exclusive to Ulaan Baatar. In general crafts and souvenirs are made solely for tourists and are expensive.

Be very careful about buying anything old. Customs officials are keen to stop any exportation of Mongolia's heritage, and may confiscate anything which looks old unless you have a receipt and/or document stating that it is not antique. Refer to the Customs section in this chapter for more information.

Many foreigners like to pick up traditional Mongolian clothing and boots. These are cheapest at the department stores and markets and several of the guest houses in Ulaan Baatar can help you get one made to order. Cashmere jumpers (sweaters) are an important export item, but are hard to find except in expensive tourist shops.

The bright landscape paintings which you will see at most tourist stops are ideal souvenirs: they are cheap, easy to carry and look great framed. Larger, more dramatic and nationalist paintings are for sale at several galleries in Ulaan Baatar. Felt carpets and cushion covers from the Kazakh areas of western Mongolia are good value.

Tapes and compact discs of traditional music are also excellent mementos of your trip, but a portable tape or CD player, to test the quality of recording before you buy, is a good idea.

If you are a philatelist, you can buy a range of extraordinarily bright and large stamps. These feature wildlife, religious dances, traditional costumes – even Princess Diana and Jerry Garcia. They are more expensive than normal stamps but make good souvenirs. The stamps you are given for postcards and letters are very boring in comparison.

Mongolian games such as *khorol*, a Mongolian form of checkers, and *shagai*, a dice game made from sheep's ankle bones, make unique gifts. Tourist shops sometimes sell chess sets with Mongolian hordes as pawns and Chinggis Khaan as, well, the King.

Other items which you may want to look out for are miniature felt gers, Mongolian dolls, Mongol calligraphy, felt waistcoats, tsam masks and snuff bottles. Definitely look out for Mongolian wrestling pants, which could also make a fine gift for that special person.

The Mongolian Artisan's Aid Foundation (☎ 311 051) in Ulaan Baatar was set up shortly after independence to support local craftspeople. It sells gers, del and hats and will ship container loads of the stuff to your home country, for a price. Check out its Web site at www.samarmagictours.com.

Getting There & Away

AIR

Flying is the main form of transport into Mongolia; the only other way into the country is by train or an inconvenient land crossing by local minibus.

Currently, all direct international flights to Mongolia go to the capital, Ulaan Baatar. Most people fly in from Beijing, Berlin or Moscow; for organised tours, there are also additional direct flights from Osaka and Seoul. Current airline schedules also allow you to fly from Ulaan Baatar to places in wider Mongolia: Irkutsk, on Lake Baikal, and Ulan-Ude, capital of Buryatia (both in 'Russian Mongolia'), and Hohhot (Khokh Khot), the capital of the 'autonomous region' of Chinese Inner Mongolia.

In July and August, most flights on most airlines are full, so book ahead, and confirm – and then confirm again.

Airports & Airlines

Ulaan Baatar's Buyant-Ukhaa International Airport is the only international hub. Only MIAT (Mongolian Airlines), Air China, Aeroflot (www.aeroflot.com) and Korean Air (www.koreanair.com) fly to Ulaan Baatar.

The international Mongolian carrier is MIAT (Mongolian Airlines), which some wags claim stands for 'Maybe I'll Arrive Today'.

High winds and fog are sometimes a problem, leading to delays and cancellations. Gales blowing in from Siberia affect smaller planes used for domestic flights more so than the larger ones on international routes; but flights to Ulaan Baatar are sometimes diverted to Irkutsk (Siberia), where you could spend the night in the transit lounge (if you don't have a Russian visa) until the wind drops.

MIAT Offices Abroad MIAT has a useful Web site at www.miat.com.mn, which displays domestic and international schedules and lists sales agents abroad.

China
Beijing: (☎ 10-6507 9297, fax 6507 7397) China Golden Bridge Bldg, East Gate, Jianguomenwai Dajie, Beijing 100020
Hohhot: (☎ 471-430 3590, fax 430 2015) Xin Cheng Qu, Ulan Aiao Qu, 5 Hao Lou
Germany
(☎ 30-2849 8142, fax 289 8140) Chaussee Strasse 84, Berlin 10115
Japan
Tokyo: (☎ 03-3237 1851, fax 3237 1853) 2F, Kudan Ashikawa Bldg 5-14, Kudan Minami 4-chome, Tokyo 102
Osaka: (☎/fax 7-2460 1402) 14 floor, Rinku Gate Tower Bldg, Izumisano City, Osaka 598
Russia
Moscow: (☎ 095-241 0754, fax 241 1052) Spasopeskovskii Pereulok D7/1
Irkutsk: (☎ 3952-344 530) Room 03, Ulistsa Lapina 11
South Korea (☎ 2-756 9761, fax 756 9762) 3F Soonhwa Bldg, 5-2 Soonhwa-Dong, Chung-u, Seoul 100-130

Buying Tickets

World aviation has never been so competitive, making air travel better value than ever, but you have to research the options carefully to make sure you get the best deal. The Internet is an increasingly useful resource for checking air fares.

Full-time students and people under 26 years (under 30 in some countries) have access to better deals than other travellers. You have to show a document proving your date of birth or a valid International Student Identity Card (ISIC) when buying your ticket and boarding the plane.

Generally, there is nothing to be gained by buying a ticket direct from the airline. Discounted tickets are released to selected travel agents and specialist discount agencies, and these are usually the cheapest deals going.

One exception to this rule is booking on the Internet. Many airlines offer some excellent fares to Web surfers. They may sell seats by auction or simply cut prices to reflect the reduced cost of electronic selling. Many

Warning

The information in this chapter is particularly vulnerable to change: Prices for international travel are volatile, routes are introduced and cancelled, schedules change, special deals come and go, and rules and visa requirements are amended. Airlines and governments seem to take a perverse pleasure in making price structures and regulations as complicated as possible. You should check directly with the airline or a travel agent to make sure you understand how a fare (and ticket you may buy) works. In addition, the travel industry is highly competitive and there are many lurks and perks.

The upshot of this is that you should get opinions, quotes and advice from as many airlines and travel agents as possible before you part with your hard-earned cash. The details given in this chapter should be regarded as pointers and are not a substitute for your own careful, up-to-date research.

travel agencies around the world have Web sites, which can make the Internet a quick and easy way to compare prices. There is also an increasing number of on-line agents which operate only on the Internet.

On-line ticket sales work well if you are doing a simple one-way or return trip on specified dates. However, on-line super-fast fare generators are no substitute for a travel agent who knows all about special deals, has strategies for avoiding layovers and can offer advice on everything from which airline has the best vegetarian food to the best travel insurance to bundle with your ticket.

You may find the cheapest flights are advertised by obscure agencies. Most of these firms are honest and solvent, but there are some rogue fly-by-night outfits around. Paying by credit card generally offers protection, as most card issuers provide refunds if you can prove you didn't get what you paid for. Similar protection can be obtained by buying a ticket from a bonded agent, such as one covered by the Air Travel Organiser's Licence (ATOL) scheme in the

UK (www.atol.org.uk). Agents who only accept cash should hand over the tickets straight away and not tell you to 'come back tomorrow'. After you've made a booking or paid your deposit, call the airline and confirm that the booking was made. It's generally not advisable to send money (even cheques) through the post unless the agent is very well established – some travellers have reported being ripped off by fly-by-night mail-order ticket agents.

Most travel agencies will offer discounted tickets to Beijing and Moscow but not to Ulaan Baatar. In fact, unless you buy a through-ticket with Aeroflot or Air China you will find it hard to even book a Moscow or Beijing to Ulaan Baatar ticket from abroad. For these you will probably have to book with a local travel agency or the airline itself. It's a good idea to budget a couple of days to get an onward ticket – both cities have plenty to see. Alternatively contact a travel agency in advance, though this is fraught with uncertainty.

Travellers with Special Needs

Most international airlines (though less so with Aeroflot, Air China and MIAT) can cater for people with special needs – people with young children, children travelling alone and travellers with disabilities. They can also cater for special dietary preferences, though they need advance warning.

Most international airports will provide escorts from check-in desks to the plane where needed, and there should be ramps, lifts, accessible toilets and phones. Aircraft toilets on the other hand are likely to present a problem; travellers should discuss this with the airline at an early stage and, if necessary, with their doctor.

Children under two travel for 10% of the standard fare, and a few airlines may carry them free of charge. The airline should provide 'skycots' if requested in advance; these will take a child weighing up to 10kg. Children aged between two and 12 can usually occupy a seat for half to two-thirds of the adult fare and will also receive a baggage allowance. Strollers (pushchairs) can normally be taken as hand luggage.

Departure Tax

If you are leaving Mongolia by air, the departure tax is T12,500 (US$12.50). A small foreign exchange counter, next to the place where you pay your departure tax, will change US dollars into *tögrög* if you don't have any left.

If you leave Mongolia by bus (not train) at Zamyn-Uud there is a T6000 departure tax, which is factored in to the price of the bus fare.

Direct Flights to Mongolia

China Air China and MIAT fly between China and Mongolia. Summer schedules are given here; there are fewer flights in winter. The times and days of these departures change regularly, especially during summer.

MIAT flies from Ulaan Baatar to Beijing and back on Monday, Wednesday, Saturday and Sunday. Air China flies from Beijing to Ulaan Baatar and back on Tuesday, Thursday and Friday. With both airlines, the fare for foreigners is US$231/400 one way/return. In Beijing, you can pay in Chinese yuan but in Ulaan Baatar you must pay in US dollars.

MIAT also flies from Ulaan Baatar to Hohhot and back every Monday and Thursday for US$103/196 one way/return. From Hohhot, in China's Inner Mongolia province, to Beijing costs the equivalent of US$80.

Russia The two carriers between Mongolia and Russia are MIAT and Aeroflot. MIAT flies to/from Moscow on Thursday and Sunday. The cheapest fare from Ulaan Baatar to Moscow is US$310/660 one way/return.

Aeroflot flies from Moscow on Monday night and arrives in Ulaan Baatar on Tuesday morning. It returns to Moscow on Tuesday and Saturday. Fares are the same as MIAT.

To combine a trip to stunning Lake Baikal, you could fly with MIAT from Ulaan Baatar to Irkutsk and back each Wednesday and Saturday for US$80/172 one way/return.

Aeroflot used to fly weekly between Ulaan Baatar and Ulan-Ude, in Russian Buryatia, but flights have ceased for the moment at least.

Germany MIAT flies between Berlin and Ulaan Baatar on Thursday and Sunday, with additional summer flights on Monday; the plane stops in Moscow. For anyone in Europe, this is a better alternative than flying to, and getting a connection from, Moscow. Tickets in Ulaan Baatar cost US$555/835 one way/return.

Japan To cater for organised tours from Japan, MIAT flies to and from Osaka up to four times a week for US$400/764 one way/return.

South Korea Both MIAT and Korean Air fly plane-loads of package tourists between Ulaan Baatar and Seoul for US$370/570 one way/return. Korean Air flies every Monday and Thursday, but only in summer; it also often offers a free night in Seoul if you need to wait for a connection. MIAT flies all year between Seoul and Ulaan Baatar on Friday and Sunday, with additional flights in summer.

Kazakhstan Irtysh Aviation, a Kazakhstani air charter company currently rents out a plane owned bg Kazakh Air and flies between Almaty and Ölgii, the capital of Bayan-Ölgii *aimag* (province), in western Mongolia, every Wednesday for US$136 one way. The manager assured us that foreigners were allowed to take these flights (and for the same price as locals). If this is your kind of thing then it's worth a try, but you must be prepared for bureaucratic immigration snags, and even the possibility that you won't be allowed to enter the country.

If you decide to try this flight you will have to arrange immigration formalities at Ölgii and you should have a Kazakhstan visa – there's an embassy in Ulaan Baatar (see the Embassies & Consulates section in the Facts for the Visitor chapter). You may need some kind of special Mongolian exit stamp so it's worth double checking with the Ministry of External Relations in Ulaan Baatar. See the Ölgii section in the Western Mongolia chapter for more details on booking the flight.

Mongolia via Beijing & Moscow

Until there are more direct flights to Ulaan Baatar, you'll probably fly firstly to Beijing, unless you are in Europe, where a flight to Moscow may be a cheaper option. You may also need to start in Beijing to collect your visa if you live in a location where there is no Mongolian embassy or consulate, or simply to save money by picking up the Trans-Mongolian train to Ulaan Baatar.

Coming from Europe, you may find the cheapest flight (probably with Aeroflot) goes via Moscow, which is well connected to every major European, North American and Asian travel centre.

Beijing Stopover Survival Information

From the airport, the cheapest way into the centre of town is on the airport bus (Y16). Buy the ticket inside the arrivals' terminal. A taxi should cost from Y70. Beijing is very spread out and the easiest way to get around is by taxi, which cost Y10 for the first 5km. Beijing also has a good subway, with three lines, which costs Y3 a ride.

Hotels are not cheap and most double rooms cost a minimum of Y300. Favourite backpacker hotels are the *Jinghua Hotel* (☎ 6722-2211, *Nansanhuan Xilu*) and the nearby *Haixing Hotel* (☎ 6721 8855, *166 Haihutun, Yongwai*) and *Lihua Hotel* (☎ 6721 1144, 71 Yangqiao, Yongding-menwai). All are in the south of the city, near the third ring road and have dorm beds for around Y30 and doubles for around Y150.

The place to get train tickets to Ulaan Baatar is the China International Travel Service (CITS) office in the Beijing International Hotel – see From China (& Hong Kong) under the Trans-Mongolian Railway entry later in this chapter for details. For air tickets head to Air China (☎ 6601 6667), Aviation Bldg, 15 Xichang'an Jie, Xicheng District. MIAT (☎ 10-6507 9297) is at the China Golden Bridge Building, Dong Men, Jianguomenwai Dajie, Beijing 100020.

The visa section of the Mongolian Embassy in Beijing (see Embassies & Consulates in the Facts for the Visitor chapter) is open weekdays from 8.30 to 11.30 for applications and 2 to 4 pm for pick-ups (enter from the south side of the embassy). It closes for all Mongolian and Chinese public holidays and shuts down completely for a few days before, during and after the Naadam Festival (July 11–13). Single entry/exit tourist visas are issued for 30 days, take three working days to process and cost US$40. An express service takes 24 hours and costs an additional US$20. For tourist visas over 30 days you will need an invitation faxed or emailed to the embassy. Two photos are required. If your passport is at the Mongolian embassy it's worth knowing that CITIC Bank will change money without a passport, but the Bank of China won't.

Note that if you are planning to enter Mongolia from China and then return to China, get a double-entry Chinese visa. Otherwise, you will need to obtain another Chinese visa in Ulaan Baatar, which isn't difficult.

If you are looking for camping equipment in Beijing, try Extreme Beyond (also known as the Adventure Travelling Mountaineering Equipments Shop; ☎ 6506 5121) at 15 Gongti Donglu, Chaoyang District, or Snowbird Camping Equipment (Xueniao Yewai Yongpin Shangdian; ☎ 6225 3630) at Deshengmen Xi Dajie. Both stock fairly good locally made Luhuan tents for around Y400, and also some Ozark brand equipment, and gas canister stoves. In Chinese *zhanfeng* means 'tent' and *meiyoulu* means 'stove'.

There are plenty of things to do in Beijing, though so thoroughly have the Chinese erased the traces of the Mongol conquest that only two major Mongol-era monuments in Beijing remain: Lama Temple (Yōnghé Gōng) and the giant white stupa in North Sea Park (Beihǎi Gōngyuán). Favourite excursions include the Forbidden City, the Lama Temple, Mao Zedong Mausoleum (Máo Zhǔxí Jiniàntáng), Temple of Heaven Park (Tiāntán Gōngyuán) and a visit to a non-touristy part of the wall, such as Simatai. For more details see Lonely Planet's *Beijing* or *China* guides.

USA The cheapest fares to Beijing are from San Francisco, Los Angeles and New York on Korean Air, Air China, Northwest Airlines and United Airlines. From the US west/east coast, return fares start at US$750/890.

The cheapest return flight to Moscow from New York will probably weigh in around US$900 return. Eastern European airlines such as CSA (Czech Airlines) and LOT (Polish Airlines) are often the cheapest.

The *New York Times*, *Los Angeles Times*, *Chicago Tribune* and *San Francisco Examiner* all produce weekly travel sections in which you will find a number of travel agency ads.

North America's largest student travel organisation, Council Travel, has around 60 offices throughout the country. Its head office (toll-free ☎ 800-226 8624) is at 205 E 42 St New York, NY. See its Web site at www.ciee.org.

STA Travel (☎ 800-777 0112) has offices in Boston, Chicago, Miami, New York, Philadelphia, San Francisco and other major cities. Check its Web site at www.statravel.com.

Canada *The Globe* and *Mail*, the *Toronto Star*, the *Montreal Gazette* and the *Vancouver Sun* carry travel agent advertisements and are a good place to look for cheap fares. Travel CUTS (toll-free ☎ 800-667 2887) is Canada's national student travel agency and has offices in all major cities. Its Web address is www.travelcuts.com. Major cities also have branches of Flight Centre.

Canadian Airlines, Air China and China Eastern sometimes run cheap offers to Beijing. In general, fares from Canada to both Beijing and Moscow cost 10% more than from the USA. Return low-season fares between Vancouver and Beijing start at around US$800.

Australia Quite a few travel agents specialise in discount air tickets. Some, particularly smaller ones, advertise cheap air fares in the travel sections of weekend newspapers, such as *The Age* in Melbourne and the *Sydney Morning Herald*.

Two well-known agents for cheap fares are STA Travel and Flight Centre. STA Travel (☎ 03-9349 2411) has its head office at 224 Faraday St, Carlton, Victoria, 3053, and offices in all major cities and on many university campuses. Call ☎ 131 776 Australia-wide for the location of your nearest branch or visit its Web site at www.statravel.com.au.

Flight Centre (☎ 131 600 Australia-wide) has a central office at 82 Elizabeth St, Sydney, and there are dozens of offices throughout Australia. Its Web address is www.flightcentre.com.au.

Low-season return fares to Beijing from the east coast of Australia start at around A$1000. Fares to Moscow are much higher, starting at around A$1500, and is only worth considering if you want to take the Trans-Mongolian train. A change of plane or stopover is normally required.

New Zealand The *New Zealand Herald* has a travel section in which travel agents advertise fares. Flight Centre (☎ 09-309 6171) has a large central office in Auckland at National Bank Towers (corner Queen and Darby Sts) and many branches throughout the country.

STA Travel (☎ 09-309 0458) has its main office at 10 High St, Auckland, and has other offices in Auckland as well as in Hamilton, Palmerston North, Wellington, Christchurch and Dunedin. The Web address is www.statravel.com.au.

Return low-season fares to Beijing start at NZ$1645 with Malaysia Airlines.

UK Advertisements for many travel agents appear in the travel pages of the weekend broadsheets and in free magazines such as *TNT*, which are widely available in London. *Time Out* is another excellent source of cheap air fares.

For students or travellers under 26, popular travel agencies in the UK include STA Travel (☎ 020-7361 6161), which has an office at 86 Old Brompton Rd, London SW7 3LQ, and other offices in London and Manchester. Visit its Web site at www.statravel.co.uk. USIT Campus Travel (☎ 020-7730 3402), 52 Grosvenor Gardens, London

SW1WOAG, has branches throughout the UK. The Web address is www.usitcampus .com. Both of these agencies sell tickets to all travellers but cater especially to young people and students.

Other recommended general travel agencies include:

Bridge the World (☎ 020-7734 7447) 4 Regent Place, London W1R 5FB.
  Web site: www.b-t-w.co.uk
Flightbookers (☎ 020-7757 2000) 177-178 Tottenham Court Rd, London W1P 9LF.
  Web site: www.ebookers.co.uk
Trailfinders (☎ 020-7938 3939) 194 Kensington High St, London W8 7RG
  Web site: www.trailfinders.co.uk

From the UK, low-season return fares to Beijing start at £430 with Air China (flying direct). Air France and British Airways also often have good deals.

Shop around and you might get a low-season return to Moscow for under £200. Aeroflot is generally cheapest and will give you a through fare to Ulaan Baatar. Most of the budget travel agencies listed in this entry don't make bookings with Aeroflot so you'll have to find a smaller company or phone the airline direct.

Aeroflot flies Ulaan Baatar to London on Tuesday for US$440 one way, with a change of planes, but no overnight stay or airport transfer required. The Saturday connection is not as convenient as it entails a night in Moscow at your own expense.

Continental Europe Most Europeans generally fly to Mongolia from Berlin or Moscow. Fares to Beijing from Western Europe are similar to those from London. The Netherlands, Belgium and Switzerland are good places to buy discount air tickets.

In The Netherlands, recommended agencies include NBBS Reizen (☎ 020 620 5071), 66 Rokin, Amsterdam, plus branches in most cities (visit its Web site at www.nbbs.nl), and Budget Air (☎ 020 627 1251), 34 Rokin, Amsterdam (visit its Web site at www.nbbs.nl).

Agencies in Germany include STA Travel (☎ 030 311 0950), Goethesttrasse 73, 10625

Berlin, and usitCampus (☎ 018 057 88336), with a Web site at www.usitcampus.de. Both these popular travel agencies have a number of branches throughout Germany.

Travel agencies in France include Usit Connect Voyages (☎ 01 42 44 14 00), 14 rue de Vaugirard, 75006 Paris and OTU Voyages (☎ 01 40 29 12 12), 39 ave Georges-Bernanos, 75005, with a Web site at www.otu.fr. Like Usit Connect Voyages, OTU Voyages is a student and young person specialist agency. Nouvelles Frontières (☎ 01 45 68 70 00), 87 blvd de Grenelle, 75015 Paris, with a Web site at www. nouvelles-frontieres.fr, also has many branches in Paris and throughout France.

LAND
Border Crossings

There are currently only two land border crossings open to foreigners; Ereen and Zamyn-Üüd, on the Chinese-Mongolian border, and Naushki and Sükhbaatar, on the Russian-Mongolian border. It's possible to cross borders by bus or train, though the latter is the most common and convenient.

There are several border crossings that may open over the next couple of years:

Altanbulag-Kyakhta This is the main road border for Russians and Mongolians. If it does opens to foreigners, they'll probably be able to drive their vehicles between Russia and Mongolia without actually taking the train across the border.
Khankh-Mondy An important trade crossing. It's rumoured that it might open by 2002; if that happens, which is unlikely, it would provide a great way to travel between Khövsgöl and Baikal lakes.
Borshoo-Handgayt It has been used a couple of times by foreign tour companies as the gateway to Tuva (western Siberia).

China

Bus Minibuses shuttle between the railway stations of Zamyn-Üüd, on Mongolia's southern border, and Ereen, the Chinese border town, for T8000 (which includes an exit tax of Y6000). There are hotels in both towns. In Ereen try the *Erlian Fandian*, which also has an office on the third floor that can issue Mongolian

Trains to/from Mongolia

train	train no	day of departure	departure time	duration (hrs)
China-Mongolia				
Beijing-Ulaan Baatar	23*	Tue	7.40 am*	30
Beijing-Moscow	3	Wed	7.40 am*	30
Hohhot-Ulaan Baatar	215	Sun, Wed	10.40 pm	30
Mongolia-China				
Ulaan Baatar-Beijing	24	Sun	8.50 am	30
Moscow-Beijing	4	Thur	8.50 am	30
Ulaan Baatar-Hohhot	216	Wed, Sun	9.15 pm	24
Mongolia-Russia				
Ulaan Baatar-Moscow	5	Tue, Fri	1.50 pm	70
Beijing-Moscow	3*	Thur	1.30 pm	100
Ulaan Baatar-Irkutsk	263	daily		36
Russia-Mongolia				
Moscow-Ulaan Baatar	6	Wed, Thur	9 pm	70
Irkutsk-Ulaan Baatar	264	-	-	-
Moscow-Beijing	4	Tue	7.55 pm	100
Moscow-Beijing	20	Fri	8.25 pm	118

* Train Nos 3 and 23 pass through Datong at 2.15 pm, Jining at 4.15 pm, Ereen at 8.45 pm and Zamyn-Üüd at 11.45 pm.

Note: schedules change from one summer to another, and services reduce in winter, and can increase in summer, depending on demand.

visas. Note that the border is currently closed on weekends.

Train Refer to table 'Trains to/from Mongolia' in this chapter outlining international train timetables.

Direct Trains Most travellers catch the direct train between Beijing and Ulaan Baatar.

There are two direct trains a week each way between Beijing and Ulaan Baatar. One of these (No 3/4) is the Trans-Mongolian train which runs between Beijing and Moscow. The other (No 23/24) is easier to get tickets for.

It is also possible to travel twice a week directly between Ulaan Baatar and Hohhot, allowing you to either bypass Beijing completely or catch a train or flight (US$80) on to Beijing from there.

The costs in tögrög for destinations in China from Ulaan Baatar are:

destination	2nd class (1/4)	1st class (2/4)	deluxe (1/2)
Datong	40,000	60,000	79,000*
Beijing	49,000	69,000	88,000*
Hohhot	43,000	60,000	78,000*

* These prices are for Chinese trains. Mongolian trains are approximately 20% cheaper for deluxe class.

Local Trains If you are on a real budget it is possible to take local trains between Ulaan Baatar and Beijing. This will save you some money but involves more hassle and uncertainty and requires more time. During the Nadaam Festival period in early July, when international train bookings are very difficult to come by, this may your only option.

The first option is train No 22/23, which runs between Ulaan Baatar and Ereen (also known as Erenhot, or Erlian in Chinese) just inside China. This Mongolian train leaves Ulaan Baatar on Monday and Thursday at 9.15 pm and arrives in Ereen at around 11.30 am the next morning, after having passed through immigration and customs formalities. In reverse, No 21 leaves Ereen on Tuesday and Friday evenings and arrives the next day. Tickets from Ulaan Baatar for 2nd/1st/deluxe class cost T23,500/32,000/44,000. The schedules of this train change regularly.

The second option is to take local trains to Zamyn-Üüd in Mongolia (see Train under Getting There & Away in the Ulaan Baatar chapter) or Ereen in China and then cross the border by minibus or jeep. This saves the time required to change bogies (wheel assemblies). Both options involve the hassle of securing onward train tickets and the ensuing wait for onward trains. From Ereen you can take a local train to Jining and then onto Beijing.

Car & Motorcycle Foreigners are not allowed to drive their own vehicle around China yet, so driving across the Chinese border is currently out of the question.

Chinese/Mongolian Border Towns If you are taking the direct train between China and Mongolia you will have up to three hours to kill in Ereen. The market at the back of the station has a great range of fruit, drinks and bread. Stock up if you are heading into Mongolia, because you won't see most of these things in the country. Upstairs in the terminal at Ereen station, a small bank is open during business hours only. If heading into Mongolia from China, you can change half your unused Chinese yuan back to US dollars here (if you have a receipt to show that you changed the money legally in the first place). Most people pass through the middle of the night though, so you'll have to change the money in Ulaan Baatar. You can also buy some

Bogies

Don't be concerned if you get off at Ereen (on the Chinese side of the border), and the train disappears from the platform. About two hours are spent changing the bogies (wheel assemblies) because the Russians (and, therefore, the Mongolians) and the Chinese use different railway gauges. Train buffs may want to see the bogie-changing operation. Stay on the train after it disgorges passengers in Ereen. The train then pulls into a large shed about 1km from the station. Get off immediately before the staff lock the doors – they really don't want you in the train anyway. It's OK to walk around the shed and take photos, but don't get in anybody's way.

yuan with US dollars, and possibly some Mongolian tögrög. Otherwise, you can use US dollars in Ulaan Baatar until you get to a bank.

Zamyn-Üüd, on the Mongolian side, is not an interesting place, so you aren't missing anything if the train stops in the middle of the countryside (often in the middle of the night), and not at Zamyn-Üüd. Mongolian customs and immigration officials take about two hours to do their stuff.

Russia

Train Besides the Trans-Mongolian Railway connecting Moscow and Beijing there is a direct train twice a week connecting Ulaan Baatar and Moscow, which is easier to book from Ulaan Baatar. The epic trip takes four days.

If you are headed to Lake Baikal, there is a daily train between Ulaan Baatar and Irkustsk, which stops en route in Darkhan. These trains stop at every village, however, and the No 263 travels past Lake Baikal at night, so if you are in a hurry or want to see the lake, take the Ulaan Baatar-Moscow (No 5) as far as Irkutsk. Note that departure and arrival times in Irkutsk are given in Moscow time, although Irkutsk is actually five hours ahead of Moscow.

Again this trip can be done more cheaply by travelling in stages on local trains, eg, from Ulan-Ude to Naushki, Naushki to Sükhbaatar, and Sükhbaatar to Ulaan Baatar, but it would involve more hassles, especially as Russian visas are more difficult to arrange than Chinese.

The approximate cost in tögrög for major destinations in Russia from Ulaan Baatar follow. Exact costs depend on whether the train is Russian, Chinese or Mongolian; we have listed the most expensive:

destination	2nd class (1/4)	1st class (2/4)	deluxe (1/2)
Naushki	21,000	-	35,000
Ulan-Ude	29,000	34,250	45,000
Irkutsk	35,000	49,000	65,420
Krasnoyarsk	60,000	74,000	110,000
Novosibirsk	69,000	85,000	113,000
Omsk	77,000	94,000	126,000
Yekaterinburg	91,000	110,000	146,000
Perm	94,000	114,000	151,000
Moscow	113,000	137,000	182,000

Car & Motorcycle As a foreigner, you cannot currently cross the border between Mongolia and Russia in your own vehicle. You are allowed to bring *in* a vehicle, but you must personally cross the border by train. This may all change if the Kyakhta-Altanbulag and Naushki-Sükhbaatar borders are opened to foreigners.

The main road crossing is currently at Kyakhta-Altanbulag. You will have to leave your vehicle at that border (or ask a trusted Mongolian or Russian to drive across the border), return to Naushki or Sükhbaatar, cross the border by train and then pick up your vehicle. However, some travellers have been told by Russian border officials that they must place their vehicle on the same train that they travel on.

Russian/Mongolian Border Towns
Customs and immigration between Naushki and Sükhbaatar can take at least four hours. You can have a look around Naushki, but there is little to see, and the border crossing usually takes place in the middle of the night. Surprisingly, you may have difficulty

finding anyone at the Naushki station to change money, so wait until Sükhbaatar or Ulaan Baatar, or somewhere else in Russia. (Try to get rid of your tögrög before you leave Mongolia, as almost no-one will want to touch them once you are inside Russia.)

The train may stop for one or two hours at, or near, the pleasant Mongolian border town of Sükhbaatar, but there is no need to look around. You may be able to buy some Russian roubles or Mongolian tögrög from a moneychanger at the train station, but the rate will be poor. If there aren't any moneychangers, you can use US dollars cash to get by until you change money elsewhere.

Trans-Mongolian Railway

Most people travel from Russia or China to Mongolia directly along the Trans-Mongolian Railway line. The following gives general information on travelling the route by rail.

The names of the rail lines can be a bit confusing. The Trans-Mongolian Railway goes from Beijing through Ulaan Baatar and onto a junction called Zaudinsky, near Ulan-Ude, where it meets the Trans-Siberian line and continues on to Moscow. The Trans-Siberian Railway runs from Moscow to the eastern Siberian port of Nakhodka – this route does not go through either China or Mongolia. The Trans-Manchurian Railway crosses the Russia-China border at Zabaikalsk-Manzhouli, also completely bypassing Mongolia.

General Train Information The stations in Mongolia never have any food; in Russia, there may be someone on the platform selling food; in the more entrepreneurial China, someone on the platform will have some delicious fruit and soft drinks for sale.

The restaurant cars on the Russian and Chinese trains have decent food (US$2 to US$4) and drinks in their restaurant cars. Staff on the Russian train to Moscow have the tendency of selling off all the food at stops in Siberia so you may find food supplies have dwindled by Novosibirsk.

Note that toilets are normally locked whenever you are in a station and for five minutes before and after. Showers are only available in the deluxe carriages. In 2nd and 1st class, there is a washroom and toilet at the end of each carriage – which always get progressively filthy. It's a good idea to bring a large enamel mug (available in most Chinese railway stations) and use it as a scoop to pour water over yourself from the washbasin.

Generally you are only allowed to take 35kg of luggage, but for foreigners, this is rarely checked, except perhaps when departing Beijing. A lot of smuggling is done on this train, so never agree to carry anything across the border for anyone else.

Don't leave unattended baggage in your cabin. A few years ago, the Trans-Mongolian had a bad reputation for theft, but militia now ride the trains and security has improved. For added safety, lock your cabins from the inside and also make use of the security clip on the upper left-hand part of the door. The clip can be flipped open from the outside with a knife, but not if you stuff the hole with paper.

If you want to get off the Trans-Mongolian at Sükhbaatar, Darkhan or Sainshand, you will still have to pay the full fare to/from Ulaan Baatar. If you are not actually getting *on* the train in Ulaan Baatar, you should arrange for someone in Ulaan Baatar to tell the attendant that you will catch the train later, so your seat is not taken.

Tickets list the departure, not arrival, times. Get to the station at least 20 minutes before *arrival* to allow enough time to find the platform and struggle on board, especially for the Beijing-Moscow trains, which only stop in Ulaan Baatar for about 30 minutes.

What to Bring US dollars cash in small denominations is useful to buy meals and drinks on the train, and to exchange for the local currency, so that you can buy things at the train stations. It's a good idea to buy some Russian roubles or Chinese yuan at the licensed moneychangers in Ulaan Baatar before you leave Mongolia.

Stock up on munchies like biscuits, chocolate and fruit and bring some bottled water or juice. You'd be wise to purchase your own alcohol before boarding the train because it is expensive on the train and the choice is limited.

A small samovar at the end of each carriage provides constant boiling water, which is a godsend for making tea and coffee, as well as instant packet meals of noodles or soup.

Other essentials include thongs (flip flops) or slippers, an enamel mug, a flannel, toilet paper, plenty of reading material and loose, comfortable long pants.

Classes With a few exceptions, all international trains have two or three classes. The names and standards of the classes depend on whether it is a Mongolian, Russian or Chinese train.

On the Russian (and Mongolian) trains, most travellers travel in 2nd class – printed on tickets and timetables as '1/4' and known as 'hard-sleeper', 'coupe' or *kupeynyy* in Russian. These are small, but perfectly comfortable, four-person compartments with four bunk-style beds and a fold-down table.

First class (printed as '2/4') is sometimes called a 'soft-sleeper', or *myagkiy* in Russian. It has softer beds but hardly any more space than a Russian 2nd class seat and is not worth the considerably higher fare charged. On Chinese trains it is nonsmoking which can be a godsend.

The real luxury (and expense) comes with Chinese deluxe class (printed as '1/2'): roomy, wood-panelled two-berth compartments with a sofa, and a shower cubicle shared with the adjacent compartment. The deluxe class on Russian trains, which is slightly cheaper than the Chinese deluxe, has two bunks but is not much different in size than the 2nd class and has no showers.

Customs & Immigration There are major delays of three to six hours at both the China-Mongolia and Russia-Mongolia borders. Often the trains cross the border during the middle of the night, when the alert Mongolian and Russian officials maintain the upper hand. The whole process is not difficult or a hassle – just annoying because they keep interrupting your sleep.

Your passport will be taken for inspection and stamping. When it is returned, inspect it closely – sometimes they make errors like cancelling your return visa for China. Foreigners generally sail through customs without having their bags opened, which is one reason people on the train may approach you and ask if you'll carry some of their luggage across the border – *not a good idea.*

During these stops, you can alight and wander around the station, which is just as well since the toilets on the train are locked during the whole inspection procedure.

Tickets The international trains, especially the Trans-Mongolian Railway, are popular, so it's often hard to book this trip except during winter. Try to plan ahead and book as early as possible.

If you are in Ulaan Baatar and want to go to Irkutsk, Beijing or Moscow, avoid going on the Beijing-Moscow or Moscow-Beijing trains; use the other trains mentioned above which *originate* in Ulaan Baatar. In Ulaan Baatar, you cannot buy tickets a few days in advance for the Beijing-Moscow or Moscow-Beijing trains, because staff in Ulaan Baatar don't know how many people are already on the train. For these trains, you can only buy a ticket the day before departure, ie, on Wednesday for trains from Ulaan Baatar to Moscow, and on Saturday for trains from Ulaan Baatar to Beijing. You will need to get to the ticket office early and get into the Mongolian scramble for tickets.

For details on buying tickets in Ulaan Baatar see the Getting There & Away section in that chapter.

From China (& Hong Kong) The best place to buy tickets in China is the China International Travel Service (CITS; ☎ 010-6512 0507), in the International Hotel, Jianguomenwai Dajie, Beijing. You can book up to two months in advance for trains originating in Beijing if you send a deposit of Y100; and you can collect your ticket from one week to one day before departure. There is a Y150 cancellation fee. The office is open weekdays from 8.30 am to noon, and 1.30 to 5 pm.

CITS will only sell you a ticket from Beijing to Moscow or Ulaan Baatar – no stopovers are allowed. Tickets to Ulaan Baatar cost Y559/778/949 in hard sleeper/soft sleeper/deluxe.

Tickets are also available at the CITS office (☎ 10-6515 0093 ext 35) in the Beijing Tourism Building, 28 Jianguomenwai, opposite the Gloria Plaza Hotel.

You can also buy train tickets privately; they will be more expensive than at CITS, but you may be able to arrange a stopover and arrange visas while you are there.

In Beijing, Monkey Business, also known as Moonsky Star (☎ 10-6356 2126, fax 6356 2127, @ MonkeyChina@compuserve.com) can put together all kinds of stopovers and home-stay programs. The office, currently in the Capital Forbidden City Hotel, 48 Guanganmen Nanjie, South Building, 3rd Floor, Xianwu District 100054, is expected to move to the move to the first floor of the expat bar The Hidden Tree (☎ 6509 3642) in the Sanlitun district. For details check out the Web site at www.monkeyshrine.com. The company has a lot of experience in booking Trans-Siberian trains for independent travellers. However, we've heard complaints from travellers of poor organisation, indifferent service and, in particular, inflated prices.

The following agencies in Hong Kong can normally book Trans-Mongolian tickets:

Monkey Business/Moonsky Star (☎ 2723 1376, fax 2723 6653, @ MonkeyHK@compuserve.com) Flat 6 4th floor, E Block, Chungking Mansions, 36-44 Nathan Rd, Tsimshatsui, Kowloon
Phoenix Services (☎ 2722 7378) Room B, 6th floor, Milton Mansion, 96 Nathan Rd, Tsimshatsui, Kowloon
Time Travel (☎ 2366 6222, fax 2739 5413) Block A, 16th floor, Chungking Mansions, 40 Nathan Rd, Tsimshatsui, Kowloon

Trains leave from Beijing Railway Station, not Beijing West Railway Station. You will need to get your baggage x-rayed and your ticket stamped before you can board the train.

If your luggage is over 35kg, you'll have to take it the day before departure to the

Luggage Shipment Office, which is on the right-hand side of the station. The excess is charged at about US$11 per 10kg, with a maximum excess of 40kg allowed.

From Russia In Moscow, you can buy tickets at the building on ulitsa Krasnoprudnaya 1, next door to the Yaroslavl train station, from where the trains to Ulaan Baatar and Beijing leave.

Infinity Travel (☎ 095-234 6555, fax 234 6556, e info@infinity.ru) at Komsomolsky prospekt 13 in Moscow is affiliated with the Travellers Guesthouse and is one of the better private sellers. Check its Web site at www.infinity.ru.

The only reliable agency in Ulan-Ude is Buryat-Intour (☎ 3012-216954, fax 219 267, e buryatia@rex.burnet.ru) at 12 Ranzhurov Sta, Ulan-Ude 670000.

In Irkutsk try Irkutsk-Baikal Intourist (☎ 3952-290 161) at the Hotel Intourist, 14 bulvar Gagarina 44, or the completely different Irkutsk Baikal Travel Inc (☎ 3952-381 938, fax 381 935, e baikalsea@pp.irkutsk.ru) PO Box 106, Irkutsk 664000.

From Other Countries Several agencies in Western countries can arrange tickets on the international trains, but their prices will be considerably higher than if you bought them from the point of departure. They often only make the effort if you also buy an organised tour from them.

Overseas branches of China International Travel Service (CITS) or China Travel Service (CTS) can often book train and plane tickets from Beijing to Ulaan Baatar.

Australasia
Gateway Travel (☎ 02-9745 3333, fax 9745 3237, e gatrav@magna.com.au) 48 The Boulevard, Strathfield, NSW 2135, Australia
Web site: www.russian-gateway.com.au
Sundowners (☎ 03-9600 1934, fax 9642 5838, e rail@sundowners.com.au) Suite 15, 15 Lonsdale Court, 600 Lonsdale St, Melbourne, 3000
Web site: www.sundowners.com.au
Suntravel (☎ 09-525 3074, fax 525 3065, e suntravel@suntravl.com) 407 Great South Road, Penrose, Auckland, New Zealand

UK
China Travel Service & Information Centre (☎ 020-7388 8838, fax 7388 8828) 124 Euston Rd, London NW1 2AL
China Travel Service (☎ 020-7836 9911, fax 7836 3121, e cts@ctsuk.com) 7 Upper St Martins Lane, London WC2H 9DL
Intourist (☎ 020-7538 8600, fax 7538 5967, e info@intourist.co.uk) 219 Marsh Wall London E14 9PD
Web site: www.intourist.co.uk
Regent Holidays (☎ 117-921 1711, fax 925 4866, e regent@regent-holidays.co.uk) 15 John St, Bristol BS1 2HR
Web site: www.regent-holidays.co.uk
The Russia Experience Ltd (☎ 0208-566 8846, fax 566 8843, e info@trans-siberian.co.uk) Research House, Fraser Road, Perivale, Middx UB6 7AQ
Web site: www.trans-siberian.co.uk

Continental Europe
Lernidee Reisen (☎ 30-786 5056, fax 786 5596) Duden Strasse 78, 10965 Berlin, Germany
Travel Service Asia (☎ 7351-373 210, fax 373 211, e tsa-reisen@t-online.de) Schmelzweg 10 88400 Biberach/Riss
Web site: www.travel-service-asia.de.

Canada
Exotik Tours (☎ 514-284 3324, fax 843 5493, e exotiktours@exotiktours.com) 1117 Ste-Catherine O, Suite 806, Montreal Quebec H3B 1H9

ORGANISED TOURS
A high percentage of travellers visit Mongolia on an organised tour. This trend is likely to continue as travel around the countryside remains time-consuming and relatively arduous. It's a country which lends itself well to expedition-style travel and hard-to-arrange travel like horse trekking and mountain biking.

Few foreign travel agencies specialise in Mongolia; they mainly sell tours organised and run by travel agencies in Mongolia (see Travel Agencies under Information in the Ulaan Baatar chapter). The costs of organised tours vary widely; they depend on the country of origin, length of trip, mode of transport, type of accommodation, current exchange rate and so on. However, you can assume that they are expensive. Below are a few places to contact about their current itineraries and prices.

USA

Boojum Expeditions (☎ 1-800-287 0125, 406-587 0125, fax 585 3474, [e] boojum@mcn.net) 14543 Kelly Canyon Rd, Bozeman, MT 59715. Runs excellent, adventurous scheduled and private horseback, mountain biking, fishing and trekking trips. Also organises specialty trips such as eagle-hunting in November and December. Boojum also has an office in Ulaan Baatar.
Web site: www.boojum.com

Geographic Expeditions (☎ 415-922 0448, 1-800-777 8183, fax 346 5535, [e] info@geoex.com) 2627 Lombard St, San Francisco, CA 94123. Horse riding trips to Khentii and jeep trips combining western Mongolia and Tuva in western Siberia.
Web site: www.geoex.com

Hidden Corners (☎ 978-371 9567, fax 369 9222, [e] discover@hiddencorners.com) 34 Hubbard St, Concord MA 01742. Small company running tours with an ecological slant.
Web site: www.hiddencorners.com

Mir Corporation (☎ 1-800-424 7289, fax 206-624 7360, [e] mir@igc.apc.org) 85 South Washington St Suite 210, Seattle WA 98104. Specialists in the former USSR, can combine Mongolia with trips to Tuva and Buryatia.
Web site: www.mircorp.com

Mountain Travel Sobek (☎ 1-888-MTSOBEK, fax 510-525 7710, [e] info@mtsobek.com) 6420 Fairmount Ave, El Cerrito, California 94530.
Web site: www.mtsobek.com

Nomadic Expeditions (☎ 609-860 9008, 1-800-998 6634, fax 860 9608, [e] info@nomadic expeditions.com) 1095 Cranbury-South River Road, Suite 20A, Jamesburg, NJ 08831. One of the best and most expensive Mongolia specialists, offering everything from palaeontology trips to eagle hunting, kayaking and camel trekking. It also has an office in Ulaan Baatar.
Web site: www.nomadicexpeditions.com

Turtle Tours (☎ 888-299-1439, fax 480-488-3406, [e] turtletours@earthlink.net) PO Box 1147, Carefree, AZ 85377. Interesting tours, including one to Bayankhongor and Khovd.
Web site: www.turtletours.com.

Canada

Concepts East (☎ 1-888-302 1222, 416-322 3387, fax 322 3129, [e] conceptseast@canada.com). Runs a combined trip to Mongolia and Inner Mongolia.
Web site: www.conceptseast.com

Hidden Trails (☎ 1-888-9-TRAILS, 604-323 1141, fax 323 1148) 5936 Inverness St, Vancouver BC, V5W 3P7. Horse riding tours to Terelj and Darkhat Valley, in conjunction with Equitour.
Web site: www.hiddentrails.com

Australia

Classic Oriental Tours (☎ 02-9261 3988, fax 9261 3320, [e] sales@hermes.net.au) 4th floor, 491 Kent St, Sydney, NSW 2000. Offers standard tours of Mongolia.
Web site: www.hermes.net.au/travel

Intrepid Travel (☎ 03-9473 2626, fax 9419 4426, [e] info@intrepidtravel.com) 11 Spring Street, Fitzroy, Victoria, 3065. Runs small group tours of Mongolia (via Beijing and the Great Wall), including a camel trek through the Gobi.
Web site: www.intrepidtravel.com.au

Peregrine Adventures (☎ 03-9662 2700) 258 Lonsdale St, Melbourne, Victoria 3000. Group tours including the Trans-Mongolian Railway.
Web site: www.peregrine.net.au

UK

Discovery Initiatives (☎ 020-9878 6341, fax 7738 1893, [e] enquiry@discoveryinitiatives.com) 21 The Bakehouse, 119 Altenburg Gardens, London SW11 1JQ. Runs environmentally friendly conservation trips to Khövsgöl, the Gobi and elsewhere in cooperation with local scientists.
Web site: www.discoveryinitiatives.com

Equitour (☎ 01865-511 643, fax 512 583) 41 South Parade, Summertown, Oxford OX2 7JP. Specialises in horse-riding tours .
Web site: www.equitour.com

Exodus (☎ 020-8675 5550, fax 8673 0779, [e] sales@exodustravels.co.uk) 9 Weir Rd, London SW12 0LT.
Web site: www.exodus.co.uk

Explore Worldwide (☎/fax 01252-760 001, [e] info@explore.co.uk) 1 Frederick St, Aldershot, Hants GU11 1LQ. Combined Inner and 'outer' Mongolia tour.
Web site: www.exploreworldwide.com

In the Saddle (☎ 01256-851 665, fax 851 667, [e] rides@inthesaddle.com) Laurel Cottage, Ramsdell, Tadley, Hampshire RG26 5SH. Runs horse riding tours.
Web site: www.inthesaddle.com

KE Adventure (☎ 017687-73966, fax 74693, [e] keadventure@enterprise.net) 32 Lake Road, Keswick, Cumbria CA12 5DQ. Organises mountain biking tours and guided ascents of Tavanbogd Uul.
Web site: www.keadventure.com.

Steppes East (☎ 01285-810 267, fax 810 693, [e] sales@steppeseast.co.uk) Castle Eaton, Swindon, Wiltshire SN6 6J
Web site: www.steppeseast.co.uk
Voyages Jules Verne (☎ 020-7616 1000) 21 Dorset Square, London NW1 6QG.
Web site: www.vjv.co.uk

Continental Europe

Eco Tour Production (☎ 498-487 105, fax 487 115, [e] janw.nomadic@gotlandica.se) Burge i Hablingbo 620 11 Havdhem, Gotland, Sweden
Ikarus Tours (☎ 06174-290221, [e] stappert@ ikarus.com) Am Kaltenborn 49-51, D-61542 Koenigstein, Germany
Kinareiser (☎ 22 11 00 57, fax 22 36 05 44) Hegdehaushveien 10, 0167 Oslo, Norway
Svensk-kinesiska Resebyran (☎ 8-108 824, fax 411 088) Sveavägen 31, 1TR 11134 Stockholm, Sweden
Voyages et Culture (☎ 41-21 312 37 41, fax 21 323 27 00, [e] cvc-travel@swissonline.ch) Rue de Bourg 10, CP 2545, 1002 Lausanne, Switzerland

Juulchin

The well regarded Mongolian travel company Juulchin conveniently has several offices abroad, which offer tours and information on the country. These offices include:

China (☎/fax 10-6525 4339) Beijing International Hotel, Room 4015, Jianguomenwai Dajie Beijing 100005
Germany (☎ 030-4405 7646, fax 4405 7645, [e] juulchin@aol.com) Prenzlauer Berg 8, D-10405 Berlin
Japan Mongol Juulchin Tours (☎ 03-3486 7351, fax 3486 7440) 8th floor, JBR Shibuya East, II 16-9, Higashi 2-chome, Shibuya-ku, Tokyo 150
South Korea (☎ 02-566 7707, fax 539 3913) 1st floor, 76-2, Kwang hee Dong 1 ka Chung-Gu, Seoul
USA (☎ 609-419 4416, fax 275 3827, [e] mongol@uno.com) 707 Alexander Road, Suite 208, Princeton, NJ 08540

Getting Around

Travelling around the countryside independently is the best way to see the country and meet the people, but there are several matters you need to be aware of. Annual outbreaks of forest fires, the plague, foot and mouth disease and even cholera may affect your travel plans if there are quarantine restrictions.

Generally, shortages of petrol and spare parts are now uncommon, except in remote regions. Accidents are not uncommon. Try to avoid travelling at night when unseen potholes, drunk drivers and wildlife can cause havoc.

Lastly, if you think Ulaan Baatar is undeveloped and lacking in facilities, think again about travelling in the countryside.

AIR

Mongolia, a vast, sparsely populated country with very little infrastructure, relies heavily on air transport. There are 81 airports, of which only 31 can be used permanently; only eight of these are paved. Just as Mongolian drivers view roads as a luxury, so paved runways are an unnecessary extravagance to Mongolian pilots.

Domestic Air Services

MIAT, the major internal airline, has flights to 17 *aimag* (provincial) capitals, major cities and tourist destinations – but not to Sükhbaatar, Erdenet, Darkhan or Sainshand, which are well serviced by train. Almost all of the destinations are served directly to/from Ulaan Baatar, so it is impossible to fly, say, between Dalanzadgad and Altai without returning to Ulaan Baatar and catching another flight.

Delayed and cancelled flights are common, and it appears that MIAT has also been getting a bad reputation for lost luggage. It seems that the aircraft is heavily overloaded by Mongolian traders who reckon this is a cargo flight. As a result, some luggage gets left behind despite being already checked in, and the longer it lies around unattended, the greater the chance

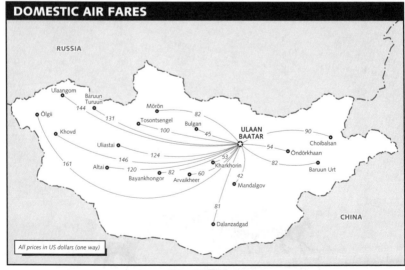

DOMESTIC AIR FARES

RUSSIA

Ulaangom
Baruun Turuun 144
Ölgii
131
Khovd
Uliastai
161
Altai 120
Bayankhongor
146
124
Mörön 82
Tosontsengel
100
Bulgan 45
82
82 60
Arvaikheer 42
ULAAN BAATAR
53
54
82
90
Choibalsan
Öndörkhaan
Baruun Urt
Kharkhorin
Mandalgov
81
Dalanzadgad

CHINA

All prices in US dollars (one way)

of it being lost or stolen. As a precaution, put your most valuable items in your hand luggage.

Longer flights to the west stop to refuel, often at Tosontsengel or Mörön, so you can sometimes combine a trip to Khovd and Khövsgöl. The problem here is that the location of these fuel stops changes regularly. Also, it can be hard to get a confirmed seat if you pick up a flight on the second leg; if the flight happens to be full, you won't get on it. At the time of research it was possible to fly between the following towns, though you'll need to check current schedules with MIAT in Ulaan Baatar: Öndörkhaan to Baruun Urt; Mandalgov to Dalanzadgad; Arvaikheer to Bayankhongor; Bulgan to Tosontsengel; Khovd-Bulgan; Khovd to Tosontsengel; Ulaangom to Mörön.

MIAT schedules change regularly, and almost weekly during the summer (14 May to 17 September) so double check your departure time the day before you fly. Pilots often use landmarks for navigation, so flights are often cancelled if there is a lot of fog. In summer, extra flights go to Dalanzadgad and the Juulchin-Gobi *ger* (traditional circular felt yurt) camp.

The only company to give MIAT any competition is the relatively new Khangard Airlines. For the same fares as MIAT, Khangard does the tourist run to Dalanzadgad (June to August) and Khatgal on Khövsgöl Nuur (mid-July to August). Khangard plans to provide a better service than MIAT (not difficult) by guaranteeing seats and by departing on time.

If you take a long-distance MIAT flight take some snacks and a bottle of water and dress lightly as there's no air-con.

Safety

There are perennial safety concerns over MIAT domestic flights. In May 1998, 28 passengers were killed in a MIAT crash near Erdenet. Overloading is common, and you may well see three people occupying two seats or people crouching in the aisles. We witnessed 16 people leave the cockpit after our flight from Khovd! Safety equipment is kept to a bare minimum, though you should

at least get a seat belt. Domestic flights are all on less-than-inspiring Soviet-built Antonov 24s (Antonov aircraft have been involved in around 120 crashes worldwide since 1962). Embassies and the Peace Corps no longer forbid their staff to fly on MIAT, but they discourage it.

Reservations & Tickets

A MIAT reservation isn't worth diddly-squat until you have a ticket in your hand. In the countryside, buy your ticket as soon as you arrive – normally at the airport or, sometimes, at the town bank. In Ulaan Baatar, MIAT staff speak some English; in the countryside, they don't.

You can buy a return ticket in Ulaan Baatar but there is no computerised reservation system connecting the various airports around the country so you will have to reconfirm your reservation at the airport as soon as you arrive at your destination. Even if you have done this, at some airports like Khovd, you need to get to the airport early in the morning of your flight in order to get a boarding pass.

If you wish to fly in one direction and return by road in the other (for example to Mörön), fly from Ulaan Baatar, where you are more likely to get a ticket and a seat, and then return overland – otherwise you may wait days or more for a flight and ticket in Mörön.

Never lose your ticket – you'll possibly get a refund in Ulaan Baatar, but nowhere else. Try not to change the date of your ticket – it is just one more headache you don't need.

Seats can be difficult to get in mid-July during Naadam and in late August as students return to college.

Costs

Domestic flights are subsidised by the government (one reason why MIAT's domestic service loses T2 trillion every year) and so foreigners must pay several times more than Mongolians for all MIAT (and Khangard) tickets. You must also pay in US dollars, and get a 'dollar-denominated ticket' or you won't get on the plane. Anyone can buy you a ticket, but you will always have to pay in US dollars (or a credit card in Ulaan Baatar). Tickets range from US$45 (to Bulgan) to US$161 for a four-hour, 1380km flight to the far west – pretty reasonable, considering the distances. Children between five and 16 years pay half; under fives fly for free.

Local volunteer workers from the Peace Corps and VSO can buy a flight pass from MIAT for about US$55, which entitles them to air tickets at local prices.

One real hassle is that the baggage limit on internal MIAT flights is 15kg and MIAT will charge you for every extra gram when you check in. When packing, remember that your baggage allowance shrinks from 60kg on Transpacific flights to 20kg on international flights to Mongolia and then 15kg on domestic flights. The cost for excess baggage is around T580 per kg, depending on the distance of the flight. To avoid this carry some heavy stuff in your small, cabin luggage (which isn't weighed) or share the load among friends.

Checking In

Go to all airports at least two hours before departure on the assumption that you will still have to struggle to get a seat on the flight, even if you have a ticket. In Ulaan Baatar, this is often less of a problem, but confusion still reigns supreme. (All flights from Ulaan Baatar leave between 8 and 10 am.) Even if you have a ticket, flight number and an allocated seat number, don't assume the plane won't be overbooked.

At the airport, you start the fun and games while queuing to exchange your ticket for a boarding pass, which you hand in when you finally get a seat on the plane. Then you have to scramble in another line to get your luggage weighed. In Ulaan Baatar you need to put your luggage through the X-ray machine and get a useless security sticker (which you can peel off and stick on any other piece of luggage!) before you can check in. After the plane has finally arrived (if travelling from anywhere other than Ulaan Baatar), scramble past the guard, through the throng of arriving passengers

and onto the tarmac. Then find a seat – there are no pre-assigned seat numbers. Try to make certain your luggage has gone on the plane. If possible, you'll save time and the worry of losing your bag by carrying your pack on as hand luggage.

Domestic Departure Tax

This is paid when you buy your air ticket and it varies from T500 to T1000, depending on the airport.

BUS

There are a few bus services around Mongolia but they are generally being replaced by private minivans. Even if you book a bus ticket you may find yourself ending up on a minivan anyway. All bus routes start and end in Ulaan Baatar; buses only travel between aimag capitals if they're on the way to or from Ulaan Baatar.

In Ulaan Baatar, it is a good idea to buy tickets in advance for all long-distance trips, though the actual time that buses leave is rarely the same as the departure times listed on your ticket or on the timetable. Always get there early, even though the bus may leave hours late. In the countryside, you just get on the bus when it arrives and pay the conductor on board.

In the countryside the post office operates postal buses or trucks, which accept passengers. They have fixed departure times, normally running once a week between an aimag capital and sum capital. They can be a useful way of getting to remote destinations, though you may have to wait a week before the next bus returns. The local post office should have a list of departure times and fares, though you'll need a Mongolian or Russian speaker to help you with this.

MINIVAN

Furgons, Russian-made 11-seater minivans, are the most common form of public transport in Mongolia. Private minivans go from Ulaan Baatar to all aimag capitals, major cities and tourist destinations except Sükhbaatar and Erdenet, which are connected by train, and the far western aimag capitals of Bayan-Ölgii and Ulaangom. Minivans do not travel around western Mongolia; the furthest west they go is to Mörön and Altai. Less frequent and reliable services operate between most aimag capitals.

The main problem with minivans is that they are privately operated and so won't leave until they are full. In the countryside most just park at the local market and wait for 11 passengers to turn up, which means that if the van isn't already mostly full you'll be waiting around all day for the seats to fill up, if they ever do. Departures from Ulaan Baatar are more reliable and have fixed departure times.

For a long distance trip bring all your own food and drink – stops will be few and far between, or at *guanz* (canteens), which have poor food. You can expect at least one breakdown and it would be a good idea to bring a sleeping bag and warm clothes just in case you have to spend the night somewhere. Long-distance travel of over 10 hours is generally fiendishly uncomfortable. Most people who take a long-distance minivan to Mörön or Dalanzadgad end up flying back. Minivan fares are reasonable, costing the equivalent of US$10 to get to Dalanzadgad (24 hours) or US$15 to Mörön (36 hours).

If there aren't enough passengers you may have to hire the whole van, for around T300 per km. Furgons are a popular way for groups of four or more tourists to travel around the countryside – they are a more spacious alternative to jeeps, and furgons can go anywhere a jeep can. Most of the rules of hiring a jeep apply to hiring a Furgon so see the Hiring a Jeep/Minivan and Driver entry under Jeep later in this chapter for more information.

TRAIN

The 1750km railway is primarily made up of the Trans-Mongolian Railway, connecting China with Russia. (Both domestic and international trains use this same line.) In addition, there are two spur lines: to the copper-mining centre of Erdenet and the coal-mining city of Baganuur. Another train runs every week from Choibalsan, the capital of Dornod aimag, to the Russian border.

North of Ulaan Baatar, express trains travel every day to Darkhan, and onto Sükhbaatar or Erdenet. To the south, there are direct trains from Ulaan Baatar to Choir twice a week, and to Zamyn-Üüd, via Choir and Sainshand, daily. You can't use the Trans-Mongolian Railway for internal transport.

When travelling in hard-seat class (see following), you will almost certainly have to fight to get a seat. If you're not travelling alone, one of you can scramble on board and find seats and the other can bring the luggage on board a little later. Young boys and girls usually travel around the train selling bread and fizzy drinks. Otherwise, there is nothing to eat or drink on local trains.

Classes

There are only two classes on domestic passenger trains: hard seat and soft seat. In hard-seat class, the seats are actually padded but there are no assigned seats nor any limit to the amount of tickets sold, so the carriages are always crowded and dirty – sometimes reminiscent of the worst Indian and Chinese regional trains. If you get the hard-seat carriage but decide that you can't stand the mass of human bodies, walk to the soft-seat carriages and ask to upgrade – spare soft-seats tickets are often available.

Soft seats are only a little bit softer, but the conditions are much better: the price difference (usually at least double the price of the hard seat) is prohibitive for most Mongolians. The soft-seat carriages are divided into compartments with four beds in each. You are given an assigned bed, and will be able to sleep, assuming of course that your compartment mates aren't riproaring drunk and noisy. If you travel at night, clean sheets are provided for about T250, which is a wise investment since some of the quilts smell like mutton. Compared with hard-seat class, it's the lap of luxury, and worth paying extra

If you're travelling from Ulaan Baatar, it is important to book a soft seat well in advance – it can be done up to 10 days before departure. There may be a small booking fee. In general, booking ahead is a good idea for any class, though there will always be hard seat tickets available.

TAXI

Mongolia claims to have 46,700km of highway – of which only 1200km is actually paved. Taxis are only useful along these paved roads, eg from Ulaan Baatar to Zuunmod, Terelj, Darkhan and possibly Kharkhorin. The general appalling quality of roads around the countryside means that most travel is by jeep or furgon.

JEEP

The ubiquitous Russian khaki-coloured jeep is nicknamed *jaran yös* (shortened to *jaris*), which means 'sixty-nine' – the number of the original model. On the terrible Mongolian roads, these jeeps are an important form of transport, and are mandatory when visiting the more remote attractions. The large and comfortable Toyota Landcruiser-style jeeps are scarcer and cost at least 30% more than a good Russian jeep.

Jeeps can typically only travel between 30 and 50km per hour. The distance table following may be helpful, especially when estimating the cost of a trip, as jeeps charge per kilometre. Along more popular routes, there are guanz along the way.

Public Jeeps

Public shared jeeps operate much the same as minivans and often wait and depart from the same stands. In larger towns shared jeeps are the main form of transport to the surrounding sum capitals. The frequency of departures depends almost entirely on demand. In the more remote areas, there are some shared jeeps, but you may have to wait a day before it leaves. Shared jeeps are dearer, but quicker and more comfortable than the public buses (and sometimes the only form of transport), though drivers will pack in as many people in the jeep as they can. Prices for a shared jeep are much the same as a minivan.

There are usually at least three passengers in the back, and two, plus driver, in front. (At a petrol station in one isolated town, we saw 11 adults and three children stagger out

of a shared jeep.) In most aimag capitals, shared jeeps leave from the market or bus/truck station. You will have to ask around; listen to distorted announcements in Mongolian over the loudspeaker at the market; or check any noticeboards at the market.

Rental

Easily the best way to see Mongolia independently is to hire your own jeep and guide. If you share the costs with others it doesn't work out too expensive and with enough time, camping equipment, water and food, and a reliable jeep and a driver, you will have the time of your life.

Renting a jeep with a driver and/or guide from Ulaan Baatar is the best way to see the countryside, but you can save some money by using public transport to major regional gateways – that is Mörön for Khövsgöl Nuur, Khovd for the west, Dalanzadgad for the south Gobi and Choibalsan for the far east. From these places, you will be able to rent a jeep fairly easily, though drivers will have little experience of dealing with tourists.

Don't expect to rent a jeep outside of an aimag capital. Most villages will have a jeep, but it may not be available or running.

If you aren't taking a guide-translator, hiring one just to negotiate the price and terms for a long and expensive trip is worthwhile. When you explain where you want to go, bear in mind that many towns and *sum* (districts) have identical or similar names, so make sure you both know exactly where you are going.

The price will include a driver (you will soon realise that you would never be able to drive around Mongolia on your own), who almost certainly won't speak anything but Mongolian and Russian (so you may need a guide to translate), and normally includes all petrol costs. On a long distance trip a rate that includes petrol is more convenient but you run the risk of your driver changing the itinerary to avoid places where petrol is expensive. A rate without petrol should be around 25% lower than that with petrol. Russian jeeps do around 5km to the litre; petrol currently costs around T330 per litre.

Road Distances (km)

	Ulaan Baatar	Tsetserleg	Ölgii	Bayankhongor	Bulgan	Altai	Choir	Darkhan	Sainshand	Choibalsan	Mandalgov	Uliastai	Erdenet	Arvaikheer	Dalanzadgad	Baruun-Urt	Sükhbaatar	Khovd	Mörön	Öndörkhaan	Zuunmod	Ulaangom	Tsagaannuur	Dornod	Khatgal
Ulaan Baatar	...																								
Tsetserleg	430	...																							
Ölgii	1636	1220	...																						
Bayankhongor	630	214	1006	...																					
Bulgan	318	289	1334	503	...																				
Altai	1001	...	635	371	874	...																			
Choir	238	537	1644	638	456	1009	...																		
Darkhan	219	630	1582	751	248	1122	457	...																	
Sainshand	463	855	1869	863	781	1234	225	682	...																
Choibalsan	655	1108	2291	1285	973	1656	439	874	531	...															
Mandalgov	260	500	1314	508	...	879	186	479	355	741	...														
Uliastai	984	531	...	459	807	195	1153	989	1322	1639	967	...													
Erdenet	371	357	1402	571	68	942	609	180	834	1026	631	809	...												
Arvaikheer	430	266	1206	200	348	571	494	596	663	1085	308	659	416	...											
Dalanzadgad	553	643	1583	577	725	948	479	772	516	1074	293	1036	793	377	...										
Baruun-Urt	560	1013	...	...	878	...	462	779	340	191	613	1544	931	990	856	...									
Sükhbaatar	311	629	...	843	340	1214	549	92	774	966	571	1147	272	688	864	871	...								
Khovd	1425	...	211	795	...	424	1489	1519	1658	2080	1303	465	1339	995	1372	...	1612	...							
Mörön	671	413	981	617	353	583	909	601	1134	1326	913	388	421	679	1056	1231	693	853	...						
Öndörkhaan	331	784	1967	961	649	1332	233	550	302	324	417	1315	702	761	710	229	642	1756	1002	...					
Zuunmod	43	496	1591	585	361	956	224	262	449	661	225	1027	414	385	518	536	354	1380	714	337	...				
Ulaangom	1336	883	301	988	1033	662	1569	1738	2223	991	1383	529	1101	1188	1585	1896	1373	238	680	1667	1379	...			
Tsagaannuur	1568	1115	69	1075	1265	704	1769	1513	1933	2223	1583	761	1333	1275	1652	1228	1605	280	912	199	1611	232	...		
Dornod	667	1120	2303	1297	985	1668	569	986	543	12	753	1651	1038	1097	1059	203	978	2092	1338	336	2003	673	2235	...	
Khatgal	772	514	1040	728	454	642	910	702	1235	1427	1014	447	522	780	1157	1332	794	942	101	1103	815	739	971	1439	...

Avoid offers of 'all-inclusive' charges by 'the day' as you will almost certainly pay more than if you pay per kilometre (though this does deal with issues like driver's accommodation costs and rest days). You can pay from T400 to T500 per km for more reliable jeeps and drivers from travel agents in Ulaan Baatar, or ger camps in the countryside. This charge may include a stove, tent and sleeping bag. At the market or bus station you may find a jeep for the taxi rate of T300 per km.

In aimag capitals, jeeps are available at very negotiable prices. The charge for Mongolians at the time of research was from T250 to T300 per km. This is about the same as the standard per kilometre rate for taxis in Ulaan Baatar, so you can use the Ulaan Baatar taxi rate as a guide for the cost of jeep rentals in the countryside.

It is vital that you and the driver agree to the terms and conditions – and the odometer or speedometer reading – before you start. Ask about all possible 'extras' such as waiting time, food and accommodation. There are several private bridges and tolls around the countryside (around T300), which is normally paid by you. If you arrange for a jeep to pick you up, or drop you off, agree on a reduced price for the empty vehicle travelling one way.

Three can sit in the back seat of a Russian jeep, but it may be uncomfortable on longer trips. If you also take a guide, rather than just a driver, you can therefore take a maximum of three passengers, though two would be more comfortable. There is usually ample room at the back of the jeep for backpacks, tents, water and so on.

In the aimag capitals, jeeps hang around the market or the bus/truck stations. In Ulaan Baatar, the best place to start looking is at the various guesthouses, the markets or at the long-distance bus station.

Hazards Flat tyres are a time-honoured tradition. Insist that your driver bring a spare and a tyre patch kit consisting of rubber patches, glue, extra tyre valves and a valve tool. Be sure the driver has a tyre pump, hydraulic jack and tyre irons. If the driver doesn't have a useable spare tyre, at least tell him to bring a spare inner tube.

The quickest distance between two points is a straight line, and the only thing that could (but not always) put off a Mongolian jeep diver from taking a shortcut is a huge mountain range or raging river. If renting a jeep by the kilometre, you will welcome a shortcut, especially to shorten an uncomfortable trip. If you have an experienced driver, allow him to take shortcuts when he feels it is worthwhile, but don't insist on any – he is the expert. The downside of shortcuts is the possibility of breaking down on more isolated roads.

Serious mechanical breakdowns are a definite possibility. To be safe, it's necessary to bring tools and whatever spare parts are available. Should your vehicle break down irreparably in a rural area, you'll be faced with the task of trying to get back to civilisation either on foot (not recommended), by hitching, or by whatever is available. The safest solution is to travel with a small group using at least two jeeps.

A warning: Russian jeeps easily overheat. There is no easy solution, but it helps to travel during the early morning or late afternoon hours when temperatures are relatively low.

Most of Mongolia is grassland, desert and mountains. You might think that mountain driving would pose the worst problems, but forests cause the most trouble of all. This is because the ground, even on a slope, is a springy alpine bog, holding huge amounts of water in the decaying grasses, which are instantly compacted under tyres, reducing a wildflower meadow to slush. Drivers in Mongolia enjoy a high status, and Mongolians are loath to dig if you become bogged – it's just not in their nomadic blood. This has been known to infuriate visitors, who expect a flurry of activity as soon as a vehicle becomes bogged. Mongolians are more inclined to sit on their haunches, have a smoke and then send word to the nearest farm or town for a tractor to come and tow you out. Just be patient.

The Gobi region generally has the best roads and here you can average 60km/h, as opposed to the 40km/h elsewhere.

Hiring a Jeep/Minivan and Driver Apart from the actual hiring of the jeep there are several other factors to consider when embarking on a jeep or minivan tour of Mongolia. Before the trip explain your itinerary in detail to the driver and make sure that he has a map and agrees to the route. If you are going to be camping, ensure that the driver and guide have the correct equipment (see Guides under the Jeep section). Both the driver and guide will need some kind of water bottle, a knife, a cup, bowl and spoon.

Your driver should supply a large petrol drum, as well as a jerry can, as a back up in case there are fuel shortages in the countryside. You'll also need at least one large water drum, preferably two if you are headed to the Gobi. (These are available in the Ulaan Baatar's Central Market for less than US$10.) Make sure it is watertight, otherwise your bags will get soaked. A wide-mouthed drum is also very useful for storing food, as boxes will rapidly disintegrate. A gunny sack is useful for vegetables and firewood (or dried dung). Resealable bags are useful for opened bags of sugar, pasta etc. Your backpacks will get filthy so it's a good idea to put them in a dust-proof and waterproof bag.

Drivers from tourist agencies will assume that you will feed them along the way. On a longer trip it's easiest for everyone to cook, eat and wash up together. If you don't want to do this you will have to agree to a fee for the driver's food or buy him the food yourself. Drivers will often not take enough food even if they have agreed to bring their own.

An experienced driver will have his own Soviet-built petrol stove, though it's a good idea to bring your own stove as a back up, and to boil water for tea while the other stove is cooking dinner. If you are cooking for a group you'll need a big cooking pot and a ladle. A cloth is useful for chopping and peeling vegetables. Bring a couple of rolls of toilet paper for cleaning and mopping up. Everyone should bring their own penknife, cutlery, bowl and torch. Drivers normally bring their own dried meat, which can be added to soups and stews.

Packaged foods, canned goods, fruit and vegetables, chocolate, and camping needs such as washing liquid and candles are all available in Ulaan Baatar, so a group shop is ideal. Many travellers organise a kitty to pay for petrol and food costs on the road. If you are travelling with strangers it's a good idea to keep everyone happy by rotating seats so that everyone (including the guide) has a go in the front seat.

To avoid confusion and frustration explain to your driver the arrangements with cooking, cleaning up, water purification and the difference between communal and private food. Don't push the driver or guide too hard; allow them (and the vehicle) to stop and rest. However, regular and lengthy stops for a chat and a smoke can add to the journey. You have the right to decide which, if any, passengers you pick up along the way and whether or not to charge them.

Lastly, if you are on a long trip, you'll find morale boosted by a trip to a bath house (hot water!) in an aimag capital. Another morale booster is the occasional meal in a decent guanz. If you are camping a lot then add in at least one night in a decent hotel to clean up and sort out your stuff.

Hiring a Guide No-one in the countryside speaks anything but Mongolian and Russian, so a guide-cum-translator is very handy, and almost mandatory. A guide will explain local traditions, help with any hassles with the police, find accommodation, negotiate jeeps, explain captions in museums and act as linguistic and cultural interpreter.

Many Mongolians in Ulaan Baatar, from students up to professors, love to earn some real money as guides during the summer holidays. The most popular foreign language (besides Russian) is English, though some speak German, Japanese, Spanish and French, although standards of fluency may not be high.

Finding a guide is not easy. In Ulaan Baatar, ask travel agencies (where guides will be more expensive), talk to anyone who approaches you in the street for any reason, find some students at the universities or nearby cafes and hotels, or check out the classified ads in the English-language newspapers. In the countryside, there is nothing to do but ask, and ask, and ask – try the hotels and schools. Guides are easier to find between June 15 and August 1, when schools and universities are on summer break.

In Ulaan Baatar, a non-professional guide or a student will cost a negotiable US$5 to US$10 per day, although guides are only really useful here if you have to deal with any bureaucracy such as extending your visa or registering. To take one around the countryside from the capital you will have to include expenses for travel, food and accommodation. If you are camping you will need to ensure your guide (and driver) has the camping proper equipment (including basics such as water bottles and eating utensils) and warm clothes; don't just leave it up to them or shrug it off if they have substandard equipment. In an aimag capital, a guide (if you can find one) costs about US$5 per day, plus any expenses. For a professional guide who is knowledgeable in a specific interest, such as birdwatching, and very fluent in your language, the bidding starts at US$20 per day. Here are a few final tips:

• Test a guide for the day.
• You can share a guide with up to four people – any more than that and it gets unwieldy.
• Guides are often little more than interpreters – they are not necessarily knowledgeable about the region you are visiting.
• Make sure the guide doesn't end up spending most of your time and money practising their language skills.
• Be careful that guides don't demand expensive meals and accommodation.

CAR & MOTORCYCLE

Travelling around Mongolia with your own vehicle is not recommended. What looks like main roads on the map are little more than tyre tracks in the dirt, sand or mud. All maps are inadequate, and there is hardly a signpost in the whole country. In Mongolia, roads connect nomads, most of whom by their nature keep moving so even the roads are semi-nomadic, shifting like restless rivers. Remote tracks quickly turn

GPS

When you are travelling around the featureless plains of Eastern Mongolia, the deserts of the Gobi or a tangle of confusing valleys in the West, a Global Positioning System (GPS) can be very useful in determining where exactly you are, as long as you have a reliable map on which to pinpoint your coordinates. We have given GPS coordinates for many hard-to-find places in this book.

A GPS won't help you every time, as you'll still need to know which road to take, even if you know the rough direction. For this you'll need to fall back on the alternative Mongolian GPS (Ger Positioning System), which involves asking directions at every ger you see and following the vague sweeps of the owner's hand until you get to the next ger.

into eight-lane dirt highways devoid of any traffic making navigation tricky – some drivers follow the telephone lines when there are any, or else ask for directions at gers along the way. Villages with food and water are few and far between, and very few people in the countryside will speak anything but Mongolian or, if you are lucky, Russian.

There is nowhere official in Mongolia to rent a car or motorcycle. If you want to buy one, you will have to ask around, or check out a couple of car yards below the bridge just south of the Bayangol Hotel in Ulaan Baatar. One traveller bought a new Ij Planeta – the Russian-made motorcycle you see all over the countryside – for the tögrög equivalent of US$900. After travelling 4000km, he was able to sell it for US$800. A new Russian jeep costs around US$5000. In markets the sign 'zarna' (Зарпа) on a jeep means 'for sale'. Russian plates and the sign 'tranzit' in the windshield are other pointers.

Travellers can use an international driving license to drive any vehicle in Mongolia; expat residents need to apply for a local license. If you buy a vehicle, inquire about registration at the local police station.

All aimag, and most sum, capitals have a petrol station. Supplies are regular, but you will probably have to come to terms with the hand pumps. Two types of Russian fuel are available: '93' is the best and the type used by Japanese jeeps, but only generally available in Ulaan Baatar; all Russian-made vehicles use '76', which is all that is available in the countryside. Petrol stations are marked by the initials 'ШТС', from the Russian for station.

BICYCLE

Now that Mongolia is opening up to the outside world, bicycles occasionally appear on the streets of Ulaan Baatar and even in the countryside, but these are generally ridden by 'eccentric' expats. Most Mongolians don't see the point in bicycles: all towns in the countryside are small enough to walk around; horses or motorbikes are the best form of transport between towns anyway; and buses run regularly around Ulaan Baatar.

Given the rough roads, a mountain bike would be a wiser choice than a more fragile 10-speed touring bike, but there are a few points to recognise: you will need to bring all your spare parts and tools; maps are inadequate and there are no road signs; the roads are appalling; taking a bike on a bus or truck (it is better on a train) is fraught with problems, and airlines have luggage restrictions; dogs will cause you headaches; the notoriously fickle weather should be taken seriously; villagers will take a lot of interest in you and your bike; and Mongolians are terrible at estimating distance – they usually grossly overestimate.

If you bring your own bike into the country by train you may have to put it in the luggage car and pay customs duty on it in Ulaan Baatar. On the plus side, once you get there nomads are often more than happy to swap a ride on your bike for a ride on their horse. Graham Taylor at Karakorum Expeditions (see Travel Agencies under Information in the Ulaan Baatar chapter) runs mountain bike tours in Mongolia and is a source of information on cycling around Mongolia.

HITCHING

Hitching is never entirely safe in any country in the world and we don't normally recommend it. People who choose to hitch will be safer if they travel in pairs and let someone know where they are planning to go.

Mongolia is different, however. Because the country is so vast, public transport so limited and the people so poor, hitching (usually on trucks) is a recognised – and, often, the only – form of transport in the countryside. Hitching is seldom free and often no different from just waiting for public transport to turn up. It is *always* slow – after stopping at gers to drink, fixing flat tyres, breaking down, running out of petrol and getting stuck in mud and rivers, a truck can take 48 hours to cover 200km.

Hitching is not generally dangerous personally, but it is still hazardous and often extremely uncomfortable. Don't expect much traffic in remote rural areas; you might see one or two vehicles a day on many roads, and sometimes nobody at all for several days. Along the road, just wave at the driver of any vehicle. In the towns, ask at the market, where trucks invariably hang around, or at the bus/truck/jeep station, police station or hotel. At the markets, sometimes there are announcements over the loudspeakers (you can make your own announcement), and notices on a noticeboard about imminent departures. You can often leave your hotel room number with a jeep driver and get him to pick you up when he is ready to leave.

If you rely on hitching entirely, you will just travel from one dreary aimag town to another. You still need to hire a jeep to see, for example, the Gobi Desert, the mountains in Khentii or some of the lakes in the far west. Hitching out of Ulaan Baatar is difficult because you must find the right truck or vehicle at the right time.

Truck drivers will normally expect some negotiable payment, which won't be much cheaper than a long-distance bus or shared jeep; figure on around T1000 per hour travelled. Rather than cash, drivers may prefer vodka or cigarettes, or anything of practical use to them. You'll need to speak either

Mongolian or Russian, or have an interpreter with you. You never know what sort of vehicle you'll be riding in – you could be riding in the back of a truck with the sheep, or you could be in an ambassador's Landcruiser next to a bunch of diplomats.

The most important thing to bring is an extremely large amount of patience and time, and a high threshold for discomfort. You must carry camping gear for the inevitable breakdowns. Bring all your own food and water, though the truck may stop at guanz enroute.

Blazing Saddles – Travelling like a Local

A surprisingly large number of intrepid travellers arrive in Mongolia each summer with plans to travel across the country on horseback and why not? The following advice stems from the experience of one such intrepid neo-Chinggis, who survived to tell the tale.

How to obtain your horses is usually the first obstacle. Horses range in price from US$60 to many thousands of dollars for a racehorse. A tourist can expect to pay US$100 to $150, though you may well be charged more. Price is not really the issue though; it's getting a good horse that is the challenge.

'Buyer Beware' is the rule of thumb and if you don't know your horses you could very well end up with a geriatric nag. Herders are very protective of their best horses and these are usually not for sale for love or money. Taking a trusted local with you to assist selection and negotiate the sale is an excellent idea.

Mongolian horses come in two varieties – 'quiet' and 'angry'. A *nomcon moir* (quiet horse) is ideal, but these are often prized by herders for use by women and children. Geldings *(moir)* are preferable to mares *(gou)* and stallions *(asarak)*. Depending on the size of the group and duration of the trip, pack horses will also likely be required (figure on one pack horse for every two to three riders). Generally, it's best to select horses that can alternate between riding and pack duties.

The saddle is possibly the single most important item of equipment, and a comfortable saddle will make or break the trip. Definitely consider bringing a Western-style saddle from home (either a stock or pony saddle). Otherwise, Russian military saddles are available at Central (Black) Market. Only a masochist on a short horse-trip should consider using a Mongolian wooden saddle. For supplies, try Shonkhor Saddles, just east of the Mobicon building in Ulaan Baatar. Horse tack such as bridles, reins, hobbles, tethers etc are best bought locally but it's worth bringing stirrup leathers from home. Other foreign items of tack make good presents for local herders, as do horse magazines.

Taking along a guide is an important consideration and is generally highly recommended. A wrangler will generally look after the horses, help load packs, navigate and deal with tricky local conditions. Just as important, a guide will offer insights into the Mongolians' close relationship with horses and will help you learn local techniques. Local horse guides normally charge between US$5 and US$15 per day. The gung-ho option of going it alone depends largely on preparation, experience, and the all important question, 'Why are we/I doing this?'

In general, it is unnecessary to be 100% stocked with food for the journey. Shops along the way stock basic foodstuffs (including beer and chocolate), and the hospitality of local herders will likely have you eating more dairy products than you ever thought possible. However, be considerate to local hospitality by not depending upon it.

A couple of simple rules apply to horse travel in the Mongolian countryside. Wherever there is water there will be herders and gers, and vice versa. A track of some sort will exist along every navigable feature in the country and if there is a trail, it will be going somewhere (this might not be where you want to go, but does it matter?) Finally look after your horses and yourself and meet lots of local people!

Graham Taylor

Graham completed a 2000km horse trek through central Mongolia in 1997. You can read the story published in the *Australian Geographic* at www.mongoliadreaming.com.

One more good idea from a reader:

The only space for my backpack was an open tray on the roof used to store oily tool boxes and jacks; add to that the rain and blood and guts from a dozen beaver carcasses, which we carried for some hunters. You may want to slip the backpack into a large plastic bag first.

Nick Winter (UK)

BOAT

Although there are 397km of navigable waterways in Mongolia, rivers aren't used for transporting people or cargo. The only two boats we have heard of in the country are the *Sükhbaatar*, which very occasionally travels around Khövsgöl Nuur, and a customs boat, which patrols the Selenge Gol on the border of Russia and Mongolia. Both can be chartered by foreigners for lots of money.

The Nature's Door ger camp in Khövsgöl Nuur has kayaks and a dinghy with an outboard motor, which are perfect for trips out on to the lake.

HORSE RIDING

Horses have provided reliable transport for Mongolians for the past few thousand years. If it worked for the Mongol hordes, it can work for you. In recent decades, many herders have acquired motorcycles, but most still use horses as their primary mode of transport. Mongolians rarely walk anywhere.

It's impossible to see everything by horse unless you have a lot of time, but it is the best way to travel around Khövsgöl Nuur, Tsagaannuur and the muddy Khentii region. Most importantly, riding a horse helps you meet locals on a level footing and experience the country as Mongolians have done for centuries.

You can rent a horse and guide in most tourist areas for between US$5 and US$20 per day (the latter at ger camps). Most foreign and local travel agencies also organise horse-riding trips. See the Suggested Itineraries in the Facts for the Visitor chapter for some good places to make a horse trip.

One thing to bear in mind is that when mounting a horse (or camel), do so only from the left. The animals have been trained to accept human approach from the left, and may rear if approached the wrong way. The Mongolians use the phrase '*chu!*' to make their horses go. If you are considering a multi-day horse trip. remember that horses attract all kinds of flies.

A few foreigners cherish the idea of buying a horse and taking off around Mongolia. It's a fine adventure (if you can get a visa long enough) but there are several pitfalls to be aware of.

Some final advice; watch and learn – Mongolians almost invented horsemanship – and be prepared for at least one good spill.

CAMEL & YAK

Don't laugh: camels and yaks are recognised forms of transport. Camels, which can carry around 250kg, carry about one-third of all cargo around the Gobi Desert. Yaks are also a useful and environmentally friendly way of hauling heavy cargo.

Why drive when you can camel?

A few travel agencies include a ride on a camel or yak in their program. In more touristy areas such as the ger camps in the southern Gobi, Khövsgöl Nuur and Terelj you may be able to ride a camel or yak for an hour or so. Otherwise, you can always ask at a ger.

LOCAL TRANSPORT
Bus, Minibus & Trolley-bus

In Ulaan Baatar, regular, and very crowded, trolley-buses, buses and minibuses ply the main roads for around T200 a ride. Cities like Darkhan and Erdenet have minibuses which shuttle from one end of town to the other but you are unlikely to need them because most facilities are located centrally.

Taxi

Ulaan Baatar is the only place with a taxi service, though in the national capital any vehicle on the street is a potential taxi – just flag down the driver and agree on a price. The current rate is a standard T300 per km, but this will certainly increase. In the countryside there are no taxis, but you can normally charter a local vehicle.

ORGANISED TOURS

See Travel Agencies under Information in the Ulaan Baatar chapter for details about recommended Mongolian travel agencies, and the Getting There & Away chapter for information about foreign travel agencies that organise tours to Mongolia.

Ulaan Baatar Улаан Баатар

With over one-third of the country's population, Ulaan Baatar is by far Mongolia's largest city. It is also the transport and industrial centre of the country. Often shortened to UB by foreigners (but not by locals), Mongolia's capital still has the look and feel of a neglected European city from the 1950s – but not for long. The old Soviet cars and buses are being replaced by newer Japanese models, apartments are being converted into flashy shops and it seems that every young Mongolian now has a mobile phone. Ulaan Baatar prides itself on being an increasingly modern (though still very laid-back) city. Despite all this, men and women still stroll along the main streets in traditional dress.

Built along the river, the Tuul Gol, and surrounded by picturesque mountains, the centre of Ulaan Baatar is dominated by Soviet-style high-rise apartment blocks. Yet about 250,000 locals live in sprawling suburbs on the outskirts of the city, opting to live in traditional *ger* (circular felt yurts).

The topography makes for good hillside views overlooking the city, however, during winter the view is frequently obscured by pollution. This environmental problem is further exacerbated by temperature inversions caused by the coal burning that powers the Soviet-built heating system.

Despite being the national capital and largest city, Ulaan Baatar retains a relaxed, small-town atmosphere. It is a very pleasant place to visit and to base yourself for trips around the country. The city has interesting monasteries and museums and excellent cultural shows, so try to spend some time here before heading out to the glorious valleys, steppes or desert of Mongolia.

HISTORY

The first recorded capital city of the recent Mongolian empire was created in 1639. It was called Örgöö and was originally located at the monastery Da Khüree, some

Highlights

- Gandantegchinlen Khiid, the largest monastery in the country, with enchanting ceremonies held daily
- Museum of Natural History, exhibiting dinosaur remains found in the Gobi during the 1920s
- National Museum of Mongolian History, with excellent exhibits of Mongol memorabilia and traditional costumes and crafts
- Winter Palace of Bogd Khaan, displaying an impressive collection of stuffed creatures, scroll paintings and costumes
- Traditional cultural shows, with must-see performances of traditional dance, song, horse-head fiddle and contortionists (!)
- Naadam Festival, famous for wrestling, archery and horse racing

RUSSIA

CHINA

Ulaan Baatar
p134-5

420km from Ulaan Baatar in Arkhangai *aimag*, or province. The monastery was the residence of the five-year-old Zanabazar who, at the time, had been proclaimed the head of Buddhism in Mongolia. The city was often moved (probably around 25 times) to various places along the Orkhon,

Selenge and Tuul rivers. Throughout such movement, the city was given some fairly unexciting official and unofficial names, including Khüree (Camp) in 1706.

In 1778 the capital was built at its present location and called the City of Felt. Later, the city became known as the Ikh Khüree, or Great Camp, and was under the rule of the Bogd Khaan, or Living Buddha.

In 1911 when Mongolia first proclaimed its independence from China, the city became the capital of Outer Mongolia and was renamed Niislel Khüree (Capital Camp). In 1918 it was invaded by the Chinese and three years later by the Russians.

Finally, in 1924 the city was renamed Ulaan Baatar (Red Hero) and declared the official capital of an 'independent' Mongolia (independent from China, not from the Soviet Union). The Khangard (Garuda) was declared the city's official symbol. In 1933 Ulaan Baatar gained autonomy and separated from the surrounding Töv aimag.

From the 1930s, the Soviets built the city in typical Russian style: lots of ugly apartment blocks, large brightly coloured theatres and cavernous government buildings.

Tragically, the Soviets also destroyed almost all of the monasteries and temples. Ulaan Baatar is still young; and unlike many Russian and European cities, there is very little that is old or glorious about the place.

ORIENTATION

Most of the city spreads from east to west along the main road, Enkh Taivny Örgön Chölöö, also known as Peace Ave. The centre is Sükhbaatar Square, often simply known as 'the Square'. Sprawling suburbia is limited by the four majestic mountains that surround the city, Bayanzurkh, Chingeltei, Songino Khairkhan and Bogdkhan. The river to the south, the Tuul Gol, also somewhat limits the growth of suburban expansion.

Useful landmarks include the Trade & Development Bank building to the northwest of the Square, the twin towers of the Bayangol Hotel to its south, and on top of the hill immediately to the south, the Zaisan Memorial. Around the Square are the Central Post Office and the Palace of Culture, and two blocks west of the Square is the State Department Store. Central Ulaan Baatar is

Camels have right of way – a typical Ulaan Baatar street scene circa the late 19th century

AM

The Khangard – the city's official emblem

defined by two ring roads; Baga Toiruu (Little Toiruu) and Ikh Toiruu (Big Toiruu).

The city is divided into six major districts, but there's a multitude of subdistricts and microdistricts. Mongolians rarely use the Western system of street names and numbers, so tracking down an address place can be difficult. A typical address might be something like: Microdistrict 14, Building 3, Flat 27. The problems with this are numerous – you are unlikely to know which microdistrict you're in, many buildings are not numbered or signed, and all street signs are in Mongolian Cyrillic. This is why most locals will give you an unofficial description, such as 'Flat 5, Floor 2, left-hand entrance of Blue Building No 44, behind the long-distance bus station'. To find your way around Ulaan Baatar, a map, phrasebook and sense of direction are vital.

Maps

There are several maps available of Ulaan Baatar, though not all are worthwhile. Besides the map in this guidebook, the best is the 1:10,000 *Ulaanbaatar City Map* (1999) on the back of the *Welcome To Mongolia* tourist map (T5000).

The best place to obtain these and other maps of Mongolia is the Map Shop on Ikh Toiruu, near the Elba Electronics shop. You can also buy good topographic maps of

Mongolia here (see Maps under Planning in the Facts for the Visitor chapter).

INFORMATION

The *UB Guide* comes out every summer and is worth a look for travel articles, restaurant lists and other tourist information. It's available at the State Department Store, most souvenir shops and a few bars and restaurants. There's an online version at www.come.to/ulaanbaatar/.

Hello! Sainbaina Uu (T1500) is a monthly local expat newsletter that has some interesting articles on local culture and sights.

Tourist Offices

The Mongolian National Tourism Center (☎ 311 102, 318 493, fax 318 492, e ntc@mongol.net) is a government agency that deals mostly in policy implementations, but there are plans to open an information centre in its offices on Chinggis Ave.

The Cultural Information Resource Center (CIRC; ☎ 316 022, fax 315 358, e circ@mol.mn), at room 202 of the Youth Palace on Zaluuchuudyn Örgön Chölöö, was recently set up as a way to exchange information on the arts in Mongolia. It's a good place to find out about Ulaan Baatar's cultural scene. Its office normally holds a small exhibit of local art and can put people in contact with local Mongolian artists.

Otherwise, staff at most of the backpacker guesthouses can answer most tourist-related queries, help with visa registration and get you a bus or train ticket.

Money

The Trade & Development Bank (T&D Bank; ☎ 327 020, fax 325 449) is the best place to change money. It's the large, modern building on the corner of Khudaldaany Gudamj and Baga Toiruu. The foreign exchange office, which is up some steps on the southern side of the building, is open weekdays from 9 am to 12.45 pm and 2 to 3.30 pm.

The T&D Bank charges no commission for changing US dollar travellers cheques (the only currency of cheque currently accepted) into tögrög. They also cash US dollars and major European and Asian

ULAAN BAATAR

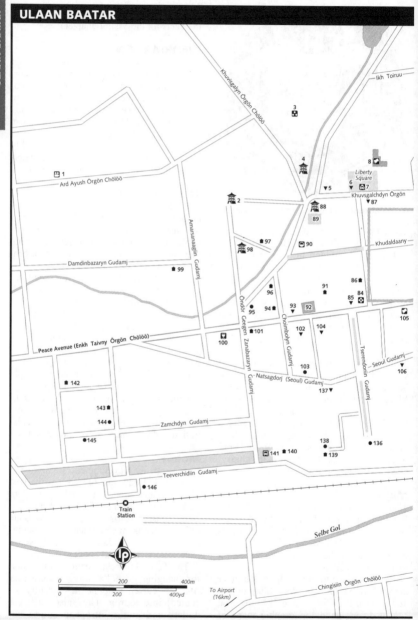

ULAAN BAATAR

Ikh Toiruu

Khuvsgalyn Örgön Chölöö

3

4

8

Liberty Square

6

7

Khuvsgalchdyn Örgön

▼5

▼87

1

Ard Ayush Örgön Chölöö

2

88

89

Khudaldaany

Amarsanaagiin Gudamj

97

98

90

Damdinbazaryn Gudamj

99

86

96

91

85

84

95

94

93

92

105

Öndör Geegen Zanabazaryn Gudamj

101

100

102

104

Chombolyn Gudamj

Peace Avenue (Enkh Taivny Örgön Chölöö)

Tserendorjiin Gudamj

Seoul Gudamj

106

142

103

Natsagdorj (Seoul) Gudamj

137 ▼

143

144

Zamchdyn Gudamj

145

138

136

139

141 140

Teeverchidiin Gudamj

146

Train Station

Selbe Gol

0   200   400m

0   200   400yd

To Airport (16km)

Chingisiin Örgön Chölöö

ULAAN BAATAR

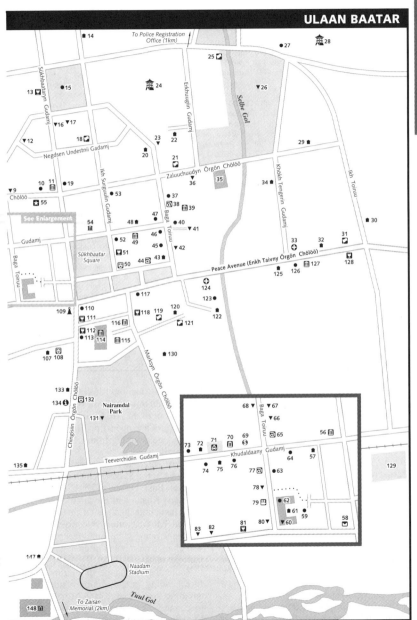

ULAAN BAATAR

PLACES TO STAY
14 Narlag Hotel
20 Zaluuchuud Hotel
22 Marco Polo Hotel
29 Flower Hotel
30 Undruul Hotel
32 New Capital Hotel
34 Chinggis Khaan Hotel
43 Ulaan Baatar Hotel;
     Protected Areas Bureau
48 Tuvshin Hotel
57 Hotel Urge
61 Nassan's Guest House
72 Khongor Guest House
75 Center Hotel; Millie's
86 Bold's Guest House
91 Mandukhai Hotel
94 Kharaa Hotel
96 Genex Hotel
97 Gana's Guest House
99 White House Hotel
101 Serge's Guest House
107 UB Guesthouse
120 Mika Hotel
122 Edelweiss Hotel
125 Negdelchin Hotel;
     Hazara Restaurant
130 Continental Hotel
133 Bayangol Hotel;
     Casablanca Café & Bar
135 Jiguur Grand; Karakorum
     Expeditions

139 Sarora hotel
140 Idre's Guest House
142 Prince Hotel
143 Batkhan Hotel
147 Zuchi Hotel

PLACES TO EAT
5 Hanamasa Restaurant; Gobi
    Original Cashmere House
6 Anatolia Turkish Restauarant
9 Axis Restaurant
12 Douala La Capitale
16 Chinggis Restaurant; Bowling
     Alley
17 Churchill's
23 Cafe De France
26 Abtai Sain Khaani Örgöö
36 Korean Restaurant
41 Taj Mahal
42 Pizza Del La Casa
60 Dorvoljin Café; Ding Chen
     Hot Pot
66 Winners Café
67 Classic Café
68 Sacher's Cafe
78 Amtat Bulag
80 BMT
82 El Latino Restaurant; Chez
     Bernard; Samar Magic Tours
83 Little Hong Kong
85 Overseas Restaurant
87 Berlin Fast Food

93 Pizza Del La Casa; Casa
     Home Video; Fine Art Shop
102 El Toro
104 Los Bandidos
106 Chin Van Khandorjiin Örgöö
131 Seoul Restaurant
137 Marco Polo Restaurant

OTHER
1 Nomin Cinema; Nomin Plaza
2 Gandantegchinlen (Gandan)
    Khiid
3 Tasgany Ovoo
4 Gesar Süm
7 Taxi Stand
8 Diplomatic Services Corps
    Bldg; Canadian Embassy;
    Czech Republic Embassy;
    French Embassy; Kazakhstan
    Embassy; Peace Corps
10 Eastern Culture Antique Shop
11 Museum of Natural History
13 Chinggis Club
15 Mongolian Art Centre for
     Children's Creativity
18 German Embassy
19 Nomadic Expeditions;
     Egshiglen National Musical
     Instrument Shop
21 Chinese Embassy
24 Dashchoilon Khiid
25 US Embassy

currencies into tögrög on a commission free basis. The bank charges 2% commission for changing US dollar travellers cheques into US dollars cash – but it won't do a similar service for any other currency.

You can also get a US dollar cash advance on your Visa, MasterCard and American Express credit cards for a 4% commission (commission free for American Express). You cannot buy tögrög with a credit card – you'll have to buy US dollars, then convert them into tögrög (no commission). The process only takes about 15 minutes.

The T&D Bank is also the place to arrange bank transfers. Transfers take three to five days and cost US$40, plus 0.01% of the amount transferred. The bank can give you a list of their correspondent banks abroad.

There are many licensed moneychangers which will legally change cash currencies at higher rates than the bank. One of the best places to do this is the row of booths on the upper floor of the Ard Cinema. These moneychangers are open from 10 am to 8 pm and change anything from Chinese yuan to Dutch gilder.

There are also convenient moneychangers at the State Department Store and Central Post Office. The Ulaan Baatar, Chinggis Khaan and Bayangol hotels have small bank branches, which are open during normal banking hours and offer standard exchange rates. Many hotel reception desks will change money but often at a lower rate than the banks.

Remember to change all your money before heading into the countryside, where anything larger than a US$20 will be hard to change. For more information, see the Money section in Facts for the Visitor.

27 Air China
28 Otochmaaramba Khiid
31 UK Embassy
33 Russian Hospital No 2
35 Cultural Information Re-
    source Center (CIRC);
    Zaluus Youth and Cultural
    Centre
37 Khan's Ger
38 Internet House Center;
    Youth Federation Building
39 Intellectual Museum
40 Central Sports Palace
44 Internet House Center
45 Ministry of Enlightenment
46 Mongolian National Modern
    Art Gallery
47 Santis Language School
49 Theatre Museum
50 State Opera &
    Ballet Theatre
51 Khan Torkh Bier Garten
52 Palace of Culture
53 French Cultural Centre
54 Government (Parliament)
    House
55 Police Headquarters
56 National Museum of
    Mongolian History
58 Central Post Office
59 Mobicom
62 Khangard Airlines

63 MIAT Office
64 Ayanchin Outfitters
65 Epsilon Internet Cafe
69 Trade & Development Bank
70 Zanabazar Museum of
    Fine Arts
71 Taxi Stand
73 Antique Shop
74 Scrolls
76 Federation for the Preserva-
    tion of Mahayana Tradition
77 Icafe
79 Ard Cinema
81 Jason's Jazz Bar
84 State Department Store
88 Bakula Rinpoche
89 Container Market
90 Truck Station
92 Peace & Friendship Building;
    Nomads; White Horse Travel
95 Map Shop
98 Lamrin Süm
100 Money Train Nightclub
103 Aeroflot Office
105 Russian Embassy
108 National Academic Drama
    Theatre; Ikra Dance Club
109 Statue of Zorig
110 Mongolian Artists' Exhibition
    Hall
111 Khanbrau Bar
112 East West Bar

113 State Central Library of
    Mongolia
114 Monastery-Museum of
    Choijin Lama
115 Wedding Palace
116 The Victims of Political
    Persecution Memorial
    Museum
117 Ministry of External Relations
118 River Sounds
119 Japanese Embassy
121 South Korean Embassy
123 DHL Couriers
124 Yonsei Hospital
126 Wrestling Palace
127 Ulaan Baatar City Museum
128 Carlsburg Pub
129 Central Market
132 State Youth & Children's
    Theatre
134 Mongolian National Tourism
    Center
136 State Circus
138 Dalai Eej & Merkuri markets
141 Long-Distance Bus Station
144 Top Ten Nightclub
145 International Railway
    Ticketing Office
146 Domestic Railway Ticket
    Office
148 Entrance to the Winter
    Palace of Bogd Khaan

Post

The Central Post Office is on the south-west corner of Sükhbaatar Square. As you enter from the main road, a door to your left leads to the Mongol Post Bank.

The Postal Counter Hall is the place to post mail and check poste restante (there's a T30 charge to pick up anything, and you'll need to show your passport). EMS express mail can also be sent from here. There is also a good range of postcards, small booklets about Mongolia in English and local newspapers for sale. The post office is officially open from 7.30 am to 9 pm weekdays and from 9 am to 8 pm weekends, though in reality most services are almost nonexistent on Sunday.

Couriers such as DHL (☎ 310 919) and TNT (☎ 313 389) will deliver and pick up door-to-door. DHL has its main office just off Peace Ave 15-A, near the Edelweiss Hotel. TNT packages can be sent through the post office.

Telephone

For local calls, you can use the telephone at your hotel (usually for free). Other hotels, including those with business centres and some of the street stalls with telephones charge a standard T100 for each call. You can also make local calls at the small booth at the back, and to the left, of the front hall of the Central Post Office.

For most Mongolians and foreigners, the only option for making long-distance and international calls is to use the Central Post Office. Approach the small booth to your left as you enter from the main road, fill out the form (written in Mongolian) requesting the number you want to call. Then pay your money up front and head to the room on the other side of the post office (to the right as you enter from the main road).

Give your form to the person behind the counter and wait for a loudspeaker announcement in Mongolian alerting you that your call has come through. Try to ask the person behind the counter to tell you when your call comes through and which telephone booth to use, otherwise you'll wait forever.

Telephones in the Bayangol, Flower and Ulaan Baatar hotels offer home country direct services to Japan, Singapore and the USA. Just press the marked button to get through to an operator in those countries.

See also Telephone under Post & Communications in the Facts for the Visitor chapter.

Fax

Most middle to top-range hotels have a fax machine which can be used by guests and anyone else who is willing to pay the high rates of between T5000 and T6000 per page. The Central Post Office offers a less user-friendly service, with cheaper rates of about T3000 per page. Hotels charge around T800 to receive a fax on your behalf.

Email & Internet Access

Ulaan Baatar now has dozens of Internet cafes where you can surf the Web and access email accounts. Hourly rates are constantly in flux but are reasonable at around T1600 per hour. There is often a minimum charge for the first 10 minutes. Connections are generally good. You can scan photos in many places for around T1000.

Epsilon, on Baga Toiruu, is a popular place. It's open daily from around 10 am to 10 pm. The Icafe, to the south and on the other side of the road, is a little more expensive but is an option if Epsilon is full or closed.

The Internet House Center has two branches, one in the Mongolian Youth Federation Building and the other in the MPRP Building, next to the Ulaan Baatar Hotel. Hourly rates are around T1500, with cheap weekend rates and a 30% discount from 9 am to noon. Both branches are open daily until 9 pm.

Travel Agencies

Of the hundred or more travel agencies which have sprung up around Ulaan Baatar in the past few years, the dozen or so listed below are recommended as generally reliable.

Only post office box addresses are listed because the postal system in Mongolia is unreliable. Many agencies run their businesses from home and their offices are notoriously difficult to find. It is far better to communicate by fax, telephone or, even better, by email. Ring in advance if you want to actually meet with someone.

Blue Sky Travel (☎/fax 312 067, e blue skytrav@yahoo.com) PO Box 181. Blue Sky run a wide range of professional tours. The office is in the National Recreation Center near Seoul Restaurant in Nairamdal Park.
  Web site: www.mol.mn/bluesky.

Boojum Expeditions (☎/fax 310 852, e boojum@mcn.net) The office is at Room 16, Bldg 13, near the Bayangol Hotel, but you are better off calling first to get someone to meet you. Contact Kent Madin.

Goviin Ogloo (☎ 315 552, fax 323 394, e gobin ogloo@magicnet.mn) A German-speaking agency, next to the Tuuvshin Hotel.

Guchtkhan Travel (☎/fax 324 770, e guchid han@magicnet.mn) PO Box 49/411. A one-man band who runs customised tours to off-the-beaten-track destinations in Bayankhongor and elsewhere. Contact Javyn Galbaatar.
  Web site: www.mol.mn/guchidhan

Juulchin (☎ 328 428, fax 320 246, e jlncorp@magicnet.mn) This former government tourist agency, now privatised, offers a wide range of tours around the country, including rafting, birdwatching, fishing, skiing, trekking and jeep trips around the Gobi. Its office is at the back of the Bayangol Hotel.
  Web site: www.mol.mn/juulchin

Karakorum Expeditions (☎/fax 315 655, mobile 9911 6729, e info@gomongolia.com) PO Box 542. Leaders in mountain bike trips and mountain treks in western Mongolia, concentrating on less-travelled areas. It also combines trips to Mongolia with hiking trips along the Great Wall in Beijing. The company has a good philosophy: a big plus is that they run snow leopard research trips and wildlife tours of eastern Mongolia. Contact Graham Taylor, 2nd floor, Jiguur Grand hotel.
  Web site: www.gomongolia.com

Mongolia Outback (☎ 311 924, fax 324 727, [e] mongoliaoutback@magicnet.mn) PO Box 695. Specialises in helifishing trips.
Web site: www.mol.mn/mongoliaoutback

Nature Tours (☎ 312 392, 311 801, fax 311 979, [e] nattour@magicnet.mn) A reliable outfit, it runs the usual range of tours around the country. It also runs ger camps in Terelj and Khogno Khan. The office is in Room 212 of the Mongolian Youth Federation Building, north-east of the UB Hotel.
Web site: www.naturetours.com

Nomadic Expeditions (☎ 313 396, 325 786, fax 320 311, [e] nomadicexp@magicnet.mn) This is the Mongolian office of the US-based travel company (see the Organised Tours section in the Getting There & Away chapter).

Nomadic Journeys (☎ 328 737, fax 321 489, [e] mongolia@nomadicjourneys.com, PO Box 479) A Mongolian-Swedish joint venture concentrating on low-impact tourism. Its trip in Terelj is unique – you ride yaks (and horses) and carry your own portable ger by yak cart. It can also arrange rafting trips on the Tuul Gol. It also runs fixed-departure yak, camel and horse treks. Contact Jan Wigsten or R Enkhtaivan.
Web site: www.nomadicjourneys.com

Nomads (☎/fax 328 146, [e] nomads@magicnet.mn) PO Box 1008. An impressive outfit run by knowledgeable German and Mongolian staff. It has a wide range of fixed departure tours, including popular horse treks in Khentii and through Terelj, visiting Gunjiin Süm. It also offers fabulous jeep trips to more remote areas in the far west and camel treks in the Gobi. Its office is in Room 21, 3rd floor, Peace & Friendship Bldg.
Web site: www.nomads.mn

Samar Magic Tours (☎ 311 051, 9611 2309, fax 327 503, [e] samartours@magicnet.mn) PO Box 329. Specialises in fishing and wildlife tours and eco-volunteer programs. The office is in the back of the El Latino Restaurant. Contact Spanish and English-speaking Christo Camilo Gavilla Gomez.
Web site: www.mol.mn/samarmagictours/.

Terelj Juulchin (☎ 324 978, fax 322 754, [e] terelj-juulchin@magicnet.mn) It runs a series of general tours but specialises in the Terelj region (central Mongolia), where it runs treks in the Khentii mountains and has a ger camp.
Web site: www.mol.mn/terelj

White Horse Travel (☎ 312 528, fax 310 729, [e] jargal@magicnet.mn) A reliable IATA-accredited agent, it can book international air tickets, including those originating out of Beijing. Its office is in Room 18 of the Peace and Friendship Bldg.

Budget Travel Agencies Most of the backpacker guesthouses offer tours to the countryside around Ulaan Baatar and further afield. Tour arrangements can be a bit ad hoc and standards vary wildly. Try to meet the driver and guide before the trip and ensure that everyone knows the itinerary and exactly what is included.

For information on arranging a trip, see the entry Hiring a Jeep/Minivan and Driver under Jeep in the Getting Around chapter. For ways to limit the impact of these tours, see the boxed text 'Responsible Tourism' in the Facts for the Visitor chapter.

Nassan's guesthouse, near Sükhbaatar Square, runs long-distance tours and local trips to Manzshir Khiid, Terelj and Gachuurt for about US$25 to US$30 per person per day, inclusive of food, transport and ger accommodation. Nassan's brother comes recommended as a driver by several travellers.

Gana's Guest House, near Gandantegchinlen Khiid, offers jeeps or minivans for US$80 per day, including a driver and petrol, plus US$10 to US$20 for a guide. A six-day inclusive tour of the Gobi costs US$300 per person in a group of three. Also on offer are day trips to Terelj, Manzshir Khiid or Moltsog Els. Check out its Web site at www.mol.mn/sanddune.

A private guide and travel fixer called Bolod wanders around Ulaan Baatar looking for clients. His folder of photos shows some fine off-beat places and activities, such as a shaman gathering in Dornod and obscure Chinggis Khaan sites in Khentii. Trips run to around US$100 per day for a jeep, driver, interpreter, tents and stove. Bolod sometimes has an apartment to rent near the Chinggis Khaan Hotel. Contact Bolod at ☎ 9919 2407 or [e] u_borchy@hotmail.com.

Bookshops

Unless you understand Mongolian or Russian you will be disappointed with the bookshops in Ulaan Baatar. However, Scrolls bookshop on Khudaldaany Gudamj has a wide range of novels in English, French and German. The ground floor of the State

Department Store has some tourist guides and other books on Mongolia. A separate stand in the building sells current-affairs magazines like *Time* and *Newsweek*.

The business centre on the 4th floor of the Ulaan Baatar Hotel sells second-hand novels in English, Japanese and German, as well as a few local guidebooks and English-language magazines.

For pricey souvenirs or art books try the souvenir shops at the Bayangol Hotel, the Monastery-Museum of Choijin Lama, the Museum of Fine Arts and the Winter Palace.

You can buy Lonely Planet's *Mongolia* guide or *Mongolian phrasebook* at Scrolls book shop or Millie's (see the Places to Eat section later).

Film & Photography

Several places along Peace Ave and the lanes around Sükhbaatar Square develop film – look for the obvious signs advertising major brands. Costs are fairly standard but the quality of developing varies from one place to another. If you have slide film, or simply care about your film, develop it elsewhere.

You can usually buy print, slide and even Polaroid film at the expensive hotels, souvenir shops around the Square, and at the major tourist attractions. Costs vary, so shop around.

See the Photography & Video section in the Facts for the Visitor chapter for information on photography restrictions and photographing people.

Be careful when taking shots of something that may be considered politically sensitive such as Parliament House.

Laundry

Almost all of the hotels in Ulaan Baatar offer a laundry service for between T500 and T1500 per kg, but they may not advertise it – so just ask. If you can be bothered, it's not difficult to do some laundry yourself – the markets and shops sell small packets of detergent and bleach.

Medical Services

If you need medical attention your embassy should have a list of reputable hospitals and doctors. There's normally at least on expat doctor in residence in the city.

The South Korean-built Yonsei Friendship Hospital (☎ 310 945), a few hundred metres east of the Square on Peace Ave, is still the best place to go. However, standards and facilities have recently dropped dramatically, and you cannot always assume that someone there will speak adequate English. The consulting rooms are open from 9 am to 12.30 pm and 1.30 to 5.30 pm on Monday, Tuesday and Wednesday, and from 9 am to 12.30 pm on Thursday, Friday and Saturday.

The only other place worth considering is Russian Hospital No 2 (☎ 458 250), just before the UK embassy, on Peace Ave.

For emergency dental treatment, try the Evada Dental Clinic (☎ 342 609), about 200m east of the Square on Peace Ave; the Arono Dental Clinic (☎ 342 609), about 100m north of the Winter Palace; or the Yonsei Hospital.

Pharmacies are poorly stocked, and you should always check the expiry dates of goods. The hospitals mentioned in this entry will stock some supplies and there are a couple of pharmacies around the markets and the mall on Khudaldaany Gudamj, but you really should bring whatever you need from home.

Dangers & Annoyances

Ulaan Baatar is a reasonably carefree and easygoing city, but treat it as you would any other mid-sized European town, and be similarly conscious of the potential risks. Be particularly careful around the railway station and Central (Black) Market. See also Dangers & Annoyances in the Facts for the Visitor chapter.

MUSEUMS
Museum of Natural History
Байгалын Түүхийн Музей
Sometimes called the State Central Museum, the Museum of Natural History (☎ 318 179) is worth a quick visit. It has exhibits featuring Mongolia's geography, flora and fauna, including the requisite section with stuffed and embalmed animals,

birds and even fish. Geologists will like the geology section (especially the awesome **meteorites**). Likewise, the birders will want to check off what they've seen at the **Ornithological Gallery**, stuffed (literally) with over 200 species.

More impressive are the two complete **dinosaur skeletons**, which were found in the Gobi – the giant flesh-eating *Tarbosaurus*, 15m tall and four to five tons in weight, and the little duck-billed plant-eating *Saurolophus* at 'only' 8m. You can see them from above on the 3rd floor, or enter room 22 on the 2nd floor (ask for it to be opened if it's locked).

The gallery next door is full of interesting knick-knacks like petrified wood, dinosaur eggs and huge leg bones, which look like something out of the Flintstones. There is also a **camel museum** on the second floor. For more on Mongolia's remarkable dinosaurs see the boxed text 'Dinosaurs' in The Gobi chapter.

The museum is old and rambling, with doors and corridors going all over the place, so trace your route using the map given out free with your ticket. The museum is on the corner of Khuvsgalchdyn Örgön Chölöö and Sükhbaataryn Gudamj, one block north-west of the Square. It's open daily in summer from 10 am to 4.30 pm (closed Monday and Tuesday in winter). The entrance fee is T3000. Photography costs T2000 *per shot*, except in the dinosaur hall which charges US$5 a pop!

The museum shop sells a pricey English guidebook to the museum (T4500).

Zanabazar Museum of Fine Arts

Занабазарын Уран Зэргийн Музей

The Zanabazar Museum of Fine Arts (☎ 326 060) has an excellent collection of paintings, carvings and sculptures, including many by the revered sculptor and artist Zanabazar. It also contains other rare – and sometimes old – religious exhibits such as scroll paintings *(thangka)* and Buddhist statues, representing the best display of its kind in Mongolia. A bonus is that most of the exhibit captions in the museum are in English.

At the top of the stairs is a glass folder with a detailed explanation of Zanabazar and his work. There are some fine examples of the sculptor's work including five Dhyani, or Contemplation, Buddhas (cast in 1683) and Tara in her 21 manifestations.

Also worth checking out are the wonderful *tsam* masks (worn by monks during religious ceremonies) and the intricate paintings, *One Day in Mongolia* and *The Airag Feast*, by renowned artist B Sharav. These depict almost every aspect of nomadic life. The ground floor has some copies of portraits of the great *khaans* (kings) and some 7th century Turkic stone carvings.

The museum, facing the taxi stand on Khudaldaany Gudamj, is open from 9 am to 6 pm. Entry is T5000. The shops inside have a good (but expensive) selection of leather goods, souvenirs and paintings. A handy little guidebook (T2750) to the museum in English and French is for sale inside, though you do get a free brochure with your ticket. English-speaking guides are also available.

National Museum of Mongolian History

Монголын Түүхийн Үндэсний Музей

Still sometimes referred to by its previous name, the Revolutionary Museum, the National Museum of Mongolian History (☎ 325 656) was renovated in 1998 and is well worth a visit.

The 1st floor has some interesting exhibits on petroglyphs, deer stones (stone sculptures of reindeer and other animals) and burial sites from the Hun and Uyghur eras. The 2nd floor houses an outstanding collection of costumes, hats and jewellery, representing most of Mongolia's ethnic groups.

The 3rd floor is a must-see for fans of the Mongol horde. The collection includes real examples of 12th century **Mongol armour**, and correspondence between Pope Innocent IV and Güyük Khaan. Written in Latin and Persian and dated November 13, 1246, it bears the khaan's seal. There is also a display of traditional Mongolian culture with, among other things, a furnished ger, traditional farming and domestic implements, saddles and musical instruments.

Also on display are Buddhist items, including the controversial **Ganlin Horn,** made from human thigh bones, and used by head monks to call and exorcise evil spirits. All the exhibits have good English captions, except for the dull gallery of Soviet-era history.

The museum is on the corner of Khudaldaany Gudamj and Sükhbaataryn Gudamj. Itís open daily from 10 am to 6 pm. Entry is T2000 and there is a US$10 photography charge.

The Victims of Political Persecution Memorial Museum

This new museum consists of a series of haunting displays chronicling the bloody communist purges of the 1930s – an aggressive campaign to eliminate ëcounter-revolutionariesí. During the campaign, intellectuals were arrested and put on trial, sent to Siberian labour camps or shot. Mongolia lost top writers, scientists and thinkers.

The museum was inspired by the former prime minister P Genden, who was executed in Moscow by the KGB in 1937 for refusing Stalinís orders to carry out the purge. The museum is now run by his daughter. The walls of the ground floor carry the names of 20,000 souls. A yellow dot by the name signifies that the deceased was a monk; red means a communist; and blue means a civilian. Unfortunately there are no English captions which makes a visit to the museum a sobering but ultimately confusing experience.

The museum (☎ 320 592) is south-west of the Ministry of External Relations. It is open from 10 am to 4.30 pm weekdays and 10 am to 2.30 pm Saturday; admission is T1000.

The large, white square building just south-west of the museum, is known as the **Wedding Palace** (Khurimyn Ordon). Built in 1976 by the Russians, it has since been used for over 150,000 weddings, including the marital vows of a few foreigners.

Zorig – The Father of Mongolian Democracy

On October 2, 1998, 36-year-old Sanjaasurengiin Zorig, a leader revered as the father of Mongolian democracy, was stabbed 18 times by masked assailants in his apartment. Zorig was a well-liked government minister and top candidate for the vacant position of prime minister. In 1990 he had taken a leading role in the pro-democracy demonstrations.

The killers have never been brought to justice, though his death is linked to a corrupt casino deal, which he helped to block. Everyone is under suspicion, from his fellow democrats to as far afield as the Macau mafia.

Zorig's murder came as a great shock to the Mongolian people, who lined the streets in their tens of thousands for the burial procession. A statue of Zorig was unveiled on April 20 1999 opposite the Central Post Office, honouring the mild-mannered, bespectacled man who helped bring democracy to Mongolia.

BRADLEY MAYHEW

Other Museums

The **Natsagdorj Museum** celebrates Mongolia's most famous poet and playwright, Dashdojiin Natsagdorj, who was an ardent nationalist. The museum is said to be built on the exact site where Natsagdorj lived. It's between the Monastery-Museum of Choijin Lama and the northern entrance of Nairamdal Park, but was closed at the time of research for remodelling.

The **Ulaan Baatar City Museum** is the green Russian-style building next to the Wrestling Palace. It has a few interesting black-and-white photos of early Ulaan Baatar and an old map of the original ger settlement, though not much else. It's open from 9 am to 5 pm daily; entry is T400.

If killing innocent animals is your thing, visit the **Hunting Museum**, on the street leading to Gandan Khiid. The **Railway Museum**, near the International Railway Ticketing Office, may satisfy train buffs. Other train-spotting options include the old engines parked in front of the Jiguur Grand hotel.

The **Mongolian Military Museum** is at the eastern end of Peace Ave – you'll need to take a taxi to find it.

The **Theatre Museum** (☎ 326 820) is worthwhile if you're interested in the dramatic arts – the collection of puppets is wonderful. The museum is on the 3rd floor of the Palace of Culture (its entrance is on the northern side of building); open daily except Monday and Tuesday.

The **Intellectual Museum**, also known as the Mongolian Toy Museum, on the 3rd floor, 44A Baga Toiruu, has a collection of puzzles and games made by local artists. Entry is T1000.

MONASTERIES

Around the start of the 19th century, over 100 temples *(süm)* and monasteries *(khiid)* served a population of only about 50,000 in Ulaan Baatar. Religious historians estimate that maybe over 50% of the population at the time were monks or nuns. During the Stalinist purges of the late 1930s, most of the city's temples and monasteries were destroyed. Several thou-

A traditional prayer wheel, circa 19th century

sand monks and nuns were murdered, while many more fled or abandoned their Buddhist life. Only since the early 1990s have the people of Mongolia started to openly practice Buddhism again.

Winter Palace of Bogd Khaan

Богд Хааны Өвлийн Ордон

Built between 1893 and 1903, the Winter Palace of Bogd Khaan is where Mongolia's eighth Living Buddha, and last king, Jebtzun Damba Hutagt VIII, lived for 20 years. For reasons that are unclear, the palace was spared destruction by the Russians and turned into a museum. The summer palace, on the banks of the Tuul Gol, was completely destroyed.

There are six temples in the grounds. The white building to the right as you enter is the Winter Palace itself. It contains a collection of gifts received from foreign dignitaries, such as a pair of golden boots from a Russian tsar, a robe made from 80 unfortunate foxes and a ger lined with the skins of 150 snow leopards (ask the curator to open the ger for you).

The Bogd Khaan's penchant for unusual live animals explains the extraordinary array of stuffed animals in the Palace – including an elephant that had to walk for

The Bogd Khaan (1869–1924)

The eighth Jebtzun Damba (Lord of Refuge) is most commonly referred to as the Bogd Khaan (partly because his real name is over 14 syllables long). He was a colourful and controversial character. One famous story tells how he hooked up a car battery to a long metal cord, hung it over the Winter Palace walls and then waited for believers to grab hold of the rope and attribute the shock to the living Buddha's great powers. His love of exotic animals (he owned a giraffe and an elephant) was matched only by his weakness for alcohol (he was sometimes drunk for days at a time).

Depending on which version of history you read, the Bogd Khaan was either a great visionary and nationalist, or a promiscuous bisexual cross-dresser who was eventually blinded by syphilis. One of his wives was the former wife of a wrestler and was well known for her sexual exploits with her hairdresser.

three months from the Russian border to Ulaan Baatar!

The entrance fee is T2000, but you'll need a permit to take photos (T5000) or to use a video camera (T10,000). The interior of the temples are often dark and the exhibits are always behind glass, so you are unlikely to get any great photos in any case. A torch is a definite advantage here. (Maybe have a look around first, then if you want to take some photos or videos pay for your permit later.)

The well-lit exceptions are the excellent scroll paintings, costumes and other items, which are upstairs in the Winter Palace and under good lighting.

Two shops sell clothes, tapes, books, paintings, leather and cashmere products, and other souvenirs – it is one of the best places to pick up a memento. The selection is excellent, but prices are somewhat high.

The Winter Palace (☎ 342 195), a few kilometres south of the Square on Chingisiin Örgön Chölöö, is open daily in summer from 10 am to 5 pm. In winter it is closed Wednesday and Thursday. It is a bit too far to walk, so take a taxi or catch bus No 7 or 19. A little pamphlet (T200), available at the entrance, gives a very brief explanation of the temples in English, and includes a handy map showing the temple locations.

Gandantegchinlen Khiid

Гандантэгчинлэн Хийд

Roughly meaning 'the great place of complete joy', Gandantegchinlen Khiid is commonly referred to as Gandan Khiid. Still the largest and most important monastery in Mongolia, this is one of Ulaan Baatar's most impressive sights.

Building was started in 1838 by the fourth Bogd Gegen, but was not finished until after his death by the fifth Bogd Gegen, Chultem Jigmid Dambijantsan. Like most monasteries in Mongolia, the purges of 1937 fell heavily on Gandan. Luckily it survived – the communists decided to keep it as a showcase to impress foreigners. Today there are over 150 monks in residence.

As you enter the main entrance from the south, a path leads towards the right to a courtyard containing two temples. On the left is the **Ochirdary Süm** and to the right is the smaller **Golden Dedenpovaran Süm**.

At the end of the main path as you enter is the magnificent white **Migjid Janraisig Süm**, the monastery's main attraction.

Migjid Janraisig Süm at Gandan Khiid

Migjid Janraisig Statue

A 20m gold and bronze statue of Avalokites-vara (Janraisig), built by the Bogd Khaan in 1911, once stood in the main temple at Gandan Khiid. The magnificent statue was destroyed by the communists in 1937, and the metal taken to Leningrad (St Petersburg) and melted down to make bullets.

In October 1996, after nearly five years of work, a new statue called Migjid Janraisig (which means 'The Lord Who Looks in Every Direction') was finally consecrated by the Dalai Lama. The 25m high, 20-ton statue is made from copper, gilded with gold donated from Nepal and Japan and covered in gold brocade and over 500m of silk. The statue contains precious stones, 27 tonnes of medicinal herbs, 334 sutras, two million bundles of mantras and, in the base, an entire ger, plus furniture!

Lining the walls of the temple are hundreds of images of Ayush, the Buddha of longevity. There is a voluntary US$1 entry charge to the temple. To the east of the temple is a small temple dedicated to Kalachakra, a wrathful Buddhist deity.

To the west of the temple is the Öndör Geegen Zanabazar Buddhist Monastery (☎ 363 831), established in 1970. If you have a genuine interest in Buddhism, you can visit the university and its library.

The souvenir shop, to the left as you enter the main southern gate of the monastery, sells non-touristy religious artefacts, including miniature copper bowls, incense and scroll paintings, as well as items like Mongolian felt hats.

You can take photographs around the monastery, but not inside the temples. The monastery (☎ 342 195), at the end of Öndör Geegen Zanabazaryn Gudamj, is open from about 9 am to 9 pm daily, and there is no entrance fee. Try to be there for the captivating ceremonies – they usually start at around 10 am, though you may be lucky and see one at another time. Most chapels are closed in the afternoon.

Pickpockets sometimes target the monastery, so take care, especially amongst crowds.

Monastery-Museum of Choijin Lama

Чойжин Ламын Хийд-Музей

This monastery is also known as the Museum of Religion. It was the home of Luvsan Haidav Choijin Lama ('Choijin' is an honorary title given to some monks), the state oracle and brother of the Bogd Khaan. The construction of the monastery commenced in 1904 and was completed four years later. It was closed in 1938 and probably would have been demolished but it was saved as a museum in 1942 to demonstrate the 'feudal' ways of the past. Although religious freedom in Mongolia recommenced in 1990, this monastery is no longer an active place of worship and will probably remain a museum.

There are five temples within the grounds. As you enter, the first temple you see is the **Maharaja Süm**. The **main temple** features statues of Sakyamuni (the historical Buddha), Choijin Lama and Baltung Choimba (the teacher of the Bogd Khaan), whose mummified remains are inside the statue. There are also some fine scroll paintings and some of the best tsam masks in the country. The *gongkhang* (protector chapel) behind the main hall contains the oracle's throne and a magnificent statue of *yab-yum* (mystic sexual union).

The other temples are: **Zuu Süm**, dedicated to Sakyamuni; **Yadam Süm**, which contains wooden and bronze statues of various gods, some created by the famous Mongolian sculptor Zanabazar; and **Amgalan Süm**, containing a self-portrait of the great Zanabazar himself and a small stupa apparently brought to Ulaan Baatar by Zanabazar from Tibet.

The museum (☎ 324 788) is only one block south of the Square. You pay T2000 at the southern gate (there is also an extra US$5 photography and US$10 video camera charge). Although not as good as the Winter Palace, there is still plenty to snap. A useful English-language booklet (T500) is available at the monastery entrance. A concrete ger inside the grounds has a good selection of reasonably priced souvenirs, and probably the best range of books about Buddhism and Mongolia in Ulaan Baatar.

Other Monasteries & Temples

Part of Gandan Khiid, **Gesar Süm**, at the junction of Khuvisgalyn Örgön Chölöö and the western part of Ikh Toiruu, is named after the mythical Tibetan king. The lovely temple is a fine example of Chinese-influenced architecture. It is a popular place for locals to request, and pay for, *puja* (a blessing ceremony).

Tasgany Ovoo, about 300m behind Gesar Süm, is worth a look if you haven't yet seen an *ovoo*, a sacred pyramid-shaped collection of stones. A 12m-high Buddhist monument is planned for the top of the hill, which is also known as Zaany Tolgoi, or Elephant's Head.

Ninth Jebtzun Damba

When the eighth Jebtzun Damba, Bogd Khaan, died in 1924 the communist government refused to allow any future 'reincarnations', ensuring their control over Mongolian Buddhism. After restrictions against religion were lifted in Mongolia, the Dalai Lama proclaimed a ninth Jebtzun Damba as the new spiritual leader of Mongolian Buddhism.

The ninth Jebtzun Damba was born in Tibet in 1932, and was accepted as the ninth reincarnation at the age of four, but his identity was kept a secret from Stalin's thugs. He fled Tibet in 1960 and, in the early 1990s, he moved to Dharamsala, in north-west India, where he is close to the current Dalai Lama.

In 1999 the 67-year-old lama surprised everyone by turning up in Ulaan Baatar after casually applying for a tourist visa in Moscow ('Occupation: Reincarnation of Tibetan deity Vajrapani'!). Mobbed by adoring crowds everywhere he went (it was his first ever visit to Mongolia), he was pressured to leave after he overstayed his visa and he finally returned to Dharamsala.

On the way to Gandan Khiid, the new **Lamrim Süm** (Stages of the Path Temple) has a small temple with statues of Tsong-khapa, the Tibetan Buddhist reformer, and Sakyamuni, the historical Buddha.

The **Pethub Stangey Choskhor Ling Monastery** also known as the **Bakula Rinpoche Temple** was founded in 1999 by the then Indian ambassador, himself a reincarnate lama from Ladakh. The monastery is used mainly as a centre for Buddhist teaching.

Dashchoilon Khiid was originally built at another location in 1890, but was destroyed in the late 1930s. The monastery was recently moved into three huge concrete gers that once formed part of the State Circus. The monastery is now used by over 100 monks. You can get to the lane running past the monastery from Baga Toiruu – look out for the orange and brown roof.

Otochmaaramba Khiid can be easily seen from the north-eastern bend of Ikh Toiruu. Although not as interesting as the others, it's still worth a visit. The monastery is the location of the **Manba Datsan** traditional medical clinic and training centre, which re-opened ten years ago.

In the north-eastern suburbs of Ulaan Baatar, **Dambadarjaa Khiid**, built in 1765, was once home to 1200 monks. Only the ruins of a few of the 30 small temples have been restored, but it is worth a look. The only way to get there is by taxi.

ART GALLERIES

As well as music, Mongolians love visual arts, and there are a few galleries worth visiting.

Mongolian National Modern Art Gallery

Монголын Уран Зургийн Үзэсгэлэн

This gallery, sometimes also called the Fine Art Gallery, contains a large and impressive display of modern and uniquely Mongolian paintings and sculptures. It has a mixture of nomadic life, landscapes and people, ranging from impressionistic to nationalistic. The artworks are always interesting, and are titled in English. The Soviet romantic paintings depicted in scroll painting style are especially interesting.

The gallery (☎ 327 177) is badly lit and poorly maintained (several birds nest in the main hall!) but it's still well worth a visit. The entrance is in the courtyard of the Palace of Culture, and the gallery is open daily from 10 am to 6 pm (T1500). The main gallery is on the 3rd floor, there are temporary exhibits on the 2nd floor and a shop on the first floor.

Mongolian Artists' Exhibition Hall

Монголын Зурадудын Үзэсгэлэн Танхим

If you want to see more Mongolian art, and maybe buy some, head into the exhibition hall immediately south of the Square and opposite the National Academic Drama Theatre. This is a private collection of modern, and often dramatic paintings, carvings, tapestries and sculptures. The displays often change and there's a good souvenir shop. The gallery (☎ 327 474) is open from about 9 am to 5 pm daily except Sunday.

SÜKHBAATAR SQUARE
СУХБААТАРЫН ТАЛХАЙ

In July 1921 in the centre of Ulaan Baatar, the 'hero of the revolution', Damdiny Sükhbaatar, declared Mongolia's final independence from the Chinese. The Square now bears his name and features a statue of him astride his horse. The words he apparently proclaimed at the time are engraved on the bottom of the statue: 'If we, the whole people, unite in our common effort and common will, there will be nothing in the world that we cannot achieve, that we will not have learnt or failed to do.'

Sükhbaatar would have been very disappointed to learn that the Square was also where the first protests were held in 1989, which eventually led to the fall of communism. Today, the Square is occasionally used for rallies, ceremonies and even rock concerts, but is generally a serene place where only the photographers – standing in a straight line selling their services – are doing anything.

As you face north from the statue, the large grey building is **State Parliament House**, commonly known as Government House – which, like every ger, was built to face south. Directly in front of it is a **mausoleum**, built in 1921, which contains the remains of Sükhbaatar, and possibly Choibalsan.

To the north-east is the tall, modern **Palace of Culture**, a useful landmark containing the Mongolian National Modern Art Gallery and several other cultural institutions. At the south-east corner of the Square, the salmon-pinkish building is the **State Opera & Ballet Theatre**.

On the north-western corner of the Square, the bright yellow building houses the Golomt Bank, with the grey **National Museum of Mongolian History** behind it. South of the Golomt Bank, the clay-red building (now with bright blue patches around the windows) is the **Mongolian Stock Exchange**, which was opened in February 1992 in the former Children's Cinema.

For a blast from the past, walk east from the south-east corner of the Square, to the **Lenin statue**. (For an even more dramatic bust of Lenin walk into the former **Lenin Museum**, on the north side of Liberty Square.)

NAIRAMDAL PARK
НАЙРАМДАЛ ПАРК

Also called the National Recreational Park, Nairamdal Park (Friendship Park) is looking a bit sad and neglected these days, but it is a nice enough place to walk around. It is quite photogenic on Sundays when hundreds of children descend upon it.

There are the usual children's rides, including a Ferris wheel (agonisingly slow, but with great views from the top) and, our favourite, the 'aerobicycle', a sort of tandem bike on a monorail track 3m high. A dirty lake in the south of the park offers boat rides in summer and ice-skating in winter.

You can enter the park from behind the Monastery-Museum of Choijin Lama, or opposite the Bayangol Hotel.

ZAISAN MEMORIAL
ЗАЙСАН ТОЛТОЙ

The tall, thin landmark on top of the hill south of the city is the Zaisan Memorial. Built by the Russians to commemorate 'unknown soldiers and heroes' from various wars, it offers the best views of Ulaan Baatar and the surrounding hills. The views are better at night, however, when you can't see the ugly power stations and the layers of dust and pollution, but there's no public transport there after 10 pm (when the sun sets in summer).

To get there, catch bus No 7, which goes past the Winter Palace. Get off at the Agricultural University, walk across the fields, up a goat trail to the car park and then up the steps to the top. A taxi would save some of the walk.

ACTIVITIES

For a swim, try the heated pool at the Zaluus Youth & Cultural Centre, on Zaluuchuudyn Örgön Chölöö. You may have to mess around with a medical check in order to use it. There's also a private gym in the building that you can use for T3000 an hour. Work has stopped on a Japanese-funded golf course near the Zaisan Memorial, so most expats swing their clubs at Gachuurt, about 20km from Ulaan Baatar.

There's a Korean bowling alley next to the Chinggis Restaurant on Baga Toiruu, near Sükhbaataar Gudamj. If you feel like a game of pool, there are dozens of billiards and pool halls around town.

Hash House Harriers, the internationally known running group, has even made it to Mongolia. Check the *Mongol Messenger* for times and location of the weekly meeting (and cleansing ales afterwards).

ORGANISED TOURS

It is not particularly easy to join an organised tour of Ulaan Baatar if you have arrived as an independent traveller. You can try to contact one of the travel agencies listed earlier in this chapter and see what they have available. However, seeing the sights of the capital can be easily done without joining an organised tour, especially if you hire a taxi for the day. Although not really necessary, a guide-cum-interpreter, especially one who speaks your language if you're not confident in English, could be handy.

SPECIAL EVENTS

The biggest event in Ulaan Baatar is undoubtedly the Naadam Festival, held from 11 to 13 July. It's a time when the city almost seems to wake up, before nodding off again when it's all over. Some visitors may not find the festival itself terribly exciting, but the associated activities during the Naadam week and the general festive mood make it a great time to visit. For more information, see the Naadam Festival special section.

Around Naadam and other public holidays, special cultural events and shows are organised. They are for the benefit of locals so any promotion (often there isn't any) will be in Mongolian. It's worth reading the local English-language newspapers and asking a Mongolian friend, guide or hotel staff member to find out what may be on.

PLACES TO STAY

There is a fairly good range of places to stay in the capital city, but rarely is there anywhere that could be regarded as good value. Accommodation may be in short supply, and prices are often higher during the week surrounding the Naadam Festival.

Places to Stay – Budget

Camping There are no official camping grounds in Ulaan Baatar, but given that nobody owns any land in Mongolia, you can technically camp anywhere.

If you wish to camp and visit Ulaan Baatar every day, catch a regular bus along the road to the airport and discreetly find a patch of ground away from the main road around Yarmag. During Naadam, Yarmag is where the horse racing takes place, and you can easily pitch your tent in the fascinating, but very noisy, temporary 'tent city' there. Be careful of thieves and drunks during this festive period and don't expect a minute of peace. The main problem, of course, is what to do with all your stuff during the day.

Guesthouses The city's private guesthouses are much like sharing an apartment. Most offer a hot shower and a kitchen. Almost all offer trips to nearby attractions, as well as visa extension and registration, laundry and the booking of train tickets. They are firmly aimed at backpackers and can be crowded and lacking in privacy over Naadam.

Nassan's (☎ 321 078, e nassan2037@ yahoo.com), near Sükhbaatar Square, has the best location of all the guesthouses. It has a choice of clean apartments (Nassan's is slowly taking over the entire apartment block), which cost between US$3 and US$5 per person. The guesthouse offers a laundry service, Internet access and local tours.

The other main budget hang-out is *Gana's Guest House (☎/fax 367 343, e ganasger@magicnet.mn)* in the ger suburb near Gandan Khiid (house number 22). Beds in a six-bed ger cost US$5, or US$3 in a large dormitory. It's more ad hoc than at Nassan's and the ramshackle showers and toilets are a little basic, especially when things get busy around Naadam. However, it's a great place to meet other travellers with a view to assembling a jeep-load of people. Breakfast and dinner are good value at T500 and T800 respectively and it has Internet access.

Bold's Guesthouse (☎ 320 455, 9919 6232, e bold777@hotmail.com) offers beds in an apartment for US$4, with a shared bathroom and kitchen. The place can get a bit cramped, especially during the Naadam Festival. The main apartment is hard to find, behind the State Department Store at Building 1, entrance 1, 2nd floor, door 8. There is a second apartment near the State Circus at Building 14A, entrance 1, block 1, apartment 1. The guesthouse will extend your visa for US$10 and buy train tickets for no commission.

UB Guesthouse (☎ 311 937, 9119 9859, e ubguest@hotmail.com) is well-run by a Korean guy and has dormitory-style bunk bed accommodation for US$4, including breakfast and free tea. The guesthouse has recently moved so is no longer correct on our map key. You will find it next to the Icafe on Baga Toiruu (opposite the MIAT office). It has a shower and laundry service, and staff can help with visa extensions. It also hires out a jeep for US$40 per day, not including petrol, and will throw in tents and a stove. Check its Web site at www.ubguest.com.

Idre's Guest House (☎ 316 749, 9916 6049, e idre9@hotmail.com) is in an apartment block just south-east of the bus station. A mattress on the floor costs US$3.50. There's a hot shower, kitchen and washing machine (T500 per load). Look for the nine-story apartment block and head for building 23, entrance 2, door 44, on the 3rd floor. Idre also has a ger at Zuunmod and can arrange horse riding trips to the area.

Khongor Guest House (☎ 329 331) is an apartment split into dorms. Beds cost from US$4.50 to US$5.50. There's a shower, kitchen and Internet access. The place is well-hidden on the second floor, apartment No 6, accessed from the north side. You are better off ringing first as the guesthouse is often only open in the high season from July to September.

A sister guesthouse, the *Azusaya,* is aimed specifically at Japanese travellers. It's at the middle entrance (No 2) of the back side of block 15, on Peace Ave and is at room No 1.

Serge's Guest House (☎ 320 267, 9919 8204, 30 Peace Ave, e asiantravel37@ hotmail.com) has a couple of dormitory rooms behind their travel agency, Asia Travel, but it only seems to get going around Naadam. Beds cost US$4.

Apartments If you are planning to stay in Ulaan Baatar for a while, have a lot of gear or you are travelling in a small group, it's worth looking around for an apartment to rent. Most owners or landlords obviously prefer long-term rentals, particularly to resident expats, but if business is slow, such as during winter, you may be able to arrange something with a short-term lease. A reasonable, furnished, two-bedroom apartment with a kitchen costs from US$200 to US$300 per month.

Like most things in Ulaan Baatar, finding an apartment is usually a matter of asking around. *UB Tour* (☎ 324 730) on the 4th floor of the Ulaan Baatar Hotel can arrange an apartment for around US$20 per day. Many of the guesthouses listed can arrange short-stay apartment rental for around US$10 a day.

Hotels Ulaan Baatar's cheap hotels are not half as good value as its guesthouses. Most are Soviet leftovers and are dark, deserted or noisy, with barely functioning facilities.

Going Underground

One result of Mongolia's recent social upheaval and rising poverty has been the appearance of street children in Ulaan Baatar. It is estimated that between 3000 and 6000 homeless children live in the city's underground sewers and heating pipes – the only places where the kids can survive in winter temperatures of -30° C.

Most of the children were abandoned by parents unable to care for them (unemployment runs to 37% in Ulaan Baatar), were sent from relatives in the countryside, or ran away from alcoholic fathers or parents (80% of street kids come from one-parent families). Many of the kids (especially boys) prefer the freedom of the streets in summer rather than the strict rules and classes of homeless shelters, but winters are brutal. Girls often end up in prostitution. Both sexes suffer from poor health, with high rates of malnutrition, syphilis, scabies and body lice.

Ulaan Baatar has around 20 shelters, many run by foreign non-governmental organisations, with beds for around 500 children. Several aid agencies work with the children, including Save the Children, the National Centre for Children and the Lotus Children's Centre. The Christina Noble Foundation operates a shelter on the edge of town and runs several education and health programs. Donors can sponsor a homeless Mongolian child for US$24 per month. For details, see the Web site at www.cncf.org for a list of offices around the world or email **e** info@cncf.org.

The often-deserted *Narlag Hotel* (☎ 350 213) is a little inconvenient and no-one speaks a word of English but the rooms are large and fairly clean, with an attached bathroom, and cost T9250 per person. Deluxe/half-deluxe rooms cost T22,350/ 12,300. It is about 50m north of the intersection of Ikh Toiruu and the extension of Ikh Surguulin Gudamj, immediately past the kindergarten.

The Soviet-style *Mandukhai Hotel* (☎ 322 204) is looking very run-down these days. Tired looking singles/doubles/quads cost T12,000/23,000/32,000 with a shared (and probably broken) bathroom and shower. It's just west of the State Department Store, hidden in apartment blocks about 100m north of Peace Ave – look for the yellow pagoda-style roof.

In a handy location on Peace Ave is the *Negdelchin Hotel* (☎ 453 230). Small dingy rooms with a shared bathroom cost US$12/18, or US$20/32 for a deluxe room (some rooms have been renovated).

A passable budget option is the huge, grey *Zaluuchuud Hotel* (☎ 324 594, fax 324 231) on Baga Toiruu, about 400m north of the Ulaan Baatar Hotel. Soviet-style rooms with a toilet and sink, but no shower, start at US$11/13.50, with suites rising to US$28. The half-deluxe rooms are a good option at US$18.

If you're waiting for the train or don't mind being woken up several times at night as trains approach along the tracks (sounds appealing, doesn't it?), try the *Railway Hotel* above the train station waiting room. Rooms cost from T3500 to T7000 per person and you can rent rooms by the hour if you are just changing trains and need to rest. Showers cost T500 but weren't working when we last checked.

Places to Stay – Mid-Range

Places in the middle range are not particularly good value, but they normally include breakfast. Ask whether the arbitrary government tax of 13% is included or not.

Center Hotel (☎ 328 731, fax 318 427, **e** centerhotel@mongol.net) has rooms on the 4th and 5th floors for US$40/50 with breakfast, TV and hot shower. Deluxe rooms cost US$60/80.

Deservedly popular because of its great location and cosy B&B feel is the *Hotel Urge* (☎ 313 772, fax 312 712, 4 Khudaldaany Gudamj). Singles/doubles with a private bathroom, fridge and cable TV cost T32,000/35,000. There are also a couple of good value doubles for T20,000, as well as more expensive suites. The hotel is to the immediate west of State Parliament House. The restaurant and bar on the ground floor are quite pleasant. (The hotel is also spelt Örgöö Hotel.)

The *Marco Polo Hotel* (☎ 310 803, fax 311 273) is a friendly, clean place and a good mid-range option. Standard rooms cost US$35/55, inclusive of breakfast and tax and the double rooms have a desk, fridge and TV. There are also deluxe rooms. Credit cards are accepted. The hotel is surrounded by apartment blocks and hard to find; approach it from Erkhuugiin Gudamj to the east.

The *Kharaa Hotel* (☎ 313 733), halfway up Choimbolyn Gudamj just north of Peace Ave, has clean but smallish rooms for US$25, US$35 and US$45 per room.

Genex Hotel (☎ 326 763, fax 323 827, Bldg 10, Choimbolyn Gudamj) is a little further north on the same street. Rooms with toilet but no shower cost US$35/50 for single/double occupancy. The half-deluxe is very comfortable at US$48/80 and the deluxe option has two double beds and a sitting area for US$75/120. Prices include breakfast. Credit cards are accepted.

The *Flower Hotel* (☎ 458 330, fax 455 652, e flower@magicnet.mn) has been nicely refurbished after plenty of Japanese investment. It's in a nice neighbourhood, with plenty of shops nearby, but is inconvenient to the Square. Standard singles/doubles are comfortable but definitely overpriced at US$44/77, when you consider that showers are down the corridor (toilets are in the rooms). Deluxe rooms run to US$71/93 and US$93/132. The Japanese-style bath house, with guaranteed warm water, is popular with Japanese tour groups. The hotel is on Zaluuchuudyn Örgön Chölöö, near Ikh Toiruu.

The *Sarora Hotel* (☎ 327 831) is a similarly Japanese-orientated place south-west of the Merkuri Market. Rooms costs US$30/40 without shower, or US$60/80 and US$70/90 for deluxe rooms.

The *White House Hotel* (☎ 367 872, fax 369 973) is a decent choice, more for the facilities than its location (it's about 20 minutes walk from the Square). The hotel has a classy English bar and French restaurant. Singles/doubles cost US$40/60, or US$65/95 for the spacious deluxe version. It's on Damdinbazaryn Gudamj, which heads west off Amarsanaagiin Gudamj, west of Gandan Khiid.

Another acceptable place in this range – but, like the others, not worth the price – is the slightly chaotic *New Capital Hotel* (☎ 458 235, fax 458 281) at US$20/30 for a small standard single/double, or US$30/50 for the deluxe option. It's near the UK embassy, at the eastern end of Peace Ave.

The *Zuchi Hotel* (☎ 343 565), in the south of town near the Winter Palace of the Bogd Khaan, has tired rooms for US$19/38, or US$38/58 for a deluxe room. The hotel is to be upgraded so expect the prices to rise to around US$50 for a standard double by 2001.

The *Jiguur Grand* (☎ 322 939, fax 322 805) has spacious, well-equipped rooms (albeit lacking in style) for US$45/60.

Undruul Hotel (☎ 455 108, fax 455 016, e undtour@magicnet.mn) has pleasant rooms for US$40 per person but has a slightly inconvenient location at the east end of town.

There are two places in the west of town near the train station. The *Prince Hotel* (☎ 300 149, fax 300 820) has clean rooms with a nice bathroom, TV and fridge for US$35/50. *Batkhan Hotel* (☎ 362 074) has similarly clean and pleasant rooms for US$35.

Places to Stay – Top End

All places in the top end include breakfast, but often they also include service and government charges of between 10 and 20%. Major credit cards are accepted and reservations are advisable in the peak season, especially around the Naadam Festival period. These places should have their own supply of hot water and electricity, which is a real bonus if normal supplies are cut off to the rest of the city.

Probably the most popular and convenient place in this range is the ***Ulaan Baatar Hotel*** (☎ *320 237, fax 324 485,* e *ubhotel@magicnet.mn),* just east of the Square. It's one of the very few hotels that was built and flourished during the former communist days. Rooms have the facilities you would expect at US$68/102 for a standard single/double, US$102/136 for a junior suite or US$136/181 for a deluxe, inclusive of tax and breakfast. The hotel also has a sauna, billiard room and a useful business centre and travel agency. You can make online reservations at www.welcome.to/ubhotel.

Popular with upmarket organised tours is the ***Bayangol Hotel*** (☎ *328 869, fax 326 880,* e *bayangol@magicnet.mn).* Standard single/double rooms start at US$72/94 (plus 13% tax), and deluxe rooms rise to US$144/178 and US$235/280. While the rooms are a little ordinary for the price, the location and hotel facilities are very good. The hotel's twin towers on Chingisiin Örgön Chölöö are very hard to miss.

The bizarre cubist pink and black ***Chinggis Khaan Hotel*** (☎ *313 380, fax 312 788)* has singles starting from US$79 and US$101/113 for a double bed/twin. Suites rise to US$170. Facilities include a gym and a pool, both of which cost extra, though the planned casino has been outlawed. It's located on Khökh Tengerin Gudamj – you cannot possibly miss it.

The cosy ***Tuushin Hotel*** (☎ *323 162, fax 325 903,* e *tuushot@magicnet.mn)* has an excellent location directly north of the Palace of Culture. Spacious, bright singles/doubles cost US$66/88 or US$77/105, depending on how sunny they are; the price is inclusive of tax and breakfast. Economy singles cost US$40, with a share bathroom.

The ***Continental Hotel*** (☎ *323 829,* fax 329 630, e *continental@magicnet.mn)* is a favourite with US business consultants on an expense account. Luxurious rooms cost US$77/105, US$90/135, or US$132/168 for a deluxe suite, including a decent buffet breakfast. Facilities include a gym, sauna and billiards.

Edelweiss Hotel (☎ *312 186, fax 325 252)* has clean rooms – nice but overpriced at US$70/90, or with a 25% discount from November to April. There's a business centre, pub, sauna and billiards.

The nearby ***Mika Hotel*** (☎ *310 566, fax 311 685,* e *xita@magicnet.mn)* is a professionally run place with small singles for US$50 and better twins starting at US$65/85 for single/double occupancy.

PLACES TO EAT

The days of food shortages are long gone, and there is now a reasonable choice of restaurants in the capital. At any place selling only Mongolian food, the menu (if there is one) will be written only in Cyrillic, and staff won't speak anything but Mongolian (and possibly Russian). Places catering mainly to foreigners will have menus in Mongolian and English, but it's likely that only half of the menu will actually be available.

The two best roads for all kinds of restaurants and cafes is the west side of Baga Toiruu or Peace Ave.

Mongolian

For a plate of greasy mutton and noodles (for around T600) or, better, some *buuz* (steamed meat dumplings) or *khuurshuur* (fried mutton pancake) for the standard price of T80 each, look for the ubiquitous sign 'Гуанз' (pronounced *'guanz'),* which means 'canteen'. Slightly more upmarket places will have the restaurant sign 'Рэсторан'. Others will only have a sign showing a steaming cup of something, or a knife and fork.

Be careful because some of the rougher places are not hygienic. (In 1996 the health authorities closed down hundreds of guanz in Ulaan Baatar.)

If you want to try some Mongolian food – but you are fussy about hygienic kitchens and want a menu in English – head for one of the middle or top-end hotel restaurants or a ger restaurant.

Dorvoljin Cafe, on Baga Toiruu, has a pleasant atmosphere and cheap soups, *tsuivan* (fried flat noodles with meat) and set meals. In true Mongolian guanz fashion it is often closed by 7 pm.

Amtat Bulag, on the north side of the Square in front of the Ard Cinema, has good khuurshuur, buuz and soups, as well as Mongolian Korean-influenced meals for around T2500.

Ger Restaurants

Two places cater for visitors on organised tours who want to taste some good – as opposed to truly authentic – Mongolian food, together with a traditional cultural show featuring some excellent music. A visit to a ger restaurant is often included in organised tours. If you are travelling independently and want to come along anyway, give them a ring or visit them to find out when they have a show, and if they have a spare table. The cost for food and the show (without drinks) is about T11,000.

The incongruous *Chin Van Khandorjiin Örgöö (☎ 320 763)* ger restaurant, on Natsagdorj Gudamj, is a mock temple and ger in the middle of suburbia.

Mongolia's biggest ger, near the US embassy, is a ger restaurant called *Abtai Sain Khaani Örgöö (☎ 453 118)*.

Asian

To cater primarily for the increasing number of Korean and Japanese tourists, several good 'Mongrean' and 'Japagolian' restaurants have sprung up. Their all-you-can-stuff-down-your-throat buffets may seem expensive, but after weeks of boiled mutton in the countryside, they are worth every tögrög, especially if you are hankering for some vegetables or salad.

The *Seoul Restaurant (☎ 326 554)*, in a building in the south of the Nairamdal Park, has Korean buffets for T11,200. There's also a barbecue on the balcony and an à la carte Korean restaurant on the ground floor.

The *Chinggis Restaurant (☎ 321 257)* is a similar Korean joint, which comes from the Chinggis Khaan school of interior design. Lunch/dinner buffets cost T7000/8000, which gets you a great salad cart and so-so *teppanyaki* (slices of meat and vegetables grilled on a sizzling hotplate).

For cheaper Korean food, local aid workers recommend the *Korean Restaurant* in the Mongolian Technical University across from the Chinese embassy, with dishes for around T3000.

For authentic Japanese cuisine, *Hanamasa Restaurant (☎ 327 544)* offers huge buffets for around US$9. It's popular with foreigners and faces Gesar Süm in a big shopping complex on the corner of Ikh Toiruu and Khuvsgalchdyn Örgön Chölöö.

The *Fuji Restaurant* in the Flower Hotel also serves pricey but really tasty *sukiyaki* (beef cooked in saki and soy sauce) and other Japanese treats.

For good Turkish food try the *Anatolia Turkish Restaurant*, though don't be fooled by the menu – most of the aubergine dishes are just there to tease you. The delicious Iskender kebab (grilled meat on bread with yoghurt and tomato sauce) is a much better option than the pre-prepared food sitting at the front of the restaurant.

Hazara (☎ 455 071), next to the Negdelchin Hotel on Peace Ave, smells fantastic and is one of the best restaurants in the city. Dishes cost around T6000, with rice an additional T1700. The lunch-time buffet is a good choice at T8000.

Taj Mahal (☎ 311 009) has a range of Tandoori and north Indian dishes such as *murgh makhni* (butter chicken). Most dishes are around T4000, or try the lunchtime *thali* (set menu) for T5900 (vegetarian) or T6500 (non-vegetarian), which gives you three curries, dahl, salad, rice, bread and desert.

For Chinese try *Ding Chen Hot Pot Restaurant* on Baga Toiruu. The only problem is that there's no English menu, so bring Lonely Planet's *China* guide, if you have it. Try the *gongbao jiding* (chicken and peanuts) or *fanqie chaodan* (egg and tomatoes).

The *Overseas Restaurant (☎ 311 219)*, run by a Malaysian woman, serves decent Chinese, Thai and Malay meals for around T3000. It's just to the west of the State Department Store.

Little Hong Kong gets mixed reviews, though it certainly has a wider menu than the other Chinese restaurants. It's also a little pricier than other Chinese places, with most dishes around T4000, but there's pleasant outdoor seating in summer.

Western

Pizza Del La Casa (☎ 324 114, 312 072) has two locations; on Peace Ave near the Peace and Friendship Building, and on the east side of Baga Toiruu, opposite the Ulaan Baatar Hotel. Both serve good pizzas, pasta, calzone and soups in a laid-back environment. Large pizzas cost between T2000 and T3000. If you have just arrived in Mongolia, try the Mongolian pizza (with mutton). The pizzeria also delivers if you pay the taxi fare.

Marco Polo has arguably even better pizzas for similar prices. The interior is dressed up like a bizarre Bavarian hunting lodge.

Churchill's (☎ 322 770), at Baga Toiruu 31, bills itself as 'a taste of England in the heart of Mongolia' and serves up fish and chips, steak and kidney pie (T2500) and English breakfasts (T6000). There's also a bakery and a bar (closed Monday).

Douala La Capitale (☎ 322 233) is an African-French joint run by an exuberant Cameroonian woman. It serves up eclectic and tasty dishes like Senegalese peanut soup, and chicken in pistachio sauce. The excellent Friday night buffet is well worth trying for T7000; otherwise a main dish and a soup will come to around T6000. It's on the north curve of Baga Toiruu.

Millie's (☎ 328 264) is currently *the* place for lunch. Get there early before it gets packed-out with consultants, aid workers and journalists sipping excellent shakes and freshly squeezed orange juice. Also excellent are the steak sandwiches, lasagne and lemon pie. It's a good place for a decadent breakfast of imported coffee and waffles. The restaurant (also known as Buna Espresso) is on the second floor of the Center Hotel; open 9 am to 7 pm, Monday to Saturday, and for Sunday brunch from 10 am to 3 pm.

Los Bandidos (318 174) is run by the same people who dreamt up Pizza Del La Casa. It's a disorientating mix of Mexico City (decor and cuisine) and Bombay (chef and music) but somehow it works, mainly due to the fine nachos, fajitas, enchiladas and vegetarian garbanzo beans. It's hidden between apartment blocks, just off Peace Ave, not far from the Peace & Friendship Building.

Nearby, across the street, *El Toro (☎ 328 517)* serves up steaks from between T4000 and T6500 in a pleasant rustic environment.

Cafe De France (☎ 351 008) is a stylish place run by a Corsican. This is the place for such Gallic treats as liver pate (T1500), Roquefort steak (T5900) and crepes (T2500), plus fine Belgian ice cream and coffee. Set lunches run to T4000, T6000 or T9000. There's a small library of French books and magazines for patrons.

El Latino Restaurant serves Cuban dishes, complemented by Cuban music, cigars, espressos and cocktails. Dishes include omelettes (T900), *huevos rancheros* (fried eggs on tortillas, with salsa), good salads, French toast with honey, and fried bananas. Mains are around T2000.

Casablanca Cafe & Bar in front of the Bayangol Hotel is an American-style grill, which serves up standard steaks, sandwiches and burgers for about T5000. There's live music and cocktails in the evenings.

For cheaper fare, *BMT* on Baga Toiruu has cheap salads, pasta and snacks for T1000 a dish. *Berlin* is a similar, but larger cafeteria-style fast food place, offering good value burgers and spaghetti.

Winners Cafe has a pleasant atmosphere and good Western-style food like roast chicken soup and salads, all at decent prices. It's also a good place for a juice or coffee. Nearby *Classic Cafe* is a carbon copy.

A nice surprise is that most hotels have reasonably priced restaurants.

Cafes

In the summer, cafes spring up on any patch of ground in areas frequented by tourists and upper-class Mongolians. These are great places to sip a coffee or Coke and watch Ulaan Baatar go about its business.

Sacher's Café (☎ 324 734) has filter coffee, German magazines and both indoor and outdoor seating. It's also home to the best bakery in north-east Asia. Blow your budget on excellent Austrian-style cakes, pretzels and breads, including Chinggis Beer bread.

Axis Restaurant has open-air seating and is a good place for a cold beer, coffee or simple Mongolian and Western food.

Self-Catering

You will soon get to know the main markets in Ulaan Baatar if you are staying in an apartment with a kitchen, stocking up for a trip to the countryside, or you happen to be a vegetarian. These days there are very few things you can't get in the city if you look hard enough, though you may have to visit several markets to track down all the things you want. Most markets are open daily from about 10 am to 8 pm, and are worth a visit, if only for the atmosphere, fresh bread and tasty ice cream.

Container Market This is the cheapest place for everyday food purchases, all sold out the back of truck containers. It's just south of the Bakula Rinpoche Temple and is also known as the Bömbögör market.

Kharkhorin Market One of the biggest food markets in Mongolia, but inconveniently situated way out in the west end of town

Merkuri Market (Мэркури) **& Dalai market** (Далай Ээж). Conveniently located next to each other, about 100m west of the State Circus. Both markets have the best range of imported goods, meat, cheese and vegetables, as well as luxuries like caviar and crab sticks. The southeast corner has Werner's Deli, which sells German sausages and sandwiches.

State Department Store The ground floor has a good selection of fruit, deli and imported goods like corn flakes and cheese, though at slightly higher prices than elsewhere.

ENTERTAINMENT

Mongolians generally haven't yet learnt the power of advertising and promotion, so trying to find out what is going on in Ulaan Baatar can be a full-time job. You'll need to try the following – look at the 'Arts Diary' on the back page of the *Mongol Messenger* newspaper, or on the front page of *The UB Post*. You could also plead with a Mongolian friend, guide or hotel staff member to make some inquiries; walk past the various theatres or galleries and hope there is an advertisement outside in English; or just buy a ticket anyway and hope for the best.

Hope is at hand however. CIRC (see the Information section at the beginning of this chapter) has just started producing a monthly cultural events calendar, which covers most theatres, galleries and museums. It also publishes an arts calendar on its Web site at www.mongolart.mn.

Pubs & Bars

What may look like a cafe during the day often turns into a bar at night, selling beer (usually imported, expensive cans) to the younger crowds, and a dozen or so varieties of vodka to the older and drunker clientele. It's better to stick to bars in the main inner city area: in the suburbs, you may come across aggressive drunks who are not used to comparatively rich foreigners.

Chinggis Club, on Sükhbaataryn Gudamj, is a pleasant German-run pub, which brews its own Chinggis Beer (you can see the huge vats through a glass wall). Light or dark beer costs around T1600 for a large glass (0.5L) and there's good German-inspired food. (The beer mats make great souvenirs!)

Khanbrau, just south of the Square, also brews its own dark and Pilsner-style beers, though not quite as well as the Chinggis. The outdoor seating gets packed out on summer evenings and it's a great place to watch the world go by. There's live music on weekend evenings.

Just south of here is the quieter *East West Bar*, which is set in a small garden.

Khan Torkh Bier Garten, on the east side of Sükhbaatar Square, between the Opera & Ballet Theatre and the Palace of Culture, is another fine place to while away a summer afternoon over a cold beer.

Two new bars that promise live music are *River Sounds*, just south of the Ministry of External Relations, with live Mongolian bands most nights from 11.30 pm, and *Jason's Jazz Bar*, a cafe-style bar with comfy armchairs and piped jazz music.

The main local expat hang-out is the *Steppe Inn*, which opens every Friday evening from 6.30 to 8.30 pm in the compound of the British embassy. It's for members and their guests only.

ULAAN BAATAR

Discos & Clubs

Nick Middleton's book, *The Last Disco in Outer Mongolia*, written about his visits to Mongolia in the late 1980s, referred to what was Ulaan Baatar's only disco at the time – in the Bayangol Hotel. Now there are plenty of places with barmen in black bow ties, expensive imported beer and thumping techno music. Places go in and out of fashion, so you'll have to ask expats what's popular. Beer costs around T2000 in most places and don't be surprised to find the odd stripper or go-go dancer in residence.

Ikra, set into the right side of the National Academic Drama Theatre, is a small-ish dance venue popular with expats. Entry is a negotiable T3000.

Money Train, set in a huge building at the west end of Peace Ave, is currently the largest club in Ulaan Baatar. It features local DJs and has a mixed crowd. Admission is T3000.

Top Ten is farther out near the train station. Admission is T1000, or T5000 if a band is playing.

Carlsburg, opposite the British embassy, pulls in a student crowd; admission is T1000.

Traditional Music & Dance

A performance of traditional music and dance will be one of the highlights of your visit to Mongolia and should not be missed. You'll see outstanding examples of the unique Mongolian throat-singing, known as *khoomi*; full-scale orchestral renditions of new and old Mongolian music; contortionists guaranteed to make your eyes water; traditional and modern dancing; and recitals, featuring the unique horse-head violin, the *morin khuur*.

One of the most popular cultural shows is the *Tumen Ekh Song and Dance Ensemble*, which performs every Tuesday at 6 pm in the State Youth & Children's Theatre (☎ 327 916, 327 379) in Nairamdal Park. Tickets costs T6000, plus US$3 to take photos or a pricey US$30 to video. You can buy tapes (T6000) and CDs (T20,000) of the performance after the show. If you have a Walkman, take it along to check the quality of the recording before

Morin Khuur

The instrument most identified with Mongolia is the horse-head fiddle, known as the *morin khuur*. It has two horse-hair strings, with the distinctive and decorative carving of a horse's head on the handle. According to legend, the instrument was created by a herdsman to sing his sorrow over his horse's death – the instrument was formed out of the ribs and mane of the horse.

Traditionally, the morin khuur often accompanies the unique long songs that regale the beauty of the countryside and relive tales of nomadic heroes. You can hear the morin khuur at ceremonies during the Naadam Festival in Ulaan Baatar, or at a performance of traditional music and dance.

you buy anything. The traditional-style hall also has a cafe and gallery.

The *Traditional Song and Dance Company* performs irregularly over summer (especially during Naadam) at the National

continued on page 163

The Naadam Festival

THE NAADAM FESTIVAL

The biggest event of the Mongolian year for foreigners and locals alike is the Naadam Festival held in July in Ulaan Baatar. It is also the main draw card on most tour programs. Part family reunion, part fair and part nomad Olympics, Naadam (meaning 'holiday' or 'festival') has its roots in the nomad assemblies and hunting extravaganzas of the Mongol armies. Even today, Chinggis Khaan's nine yak tails, representing the nine tribes of the Mongols, are ceremonially transported from Sükhbaatar Square to Naadam Stadium to open the festivities.

The communists renamed the festival People's Revolution Day and fixed it to July 11 to 13, on the anniversary of the Mongolian Revolution of 1921. However, in country centres close to Ulaan Baatar, Naadam festivities may be held before or after the major festival in Ulaan Baatar. Some people like to attend both the local and national celebrations. The quality and number of sports and activities at Naadam festivals in the countryside will be lower than in Ulaan Baatar, but at a country Naadam you are more likely to get better seats, witness genuine festivals tainted without the tourist's brush, and even make up the numbers during a wrestling tournament! Watch out!

Some travellers visit the smaller Naadam at Zuunmod, an hour's drive from Ulaan Baatar, which is held at the same time as the capital's. Naadam festivities are also held at different times in the Kazakh and Buryat regions (a large Buryat Naadam was held in Dashbalbar in Dornod in late July 2000).

Unless you are really keen on the three main (and manly) sports, the festival itself can be a little disappointing and may not be worth coming specially to Mongolia to see. The opening and closing ceremonies, the associated activities and shows, and the general joy around the country, though, are reasons enough to base a visit around the

Title Page: Archery mosaic, Naadam stadium. (Photograph by Bradley Mayhew)

Icon: A wrestler performing the eagle dance before a bout. (Photograph by Graham Taylor)

Left: Wrestlers training for the big event.

Naadam Festival. Bear in mind that accommodation can be scarce during Naadam, and prices are often higher than normal. Book your hotel in advance or get there a few days early to tee up your room.

You may not bother seeing everything that Naadam has to offer. However you should try to make it to the following: the ceremony in the Sükhbaatar Square, from there go down to the stadium to see the opening ceremony. Wait for the first few rounds of the wrestling, then maybe wander off to see the archery and watch the Mongolians outside the stadium. Perhaps watch the horse racing on day two, and see the closing ceremony later that day.

On or about August 9, another tourist-oriented Naadam Festival called Baga Naadam (Small Naadam) is held. Some travel agents may sell you a program including this inferior festival. The best and original Naadam Festival will always be held from July 11 to 13 in Ulaan Baatar.

Ulaan Baatar's Naadam Festival

Wrestling, archery and horse racing are held during the first and second days. Very little happens on the third day, so get drunk the day before, and use it to recover from a hangover like everybody else does. During the three days, few restaurants and shops open and virtually no-one works.

Day one starts at about 9 am with a fantastic, colourful ceremony outside the State Parliament House at Sükhbaatar Square (often missed by visitors). Hundreds of soldiers in bright uniforms play stirring warlike music on brass instruments. Mongolians – dressed in Chinggis-style warrior outfits – parade around the square, then circle Parliament House before marching to the Stadium.

The opening ceremony, which starts at about 11 am at the Naadam Stadium, includes an impressive march of monks and athletes, plenty of music and even parachute displays. The closing ceremony, with more marches and dancing, is held at about 7 pm on the second day, but the exact time depends on when the wrestling finishes.

The first round of the wrestling, which starts at about noon on day one in the main stadium, is the more interesting and photogenic. Later rounds can get boring – most Mongolians don't bother returning to the stadium until the final rounds on the second day. If the wrestling gets too much, walk around the outside of the stadium and watch the interaction between Mongolians. This can be far more interesting than what is happening in the stadium. Also worth a look is the changing of the guards.

Archery is held in an open stadium next to the main stadium. The judges, who raise their arms and utter a traditional cry to indicate the quality of the shot are often more entertaining than the archery itself. Remember to watch out for stray arrows!

The horse racing can attract well over 1000 horses (so watch your step; this is dung city). During the festival, you may see dozens of horses being herded down the main streets of Ulaan Baatar, as if they were on the steppes. The horse racing is held at the village of Yarmag (Ярмаг), about 10km along the main road to the airport – it is very easy to spot. The atmosphere is electric, and there is always plenty to watch.

To get to Yarmag, you will need to catch one of the very regular buses or minibuses (T200) to Buyant-Ukhaa (Буянт-Ухаа), from along the road to Naadam Stadium. A taxi there will cost around T4000.

The best and busiest time to watch the horse racing is at the final race, late on the second day. You will be hard-pressed to see what is going on, and it is unlikely that you will be able to take any good photos. Get there really early for the final, go to other races on both days, or walk up a few hundred metres along the track where the crowds thin out.

A recent addition to the Naadam program is anklebone shooting. This entails using a hand-propelled mini crossbow to flick sheep anklebones, a row of which are set up as a target. The competition is held in a separate hall, normally near Naadam Stadium, but the location is never fixed so ask around.

Tickets to the stadium (except for the two ceremonies), and to the archery and horse racing are free, but to the opening ceremony foreigners pay US$12, and US$8 for the closing ceremony. A ticket does not usually give you a seat number, so get there in plenty of time for a good position, especially for the closing ceremony, when good seats may have been taken during the afternoon.

If on a package tour, your travel agency will arrange tickets. If travelling independently, getting a ticket to the opening and closing ceremonies can be tricky. From 4 to 10 July, you can buy tickets from the Central Stadium Company (☎ 343 123, fax 343 320) and you can normally buy tickets at the stadium before the two ceremonies. Guesthouse owners normally help their guests buy tickets.

To find out what is going on during the festival, look for the events program in the two English-language newspapers, which list the times and locations of the wrestling, archery and horse racing.

You can find plenty of warm drinks and cold *khuurshuur* (fried meat pancakes), as well as ice cream, bread and *airag* (fermented mare's milk) around the outside of the stadium. Take an umbrella or hat, because most seats are not undercover, and it will either rain or be hot.

The Three Manly Sports of the Naadam Festival

Naadam is properly known as Eriyn Gurvan Naadam, after the three 'manly' sports of wrestling, archery and horse racing (though women participate in the first two events). Winning at Naadam carries great prestige and financial reward. The 2000 Naadam offered T1.5 million of prize money to the winning wrestler and T600,000 to the winner of the main horse race.

Day one, Naadam Festival

A jockey relaxes after a race.

A musician plays the *yattak*, adding to the festivities.

Naadam archery competitors compete in traditional dress of *del* (long robe) and *loovuuz* (hat).

The most 'manly' of sports – wrestling

Chinggis Khaan-style costumes add to the scene.

Riding to the starting line of a horse race

Watch out for stray arrows during the archery!

Full house – spectators at the festival

BRADLEY MAYHEW

BRADLEY MAYHEW

FELICITY VOLK

BRADLEY MAYHEW

FELICITY VOLK

Wrestling Mongolian wrestling is similar to wrestling found elsewhere, except there are no weight divisions, so the biggest wrestlers (and they are big!) are often the best. Mongolian wrestling also has no time limit – the bout will continue with short breaks. It will end only when the first wrestler falls, or when anything other than the soles of the feet or open palms touch the ground.

Before each elimination bout, wrestlers limber up and honour the judges and their individual attendants (*zasuul*) with a short dance called a *devekh*, or 'eagle dance'. After the bout, the loser must perform the *takhimaa ogokh*, walking under the right arm of the winner, who then makes a lap of honour around the flag on a pedestal and does some more eagle dancing. The gesture signifies peace between the two wrestlers.

Wrestlers wear heavy boots called *gutul* – similar to the traditional boots worn by ordinary Mongolians. The tight, unflattering pants are called *shuudag*, and the small vest across the shoulders is a *zodog*. The open-fronted vest was allegedly introduced after one Amazonian-sized female wrestler floored all the male wrestlers. When it was discovered she was a woman the vest was introduced to ensure that women would no longer take part in bouts (and thrash the men!).

Winners are bestowed glorious titles depending on how many rounds they win. These are *nachin* (falcon) – five rounds; *zaan* (elephant) – seven rounds; and *arslan* (lion) – given to the winner of the tournament. When an arslan, or lion, wins two years in a row he becomes an *avarga*, or titan. One renowned wrestler was given the most prestigious, and lengthy, title of the 'Eye-Pleasing Nationally Famous Mighty and Invincible Giant'. Mongolia's most famous wrestler is currently Bat-Erdene.

You will see plenty of wrestling if you are in Mongolia during the Naadam Festival, or during the Ikh Sorilgo (Major Test) tournaments in the weeks before Naadam.

Right: Two opponents face-off during a wrestling event at the Naadam Festival in Ulaan Baatar.

GRAHAM TAYLOR

THE NAADAM FESTIVAL

Archery Like horse racing, the sport of archery originates from the warring era, starting from around the 11th century.

Archers use a bent composite bow made of layered horn, bark and wood. Usually, arrows are made from willows and the feathers are from vultures and other birds of prey.

Traditionally dressed male archers stand 75m from the target, while women archers stand 60m from it. The target is a line of up to 360-round grey, red and/or yellow leather rings (known as *sur*) on the ground. Usually there are only about 20 or 30 rings. After each shot, special judges who stand near the target (but miraculously never get injured) emit a short cry called a *uukhai*, and raise their hands in the air to indicate the quality of the shot. The winner who hits the targets the most times is declared the best archer, or *mergen*.

Horse Racing There are normally six categories of horse racing, depending on the age of horses: for example, a two-year-old horse, called a *shudlen*, will race for 15km, while six and seven-year-old *azrag* and *ikh nas* horses race for up to 30km. There are no tracks or courses; it is just open countryside, which leaves great scope for cheating. Jockeys – boys and girls aged between five and 13 years old – prepare for months for special races, particularly at Naadam. Horses are fed a special diet for weeks beforehand. The competition is not without its dangers: in 1999 a young rider was tragically killed during one of the horse races.

Before a race, the audience, all decked out in traditional finery, often sings traditional songs. The young riders sing a traditional anthem called a *gingo* before the race, and scream '*goog*' at the horses during the race.

The winner is declared *tümnii ekh*, or 'leader of ten thousand'. Riders and spectators rush to comb the sweat off a winning horse with a scraper traditionally made from a pelican's beak. The five winning horses are admired and talked about in reverence by the crowd, and traditional poems are read out, extolling the virtues of the riders and trainers. The five winning riders must drink some special airag, which is then often sprinkled on the riders' heads and on the horses' back-sides. During Naadam, a song is also sung to the two-year-old horse that places last.

BRADLEY MAYHEW

Left: The hard-fought race to the line.

continued from page 156

Academic Drama Theatre. You can buy tickets at the theatre on the day of the performance. Get to the show 30 minutes early to ensure a good position at the front. Several souvenir shops sell a video of the troupe in action.

The *Palace of Culture* (☎ 321 444) is a large, modern complex on the north-east corner of Sükhbaatar Square. It is occasionally used by the State Philharmonic Society, which performs both classical and folk music, and also by Mongolian and international orchestras and pop groups. A huge cloth banner outside, written in Cyrillic, is a sign that something's on; otherwise you'll probably never know unless you ask. The building is also sometimes called the Central House of Culture.

Opera & Ballet

Built by the Russians in 1932, the *State Opera & Ballet Theatre* (☎ 322 854) is the salmon-pinkish building on the south-east corner of Sükhbaatar Square. Throughout the year on Saturday and Sunday evenings, and sometimes also on weekend afternoons in the summer, the theatre holds stirring opera (in Mongolian) and ballet shows. Tickets for foreigners cost US$5 and are worth it.

One of the best operas is *Three Fateful Hills* – sometimes known as *The Story of Three Lives* – by Mongolia's most famous poet and playwright, D Natsagdorj. Other productions include an exhilarating (but long) rendition of *Carmen*, plus plenty of Pucinni and Tchaikovsky.

A board outside the theatre lists the shows for the current month in English. Advanced bookings are possible at the ticket office (☎ 323 881) on the ground floor, which is open from about 10 am to 5 pm daily, except Tuesday. Advance purchase is worthwhile for popular shows because tickets are numbered, so it's possible to score a good seat if you book early. If you are a little cheeky, you can have a look around inside the theatre during the day on weekdays (when there is no show in the evening).

Theatre

During most of the year the large, bright orange-brown *National Academic Drama Theatre* (☎ 324 236), on the corner of Natsagdorj Gudamj and Chingisiin Örgön Chölöö, shows one of a dozen or so Mongolian-language productions. These productions are penned by, among others, William Shakespeare and Jean-Paul Sartre, as well as various Mongolian playwrights. There are only between six and 10 performances every month – maybe a few more in summer.

A list of upcoming shows is painted in Cyrillic on a board to the right as you look at the theatre. You can buy tickets in advance at the booking office (☎ 323 213), which is on the right-hand side of the theatre, between 9 am and 8 pm (except during lunch from 1 to 2 pm), daily except Tuesday.

On the left-hand side of the theatre, as you approach it from the road, is a door that leads to a *puppet theatre* (☎ 321 669). Unfortunately, there are very few performances, but invariably something is organised during the week of the Naadam Festival.

Circus

Formed in 1940, the *State Circus* (☎ 324 357) has been housed in the recognisable round building with the blue roof at the end of Tserendoriin Gudamj since 1971.

The circus is perhaps the most disappointing attraction in Ulaan Baatar. There are some impressive acrobatics and juggling, and extraordinary contortionists, but watching a poodle do the lambada in a tutu was not a highlight. Animal lovers will probably not be impressed.

Performances are sporadic and it can be hard to find out exactly when a performance is on. Advance bookings (☎ 324 517) are possible on the day of performance, but not really necessary. Buy tickets (T2500) at the salmon-coloured building, south of the circus building. The circus is closed during August.

Performances usually start at about 5 pm, and sometimes matinees are held in summer (but not in August). Try to get there 30 minutes before the show starts to find a good seat. Nobody warns you, but flash photography is strictly prohibited.

Cinemas

In general the quality of films shown in the city is disappointing. Most are either kung fu classics or sleazy flicks (or both), and anything that isn't in Russian will be massacred by appalling overdubbing in Mongolian. There are a few exceptions to the rule.

Nomin Cinema (☎ 367 445, 324 187), on Ard Ayush Ave, way out in the 3rd/4th microdistrict, in the north-western suburbs, shows foreign films in English. Tickets cost around T1000.

Casa Home Video (☎ 324 114), part of the Casa Del la Pizza chain, operates its own 'mini movie theatre', meaning it will rent videos and a player. Watching a video costs T2000 per person, with a minimum of three people. You can also rent videos for US$2 plus a deposit. The theatre is open weekdays from 2 pm to 9 pm (except Thursday when it opens from 3.30 pm to 9 pm), and weekends from 1 to 9 pm.

The *French Cultural Centre* (☎ 310 565), on the 3rd floor of the Humanities Faculty, just north-east of Sukhbataar Square, shows French-language films every Friday at 6.30 pm.

SPECTATOR SPORTS

Besides archery, horse racing and wrestling, some of the local populace enjoy other sports. Fiery games of basketball are often held on summer evenings at the Central Sports Palace, which is the long, unsigned, yellowish building facing the lane behind the Ulaan Baatar Hotel.

For wrestling check out the schedule at the new Wrestling Palace (☎ 456 978) on Enkh Taivny Örgön Chölöö. Tickets normally cost between T1000 and T2500.

Wrestling, boxing and dog-fighting (a curious mix of boxing and wrestling for humans, not dogs) are also held at the Central Sports Palace during the year. These tournaments are rarely advertised, so check the local English press or ask a Mongolian friend, guide or hotel staff member.

On weekends during the short summer (but not around the time of the Naadam Festival), the newly formed Mongolian Football League plays football (soccer) matches at the Naadam Stadium. In the lead up to Naadam, you should be able to catch some informal, but still competitive, wrestling at the Naadam Stadium. Another venue is at the stadium in the southern part of Nairamdal Park, with events on weekend afternoons. During Naadam, you may also stumble across dog-jumping exhibitions and training here as well.

SHOPPING

The closest thing that Ulaan Baatar has to a shopping mall is the western half of Khudaldaany Gudamj, which is lined with clothing and second-hand book stalls and some useful shops, including hairdressers and pharmacies.

Cheap, easy to take home and unique to Mongolia are the bright landscape paintings which you will see in all the souvenir shops. The ones for sale from the art students (who sometimes hang around the Square) are far better and cheaper (from T550 to T2750). Some days, students may pester you a dozen times in one afternoon; then you won't see one for days. Gandan Khiid and the State Department Store are also good places to buy these types of paintings.

If you want to pick up some Mongolian cashmere, the shops in the upmarket hotels and at the Winter Palace sell jumpers (sweaters), rugs and gloves – but prices are high and non-negotiable (so try other smaller shops). The major cashmere factories are the government-owned Gobi Corporation, joint US-Mongolian company Mon-Forte, and a company called Buyan. The major showrooms are the Gobi Original Cashmere House, near the Hanamasa Restaurant, and Gobi Cashmere, just southwest of the Bayangol Hotel.

If you are serious about your musical instruments try the Egshiglen National Musical Instrument Shop (☎ 312 732), opposite the Museum of Natural History. *Morin khoor* (horse-head fiddles) range from T40,000 to T100,000 and there are *yattag* (zithers) and two-stringed Chinese fiddles.

If you are interested in Mongolian boots, try the tiny Buriyat boot *(buriad gutal)* workshop, just behind the west end of the Tuushin Hotel. It was closed when we visited during Naadam but should normally be open.

For modern goods, expats recommend the row of shops out in Nomin Plaza, along Ard Ayush Örgön Chölöö, in the 3rd/4th microdistrict.

Souvenir Shops

The art and souvenir shops in, and near, the Ulaan Baatar and Bayangol hotels are naturally more expensive than they should be, but they do have a reasonable selection of paintings, cashmere products, books, postcards, stamps and music. Several shops are actually in gers mounted on carts, notably outside the Bayangol Hotel and National Museum of Mongolian History. For price and selection, one of the best places to check out is in the yellow Golomt Bank building on the north-western side of the Square – look for the word 'souvenir' painted on the window.

Other places to look around are the 4th floor of the State Department Store, and the shops in the Winter Palace and the Monastery-Museum of Choijin Lama.

Khan's Ger (☎ 328 410), next to the Youth Federation Building on Baga Toiruu, has one of the best (though not cheapest) selection of handicrafts in the city. Souvenirs include bags, boots, mini tsam masks, chess sets, shirts, Mongolian games, paintings, cashmere, books and even wrestling pants. Credit cards are accepted.

For paintings and felt products try the Fine Art Shop on Peace Avenue, just east of Pizza Del La Casa.

The Antique Shop diagonally opposite from Scrolls has boots and pricey Buddhist artwork. Next door, the art shop has cheaper souvenirs like hats, paintings, figurines and Kazakh felt carpets. For more antiques try Eastern Culture (Dornyn Soyel), just west of the Natural History Museum.

A shop in the foyer (to the side) of the Zanabazar Museum of Fine Arts has some nice antiques, as well as Kazakh carpets and nomad accessories. It also provides customs stamps.

Camping Gear

Open air stalls outside the Bayangol Hotel and State Department Store sell cheap Chinese-made tents of barely acceptable quality.

Ayanchin Outfitters (☎ 327 172) sell good quality camping and fishing gear, including American brand sleeping bags, fleeces, tents, stoves, GPS, binoculars, jackets and first-aid kits at Western prices.

State Department Store

Улсын Их Дэлгуур

Known as *ikh delguur*, or 'big shop', the State Department Store (☎ 320 506) is virtually a tourist attraction in itself, an anachronism from the communist days of not so long ago. It's open between 9 am and 8 pm Monday to Saturday, and from 10 am to 6 pm Sunday.

The 1st floor has a good selection of food, books, maps and magazines and things like pots and pans, useful if you are planning an overland trip. The 3rd floor sells normal clothes and has one of the best collections of traditional clothes. Here you could be fully decked out in the traditional *del* (long robe), *loovuuz* (hat) and *gutul* (boots).

Most visitors head straight to the 4th floor, which has one of the best collections of souvenirs in the country, many at reasonable prices. If you can't pick up one from an art student in the street, the landscape paintings here are still good value. Other souvenirs you may wish to pick up include carvings, wall hangings of the great Chinggis Khaan, authentic Mongolian coats, incense bags and a good, but expensive, range of cashmere and leather products. This is also one of the better places to pick up postcards, shirts, and recordings of traditional and new Mongolian music (though these are pricey at around US$8 for a tape or US$25 for a CD). A foreign exchange counter on this floor changes US dollars only at standard bank rates.

Central Market

Төвийн Зах

The central market is actually called the Black Market (Khar Zakh), but it's not the sort of place where you go to change money illegally and smuggle goods – though this certainly happens.

First established about 60 years ago, and run by Chinese traders in different parts of the city, the market is now in the south-eastern corner of the city, at the corner of Teev-erchidiin and Ikh Toiruu. In summer up to 60,000 people a day squeeze into the market.

There's a T50 entrance fee. Once inside, there's an indoor area which contains a food market and few guanz. Prices are certainly lower than at the shops and markets in the city, but it's hardly worth the effort to come to this market just to save a few tögrög.

An undercover area has a decent selection of clothes, such as bags, sunglasses, leather boots and fake North Face jackets. This is also one of the cheapest places to get traditional Mongolian clothes like a del (T25,000), jacket (T20,000) and hat (T3,500). There's little else in the way of souvenirs.

The market is notorious for pickpockets and bag slashers so visit with a minimum of valuables. Hang on desperately to all your belongings; don't carry anything on your back, and strap your money belt to your body. Even Mongolians are scared of theft here. Some travellers have also reported being abused and some have had rocks thrown at them for taking photos in the market.

To get to the market, a taxi should cost around T1000 from the centre of town. Minibuses leave from the corner of Ikh Toiruu and Khudaldaany Gudamj (T200). To walk will take about 45 minutes.

The market is open 9 am to 6 pm on Wednesday, Thursday, Saturday and Sunday. Try to avoid Saturday and Sunday afternoons, when the crowds can be horrendous.

GETTING THERE & AWAY
Air
The main MIAT airline office is on the southern end of Baga Toiruu – there is a huge 'МИАТ' sign on the roof, and a notice with the words 'ticketing and reservation office' in English by the door. Once you get inside the building , turn left (north) for international flights, or right (south) for internal flights. Both sections accept credit cards. Both offices are open from 9 am to 5 pm weekdays (closed for lunch from 1 to 2 pm), and until 1.30 pm Saturday.

Most staff have a smattering of English (certainly Russian and possibly German) so it is sometimes worth ringing them, but you are far more likely to get what you want if you visit their head office. Numbers you may need are – arrivals/departures (☎ 119), international bookings (☎ 325 633), domestic bookings (☎ 322 144, 322 273) and information (☎ 320 221, 313 163).

If only as an alternative to the unreliable MIAT, the other internal airline, Khangard, is worth trying. Their booking office (☎ 379 851) is 100m south of MIAT, on the corner of an apartment block and is open 9.30 am and 1 pm and 2 and 5 pm daily except Sunday.

Foreign airline offices include:

Aeroflot (☎ 320 720) On Natsagdorj (Seoul) Gudamj, the office is open 9 am to 4 pm weekdays (noon to 6 pm Tuesday) and noon to 3 pm on Saturday. The staff are helpful, though it helps if you speak some Russian. Tickets can be reserved in advance but must be paid 15 days before departure in US dollars only.
Air China (☎ 328 838, fax 312 324) On Ikh Toiruu, in the north-east corner of town. The office is open 9 am to 5 pm (closed from 1 to 2 pm) weekdays and until noon Saturday.
Korean Air (☎ 326 643, fax 326 712) 1st floor, Chinggis Khaan Hotel. The office is open 8.30 am to noon and 1.30 to 5 pm weekdays and 8.30 am to noon Saturday.

Get to the airport early as departure times often change without warning. You need to put your bags through a useless security check before checking them in.

Minivan & Bus
Minivans travel at least once a week (to all but the three provinces in the far west) from the long-distance bus station (Тэврийн Төвчоо) at the southern end of Öndör Geegen Zanabazaryn Gudamj. The station is fairly chaotic; if you are new to Mongolia, don't speak the language and can't read Cyrillic, it may be a bit overwhelming at first. A Mongolian friend or guide would

make buying a ticket, and finding your bus, a lot easier. Local bus No 15 or 20, and trolley-bus No 2, 4 or 7, link the long-distance bus station with Sükhbaatar Square.

The station is divided into several sections. Most buses park impatiently under specific destination signs – but not necessarily the *right* signs. Ask, and keep asking, other passengers where the bus is going and look for destination signs (in Cyrillic) in the front window of the bus. Mongolian speakers can get information by calling ☎ 321 730.

Most departures are between 8 and 9 am. If you're taking a long trip, get to the station at least 60 minutes before your bus is scheduled to leave so you can find your minibus, and be ready to scramble on board to get a seat when the driver finally decides to open the doors. Always remember that, as with MIAT airlines, a ticket never guarantees you a seat. Most services are in minivans, though local destinations are served by bus.

Tickets for places close to Ulaan Baatar – namely Nalaikh (T500), Baganuur (T2500), Darkhan (T3500) and Zuunmod (T700) – are bought on the bus, so jump on and get a seat; the conductor will sell you a ticket. These buses go every hour or so, or when full. For longer trips you can, and should, book as early as possible, which is usually only one day in advance. The ticket office and waiting room is in the blue building in the eastern part of the middle section of the station. It's open weekdays from 8 am to noon, and 1 to 3.30 pm. See the bus timetable later in this entry.

Public shared jeeps occasionally wait at the bus station for passengers and operate much like the minivans. See the entry Hiring a Jeep/Minivan and Driver under Jeep in the Getting Around chapter for information about renting jeeps or minivans for private trips around the countryside.

In summer, minibuses also go to Terelj and other nearby resort areas like Khandgait. They leave from the truck station just south of the Container Market on Khudaldaany Gudamj and have no schedule at all; getting a ride involves a lot of waiting, asking and then scrambling aboard when the damn thing arrives out of nowhere.

The following is an approximate bus timetable. It gives an idea of frequencies, rather than fixed departures. Few minivans will go until they are full. All departures are theoretically between 8.30 and 9.30 am.

destination	frequency	cost
Altai	daily	T18,000
Altanbulag	daily	T4000
Arvaikheer	daily	T8000
Bayankhongor	daily	T11,500
Bulgan	Mon, Thur	T6000
Choibalsan	daily	T15,000
Dalanzadgad	Mon, Fri	T10,000
Darkhan	daily	T3500
Kharkhorin	daily	T6770
Khujirt	Mon, Fri*	T7800
Mandalgov	Mon, Thur, Sat	T5000
Mörön	daily	T15,000
Öndörkhaan	Mon, Fri	T6000
Sükhbaatar	Fri	T8500
Tariat	Wed	T11,750
Tsetserleg	Mon, Fri	T9070
Uliastai	Mon	T18,000

* and sometimes Wednesday

Apart from these, there are also private minivans which wait around, often most of the day, for enough passengers.

Train

The train station has an information office, a left-luggage department, a telephone office, a hotel and a restaurant.

From Ulaan Baatar, daily trains travel to northern Mongolia and on to Russia, via Darkhan and Sükhbaatar, and south-east to China, via Choir, Sainshand and Zamyn-Üüd. There are also lines between Ulaan Baatar and the coal mining towns of Erdenet and Baganuur.

Domestic Tickets for domestic trains are available from a modern-looking building directly east of the Square outside the train station. Unfortunately, no one inside speaks anything except Mongolian or Russian. Boards inside the office show departure times (in Cyrillic) and ticket prices for hard seats and soft seats. There's also a full timetable at the information desk on the station platform.

Domestic Train Timetable

destination	train no	frequency	departure time	duration (hours)	fare (hard/soft class)
Zamyn-Üüd	276	daily	4 pm	15½	T3900/9300
Darkhan	211	daily	3.40 pm	5	T2000/5100
Darkhan	271	daily	10.30 am	8	T2000/5100
Erdenet	273	daily	7.34 pm	13½	T2800/6800
Sükhbaatar	263	daily	9.05 pm	7¾	T2500/6400
Sükhbaatar	271	daily	10.30 am	7¾	T2500/6400

The domestic booking office (☎ 94 137, 94 135) is open every day between 8 am and 12.30 pm, and from 2.30 to 9 pm. You can book a ticket up to a month in advance for an extra T450, which is not a bad idea if you have definite plans and want a soft seat during peak times (mainly July-August). If you speak Mongolian, there is an inquiries number (☎ 94 194, 194).

For Choir (T1900/5000) take the Zamyn-Üüd train.

International Trains link Mongolia with its powerful neighbours, China and Russia. Getting a ticket in Ulaan Baatar isn't the ordeal it once was, but you should still plan ahead.

The yellow International Railway Ticketing Office is about 200m north-west of the train station. Inside the office, specific rooms sell tickets to Beijing, Irkutsk (Russia), Moscow, and Ereen and Hohhot (both in China). The easiest place to book a ticket is in the foreigners booking office, in Room 212 upstairs; staff here speak English. The booking office (☎ 94133, inquiries ☎ 944 868) is open 9 am to 1 pm and 2 to 5 pm weekdays, and 9 am to 2 pm weekends. You'll need your passport to buy a ticket. You can book the ticket by phone for a T4500 booking fee. If you cancel a ticket there is a minuscule T1000 charge.

You can book a ticket for international trains out of Ulaan Baatar up to one month in advance – but for the Moscow-Beijing or Beijing-Moscow trains you will have to scramble for a ticket on the day before departure. For train times and details see the Getting There & Away chapter.

If you have troubles booking a berth, UB Tour (☎ 324 839, fax 324 730, ⓔ ubtour@ magicnet.mn), on the 4th floor of the Ulaan Baatar Hotel, can often book train tickets when others can't, though it charges a painful US$15 commission. It's open daily until 11 pm.

Taxi

Taxis (shared or private) can only travel along paved roads, so they are only useful for trips around Töv aimag, to the towns along the main road to Russia (Darkhan, Erdenet and Sükhbaatar) and to the tourist site of Kharkhorin.

The cost of hiring a taxi to these places should be the same as the cost around Ulaan Baatar – currently T300 per km. Taxi drivers may want more for waiting if you are, for example, visiting Manzshir Khiid, or because they may return with an empty vehicle if dropping you off to somewhere remote. This is not unreasonable, but it *is* negotiable.

To avoid any argument about the final charge make sure that you and the driver have firstly agreed on the cost per kilometre, and have discussed any extra charges. Then write down the number shown on the odometer/speedometer before you start.

Hitching

Hitching is a necessary form of transport in the countryside, but is less certain and more difficult to organise out of Ulaan Baatar. Most Mongolians get out of the capital city by bus, minibus, train or shared jeep/taxi, and then hitch a ride on a truck for further trips around the countryside, where there is far less public transport. See the Hitching section in the Getting Around chapter for more information about hitching on trucks in the provinces.

In Ulaan Baatar, some trucks congregate around the station south of the Container Market, on the corner of Khudaldaany Gudamj and the south-west section of Ikh Toiruu. These primarily wait for cargo, but will take passengers if you are lucky enough to be there when one is leaving. You can pre-arrange something, but you may be waiting for days and days.

GETTING AROUND
To/From the Airport

The Buyant-Ukhaa International Airport, 18km south-west of the city, has been renovated to bring it up to international standards. You can change money at a branch of the T&D Bank, and there's a post office and Internet access for T50 per minute.

Between the airport and city (T200), bus No 11 stops at the Ard Cinema on Baga Toiruu and opposite the Bayangol Hotel, and bus No 22 stops near Liberty Square and Ikh Toiruu, near the Map Shop. To find the bus stop near the airport, head out of the terminal, walk north for a few hundred metres and look for a group of locals mingling around a tin shelter.

If you have a lot of gear, or have just arrived in Mongolia, it's worth paying extra for a taxi. Make sure that you pay the standard rate, currently T300 per km, which works out around US$5 one-way to Sükhbaatar Square.

Bus

While old Soviet rustbuckets still rattle around the countryside, shiny new buses, donated by the Japanese government, travel around most of the capital city. The inner-city area is also serviced by a few trolley-buses.

Local public transport is reliable and departures are frequent, but buses can get crowded. Sometimes, you can count yourself extremely fortunate if you even see a seat, let alone sit on one. Conductors collect fares (currently T200 for a bus or T100 for a trolley-bus for any trip around Ulaan Baatar, including to the airport) and usually have change. Pickpockets and bag slashers

occasionally ply their trade on crowded routes. It is not as bad as in China, but you should be careful. For short trips it's just as cheap to take a taxi, especially if there is more than one of you. Some of the useful buses and trolley-buses are listed below:

destination	bus no	trolley bus no
Airport	11 & 22	-
Peace Ave (west)	4, 17, 22 & 24	1
Peace Ave (east)	2 & 13	1, 4 & 5
Long-Distance Bus Station	9, 10 & 20	-
Train Station	15 & 20	2, 4 & 7
Winter Palace	3 & 19	-
Zaisan Memorial	7	-

All destinations of trolley-buses and buses will be in Cyrillic; the route number is next to the destination sign on the front of the trolley-bus or bus. The route is often marked on the side of the bus.

Car

There is nowhere in the city to rent a car or motorbike, and it's unlikely there will be for some time. The cheapest way to have your own wheels is to rent a taxi by the day. You'll be expected to pay the standard T300 per km, plus a daily rate if you are not doing many km. Most travel agencies and guesthouses can help to arrange this, or a cheaper alternative is to talk directly to a driver.

Taxi

In Ulaan Baatar, there are official and unofficial taxis; in fact, just about every vehicle is a potential taxi. All charge a standard T300 per km, though you'll need to check the current rate as this will increase regularly. Don't agree to a set daily price because you will always pay more than if you pay the standard rate per kilometre.

Taxi drivers are generally remarkably honest, and within the city you won't be overcharged too much or too often. Most reset the meter as soon as you get in. If they don't reset it, make a note of the reading so you know how many kilometres you've covered.

Getting a taxi is just a matter of standing by the side of a main street and waving your arms about. Within a minute or two a vehicle – either a taxi (some with a 'taxi' sign in English) or a private car – will stop. Alternatively, you can find them at designated taxi stands opposite the Zanabazar Museum of Fine Arts, outside the train station, and in Liberty Square. After dark, women should generally avoid using a private car, rather than an official taxi.

The most visible official taxi is City Taxi which runs a fleet of modern yellow Hyundai Accents. They all have meters and are the most comfortable and reliable choice, but can be devilishly hard to find at rush hour. Smaller companies include Ulaan Baatar Taxis and Mon-Kor Taxis.

Avoid using obvious landmarks such as the Ulaan Baatar and Bayangol hotels to catch, or get off, local taxis: taxi drivers will almost always assume that you are staying at these expensive places and can therefore afford to pay more than you should for your fare.

Bicycle

Ulaan Baatar is reasonably flat and the streets are wide, so it's a good place for bicycles – except that almost no-one in the city rides them or hires any out (what a pity!). A mountain bike would give you a wonderful opportunity to explore the nearby countryside.

Karakorum Expeditions (see Travel Agencies under Information earlier in this chapter) are currently the only people who rent mountain bikes. A 21-speed Western bike will set you back US$25 per day. You could buy a Chinese-made bike locally but you'd have trouble finding spare parts.

Central Mongolia

The central *aimags*, or provinces, of Töv, Arkhangai and Övörkhangai are the most visited areas in the countryside for several reasons: the roads and transport are far better than the rest of Mongolia, the region is closer to Ulaan Baatar, and there is plenty to see, including ancient monasteries, gorgeous lakes and several national parks.

The central region has varied and dramatic scenery, from the mountain ranges of the Khentii Nuruu in the north and the Khangai Nuruu in the mid-west, to the Gobi Desert in southern Övörkhangai. The rest is steppe with forests or desert, and there are several volcanoes, as well as many rivers, especially in the wet aimag of Arkhangai. This is classic Mongolian landscape and the heartland of the nation.

Töv Төв

pop 111,900 • area 81,000 sq km
Ulaan Baatar is an autonomous municipality; the aimag which surrounds it is called Töv, which means 'central'. Just an hour's drive from Ulaan Baatar are restored monasteries in beautiful valleys, and mountains with some wonderful hiking. A large section of the aimag is part of the Gorkhi-Terelj, Khan Khentii and Bogdkhan Uul national parks. The ethnic groups include the Khalkh, the Kazakhs, and the Barga.

Töv may not be the wildest or most spectacular aimag in Mongolia, but it's an excellent place to start your exploration, or to see some of the countryside if your time is limited. It has a network of good unpaved and paved roads, so you can easily use public transport to make day or overnight trips from the capital.

ZUUNMOD
ЗУУНМОД
pop 17,000 • elevation 1529m
Nestled in a valley some 40km south of Ulaan Baatar, Zuunmod – the capital of Töv

Highlights

- Bogdkhan Uul Strictly Protected Area, a superb hiking area; an overnight trek back to the capital is possible
- Terelj, a popular place to see the countryside around Ulaan Baatar; excellent hiking and horse riding
- Khustai National Park, home to the *takhi*, the Mongolian wild horse, with good hiking and horse riding
- Kharkhorin, home to the magnificent monastery Erdene Zuu Khiid and the site of the former Mongol capital of Karakorum
- Terkhiin Tsagaan Nuur, one of the best lakes in the country, with lovely sunsets and great camping

– is a laid-back town. If travelling independently, you may need to stay in Zuunmod to visit the nearby monastery, Manzshir Khiid, or hike in the nearby mountains. Otherwise there's little reason to linger.

Things to See
The chief attraction in Zuunmod is the **Central Province Museum**, opposite the

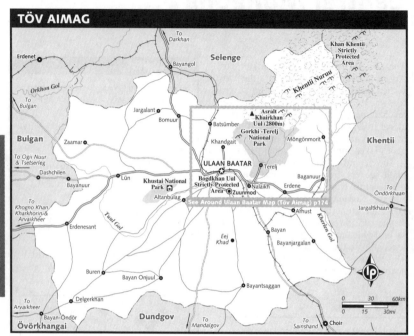

TÖV AIMAG

See Around Ulaan Baatar Map (Töv Aimag) p174

southeast corner of the park – look for the sign in English. Like most aimag museums, it gives a good summary of the local geology, flora and fauna, and has a stuffed-animals section – the moose is gigantic. There are also some interesting black and white photos of Manzshir Khiid, including the once-regular *tsam* dances. The museum (T1000) is open daily, except Tuesday, from 9 am to 4 pm (closed from 1 to 2 pm). The nearby **Ethnography Museum** is currently closed.

Not in the same league as Manzshir Khiid but worth a brief visit, **Dashichoinkhorlon Khiid** (Дашчоынхорлон Хийл) is a 500m walk directly east of the department store and across the creek. If you ask the monks, you can go inside the temple. Ceremonies start at around 11 am on most days.

Places to Stay

You can *camp* anywhere near town, although Manzshir Khiid and the area around it is better than Zuunmod.

Chronically overpriced (for foreigners), the **Zuunmod Hotel** has drab rooms for T9492 in a deluxe with bathroom, or T6780 per person in a four-bed room, without running water. The hotel is actually in what is marked as the bar, behind the crumbling main building.

Travellers have recommended the **Government Hotel**, opposite the Zuunmod Hotel, though it was closed when we visited.

Places to Eat

Zuunmod epitomises the poor choice of restaurants in the countryside: although it's the capital of one of the most populous provinces in the country, and only an hour's drive from Ulaan Baatar, Zuunmod has no decent place to eat. Your best bet is to track down an open *cafe* on the main north-south street, where you might get some milky tea and *khuurshuur* (fried mutton pancakes). The most reliable option looks to be the **Dölgöön Café**, on the east side of the central park.

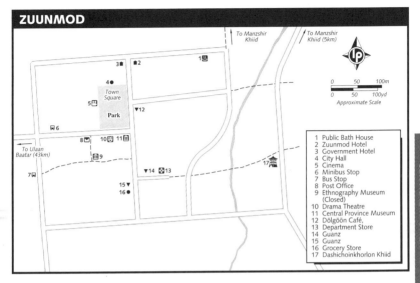

ZUUNMOD

To Manzshir Khiid
To Manzshir Khiid (5km)

Town Square
Park

To Ulaan Baatar (43km)

0   50   100m
0   50   100yd
Approximate Scale

1 Public Bath House
2 Zuunmod Hotel
3 Government Hotel
4 City Hall
5 Cinema
6 Minibus Stop
7 Bus Stop
8 Post Office
9 Ethnography Museum (Closed)
10 Drama Theatre
11 Central Province Museum
12 Dölgöön Café,
13 Department Store
14 Guanz
15 Guanz
16 Grocery Store
17 Dashichoinkhorlon Khiid

Getting There & Away

Minibus These run through the pretty countryside between Zuunmod and Ulaan Baatar (one hour, hourly, T700) between 8 am and 6 pm, from Ulaan Baatar's long-distance bus station. The road is paved and in good condition. The bus stop in Zuunmod is just a short walk west of the main street.

Taxi Shared taxis (jeeps are not needed) also ply the route between Ulaan Baatar and Zuunmod. They are more expensive but more comfortable than the sardine-can minibuses. You'll find shared taxis easily on the streets of Zuunmod; in Ulaan Baatar, they leave occasionally from the long-distance bus station.

A chartered taxi from Ulaan Baatar will cost between US$10 and US$13 one-way. It is surprisingly difficult in Zuunmod to find a taxi, or any vehicle, interested in being chartered. The fare should be the standard rate paid in Ulaan Baatar. Some drivers may want a waiting fee for hanging around the monastery Manzshir Khiid if you are going up there. This is reasonable as you may be there for an hour or two.

MANZSHIR KHIID
МАНЗШИР ХИЙД

Only 5km on foot to the north-east of Zuunmod, and 46km from Ulaan Baatar, is Manzshir Khiid. Established in 1733, the monastery had over 20 temples and was once home to 350 monks. Tragically, it too was reduced to rubble during the Stalinist purges of 1937.

The main temple has been recently restored and converted into a museum, but the other buildings in the area remain in ruins. The monastery and museum are not as impressive as those in Ulaan Baatar – it is the beautiful setting which makes a visit worthwhile. Many brochures about Manzshir, which you may pick up from travel agencies, still claim that religious tsam dances are held once a year at the monastery. In fact, they haven't taken place here for decades.

Manzshir Khiid overlooks a beautiful valley of streams, and pine, birch and cedar trees, dotted with granite boulders. The monastery, and most of the area between it and Zuunmod, is part of the Bogdkhan Uul Strictly Protected Area, where wildlife, including wolves and foxes, is abundant.

Endangered species of hare and deer are theoretically protected from hunting.

As you enter from the main road from Zuunmod you'll be required to pay an admission fee of T1000 per person and T500 for any car, including a taxi if you take one at the main gate. The entrance fee also allows entry to Bogdkhan Uul Strictly Protected Area (though you are already in it). From here it's a couple of kilometres to the main area, where there is a shop, a museum, a restaurant and several gers offering accommodation. Look for the huge two-tonne **bronze cauldron**, which dates from 1726.

The remains of the monastery are about 800m uphill from the museum. The caretaker lives in the compound next door and will open up the main building for you. The **monastery museum** has exhibits on the layout of Manzshir and some photos which show what the it looked like before Stalin's thugs turned it into rubble. The museum also has some fine Buddhist art and tsam masks, as well as several examples of the controversial **Ganlin Horn**, made from human thigh bones.

If you have time, it's worth climbing up the rocks behind the main temple, where

AROUND ULAAN BAATAR (TÖV AIMAG)

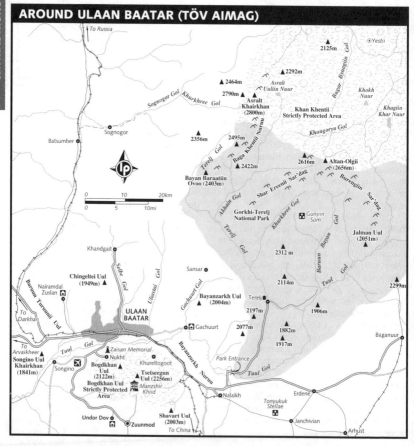

there are some Buddhist **rock paintings**. At the top, the views are even more beautiful, and you'll find yourself in the midst of a lovely pine forest. You can continue from here all the way to Ulaan Baatar if you are equipped for an overnight trip. See the Tsetseegun Uul entry under Four Holy Peaks later in this chapter for more information on this route.

Places to Stay & Eat

Camping The area around the monastery is one of the best camping spots near Ulaan Baatar. You should get permission from the caretaker at the monastery if you are camping nearby, or just hike off into the woods.

Ger Camps If you've wanted to stay in a ger camp but have avoided it because it's expensive, the gers at the monastery may be what you're looking for. Only a handful are available at a comparatively reasonable US$15 per person, including meals. There's a restaurant in the grounds, but it may only be open if a tour group is staying there, so take some food. The problem is that you can't book ahead, and the gers may be occupied, but it is worth asking anyway.

Getting There & Away

The monastery is easy enough to visit in a day trip from Ulaan Baatar or Zuunmod (from where it's a 7km drive). If you are walking from Zuunmod, you can either walk along the main northern road after visiting Dashichoinkhorlon Khiid, or you can save some time by walking directly north from Zuunmod, eventually joining up with the main road.

The perfect way to get to Manzshir and explore the area is by horse, but finding one with all the right gear and, if necessary, a guide, is not easy – Zuunmod is not set up for tourists. You could ask around the ger suburbs of Zuunmod, but it's probably best to arrange something from Undor Dov, about 22km from Manzshir Khiid, or via one of the guesthouses, like Idre's, in Ulaan Baatar.

UNDOR DOV
ӨНДӨР ДОВ

The ***Undor Dov Tourist Camp*** (☎ 457 970) is about 8km directly west of Zuunmod. Opened in 1991, the camp contains a large concrete restaurant and a couple of dozen gers in a row. A night in a ger is US$45 per person, with meals, sauna and hot shower. Bookings can be made at Room 105 of the Undruul Hotel (☎ 455 108, fax 455 016, e undtour@magicnet.mn) in Ulaan Bataar.

The main attraction is a lovely horse ride from Undor Dov to Manzshir Khiid (22km). The ride, with a guide, costs a reasonable US$10 per day; inquire at the camp.

The only way to Undor Dov is by taxi from Zuunmod. There is an obvious turn-off on the paved road between Ulaan Baatar and Zuunmod. You may even want to walk from Zuunmod, either along the road or across the fields.

EEJ KHAD
ҮҮЖ ХАД

Near the village of Khöshigiin Ar in the *sum* (district) of Sergelen, 15km south of Zuunmod, is the sacred rock known as Eej Khad, or Mother Rock. Mongolians often come here to seek solace and advice, and make offerings of vodka, milk and silk scarves called *khatag*. Pilgrims ask for three wishes to be granted, circle the rock three times and make three separate visits. The earth around the rock is sacred, so any rubbish that is dropped cannot be picked up; unfortunately, the area is now extremely dirty, with rubbish and broken bottles lying everywhere.

There are several other sites which are thought to generate good luck. One is **Dog Rock**, which Mongolians rub their body against to cure ailments. The other, a few kilometres north of Mother Rock, is called **Rich Rock** and locals touch their wallet to it to ensure financial security.

Daily buses are supposed to leave from the long-distance bus station in Ulaan Baatar at around 8 am (T2000, or T4000 return with a two hour wait at Eej Khad). Otherwise, try to get a taxi from Zuunmod, or include it in a day trip by taxi to Manzshir Khiid from Ulaan Baatar.

Mother Rock

During communism, visiting Eej Khad (Mother Rock) was a political crime, though some people still went in secret. Sometime in the late 1970s the communists decided to do away with the 'feudal' site once and for all. Workers tried dynamite to blow it up, and a tractor to haul it away, both to no avail. The next day workers awoke to find their tractor burnt and destroyed. Soon after the incident the official that ordered Eej Khad's destruction died and his family members became ill. It is said that all the other members of the team suffered a string of bad luck. Most Mongolians can recite a similar tale of provocation and retribution at the holy rock.

There is nowhere to stay near Eej Khad. You can *camp* but make very sure that you are well away from the drunks who congregate here.

BOGDKHAN UUL
БОГДХАН УУЛ

The mountain Bogdkhan Uul (2122m) was proclaimed a national park as far back as 1778. During the Soviet period the park's status was formalised and it was renamed after Choibalsan. It is now designated the Bogdkhan Uul Strictly Protected Area (42,651 hectares). Unesco has also proposed to establish a wildlife park in the region, of up to 65,000 hectares. It seems that early legislation has ensured that the park won't become part of Ulaan Baatar's awful urban sprawl.

The protected area is immediately south of the river, the Tuul Gol, south of Ulaan Baatar and west of Nalaikh. It surrounds Tsetseegun Uul and contains the Zaisan Memorial, Nukht and Manzshir Khiid.

The main activities in the park are hiking and horse riding. The most accessible entrances are via Zaisan, the Ikh Tenger Valley, and from Manzshir. There is another entrance from the camp, Chinggis Khaani Khüree. For information on hiking to the main peak from Zaisan or Manzshir, or combining the two in an overnight hike from Manzshir to Ulaan Baatar, see the Four Holy Peaks section later in this chapter.

Entrance to the park costs T1000 per day for foreigners, and T3000 for any type of vehicle. If you don't enter the park from the two gates – ie, on the main road near Chinggis Khaani Khüree or at Manzshir Khiid – you should in theory get a permit from the Protected Areas Bureau (☎ 326 617, fax 328 620), Ministry of Nature & Environment, Baga Toiruu 44, Ulaan Baatar.

Places to Stay
If you just want to do some walking, and then stay in a comfortable place outside of the city there are a couple of choices.

At the western entrance to the park, near the turn-off to the left at the unlikely traffic light along the main road between Ulaan Baatar and Zuunmod, the *Chinggis Khaani Khüree* ger camp can justifiably claim to be 'different'. It goes the whole hog with the Chinggis Khaan theme: there's a museum with leftovers from the movie about the great man and it includes costumes, weapons, armoury and ger carts. The restaurant has to be seen to be believed: each seat is an enormous throne, set inside a huge ger with a bear-skin welcome mat, and the walls are lined with the skins of 84 unfortunate snow leopards.

Considering the opulence, the price of US$35 per person per night for a standard ger with three meals is not unreasonable (though tacky and not for animal lovers). You can book at Tsagaan Shonkhor Holding Travel Company (☎ 379 923, 311 783).

The *Nukht Hotel (☎ 310 421)*, sometimes called the Nukht EcoTourism Centre, is in another agreeable place for hiking, only 10km from Ulaan Baatar. It caters almost exclusively for organised tours, though if you ask nicely, and business is quiet (and they are open), they may offer you a ger for as little as US$10 a night, excluding meals. Hotel rooms start at US$20, excluding meals, and go a lot higher if you want any luxuries. The place is sometimes booked solid by plane loads of Japanese golfing enthusiasts. The turn-off for the road to Nukht is south from

CENTRAL MONGOLIA

the main road to the airport; on the corner are the remains of the tiny **stadium** used for the Naadam Festival in the 1940s.

FOUR HOLY PEAKS

The four peaks surrounding Ulaan Baatar are considered holy. Tsetseegun, Chingeltei, Songino Khairkhan and Bayanzurkh mountains correspond, more or less, to the four points on the compass. These peaks are great for hiking, and they're popular for their forests of larch trees, grasslands and stunning bird and other animal life, including red deer, ibex and sable. The forest is the southernmost limit of the Siberian larch forests. There is no shortage of thunderstorms in summer, so be prepared, and there's heavy snow in winter.

Tsetseegun Uul

Цэцээгүн Уул

Of the four, easily the most magnificent mountain is Tsetseegun. At 2256m, Tsetseegun is the highest point in the Bogdkhan Uul range, which dominates the skyline to the south of Ulaan Baatar. From the city, you can't get an idea of just how beautiful this area is, but once you're in the forest it has a whole different feel.

If you are hiking around this mountain, you need a permit – that is, you must pay an admission fee. You can do this at the gate to the Bogdkhan Uul Strictly Protected Area or at Manzshir Khiid. If you aren't hiking to the mountain through these entrances, you should get a permit from the Protected Areas Bureau in Ulaan Baatar, though in reality the chances of being checked are minimal.

There are numerous approaches to the summit, some easier than others, and you may want to go up one way and descend by another route. One popular option is to hike from Manzshir Khiid to Ulaan Baatar, either to the Zaisan Memorial or the Ikh Tenger Valley. This takes about 10 hours' hiking, so you'll need to camp overnight in the park.

The trip is only sensible from the beginning of June to the end of September. During the rest of the year, no matter how pleasant the weather is in the morning, sudden thunderstorms and icy winds can come out of nowhere (even during summer). It's important to take a compass and know how to use it, as it's easy to get lost in the forest. You'll need to make an early start and, as there is little or no water on top of the ridge, carry all the water you will need, plus extra food.

Some scrambling over fields of granite boulders is necessary, and the chance of slipping and injuring yourself should not be taken lightly. It would be wise to inform a friend or guesthouse owner in Ulaan Baatar of your itinerary and the time of your expected return.

Manzshir Khiid Route This approach to Tsetseegun from the south side is the easiest route by far. As you face the monastery, cut over to your right (east) until you get to the stream. Just follow the stream until it nearly disappears and then head north. About three hours' walking should bring you out over a ridge into a broad boggy meadow, which you'll have to cross. If you've walked straight to the north, the twin rocky outcrops of the summit should be right in front of you. When you start to see Ulaan Baatar in the distance, you're on the highest ridge and close to the two large *ovoo* (sacred pyramid-shaped collection of stones) on the summit.

From the ovoo you can return to Manzshir or descend to Ulaan Baatar. If you head down to Ulaan Baatar it's difficult to find the right way; you'll just have to estimate from your visual reference of the city. The easiest route takes you to the Ikh Tenger Valley, on the southern fringe of the city, from where you can hitch or take a taxi into the city centre. Beware about hiking too close to the Presidential Palace, between the Zaisan Memorial in Ulaan Baatar and the Ikh Tenger Valley, as one reader warns:

There is a ring of army guards on the hills surrounding the palace. On my first hike, I had a couple of young soldiers with AK-47s running up the hill trying to catch me. They held me for a couple of hours before letting me go. But not before I was subjected to a stern 15-minute lecture in Russian, which ended with a sweep of the commanding officer's arms towards the hills and a shout of *'nyet!'*.

CENTRAL MONGOLIA

Zaisan Route This is the most scenic route of all, but also the most difficult. It's a good six hours each way and the boulders near the summit make it hard going.

From the Zaisan Memorial, move past the huts and head up the valley 100m or so, then cut into the forest to your left. It's a very steep slope until you get to the top of the first ridge (about a 30-minute walk). On top of the ridge, you should find a large ovoo and an obvious path. From here, the slope levels off and becomes an easy walk through a pleasant forest for the next two hours.

Eventually, the path disappears into an area of boulders, and you should come out to a point where you have a good view. You should be able to see the summit clearly at this point, but the climb is not yet half over. Take a compass reading on the summit, then descend into a valley before climbing the final ridge. There is no path, though there are many false paths made by pine nut gatherers. You'll hit plenty of boulder fields on this last ridge, but you can avoid the worst of them by keeping a little to the east of the summit. Finally, you come out into a broad meadow where the two rock pinnacles of the summit should be visible.

Shavart Route Shavart Uul, which appropriately means 'muddy mountain', is a lesser peak of 2003m on the south-east side of Tsetseegun. As you climb, you'll note seven large rocks on your left. This route takes five hours in each direction. Getting to the starting point requires a car or taxi.

Khureltogoot Route This is the easiest route on the Ulaan Baatar side, mainly because you hit the fewest boulders. However, this route is also the least interesting. The walk takes about three hours in each direction.

The problem is that getting to Khureltogoot is difficult. At about 8 am every morning a bus for workers at the Astronomical Building in Khureltogoot leaves from the long-distance bus station in Ulaan Baatar; you may be able to hitch a ride on this. Otherwise, you'll have to take a taxi.

Chingeltei Uul
Чингэлтэй Уул
On the north side of Ulaan Baatar, Chingeltei Uul (1949m) has some pretty forests near the top. You can reach the base of the mountain by bus No 3, 16 or, best of all, 18 from the centre of Ulaan Baatar. By taxi, you can go all the way up to a gate from where it's a 2km walk to the summit.

Songino Khairkhan Uul
Сонгино Хаирхан Уул
This small mountain to the west of Ulaan Baatar has the unusual name of 'onion mountain'. There is no bus to it, so you need to take a taxi to the base, passing through a park with concrete animal statues. Getting back to Ulaan Baatar could be a hassle if you haven't made prior arrangements, though on a Sunday it should be easy enough to hitch a ride.

Bayanzurkh Nuruu
Баянзурх Нуруу
The name of this range of peaks to the east of Ulaan Baatar means 'rich heart mountains'. There's a little forest at the top and views from the summit are good. You can reach the base of the mountains by taking the bus to Nalaikh and getting off before the women's prison. Of the four holy peaks, these are the least impressive.

TERELJ
ТуРуЛЖ
Terelj, about 80km north-east of Ulaan Baatar, is a deservedly popular destination. At 1600m, the area is cool and the alpine scenery is magnificent, and there are great opportunities for hiking, rock climbing, swimming (in icy water), rafting, horse riding and, for hard-core extreme sports fanatics, skiing in the depths of winter.

Terelj was first developed for tourism in 1964 and 30 years later it became part of the Gorkhi-Terelj National Park. To the north-east, the park joins onto the Khan Khentii Strictly Protected Area, comprising over 1.2 million hectares of the Töv, Selenge and Khentii aimags. The Khan Khentii park is almost completely uninhabited by humans, but it is home to **endangered species** of moose, brown bear and weasel, to name but a few, and to over 250 species of **birds**.

Parts of the tiny section of the Gorkhi-Terelj National Park developed for tourism are a bit touristy: some ger camps have concrete car parks, ugly electricity poles, TV antennae and discos at night; and locals overcharge for goods and services. But you can easily get away from all this if you want.

In later summer, the mosquitoes at Terelj can be appalling – at times, the worst in the country – so make sure you have insect repellent with you.

There is a daily T1000 entry fee for each person and T3000 for each car, which you'll have to pay at the entrance to the park, 6km from the main road, where a visitors centre is being built. If you don't enter on the normal road to Terelj, you should get a permit from the Protected Areas Bureau at the Ministry of Nature & Environment in Ulaan Baatar.

Gunjiin Süm
Гунжийн Сүм

Surrounded by magnificent forests, not far from the lovely river, the Baruun Bayan Gol, the temple was built in 1740 by Efu Dondovdorj to commemorate the death of his Manchurian wife Amarlangui. Once part of a huge monastery containing about 70 sq metres of blue walls, five other temples and a tower, Gunjiin Süm is one of the very few – if not the only – Manchurian-influenced temple in Mongolia to survive over the centuries.

Unlike most other monasteries in Mongolia, Gunjiin was not destroyed during the Stalinist purges, but just fell into ruin from neglect, vandalism and theft. Only the main temple, and some of the walls of the monastery, remain. Although you wouldn't know it, extensive restoration has been carried out – and is still being carried out – which gives you some idea of how damaged it must have been.

The temple is not a must – there are several better and more accessible temples and monasteries in Ulaan Baatar and Töv – it's more of an excuse for a great **overnight trek**, on horse or foot, from the ger camps

at Terelj, or as part of a longer trip around the national park.

Gunjiin is about 30km (as the crow flies) north of the main area where most of the ger camps are situated in Terelj. With a guide you can hike directly over the mountains, or take the easier but longer route along the Baruun Bayan Gol to get there. You can reach it in a day on horseback, while trekkers should allow two days each way for the journey.

Activities

Hiking If you have good maps, a compass and some experience (or a proper guide), hiking in Terelj is superb in summer, but be careful of the very fragile environment, and be aware of the mosquitoes and unpredictable weather. The fact that helicopters are sometimes used by travel agencies to start or finish treks in this area shows you how remote the terrain can be.

For more sedate **walks** around the Terelj ger camp area, just follow the main road and pick a side valley to stroll along at your leisure. From the main road, look out for two interesting rock formations: **Turtle Rock** (Melkhi Khad), in a side valley, which really looks like one at a certain angle, and the **Old Man Reading a Book**, on top of a hill.

Some suggested **easier hikes** are to Gunjiin Süm or along the Terelj or Tuul rivers towards Khentii Nuruu. This is a great area for wildflowers, particularly rhododendron and edelweiss.

Places of interest on more difficult, longer treks in Khentii Nuruu are:

Khagiin Khar Nuur A 20m-deep glacial lake, about 80km up the Tuul Gol from the ger camps at Terelj.
Yestii Hot Water Springs These springs reach up to 35°C, and are fed by the Yuroo and Estiin rivers. Yestii is about 18km north of Khagiin Khar Nuur.
Altan-Ölgii Uul (2656m) The source of the Akhain Gol.
Baga Khentii Nuuru North of Akhain Gol.

Horse Riding Travelling on a horse is the perfect way to see a lot of the park, including Gunjiin Süm and the side valleys of the

Tuul Gol. To travel any long distances, you will need to have experience, or a guide, and to bring most of your own gear. Horses can be hired through any of the ger camps, but you'll pay high tourist prices. A mob of horse boys hang outside the UB2 ger camp complex offering horse riding at US$5 per hour, or somewhere between US$12 and US$20 for the day. Alternatively, approach one of the Mongolian families who live around the park and hire one of their horses, though they may not be much cheaper.

Rafting Tuul Gol, which starts in the park and flows to Ulaan Baatar and beyond, is one of the best places in the country for rafting. The best section of the river is a 40km stretch from an area known as Dorgontiin Gatsaa, north of the Terelj ger camp area, to Gachuurt, near Ulaan Baatar. Boojum Expeditions runs rafting trips here (see Travel Agencies under Information in the Ulaan Baatar chapter).

Skiing If you're unlucky enough to be in Mongolia during the -30°C winter, and can stand leaving your heated hotel (if there hasn't been an electricity failure), you might as well make the most of it and enjoy some outstanding cross-country skiing around Terelj. There are no set trails, so just take your own gear and ask the locals, or any ger camps that are operating, for some good, safe areas to try.

Organised Tours

Most foreign travel companies and local agencies include a night or two in a tourist ger at Terelj in their organised tours. Several local agencies based in Ulaan Baatar, such as Terelj-Juulchin, Nomadic Journeys and Nomads run some of the more interesting trips around Terelj (see Travel Agencies under Information in the Ulaan Baatar chapter for more information).

Places to Stay

Camping Although the area around Terelj and the national park would appear to be a good place to camp, it's not actively encouraged by park authorities for several rea-

sons: the potential damage to the pristine environment; the genuine risk of forest fires from careless campers; and the fact that no money can be made from campers.

Unless you hike out into the hills it's best to get permission to camp, either from the nearest ger or, for a fee, a ger camp. Pitch your tent away from the main road, don't use wood fires and please take all of your rubbish out.

Ger Camps During the peak season of July and August (and at the more popular camps), it's not a bad idea to book ahead, although some places don't have telephones. Outside of the normal tourist season (July to September), it's also a good idea to ring ahead to make sure the camp is open and serves food. A few places are open in winter, catering mainly to expats who want to ski.

Most ger camps cater mainly for organised tours and may not be so interested in independent travellers, but it is certainly worth asking anyway. If you are the only guests at a camp you may have to find staff to open up the restaurant, showers etc. The ger camps offer almost identical facilities and prices – about US$40, including three good, Western meals, or US$10 without food.

Aside from the ger camps listed, many *individual families* rent out a spare ger, and/or hire horses, normally at cheaper rates than the ger camps. You'll have to ask around as none advertise.

Bolor, 10km along the main road from the park entrance, has pleasant gers for a negotiable T15,000 per ger, or T3500 per person; extra for food. They don't mind if you bring your own food. There's a large children's camp nearby.

Tsolmon (☎ 322 870), 13km along the main road from the park entrance, is in a beautiful secluded valley 3km east of the main road. Beds in a ger cost from US$12 to US$20, excluding food, depending on the number of people in a group. They also have beds in a cabin for between US$14 and US$24, for up to three people. Three meals cost a further US$18. All prices are per person.

Miraj (☎ *325 188)*, 14km along the main road from the park entrance, is in a good location for hiking. It charges US$17/10 per person with/without three meals. Horses cost US$5 per hour or US$10 per day. Hot showers are available.

Gorkhi, 15km along the main road from the park entrance, is in a lovely secluded valley, 5km west of the main road, past Turtle Rock and the Javkhlant childrens' camp. Prices are US$22/12 with/without three meals. A monastery is being built nearby.

Temuujinin Otog (☎ *456 087)*, also known as Naiman Sharga, is easy to identify by the huge, concrete dinosaurs out the front. It's a bit overpriced at US$30 per person with three meals and hot shower, or US$20 without meals, but it's a good place to stop if you have kids. It's 15.5km along the main road from the park entrance.

San, 18.5km along the main road, is aimed more at Mongolian visitors, which is good as it's cheaper at US$5 per person in a ger or simple hotel room, plus an additional US$12 for three meals. There's nice hiking nearby but no hot showers.

Terelj-Juulchin (☎ *324 978)*, jointly run by Juulchin, is a huge complex on the main road – you can't miss it. The camp looks like a few gers set up in the middle of a car park, but the camp facilities are good (hot shower, sauna, restaurant), or you can stay at the comfortable hotel nearby. Gers cost US$14 per person, basic cabins cost US$10 per person and pleasant rooms cost around US$14 per person. It's 25.5km from the park entrance.

UB2 (☎ *309 016)* is a large hotel complex at the end of the road, 27km from the park entrance, next to the village of Terelj. Beds in a ger cost T5600 or you can get a room for T11,300 per person. Deluxe rooms cost T22,600/33,900 for a single/double. It has a good restaurant.

In addition to the ger camps, the Khan Khentii Protected Areas Administration is running a pilot *'ecoger'* project. Three gers have been set up further in the park at Sain Ovoo (the junction of the Tuul and Baruun Bayan rivers), Buutiin Khoshuu (in the Baruun Bayan Valley) and Khalzangiin Adag, further up the Tuul Gol. The gers are around 10km apart so it's possible to hike or ride between them to create a multi-day trip.

The gers cost US$20 per person and food is extra. Horses are available for rent at a reasonable US$5 per day, plus US$5 for a guide. The money goes to local income-generating projects and conservation efforts. For details of the project in Ulaan Baatar contact T Selenge (☎ 329 323, **e** gtznaturecom@magicnet.mn).

Nomadic Journeys run the remote and low-impact *Jalman Meadows* ger camp in the upper Tuul Valley, which makes a good base if you are headed to Khagiin Khar Nuur, an eight-hour horse ride away. Four-day packages from Ulaan Baatar, including transfers, cost a reasonable US$165 per person.

Getting There & Away

Bus The road from Ulaan Baatar to Terelj, which goes through part of the national park, is in pretty good nick. Buses depart Ulaan Baatar's long distance bus station daily at 3 pm, returning to the capital from near the UB2 ger camp at around 8 am. If this doesn't pan out you'll have to hitch.

Taxi A taxi from Ulaan Baatar is easy to organise; jeeps aren't necessary because the road is paved all the way. You should only pay the standard rate per kilometre, which works out at about US$25 one way, but the driver may understandably want more because his taxi may be empty for part of the return journey. You can also arrange with your taxi to pick you up later. Try to share the cost of the taxi with other travellers.

When there's enough demand, shared taxis to Terelj sometimes leave from the long-distance bus station in Ulaan Baatar. This is more likely on summer Sundays when locals make a day-trip to the area.

Hitching Hitching *out* of Ulaan Baatar can be difficult because vehicles going out to Terelj could leave from anywhere; try asking around the truck stations. The cheapest way to hitch to Terelj is to take the bus to Baganuur or Nalaikh and get off at the turnoff to Terelj, where you are far more likely to get a lift.

Hitching *back* to Ulaan Baatar from along the main road through Terelj is not difficult, as almost every vehicle is returning to the capital.

Bicycle A mountain bike would be an excellent way of getting around some of Terelj if you could stand the 80km of uphill riding to get there and cope with the traffic in Ulaan Baatar along the way. Karakorum Expeditions in Ulaan Baatar are the only outfit to rent bicycles (US$25 per day).

KHANDGAIT
ХАНДГАЙТ

About 40km north of Ulaan Baatar, Khandgait is another lovely area of cow pastures, small mountains, pine forests and wildflowers, surrounding the small village of the same name. Like Terelj, there are plenty of opportunities for hiking, rock climbing, fishing in the nearby Selbe Gol and, in winter, ice-skating and cross-country skiing (it's possible to rent skis and sleds here in winter).

Khandgait is a cheaper and less touristy alternative to Terelj but, because of this, Khandgait suffers from a lack of transport and good facilities. Khandgait is not part of a national park, so no permit is required.

The first half of the road between Ulaan Baatar and Khandgait is paved; the second half is reasonably rough. The road goes past Khandgait and continues north to smaller, lovelier and more secluded valleys.

On the road to Khandgait, you'll pass hundreds of wooden huts built in a haphazard fashion around the valleys. These were used by residents of Ulaan Baatar as summer houses – somewhere cool and quiet to escape the heat. However, with the advent of capitalism, many Mongolians are now poorer and can no longer afford the huts, so most of them lay abandoned. (They cannot be used by travellers.)

Places to Stay

This is great countryside for *camping*. Just pick any site, preferably near a river, and enjoy; but be careful about wood fires and make sure to take your rubbish out.

To find somewhere to stay, get off your taxi, truck or minibus at any group of *cabins* or *huts* that haven't been abandoned and ask the caretaker if you can stay. If you are unsuccessful, then hike one or 2km to the next group of *huts* along or just off the main road.

Getting There & Away

Minibus There is no scheduled public transport to Khandgait, but if you hang around long enough at the truck stop south of the Container Market on the corner of Khuldaany Gudamj and Ikh Toiruu in Ulaan Baatar, you may be lucky enough to catch a public minibus bound for Sharga Morit, about 5km before Khandgait. Otherwise, take bus No 16 to the Zendmene terminal in the north of Ulaan Baatar and try to get a shared minibus further north. If that fails, you may need to hitch.

Taxi A taxi (jeeps aren't necessary) from Ulaan Baatar is easiest but, naturally, more expensive at around US$25 return, plus waiting time. You can arrange for the taxi to pick you up later.

Hitching Hitching *to* Khandgait from Ulaan Baatar is almost impossible. But it is fairly easy to hitch a ride *from* Khandgait within an hour or two – just about every vehicle going along the main road at Khandgait is going to Ulaan Baatar.

GACHUURT
ГАЧУУРТ

East of Ulaan Baatar, the village of Gachuurt is nothing special but the area near the village is delightful. If you're tired of the comparative hustle and bustle of UB and crave some serenity and clean air, Gachuurt is definitely the place for you. You can hire horses from nearby gers, catch fish, and go rafting in the Tuul Gol (check out Boojum Expeditions or Nomadic Journeys in Ulaan Baatar), hike in the nearby valleys, and camp anywhere you want. And all of this is only 21km from Ulaan Baatar.

There is no hotel or restaurant in the village, so bring your own food and tent if you want to stay nearby. About 2km before the

Takhi – The Reintroduction of a Species

The Mongolian wild horse is probably the most recognised and successful symbol of the preservation and protection of Mongolia's diverse and unique wildlife. The *takhi*, also known as the Przewalski horse (named after the Polish explorer who first 'discovered' the horse in 1878), used to roam the countryside in great herds.

They finally became extinct after poachers killed them for meat, and overgrazing and development reduced their fodder and breeding grounds. The last wild Mongolian takhi was spotted in the western Gobi in 1969.

At that time, only about a dozen takhi remained alive, living in zoos in Russia and Europe. Special breeding programs in Australia, Germany, Switzerland and the Netherlands have brought the numbers of takhi outside of Mongolia to about 1500. The entire global population of takhi are now descended from the bloodline of three stallions and so computerised records have been introduced to avoid inbreeding.

Between 1992 and 2000, with assistance from international environmental agencies, takhi were reintroduced into Mongolia at Khustai Nuruu, and Takhiin Tal, in the south Gobi. Today there are currently 107 takhi in Khustai and 59 in Takhiin Tal.

The takhi are the last remaining wild horse worldwide, the forerunner of the domestic horse, as depicted in cave paintings in France. They are not simply horses that have become feral, or wild, as found in the USA or Australia, but a genetically different species, boasting two extra chromosomes in their DNA make-up. The takhi are sandy coloured except for a dark dorsal stripe. The tail and legs are dark and the legs have zebra stripes. The skull and jaw is heavier than a horse's, there is no forelock and the mane is short and erect.

New arrivals are kept in enclosures for a year to help them adapt to a new climate. The laws of nature are allowed to run their course; an average of five foals are killed by wolves every year in Khustai. The park gets locals onside by hiring herders as rangers, offering cheap loans to others and offering employment at the park's cheese-making factory on the outskirts of the park.

CENTRAL MONGOLIA

village there are plenty of serene spots to pitch your tent – just look for somewhere nice from the window of your bus or taxi.

The new Japanese-Mongolian ger camp called **Daisogen** (*☎/fax 358 373)* is in a great location along the river. The cost is US$45 per person, including meals.

A small *ger camp*, 3km up the Tuul Gol from town, was set up in late summer 2000 by a German woman and her Mongolian husband. Beds cost around US$5 per person and you can hire horses for US$10 per day. Contact Gana's Guest House in Ulaan Baatar for details.

Getting There & Away

Buses pick up passengers every hour or so from the east end of Peace Ave, near the Jukov statue, a couple of kilometres east of the city centre, bound for Gachuurt. You can also easily get a taxi from Ulaan Baatar. The paved road continues past Gachuurt,

up the Gachuurt Gol as far as Sansar, but public transport doesn't go this far.

KHUSTAI NATIONAL PARK

ХУСТАЙН НУРУУ

Established in 1993, this park, also known as Khustai Nuruu (Birch Mountain Range), is about 100km south-west of Ulaan Baatar. The 50,620 hectare reserve protects the *takhi*, Mongolia's wild horse, and its steppe and forest-steppe environment. In addition to the takhi, there are populations of maral (Asiatic red deer), steppe gazelle, deer, boar, manul wild cat, wolf and lynx. A visit to the park has become a popular overnight excursion from Ulaan Baatar in recent years.

Entry to the park is a one-time fee of US$5 (T500 for locals). It's worth spending at least one night in the park, as you are most likely to see takhi and other wildlife at dusk or dawn.

The park is run by the Mongolian Association for the Conservation of Nature and the Environment (MACNE), with the cooperation of the Foundation Reserves for the Przewalski Horse (FRPH) and the support of the Dutch government.

To book accommodation contact MACNE (☎/fax 321 426, e macne@magicnet.mn) in Ulaan Baatar. The office is hard to find, in Flat 4, 2nd floor, Building 28, in an apartment block south-west of the Bayangol Hotel, so ring first.

Orientation & Information

The information centre at the entrance to Khustai National Park has a ger with displays on the park and the takhi horse, as well as a small souvenir shop. Ten kilometres south into the park's core area is the former park headquarters, where there is a takhi enclosure. Another 10km or so west is the Moilt camp, where there is cabin-style accommodation.

Things to Do

The park is starting to offer horse riding, hiking, jeep excursions and fishing in an effort to make the park self-financing. Several hiking routes have been established. One good **hike** takes you from the visitors centre to Moilt camp in about four to five hours.

A good **horse riding trip** takes you to some Turkic graves in the south-east of the park and then on to the Tuul Gol. Horse rental is US$10 per day. Contact the park for details.

With your own jeep you can drive to the Moilt camp, stopping at **takhi enclosures** en route. Park regulations require you to take a park guide and stick only to existing tracks.

Wildlife watching is best at dusk and at dawn. One of the best places to head for is the Tuul Gol, where **takhi** usually come to drink in the evening.

The park runs a three-week eco-volunteer program where you pay to help with research. See the Web site at www.ecovolunteer.org or contact Samar Magic Tours for details (see Travel Agencies under Information in the Ulaan Baatar chapter).

Places to Stay

Camping on your own is not allowed inside the park so have to camp outside the park boundary.

There is a small *ger camp* at the entrance to the park, which costs US$15 per person, plus another US$15 for three meals. Rooms are available in the main building for US$20 per person. There are also *cabins* at the Moilt camp.

Getting There & Away

To get to the park you have to travel 100km west of Ulaan Baatar, along the road to Kharkhorin, where there is a signpost pointing you the 10km south to the park entrance. There is no scheduled transportation to the park. You could hitch or take a bus to the the turn-off and walk.

NAIRAMDAL ZUSLAN

НАЙРАМДАЛ ЗУСЛАН

Only 30km from Ulaan Baatar in the lovely Bayangol Valley, the Nairamdal Zuslan International Children's Centre (☎ 332 776) is an interesting alternative to Terelj. It may be full of hundreds of screaming kids from all over the world in summer, but you can easily avoid them and enjoy the serenity of the countryside.

Built in the 1970s, the centre was the brainchild of Filatova, the powerful Russian wife of former Communist leader, Tsedenal. The idea was to enhance Mongolia's prestige by hosting international summer youth exchange programs with both Eastern bloc and Western countries. (*nairamdal* means 'friendship' in Mongolian).

The centre contains buildings constructed in styles from Central Asia, Latin America, Scandinavia and the Balkans. The *hotel* is palatial, the rooms are spotless and the staff are courteous.

You can enjoy some **cultural displays**, **archery** competitions and **horse riding** during the day, and in the winter, **cross-country skiing** is as good at as Terelj.

The centre (which is open all year) is sometimes full in July and August, so it's worth ringing ahead. Prices are high – they range from US$15 to US$30 for children and US$40 to US$80 for adults – but include all meals, guides and transport from the city. Nonguests are not particularly welcome, but you can have a look if you've got your own vehicle.

NALAIKH
НАЛАЙХ

The poor village of Nalaikh, 35km southeast of the capital, is part of the Ulaan Baatar autonomous municipality because it once jointly supplied the capital city with its coal. Coal is now primarily supplied by Baganuur; Nalaikh's coal mine has closed down, leaving the place with little purpose. There's little reason to visit except to see a **Kazakh community**.

In the 1950s many Kazakhs from Bayan-Ölgii were 'persuaded' to work in Nalaikh's mine, only to see the mine completely close down in 1990 when the Russians left.

To find Nalaikh's **mosque**, face the bright-blue town hall, turn 180° and walk about 25 minutes over a small hill. The mosque is a disappointment if you have been to Kazakhstan or other Central Asian countries.

Crowded buses leave Ulaan Baatar every 30 minutes (45 minutes, T230) during the day.

AROUND NALAIKH

Around 17km south-east of Nalaikh is an 8th century Turkic **stele of Tonyukuk**. The stele is covered in runic script and there are *balbal* (stone figures) and grave slabs nearby.

To get there you'll need your own transport. Drive south-east from Nalaikh, following the track south of the military airfield towards Janchivian (careful – there

A kid's best friend – the humble camel

are two villages by this name within 30km of each other!). Just past the last hangar, isolated from the others, you drop down a hill to the small enclosure.

Övörkhangai
Өвөрхангай

pop 118,400 • area 63,000 sq km

Övörkhangai contains what is probably Mongolia's most popular attraction: the magnificent monastery Erdene Zuu Khiid, built from the ruins of the ancient Mongol capital of Karakorum (now the modern town of Kharkhorin). Övörkhangai means 'south Khangai', a reference to the spectacular mountains of central Mongolia known as the Khangai Nuruu, which dominate the north-western part of Övörkhangai. The southern part of the aimag, past Arvaikheer, is uninteresting desert steppe. The main ethnic group is the Khalkh.

If travelling by rented jeep, it is easy to combine a visit to Kharkhorin with other places clustered near the borders of Arkhangai, Bulgan and Töv aimags: Khogno Khan Uul, the Mongol Els sand dunes, the Batkhaan Uul Natural Reserve, Shankh Khiid and the waterfall, Orkhon Khürkhree. The paved road, which reaches Kharkhorin and the aimag capital of Arvaikheer, is also a definite attraction – but the road to the waterfall Orkhon Khürkhree is often atrocious.

ARVAIKHEER
АРВАЙХ‍Ү‍Р
elevation 1913m

A nondescript but friendly aimag capital, Arvaikheer is of little interest except as a place to eat and rest, refuel the jeep or arrange onward public transport to places further west. Arvaikheer has the requisite hotel, bar, cinema, school and administrative building, and the monastery and museum are worth a look.

There is no need to go to Arvaikheer if you only want to visit Kharkhorin and other sights in northern Övörkhangai, as a paved road reaches Kharkhorin from Ulaan Baatar.

CENTRAL MONGOLIA

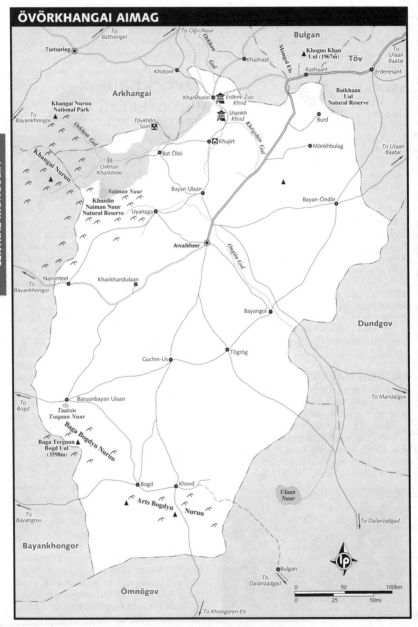

ÖVÖRKHANGAI AIMAG

To Battsengel
To Ogii Nuur
Bulgan
To Ulaan Baatar

Tsetserleg

Khashaat

Khogno Khan
Uul (1967m)

Töv

Khotont

Rashaant

Erdenesant

Arkhangai

Kharkhorin

Erdene Zuu
Khiid

Batkhaan
Uul
Natural Reserve

Khangai Nuruu
National Park

To
Bayanhongor

Orkhon Gol

Tövkhön
Süm

Shankh
Khiid

Burd

Khujirt

To Ulaan
Baatar

Khangai Nuruu

Bat Ölzii

Mönkhbulag

Orkhon
Khürkhree

Naiman Nuur

Bayan Ulaan

Khuislin
Naiman Nuur
Natural Reserve

Uyanaga

Bayan-Öndör

Arvaikheer

Ongiin Gol

Nariynteel

Khairkhandulaan

To
Bayankhongor

Bayangol

Dundgov

Tögrög

Guchin-Us

To Mandalgov

Baruunbayan Ulaan

To
Bogd

Taatsin
Tsagaan Nuur

Baga Bogdyn Nuruu

Baga Terguun
Bogd Uul
(3598m)

Bogd

Khovd

Ulaan
Nuur

To Dalanzadgad

To
Bayangovi

Arts Bogdyn

Nuruu

Bayankhongor

Bulgan

To
Dalanzadgad

Ömnögov

0   50   100km

0   25   50mi

To Khongoryn Els

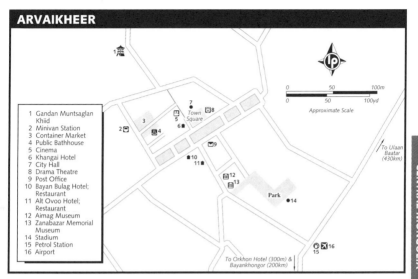

ARVAIKHEER

1 Gandan Muntsaglan
   Khiid
2 Minivan Station
3 Container Market
4 Public Bathhouse
5 Cinema
6 Khangai Hotel
7 City Hall
8 Drama Theatre
9 Post Office
10 Bayan Bulag Hotel;
   Restaurant
11 Alt Ovoo Hotel;
   Restaurant
12 Aimag Museum
13 Zanabazar Memorial
   Museum
14 Stadium
15 Petrol Station
16 Airport

Information

The public bath house, just south of the market, is the place for a hot shower (T300). It's *theoretically* open daily, except Tuesday, from 10 am to 9 pm (though it was shut when we begged for a shower at 3 pm on a Wednesday).

The bustling daily container market is just north-east of the centre and has yoghurt, airag (after June) and sheepskins, as well as the normal range of packaged foods.

Gandan Muntsaglan Khiid

Гандан Мунтсаглан Хийд

This comparatively large monastery, about 300m north of the town square, contains a fine collection of scroll paintings *(thangka)*, including one depicting the original monastery, which was destroyed in 1937. The current monastery was opened in 1991, and now has about 50 monks in residence. Visitors are welcome. To the left of the temple is a small **shop** selling religious items.

Museums

Since Övörkhangai lies partly in the forested Khangai region and the Gobi Desert, the **Aimag Museum** boasts a better-than-average selection of stuffed mountain and desert animals. There are also some fossils and arrows, local artwork and leftovers from Karakorum. Upstairs are intricate carvings.

Just around the corner is the **Zanabazar Memorial Museum**, which has a collection of religious artwork connected to the master sculptor.

Both museums open from 9 am to noon and 2 to 6 pm weekdays. Tickets cost T1000 and photography is a ludicrous T10,000 per shot.

Places to Stay

Camping Like most aimag capitals, camping is a better option than the dreary hotels, but in Arvaikheer you'll have to walk a kilometre or so to find a quiet place to pitch your tent. It's best to head out to the area north of the monastery or drive 5km south to the Ongiin Gol.

Hotels The *Khangai Hotel* looked like it had just been hit with a scud missile when we visited, though apparently it was actually under restoration. It's due to reopen by the end of 2000 as the biggest hotel in town.

The **Bayan Bulag Hotel** has five clean, carpeted but overpriced rooms for US$15 per person. The bathrooms are a bit grim and there's no hot water. The attached restaurant is pretty good, though, and serves its own Bayan Brau beer.

The privately-run **Alt Ovoo Hotel** (☎ 236 55, 237 55) has standard three-bed rooms with a common bathroom for US$15 person. If the hotel isn't busy solo travellers should be able to pay for just one bed; at other times you'll have to pay for at least two beds. Half-deluxe and deluxe rooms with bathroom and shower cost US$25/30 per person. Hot water comes on for a couple of hours in the morning and evening – check the times with reception. The place is clean and bright but overpriced so try for a discount.

A better value but more inconvenient choice is the **Orkhon Hotel**, out on the edge of town near the main road. Beds in a dormitory or double room cost between T3800 and T4200, with an extra T500 for a hot shower in the common bathroom. Deluxe rooms cost T12,000 and come with a hot shower and toilet.

Places to Eat

The **restaurants** at the Bayan Bulag and Alt Ovoo hotels are both good but you'll need to give them a couple of hours' advance notice. You can try the **Khangai Hotel** when it reopens. Otherwise there are plenty of **guanz** and **noodle stalls** (tsuivan gazar) near the market.

Getting There & Away

You can travel quickly along the 430km paved road between Ulaan Baatar and Arvaikheer. (There are plenty of guanz along the way.) The paved road finishes just west of Arvaikheer; from there it is about another 200km along the usual rough road, with the occasional collapsed bridge, to the next aimag capital of Bayankhongor. With a jeep, an experienced driver and lots of time you could venture south to Dalanzadgad, 377km away in Ömnögov aimag, either via Saikhan-Ovoo or, more adventurously, via Guchin Us, Hovd and Khongoryn Els.

Air MIAT is scheduled to fly between Ulaan Baatar and Arvaikheer every Monday for US$60/106, en route to/from Bayankhongor. The airport is less than 1km south of town.

Minivans Minivans and smaller microbuses run along the paved road between Arvaikheer and Ulaan Baatar every day except Sunday (seven hours, T9000). Look for them just east of the market. Post office vans run to Kharkhorin every Wednesday and Friday from the post office.

Jeep If you want to hire a jeep to see the sights around northern Övörkhangai, it's better to catch a bus to Kharkhorin and hire a jeep there, rather than go to Arvaikheer. Shared and charter jeeps are rare in Arvaikheer, but you could try around the market. You can also hire a motorbike and sidecar for shorter trips.

Hitching The Ulaan Baatar-Arvaikheer road is one of the busiest in the country – at least one vehicle goes in both directions every minute. Hitching a ride on a truck or in a private car should be comparatively easy. Going further west along the main road to Bayankhongor won't be as easy, but it is possible. In Arvaikheer, trucks hang around the market, so try there or at the petrol station on the main road.

KHARKHORIN (KARAKORUM)
ХАРХОРИН (КАРАКОРУМ)

In 1220 Chinggis Khaan decided to move his capital from the Onon Valley in Khentii to Karakorum, 373km south-west of modern-day Ulaan Baatar. Building only began after Chinggis' death by his son Ögedei Khaan. Karakorum served as the political, cultural and economic capital of the Mongols for only 40 years, before Kublai Khaan moved it to Khanbalik, in what is now Beijing.

Following the move to Beijing, and the subsequent collapse of the Mongolian empire, Karakorum was abandoned and then destroyed by vengeful Manchurian soldiers in 1388. Whatever was left of Karakorum was used to help build Erdene Zuu Khiid in

The Ancient Capital

Hardly a single stone remains of ancient Karakorum, the Mongol capital, but an intriguing picture can be painted using contemporary accounts of visiting missionaries ambassadors and travellers.

The city was situated at the crossroads of trade routes and was surrounded by walls with four gates; each had its own market, selling grain in the east, goats in the west, oxen and wagons in the south and horses in the north.

The surrounding town of gers was an impressive sight, though the missionary William of Rubruck (1215–1295) dismissed the city as no bigger than the suburb of Saint Denis in Paris. Giovanni de Piano Carpine (1180–1252), an envoy sent to the Mongols in 1245 by Pope Innocent IV, described the city vaguely as 'at the distance of a year's walk' from Rome. Marco Polo gave a brief description of the city, though he never made it there.

The Mongol khaans were famed for their religious tolerance and split their time equally between all the religions; hence twelve different religions co-existed within the town. Mosques, Buddhist monasteries and Nestorian Christian churches competed for the Mongol's souls. Even powerful figures such as Ögedei's wife and Khublai's mother were Nestorian Christians.

The centrepiece of the city was the Tumen Amgalan, or Palace of Worldly Peace, in the southwest corner of the city. This 2500 sq metre complex, built in 1235, was the palace of Ögedei Khaan. The two-storey palace had a vast reception hall for receiving ambassadors, and its 64 pillars resembled the nave of a church. The walls were painted, the green-tiled floor had underfloor heating, and the Chinese-style roof was covered in green and red tiles. Whenever he was at court, the khaan sat on a panther skin atop a great throne, to which stairs ascended from one side and descended from the other. You can see a model of the palace in the Museum of Mongolian History in Ulaan Baatar.

The most memorable highlight of the city was a fountain designed in 1253 by the French jeweller and sculptor Guillaume Bouchier (or Bouchee) of Paris, who had been captured by the Mongols in Hungary and brought back to embellish Karakorum. The fountain was in the shape of a huge silver tree, which simultaneously dispensed mare's milk from silver lion's heads, and wine, rice wine, *bal* (mead) and airag from four golden spouts shaped like snake heads. On top of the tree was an angel. On order a servant blew a pipe like a bugle that extended from the angel's mouth, giving the order for other servants to pump drinks out of the tree.

Mongolian noblemen lived in the north of town, near the Orkhon Gol. Rubruck disparagingly describes various pleasure domes and epic feasts (during one of which the Mongol guests guzzled 105 cartloads of alcohol). There were also quarters of craftsmen and traders, populated by a great mix of people brought back to Karakorum from all over Asia. So cosmopolitan was the city that both foreign and Mongol coins were legal tender.

the 16th century, which itself was badly damaged during the Stalinist purges.

There is virtually nothing left of Karakorum; the neglected modern town of Kharkhorin (and its huge flour factory) was built on the same spot. It is, however, the hidden history of Karakorum and the restored temples at Erdene Zuu Khiid that justifiably attract visitors.

There are calls to transfer Mongolia's capital from Ulaan Baatar to Kharkhorin between 2020 and 2030, to echo the 800th anniversary of Chinggis' transfer of the Mongol capital from 1220–1236. Who knows, in 30 years the sleepy town of Kharkhorin may just become Mongolia's version of Brasilia, Canberra or Islamabad.

Information

Kharkhorin has surprisingly few tourist facilities (most groups stay in ger camps in the surrounding countryside). A container market *(khudaldaany töv)* in the centre of the town has most things you might need.

The Kharkhorin Community Information Centre is trying to set up an email service on the first floor of the government building in the old town square, about 1km from the market.

The public bath house, next to the market on the main central road, is open from 10 am to 8 pm weekends. Showers cost T300.

Erdene Zuu Khiid

Үрдэнэ Зуу Хийд

Erdene Zuu (Hundred Treasures) was the first Buddhist monastery in Mongolia. The monastery was started in 1586 by Abtai Khaan, but wasn't entirely finished until about 300 years later. It had between 60 and 100 temples, about 300 gers were set up inside the walls and, at its height, up to 1000 monks were in residence.

Like Karakorum, the monastery was abandoned and then vandalised by invading Manchus. Attempts at restoration were made in about 1760 and, again, in 1808 under the direction of the famous architect Manzshir, but then came the Stalinist purges of the 1930s. All but three of the temples in Erdene Zuu were destroyed and an unknown number of monks were either killed or shipped off to Siberia and never heard from again.

However, a surprising number of statues, tsam masks and scroll paintings were saved from the monastery at the time of the purges – possibly with the help of a few sympathetic military officers. These were buried in nearby mountains, or stored in local homes (at great risk to the residents). Sadly the statues are still not safe: a security system was installed in the monastery halls in early 2000 after several statues were stolen.

The monastery remained closed until 1965 when it was permitted to reopen as a museum, but not as a place of worship. It was only with the collapse of communism in 1990 that religious freedom was restored and the monastery became active again. Today, Erdene Zuu Khiid still retains much of its former glory, though no doubt it's a shadow of what it once was. Restoration of the monastery is one of Mongolia's top cultural projects, but few funds are available from the government or international agencies.

Temples The monastery is enclosed in an immense walled compound. Spaced evenly along each wall, about every 15m, are 108 stupas (108 is a sacred number to Buddhists). The three temples in the compound, which were not destroyed in the 1930s, are dedicated to the three stages of Buddha's life: childhood, adolescence and adulthood. See the boxed text 'Important Figures of Tibetan Buddhism' in the Facts about Mongolia chapter for a brief description of some of the gods you will see in the monastery.

Dalai Lama Süm was built to commemorate the visit by Abtai Khaan's son, Altan, to the Dalai Lama in Tibet in 1675. The room is bare save for a statue of Zanabazar and some fine 17th-century scroll paintings depicting the dalai lamas and various protector deities.

Inside the courtyard, the temple to the west, built by Abtai Khaan and his son, is dedicated to the adult Buddha. Inside, on either side of Sakyamuni (the historical Buddha), are statues of Sanjaa (Sanskrit: Dipamkara), the past Buddha, to the left; and Maidar (Sanskrit: Maitreya), the future Buddha, to the right. Other items on display include some golden 'wheels of eternity', *naimin takhel* (the eight auspicious symbols), figurines from the 17th and 18th centuries, and *balin* (wheat dough cakes, decorated with coloured medallions of goat or mutton fat), made in 1965 and still well preserved. Look out for the inner circumambulation path leading off to the left, just by the entrance.

The main and central temple is called the **Zuu of Buddha**. The entrance is flanked by the gods Gonggor on the left and Bandal Lham (Sanskrit: Palden Lhamo) on the right. Inside, on either side of the statues of the child Buddha, are (to the right) Otoch Manal, the Medicine Buddha and (to the left) Holy Abida, the god of justice. The temple also contains statues of Niam and Dabaa, the sun and moon gods respectively, a few of the tsam masks that survived the purges, some carved, aggressive looking guards from the 16th and 17th centuries, and some displays of the work of the revered sculptor and Buddhist, Zanabazar.

In the temple to the east, there's a statue depicting the adolescent Buddha. The statue on the right is Tsongkhapa, who founded the yellow Hat sect of Buddhism in Tibet. The figure on the left is Janraisig (Tibetan: Chenresig; Sanskrit: Avalokitesvara), the bodhisattva of compassion.

As you walk north you will pass the **Golden Prayer Stupa**, built in 1799. The temple next to this is said to be the first temple built at Erdene Zuu. Look out for the **mandala** on the ceiling.

The large white temple at the far end is the Tibetan-style **Lavrin Süm**, where ceremonies are held every morning.

Apart from the main temples, there are several other interesting things to see. The **gravestones** of Abtai Khaan (1554–1588) and his grandson Tüshet Khaan Gombodorj (the father of Zanabazar) stand in front of the Dalai Lama Süm and are inscribed in Mongol, Chinese, Tibetan and Arabic scripts. In the north-east of the monastery are the base stones of a gigantic ger (now called the **Square of Happiness and Prosperity**), set up in 1639 to commemorate Zanabazar's birthday. The ger was reported to be 15m high and 45m in diameter, with 35 concertina-style walls, and could seat 300 during the annual assemblies of the local khaans. The hollow of what was once an artificial lake can be seen next to the foundations.

Entrance to the monastery grounds (open 9 am to 9 pm daily) is free. If you want to see inside the temples, however, you'll have to go to the administration office on your left as you enter the grounds from the south and buy a ticket for T3000, which includes a guided tour of the site. The museum is open from 9 am to 6 pm daily. The monastery is an easy 2km walk from the centre of Kharkhorin.

Ceremonies in Lavrin Süm usually start at around 11 am, though the times vary so ask at the office. Visitors are welcome, but photographs during ceremonies are not. A shop next to the administration office sells some good but expensive souvenirs.

There is a US$5 charge to take photographs inside the temple, while using a video camera costs US$10. Outside of the temples, you may take as many photos as you wish.

Turtle Rocks

Outside the monastery walls are two 'turtle rocks'. Four of these sculptures once marked the boundaries of ancient Karakorum, acting as protectors of the city (turtles are considered symbols of eternity). The turtles originally had an inscribed stone stele mounted vertically on their back.

One is easy to find: just walk out of the northern gate of the monastery and follow the path north-west for about 300m. Often, an impromptu **souvenir market** is set up here next to the turtle rock. You'll need a guide or directions to find the other turtle rock.

Phallic Rock

If you have some time, it is worth looking for the bizarre 'phallic rock', which points erotically to something interestingly called a 'vaginal slope'. It is surrounded by a stone fence, hidden up a small valley, and visible from the main road to Ulaan Baatar, about 1km from Kharkhorin. It's a 30- or 40-minute walk from Erdene Zuu Khiid. You will have to ask for exact directions at the monastery, or at your hotel, that is if you can describe in Mongolian what you want to see (and exactly why!).

Legend has it that the rock was placed here in an attempt to stop frisky monks, filled with lust by the shapely slope, from fraternising with the local women.

Places to Stay

Camping It's very easy to find a perfect camping spot along the Orkhon Gol, only a kilometre or two from Kharkhorin. From the road heading out west, turn left before the bridge and walk or drive a kilometre or so to a small island in the river, which is perfect for camping.

Hotels There are surprisingly few places to stay in Kharkhorin because most travellers stay in upmarket ger camps. Sometimes the water supplies in Kharkhorin are not reliable.

CENTRAL MONGOLIA

Bayan Burd (☎ 2315), meaning 'rich steppe', is 400m north-east of the market; look for the red sign. Beds in a clean room with a shared bathroom cost US$6 per person, or US$15 for a deluxe with private bathroom. There's a sauna in the basement that costs T2500 per person per hour.

Möngön Mod (☎ 2777), which means 'silver tree', has smoky triples for T4000 per person and excellent value doubles, with hot shower for T5000 per person.

A woman called Monkhsuuri runs a private *guesthouse* (☎ 2031) in the suburbs north-west of the market. Beds in a ger cost US$5 per person, inclusive of breakfast and dinner. There's a washbasin (the owner can boil up hot water) and basic pit toilet. Monkhsuuri works as a guide at Erdene Zuu and is most easily contacted there.

The rough and ready *Zon Hotel* (☎ 2945), next to the Möngön Möd Hotel, has basic rooms with a washbasin and pit toilet for T3000 per person.

Ger Camps Seven kilometres north of town past the airstrip, there are three large ger camps, *Kharkhorum*, *Khan Bayan* and *Oggodei*, all within 1km of each other. All are fairly charm-free and cater to groups for about US$30 per person, including meals.

The second bunch of camps are in a better location south-west of town. The first of these is the *Daniel Ger Camp*, the cheapest of the bunch, and the only one aimed at independent travellers. Beds in one of the five gers are good value at US$4. There's a solar-heated shower.

Continuing away from town, next comes the *Nomin* camp, which costs around US$15 with meals.

The next one you come to is the *Orhon Hotel*, along the Orkhon Gol, which might be worth a splurge. The hotel has nice rooms and gers, set in a lovely wooded area, for around US$35 per person, with meals. You can see the hotel from the main road as you head west.

The *Anar* (☎ 2376), the furthest camp, has a great location in the south-west corner of the valley, where there is plenty of walking and horse riding opportunities. The

camp charges US$35 per person, or US$25 without meals.

The *Khublai Khan* camp is up on a hill to the south-east of town and charges US$30, including meals.

There are a couple of camps out of town on the road to the monastery, Shankh Khiid. In a nice location in a lush valley, the *Chandmam* camp charges US$30 per person, including meals, and offers a few interesting gimmicks like how-to exhibitions on making a ger and wearing traditional costumes. The camp is about 18km from Kharkhorin, on the main road to Khujirt.

The *Möngön Möd* camp, a couple of kilometres away, offers much the same deal for US$35, but has better service and is one of the better ger camps in the region.

Places to Eat
The best bet is to eat in your hotel or ger camp, or cook if you're camping. Otherwise there are some *guanz* at the entrance to the container market, which offer decent khuurshuur and goulash dishes.

On the main road, the *Naran Restaurant* is the town's main restaurant and *might* have food, *if* it's open.

The *Möngön Mod Hotel* has a nice restaurant, which can cook up meals if you give it an hour's warning.

Getting There & Away
Air MIAT has occasional flights in summer between Ulaan Baatar and Kharkhorin for US$53/92. The landing strip is 3km from Kharkhorin, so you can either walk or take a jeep, if available.

Minivan Minivans run daily to Ulaan Baatar (eight hours, T8000) from the container market, leaving sometime after 8 am, whenever they are full. As the road is all but sealed, this is one of the more bearable long-distance bus trips in the countryside. In summer, it's best to book a ticket the day before departure, if that's possible.

A post office van runs every Wednesday and Friday afternoon to Khujirt (T1500) and Arvaikheer (T4500). Inquire at the post office for details.

Taking a fresh milk break

The pride of the Mongolian nomad – the horse

A *ger* camp near Ulaan Baatar

Too cute: a herder's son with lamb, Töv aimag

Gutul (boots) – perfect for surviving the winter

Trained eagles are used by the Kazakhs to hunt marmots, foxes and wolves during winter.

BRADLEY MAYHEW

Khar Nuur, shadowed by the 3943m-high Tsengel Khairkhan Uul, Bayan-Ölgii

BRADLEY MAYHEW

Mongolians have over 300 words to describe horses, mostly relating to colouring.

PAUL GREENWAY

Jeep A few jeeps are available for charter in Kharkhorin, but in the tourist season they may be hard to find. Ask around the jeep/truck station, or at the hotels.

The road from Kharkhorin to Khujirt (54km) is rough but scenic, and there are many hawks and falcons to admire and attempt to photograph. The aimag capital, Arvaikheer, is 138km to the south-east. The 160km road between Kharkhorin and Tsetserleg is being rebuilt, which should cut down the current four hours' driving time (though until it's finished, the road is in even worse condition than before).

Hitching Hitching along the main road between Ulaan Baatar and Kharkhorin is fairly easy, but remember that a lot of vehicles will be carrying tourists, so they may not want to pick up a hitchhiker. Getting a lift between Arvaikheer and Kharkhorin is less likely, but if you're determined to wait something will come along.

Hitching between Khujirt and Kharkhorin shouldn't be too much of a hassle; many Mongolians take the Ulaan Baatar to Kharkhorin road to reach the popular spa town of Khujirt. In Kharkhorin, ask around the container market, or just stand by the road.

SHANKH KHIID
ШАНХ ХИЙД

Shankh Khiid, once known as the West Monastery, is the only one of the region's monasteries other than Erdene Zuu to have survived. Shankh was renowned because of its connections with the great Zanabazar and is said to have once housed Chinggis Khaan's black military banner. At one time the monastery housed over 1500 monks. As elsewhere, the monastery was closed in 1937, temples were burnt and many monks were shipped off to Siberia.

During the years of repression, five monks secretly kept the monastery alive in a local ger at great risk to themselves. One of these monks reopened the monastery in 1990. It is currently trying to raise funds to build a stupa in his honour.

Of the three main buildings only the central main temple has been restored.

Photographs are not normally allowed inside the temple, but if you ask, it may be possible. Ceremonies usually start at 9 am and visitors are welcome. There are presently 30 monks in residence, mostly young students. There is a T2000 entry fee.

There is nowhere to stay in the village, but it's easy enough to walk over the other side of the main road and find a discreet patch of ground to pitch a tent if you have one. Otherwise, you'll have to go on a day trip from Kharkhorin or Khujirt.

The monastery is exactly halfway along the main road between Kharkhorin and Khujirt, in the village of Shankh. If you have your own transport, it's a perfect place to stop between both towns.

The twice weekly Khujirt-Ulaan Baatar bus and postal truck go past the monastery, but with the amount of traffic along the road in summer it's probably just easier to hitch a ride. The monastery is now firmly part of the tourist trail, so don't be surprised to see a few coaches parked outside.

KHUJIRT
ХУЖИРТ

South of Erdene Zuu, Khujirt is a small, soporific town noted for its mineral hot springs and health resort. There's not much else to see here, except for the tiny **Gandan Piljeling Khiid**, which has a contingent of 15 part-time monks. Most travellers pass through the town en route to the waterfall Orkhon Khürkhree. There are some interesting grave sites worth looking out for a couple of kilometres out of town on the road to Kharkhorin.

The road between Kharkhorin and Khujirt (a bumpy 54km) is one of the best places in the country to see **falcons** and **hawks**, particularly the *saraa* (moon) hawk. If you are ever likely to get a photo of one of these birds, this is the place.

Spas

During the summer, Khujirt used to be chock-a-block with Mongolians enjoying mud baths and hot springs at the Russian-style all-inclusive spa resort. At the time of research the spa was undergoing extensive renovations, which, in all likelihood, should make the resort much more of a draw to foreigners.

Places to Stay & Eat

Camping There are no obvious camping spots, but if you walk 1km in any direction you will find somewhere secluded and decent.

Hotels With the renovations at the spa should come a renovated *hotel*, though prices were unavailable at the time of research. There is also talk of building a five-star hotel next to the spa, though it's hard to see who on earth would ever stay there.

Ger Camps The *Khujirt Tur* ger camp has 20 gers next to the sanatorium. A bed costs US$25 per person with three meals, or US$10 without meals. There are hot showers and a restaurant, but the setting is poor compared with others nearby.

Getting There & Away

Air During the summer (July to September), MIAT flies occasionally between Ulaan Baatar and Khujirt for US$54/US$95, normally via Kharkhorin.

Bus & Minivan Buses run every Tuesday and Thursday to Ulaan Baatar (T8000), passing within 5km of Kharkhorin. Faster minivans also do the run occasionally for T10,000.

Hitching With the number of Mongolians using the Ulaan Baatar-Kharkhorin road to get to Khujirt in summer, it shouldn't be hard to hitch a ride between Kharkhorin and Khujirt.

AROUND KHUJIRT
Orkhon Khürkhree

Орхон Хүрхрээ

Apart from the springs at Khujirt, the main attraction in the area is the Orkhon waterfall (GPS: N46° 47.234', E101° 57.694'). The waterfall is situated in the historically significant Orkhon Valley, whose river flows an incredible 1120km to the north before it joins the mighty Selenge Gol. Also called Ulaan Tsutgalan (Улаан Цутгалан), the waterfall was formed by a unique combination of volcanic eruptions and earthquakes about 20,000 years ago. The fall is naturally most impressive after heavy rain.

Ironically, these rains will also make the 82km road from Khujirt almost impassable: the river floods, the road is prone to mud slides and bridges often collapse. You should always ask around Khujirt for information about the current state of the road before heading out there. You can expect the drive to take three hours from Khujirt.

A little way downstream from the waterfall, you can climb down to the bottom of the **gorge**. The gorge itself is only 22m deep, but it is dotted with pine trees and is quite scenic from the bottom. Hardly anyone lives in the area near the falls, and the only sign of civilisation you'll see along the way are a few gers. There are said to be **hot springs** about 10km from the falls, on the south side of the valley. You'll have to ask locals for directions.

There is a designated *camping* area here, but it is always very cold at night, so be prepared.

If you haven't brought a tent, you can stay at the *Orkhon Old Government House* set on a gorgeous, secluded island. It is difficult to find: 500m before the bridge, turn left and drive parallel to the river (ie, upstream) and ask for further directions. You can stay in the house (US$25 per person) or there may be a few gers (US$20) set up as well – prices include all meals. The people running the place are friendly and they can arrange horses, which is probably the best way to see this region.

Tövkhön Süm

Төвхөн Сүм

High in the mountains marking the north side of the Orkhon Valley lie the ruins of this ancient temple and retreat. Zanabazar founded the site in 1653 and lived, worked and meditated here for 30 years. Several **pilgrimage sites** have grown up around the temple and hermit's caves, including one that is said to be Zanabazar's boot imprint.

The remains of the temple are hard to reach. There is an indirect road which runs around 30km from the north bank of the Orkhon Gol, but you might be better off on horseback. The ruins are around 50km from the centre of Bat-Ölzii sum centre.

Naiman Nuur
Наиман Нуур

Also worth visiting if you have a jeep is the area known as Naiman Nuur (Eight Lakes), which was created by volcanic eruptions centuries ago and is now part of the 11,500 hectare Khuisiin Naiman Nuur Natural Reserve. The lakes are 70km south-west of the Orkhon waterfall, but the roads are often virtually impassable. Companies like Nomads and Nomadic Expeditions runs tours here, including horse-riding trips.

ULAAN BAATAR TO KHARKHORIN

There are several interesting places en route to Kharkhorin, which together make a good three- or four-day trip from Ulaan Baatar, or tagged onto a longer trip to Arkhanghai aimag. For information on one of these, see the Khustai National Park section earlier in this chapter.

Khogno Khan Uul
Хогно Хан Уул

You can see this 1967m peak to the north of the main road. At the southern foot of the mountain are the ruins of **Uvgun Khiid**, built in 1660 after the existing monastery was destroyed and the monks were massacred by the armies of Zungar Galdan Bochigtu, a rival of Zanabazar's in 1640. The monastery reopened in 1992 and there are a couple of monks from Ulaan Baatar. The head lama is a charming lady who professes soothsaying abilities.

The ruins of the earlier destroyed monastery are a lovely 45-minute walk along a well-defined path up the valley to the right. The surroundings belong to the 46,900 hectare **Khogno Khan Natural Reserve** and you might spot ibex, wolves and many varieties of hawk. There are lots of **hiking** possibilities around here.

The mountain is actually in Bulgan aimag but is most easily accessed from the Ulaan Bataar-Arvaikheer road.

Places to Stay There are several places to stay. A family living at the base of the monastery have a **ger** that they rent for US$10 per person, which includes three basic meals. You can also rent **horses** here for a few dollars a day. If you bring some supplies with you, it's a great place to spend a day or three exploring the surrounding hills.

A kilometre or so from the monastery is the nicely situated **Batkhan** ger camp, which, at the time of research, was offering discounted rates of US$15 per person with meals, or US$7 for lodging only (the full rate is US$25 with meals).

Camping is excellent in the valley, though the only water comes from a hard-to-find well at the lower end of the valley.

Further away in the valley to the west, in a lovely location perfect for hiking, the **Nature Tours** ger camp charges between US$30 and US$40 with meals, or US$18 without meals. You can rent **horses** for US$3 per hour.

If you get stuck travelling on public transport, there is a small private **hotel** in Rashaant sum centre, right on the main highway.

Getting There & Away To get there from Ulaan Baatar by jeep turn north off the main road, 80km before Kharkhorin. The road passes several ger camps until after 8km you reach Nature Tours camp, where you turn right for the remaining 4km or so to the monastery ruins. There is a short cut if you are coming from Ulaan Baatar, but your jeep driver will need to know it.

There is no public transport to the monastery but you can take a Kharkhorin, Khujirt or Arvaikheer-bound minivan from Ulaan Baatar, get off at the turn on the main road (T5000) and then hitch (or more likely walk) the remaining 12km.

Mongol Els
Монгол Улс

As you approach the border of Övörkhangai from Ulaan Baatar, one surprising sight that livens up a fairly boring stretch of road are the Mongol Els sand dunes. If you don't have the time to visit the Gobi (where there are not a lot sand dunes anyway), these are certainly worth wandering around.

Batkhaan Uul
Батхаан Уул
The sum of Burd, in the north-east corner of Övörkhangai aimag, is host to some spectacular birdlife. Some of the area is part of the 22,000 hectare Batkhaan Uul Natural Reserve. The Mongol Els sand dunes are also nearby.

The area is just south of the main road between Ulaan Baatar and Arvaikheer, not far from the border of Övörkhangai and Töv aimags. With your own jeep, it is an easy day trip from Khujirt or Kharkhorin.

To take advantage of this and other sights in the north-eastern part of Övörkhangai, stay at the *Bayangobi* ger camp which costs US$40 per person, including meals. Some travellers have stayed for around US$15 without meals, when the camp isn't busy. The camp can be reached by branching south for 6km off the main road, 3km west of the turn-off to Khogno Khan Uul.

Arkhangai Архангай

pop 104,300 • area 55,000 sq km
Arkhangai has astounding scenery: wide rivers full of fish (the best times for fishing are in August and September), several volcanoes and volcanic lakes, extensive forests, and pastures where yak thrive. It also boasts the stunning lake Terkhiin Tsagaan Nuur, the ruins of several ancient kingdoms and probably the nicest aimag capital in the country. The ethnic groups are the Khalkh and the Oold.

Much of Arkhangai, which means 'north Khangai', is on the northern slope of the spectacular Khangai Nuruu mountain range. These are the second-highest mountains in Mongolia and are protected by the Khangai Nuruu, Noyon Khangai and Tarvagatain Nuruu national parks. The range is well watered, so expect lovely forests, meadows and

plenty of streams to quench your thirst, but it also floods, so expect muddy roads and even snowfalls in the summer.

Another drawback is that the aimag, particularly along the road between Tsetserleg and Ulaan Baatar, is notoriously bad for flies in summer – take repellent or you will live to regret it. If the flies make your life a misery, you can always indulge in fermented mare's milk, *airag* (Arkhangai is renowned for the quality of its airag).

One jeep road runs in an east-west direction through the aimag between Ulaan Baatar and Tosontsengel in Zavkhan aimag via Tsetserleg; another from Kharkhorin joins at Tsenkher. The Kharkhorin to Tosontegel road is currently being upgraded with World Bank money. From the roads in Arkhangai look out for small rock formations. These are **ancient gravesites**, which may even predate Chinggis Khaan.

TSETSERLEG
Цэцэрлэг
elevation 1691m
Tsetserleg is the only aimag capital in Mongolia that could, at a pinch, be called beautiful (*tsetserleg* means garden). The town is ringed by scenic mountains, the streets are tree-lined and a lovely little temple overlooks the town.

Tsetserleg is a good place to break up your journey if you are combining a visit to Kharkhorin and/or Khujirt with a trip to Terkhiin Tsagaan or Khövsgöl Nuur. Maybe it's the mountain air, but the people of Tsetserleg seem to be friendlier than in other aimag capitals. There's even a huge, rusting sign in English, next to the main square, saying 'Welcome to Arhangai' (sic).

The daily market *(khunsnii zakh)*, on the corner of the main road and the road to Ulaan Baatar, is pretty good and you can stock up on most supplies. There is nowhere else in the aimag with a similar selection.

Things to See
The **Museum of Arkhangai Aimag** is one of the best in the country. It's housed in the temple complex **Zayayn Gegeenii Süm**, which was first built in 1586 but expanded

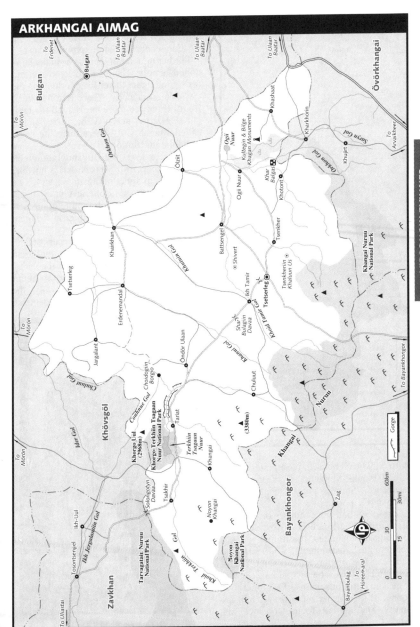

CENTRAL MONGOLIA

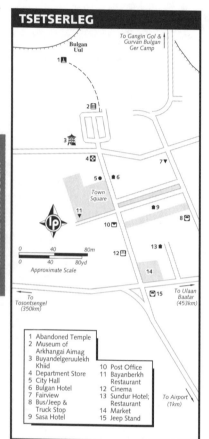

TSETSERLEG

To Gangin Gol &
Gurvan Bulgan
Ger Camp

Bulgan
Uul

Town Square

| 0 | 40 | 80m |
| 0 | 40 | 80yd |

Approximate Scale

To
Tosontsengel
(350km)

To Ulaan
Baatar
(453km)

To Airport
(1km)

1 Abandoned Temple
2 Museum of
   Arkhangai Aimag
3 Buyandelgeruulekh
   Khiid
4 Department Store
5 City Hall
6 Bulgan Hotel
7 Fairview
8 Bus/Jeep &
   Truck Stop
9 Sasa Hotel
10 Post Office
11 Bayanberkh
   Restaurant
12 Cinema
13 Sundur Hotel;
   Restaurant
14 Market
15 Jeep Stand

Entry is T2500, plus T3000 for a still camera or T10,000 for a video camera. The museum is open 9 am to 4pm weekdays.

Further up the hill there is a small **abandoned temple**. There's nothing to see, but the setting under the cliffs, overlooking the town, is spectacular. There is a trail to it from behind the museum. Behind the temple is a large, nearly vertical, rocky hill called Bulgan Uul, where there are some **Buddhist inscriptions**.

At street level the **Buyandelgeruulekh Khiid** (Буяндэлгэруулэх Хийд) is now the town's main functioning monastery. The temple has an atmospheric clutter of assorted religious artefacts, and religious services are held regularly, either in the main hall or in a ger next door.

In the north-east of town a trail leads to the pretty Gangin Gol, which offers great **hiking** potential. At the mouth of the valley is a ger camp and a pitiful **nature museum** of stuffed animals, which isn't worth the T1000 or T2000 the caretaker will demand.

in 1679, when it housed five temples and up to 1000 monks. Miraculously, the monastery escaped the Stalinist purges because it was made into a museum.

The main hall concentrates on features of traditional Mongolian lifestyle, with exhibits of costumes, traditional tools, a ger, musical instruments, weaponry and saddles. The displays have some useful English captions. The second hall concentrates on religious icons. The other two rooms of the former main prayer hall are empty. The last hall focuses on local artwork.

Decorative Khalkh saddle

Places to Stay

Camping The Gangin Gol has some great camping spots, though someone may come and collect a dubious 'fee' for camping in a 'nature reserve' (it's not). A few hundred metres past the ger camp is a grassy enclosure perfect for camping.

If you have a vehicle there are some nice spots a few kilometres south of town on the banks of the river.

Hotels The *Bulgan Hotel (☎ 2233)* is the old Communist-era stalwart. Simple four-person rooms cost T1500, or T3000 for a similar-looking half-luxury option. Solo travellers and even couples may have to pay for all the beds in the room if they don't want to share it with others. Luxury rooms cost T7000, which gets you a bathroom and two rather pointless additional rooms. The hotel has a separate shower room, which has continuous hot water for T400 a go. Part of the hotel is a teachers college so you should be able to find English-speakers here.

The flashiest hotel in town is the *Sundur Hotel (☎ 2359)*, which has a variety of singles/doubles for US$10/20, US$12/22, US$15/25 or US$30. The cheapest rooms have only a toilet and no shower, but all others have nice bathrooms with hot water (at fixed times of the day only – check the times with reception).

The *Sasa Hotel*, above a shop just off the main street, is probably the best value you'll get in Tsetserleg at T3000 a bed (though solo travellers will have to buy both beds). The water supply is a bit hit-and-miss but the staff are friendly and the rooms are decent enough. If there is no-one around ask at the shop downstairs.

Ger Camps The *Gurvan Bulgan* ger camp has a nice location in the Gangin Valley, though it's a little disorganised. A bed in one of the six gers costs US$10, or US$20 with food. The camp has a water problem so don't expect a shower here.

Places to Eat

One of the most bizarre and welcome restaurants in Mongolia is *Fairview*, on the east edge of town. Run by an expat British couple (in Tsetserleg?!) the well-run cafe serves up pizza, lasagne, steak sandwiches, and beef in beer sauce, all for less than T1000 each. Finish this off with a mug of English tea, a warm cinnamon bun (T100) and an old copy of the *Economist* and you may well think you've just died and gone to heaven. (Our minivan bought up the entire week's supply of cinnamon buns!) The only tragedy is that the place is open only from 10 am to 3 pm, Monday to Saturday (closed Sunday). This restaurant is worth rearranging your whole itinerary around if you are on a long trip!

Apart from the Fairview, the best place in town is the restaurant at the *Sundur Hotel*, which has main courses for around T900 and tasty salads for about T300. As with all hotel restaurants in Mongolia, give them as much advance warning as possible.

If you just can't get enough of cavernous Soviet-style canteens doling out government-regulation goulash, then try the *Bayanberkh Restaurant*, just south-west of the square.

Getting There & Away

Air There are currently no flights running to Tsetserleg, though this may change in the future. The airport is only 1km south of town.

Bus & Minivan Microbuses and minivans run between Tsetserleg and Ulaan Baatar (except Tuesday) at about 8 am daily if there are enough passengers (nine hours, T10,000,). The unofficial and unsigned bus/truck station is at the east end of town. If you have no luck here try the minivans at the jeep stand opposite the market, though this stand is generally for local destinations such as Ikh Tamir and Kharkhorin.

Jeep Tsetserleg is a pretty good place to arrange transport to nearby sights. Jeeps for hire hang around on the main highway, across from the south entrance of the market. Several jeep drivers offered us a good rate of around T200 per km, or between T40,000 to T60,000 for a return trip to Terkhiin Tsagaan Nuur, depending on the number of days of the trip.

There are two routes between Tsetserleg and Ulaan Baatar – directly east via Ogii Nuur (453km) or along the longer but better road via Kharkhorin (493km).

Heading west, the road from Tsetserleg to Tosontsengel (350km) goes through some wonderful mountain and wildflower scenery, and is in reasonably good condition.

If you are travelling between Tsetserleg and Mörön (for Khövsgöl Nuur), it's quicker to go on the road through Erdenemandal to the north, even if it means backtracking if you plan to visit Terkhiin Tsagaan Nuur (which is worth it).

Hitching All types of vehicles go to and from Tsetserleg and, generally, along the main road through Arkhangai. Hitching opportunities, however, are limited because the primary roads to the north-west (via Khövsgöl aimag) and to the south-east (through Övörkhangai) bypass Arkhangai's main sights. If you want to hitch, hang around the bus/jeep station and something will come along eventually. A useful sign listing fixed fares for a ride in a truck to various destinations is posted in the window of the ticket office.

OGII NUUR
ОГИЙ НУУР

On the road between Ulaan Baatar and Tsetserleg, near the border with Bulgan aimag, the lake Ogii Nuur is a wonderful place for birdlife – cranes and ducks, to name just a few species, migrate to the area around late April. The lake is also renowned for its fishing (and the bugs by the lake shore!).

The lake and Khar Balgas ruins can only be reached from the direct road linking Tsetserleg with Ulaan Baatar. You can visit them on a day trip from Khujirt or Kharkhorin if you have your own transport, but they're not easy detours. The lake makes a nice overnight break between Ulaan Baatar and Tsetserleg.

KHAR BALGAS
ХАР БАЛГАС

The ruined citadel of Khar Balgas (Kara Balgasun in Turkic) is in Khotont sum on the banks of the Orkhon Gol. The city was founded in AD 751 as the capital of the Uighur khanate, which ruled Mongolia from 745–854.

There's not much to see except the outer walls (with gates in the north and south), a **Buddhist stupa** and the ruler's *kagan*, or **castle**, in the south-west corner. From the walls you can see the rows of stupas on either side of the walls and the remains of irrigated fields in the surrounding countryside. The city had an elaborate plumbing system, which brought water into the city from several kilometres away.

The ruins (GPS: N47° 25.782', E102° 39.490') lie east of the road connecting Ogii Nuur and Khotont and aren't easy to get to.

KULTEGIN MONUMENT

When Chinggis Khaan decided to move his capital to Kharkhorin, he was well aware that the region had already been capital to successive nomad empires. About 20km north-east of Khar Balgas (as the crow flies) lies the remainder of yet another of these pre-Mongol empires, the Turkic khaganate. All that's left of the khaganate is the 3m-high inscribed **monument of Kultegin** (684–731), the *khagan* (ruler) himself. The monument (GPS: N47° 33.837', E102° 49.931') was raised in AD 732 and is inscribed in Runic and Chinese script. You can see a copy of the stele in the entrance of the National Museum of Mongolian History.

Just over 1km away is another **monument** to Bilge Khagan (683–734), younger brother of Kultegin. Ten years after the death of Bilge the Turkic khaganate was overrun by the Uighurs.

The two monuments are 25km north-west of Khashaat in a region called Tsaidam, about 47km north of Kharkhorin, and are hard to find. Amateur historians who relish a challenge are best off packing a GPS into their jeep; otherwise ask at gers en route from either Khashaat or Ogii Nuur.

TAIKHAR CHULUU
ТАЙХАР ЧУЛУУ

The nondescript town of **Ikh Tamir** is 22km along the main road west of Tsetserleg. The reason to stop here is to inspect the enormous Taikhar Chuluu rock formation. The rock is the subject of many local legends, the most common one is that a great *baatar*, or hero, crushed a huge serpent here by hurling the rock on top of it. Locals claim there are some ancient Tibetan inscriptions on the rock, though you'll be lucky to spot them through 30 years of Mongolian graffiti. There is even an **ovoo** at the top.

Taikhar Chuluu is about 2km north of Ikh Tamir along the river – you can see it from the main road.

There is a *ger camp*, run by MAT Outdoor Safaris, next to the rock. Prices are US$35 including three meals, or US$15 just for lodging. In summer, a local school-teacher sometimes sets up a cheaper *private ger* by the river to the north-east. You could *camp* anywhere along the Khoid Tamir Gol, or wait until Tsetserleg.

Locals recommend the three-hour **hike** to the large wooden ovoo at the top of the forested peak to the south-west of Ikh Tamir.

TERKHIIN TSAGAAN NUUR
ТУРХИЙН ЦАГААН НУУР

Known in English as the Great White Lake, this freshwater lake (and the volcanic area around it) is certainly the highlight of Arkhangai, and one of the best in a country full of beautiful lakes. Surrounded by extinct and craterous volcanoes (part of the Tarvagatain Nuruu range), Terkhiin Tsagaan Nuur is not as forested or as large as Khövsgöl Nuur, but it is closer to Ulaan Baatar, completely undeveloped and just about perfect for camping (though there are a few flies in summer). The lake, birdlife and mountains are now protected within the 77,267 hectare Khorgo-Terkhiin Tsagaan Nuur National Park.

The lake, which was formed by lava flows from a volcanic eruption many millennia ago, is excellent for **swimming**, though a bit cold in the morning – try the late afternoon, after the sun has warmed it. It even has what may be Mongolia's only truly sandy beach. The **fishing** is good, though you should get a permit for around T2000 per day. There are several park

rangers who sell permits but they can be hard to find. Dramatic sunsets round off the day perfectly.

One good excursion takes you to the top of **Khorgo Uul** volcano (2965m). A road leads 4km from **Tariat** (also known as Khorgo) village to the base of the volcano, from where it's a 10-minute walk up to the cone (GPS: N48° 11.695', E99° 51.054'). The volcano is in the park so you'll need to pay the park fee of T1000 per person per day, plus T3000 if you have your own car. The park entrance is by the bridge.

Places to Stay & Eat
Camping Except for a few annoying flies, Terkhiin Tsagaan Nuur is one of the best camping spots in Mongolia. There is good fishing, endless fresh water, and flat ground for pitching a tent. The western end of the lake, where it joins the Khoid Terkhiin Gol, is muddy. The best place to camp is the eastern part where there are some pine trees and lovely side valleys (in case the flies near the lake get too much). The lake is right on the main road, so just pick your camping spot anywhere around 8km west of Tariat.

The other main place to camp is in the north-east corner of the lake, where there are some nice sandy beaches past the volcano as well as the Khorgo I ger camp. You'll have to pay the daily park fee if you camp here. The area is cold all year round, and often windy, so a good sleeping bag is vital.

Hotels There are no hotels right on the lake; the nearest accommodation is in Tariat village, about 6km east of the lake, and just a little off the main road. The one *hotel* in Tariat is the unnamed, yellow building facing the main road. The rooms are good value at T1500/3000 per person for a simple/deluxe room. You may have to track someone down to open it up. The town is really too far to commute to the lake without your own transport.

Ger Camps The *Khorgo I* camp in a lovely location in the Zurkh Gol Valley (Heart River Valley) in the north-east section of the lake is run by the Tsolmon travel company in Ulaan Baatar (☎ 01-322 870). The camp officially costs US$25 per person but, at the time of research, staff were willing to let us stay at a discounted rate of US$12/14 in a two/four person ger. Three meals cost an extra US$14. The camp has hot showers and there is excellent hiking nearby. To get there take the road north of Tariat into the park and take the branch to the right when you get near the volcano.

If you want lake views then **Khorgo II**, the sister camp, is just over the pass to the south-west, on the lakeshore. Prices are the same as Khorgo 1.

Getting There & Away

There are occasional minivans to/from Ulaan Baatar and Tsetserleg. From anywhere else you are better off hitching. About 30km east of Tariat is a dramatic gorge, which makes a nice picnic stop. Cyclists might want to note that 89km from Ikh Tamir, and around 60km east of Tariat, is a kitsch **guanz** and **hotel**, decorated with various dead animal heads, where you can get basic food and accommodation.

From the lake to Tosontsengel (179km), the main road climbs over Solongotyn Davaa pass, a phenomenally beautiful area, which is also steep and very rough. You can see patches of permanent ice from the road. The road is currently being upgraded and there are a few guanz along the way, as well as a couple of basic places to stay on either side of the pass.

NOYON KHANGAI
НОЬЮН ХАНГАЙ

A few intrepid souls push on to Noyon Khangai, a remote camping and hiking area in the mountains south-west of Terkhiin Tsagaan Nuur. It's a very difficult place to reach, but may be worth the effort if the jeep road, which is either muddy or potholed, is passable. The mountainous region on the aimag border to the south is the 59,088 hectare Noyon Khangai National Park.

From Khunt, the capital of Khangai sum, you need to follow the river west (upstream) into the mountains.

CHOIDOGIIN BORGIO
ЧОИДОГИЙН БОРГИО

To the east of **Tariat** village and in Tariat sum, Choidogiin Borgio, where the Chuluut and Ikh Jargalantiin rivers converge, is a good **hiking**, **fishing** and **camping** area. Some companies run tours in the area but the place is difficult to reach by yourself, even with a jeep, as the roads are awful.

Northern Mongolia

Hugging the Siberian border are the northern *aimag*, or provinces, of Bulgan, Khövsgöl and Selenge. If you are travelling by train to or from Russia, you'll pass through Selenge. If you are staying in Mongolia for a while, you will undoubtedly want to visit stunning Khövsgöl Nuur, fast becoming the number one attraction in the country.

In the region around Khövsgöl aimag, the terrain is mainly taiga (subarctic coniferous) forest of Siberian larch and pine trees, where there's plenty of rain (often about 40cm a year). The rest of northern Mongolia is mountain and forest steppe. The steppes teem with elk, reindeer and bears, and the rivers and lakes are brimming with fish.

Khövsgöl Хөвсгөл

pop 124,500 ● area 101,000 sq km
Mongolia's northernmost aimag, Khövsgöl is – with the possible exception of Arkhangai – the most scenic in Mongolia. This is a land of tall taiga forest, crystal-clear lakes, icy streams and lush grass. It does rain a lot during summer, but this only adds to the scenery: rainbows hang over meadows dotted with white gers and grazing horses and yaks. The best fishing is in the south, where the Ider, Bugsei, Selenge, Delger Mörön and Chuluut rivers converge.

The aimag is dominated by the magnificent Khövsgöl Nuur, one of the most scenic spots in Mongolia. The lake is surrounded by several peaks of almost 3000m in height. To the west, there is the Darkhadyn Khotgor Depression, with plentiful forests and lakes. In this region, around Tsagaannuur, live the fascinating, but fast disappearing, Tsaatan people, whose lives revolve around domesticated reindeer. Other ethnic groups include the Khalkh, Buryat, Uriankhai and Darkhad.

Highlights

- Khövsgöl Nuur, a gorgeous alpine lake area offering excellent fishing, swimming and hiking
- Amarbayasgalant Khiid, a remote but important monastery and the architectural highlight of the country
- Bugat, a small but accessible region of forests and wildflowers; ideal for hiking and horse riding

NORTHERN MONGOLIA

MÖRÖN
МӨРӨН
pop 28,000 ● elevation 1283m
This rather scruffy aimag capital is cooler than most Mongolian cities, and has relatively few gers because nearby forests supply abundant timber. Mörön (which means river) has few sights and most travellers just drive through en route to Khatgal at the southern end of Khövsgöl Nuur.

The market, about six blocks north of the museum, is said to be the largest outside of Ulaan Baatar.

Orientation & Information
The grey building north-east of the square is the Daatgal Bank. It will change only US

KHÖVSGÖL AIMAG

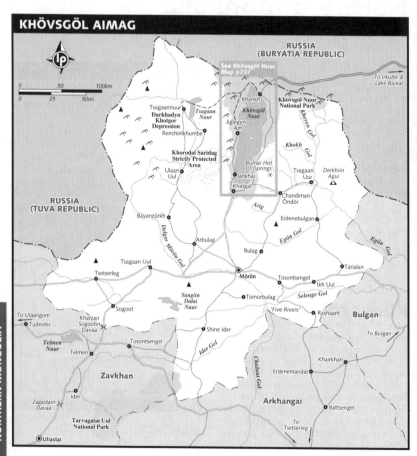

dollars cash. It's open from 9 am to 4 pm weekdays, 9 am to noon Saturday.

The public bath house in the north-west edge of town is open daily, except Monday, and costs T300 for a hot shower. Look for the tall chimney stacks.

The Huvsgul Travel Company (☎ 41-21 028, fax 01-687 626, e hovsgol-travel@mongol.net) is the only travel agency in Mörön or the Khövsgöl Nuur region. It can organise fishing, horse riding and jeep tours, and trekking trips around the lake and to the Tsaatan people. Seemingly well organised (if you speak to the right person)

and with English-speaking staff, the office is in a wood cabin north-west of the central square.

The remarkable-looking wrestling stadium in the east of town has run out of funds and is to be turned into a shopping plaza.

Museum

Given the variety of wildlife in the aimag, stuffed animals are, not surprisingly, the main feature of the museum. There's a large tusk from a woolly mammoth, but you won't see one of those in the flesh – they

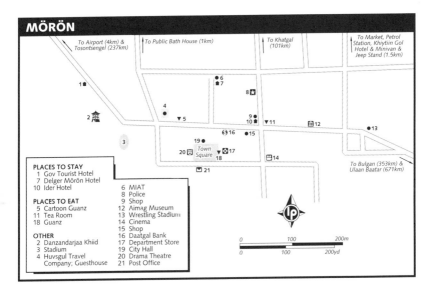

MÖRÖN

To Airport (4km) & Tosontsengel (237km)
To Public Bath House (1km)
To Khatgal (101km)
To Market, Petrol Station, Khiytiin Gol Hotel & Minivan & Jeep Stand (1.5km)

To Bulgan (353km) & Ulaan Baatar (671km)

Town Square

PLACES TO STAY
1 Gov Tourist Hotel
7 Delger Mörön Hotel
10 Ider Hotel

PLACES TO EAT
5 Cartoon Guanz
11 Tea Room
18 Guanz

OTHER
2 Danzandarjaa Khiid
3 Stadium
4 Huvsgul Travel Company; Guesthouse

6 MIAT
8 Police
9 Shop
12 Aimag Museum
13 Wrestling Stadium
14 Cinema
15 Shop
16 Daatgal Bank
17 Department Store
19 City Hall
20 Drama Theatre
21 Post Office

haven't inhabited this region for over 40,000 years. Photographic exhibits of the Tsaatan people are also intriguing.

The museum is open from 9 am to 6 pm daily except Monday (T500) and is about 150m east of the Ider Hotel.

Danzandarjaa Khiid
Данзандаржаа Хийд
The history of this *khiid* (monastery) is unclear, but the original monastery (Möröngiin Khüree) was built around 1890 and was home to 2000 monks. It was rebuilt and reopened in June 1990, and now has 30 monks of all ages. It's a charming place, designed in the shape of a concrete ger, and contains a great collection of **scroll paintings** *(thangka)*.

The monastery is just back from the main road, on the way to the airport. Visitors are always welcome.

Places to Stay
Camping Mörön is not a great place to camp, so head up to Khövsgöl Nuur or into the countryside as soon as you can. Otherwise, the best spots are by the river, the Delger Mörön Gol.

Twenty-seven kilometres east of Mörön, on the road to Bulgan city, a tiny, unmapped and unnamed lake offers good camping. A lush valley, 13km further east, is peppered with gers in summer and makes a great place to camp if you want to meet local herders.

Hotels The *Delger Mörön Hotel* is a Soviet dinosaur with some funky rooms from T2000 per person, including one decorated like the interior of a ger. The downside is that the toilets are often filthy and the showers nonexistent. The hotel is at the end of the street that starts north of the square.

Gov Tourist Hotel (☎ 41-3479, fax 41-210 20), on the north-western outskirts, is professionally run but overpriced. Rooms in the main building cost from US$23 to US$28, though you might be able to get a bed for as low as US$15. Outside cabins cost US$15 to US$20 per person. You can get food and hire vehicles here. The hotel is owned by the Gobi Cashmere Company.

Huvsgul Travel Company recently opened a guesthouse in its compound. It's mainly for its clients, though anyone can use it if there is space. Rooms cost US$16 per person, or US$35 with three meals.

NORTHERN MONGOLIA

Davaadorj

It seems that every aimag needs a local hero, and Khövsgöl gets Davaadorj. Unlike most heroes, he didn't fight in the 1921 Revolution – he was too young. Instead he was noted for his bravery while fighting the Japanese along Khalkhin Gol in 1939 (in Dornad aimag), although he must have been about 13 years old at the time.

Davaadorj didn't live long: he died in 1948, at the tender age of 22. Like Sükhbaatar, another Mongolian hero, his death is a mystery. His statue now dominates the town square in Mörön.

The **Ider Hotel**, 100m north-east of the square, was closed when we researched the previous edition of this guide and was closed again when we researched this edition, though locals swear the hotel was open all the time in between! It might be worth checking out.

The green **Khiytiin Gol Hotel**, just south of the market, has basic rooms for T1600 per person, but it's more of a truck stop and bar than a proper hotel.

Places to Eat

The best **guanz** (canteen or cheap restaurant) is the one with the cartoon sign above the entrance, just north-west of the square. The team of women who run the place rustle up good schnitzel, but the place closes around 6 pm, just as people start getting hungry.

Another good bet is the **tsain gazar** (tea room) just opposite the Ider Hotel, which has decent potato salad, *khuurshuur* (fried mutton pancakes), goulash and Mongolian tea. There are a couple of well-stocked **shops** nearby.

A **guanz** on the east side of the square serves up more khuurshuur, *buuz* (steamed mutton dumplings) and tea.

The **market** has a reasonable choice of fresh food. The large hall in the southern section has vegetables. The north is made up of a **clothes market**, which sells some fine leather boots and all the marmot skins you could ever need.

Getting There & Away

Air MIAT (Mongolian Airlines) run direct flights between Ulaan Baatar and Mörön on Monday, Wednesday and Friday for US$80/143. The other domestic airline company, Khangard, flies to Mörön on Thursday for the same price as MIAT. Khangard can also arrange charters.

MIAT flights between Ulaan Baatar and Ulaangom city, and other places in the west, often stop at Mörön to refuel, so you could theoretically combine a trip to the west with Khövsgöl Nuur. Check MIAT for details.

The MIAT office is just north of the Delger Mörön Hotel. If you don't have any luck there, try the Huvsgul Travel Company, which often has extra seats. Buy your ticket as early as possible.

Mörön airport is about 4km from the centre of town. You will have to take a jeep or taxi there (T1000), or hop on the crowded bus.

Minivan & Jeep Minivans run between Ulaan Baatar and Mörön daily (25 hours, T15,000). Minibuses and jeeps leave most afternoons to Khatgal (four hours, T5000). There are occasional jeeps to Erdenet (T10,000) and Darkhan.

Transport to Ulaan Baatar, Erdenet and Darkhan leaves from the south side of the market. A loudspeaker announcement (in distorted Mongolian) will be made at the market when a jeep is planning to head off. Transport to Khatgal and elsewhere leaves from north of the market.

From Mörön it is 273km to Tosontsengel in Zavkhan aimag, 353km to Bulgan city and 671km to Ulaan Baatar. You can cut down on the time spent bumping around in a van by taking the sleeper train between Ulaan Baatar and Erdenet.

Hitching The Ulaan Baatar–Bulgan–Mörön road is fairly busy, so hitching a ride shouldn't be a problem. But be warned: the trip by truck between Ulaan Baatar and Mörön is a *very* tough 30 non-stop hours (expect to pay T5000 to T10,000 for a lift). Some travellers do it one way for the 'experience' – and then gratefully fly back.

To get information about hitching a ride from Mörön, hang around the market or the petrol station.

KHÖVSGÖL NUUR
ХӨВСГӨЛ НУУР

Try to imagine a 2760 sq km alpine lake, with water so pure you can drink it. Then add dozens of mountains 2000m high or more, thick pine forests and lush meadows with grazing yaks and horses, and you have a vague impression of Khövsgöl Nuur, Mongolia's top scenic attraction. In surface area, this is the second-largest lake (136km long and 30km wide) in Mongolia, surpassed in size only by Uvs Nuur, a shallow, salty lake in the western part of the country.

Khövsgöl Nuur is the deepest lake (up to 262m) in Central Asia, and the world's four-teenth-largest source of fresh water – containing between 1% and 2% of the world's fresh water (that's 380,700 billion litres of water!). Geologically speaking, Khövsgöl is the younger sibling of Siberia's Lake Baikal, only 195km to the north-east, and was formed by the same tectonic forces.

It is full of fish, such as lennok and sturgeon, and the area is home to argali sheep, ibex, bear, sable and moose, as well as over 200 species of birds, including the Baikal teal, bar-headed goose *(kheeriin galuu* in Mongolian), black stork and Altai snowcock.

The region also hosts three separate, unique peoples: Darkhad, Buryat and Tsaatan. For more information on Buryats, see the boxed text 'The Buryat People' in the Facts about Mongolia chapter.

The lake is now part of the Khövsgöl Nuur National Park (established in 1992). Of its 838,000 hectares, 251,000 are forest (though tree cover is starting to disappear around the lakeshore). The 188,634 hectare Khoridol Saridag Nuruu Strictly Protected Area was added to the park in 1997. An amazing 96 rivers flow *into* the lake, while only one river flows *out* – the Egiin Gol, which flows into the Selenge Gol and finally reaches Lake Baikal in Siberia.

One Tsataan family has moved into the national park, drawn by the money created by tourism. The family offers tourists a

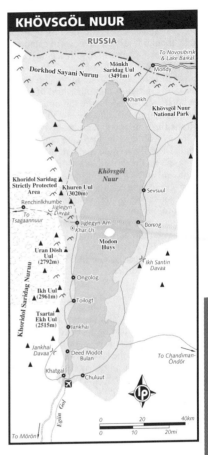

shamanic consultation (for around US$5) and charges for any photos. Their camp keeps getting moved on by the park authorities, who don't like the disruption to the environment caused by their reindeer.

Khövsgöl Nuur freezes in winter with 120cm of ice (and may not completely thaw out until early June), allowing huge trucks carrying fuel to cross from Siberia. This practice was officially prohibited in the 1980s (but still continues regardless) when it was realised that leaking oil from the trucks was polluting the lake. Around 40 trucks have fallen through the ice over the years.

There are numerous caves around the lake, so speleologists are interested in the area, though finding a cave worth exploring in the thick forests will require a guide, considerable time and a lot of luck. Visitors also come to fish, swim in the icy water, watch the ducks, seagulls and other bird life, hike or horseback ride along the shoreline, or just find a comfortable spot to stay and soak in all the fresh air and natural beauty.

Khövsgöl Nuur is a pristine but increasingly heavily visited part of Mongolia. Please see the boxed texts 'Responsible Tourism' and 'Minimum Impact Camping' in Facts for the Visitor for suggestions on how you can minimise your impact on this beautiful region.

Discovery Initiatives produces a useful booklet on the park entitled *Lake Hovsgol National Park: A Visitors Guide*, which you can get in Ulaan Baatar and, maybe, in the national park office.

Information

The best time to visit the lake is in spring, when it rains less and the flowers and bird life are often at their best – but it will still be very cold (there will be plenty of snow on the ground), and the lake may still be frozen.

The summer is a little more crowded (not so crowded that it would spoil your trip), but it can still be cold, and it often rains. The meadows around the lake are sprinkled with beautiful wildflowers during this time. Autumn is another good time to visit, when the leaves are turning colour.

Winter is amazingly cold, though blue skies are the norm. The lake freezes over and you can drive up over the lake and enjoy the disorientating feeling of looking down through the ice to the lake floor. Locals say that the lake is at its most beautiful during this time.

Permits On the main road, 12km before Khatgal, you'll be required to pay an entrance fee at a gate to Khövsgöl Nuur National Park. The cost is T1000 per night for foreigners, plus T3000 per vehicle. If there's no-one there you can buy permits off the ranger, who scoots around Khatgal and

the park on a motorbike. With your permit you should receive a useful visitors pamphlet explaining the permits and how to limit your impact on the lake.

You'll be asked how long you intend to stay in the park, which is not always easy to estimate. You can always pay one of the park's rangers for any extra days you stay, which you can do on your return to Khatgal.

Khatgal
Хатгал

As the southern gateway to Khövsgöl Nuur, Khatgal is the largest town on the lake. With some of the best budget accommodation in Mongolia, it is a good launch pad for the lake and most people spend at least a day here preparing for or relaxing after a trip. The town is actually on the river, the Egiin Gol, at the mouth of the lake, so you don't get much of an idea of the lake's size from here.

Khatgal used to be a busy depot for trucks headed to and from Russia, but the town's economy has since ground to a halt.

The national park has set up a couple of marked walking trails starting from Khatgal. A shoreline trail leads 10km until it hits the jeep road. A 12km loop ridge trail branches off the shoreline trail and heads up and along a ridge, offering fine views of the lake. For an easier view of the lake just climb the hill immediately north of Nature's Door camp.

Information A new national park office is being built at the southern end of town, which should offer hiking information and a video and slide show on the park. Khatgal's public bath house is open from 9 am to 1 pm and 2 to 6 pm, Wednesday, Saturday and Sunday only (T500). Unfortunately the hot water isn't all that reliable.

Places to Stay & Eat Food supplies in Khatgal are limited but you can get beer, soft drinks and chocolate bars. Otherwise, stock up in Mörön or Ulaan Baatar.

A local women's craft cooperative operates a ger shop next to the Blue Pearl Hotel. Saleswomen also do the rounds of the guesthouses, selling camel hair jumpers, traditional clothes and knucklebone games.

If you have a tent and are hanging around for a lift to the lake or to Mörön, you can camp in the forests along the shores of the Egiin Gol, either in town or in the beautiful valleys further south.

Nature's Door (Baigal Uud; ☎ 01-323 957) is an ambitious new initiative, combining tourism with income-generating projects for the local community. It has two well-run guesthouses, one in Khatgal (Thyme 3), the other in Toilogt (Thyme 1).

The base camp at *Thyme 3* is firmly aimed at backpackers, with dormitory accommodation in bunk beds for around US$4. It also has solar-heated showers, a laundry service, a kitchen and bakery, and plans to grow its own vegetables. The camp is in the north of town, at the base of the hill, not far from the storage drums of the petrol station.

Jambal's Guest House is smaller, with accommodation in a ger for US$5 per person. Jambal is a local park ranger and can arrange horses for US$6 per day and guides for US$8 per day. A sauna is being built on the grounds.

The *Monkh Saidag* camp in the extreme south of town is the first collection of gers you see when arrive in town. Beds in a ger cost around T3000, and a toilet and shower block should be finished by now. The place closes if there aren't many tourists around. Ask for Ganbaatar or Batzorig.

The *Hovsgol Lake Hotel* is run by the national park, primarily for its staff, but it does have a couple of pleasant rooms for around T2500 per person. Look for the green sign.

The government-owned *Blue Pearl Hotel* has pretty good rooms for T3000 per person, though the indoor showers and toilet were broken when we visited. There are some nice picnic tables in front of the hotel.

The *Tsagaan Uul Hotel*, near the post office, is really more of a bar and guanz but there are a couple of basic rooms for T2500 per person.

Western Shore

From Khatgal, a reasonable road first heads south-west before swinging north-east across several dry river beds and over the pass, Jankhai Davaa, 17km from Khatgal, where you receive your first magical glimpse of the lake. The road continues past the gorgeous headlands of **Jankhai**, once a Russian village, and **Toilogt** (routinely mispronounced 'toilet' by most travellers), where there is a rash of ger camps. The road then gradually deteriorates. Very few vehicles venture past Toilogt, so no road maintenance is deemed necessary.

Around 30km north of Toilogt is **Khar Us**, a series of springs surrounded by meadows of beautiful wildflowers. In June locals flock here to eat the bailius fish for its medicinal properties. This makes a great destination to reach on horseback.

A jeep can travel as far as **Jiglegyn Am**, almost exactly halfway up the western shore, before the trail disappears into mud and forest. Only horses can go further north or take the western trail from Jiglegyn Am to Renchinlkhumbe, on the way to Tsagaannuur.

Eastern Shore

The eastern shore is not as good because the road rarely hugs the lake, the scenery isn't as pretty, there are only a handful of gers between Chuluut and Borsog, almost no wildlife, and the flies can be appalling. If that doesn't put you off, it might if we said that this is the worse stretch of road we encountered in 15,000km of overland travel! There are some plans to improve the trail: we saw chain gangs of prisoners busily building pretty bridges – which are likely to collapse after the first decent rain or heavy vehicle crosses them.

From Khatgal, head for the bridge over the Egiin Gol, where you may need to ask directions. The trail meanders over some hills and past a collection of huts known as **Chuluut** – if in doubt, follow the line of electricity poles. The trail continues past an interesting *ovoo* (a shamanistic collection of stones, wood or other offerings) at the pass **Ikh Santin Davaa** to a gorgeous spot called **Borsog**, six hours by jeep and 103km from Khatgal.

With a tent and your own food, you could have a lovely time in Borsog picking wildflowers, swimming, hiking and fishing, with just a few yaks and a ger with a slightly loony family for neighbours.

If your spine hasn't suffered permanent damage by now, you could carry on further to a couple of gers known as **Sevsuul**. The road actually improves a little here, then hugs the lake and is usually passable all the way to Khankh. Surprisingly, a few sand dunes dot the landscape.

From Khatgal, allow at least 12 hours by jeep to travel the 200 or so kilometres to **Khankh** (Turt), a former depot for oil tankers headed to and from Siberia. Khankh is more Buryat and Russian than Mongolian, because it is closer to its northern neighbour than to Ulaan Baatar. Don't stray too far from Khankh; nearby is the Russian border, where smugglers may be arrested or shot. There is nowhere to stay or eat here, so you will have to be completely self-sufficient.

Remember that if you reach Khankh, you will have to come *all* the way back along the same bone-crunching, eastern road: there is no way any vehicle could get from Khankh to Jiglegyn Am, halfway up the western shore. At the moment going all the way around the lake is only possible by boat or horse.

Activities

Hiking This is one of the best ways to see the lake and the mountains surrounding it. You will need to be self-sufficient, although there are a few gers in the area to buy some meat or dairy products from. The trails around the lake are easy to follow, or just hug the shoreline as much as you can.

Of the mountains in the south-western region, the most accessible is Tsartai Ekh Uul (2515m), immediately west of Jankhai, where the hiking is excellent. Also try the numerous other mountains in the mountain range Khoridol Saridag Nuruu, such as Khuren Uul (3020m), not far north of the trail to Renchinlkhumbe; Ikh Uul (2961m), a little north-west of Toilogt; and the volcano of Uran Dösh Uul (2792m).

Longer treks are possible around the Dorkhod Sayani Nuruu range, which has many peaks over 3000m. It is right on the border of Russia, so be careful.

Thyme 1 has trained some local hiking guides in first aid, route finding and low impact trekking and has scouted out some good treks in the surrounding mountains. Contact them for route ideas and/or guides.

Alternatively, several travel agents in Ulaan Baatar and abroad arrange organised treks in the area.

Kayaking & Boating Travelling by kayak would allow you to see the lake without the strain of driving along the appalling roads. The lake is full of glorious little coves, perfect for camping and fishing, and you could even check out the only island, **Modon Huys**, almost exactly in the middle of the lake. Nomadic Expeditions (see Travel Agencies under Information in the Ulaan Baatar chapter) runs kayaking trips in the region.

Nature's Door has a inflatable dinghy and is planning to run travellers up to its camp and beyond to the island and the northern reaches of the lake. A few ger camps, such as Toilogt, can arrange the rental of a boat for high tourist prices.

Several large boats remain moored at Khatgal docks. They *very* occasionally take passengers up to Khankh but these days they will only move when chartered, which will cost an arm and a leg. If you do charter a boat to Khankh, you'll still have to share it with a boatload of nonpaying passengers who have been waiting for some tourist or trader to fork out the money.

Horse Riding The only place to organise a horse trek around the lake is at Khatgal. Nature's Door and Jambal's Guest House can arrange everything within 24 hours. Prices are negotiable but reasonable at about US$5 per horse per day, and about US$5 to US$8 per day for a guide.

If you just want to hire a horse for a few hours you could arrange this with a family at the lake. All ger camps can arrange horse riding for anyone willing to pay high tourist prices of around US$10 to US$20 per day, plus a guide.

A guide is recommended for any horse-riding trips in the region and, in fact, park regulations stipulate that foreigners should have one local guide for every four tourists. Guides will expect you to provide food while on the trail.

A complete circuit of the lake on horseback will take from ten days to two weeks. A return trip by horse from Khatgal to Tsagaannuur, and a visit to the Tsaatan people, will take from 10 to 12 days. An interesting 10-day trip could take you east of the lake to Chandiman Öndör and Dayan Derkhiin Agui cave. You'll definitely need a guide for these last two trips.

Shorter trips include one to Toilogt, through the mountainous Khoridol Saridag Nuruu Strictly Protected Area, or up to Khar Us and back in a couple of days.

If you want something really different, challenging and uncomfortable, the Jankhai Resort can arrange some yak riding.

Fishing If you love fishing, then you'll get excited about Khövsgöl Nuur. Bring your own fishing gear – or beg, borrow or steal some. Nature's Door might be able to rent you some gear. A rod would be better, but you can still have success with a handline and a simple lure. You can fish from headlands along the shore, from bridges or, if you are keen, wade into the lake for a few metres. After weeks of mutton you'll be desperate for some fish – incredibly, none of the guanz or restaurants in the aimag serve it.

Some of the best spots we found were the bridge at the southern end of Khatgal (which leads to the road going up the eastern shore), Borsog on the west shore, and at several coves where the eastern road meets the south-east shore. Around a dozen species of fish inhabit the lake, including salmon, (bony) sturgeon, grayling and lennok.

A fishing permit costs US$5 and is valid for two days and 10 fish. You can get them from the national park rangers or from Khatgal government house. Fishing is not allowed before July 10. The fine for fishing illegally is US$40.

Staff at Huvsgul Travel in Mörön and at Toilogt I ger camp can give information on their fishing camps in the region.

Places to Stay

Camping Khövsgöl Nuur is possibly the best place in Mongolia to camp. There is endless fresh water, plenty of fish; and the hiking is outstanding. On the down side, it often rains in summer and flies abound.

There is some confusion as to whether tourists can camp anywhere. There are designated camp sites, marked by often obscured blue signs, which read 'Хоног Цэг' (camping ground). There are *camp sites* near the Thyme 1 camp, just past Jankhai camp and two in the bay between Jankhai and Toilogt. These seemed aimed primarily at Mongolian tourists and groups.

Away from these areas you can pretty much pitch your tent anywhere you want, though try to stay 100m from other gers. You should never camp, wash or build fires within 50m of the shore.

The best camping spots on the western shoreline are anywhere between Jankhai and Ongolog, 10km north of Toilogt. If you have your own jeep, and want to experience one of the worst roads in Mongolia, the best spot to camp on the eastern shoreline is at Borsog.

The lake water is still very clean but a rise in livestock using the area for winter pasture has led to some pollution of the shore and feeder rivers, so you are better off purifying your water.

Ger Camps There are several ger camps in stunning locations on the western shore (none on the east). Most ger camps have electricity, running water, toilets and showers, though many are dangerously near the shoreline and have little environmental regard for the lake. Most places will offer a lower price if you bring and cook your own food. The majority only open in mid-June.

Several families also accept guests in a *guest ger*. They are not registered with the park and so don't advertise, but if you ask around you can probably find a family who will let you stay for a couple of US dollars.

The ***Khangard*** and ***Khantaiga*** camps, a couple of kilometres north of Khatgal, cater mostly to organised groups. They are reached from the road north of Khatgal, not

NORTHERN MONGOLIA

the main road which heads to the lake over the pass, Jankhai Davaa.

The main group of camps start where the road meets the lake, after descending from Jankhai Davaa. The **Dalain Turleg** (or Jankhai Tsaram) camp has beds in a basic but clean cabin for US$17, plus US$8 for three meals. A sauna and hot showers are available.

Just a little further is **Erden Uul** (or Dalai Tur), which offers beds in a ger for US$10 per person, though doubles sometimes go for US$15 for two. Bring your own food, as meals are a pricey US$20. Saunas and hot showers are available.

Just next door is **Thyme 1**, the backpacker camp run by Nature's Door. Beds in a five-bed ger cost US$10 and there is an eco-friendly toilet and shower block. The food is the best on the lake. You can camp on the site for US$3. It's a great place to hang out or arrange horse, boat and trekking trips.

Another kilometre or so is a fabulous **camping area** in a majestic location on a headland surrounded by pine trees. It is part of the main resort at Jankhai, and a bed in a ger costs US$15, or US$30 with food. If you are here early in the season there may be no gers set up and you can probably get away with camping here.

From here, it is another 5km to the main **Jankhai Resort**, a huge and charmless concrete complex on the western side of the road. Beds range from US$8/12/15 in an ordinary/half-deluxe/deluxe room, or US$19/ 27/30 with meals.

A further 5km north of Jankhai, two ger camps are set up at the Toilogt headland, around two lovely, tiny lakes immediately adjacent to Khövsgöl Nuur. **Toilogt I** (or Khuvsgol Juulchin) is run by the Huvsgul Travel Company (in Mörön) and costs US$35 per person including meals, or a reasonable US$10 without meals. The camp sometimes has music shows for guests and hires out a motor boat. Look for the sign in English on the main road.

The other one, **Toilogt II**, is set up on an isthmus linking the two lakes and is the first of the two camps you reach after branching off the main road.

A couple of kilometres past here are the last two camps, **Eder Tour** and **Gants Nuur** ger camps, both of which are fairly basic, with pit toilets.

Getting There & Away

Air Khatgal has a dirt runway but only the occasional flights from Mörön or Ulaan Baatar operate. Khangard Airlines flies to/from Ulaan Baatar on Monday, Wednesday and Friday from July 10 to August 15. Schedules are continually in flux so check with Khangard in Ulaan Baatar. MIAT and Khangard have ceased flights to Khankh.

Boojum Expeditions, a US-based company with an office in Ulaan Baatar, occasionally operates helicopter trips from Ulaan Baatar to the lake and will sell travellers any remaining seats. Contact their office in Ulaan Baatar.

Jeep Minivans and jeeps regularly make the trip between Mörön and Khatgal (three hours) for T5000 per person, or T20,000 for the jeep. Inquire at the stand at the north end of the market in Mörön.

Transport also meets the Ulaan Baatar flight at Mörön airport to take passengers directly to Khatgal. Some jeep owners will try to charge foreigners up to US$50 for the run; local drivers with the 'Хөл' license plate are likely to be fairer. Nature's Door will normally pick up and drop travellers at Mörön airport for T5000 per person.

A chartered jeep should not cost more than the normal T300 per kilometre. There are plenty of jeeps in Mörön but few in Khatgal, where you are best asking at the guesthouses. In the peak season of July and August, it may be difficult to charter a jeep for a reasonable price. If you are headed north of Khatgal it is also important to find a reliable jeep that can handle the terrible roads. From Khatgal to Khankh, at the top of the lake, it is about 200km. You need to be aware of this if you are chartering a jeep by the kilometre.

Khatgal is a rough 101km from Mörön – the valleys of the Egiin Gol, along the way, are particularly beautiful and worth a visit in their own right.

Hitching For lifts from Mörön, hang around the market or the petrol station – and keep asking. Once in Khatgal, most trucks will stop in front of the post office.

From Khatgal, hitching a ride to Jankhai or Toilogt shouldn't be difficult in summer, but you'll probably end up paying a fair bit for a lift anyway. You should be self-sufficient with camping gear and food.

Hitching around the eastern shore is much more difficult and you could wait for days for a lift to come along.

TSAGAANNUUR
ЦАГААННУУР

About 50km west of Khövsgöl Nuur, in Renchinlkhumbe *sum* (district), is a large depression called Darkhadyn Khotgor, often referred to as Tsagaannuur (White Lake), after the main village in the area. The Darkhadyn Depression is roughly the same size as Khövsgöl Nuur and was indeed originally formed as a glacial lake.

The difficulty in reaching the region ensures that the unique Tsaatan people who inhabit the valleys are able to continue their traditional lifestyle – but tourism is slowly making an impact. Darkhadyn is one of Mongolia's strongest centres of shamanism.

This is one of the best-watered regions in Mongolia: the aimag has about 300 lakes and 200 of them are in this area. The lakes are a vital part of Mongolia's very limited commercial fishing industry – white carp and trout are packed in salt and flown out to Ulaan Baatar to be served in the fancier hotels. Salmon and huge taimen can also be found in the region.

One definite drawback to visiting the region is the insects that invade the area. Be warned: these little critters have insatiable appetites for foreign skin and will ruin your trip if you are not fully prepared with mosquito nets and repellent.

Permits
Tsagaannuur and the region inhabited by the Tsaatan is not part of Khövsgöl Nuur National Park. However, authorities in Ulaan Baatar are currently considering a plan to limit the effects of tourism on the

The Tsaatan

Not far from Khövsgöl Nuur, live the Tsaatan people, named from the Mongolian word for reindeer, *tsaa*. Their entire existence is based around the reindeer, which provide milk, skins for clothes, transport and, occasionally, meat.

The Tsaatan are part of a Tuvan ethnic group, which inhabits the Tuvan Republic of Russia. There are only about 60 Tsaatan families, spread over 100,000 sq km of northern Mongolia. They are truly nomadic, often moving their small encampments, called *ail*, every two or three weeks – looking for special types of grass and moss loved by the reindeer. The Tsaatan do not use gers, but prefer tents made from reindeer skin. The Tsaatan practise shamanism.

Visiting the Tsaatan is difficult, exhausting and not recommended. The mosquitoes are legendary, the climate is exceedingly harsh, and the lack of responsible tourism guidelines means that tourism currently has only a negative impact on the Tsaatan. Few, if any, of the companies who arrange trips to the Tsaatan take any ethical stance to support Tsaatan culture. Until they do, tourism will only further erode a culture on the brink of extinction.

Tsaatan by implementing a permit system. These permits are likely to be expensive and only available to organised tour groups.

At the time of research, there were no restrictions on travelling to Tsagaannuur, though some travellers have reported requiring a permit from the border police. It is best to check with the police in Mörön before starting the long trek out there.

Places to Stay
There is a tiny *hotel* in Tsagaannuur, but it was closed at the time of research. Until it reopens, you'll have to take a tent. Bring all your own food. There are plenty of lakes and rivers with fresh water and fish in the area.

Getting There & Away
Air Tiny chartered planes can land at the dirt runway at Tsagaannuur, but it will still

take a couple of days on horseback to reach the Tsaatan people. Staff from foreign embassies and development agencies in Ulaan Baatar sometimes take a helicopter directly to the Tsaatan encampments and land like some spacecraft from outer space.

Jeep By chartered jeep, you can get to Tsagaannuur from Mörön (but not from Khatgal) in a bone-crunching 12 to 15 hours, depending on the state of the road. You will have to negotiate hard and long for a reasonable price. There are no scheduled public shared jeeps to Tsagaannuur.

Hitching Traffic between Mörön and Tsagaannuur is extremely sparse, but if you have your own tent and food, and don't mind waiting for a day or two, something may come along during summer – or it may not.

Horse There is really only one way to get to Tsagaannuur and the area: by horse. It is best to arrange things at Khatgal.

From Khatgal to Jiglegyn Am, about halfway up the western shore of Khövsgöl Nuur, will take three leisurely days (four hours' riding each day). From Jiglegyn Am, there are several easy-to-follow horse trails to Renchinlkhumbe – just make sure you are heading west. You will need to allow two days to get from Jiglegyn Am and over the pass, Jiglegyn Davaa (2500m). From the pass, the trail to Renchinlkhumbe is easy; it then heads north-west to Tsagaannuur. From there, it will probably still take a couple of days to reach some Tsaatan encampments.

A return trip from Khatgal to Tsagaannuur, with a visit to the Tsaatan, will take from 10 to 12 days. You could go from Khatgal to Tsagaannuur on an easy trail in about five days (bypassing Jiglegyn Am), but your back would not appreciate the hard ride and you would miss Khövsgöl Nuur.

CHANDIMAN-ÖNDÖR & SURROUNDS
ЧАНДИМАН-ӨНДӨР

The village of Chandiman-Öndör, a day's drive east of Khatgal, is in a beautiful area, which would make a good exploratory trip

for hardy travellers. There are few amenities here, though some locals have received training in ecotourism from a local Peace Corps volunteer.

There is no formal accommodation in town but a couple named Oyunchimeg and Enktuvshin operate two *wood cabins* in their *hashaa* (ger suburb) in the south-east edge of town. The town also has a decent **museum** and *guanz*.

Shared jeeps to Chandiman-Öndör (T5000) occasionally leave from the north side of the market in Mörön. From Khatgal you need your own jeep, though the two- or three-day horse ride is said to be wonderful.

Surrounding sites include the **Bulnai hot springs**, about 50km north-west of town, which offers simple cabins around a former Soviet resort. Further east, 30km south-east of Tsagaan-Uur, is the **Dayan Derkhiin Agui** cave, considered holy by local Buddhists and shamanists, and a nearby ruined monastery. Many **Buryats** live in this area. With a few days up your sleeve this could make a rough but beautiful alternative route from Khövsgöl to Bulgan.

In the north-east of the aimag, the area around the Khokh, Arig and Kheven rivers, is particularly good **fishing**. The Huvsgul Travel Company in Mörön organises trips to the best fishing spots in the area.

FIVE RIVERS
About 50km south of Mörön, on the border with the Arkhangai aimag, is an area where the Ider, Bugsei, Selenge, Delger Mörön and Chuluut rivers converge. In September and October this is one of the best **fishing** spots in the country.

Bulgan Вулган

pop 67,300 • area 49,000 sq km
Bulgan aimag is a curious mixture: the south is dry grassland and the north is green and has enough forest to support a small timber industry; scattered in between are about 50,000 hectares of wheat and vegetable crops – Mongolia's agricultural heartland – and Erdenet, Mongolia's largest

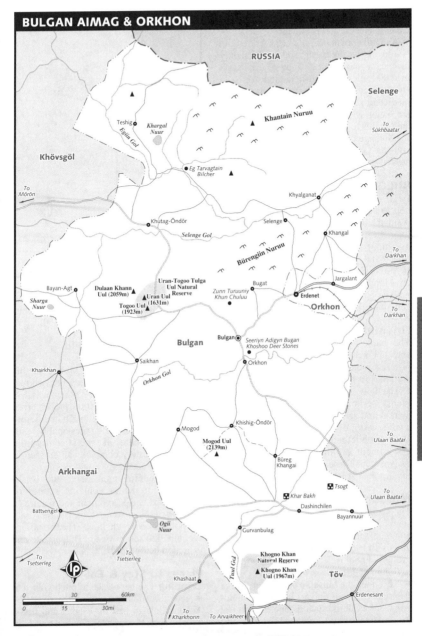

BULGAN AIMAG & ORKHON

RUSSIA

Selenge

Khövsgöl

To Sükhbaatar

Teshig

Khargal Nuur

Egiin Gol

Khantain Nuruu

To Mörön

Eg Tarvagtain Bilcher

Khyalganat

Khutag-Öndör

Selenge Gol

Selenge

Khangal

To Darkhan

Bürengin Nuruu

Bayan-Agt

Dulaan Khann Uul (2059m)

Uran-Togoo Tulga Uul Natural Reserve

Zunn Turuuniy Khun Chuluu

Bugat

Jargalant

Sharga Nuur

Uran Uul (1631m)

Togoo Uul (1923m)

Erdenet

Orkhon

To Darkhan

Bulgan

Seeriyn Adigyn Bugan Khoshoo Deer Stones

Bulgan

Saikhan

Orkhon

Khairkhan

Orkhon Gol

Mogod

Khishig-Öndör

To Ulaan Baatar

Mogod Uul (2139m)

Büreg Khangai

Arkhangai

Tsogt

Khar Bakh

To Ulaan Baatar

Battsengel

Dashinchilen

Bayannuur

Ogii Nuur

Gurvanbulag

To Tsetserleg

To Tsetserleg

Khogno Khan Natural Reserve

Töv

Khashaat

Khogno Khan Uul (1967m)

Tuul Gol

Erdenesant

0   30   60km

0   15   30mi

To Kharkhorin   To Arvaikheer

NORTHERN MONGOLIA

copper mine. The ethnic groups comprise Khalkh, Buryat and Russians.

A small mountain range, the Bürengiin Nuruu, bisects the aimag, and though it only reaches a maximum altitude of 2058m, it provides plenty of lush habitat for wild animals and livestock. Herbs, often used for medicinal purposes, are being cultivated in the region with some success. Elk are abundant in this region. Mongolia's largest river, the Selenge Gol, crosses the aimag's north, and the Orkhon and Tuul rivers meander around the southern parts.

BULGAN
БУЛГАН

pop 13,000 • elevation 1208m

A small aimag capital, the city of Bulgan has long been known to foreigners as an overnight stop midway between Ulaan Baatar and the ever-popular Khövsgöl Nuur. If you've been travelling in central or southern Mongolia, Bulgan city may impress you with its conifers, log cabins and absence of gers, though there's little reason to linger.

Orientation & Information
The bank along the main street might change US dollars. Alternatively, there may be a few moneychangers hanging about the market, just behind the bank.

The daily market is small but interesting. Plenty of horses are hitched outside the market and around town, like a scene from a wild west movie.

The public bath house, behind the pink government building, is officially open daily except Tuesday, though weekends are the best bet. A hot shower costs T300.

Museums
The **Aimag Museum** on the main street has some information on obscure sights in the aimag, a display on J Gurragcha, Mongolia's first man in space, and some interesting old photos. It's open daily from 9 am to 6 pm (T500).

Next door, the **Museum of Ancient Things** (Ugsaatny Zizuyn Salvar) has a few ethnographical exhibits, such as ancient surgical instruments, *airag* (fermented mare's milk)

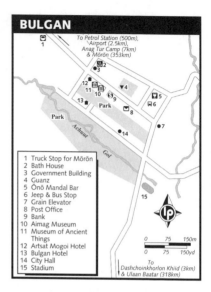

BULGAN

To Petrol Station (500m),
Airport (2.5km),
Anag Tur Camp (7km)
& Mörön (353km)

1   Truck Stop for Mörön
2   Bath House
3   Government Building
4   Guanz
5   Önö Mandal Bar
6   Jeep & Bus Stop
7   Grain Elevator
8   Post Office
9   Bank
10 Aimag Museum
11 Museum of Ancient
    Things
12 Artsat Mogoi Hotel
13 Bulgan Hotel
14 City Hall
15 Stadium

To
Dashchoinkhorlon Khiid (3km)
& Ulaan Baatar (318km)

churners and saddles, but was undergoing repairs, following the theft of several Buddhist statues in spring 2000. Entry is T500.

Dashchoinkhorlon Khiid
Дашоинхорлон Хийд

Like most monasteries in Mongolia, this one (built in 1992) replaces the original monastery, Bangiin Khüree, which was destroyed in 1937. About 1000 monks lived and worshipped at Bangiin Khüree before they were arrested and, presumably, executed. The remains of several stupas from the old monastery complex can be seen in the surroundings.

The modern monastery of Dashchoinkhorlon Khiid contains statues of Tsongkhapa and Sakyamuni and features a painting of the old monastery layout. About 30 monks now reside there. The monastery is about 3km south-west of Bulgan city and is hidden behind some hills.

Places to Stay & Eat
Camping The best place to pitch your tent is over the southern side of the river, the Achuut Gol; go past the market and find a discreet spot. If you have your own transport,

consider camping a few kilometres north of town, along the road to Mörön.

Hotels The *Bulgan Hotel*, in the park, is one of the best of Mongolia's aimag capital hotels (though, admittedly, this isn't saying a lot). Large, clean deluxe rooms with a clean bathroom are a bargain at between T3800 and T4200 per person. Beds in a triple/quad without bathroom cost T2300/2000.

The *Artsat Mogoi*, or Snake Hotel, on the 3rd floor of an anonymous-looking apartment block, has beds for T1500 in an apartment-style room, with a toilet and sink but only cold water. If no-one's there, inquire in the next door shop.

The *restaurant* at the Bulgan Hotel may be able to rustle up some mutton and noodles if you can find anyone in the kitchen. Otherwise try the *guanz* by the entrance to the market.

The *Anag Tur Camp (☎ 67-22 550)*, also known as the Jargalant Camp, is a tourist camp (no gers), popular with locals, 7km north-west of Bulgan.

Getting There & Away
Air Each Tuesday and Friday, MIAT flies from Ulaan Baatar to Bulgan for US$45/79. In theory at least you might be able to catch onward flights to Khovd and Tosontsengel and back again, but only if there are seats when the plane arrives. The airport is 2.5km north of town.

Bus & Minivan A few direct buses go between Bulgan and Ulaan Baatar, but most people take a minivan to Erdenet and then take the overnight train. Minivans depart Ulaan Baatar on Monday and Thursday (T6000). A post office van departs for Ulaan Baatar every Tuesday at around noon (T7000).

Minivans headed to Mörön pass through the outskirts of Bulgan city but are normally crammed full of people.

Jeep Locals say that a public shared jeep goes to Ulaan Baatar every Wednesday, but Bulgan city is not somewhere you want to hang around, so do what the locals do: catch a crowded public jeep or taxi direct to Erdenet train station (two hours, T3000 for a seat or T10,000 for the car), and then take the 7.45 pm train to Ulaan Baatar. Jeeps hang around the Önö Mandal Bar, northeast of the post office.

Chartered jeeps were asking around T70,000 for a one-way trip to Khövsgöl Nuur, or T130,000 for a return trip, including a day or two's waiting time.

There are two routes between Ulaan Baatar and Bulgan city. The southern route is the most direct (318km), but it's mostly a dirt road, though not in bad condition as long as it isn't raining. Take this road if you are going straight from Ulaan Baatar to Khövsgöl Nuur.

The northern route (467km), through Darkhan (in Selenge aimag) and Erdenet, is on a good, often sealed, road – except for the Bulgan-Erdenet leg. If you want to visit Darkhan, Erdenet or Amarbayasgalant Khiid (north of the Darkhan-Erdenet main road), the northern route is the way to go.

Bulgan city is 68km from Erdenet, 248km from Darkhan and 353km from Mörön.

Hitching Plenty of vehicles go along the Ulaan Baatar–Bulgan-Mörön road, including a few with foreign tourists, so it should not be too much of a headache hitching a ride. At a cafeteria near the bridge a few kilometres south of Khutag-Öndör – which is about 80km north-west of Bulgan city – you will be able get some food and a bed for the night. A few trucks stop there, so it's a good place to hang around and ask for a lift.

To take advantage of the traffic between Erdenet and places to the west (which often bypass Bulgan city), you need to hang around the petrol station about 500m northwest of Bulgan city. A lift to Mörön will probably cost around T13,000.

AROUND BULGAN
There are a couple of obscure historical monuments around Bulgan. About 20km south of Bulgan, just east of Orkhon are seven standing **deer stones**, so called because the stones are carved with reindeers and other animals. The stones, known as

Seeriyn Adigyn Bugan Khoshoo, mark what are thought to be Neolithic grave sites.

About 25km north of Bulgan is a 1m-tall Turkic **balbal** (Turkic grave markers), known as Zunn Turuuniy Khun Chuluu.

URAN UUL & TOGOO UUL
УРАН УУЛ & ТОГОО УУЛ

About 60km directly west of Bulgan city is the extinct volcano of Uran Uul (GPS: N49°59.855', E102°44.003') and nearby Togoo Uul, now part of the 1600 hectare Uran-Togoo Tulga Uul Natural Reserve in the *sum* (district) of Khutag-Öndör.

Uran Uul is a pretty good place to break the journey to Khövsgöl, though the flies in this area can be intensely irritating. Trails to the top of the relatively unimpressive volcano lead up from the west side, which also has some nice camping areas. Jeep tracks lead to the volcano from the main road.

EG TARVAGATAIN BILCHER
УГ ТАРВАГТАИН БИЛЧҮР

This is a scenic area of rivers, forests and mountains, suitable for hiking and camping, though there are no tourist camps as yet. It is in Teshig sum. Access roads are very poor in this region. Just east of Teshig is the pretty Khargal Nuur.

BUGAT
БУГАТ

If you have rented a jeep with a driver, the best way to travel between Erdenet and Bulgan city is via Bugat village. It is rough going, but the 40km jeep trail goes through some of the most picturesque forests and gorgeous wildflowers in northern Mongolia (Bugat means 'Place of Elk'). You will have to ask directions to find the start of the trail from Erdenet as the trail can be tricky to follow; it's easier to find from Bulgan city.

ERDENET
УРДҮНҮТ
pop 74,000

In the autonomous municipality of Orkhon, and not technically part of Bulgan aimag, Erdenet is Mongolia's third-largest city. The reason for Erdenet's existence is the copper

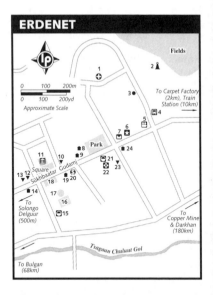

mine, which employs about 8000 people and is the lifeblood of the city. Erdenet is modern (built in 1974) and a bit soulless, but far nicer than most towns in the countryside. It is comparatively wealthy, so the facilities are the best outside of Ulaan Baatar. There is also a significantly large Russian community. Up to a third of the population of Erdenet was Russian during Communist times, though now only about 1000 Russians still work as technical advisers at the mine.

There is evidence that Mongolians were making copper pots in the Erdenet area at least 200 years ago. Russian geologists initially recognised the area's potential during the 1940s. The copper was first seriously prospected during the 1960s, and by 1977 a train line to Ulaan Baatar was installed for hauling the ore. In 1981 an ore-processing plant was commissioned and Erdenet began exporting copper concentrate (30% copper), mostly to the former Soviet Union.

There are rumblings about privatisation, but the cash-strapped Mongolian government isn't keen to sell off the mine, as it currently generates about 70% of Mongolia's hard-currency earnings (depending on

ERDENET

PLACES TO STAY
8 Bolor Hotel
9 Togos Hotel
14 Aladdin Hotel; Restaurant
19 Chandman Hotel
24 Selenge Hotel; Restaurant;
   Onet Internet Centre

PLACES TO EAT
10 Tost Café
12 Nomin Cafe
13 Khooln Ches
23 Naran 1 Café

OTHER
1 Hospital
2 Friendship Monument
3 Train Ticket Office
4 Local Bus Station
5 Cinema
6 Police Station
7 Post Office
11 Culture Palace; Mining Museum
15 Jeep and Minivan Stand
16 Market
17 Stadium
18 Sports Palace
20 Bank
21 Transport for Bulgan
22 Department Store

the current price of copper). In 1995, 208,000 tons of iron ore and 11,000 tons of molybdenum produced at the mine generated US$900 million for Mongolia. The mining and processing operation consumes nearly 70% of Mongolia's electricity.

Orientation & Information

Erdenet is a sprawling city, though everything you will need is along the main street, Sükhbaatar Gudamj. Erdenet's train station is inconveniently located more than 10km east of the centre.

The couple of banks along Sükhbaatar Gudamj are reluctant to change money, but many shops along the street will change US dollars cash only. Exchange rates are about 2% lower than in Ulaan Baatar, and differ from shop to shop, so check around.

The Onet Internet Centre, on the 2nd floor of the Selenge Hotel offers Internet access for T30 per minute, or T300 for an email message, plus T20 per minute spent writing it. The centre is open weekdays from 8 am to 5 pm.

Friendship Monument

This Communist monument, about 200m north-east of the Selenge Hotel, is worth a quick look. On the way you pass a fine Marx mural and a picture of Lenin bolted to the wall. A little further to the east, the ovoo is impressive if you haven't seen too many before. The hills north of the monument and south of the stadium are great for short hikes.

Mining Museum

This Soviet-built museum belongs to the copper-mining company, Erdenet Concern. It's on the 2nd floor of the Culture Palace, and is worth a look. Entry is free; open from about 10 am to 5 pm weekdays.

Copper Mine

The open-cut mine (thankfully, several kilometres from the city) is one of the 10 largest copper mines in the world. You can see it from the south of town.

Open-cut mining is more damaging to the environment but infinitely safer than digging mine shafts below the surface. Also, since this particular mountain is almost solid copper and molybdenum ore, this is the only practical way to reach it. The mine operates 24 hours a day, 365 days a year.

The mine is worth a visit if you've never visited one like this before. We were able to take a taxi to the mine and persuade the guard at the gate to take us to the look-out platform, though it was hard work. It would be better to contact the boss Darvaa Suren (☎ 71 514) to get permission, after which a guide will then be assigned to you. Tours are only allowed on weekdays. The views from the lookout over the gigantic open-cut mine, and of the city, are impressive. A taxi to the mine from the town centre costs about T4000, including waiting time.

Places to Stay

Camping Although the city is comparatively large, it is still possible to camp near Erdenet. The best places to try are north of the Friendship Monument, or south of the stadium, over the other side of Tsagaan Chuluut Gol and among the pretty foothills.

Hotels Erdenet has the best choice of hotels outside Ulaan Baatar and is a good place to spoil yourself if on a long distance camping expedition.

The *Selenge Hotel* (☎ 20 474) is a classic Soviet-style hotel with large, clean rooms with bathroom, TV and hot water. Ordinary rooms cost between T3000 and T4800 per person, half-deluxe doubles cost around T10,000 and deluxe doubles cost T26,000 or T40,000, less for single occupancy. The hotel is also signposted as the Erdenet Hotel.

The *Chandman Hotel* (☎ 20 808) is better value than the Selenge. A large, clean half-deluxe room with great bathroom and hot water costs T4500 per person. Other rooms are less clean and more Soviet in style but cheaper at T3500 per person, or T5000 for a single. The hotel is across from the main square; look for the 'Hotel Bar' sign. Reception is on the upper floor.

The *Aladdin Hotel*, on the west end of town, has nice, clean and modern rooms with bathroom and hot water for T4000 per person, or T6000 for a larger deluxe. The place can get a bit noisy when it's busy but it's good value.

The apartment block that holds the *Togos Hotel* (☎ 30 555) looks worryingly like a bad part of the Bronx but once you get inside it's bright and clean. Ordinary rooms cost T7000 per person, or you can get a deluxe suite with balcony and cable TV for T12,000 per person. Groups of three rooms share a clean bathroom with hot water. The hotel is signposted from Sükhbaatar Gudamj and is on the 3rd floor of an apartment block.

The *Bolor Hotel* (☎ 25 361), across the courtyard from the Togos, is a cheaper and rougher looking place. Double and triple rooms cost T3000 per person and there are deluxe rooms for T5000 per person, all sharing common bathrooms. Reception is in the attached guanz/bar.

Places to Eat

The daily *market* behind the Sports Palace is surprisingly small and scrappy, though there's a good selection of (nonrefrigerated) dairy products here. Most locals buy their food from the selection of good shops along the main drag.

The *Naran 1* cafeteria is a good choice for lunch and serves up good potato salad and beefsteak for around T1000. It tends to close early in the evening. Buy your drinks in the shop next door.

The *Selenge Hotel* has a good restaurant, serving up standards like beefsteak with an egg on top (T1250), schnitzel (T1000), salad, soup and, maybe, just maybe, fried chicken. You can top this off with a large draught Chinggis Beer (T1600).

The bar at the *Chandman Hotel* is a good place to grab a beer, especially when the open-air seating area is set up.

Just south-west of the main square are a couple of cafes such as the *Khooln Ches*, the *Nomin Café* and the restaurant in the *Aladdin Hotel*. There are more *cafes* along Sükhbaatar Gudamj between the main square and the park, including the *Tost Café*. All serve noodles, salads and other Mongolian staples for around T800 a main dish.

Entertainment

The *Culture Palace*, on Sükhbaatar Gudamj, always has something on: a pop concert, some Russian and Chinese films, or a classical music recital. There is even a disco on the weekends.

If you have some time to kill, check out the impressive *Sports Palace*, also on the main street. You can take a hot shower (T500) or sauna (T1000 per hour), watch some wrestling or, in winter, go ice-skating at the stadium at the back. There's an indoor pool (T2000), open weekdays only, but the staff may make life difficult by insisting on a medical examination before they let you swim. The Sports Palace is open daily from 8 am to 10 pm.

Shopping

If a couple of tons of copper is a bit inconvenient to carry around, a carpet would make a good souvenir. The city's **carpet factory** produces over one million square metres every year using machinery from the former East Germany. About 98% of the carpets are exported, mostly to Russia, but now increasingly to China and places beyond.

The carpet factory is closed during the summer (June–August) when staff take holidays and supplies of wool are scarce. If you are in Erdenet during the rest of the year, you can go on a tour and see the entire operation. The factory is just off the main road to the train station, about 2km from the Friendship Monument.

You can also buy carpets and rugs at the **Solongo Delguur**, about 500m west of the Sports Palace. A huge Chinggis Khaan wall carpet costs from T79,000 and smaller, towel-sized carpets are T12,000 to T20,000.

Getting There & Away

Travellers often bypass Erdenet and go straight from Ulaan Baatar to Mörön via Bulgan. If you have the time, and want a little luxury, take the sleeper train from Ulaan Baatar to Erdenet. From Erdenet, catch a public shared jeep to Bulgan – but then you'll have to wait for whatever comes along to Mörön.

Air Although it is Mongolia's third-largest city, there are no flights to or from Erdenet: everyone travels by train, jeep and, to a lesser degree, bus. The airport is used almost exclusively by helicopters carrying executives to and from the mine.

Bus, Minivan & Jeep Because of the popularity of the train, buses from Erdenet to Ulaan Baatar, Darkhan and Sükhbaatar only leave when there is enough demand. If there is a bus, it will leave from the market, or from the local bus station diagonally opposite the cinema.

Occasional cars to Ulaan Baatar leave from the local bus station at around 6 pm and charge T5000 for the six-hour ride. The local rate for a chartered minibus to Ulaan Baatar is T60,000.

Minivans, Korean microvans and jeeps to Mörön (10 hours, T10,000) leave most mornings from the market. Jeeps can also be chartered from here for about T350 per km.

Occasional minivans and jeeps to Bulgan leave from opposite the department store.

The good but unpaved road between Erdenet and Darkhan (180km) will become fully paved with the help of a loan from, of all countries, Kuwait. The road between Erdenet and Bulgan city (68km) is unsealed and rough – or you could go via Bugat. Ulaan Baatar is 371km from Erdenet.

Train The train between Ulaan Baatar and Erdenet, via Darkhan, takes 14 hours and costs T3000 for a hard seat and T7200 for a soft-seat sleeper. The sleeper is definitely worth the extra tögrög: the hard-seat carriages are packed to the roof. Daily trains to Ulaan Baatar depart at 7 pm. A weekend express train leaves at 10.30 am and takes 10 hours for the same fare.

The trip between Erdenet and Darkhan (5½ hours) goes through some lovely countryside, though most of the ride takes place in darkness. To Darkhan, the train costs T1800 for a hard seat and T4400 for a soft seat. For Sükhbaatar in Selenge aimag, change in Darkhan.

The station has a small quota of tickets on the Trans-Siberian Railway and sells tickets to Ulaan Ude (T28,200), Novosibirsk (T68,000) and Moscow (T112,900).

If travelling hard seat, get to the station a couple of hours before departure, sharpen your elbows and huddle outside the train – the doors of the carriages open about 30 minutes before departure.

Buses meet arriving trains, but the stampede of passengers quickly fills these to overflowing. Also, not every bus you see at the train station is going to the centre – many are headed to industrial areas surrounding the city, so don't just get on any bus. It's best to get off the train as soon as you can and find a taxi (about T4000) before the crush starts.

It is a more sedate going by bus *to* the train station. Buses (T300), cars (T500 per person) and taxis (T4000) leave from the local bus station, south of the train ticket office.

You can buy tickets at the train station, but it's better to queue on the day of, or before, departure at the train ticket office (☎ 225 505) in the north-east end of town. The office is open from 9 am to noon and 2 to 6 pm – look for the small train sign on the side of an apartment block, north of the local bus station. After 3 pm on the day of departure, it's best to go straight to the train station.

DASHINCHILEN
ДАШИНЧИЛ_ҮН

There are a couple of minor monuments in Dashinchilen sum, in the south of the aimag, which might be of interest if you are travelling between Ulaan Baatar and Tsetserleg, via Ogii Nuur.

On the west side of the Tuul Gol, about 35km north-east of Dashinchilen, are the ruins of **Tsogt** (Tsogt Tayjiin Tsagaan Balgas), a 17th century fort which was the home of the mother of Prince Tsogt, a 17th century poet who fought against Chinese rule. There is a **stone stele** nearby.

Closer to the sum capital, the ruined **Khar Bukh Fortress** (Khar Bakhin Balgas), might be worth exploring as it's just a few kilometres north of the main road.

Selenge Сэлэнгэ

pop 108,500 ● area 42,800 sq km

Selenge is the first – or last – aimag seen by train travellers shuttling between Ulaan Baatar and Russia. There is not a lot to attract visitors to Selenge except the majestic, but remote, monastery Amarbayasgalant Khiid and some beautiful scenery.

Ethnic groups in the aimag include Khalkh, Buryat, Dorvod, Oold and Russians. Buryats, Kazakhs, Russian and even Chinese live in wooden huts in villages hugging the train line and the main paved road that bisect the aimag. They look after some of the 300,000 hectares of grains, fruits and vegetables. Many others live in Darkhan, Mongolia's second-largest city. In the south-east, the open-pit coal mine at Sharyn Gol produces about two million tons of coal each year to provide electricity for the Erdenet mine in Bulgan aimag.

The mighty Selenge Gol starts from the mountains of western Mongolia and flows into Lake Baikal in Siberia, draining nearly 300,000 sq km in both countries. The other great river, the Orkhon, meets the Selenge near the aimag capital of Sükhbaatar.

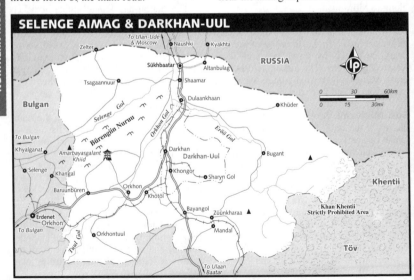

SELENGE AIMAG & DARKHAN-UUL

SÜKHBAATAR
СУХБААТАР
pop 20,000 • elevation 626m
Near the junction of the Selenge and Orkhon rivers, the capital of Selenge aimag, Sükhbaatar, was founded in the 1940s. Although Mongolia's chief border town, it is a quiet, pleasant place. There is little reason to stay, however, unless you want to break up the train journey to or from Russia, you want to save money by travelling on local trains rather than on the more expensive international train, or you are smuggling goods.

Orientation & Information
Just north of the train station is the centre of town, where you'll find the main hotel, market and town square. The daily market, behind the Selenge Hotel, is lively and friendly and, as a border town, well stocked.

Money When the international train arrives and stops for an hour or two, a few moneychangers come out of the woodwork. They will change Mongolian tögrög, US dollars and Russian roubles. Otherwise the bank, which is open during normal banking hours (which is *not* when the train normally arrives), is in a round, orange building just south of the train station.

If you are leaving Mongolia, get rid of your tögrög – they are worthless anywhere in Russia (including on the Trans-Mongolian train in Russia).

Places to Stay
Camping Selenge aimag is particularly pleasant for camping. At Sükhbaatar, the best place to try is across the train line and among the fields, just west of town. Alternatively, there are great spots among the hills north-east of the market.

Hotels Probably the best place in town is the *Selenge Hotel*, a yak's spit from the train station. Dark, musty rooms with toilet cost T3000 per person without running water, or T5000 with.

The *Orkhon Hotel* is in the southernmost corner of town, next to the grain elevators. These generate a lot of noise, but the rooms

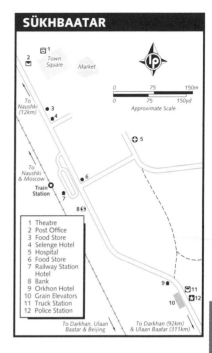

SÜKHBAATAR

To Naushki (12km)
To Naushki & Moscow
Town Square
Market
Train Station

0   75   150m
0   75   150yd
Approximate Scale

1 Theatre
2 Post Office
3 Food Store
4 Selenge Hotel
5 Hospital
6 Food Store
7 Railway Station Hotel
8 Bank
9 Orkhon Hotel
10 Grain Elevators
11 Truck Station
12 Police Station

To Darkhan, Ulaan Baatar & Beijing
To Darkhan (92km) & Ulaan Baatar (311km)

are nicer than at the Selenge. Rooms cost T6000 per person, or T16,000 for a deluxe with running water. You may have to spend half a day looking for someone who works there, then persuade them to give you a room.

The *Railway Station Hotel*, at the station, is pretty grotty but comparatively good value at T1500 per person in a dormitory or T4000 in a private room.

Places to Eat
The restaurant on the ground floor of the *Selenge Hotel* serves barely edible mutton-goulash and undrinkable Chinese beer. The only decent place to eat is the *guanz* above the train ticket office at the station. You can dine out here on a reasonable mutton and noodle dish for T400, and the beer is tasty, but warm.

Getting There & Away
Train Sükhbaatar is the first (or last) Mongolian stop on the regular services of Ulaan

Sükhbaatar, the Hero

It won't take long before you wonder who Damdin Sükhbaatar is – a statue of the man astride a horse dominates the square named after him in Ulaan Baatar, his face is on many currency notes, and there is a provincial capital and aimag called Sükhbaatar.

Born in 1893, probably in what is now Ulaan Baatar, Sükh (which means 'axe'), as he was originally named, joined the Mongolian army in 1911. He soon became famous for his horsemanship but was forced to leave the army because of insubordination. In 1917 he joined another army, fought against the Chinese and picked up the added moniker of *baatar* or 'hero'.

In early 1921, Sükhbaatar was appointed Commander-in-Chief of the Mongolian People's Revolutionary Army which defeated the Chinese, and, later, the White Russians. In July of that year, he declared Mongolia's independence from China at what is now known as Sükhbaatar Square.

He packed a lot in a short life – he was dead at 30. The exact cause of his death has never been known, and he did not live to see Mongolia proclaimed a republic.

Baatar to Irkutsk, Ulaan Baatar to Moscow or Beijing to Moscow. Trains stop here for two or more hours while Mongolian customs and immigration are completed. This usually takes place late at night or very early in the morning – not the best time to wander around Sükhbaatar. See the Trans-Mongolian Railway entry under Land in the Getting There & Away chapter for more information about international trains.

Direct, local trains travel between Ulaan Baatar and Sükhbaatar, with a stop at Darkhan. Tickets from Ulaan Baatar to Sükhbaatar cost T2500/6400 for a hard/soft seat. Trains leave Ulaan Baatar every day at 9.05 and 10.30 am, and return from Sükhbaatar at 9.30 pm and 6.10 am.

Taxi The road to Ulaan Baatar (311km) through Darkhan (92km) is well paved, so jeeps are not necessary. Because of the popularity and regularity of the train, public shared taxis between Sükhbaatar and Darkhan, and onto Ulaan Baatar, are irregular and only leave when there is enough demand.

If you want to explore the nearby countryside, the best place to hire a taxi or jeep is outside the train station.

Hitching Because of the regular public transport along the main road between Ulaan Baatar and Sükhbaatar, you'll get a lift pretty easily along this road. From Sükhbaatar, trucks, which congregate outside the grain elevators, could give you a lift to Ulaan Baatar – but definitely not across the Russian border.

DULAANKHAAN
ДУЛААНХААН

Sixty-two kilometres south of Sükhbaatar, this tiny village in the sum of the same name is worth a stop if you have your own vehicle. Dulaankhaan is home to Mongolia's only **bow and arrow factory**. Bows and arrows are made from ibex, reindeer horn, bamboo and, even, fish guts. Only 30 to 40 sets are crafted every year because they take about four months to complete. Each set sells for about US$200. It is thought that today less than 10 people in Mongolia know how to make a traditional Mongol bow.

There is nowhere to stay in the village so carry on to Sükhbaatar or Darkhan, or camp nearby.

ALTANBULAG
АЛТАНБУЛАГ

Just 24km to the east of Sükhbaatar is Altanbulag, a small, peaceful border town in the sum of the same name. Just on the other side of the border is the Russian city of Kyakhta. From the border, you can easily see the abandoned, but once opulent, **Kyakhta Cathedral**. The Mongolian government recently decided to allocate 500 hectares at Altanbulag as a **Free Trade Zone** for the development of trade with Russia. Hopefully, this will be more successful than the Free Trade Zone in Choir, in Dornogov aimag.

Altanbulag is worth a look if you have some spare time in Sükhbaatar but don't go too close to the border. Minivans run between Sükhbaatar and Altanbulag at various times during the day, and also to Ulaan Baatar. There is no fixed schedule, so make local inquiries. Otherwise, charter a taxi.

At the time of research, foreigners could not cross the border by road through Altanbulag; you can take a vehicle over the border, but you personally have to go through customs on the train between Naushki and Sükhbaatar. However, there are future plans to open the road border at Altanbulag for foreigners. (See the Land section in the Getting There & Away chapter for more details.)

Both Kyakhta and Altanbulag are of some historical importance to Mongolians. In 1915 representatives from Russia, China and Mongolia met in Kyakhta to sign a treaty granting Mongolia limited autonomy. This was later revoked when China invaded again in 1919. At a meeting in Kyakhta in March 1921, the Mongolian People's Party was formed by Mongolian revolutionaries in exile, and the revolutionary hero Sükhbaatar was named minister of war.

DARKHAN
ДАРХАН
pop 95,500

Darkhan is the second-largest city in Mongolia. This city is, in fact, not part of Selenge aimag, but an autonomous municipality, Darkhan-Uul. The city was built in the middle of nowhere in 1961 as a satellite town to take pressure off the sprawling Ulaan Baatar, and as a northern industrial centre. Darkhan, which means 'blacksmith', is a modern, sterile place. Fortunately, Darkhan's designers put a little thought into urban planning, so the industrial smokestacks are on the south side of town and the pollution is carried away from residential areas by the relentless northern wind. The Russians designed the city in their image and a sizeable Russian community still lives in Darkhan.

It is not somewhere you would rush to see, but you may need to stay here while you arrange transport to Amarbayasgalant Khiid.

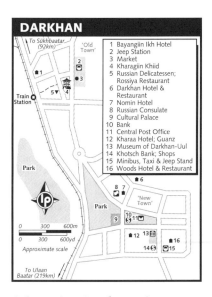

DARKHAN

1	Bayangiin Ikh Hotel
2	Jeep Station
3	Market
4	Kharagiin Khiid
5	Russian Delicatessen; Rossiya Restaurant
6	Darkhan Hotel & Restaurant
7	Nomin Hotel
8	Russian Consulate
9	Cultural Palace
10	Bank
11	Central Post Office
12	Kharaa Hotel; Guanz
13	Museum of Darkhan-Uul
14	Khotsch Bank; Shops
15	Minibus, Taxi & Jeep Stand
16	Woods Hotel & Restaurant

Orientation & Information

Darkhan is spread out. The city is divided into an 'old' town near the train station and a 'new' town to the south. Near the Central Post Office in the new town is Darkhan's pride and joy: a 16-storey building, for a long time Mongolia's tallest.

The modern Khotsch Bank in the suburbs, just behind the museum, or the bank just north of the Kharaa Hotel might change US dollars cash, otherwise try the market for US dollars and roubles.

Kharagiin Khiid
Харагийн Хийд

Probably the most interesting sight in Darkhan is the Kharagiin monastery. Housed in a pretty log cabin in the old town, it has recently become very active. With a host of protector deities and a tree encased in blue *khatag* silk scarves, the monastery has the feel of a pilgrimage centre. As elsewhere, photography is forbidden inside unless special arrangements are made.

Museum of Darkhan-Uul

This museum, also named the Traditional Museum of Folk Art, contains a well laid

NORTHERN MONGOLIA

out collection of archaeological findings, traditional clothing, religious artefacts and a few obligatory stuffed animals. The museum is upstairs in a building on the north side of the shopping square, opposite the minibus, taxi and jeep stand. It's open daily from 9 am to 5 pm (T500).

Places to Stay

Camping Despite the size of Darkhan, it isn't hard to get away from the town and find a nearby secluded spot to camp. Southwest of the train station are some empty fields – but get away from the drunks who hang around the station. The fields to the north of the Darkhan Hotel are also good.

Hotels In the new town area, the decent *Nomin Hotel*, is on the 5th floor of the Nomin Kompani building. Clean doubles, with an ensuite or sometimes common bathroom (with hot water) cost T3400 or T3900. Dormitories cost T2300 per bed. To find the hotel go in the building, turn right and then go up the stairs by the Millennium Restaurant.

The *Darkhan Hotel (☎ 20 001)*, a Soviet-era monster, charges T6000/10000 for a pleasant single/double – but the attraction is a private bathroom with hot water, and even an intact toilet seat! Deluxe options range from T12,000 to T16,000 a bed. Pay for your room when you register to avoid a possible increase in the check-out price.

Kharaa Hotel (☎ 23 970) has singles/doubles with a sink, toilet and hot water for T4300/8000. For a shower you'll need the half-deluxe room for T13,000. The entrance is through the Chinggis Beer Bar.

Woods Hotel (☎ 24 367) is a small, modern hotel with rooms for around T15,000/20,000. It's behind the new town minivan stand.

In the old town area, *Bayangiin Ekh (☎ 33 841, fax 37 344, e bayanekh@ mongol.net)* is a private hotel, 150m north of the train station. Spacious, clean, modern rooms with a balcony cost a negotiable US$16 to US$$18, or US$25 for a suite. Prices are per person and include breakfast. There's a restaurant and Internet connection. It's all a bit of a trade secret; there's no

visible sign that the place is a hotel and staff can be very cryptic. Look for the five-story red building and press the buzzer at the main gate.

If you are desperate, and don't want to walk in the middle of the night to catch that damned connection to Erdenet, you could try one of the dorm beds at the *train station* for T700 per person. As you enter the terminal, the doors to the right lead to this grimy 'hotel'.

Places to Eat

The restaurant at the *Darkhan Hotel* is pretty good and actually has a choice (though not as much as the menu would fool you into believing), with such trusty standards as beefsteak, schnitzel and, would you believe it, goulash (T800 each).

The *Woods Hotel* has the city's only proper restaurant and is the best place in town, with dishes like potato salad (T350), spaghetti (T850), Russian and Asian dishes, plus cold beer on tap. There's also a good canteen on the ground floor of the *Kharaa Hotel.*

If you are self-catering, the *market* in the old town is large, well stocked and worth a quick look. There are lots of different sections and a few hard-to-find things like vegetables and watermelons.

A *delicatessen* and cafe run by, and catering for, local Russians is across the road from Kharagiin Khiid. You can stock up on vegetables, yoghurt, sausage and vodka, and there's even fish for those Russians who are just a little fed up with endless mutton. The *Rossiya Restaurant* is next door and might be worth a try.

The best range of imported *food shops* are in the museum square, near the Khotsch Bank, in the new town.

Getting There & Away

Train Darkhan is the only train junction in Mongolia: all northern trains to/from Ulaan Baatar, and all trains to/from Erdenet, stop here. If your time is short, and you want to see some scenery in comfort (ie, in a soft seat), take the train between Darkhan and Ulaan Baatar: the train travels during the day, the trip is short and the scenery is interesting in Töv aimag (but is a little boring in Selenge).

All trains to Ulaan Baatar and Erdenet are jam-packed, reminiscent of the worst squalor you'll see on regional Indian and Chinese trains. It is definitely worth spending a few extra tögrög for a soft seat. The domestic ticket office at Darkhan train station is open daily from 8 am to noon, 4 to 6 pm, and 10 pm to 2 am. There is a timetable here (in Cyrillic). A separate international ticket office deals with tickets to Irkutsk and beyond.

The daily five-hour trip between Darkhan and Erdenet (T1600/4000 for hard/soft seat) goes through some lovely countryside, but you'll miss it as the train leaves Darkhan sometime between midnight and 4 am.

The daily Ulaan Baatar–Sükhbaatar train (No 271) leaves Darkhan for Sükhbaatar at 5.40 pm (two hours, T900/2300), or an ungodly 2.50 am.

Between Darkhan and Ulaan Baatar, a daytime train (No 272) leaves at 8.20 am, arriving in the capital at around 4 pm. An overnighter (No 264) departs at 11.40 pm, arriving at 6 am. Other trains leave in the middle of the night. Tickets cost T2000/5100.

See the Trans-Mongolian Railway entry under Land in the Getting There & Away chapter for details about international trains to/from Russia and China that stop at Darkhan.

Minivan & Taxi Constant demand ensures that public shared taxis (T5000) and minivans (T3000 to T4000) regularly do the five-hour run to Ulaan Baatar. They go less often to Sükhbaatar (T2000) because of the popularity of the train. These vehicles depart from the bus stand opposite the shopping square in the new town.

Being a major city, Darkhan enjoys the privilege of having a paved road to Ulaan Baatar (219km) and Sükhbaatar (92km). Many *guanz* along the way sell airag and basic meals.

Surprisingly, there is no scheduled transport between Darkhan and Erdenet. This leaves the train, which isn't much better as

it leaves in the middle of the night. The road to Erdenet (180km) is not paved but in good condition and being upgraded (with aid money from Kuwait).

Jeep Shared jeeps for surrounding aimag capitals, and jeeps which can be chartered, normally hang around the market. You'll need a Mongolian friend to listen out for the incomprehensible announcements over the loudspeaker. Shared jeeps leave for Bugant (T4000), Sharyn Gol, Khötöl and Selenge. For Amarbayasgalant Khiid you'll have to hire a jeep, at around T300 per km. Shared jeeps to Erdenet are very infrequent.

Getting Around
Darkhan is spread out, so you will probably have to take a taxi or two, or rent a motorcycle and sidecar (with driver) from the market. Taxis charge a reasonable T400 from the new town's shopping square and old town's train station.

BUGANT
БУГАНТ

Most of Selenge consists of fields and flood plains, but Bugant is an area of birch and pine forests, mountains and abundant wildlife. At one time, the town was known for its sawmill and nearby gold mine, but these industries are on their way out. The crystal-clear Eröö Gol flows through the town, and one possible journey on horseback would be to follow the river upstream to its source in the Khentii Nuruu range. **Trekking** is a possibility, but if you go wandering through the forest during the hunting season, wear bright colours to avoid being mistaken for an elk.

Bugant is in Eröö sum, a remote area about 110km south-east of Dulaankhaan. Access is strictly by jeep or truck over a bad, often muddy, road. Shared jeeps run when full from Darkhan for T4000 per person.

AMARBAYASGALANT KHIID
АМАРБАЯСГАЛАНТ ХИЙД

The star attraction of Selenge aimag, this monastery is considered the second most important in Mongolia (after Erdene Zuu

Khiid in Kharkhorin) and the most intact architectural complex in Mongolia. It is well worth visiting on the way to or from Khövsgöl Nuur or other areas in northern or western Mongolia, but it is difficult to reach. It's probably not worth the effort of coming here all the way from Ulaan Baatar just to see the monastery – you are better off incorporating it into a short three- or four-day countryside trip to take in the surrounding scenery, or a longer cross-country trip.

Amarbayasgalant Khiid was originally built between 1727 and 1737 by the Manchu emperor Yongzheng, and dedicated to the great Mongolian Buddhist and sculptor, Zanabazar, whose mummified body was moved here in 1779. The monastery is in the Chinese style, down to the inscriptions, symmetrical layout and imperial colour scheme.

The communists found a way out here in the late 1930s, but 'only' destroyed 10 out of the 37 temples and statues, possibly because of sympathetic and procrastinating local military commanders. The monastery was extensively restored between 1975 and 1990 with the help of Unesco. These days, around 50 monks live in the monastery, compared to over 2000 in 1936.

The temples in the monastery are normally closed, so you'll have to ask the head monk to find the keys and open them up if you want to see any statues or scroll paintings. There are around five halls open to tourists.

The main hall has a life-size statue of **Rinpoche Gurdava**, a lama from Inner Mongolia who lived in Tibet and Nepal before returning to Mongolia in 1992 and raising much of the money for the temple's restoration. It's normally possible to climb up to the roof for fine **views** of the valley.

To help with the restoration work, foreigners are charged an entry fee of T3000, plus T5000 to take photos inside the temples. Ceremonies start at around 9 am.

Some travellers have raved about the scenery of the mountain range, Bürengiin Nuruu, north of Amarbayasgalant. One traveller wrote:

This is probably the most spectacular and beautiful piece of countryside I saw in Mongolia. It is alpine forest of birch and conifer, with knee-high grass, full of wildflowers. Anyone travelling to the Amarbayasgalant monastery should definitely try to make their way to the Selenge River over this mountain range.

Ben Perry

Places to Stay
Camping The area surrounding Amarbayasgalant Khiid is an excellent camping spot, though water is scarce – you'll have to search hard for a campsite with any, or stock up before you head out.

AMARBAYASGALANT KHIID

1 Screen Wall
2 Entrance Temple
3 Drum Tower
4 Bell Tower
5 Temple of Protector Gods
6 Pavillion
7 Pavillion
8 Tsogchin Dugan (Main Temple)
9 Sakyamuni Buddha Temple
10 Tomb of 4th Bogd Gegen
11 Tomb of Zanabazar
12 Manal Temple
13 Ayush Temple
14 Living Rooms of Bogd Gegen
15 Narkhajid Temple
16 Maider (Maitreya) Temple
17 Monk's Accomodation

0   40   80m
0   40   80yd

NORTHERN MONGOLIA

Zanabazar

Born in 1635, Zanabazar is one of Mongolia's most remarkable and versatile figures. At the tender age of three, he was deemed to be a possible *gegen*, or saint, so at the age of 14 he was sent to Tibet to study Buddhism under the Dalai Lama. A descendent of Chinggis Khaan, he was also proclaimed the reincarnation of the Jonangpa line of Tibetan Buddhism and became the first Bogd Gegen. He is also known in Mongolia as Öndür Gegen.

While in Tibet, Zanabazar learnt the skills of bronze casting. He returned to kick-start a Mongolian artistic renaissance and become Mongolia's greatest sculptor. In his spare time he invented the *soyombo*, the national symbol of Mongolia, and reformed the Mongolian script. Zanabazar was also a political figure and his struggle with the Zungar Oirad leader Galdan led to Mongolia's submission to the Manchus in 1691.

SJ   Zanabazar died in Beijing in 1723. His body was taken to Urga (modern Ulaan Baatar) and later entombed in a stupa in Amarbayasgalant Khiid. You will see many of Zanabazar's creations in monasteries and museums in Mongolia, and there is a fine collection of his art (particularly his Tara and Dhyani Buddha statues) in the Zanabazar Museum of Fine Arts in Ulaan Baatar. His sculptures of Tara are supposedly based on his 18-year-old lover. You can recognise images of Zanabazar by his bald, round head and the *dorje* (thunderbolt symbol) he holds in his right hand and the bell in his left hand.

Hotel The monastery has three buildings outside of the monastery grounds that serve as a basic *guesthouse* for up to 20 people. Beds cost T3000 per person.

Ger Camps *Amarbayasgalant (☎/fax 01-683 025)* camp is about 7km south of the monastery – you'll pass it on the main road. The midges around this area can be appalling in late summer. The camp charges the standard US$30 per person including meals and a hot shower, or between US$15 and US$20 without food.

Getting There & Away

Jeep To go on a day trip from Ulaan Baatar would take a horrendous 15 hours (there and back, including time to look around). It's far better to stay near the monastery so you can witness a ceremony in the morning and appreciate the place in the evening light.

Even with an experienced driver you may need directions to find the monastery. From the west, roads lead north-east from Baruunbüren. From the south, tracks branch off north from the Orkhon-Baruunbüren road.

Hitching Vehicles to the monastery are few and far between, though with a tent, enough food and water and some determination, you will probably get there. The cheapest and best way from Ulaan Baatar is to catch a train to Darkhan, take a shared jeep to Khötöl, hitch (which is easy) from there to the turn-off, then hitch another ride (much more difficult to the monastery. The problem is finding the correct jeep track – compounded by the fact that jeeps all take different routes to the monastery.

When all is said and done you are better off visiting the monastery as part of a jeep or minivan trip to Khövsgöl, or chartering a jeep (about US$100 return) from Darkhan.

NORTHERN MONGOLIA

Eastern Mongolia

Nestled along the borders of China and Russia are the three *aimags* (provinces) of Dornod, Khentii and Sükhbaatar, which were all part of the giant Tsetsenkhaan aimag before it was split in 1921. Except for the spectacular Khentii Nuruu mountain range, and some forests surrounding it, eastern Mongolia is pure steppe plain. The area is almost uninhabited by people, but home to hundreds of thousands of Mongolian gazelle, which make it, according to the famous biologist George Schaller, 'one of the last great unspoiled grazing ecosystems in the world'.

Most travellers head out west from Ulaan Baatar, but those who go east are rewarded with some stunning scenery, one of the world's last great undisturbed grasslands and several historical sites closely linked to Chinggis Khaan. All of these sites enjoy the advantage of being closer to Ulaan Baatar, meaning shorter trips and less arduous travel.

Khentii Хэнтий

pop 78,300 • area 82,000 sq km

Khentii is named after the impressive Khentii Nuruu mountain range, which covers the north-west corner of the aimag and is part of the giant 1.2 million hectare Khan Khentii Strictly Protected Area (most of which is in the adjoining Töv aimag). Although none of the peaks are over 2000m, these mountains are well watered and heavily forested. The aimag has over 70 rivers, including the Kherlen Gol, which flows through the aimag capital of Öndörkhaan, and the Onon Gol in the far north-east. There are also over 30 sources of mineral water.

All this means that the scenery is lush and the travelling is very difficult. Jeeps have a hard time and often get bogged; access through the thickly forested regions is mainly on horseback or on foot. The water attracts an abundance of wildlife and is responsible for the stunning wildflowers that

Highlights

- Dadal, with majestic streams and forests and great hiking around the birthplace of Chinggis Khaan
- Dariganga, a superb area of lakes, sand dunes and steppe
- Shilin Bogd Uul, a sacred mountain with awesome views across to China

seem to carpet hills and valleys with a profusion of purple, red and yellow.

Khentii is the land of the ethnic groups Khalkh and Buryat, and also of the famed Chinggis Khaan. It is where he was born, grew up, rose to power, was crowned and (probably) where he was buried.

The land is the source of the Kherlen and Onon rivers, both of which are mentioned extensively in the epic history of the life and deeds of Chinggis Khaan, *The Secret History of the Mongols*. The authorities have decided that Chinggis Khaan is the aimag's greatest tourist attraction and have so far identified 43 historical sites.

This historical Mongol heartland, and specifically the town of Galshar in the far south of the aimag, is famed as the source of Mongolia's fastest horses.

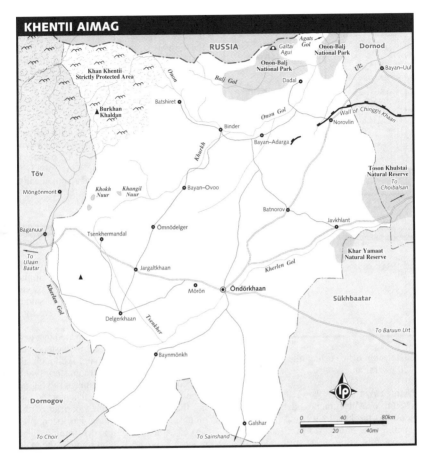

ÖNDÖRKHAAN
ӨНДӨРХААН

pop 17,000 • elevation 1027m

The aimag capital, Öndörkhaan, which means 'high king', is in one of the flattest and driest parts of Khentii aimag. The river, the Kherlen Gol, flows through the southern part of Öndörkhaan, however, providing the cattle with water and grass, and the locals (and brave foreigners) with a good swimming hole in the hot summer months. Most of the residents live in wooden buildings, so gers are relatively few in number.

Öndörkhaan, a sleepy place, is far nicer than the other two eastern aimag capitals. It is perfectly located as a gateway to eastern Mongolia, so you may need to stay here to arrange onward transport or to break up a journey if you are heading to/from other places in the east.

Orientation & Information

The town is fairly compact and centred on a desolate central park. You can change US dollars only in the bank opposite the Kherlen Hotel (the counter is to your right as you enter). A small Internet cafe inside

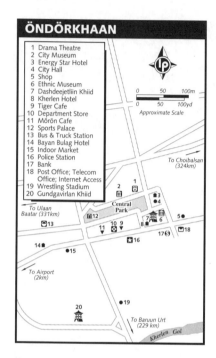

ÖNDÖRKHAAN

1 Drama Theatre
2 City Museum
3 Energy Star Hotel
4 City Hall
5 Shop
6 Ethnic Museum
7 Dashdeejetliin Khiid
8 Kherlen Hotel
9 Tiger Cafe
10 Department Store
11 Mörön Cafe
12 Sports Palace
13 Bus & Truck Station
14 Bayan Bulag Hotel
15 Indoor Market
16 Police Station
17 Bank
18 Post Office; Telecom
   Office; Internet Access
19 Wrestling Stadium
20 Gundgavirlan Khiid

0   50   100m
0   50   100yd
Approximate Scale

To Choibalsan
(324km)

Central
Park

To Ulaan
Baatar (331km)

To Airport
(2km)

To Baruun Urt
(229 km)

Kherlen Gol

the telecom office offers Internet access for T20 per minute.

Museums

The **Ethnic Museum**, next to the City Hall, is one of the best of its kind in the country and is certainly worth a look. It contains a few ethnic costumes, Mongolian toys and some religious artefacts, such as statues, scroll paintings *(thangka)* and books that must have been rescued from Stalin's thugs in the late 1930s. The four museum buildings were the 18th-century home of the Tsetseg Khaan, a Mongol prince who governed most of eastern Mongolia during the Manchu reign. (As you enter the complex, the building on the left holds a portrait of the last Tsetseg Khaan, painted in 1923.)

The museum is open 8 am to 1 pm and 2 to 6 pm weekdays, and on Saturday morning (T500) – if it's closed ask someone at the hut at the back to open it up.

The small **City Museum**, north of the park, was recently renovated. Apart from the normal exhibits, the museum has a huge mastodon tusk (an extinct elephant-like mammal) and some Chinggis Khaan-era armour. Entry is T500.

Dashdeejetliin Khiid

Дашдээжэтлийн Хийд

This small monastery is in an 18th-century building next to the Ethnic Museum. Originally part of the Tsetseg Khaan's palace, it was converted into a temple in 1994. It is served by five lamas and opens sporadically.

Gundgavirlan Khiid

Гундгавирлан Хийд

The original Gundgavirlan monastery was built in 1660 and housed the first Buddhist philosophy school in Mongolia. At its peak, the monastery was home to over 1000 monks. In the spring of 1938, the Stalinist purge reached Khentii and the monks were all arrested. The buildings remained standing until the 1950s, when they were torn down.

In 1990 the monastery reopened in a ger. Two years later, the present monastery was opened on the original site. Although all photos of the original monastery were burned, some of the old people – relying on memory alone – worked with a painter during the 1960s to recreate a portrait of the monastery. This painting has been preserved and hangs in the temple. The monastery is about 300m south of the main street. The monastery has 30 lamas, and foreigners are welcome to see the ceremony that takes place most mornings.

Places to Stay

Camping If you want to camp, head south past the wrestling stadium, and walk along the Kherlen Gol to the west until you've found a quiet spot.

Hotels The best bet is the good value *Kherlen Hotel*. Dorm-style rooms are T3500 per person, and double rooms are T6000 per person. It is on the main street above some shops.

The spacious but run-down *Energy Star Hotel* has simple rooms for T3000 per person and bigger, but not necessarily cleaner, deluxe rooms for T6000. The entrance is around the back of the government building.

There is also a small *hotel* on the second floor of the post office. A bed will cost you T3500, but the pit toilets outside are pretty grim.

At the time of research the *Bayan Bulag Hotel* (also known as Nedgelchin Hotel) was under renovation. It is just past the food market on the main street and may be worth checking out.

Places to Eat

The flashiest place in town is the *Tiger Cafe*. The food is OK but most locals just come for a beer. It is on the second floor of a distinctive green building on the main street.

A bit further down the road is the *Mörön Cafe* (*mörön* means 'river'). Alternatively you could scare the wits out of the restaurant staff of the *Kherlen Hotel* by actually ordering some food. A couple of *guanz* (cheap restaurant/canteen) on the main street offer *buuz* (steamed meat dumplings) and *khuurshuur* (fried meat pancake).

The market near the Bayan Bulag Hotel is a good place to stock up on supplies. And if you have some time on your hands, you could shoot a game of pool next door at the 'Bilyards Klub.'

Getting There & Away

Air On Thursday MIAT (Mongolian Airlines) flies to/from Ulaan Baatar, en route from Baruun Urt, for US$54 one way. Öndörkhaan's airport is 2km west of the city.

Minivan A comparatively large number of minivans and jeeps go from Ulaan Baatar to Öndörkhaan, and on to the other two aimag capitals in eastern Mongolia. Direct minivans leave Ulaan Baatar on Monday and Friday (T6000 to T7000) and return the next day. You can also get a ride on the minivans from Ulaan Baatar that go through Öndörkhaan on the way to Baruun Urt and Choibalsan.

Jeep Pubic shared jeeps and vans from Ulaan Baatar cost T10,000 and take eight hours in dry weather and 12 hours when it rains. Most vehicles at the bus/jeep stand are bound for Ulaan Baatar, but some will go on to Dornod, Sükhbaatar or other parts of Khentii.

Postal trucks run to Dadal on Thursday and to Delgerkhaan on Friday; check timings at the post office. You could hire your own jeep at the stand, but many private cars also seem to hang around on the main street, near the food market.

Öndörkhaan is 331km east of Ulaan Baatar, 324km south-west of Choibalsan and 229km west of Baruun Urt. The road to each of these destinations is unpaved but fairly rea sonable.

Hitching Öndörkhaan is the gateway for eastern Mongolia, so all vehicles heading to Dornod aimag and Sükhbaatar aimag will come through here. Getting a lift to Ulaan Baatar, Choibalsan and Baruun Urt is comparatively easy. Hitching north is far harder. Like most aimag capitals your best bet is to wait at the petrol station, at the eastern edge of town. Alternatively, you could ask the drivers at the bus stand or on the main street.

DADAL
ДАДАЛ

As written in *The Secret History of the Mongols*, it is now generally accepted that the great Chinggis was born at the junction of the Onon and Balj rivers (though his date of birth is still subject to great conjecture). The assumed spot is in Dadal *sum* (district), near the town of the same name (also known as Bayan Ovoo).

Dadal is a gorgeous area of lakes, rivers, forests and log huts (very few people live in gers) – reminiscent of Siberia, which is only 25km to the north. Even if you are not a Chinggisphile, there is no shortage of scenery to admire and hike around in. It wouldn't be hard to stay here a few days (which may be necessary anyway unless you have rented a jeep). The downside is that it often rains here in summer.

The 415,752 hectare Onon-Balj National Park was established in the region in March 2000. There was little infrastructure in place at the time of research, but you can expect national park charges to apply if you go hiking north of Dadal.

Information

Dadal is in a sensitive border area so it would be wise to register with the police (T2000). If you are heading any further out of town it would also be a good idea to register with the border guards, on the west side of Dadal. Don't expect anyone to speak English.

Things to See

Three kilometres north of Bayan Ovoo is a collection of hills known as **Deluun Boldog**. On top of one of the hills is a stone marker, built in 1990 to commemorate the 750th anniversary of the writing of *The Secret History of the Mongols*. The inscription says that Chinggis Khaan was born here in 1162. Some historians may not be entirely convinced about the exact date or location of his birth, but it's a great place to come into the world: the scenery and hiking around the valleys and forests are superb.

There's a more impressive **Chinggis Khaan Statue** in the Gurvan Nuur camp, built in 1962 to commemorate the 800th anniversary of his birth.

About 1km west of the statue is the **Khajuu Bulag** mineral water springs, where the great man once drank. Take your water bottles and fill them to the brim, because this is the freshest (flowing) spring water you will ever taste. You could also hike up into the hills behind town, where there is a large **ovoo** (sacred pyramid-shaped collection of stones).

Activities

There are several **trekking** routes out of Dadal. Locals recommend the 30km hike to the junction of the Onon and Balj rivers, or the 45km trek further along the river to the gorge at the confluence of the Onon and Agats rivers. You'll need to in-

Chinggis Khaan Statue

The statue at Gurvan Nuur is odd, if only because it was built at the time of the communist reign and managed to survive. Construction of the statue was authorised by Tomor-Ochir, a high-ranking member of the Central Committee of the Mongolian Communist Party in 1962. Construction was completed on the 800th anniversary of Chinggis' birth, and was seen as a reaction to Chinese efforts to promote nationalist pride in Inner Mongolia after a Chinggis Khaan mausoleum was constructed there. Tomor-Ochir was also instrumental in issuing a set of Chinggis Khaan stamps and organising the 1962 Chinggis Khaan symposium. He was considered a loyal communist and an ardent nationalist.

After the statue was finished, Tomor-Ochir was suddenly stripped of his official position. Davaatseren, the man who sculpted the monument, also lost his job and was jailed. Tomor-Ochir was sent to work in a timber mill in Bayankhongor and was then exiled again to Khankh in northern Khövsgöl to work as a customs official. He later became a museum director in Darkhan. In 1985 he was axed to death and the killer was never found.

It is thought that as officials in both Moscow and Ulaan Baatar grew nervous over the rising nationalistic pride in Chinggis Khaan, President Tsedenbal was told to clamp down on all those involved. Why the statue remained, and what exactly happened to those involved with the construction of the statue, remains a mystery.

form the border patrol of your itinerary and it would be wise to take a guide (this is not a good place to get lost!). Ask at the ger camps or try to track down an English-speaking local.

Fishing is excellent in the entire Dadal region, with huge taimen growing up to 1.5m in length! Taimen are one of the largest freshwater fish on earth and can be very ferocious.

You are supposed to get a fishing permit (T200) from the town hall.

Places to Stay & Eat

Camping This is perfect camping country, so if you have your own tent and food supplies there is no need to stay in a hotel or ger camp. Just walk about 200m in any direction from Bayan Ovoo and set up camp.

Ger Camps The *Gurvan Nuur* (Three Lakes) resort is in the nicest location, and is the best value. On the shore of a lake about 2km from Bayan Ovoo, the setting in a pine forest is superb. Beds in a basic but clean five-bed cabin (there are no gers) cost around T3000 per person, plus T1000 to T1500 per meal. A good **hiking trail** starts from the back of the camp.

One kilometre from Bayan Ovoo, the *Onon* ger camp is owned by the Joshi company from Ulaan Baatar. Prices are high at around US$30 per person, or US$40 with meals, but it's probably the best camp in the area.

Getting There & Away

Air Dadal has an airfield, 14km from Bayan Ovoo, but a chronic lack of small planes means that there is currently no scheduled service to/from Ulaan Baatar. Flights may resume at any time so it's worth checking at the MIAT office in Ulaan Baatar.

Jeep There is no formal public transport to Dadal but jeeps go to Ulaan Baatar every few days, taking passengers for T16,000 to T18,000. Jeeps take the quicker and more scenic road via Ömnödelger and Binder. The journey takes anywhere from 12 hours up to 35 hours after heavy rains.

In summer, along the road between Ömnödelger and Dadal (about 236km) you'll see plenty of nomadic families moving home with heavily-laden carts pulled by camels or yaks (the best form of transport in muddy Khentii).

A postal truck travels to Öndörkhaan (T8000) every Thursday morning at around 8.30 am. Ask at the post office for current timings. Most traffic to Öndörkhaan takes the road via Norovlin (also known as Uls), which is on the main road between Öndörkhaan and northern Dornod.

As there are virtually no vehicles available for hire in Bayan Ovoo, the only option is to contact the Onon ger camp, which should be able to arrange something for around T300 per km.

Dadal is 254km north-east of Öndörkhaan; 301km north-west of Choibalsan; and 585km north-west of Ulaan Baatar – or exactly 500km if you have an experienced driver who knows the right shortcuts.

Hitching Getting a lift to Dadal from Ulaan Baatar is difficult and will take several days, but the whole experience is great fun. Quite a few vehicles travel between Baganuur, Tsenkhermandal and Ömnödelger every day, so this stretch shouldn't be difficult. One good place to wait for a ride is the bridge over the Kherlen Gol, 16km south of Baganuur, where traffic stops briefly at a checkpoint. There is also a *guanz* here with basic *accommodation*.

From Ömnödelger (a pleasant village with wooden huts and a *hotel*), fewer vehicles travel to Binder, another pretty, forested area. From Binder to Dadal, you could even trek (about 60km) along the Onon Gol to the north-east. Otherwise, a vehicle to Dadal will eventually come along, but it might take a few days.

Alternatively, you could try to hitch a ride from Öndörkhaan to Norovlin (also known as Ulz), where you can see the remains of the **Wall of Chinggis Khaan**, though traffic along this road is also sparse and there is nowhere to stay along the way.

GALTAI AGUI
ГАЛТАЙ АГУЙ

Seventy kilometres north-west of Dadal is the Galtai Agui, a cave set in some beautiful countryside. It is an amazing 80m deep; apparently the deepest in Mongolia. There are also **healing rocks** in the area called Tsagaan Cholor, which are rich in shamanic lore. The cave is very close to the Russian border, hence you should get permission from the border police (see the Information entry under Dadal earlier). You'll need a good driver or guide to find it.

DELGERKHAAN

ДУЛГУРХААН

Despite the historical significance of the area, there's little to actually see in Delgerkhaan, the sum capital, though it's an easy enough detour to or from Öndörkhaan.

Locals, and some historians, claim that Avarga, not Karakorum, was the first capital of the Mongolian empire. The ancient city is located on a 20km-wide plain, **Khodoo Aral** (Countryside Island), so named because the area is encircled by the Kherlen and Tsenheriin rivers.

Things to See

The biggest and most impressive of the various statues and monuments in the area is the **Chinggis Statue**, 13km south of Delgerkhaan village. It was built in 1990 under the sponsorship of Unesco, to commemorate the 750th anniversary of the writing of *The Secret History of the Mongols*. The symbols on the side of the statue are the brands used by about 300 different clans in the area for marking their livestock.

One kilometre east of the statue is the **Avarga Toson Mineral Spring**, from which Ögedei Khaan drank and was cured of a serious stomach ailment. Locals claim the water can cure up to 13 known diseases including ulcers, hepatitis and any pancreatic problems, and acts as a male aphrodisiac (who says the Mongolians don't understand marketing?). The spring is covered by an ovoo, and a pump house has been built near the site. A guard lives in the ger nearby and can open up the pump and sell you a litre of fizzy spring water for T100 (bring some water bottles). A handbook is also for sale (T250), which explains the significance of the spring and of the area.

Between the statue and the spring lie the underground remains of the ancient city of **Avarga** (see the boxed text 'Avarga' earlier).

If you've had enough of Chinggis, you can always go for a swim in the tiny lake, **Avarga Toson Nuur**, 4km west of Delgerkhaan.

Places to Stay & Eat

Camping You can camp anywhere near the lake, though it would help to have your own transport. Delgerkhaan has limited supplies of food, so bring your own, or order meals in advance at the resort.

Ger Camps On the shore of Avarga Toson Nuur is the large *Avarga Resort*, which was set up as a holiday resort and spa for Mongolian families. The resort offers hot-water baths or you could bury yourself in mud on the shores of the lake. The two small lakes behind the resort are said to contain curative properties. The place is crowded in the summer and a bit run-down but the price is right at T2400 per person (including meals). The resort is 4km west of Delgerkhaan.

Juulchin runs a ger camp called *Ondor Givant* (or Khuduu Aral), 8km west of the resort. It charges US$30 a night per person, has hot showers and, if you face the right direction, you don't see the power poles.

Getting There & Away

The major advantage of Delgerkhaan is its proximity to Ulaan Baatar (260km). It's also close to the regional centres of Öndörkhaan (124km) and Baganuur (95km). However, there are no flights or public transport to Delgerkhaan or Avarga.

Jeep Chartering a jeep to Delgerkhaan from Ulaan Baatar, Öndörkhaan or Baganuur is easy – you could even go on day trips from the latter two places. You *might* be able to hire a jeep to see the local

---

Avarga

Avarga is where Chinggis Khaan is believed to have established the armies that tore through Central Asia and Europe, and where Chinggis' third and favourite son, Ögedei, was later proclaimed khaan of the Mongolian empire. In the mid-1990s computer findings from a Japanese-Mongolian expedition apparently proved the existence of an entire city underground, including nine temples and a palace belonging to Chinggis' first wife, Bortei. This seems a little far-fetched, but future excavations may convince the unbelievers.

sights at the Avarga Toson Resort, or in Delgerkhaan village. You could also ask around both places for onward transport to Öndörkhaan or Ulaan Baatar.

Hitching Delgerkhaan is popular with domestic tourists, but getting there is still a matter of luck. Some cars (and the Friday postal truck) come here from Öndörkhaan. Cars from Ulaan Baatar turn off the main road at Erdene (the end of the paved road in Töv aimag), or sometimes turn off at the bridge over the Kherlen Gol, 16km south of Baganuur. There is a road from Tsenkermandal, but not many cars use it. The best idea is to get off the bus to Öndörkhaan at one of these turn-offs, or try the busier road junction of Jargalthaan. And wait...

KHÖKH NUUR
ХӨХ НУУР

About 35km north-west of Tsenkhermandal, the small Khökh Nuur (Blue Lake) is said to be where Temujin was crowned Chinggis Khaan in 1206. There is a small plaque that marks the **coronation spot**, which some say was attended by 100,000 soldiers. It's not a required stop on the Chinggis Khaan pilgrimage trail but it provides a nice place to break a jeep trip.

You'll need your own transport and a driver who knows where it is. Someone from nearby **Modot** might take you there by jeep or motorcycle, or you could organise an overnight horse trip if you or your driver/guide has some contacts in the area. The area is sometimes labelled Khar Zurkhen (Black Heart) on maps, which refers to a mountain behind the lake.

A further 30km away is the larger and prettier lake of **Khangil Nuur**.

BALDAN BAREVEN KHIID
БАЛДАН БАРУВУН ХИЙД

This monastery in Ömnödelger sum was first built in 1777. At its peak it was one of the three largest monasteries in Mongolia and home to 1500 lamas. It was destroyed by thugs in the 1930s and by fire in the 1970s. Now only ruins remain.

The Search for Chinggis Khaan's Grave

Mongolians, and some historians, have agreed that the birthplace of Chinggis Khaan is at Deluun Boldog, in northern Khentii aimag – although the date of 1162 is not universally accepted. But where was he buried?

Chinggis' grave is probably in Khentii aimag, and not too far from his birthplace, but the exact location is not known. According to diaries kept by Marco Polo, at the time the Mongols wanted to keep the location of the grave a secret – which they have managed to do to this day. According to legend, the 2000 or so people who attended Chinggis' funeral were killed by 800 soldiers, who were in turn slaughtered themselves – so total secrecy was ensured. It is said that 1000 horsemen trampled the earth over the grave after the burial to conceal its location.

Various expeditions, often with Japanese and American assistance and technology, have failed to shed any light on the mystery, though a recent Chinese expedition claims to have found the tomb in the Altai region of Xinjiang province. Others claim that the site is in Gov-Altai aimag. His tomb may contain millions, if not billions of dollars worth of gold, silver, precious stones and other priceless religious artefacts (as well as many women, men and horses who were buried alive with the khaan), so the search is sure to continue.

However, the vast amount of money spent so far, which could be better used to assist regional development, and the fact that discovery of the grave is against the obvious wishes of Chinggis Khaan himself, has created resentment among many Mongolians.

The monastery is currently being restored by tourist-volunteers under the auspices of the American-based Cultural Restoration Tourism Project (CRTP). The project is due to be completed by 2006. For details contact the CRTP (☎ 415-563 7331, email crtp@earthlink.net) in the US or try the Web site at www.home.earthlink.net/~crtp.

BURKHAN KHALDAN
БУРХАН ХАЛДАН

This remote mountain, known as God's Hill, in the Khentii Nuruu is one of the sites mooted as the burial place of Chinggis Khaan. Over 800 burial sites have been found in the region, though the main tomb has yet to be located. Whether or not Chinggis was buried here, *The Secret History of the Mongols* does describe how the khaan hid here as a young man and later returned to give praise to the mountain and give thanks for his successes.

Because of its auspicious connections, Mongolians climb the mountain, which is topped with many **ovoo**, to gain strength and good luck. The hill is very remote, in the Khan Khentii Strictly Protected Area. To get there, head to Möngönmorit in Töv, then travel north along the Kherlen Gol. This is also a great place to reach by **horse**.

Zavia Tourism (☎ 1-458 869, e zavia@magicnet.mn) run the *Mongon Morit* ger camp in the region. Nomads also run trips here (see Travel Agencies under Information in the Ulaan Baatar chapter).

Dornod Дорнод

pop 84,500 • area 123,500 sq km

Dornod, which means 'east', is not the most remote aimag in Mongolia, but it probably receives the least visitors. If you have the time, and a jeep to cross the vast treeless sparsely populated steppes, there are a few places of interest.

These include Buir Nuur and Khalkhin Gol – both the scenes of fierce fighting against the Japanese; Khökh Nuur, the lowest point in the country; and some lovely natural reserves. If you've already visited other more popular areas of Mongolia, Dornod offers good scope for some offbeat exploration.

The northern sums of Bayan Uul, Bayandun and Dashbalbar are home to the Buryats, who still practise shamanism. If you ask around you may be able to meet a shaman or, if you are lucky, watch a shaman ceremony in these areas.

Gazelle & Antelope

One of the most magnificent sights in Mongolia, especially in the flat eastern provinces, is the hundreds of white-tailed gazelle and saiga antelope that almost seem to float across the plains. They collect in huge migratory herds that rival the Serengeti in Africa.

In the year of 1942 alone, 100,000 gazelle and antelope were slaughtered for meat by Russian troops. While wholesale slaughter is now outlawed, they are still at risk from development and mining. Gazelle continue to be poached at the rate of one a day.

Antelopes are especially prized by Chinese and Mongolians for meat, skins and their horns – each one fetches from Y70 to Y100 (US$8.50 to $12). Hunting, both illegal and legal, continues: in 1996, several Mongolian and Chinese poachers, armed with submachine guns, were arrested in Dornod.

National Parks

Thankfully, authorities have been convinced that the area's fragile environment and endangered fauna and flora need to be conserved. Dornod is currently the base of a multi-million dollar environmental protection project, which is researching everything from fires to field mice in an attempt to protect one of the world's last undisturbed grasslands. Three large Strictly Protected Areas (SPA) were established in the aimag in 1992:

Dornod Mongol (570,374 hectares) Holds one of the last great plain ecosystems on earth, protecting seas of feather grass steppe and 70% of Mongolia's white-tailed gazelle, which roam in herds of up to 20,000.

Nomrog (311,205 hectares) An unpopulated area, which contains rare species of moose, cranes, otter and bears. Ecologically distinct from the rest of Mongolia, the area takes in the transition zone from the Eastern Mongolian steppe to the mountains and forest of Manchuria. It is proposed that the park expand eastwards.

Mongol Daguur (103,016 hectares) The reserve is divided into two parts; the northern half is hill steppe and wetland bordering on Russia's Tarij Nuur and Daurski Reserve, protecting endemic species like the Daurian hedgehog; the southern area along the Ulz Gol protects white-naped

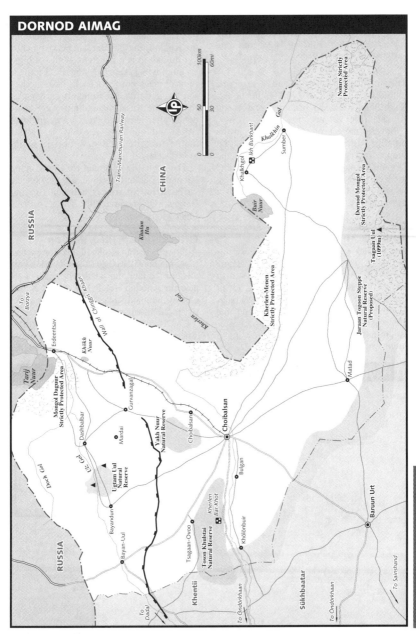

DORNOD AIMAG

EASTERN MONGOLIA

crane (*tsen togoruu*) and other endangered birds. The area is part of a one-million hectare international reserve, linking the Siberian taiga with the Inner Asian steppe.

The aimag also has several natural reserves, including Ugtam Uul (46,100 hectares), Yakh Nuur (251,388 hectares) and Toson Khulstai (469,928 hectares).

Several more protected areas are in the pipeline, including the Jaraan Togoon Steppe reserve, which will join onto the Dornod Mongol Strictly Protected Area and the Kherlen-Menen Strictly Protected Area, hugging the Chinese border in the east of the aimag.

CHOIBALSAN
ЧОЙВАЛСАН
pop 47,000 • elevation 747m

Named after the Stalinist stooge Khorloogiyn Choibalsan, this charmless aimag capital is easily Mongolia's largest (after the autonomous cities of Ulaan Baatar, Darkhan and Erdenet). Centuries ago, the city was a trading centre and part of a caravan route across central Asia. It grew into a town in the 19th century, and is now the major economic centre for eastern Mongolia. The ethnic groups that reside here are the Khalkh, Buryat, Barga, and Uzemchin.

Choibalsan is a poor city with the highest employment rate in Mongolia. From the ruins of many houses, it looks like Choibalsan has suffered a horrendous earthquake. In fact, the Russian buildings were abandoned after 1990 and the bricks, windows, gates and anything useable have been looted to help build new houses in the town's east.

The capital is inhabited by a large number of dark-skinned people, a legacy of centuries of intermarriages between Buryats, Bargas, Uzemchins, and Chinese from Inner Mongolia.

Orientation & Information

Although the city is spread out along a narrow 5km corridor north of the Kherlen Gol, most of the facilities needed by visitors are near the Kherlen Hotel. The market is 3km east of the main square, about halfway between the town and the train station.

The Eastern Mongolia Strictly Protected Areas Office (☎ 61-1257, fax 2217, 🅔 esbp@ magicnet.mn), next to the Tovan Hotel, has

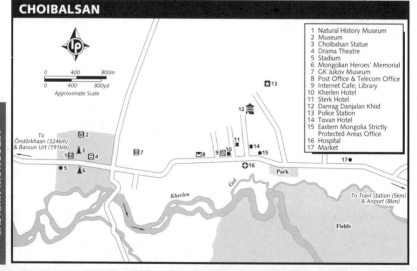

CHOIBALSAN

0   400   800m
0   400   800yd
Approximate Scale

To Öndörkhaan (324km) & Baruun Urt (191km)

Kherlen Gol

To Train Station (5km) & Airport (8km)

Fields

Park

1 Natural History Museum
2 Museum
3 Choibalsan Statue
4 Drama Theatre
5 Stadium
6 Mongolian Heroes' Memorial
7 GK Jukov Museum
8 Post Office & Telecom Office
9 Internet Cafe; Library
10 Kherlen Hotel
11 Sterk Hotel
12 Danrag Danjalan Khiid
13 Police Station
14 Tovan Hotel
15 Eastern Mongolia Strictly Protected Areas Office
16 Hospital
17 Market

EASTERN MONGOLIA

several foreign staff and can supply information on visiting protected areas in both Dornod and Sükhbataar aimags.

The police station, 500m north of the Sterk Hotel, is the place to inquire about permits if you are headed out to Sümber (also known as Tsagaannuur) and Nomrog near the sensitive border with China.

The city library offers Internet access for T600 per hour.

Museums & Memorials

The **City Museum**, in the former government house in the old part of town, is probably the best of its kind outside of Ulaan Baatar. It contains some interesting paintings, fascinating old photos, some Choibalsan memorabilia and a giant bowl, made in 1861, which is large enough to boil mutton for 500 people. (The mind boggles, the stomach churns.) The aimag map marks the location of the many ruined monasteries. The museum is open weekdays from 9 am to 6 pm (T500).

If you desperately miss the requisite stuffed animals in the City Museum, head for the **Natural History Museum**, on the west side of the square (T500).

The **GK Jukov Museum** chronicles the war with the Japanese along the Khalkhin Gol in 1939. It is in the ger suburbs, about 1.5km north-east of the Drama Theatre and 200m north of the main road. The caretaker (with the key) lives next door.

Choibalsan's Mongolian Heroes' Memorial is one of the more dramatic pieces of Stalinist architecture in Mongolia. It is a large arch with a soldier on horseback charging towards the enemy. A Soviet tank next to the monument adds a quaint reminder of who really was boss. Presumably, they are too big to destroy.

Danrag Danjalan Khiid

Данраг Данжалан Хийд

According to the chief monk, this monastery was built around 1840 and was once very active. It contained three northern temples and four southern temples, but less than half the 800 monks could be accommodated at one time, so most had to

Khorloogiyn Choibalsan

Choibalsan was born in Dornod aimag, northeast of what is now Choibalsan. A former monk at Gandantegchinlen Khiid and later a great hero of the 1921 Revolution, he became Mongolia's leader in 1928, allegedly assassinating rivals in the process. Like his Russian mentor, Joseph Stalin, Choibalsan was ruthless, and is credited with launching the purge in 1937, which cost up to 30,000 lives. The victims, mostly monks, were forced to dig their own graves before being shot in the back of the head. Thousands of others were arrested and sent to Siberian labour prisons. Even after the purge, Choibalsan kept the country in a state of fear. Midnight arrests and executions for anyone suspected of treason continued for decades afterwards.

Although Choibalsan's regime has been heavily criticised by modern Mongolians, he is still surprisingly well regarded because of his efforts to protect Mongolia's independence. In 1945, against Stalin's orders, he launched an attack into Inner Mongolia. It was an attempt to reclaim the lost province during the political vacuum of the Japanese retreat near the end of World War II. The 80,000 Mongolian troops only withdrew after a strong rebuke from the Soviet Union.

Following the war, pressure was mounting for Mongolia to join the USSR. In 1944, Mongolia's north-west neighbour Tannu Tuva gave up its independence and joined the Soviet Union. The Tuvan leader Salchack Toka met Choibalsan and urged him to do the same. Choibalsan is said to have slapped Toka across the face for suggesting so and berated him for giving up Tuva's independence.

Choibalsan died of cancer in 1952, one year before Stalin. While images of Stalin have all but disappeared from Russian streets, statues of Choibalsan remain in Mongolia, and his name is still used for streets, cities and sums.

pray outside. The Mongolian security forces descended on the place in 1937, destroyed all records and arrested most of the monks, none of whom has ever been heard from since.

In June 1990 the monastery reopened and it now has two small temples where about 35 monks worship. The monks are particularly friendly; we were warmly welcomed and allowed to watch a ceremony. The monastery is about 400m behind the Sterk Hotel.

Places to Stay

Camping The best place to camp is anywhere south of the main street – walk for a few hundred metres and you will be sharing some great spots along the Kherlen Gol with a few curious cows.

Hotels The *Kherlen Hotel* is friendly and much improved. The rooms are comfortable and are currently the cheapest in town at T7700/11,600 per person for a standard/deluxe room. There is a common shower room with hot water and also a sauna for an extra T1200.

The *Tovan Hotel* is the other main option. Rooms are clean and decent for US$16/20/25 per person in a standard/half-deluxe/deluxe room. Most rooms have a shower and hot water.

The only other place is the unlikely-sounding the *Sterk Hotel* (previously known as the Scorpion Corporation Hotel), part of (and located behind) the grandly named, and very quiet, Business Development Center of Eastern Mongolia. The hotel has large double rooms for T14,000, although this is negotiable. Facilities include TV, billiards, a sauna and (would you believe it?) a swimming pool.

Places to Eat

The *Kherlen Hotel* has pretty good food, though the restaurant in the *Tovan Hotel* is probably the best in town. Other choices include the *guanz* next to the telecom office and the cafeteria on the ground floor at the front entrance of the Business Development Center.

The well-stocked market has most things a self-caterer could want.

Getting There & Away

Air MIAT flies between Ulaan Baatar and Choibalsan on Monday, Wednesday and Friday (US$90/158). Choibalsan boasts a top-notch runway (by Mongolian standards). It is the legacy of the large Soviet military base which existed until 1990. The airport terminal is currently being upgraded. The airport is about 8km east of the centre; buses, jeeps and minivans sometimes go there.

Minivan & Jeep Minivans and jeeps run along the good road between Ulaan Baatar and Choibalsan daily (T15,000). Minivans returning to Ulaan Baatar leave from the market. Daily vans and the odd jeep to Öndörkhaan (T7000), Baruun Urt (T6000) and, less frequently, nearby sums like Bayan Uul, also leave from the market. It's relatively easy to charter a jeep here to visit the national parks and lakes in the aimag.

Choibalsan is 191km north-east of Baruun Urt, 324km north-east of Öndörkhaan and 655km north-east of Ulaan Baatar. The roads in the northern part of Dornod are often buried under mud in late summer, but roads to the other eastern aimag capitals are OK.

Train A direct rail line from Choibalsan to Russia was built in 1939 to facilitate the joint Soviet-Mongolian war effort against Japan. It still functions, albeit only twice weekly. As a foreigner, you can go as far as Erdeentsav on the Mongolian side of the border (no permit is apparently required) – but the train only travels to Russia to pick up fuel and no longer carries any passengers.

The train leaves Choibalsan every Tuesday and Thursday at 5 pm and takes seven hours. The return trip leaves Erdeentsav on Wednesday and Friday at 10 am. Tickets cost T1800 for hard seat (the only class). Take food and plenty of water as the carriage can get stiflingly hot during the day.

The train station is about 7km north-east of the centre. You can reach the station by bus, but go early, because close to departure time the buses can make a sardine tin look spacious.

Hitching Choibalsan is a large city by Mongolian standards, so hitching a ride on a truck or any other vehicle in or out of the

EASTERN MONGOLIA

city should not be difficult. Hang around the market and keep asking.

KHERLEN BAR KHOT
ХУРЛҮН БАР ХОТ

Kherlen Bar Khot is the location of some small-scale ruins and a 3m-high tower from a 12th century city, once part of the ancient state of Kitan. There are also some **balbals** (Turkic stones believed to be grave markers) and, predictably, a Chinggis Khaan memorial of sorts: a rock called the **'Chinggis Bed'**, which commemorates his stay here. You can see a picture of the tower in the Choibalsan History Museum.

Kherlen Bar Khot is about 90km west of Choibalsan, in the sum of Tsagaan Ovoo. It is on the main road between Choibalsan and Öndörkhaan, and is worth a look if you have your own vehicle.

WALL OF CHINGGIS KHAAN

Stretching over 600km from Khentii aimag to China, and through all of Dornod, are the ruins of the Wall of Chinggis Khaan. This is not promoted by Mongolian tourist authorities because it was not built, or used, by Chinggis Khaan, but almost certainly created by the Manchu to limit (unsuccessfully) frequent raids from rampaging Mongolian hordes. Locals know it as the Chinggisiin Zam, or Chinggis' Road.

You will need a guide and jeep to find what little remains from the ravages of vandals and time, though it's doubtful whether it's worth the effort. The best place to start looking is about two-thirds along the northern road from Choibalsan to the Russian border, near the village of Gurvanzagal (also known as Sümiin Bulag).

UGTAM UUL
УГТАМ УУЛ

Ugtam mountain is part of the Ugtam Uul Natural Reserve (46,160 hectares), which also includes the nearby Khairkhan Uul and the ruins of some monasteries, one of which has recently reopened. The park is situated along the Ulz Gol in the north-west of the aimag, about 35km from the village of Bayandun (also known as Naranbulag).

KHÖKH NUUR
ХӨХ НУУР

The lowest point in Mongolia is Khökh Nuur (Blue Lake), a medium-sized freshwater lake at 560m altitude. Other than the thrill of standing in the lowest part of the country, there isn't much to keep you here, though the lake has a subtle beauty and you could combine it with an exploration of the Wall of Chinggis Khaan. The lake is also an important migration point for birds and you can spot many waders and shore birds here.

Khökh Nuur is visible from the railway line; you can get off the train at a stop near the lake, and then reboard the train the next day in the afternoon. There's no accommodation, so you'd need camping gear and all your food. Otherwise the lake is an hour's drive from Erdentsav, the rail terminus, where you can hire a motorbike or jeep. There is no accommodation in Erdentsav.

BUIR NUUR
БУИР НУУР

This beautiful lake is the largest in eastern Mongolia (the northern shore is actually in China). The surrounding countryside is mostly grassland, though there are a few trees. The lake has a maximum depth of 50m and, if you're equipped with the proper paraphernalia, is a good place to fish. The area is especially popular with mosquitoes so bring lots of repellent, or you'll need a blood transfusion. A dilapidated Soviet-era *tourist holiday camp* here will probably open its creaking doors if a tourist ever turns up.

The only way to Buir Nuur is by chartered jeep from Choibalsan, 285km away over a flat dirt road, which occasionally gets flooded.

KHALKHIN GOL
ХАЛХИН ГОЛ

The banks of the Khalkhin Gol, in the far eastern part of Dornod, are of particular interest to war historians because of the battles against the Japanese in 1939. The dry, unpolluted air ensures that most of the relics, which are just lying around, have been well preserved.

Numerous **war memorials** line the banks of the river. The memorials are real socialist masterpieces, built to honour the Russian and Mongolian soldiers who died here. The largest memorial is the 50m **Khamar Davaa**. A **museum** in Sümber (also known as Tsagaannuur), and a smaller one in Choibalsan, offer some explanations (in Mongolian) about the history of the battles. Sümber has a basic, unnamed *hotel*.

Another interesting site in the region is **Ikh Burkhant**, where there is a huge image of Janraisig (Sanskrit: Avalokitesvara) carved into the hillside. The carving was commissioned in 1864 by local regent Bat Ochiriin Togtokhtooriin, or Tovan (*van* means 'lord') and was reconstructed between 1995 and 1997. The carving is right on the roadside, about 10km south-east from Khalkhgol town.

From here the spectacular but remote Nomron Strictly Protected Area is around 100km south-east.

Khalkhin Gol is near the border and a military base, so you will need permission from Choibalsan police station to visit. You might get permission at Khalkhgol, the sum capital, but they may just as well send you back. The region is a nine-hour drive from Choibalsan.

War at Khalkhin Gol

After the Japanese moved into north-east China in 1931 to create the puppet state of Manchukuo, hundreds of thousands of Soviet troops moved into Dornod, along with 80,000 Mongolian soldiers. When the Japanese attacked the banks of the Khalkhin Gol in May 1939, the Russians were ready.

By September 1939, the tally was 61,000 Japanese, 10,000 Russians and over 1000 Mongolians killed, wounded or captured in battles involving tanks, bombers and ground troops. War historians believe the result probably prompted the Japanese generals to change their strategies, avoid further war with Russia, and concentrate on eastern Asia and the Pacific.

Sükhbaatar
Сухбаатар

pop 59,700 • area 82,000 sq km

At the eastern edge of the Gobi Desert, Sükhbaatar aimag is one of the least visited and least interesting parts of Mongolia. Almost the entire aimag is flat grassland – there are no forests at all, and only a few hills masquerading as mountains. The sparsely populated aimag is named after Sükhbaatar, the canonised hero of the communist revolution of 1921. Sükhbaatar did not actually live in this part of the country – it was his father who came from here. Ethnic groups residing here are the Khalkh, Dariganga and the Uzemchin.

The best thing about the aimag is the far south-eastern region, known as Dariganga, and the nearby mountain, Shiliin Bogd Uul. Both are definitely worth a visit, but getting there will involve some effort.

BARUUN URT
БАРУУН УРТ

pop 17,000 • elevation 981m

Baruun Urt is a scruffy, dusty and sometimes rowdy town in the middle of absolutely nowhere. Most people live in large ugly apartment blocks and work in a new Chinese-invested zinc mine, or in another coal mine 7km to the north-west. The water in Baruun Urt has high levels of sulphur so you are better off buying bottled water or filtering the tap water. Some maps refer to the town as Sükhbaatar, which is confusing because this is the name of the capital of Selenge aimag.

Information

The police station on the west edge of town is the place to get a permit to visit Dariganga and Shiliin Bogd. Surprisingly, public Internet access is available at the post office.

Museum

If you are stuck in Baruun Urt, the museum in the dusty southern part of town is worth a look. It has a reasonable collection of costumes representing the three ethnic groups

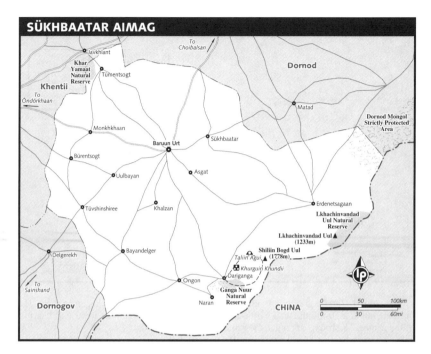

SÜKHBAATAR AIMAG

Javkhlant
Khar Yamaat Natural Reserve
Tümentsogt
Khentii
To Choibalsan
To Öndörkhaan
Dornod
Matad
Dornod Mongol Strictly Protected Area
Monkhkhaan
Baruun Urt
Sükhbaatar
Bürentsogt
Asgat
Uulbayan
Erdenetsagaan
Khalzan
Tüvshinshiree
Lkhachinvandad Uul Natural Reserve
Lkhachinvandad Uul (1233m)
Shilin Bogd Uul
Delgerekh
Bayandelger
Taliin Agui
Shiliin Bogd Uul (1778m)
Khurguin Khundii
Dariganga
To Sainshand
Ongon
Ganga Nuur Natural Reserve
Dornogov
Naran
CHINA

0   50   100km
0   30   60mi

---

that inhabit the region: the majority Khalkh, Dariganga (30,000 live in the south of Sükhbaatar aimag) and Uzemchin (about 2000 live in Dornod aimag and Sükhbaatar aimag). Look out for the interesting Uzemchin wrestling jacket.

There are also fine examples of products from Dariganga's renowned silversmiths and blacksmiths, some stuffed gazelle (which is probably about as close as you will ever get to one), a map showing the locations of the 'man' and 'woman' balbal statues in the aimag and some memorabilia of Sükhbaatar. The museum is open weekdays from 8 am to 5 pm and, if you're lucky, weekends from 8 am to 2 pm; entry is T1000.

Erdenemandal Khiid
Үрдэнэмандал Хийд

According to the monks at the monastery, Erdenemandal Khiid was originally built in 1830, about 20km from the present site. At the height of its splendour, there were seven temples and 1000 monks in residence, but the Stalinist purges of 1938 had the same result as elsewhere. The monastery is about 200m west of the square.

Places to Stay

Camping Baruun Urt is the only aimag capital where camping is not a good idea. The town is in the middle of dusty plains and there is no river nearby. The only passable option is by a creek in the north-east of town.

Hotels For such a dismal town, the three hotels are astoundingly good. The simple rooms at the *Sharga Hotel*, next to the town square, are passable at T3000 per person; the deluxe rooms, which have a sitting room, TV room, bedroom and private bath (but no hot water), are a better bet at T6000 per person. Try to get a room that doesn't face the square – it's full of loud drunks during the evening.

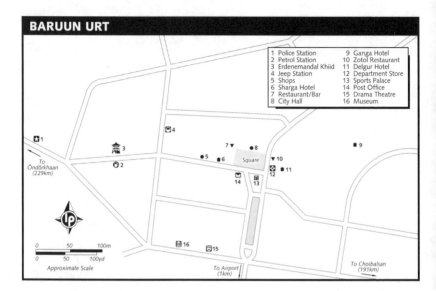

BARUUN URT

1 Police Station
2 Petrol Station
3 Erdenemandal Khiid
4 Jeep Station
5 Shops
6 Sharga Hotel
7 Restaurant/Bar
8 City Hall
9 Ganga Hotel
10 Zotol Restaurant
11 Delgur Hotel
12 Department Store
13 Sports Palace
14 Post Office
15 Drama Theatre
16 Museum

To Öndörkhaan (229km)

To Airport (1km)

To Choibalsan (191km)

Approximate Scale

The **Ganga Hotel** is the square, crimson building about a 10-minute walk north-east of the centre. The rooms are much the same as the Sharga and cost T2800 per person for a simple room and T5000 for the deluxe room with a bathroom.

The **Delgur Hotel** is a small private hotel, also known as the Titem. Rooms look good at T3500 per person with a bathroom and TV, though no-one could find a key to any of the rooms when we visited!

Places to Eat

The **Sharga Hotel** is the best option: it actually serves up an edible mutton and potato dish and, if you ask, will provide some hot water for tea, coffee or soup. The **Ganga Hotel** has a plush-looking restaurant, but doesn't offer anything to get excited about.

The other alternatives are the **Zotol Restaurant**, on the eastern side of the square, and an unnamed **restaurant/bar** on the north-western side. The town has no market, and the shops are poorly stocked.

Getting There & Away

Air MIAT has flights to and from Ulaan Baatar every Thursday for US$82/144, normally stopping in Öndörkhaan en route. The airport is 1km south of town and has just been upgraded.

Bus & Minivan Buses and minivans leave Ulaan Baatar and Baruun Urt every Monday, Wednesday and Friday (T13,000) and return about two days later, depending on how long it takes to get to Baruun Urt. Buses arrive and leave from next to the petrol station, opposite Erdenemandal Khiid.

Jeep Don't expect to be able to charter a jeep in Baruun Urt. A few public shared jeeps leave from the jeep station in the west of town for Choibalsan and even fewer to Dariganga. Most people hitchhike or take the bus.

Baruun Urt is 191km south-west of Choibalsan, 229km south-east of Öndörkhaan and 560km south-east of Ulaan Baatar. The roads in eastern Mongolia are in pretty good condition, but the scenery in Sükhbaatar aimag is monotonous. Only the sight of thousands of gazelles galloping across the steppes can liven up a dull trip.

EASTERN MONGOLIA

Erdes Uranium Mine

Erdes (known locally as Mardai) was once a unique town in Mongolia. Built in the early 1980s for Russian miners brought in to work in the nearby Russian uranium mine, Mardai resembled a Western suburb – complete with footpaths, front lawns, quaint homes and lots of trees. The Russians wanted uranium for their warheads during the mid-1980s, so output at the mine was expected to hit one million tons a year. Simultaneously the population of Mardai was expected to reach 25,000 by the year 2000. Despite its remoteness, the shops were stocked with new supplies from Moscow. The town and mine were kept a state secret until late in 1989.

With the collapse of the Soviet economy in 1990, money for Mardai ran out. The Russian Government pulled out and production stopped. In 1997 a Canadian-Mongolian-Russian consortium announced it would buy the mine but it too pulled out in 1998, leaving hundreds of Russians and Mongolians unpaid and unemployed.

By September 1999, all the Russians had left and, amidst much resentment and despair, the town was slowly stripped by vandals and looters. The Mongolian government has assumed control of the mine and troops have been deployed to protect the town, though there isn't much to save any more. Despite the closure of the local school, police station and government office, around 60 Mongolian families still live in the once prosperous town.

Hitching This is difficult because few vehicles come here. Still, with some patience you'll get a lift to Choibalsan, Öndörkhaan, Dariganga and even the bleak ride to Zamyn-Üüd. In Baruun Urt, ask around at the hotels or the police station.

DARIGANGA
ДАРИГАНГА

Dariganga sum in the south-east of Sükhbaatar is by far the most interesting place in the aimag to visit. Famous for its **silversmiths** and **blacksmiths**, friendly Dariganga is also where the sand dunes of the Gobi and the grassy plains of the northern steppe converge to create what looks like thousands of hectares of perfect natural golf courses – but don't let any developer know!

To reach the sights in the area you will need a jeep and a good driver or guide. It's the only way to, firstly, get to Dariganga village (also known as Ovoot), and then to explore the lakes, volcanoes, mountains, sand dunes and ancient stones nearby. The sacred mountain of Shiliin Bogd is also not too far away.

Permits

According to authorities in Erdenetsagaan (also known as Chinogol) and Dariganga (but not in Ulaan Baatar), foreigners need a permit to visit the area around Dariganga and Shiliin Bogd because it is so close to the Chinese border.

The police in Dariganga are unpredictable; some people have been allowed to stay without a permit, others have been issued a permit on the spot and others have been thrown out of town. Your best bet is get a permit at the police station in Baruun Urt. The permits are free and take about five minutes to process if all goes smoothly. It *might* be possible to get a permit in Erdenetsagaan if you are approaching from that direction but it's not worth the risk.

Our permit was checked in Dariganga but not on the road to or from Shiliin Bogd.

Things to See

The skyline of Dariganga is dominated by **Altan Ovoo** (Golden Ovoo), a wide former crater topped by a new **stupa**, which only men are allowed to visit. The stupa was built in 1990 on top of the ruins of the original Bat Tsaagan stupa, which was built in 1820 and destroyed in 1937.

In the area around Altan Ovoo, there are dozens of broken **balbal** – their exact origins are not clear. According to local tradition, you should place an offering of food in the cup held in the statue's left hand. There are also three balbals known as the king, the queen and the prince, in the north edge of town, near some hay sheds.

EASTERN MONGOLIA

The ruins of **Ovoon Khiid** can be seen in the south-east edge of town. Built in 1820, it housed 600 monks before it was burned to the ground. The new Ovoon Monastery was built in 1990 and is served by six monks.

There are six lakes in the vicinity of Dariganga; all are part of the 28,000 hectare Ganga Nuur Natural Reserve. The three main lakes, Kholboo Nuur, Tsagaan Nuur and Ganga Nuur, are good for swimming, though a bit muddy.

The magnificent **Ganga Nuur** is about 13km south-east of Dariganga. Between the start of August and the end of October, the lake is home to thousands of migrating swans. Along the shore, in a fenced compound, is delicious and safe spring water.

The sand dunes in the region are known as **Moltsog Els** and stretch for 20km, coming to within walking distance of Dariganga.

Places to Stay

The town's only hotel is the ***Dagshin Hotel***, a collection of quaint cabins next to tiny Dagshin Bulag Nuur, 1km north of the village. Beds in a large dorm-style room cost T2500 per person and they serve reasonable mutton soup dishes for T700.

About 10km east of Ganga Nuur, the Juulchin-run ***Shiliin Bogd*** ger camp costs about US$20 per person including breakfast, but it's often closed due to lack of guests.

There is nothing stopping you camping anywhere you want as long as you stay away from the ger camp and hotel. If you have a vehicle, camp on the shores of Ganga Nuur.

Shopping

Dariganga is renowned throughout Mongolia for the kettles, plates, jewellery and other products made by its blacksmiths and silversmiths. Examples of their excellent work can be seen in the museum in Baruun Urt. You can commission work from craftsmen in the town but this is easier said than done. Firstly you'll have to track a craftsman down. Secondly, the economic situation means that there is no silver in town, so you'll have to bring your own from Ulaan Baatar. Thirdly, you'll have to wait around long enough for the work to get done.

Dariganga's shops are poorly stocked so bring food with you.

Getting There & Away

The occasional chartered tourist flight comes to Dariganga but you'll be lucky to get on it.

Your best bet is to look out for the occasional shared jeep (T4000) that connects Dariganga with Baruun Urt (153km, four hours). A postal truck runs every Thursday from Baruun Urt; ask the post office for timings. You should be able to hitch a ride from Baruun Urt to Dariganga without too much trouble in summer.

One or two jeeps and even motorbikes with sidecars are available for charter in Dariganga. Rates are some of the cheapest in Mongolia at around T150 per km for a jeep.

SHILIIN BOGD UUL
ШИЛИЙН БОГД УУЛ

At 1778m, Shiliin Bogd Uul, about 70km east of Dariganga, is the highest peak in Sükhbaatar aimag. The extinct volcano is sacred to many Mongolians: the spirit of any man (and man only!) who climbs it, especially at sunrise, will be revived. The region is stunning, isolated and close to the Chinese border – so be careful.

A jeep can drive about halfway up the mountain, and then it's a short, but blustery, walk to the top. There are plenty of ovoo and awesome views of craters across the border to China, 3km away. If you are camping, Shiliin Bogd offers one of the greatest sunrises in a country full of great sunrises.

On the road between Dariganga and Shiliin Bogd, 8km past Ganga Nuur, look out for the new statue of **Toroi-Bandi**, the 'Robin Hood' of Mongolia, who had a habit of stealing the horses of the local Manchurian rulers, then eluding them by hiding near Shiliin Bogd Uul. The statue, dedicated in 1999, pointedly faces China.

Getting There & Away

The only two roads to Shiliin Bogd start from Erdenetsagaan (70km) and Dariganga

(70km). It's better to go to Dariganga first, where you are more likely to find a jeep for rent or a lift.

AROUND SHILIIN BOGD UUL

Assuming that you have a jeep to get to Shiliin Bogd Uul in the first place, you can make a good loop from Dariganga, to take in Ganga Nuur on the way to Shiliin Bogd Uul, and Taliin Agui and Khurguin Khundii on the way back to Dariganga.

Taliin Agui (Талийн Агуй), 15km northwest of the mountain, is one of the largest caves in Mongolia. If the ice covering the entrance has melted (it's normally covered until August) you can squeeze through the narrow entrance. The large, and a little claustrophobic, cave has seven chambers to explore. You'll need a torch (flashlight) to see anything, and be careful on the icy floor. A small sign in Mongolian identifies the entrance.

Khurguin Khundii (Хургуин Хундий) is in a valley 40km west of Shiliin Bogd Uul, on the way back to Dariganga. Here a dozen or so ancient (pre-Chinggis Khaan) stone statues lay on the ground. The origins of these statues are debated: they are thought to either represent famous people from the region, or they were built to commemorate local women who jumped off a nearby mountain because they were forced to marry men they didn't love. You will have to rely on your driver to find the statues and to locate **Bichigtiin Skhakhaa** (Бичигтийн Схахаа), a pretty canyon about 2km away.

LKHACHINVANDAD UUL NATURAL RESERVE
ЛХАЧИНВАНДАД УУЛ

If you are visiting Shiliin Bogd by jeep, you may wish to carry on east for another 120km to the 58,500-hectare Lkhachinvandad Uul Natural Reserve, on the border with China. This reserve contains Lkhachinvandad Uul (1233m) and is full of **gazelle** and **elk**. Access is through the town of Erdenetsagaan, where there is a basic *hotel*. You will need a police permit to visit the reserve (See the Permits entry in the Dariganga section earlier).

Western Mongolia

In 1931 the giant western *aimag* (province) of Chandmani was divided into three: Bayan-Ölgii, Khovd and Uvs. The dominant feature of western Mongolia is the Mongol Altai Nuruu, Mongolia's highest mountain range, which stretches from Russia through Bayan-Ölgii and Khovd, and on to the adjacent Gov-Altai aimag. It contains many challenging and popular peaks for mountain climbers, and is the source of several rivers which eventually flow into the Arctic and Pacific oceans.

There are some important points to note when travelling in western Mongolia. Transport between western Mongolia and Ulaan Baatar is mainly by plane – so flights are often very full. No long-distance buses travel from Ulaan Baatar to these three aimags, or between the aimags. The only form of travel around western Mongolia is by shared or private jeep, or by truck. As the three capitals are joined by road, it is easy to see all the sights by jeep.

Western Mongolia is on a different time zone than Ulaan Baatar – one hour earlier than the rest of the country. In some parts, especially Bayan-Ölgii, Kazakh is a dominant language. Western Mongolia's electricity is connected to the Russian grid and the Russians occasionally cut the power when Mongolia forgets to pay its bills, even in winter. You should also be aware that an occasional outbreak of the plague can restrict travel, and that rabid dogs are not uncommon in the region.

Bayan-Ölgii
Баян-Өлгий

pop 100,000 • area 46,000 sq km
The Mongol Altai Nuruu is the backbone of Bayan-Ölgii. The highest peaks, many over 4000m, are permanently covered with glaciers and snow, while the valleys have a few green pastures, which support about two

Highlights

- Achit Nuur, a pleasant lake for swimming, fishing, camping, with superb sunsets and bird life

- Kazakh culture and its brightly-decorated gers and unique practice of eagle-hunting

- Kharkhiraa Valley, a stunning area of forests and streams, inexpensive resorts, and superb hiking

- Üüreg Nuur, a lovely, accessible freshwater lake, with excellent camping and hiking

- Uvs Nuur, Mongolia's largest lake, with impressive (but hard to find) bird life; nearby sand dunes and mountains are great for exploration

- Tavanbogd National Park, with stunning mountains and lakes, and Mongolia's highest peak

million livestock, as well as bears, foxes and lynxes. These valleys are dotted with small communities of nomadic families enjoying the short summer from mid-June to late August, as well as some beautiful alpine lakes.

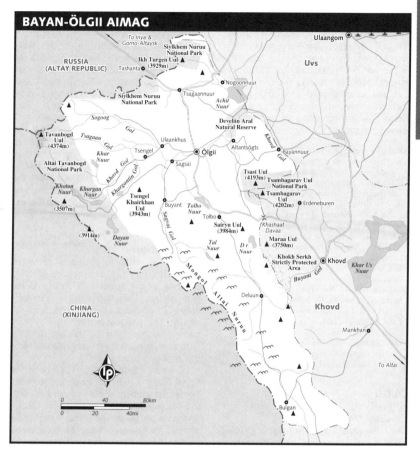

BAYAN-ÖLGII AIMAG

The ethnic groups who call Bayan-Ölgii home are comprised of the Kazakh, Khalkh, Dorvod, Uriankhai, Tuva, and Khoshuud. Unlike the rest of Mongolia, which is dominated by the Khalkh Mongols, about 90% of Bayan-Ölgii's population are Kazakh, almost all of them Muslim. The remaining 10% are mostly obscure minority groups.

Many people in the aimag speak Kazakh, so if you have spent time perfecting some conversational Mongolian, you may be devastated because many Kazakhs won't be able to understand you. There is bound to be someone nearby, however, who speaks Mongolian and, possibly Russian, but certainly nothing else.

The aimag has a rich collection of archaeological sites, with many *balbal* (Turkic stone figures believed to be grave makers), deer stones, *kurgans* (burial mounds) and a remarkable collection of 10,000 petroglyphs near the Russian border at Tsagaan Sala (also known as Baga Oigor). If you are particularly interested in these remote and obscure sites contact the Mongol Altai Nuruu Special Protected Area office in Ölgii.

Protected Areas

Most of the parks come under the jurisdiction of the Mongol Altai Nuruu Special Protected Area. Environmentalists hope that further sections of Bayan-Ölgii will become national parks to preserve the argali sheep, ibex and snow leopard, as well as the important sources of lakes and rivers in the Great Lakes Depression in the Uvs and Khovd aimags.

Altai Tavanbogd National Park (636,161 hectares) Takes in Tavanbogd Uul, Mongolia's highest mountain, and the stunning lakes of Khoton, Khurgan and Dayan. Fauna includes argali sheep, ibex, maral (Asiatic red deer), stone marten, deer, elk, Altai snowcock and eagles.

Khokh Serkh Strictly Protected Area (65,920 hectare) A mountainous area on the border with Khovd, which protects argali sheep and ibex.

Siylkhem Nuruu National Park (14,080 hectares) This new park, created in 2000, has two sections, one around Ikh Türgen Uul, the other further east.

Develiin Aral Natural Reserve (10,300 hectares) A remarkable habitat around Develiin Island in the Usan Khooloi and Khovd rivers. Established in 2000, it is home to pheasants, boars and beavers.

Tsambagarav Uul National Park (110,960 hectares) Established in 2000 to protect glaciers and the snow leopard habitat; borders on Khovd.

ÖLGII
ӨЛГИЙ
elevation 1710m

Ölgii, the capital of the aimag, is an ethnically Kazakh city that happens to be in Mongolia. You can certainly feel that you are in a Muslim-influenced Central Asian region, rather than in Mongolia: many places have squat toilets; in the city, there are signs in Arabic and Kazakh Cyrillic; the market, which is called a *bazar* rather than the Mongolian *zakh*, sells the odd kebab *(shashlyk)* and is stocked with goods from Kazakhstan. Ölgii is 1645km from Ulaan Baatar but only 225km from Russia.

Ölgii is suffering from the outflow of Kazakhs to Kazakhstan following the break up of the Soviet Union. Ölgii is the only aimag capital to have a serious decline in population: about 9000 Kazakhs left the city in 1992 and 1993. Many have since returned, disillusioned with life in the ex-Soviet republic and the population is rising once again.

Information

The Mongol Altai Nuruu Special Protected Area office (☎ 2111) is in the government building at the south-east corner of the main square. The office can give information and sell permits for any park in the aimag. The parks director, Atai, is very knowledgeable about the area and can help with both general travel and mountaineering arrangements.

If you are headed to Altai Tavanbogd National Park you will need a permit from the border detachment. First you need to go to the Intelligence Bureau (Tagnuul Gazar) and get permission. Then head to the border army barracks out on the north-western outskirts. If you have been in Mongolia for more than 30 days you will need to show

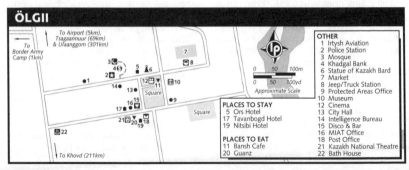

ÖLGII

To Airport (5km), Tsagaannuur (69km) & Ulaanggom (301km)

To Border Army Camp (1km)

To Khovd (211km)

0   50   100m
0   50   100yd
Approximate Scale

OTHER
1 Irtysh Aviation
2 Police Station
3 Mosque
4 Khadgal Bank
6 Statue of Kazakh Bard
7 Market
8 Jeep/Truck Station
9 Protected Areas Office
10 Museum
12 Cinema
13 City Hall
14 Intelligence Bureau
15 Disco & Bar
16 MIAT Office
18 Post Office
21 Kazakh National Theatre
22 Bath House

PLACES TO STAY
5 Ors Hotel
17 Tavanbogd Hotel
19 Nitsibi Hotel

PLACES TO EAT
11 Bansh Cafe
20 Guanz

your registration and possibly your permission to travel in the countryside.

A small travel agency Altai Tours can help organise permits. Contact the director, Kazbek (☎ 1245 2169). Its office is in a building south of the square.

The public bath house is open daily from 10 am to 10 pm and a hot shower costs T400 (*monsha* is 'hot water' in local Kazakh dialect).

Things to See

The **aimag museum** gives an excellent overview of Kazakh culture and of the geography of Bayan-Ölgii. The 2nd floor is devoted to history, and the 3rd floor has some interesting displays; entry costs T1000. It is open on weekdays from 9 am to 1 pm, and from 2 to 5 pm.

Ölgii's **mosque** and madrasah (Islamic place of learning) is worth a quick look, especially on Friday at lunch time when weekly prayers are held, though you may not be allowed inside. The mosque holds the offices of the Islamic Centre of Mongolia. Its unusual angle is due to its orientation to Mecca.

Places to Stay

Camping If you want to camp, walk east of the square to Khovd Gol and then head southeast, away from the market and ger suburbs.

Hotels Opposite the National Theatre, the Kazakh-run *Tavanbogd Hotel* is the best in town. Rooms are comfortable and clean, and have a toilet and sink (though hot water is limited to winter). Clean and fairly pleasant

Kazakhs

Kazakh nomads have lived in Central Asia for 400 years, but first started to come to the Bayan-Ölgii area in the 1840s to graze their sheep on the high mountain pastures during summer. They then returned to Kazakhstan or Xinjiang for the winter. After the Mongolian Revolution in 1921, a permanent border was drawn by agreement between China, Russia and Mongolia, but the Kazakhs remained nomadic until the 1930s, crossing the border at will.

The word 'Kazakh' is said to mean 'free warrior' or 'steppe roamer'. Kazakhs trace their roots to the 15th century, when rebellious kinsmen of an Uzbek khaan broke away, and settled in present-day Kazakhstan. Traditional costume for Kazakh women is a long dress with stand-up collars, or a brightly-decorated velvet waistcoat with heavy jewellery. Older married women often wear a white headscarf. The men still wear baggy shirts and trousers, sleeveless jackets, long black cloaks (not traditional Mongolian *del*), a skullcap, or a fox-fur hat. The Kazakh culture of Mongolia is far more intact than that of strongly Russified Kazakhstan.

Kazakh culture is quite different from Mongolian; even Kazakh saddles are a different shape. Music is commonly sung by bards who accompany their singing with a *dombra*, a two-stringed lute. Kazakh gers are taller, wider and more richly decorated than the Mongolian version. Wall hangings known as *tush* and felt carpets *(koshma)*, decorated with stylised animal motifs, are common. Traditional reed screens called *chiy* are becoming less common.

Kazakhs generally adhere rather loosely to Sunni Islam, but religion is not a major force. This is because of their distance from the centre of Islam, their nomadic lifestyle, and the suppression of Islam by Stalinism. Islam is making a comeback in Bayan-Ölgii, however, following the lifting of restrictions against religion, aid packages from other Muslim countries, the construction of a mosque in Ölgii, and the first hajj or pilgrimage to Mecca in 1992. Islamic law has always sat lightly with the many Kazakhs, however, who enjoy a bottle of vodka as much as the next Mongolian. The main Kazakh holiday is the pre-Islamic spring festival of Nauruz, celebrated on March 21.

Kazakhs speak a Turkic language with 42 Cyrillic letters, similar to Russian, and a little different to Mongolians. The Mongolian Government is trying to placate the Kazakh minority, and stop them returning to Kazakhstan, by encouraging the Kazakh language in schools in Bayan-Ölgii.

standard rooms with a toilet and basin range from T3500 to T5600 per person, or splash out on a gigantic deluxe suite for T10,500 (per person). This is one of the few hotels that keeps your passport while you stay there.

The two other hotels, the *Ors Hotel* and *Nitsibi Hotel* are both pretty rough and not recommended.

Places to Eat

The restaurant in the *Tavanbogd Hotel* serves standard food, given some notice. A large *Kazakh restaurant* at the western end of the main street, and another east of the post office, are worth trying for some Kazakh-style boiled mutton rather than the Mongolian variety (unfortunately, there is no difference).

Otherwise, try the five or six *shaykhana* (teahouses) or *ashkhana* (restaurants) in abandoned train wagons around the market and town squares. They usually serve delicious tea (*shay* in the Kazakh language) – not the milky and salty stuff loved by Mongolians. They also serve some *khuurshuur* (fried meat pancakes). There is a decent *shaykhana* opposite the Tavanbogd Hotel run by three Kazakh sisters.

Entertainment

The rowdy *bar* next to the Tavanbogd Hotel might be worth a visit, though the atmosphere can be a little rough.

The incongruous ochre-coloured *Kazakh National Theatre* has the odd dombra recital.

Shopping

The market has a decent selection of food supplies, with the emphasis on Russian imports. If you are very lucky you might spot some traditional Kazakh skullcaps or boots. There's a small charge to get into the enclosed part of the market where all the food is.

If you have a local guide, you may be able to look around the small Kazakh factories in Ölgii which churn out these traditional products, as well as felt carpets and leather products.

The Special Protected Area office also sells a selection of reasonably priced Kazakh handicrafts such as felt cushions, carpets and skullcaps.

Getting There & Away

Air MIAT flies between Ölgii and Ulaan Baatar, with a refuelling stop (often at Mörön), every Tuesday, Thursday and Saturday for US$161/281. The four-hour flight provides breathtaking views of glacier-capped peaks as you approach Ölgii.

The airport is 5km north of the centre, on the opposite side of the river. There is no bus, but it's usually possible to hitch a ride in a truck or on the back of a motorcycle.

The MIAT office is next to the Tavanbogd Hotel, up the stairs and to the right. The office is open weekdays from 8 am to noon and 1 to 4.30 pm. Remodelling might mean that the entrance is around the back of the building.

MIAT has stopped flying between Ulaan Baatar and Almaty (the capital of Kazakhstan), via Ölgii, after losing T180 million in one year. Each Wednesday afternoon, a chartered aircraft (Kazakh Air) flies between Almaty and Ölgii – but this flight (US$136) is a little unreliable. For more information in Ölgii visit the Irtysh Aviation office, not far from the police station. Your biggest obstacle to this flight is immigration procedures, which will have to be cleared either at an immigration office next to the MIAT office, or at the airport.

Jeep Ölgii is not blessed with a lot of jeeps for hire but those that exist charge a reasonable T250 per km, including petrol. For a trip around western Mongolia, it's better to start from Ulaangom or Khovd city.

Public shared jeeps to Tsagaannuur (T7000) and, less frequently, to Khovd (T5000) and Ulaangom (T10,000) leave from the Ölgii market. Drivers have a nasty habit of charging foreigners double here, so check to see what others are paying.

The road from Ölgii to Khovd city (211km) is pretty good. The 300km road to Ulaangom, via Achit Nuur is also good. The road passes the surprisingly lush riverside forests of the Develiin Aral Natural Reserve. Look out for the canyon to the left, marked by ancient graves, some 21km from Ölgii.

Hitching A few vehicles, most of which are petrol tankers, travel the road between Ölgii and Khovd city. The Ölgii-Ulaangom road is not as busy because most vehicles head east towards Ulaan Baatar and use the southern road via Khovd city. Some vehicles travelling between Ölgii and Ulaangom will bypass Tsagaannuur and take the short-cut via Achit Nuur.

Check out the noticeboard and loud-speaker at the market for information (this could be a challenge as you'll hear it in Mongolian, Kazakh or Russian) about lifts around the aimag. If you can't read the notices, just ask anyway. A lot of Russian trucks hang around the market, waiting for cargo to take to Russia via Tsagaannuur. There is also quite a lot of traffic, with jeeps being driven from Russia and elsewhere and sold locally.

TSAGAANNUUR
ЦАГААННУУР

Yet another place called Tsagaanuur (White Lake); the town is less famous for its lake (there are several bigger and nicer ones nearby) than as the starting point for travel by road into Russia.

The Ölgii-Ulaangom road is generally not busy, and some vehicles take a short-cut via Achit Nuur, but you can get a ride on a shared jeep to Tsagaannuur (five hours, T7000) easily enough. There are no hotels in Tsagaannuur, so if you are waiting for a lift, ask some Russian drivers, or someone at the petrol station, about a place to stay.

TSAST UUL
ЦАСТ УУЛ

The two *sums* (districts) of Altantsögts and Bayannuur are about 50km south-east of Ölgii, on the border with Khovd aimag. They are full of lush valleys with friendly Kazakh and Mongol nomads in summer, dozens of tiny unmapped lakes and soaring,

permanently snowcapped peaks, such as Tsast Uul (4193m).

If you have your own vehicle and tent, take a detour between Khovd city and Ölgii and spend a few peaceful days around Tsast Uul (meaning 'mountain of snow'). It is always cold up here (it only stops snowing between about mid-June and late August), so be prepared. Just to the south, in Khovd aimag, Tsambagarav Uul (4202m) is slightly higher and equally as stunning (see the Tsambagarav Uul section later).

Eagle-Hunters

While travelling around Bayan-Ölgii, you may come across Kazakh eagle-hunters. If you ask gently, the Kazakhs may proudly show you their birds, though actual hunting only ever takes place in November and December.

Eagle-hunting is a Kazakh tradition dating back about 2000 years (Marco Polo mentions it in his *Travels*). Female eagles are almost always used as they are one-third heavier than the males and far more aggressive. Young birds, around two-years-old, are caught in nearby valleys, fattened up and washed, and then 'broken' by being tied to a wooden block so that they fall when they try to fly away. After two days they are exhausted and ready for training, which involves being kept on a pole called a *tugir*, and catching small animal skins or lures called *shirga*. The eagles are trained to hunt marmots, small foxes and wolves (eagles have vision eight times more acute than humans), and release them to the hunter, who clubs the prey to death. Part of the meat is given to the eagles as a reward.

Tools of the trade include the *tomaga* (hood), *bialai* (gloves) and *khundag* (blanket to keep the bird warm). If well trained, a bird can live, and hunt, for about 30 years. Most hunters train several birds during their lifetime and release their birds into the wild after 10 years.

The most likely places to find a Kazakh eagle-hunter are in the Tsast Uul mountain region between Khovd and Bayan-Ölgii, and the Deluun, Tsengel and Bayannuur regions of Bayan-Ölgii aimag.

ALTAI TAVANBOGD NATIONAL PARK
АЛТАЙ ТАВАНБОГД

This stunningly beautiful park stretches south from Tavanbogd Uul and includes the three stunning lakes of Khoton Nuur, Khurgan Nuur and Dayan Nuur. It's a remote area, divided from China by the high wall of snowcapped peaks, and known to local Kazakhs as the Syrgali region.

All three lakes are the source of the Khovd Gol, which eventually flows into Khar Us Nuur in Khovd aimag. It's possible to make rafting trips down river from Dayan Nuur, though no agencies offer this at present.

There are many archeological sites in the region. As the main road through the region swings towards the southern shore of Khurgan Nuur you can see a stupa-like construction and several burial sites. Nearby is a **balbal** (Turkic stone statue) and the remains of a **processional pathway** (GPS: N 48° 31.908', E 86° 28.926'). Further along the road is a wooden **Kazakh mosque**, with a ger-shaped roof.

Further north-west, along the south-western shore of Khoton Nuur, the road deteriorates and there are several rivers to cross as they flow into the lake. North-west of Khoton Nuur the mountains close in and there's some fine trekking possibilities.

One local environmental concern is the US$10 million hydroelectric project, which plans to siphon water from nearby Khar Nuur through a 3.4km pipeline. It is planned that water will be replaced by diverting the Khargant Gol, though the environmental impact report had not even been completed before construction started.

Permits
Park entry fees are the standard T1000 per person per day, plus T3000 per car. Fishing permits cost T500 per day, but fishing is not permitted between 15 May and 15 July (there is a US$50 fine). The main entry to the park is by the bridge over the Khovd Gol, south of Tsengel. You can pay for permits here, or at the Mongol Altai Nuruu Special Protected Area office in Ölgii, or from rangers around the lake.

You need to get a border permit from the border guards at Ölgii. This will be checked by the border guards at the point where Khoton Nuur meets Khurgan Nuur. If you don't have a permit the guards say that you will be fined around US$100 and given 72 hours to leave the area. Note that your guide and driver will need their Mongolian passports.

You don't need a park permit or border permit if you just visit Dayan Nuur from the Khargantin Valley.

Places to Stay & Eat
There's no formal accommodation or places to eat in the park, though the park has plans to build an **ecoger** somewhere between the two lakes. Costs will be between US$5 and US$8 per night, or US$10 with dinner.

There are beautiful camping spots all around the lakes. Dayan Nuur has some nasty mosquitoes but the other two lakes are largely bug-free. The lakes are teeming with fish.

Getting There & Away
The main road from Tsengel leads 50km south to the bridge over the Khovd Gol (there's a T400 toll) and then continues 33km to the junction of the Khoton and Khurgan lakes, where you will have to cross the 200m-wide water channel between the two lakes. Your jeep will never make it alone so you need to get the truck stationed at the border guard camp to pull you across for the equivalent of 10 litres of petrol (around US$3.50). There is a **guanz** (cheap restaurant or canteen) but no hotel in Tsengel.

A more scenic route takes you from Sagsai, over a pass and up the beautiful Khargantin Gol Valley, past the 3943m-high Tsengel Khairkhan Uul and Khar Nuur, and then down to Dayan Nuur. A good option would be to enter the park this way and exit via the main road. It's possible to drive from Dayan Nuur to Buyant by jeep but you'd need a good driver who knows the way.

Tavanbodg Uul
ТАВАНЬОГД УУЛ

Tavanbogd (Five Saints) mountain rises 4374m above the borders of three nations,

The 'Flaming Cliffs' of Bayanzag, in the Gobi Desert, are renowned worldwide for dinosaur finds.

Revered by nomads, the two-humped Bactrian camel is perfect for long-distance travel.

Stunning valley scenery of Tosontsengel, Zavkhan aimag, western Mongolia

A nomad family takes an enforced break en route.

A solitary 'petrol station'

Runic script of Tonyukuk stellae

The reindeer herd of a Tsaatan family, Khövosgöl Nuur

A typical *ovoo*, a sacred pile of stones found on hilltops and passes

A *balbal*, a Turkic grave marker

and for this reason it is also known as Nairamdal (Friendship) Peak. If you sit on the summit, you can simultaneously be in Mongolia, China and Russia (though you won't need a visa for all three).

Tavanbogd is one of Mongolia's most spectacular peaks, of interest to professional climbers, and the only one in Bayan-Ölgii to be permanently covered with large glaciers (including the 19km long Potanii Glacier, the longest in Mongolia). It's fairly dangerous, and to climb it you need to be with an experienced group properly equipped with ice axes, crampons and ropes. Don't even consider attempting it solo. The best time to climb is August and September, after the worst of the summer rains.

The massif is made up of five peaks (the 'five saints') – Khuiten, Naran, Ölgii, Burged and Nairamdal – the highest of which is Khuiten (meaning 'cold') at 4374m.

Getting There & Away To get to the mountain, you should be able to hitch a ride to Tsengel sum centre (also known as Khöshööt), but from there you will have to trek about 110km along the Tsagaan Gol. If you have your own vehicle, you can drive to within about 40km of the base of the mountain, where there are fine views of the glaciated mountains. Even if you are not a climber it's worth making it here for the views and hiking potential.

From the end of the road, it's a 15km trek to the first glacier, where most climbers set up base camp. The climb up the glacier is about 25km, and you can expect to encounter icy temperatures, crevasses and very volatile weather.

It is also possible to access the mountain by road along the Sogoog Gol and, in fact, in rainy weather this is often the most reliable route. For advice on access and climbing talk to Atai at the Mongol Altai Nuruu Special Protected Area office in Ölgii city. You will need border permits to visit the mountain (see the Altai Tavanbogd National Park section previously) and will have to pay national park fees.

TOLBO NUUR
ТОЛБО НУУР

Tolbo Nuur (Frog Lake) is about 50km south of Ölgii, on the main road between Ölgii and Khovd city, so it's an easy day trip or stopover. The saltwater lake is high (2080m), expansive and eerie, but a bit disappointing because the shoreline is treeless. There are a few gers around the lake, and the water is clean enough for swimming if you don't mind icy temperatures. If you want to see, and camp at, some better lakes, keep travelling on to Uvs aimag.

A major battle was fought here between Bolshevik and White Russians, with the local Mongolian general, Hasbaatar, siding with the Bolsheviks. The Bolsheviks won and so there are a couple of memorial plaques by the lake.

Khovd ХОВД

pop 94,500 • area 76,000 sq km

Khovd is one of Mongolia's most heterogeneous aimags, with a Khalkh majority and minorities of Khoton, Kazakh, Uriankhai, Zakhchin, Myangad, Oold and Torguud peoples. It is the most visited aimag in western Mongolia and the most popular place for tourists west of Khövsgöl Nuur, mainly because it's a good place to start a tour of the west, and it's cheaper to fly to than Bayan-Ölgii.

Khovd aimag is almost cut in half by the mighty Mongol Altai Nuruu range; away from the mountains the land is a barren semi-desert dotted with salt lakes and smaller mountains. The melting snow from the mountains recharges the water table every spring, providing Khovd with more than 200 fast-moving rivers (and dozens of lakes), none of which has an outlet to the sea. All the rivers simply disappear beneath the sands or run into large saltwater marshes, which serve as giant evaporating ponds.

The mix of desert rock, salt lake, snowy peaks and Kazakh culture makes Khovd one of the most beautiful and appealing aimags in Mongolia.

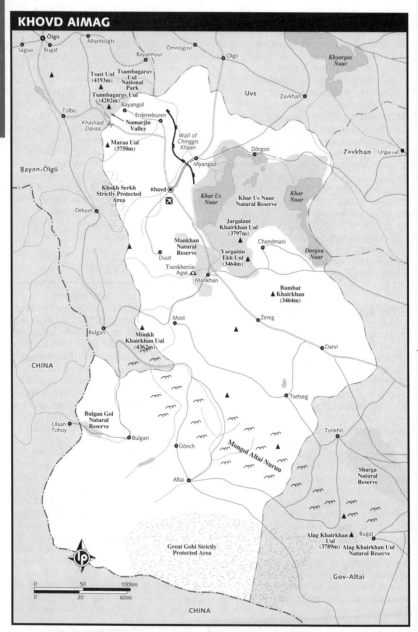

KHOVD AIMAG

Ölgii
Sagsai Bugat
Altantsögts
Bayannuur
Ömnögovi
Olgii

Khyargas Nuur

Tsast Uul (4193m)
Tsambagarav Uul National Park
Tsambagarav Uul (4202m)
Bayangol
Erdeneburen
Namarjin Valley

Uvs

Zavkhan

Tolbo

Khashaat Davaa

Maraa Uul (3750m)

Wall of Chinggis Khaan

Dörgon

Zavkhan   Urgamal

Bayan-Ölgii

Myangad

Khokh Serkh Strictly Protected Area
Khovd

Khar Us Nuur

Khar Us Nuur Natural Reserve

Khar Nuur

Deluun

Jargalant Khairkhan Uul (3797m)

Mankhan Natural Reserve
Duut

Chandmani

Yargaitin Ekh Uul (3464m)

Dorgon Nuur

Tsenkheriin Agui
Mankhan

Bumbat Khairkhan (3464m)

Most
Zereg

Bulgan
Mönkh Khairkhan Uul (4362m)

Darvi

CHINA

Tsetseg

Bulgan Gol Natural Reserve
Ulaan Tohoy
Bulgan

Tonkhil

Üönch

Mongol Altai Nuruu

Sharga Natural Reserve

Altai

Great Gobi Strictly Protected Area

Alag Khairkhan Uul (3789m)
Bugat
Alag Khairkhan Uul Natural Reserve

Gov-Altai

0   50   100km
0   30   60mi

CHINA

WESTERN MONGOLIA

Protected Areas

There are several important protected areas in Khovd aimag:

Bulgan Gol Natural Reserve (1840 hectares) On the south-western border with China, it was established to help preserve *minj* (beavers), sable and stone marten.

Great Gobi Strictly Protected Area (also known as 'Gobi B') Created to protect *khulan* (wild asses), gazelles, jerboas and *takhi* (wild horses).

Khar Us Nuur National Park (850,272 hectares) Protects the breeding grounds for antelopes and rare species of migratory pelicans, falcons and bustards.

Khokh Serkh Strictly Protected Area (65,920 hectares) On the north-west border with Bayan-Ölgii, helps protect argali sheep, ibexes and snow leopards.

Mankhan Natural Reserve Directly south-east of Khovd city, preserves an endangered species of antelope.

Tsambagarav Uul National Park (110,960 hectares) Established in 2000, on the border with Bayan-Ölgii, it protects the snow leopard habitat.

Organised Tours

Nomads in Ulaan Baatar are specialists in the Khovd region and run fascinating tours to the aimag. These tours include horse riding and trekking trips to Tsambagarav Uul, visits to Kazakh families and exploration of the magnificent Üüreg, Achit and Uvs lakes.

KHOVD
ХОВД

pop 35,000 • elevation 1406m

Once a small farming community, and later a centre for trade with Russia, Khovd city is the major industrial centre of western Mongolia. It was one of the last cities to be liberated from the Chinese, in 1912 (and again in 1921), by the forces of the Mongolian commanders Dambijantsan, Magsarjav and Damdinsüren.

A pleasant and easygoing city built near the fast-flowing Buyant Gol, Khovd is a good place to start a trip around western Mongolia. The city is not prosperous but survives on an agricultural economy, food processing and some light manufacturing of building materials. It also boasts an agricultural institute and the main university in

KHOVD

To Ulaangom (238km) & Red Goat Mountain (3km)
To Ölgii (211km)
Buyant Gol
Approximate Scale
Square
Park
To Altai (424km)
To Airport (5km)
To Stadium (500m)

PLACES TO STAY	3 Post Office
11 Khovd Hotel	4 Museum
17 Buyant Hotel	6 Police Station
	9 Tureemel Amarjuulagai Khiid
PLACES TO EAT	12 Drama Theatre
5 Guanz	13 City Hall
7 Guanz	14 Hospital
8 Guanz	15 Magsarjaw Theatre
10 Guanz	16 Shop
	18 Mini Delguur Shop
OTHER	19 Altan Luu shop
1 Sangiin Kherem	20 Bath House
2 Protected Areas Office	21 Market & Jeep/Truck Station

western Mongolia. About 300 Kazakhs live in the town and more live in the sum centre of Buyan, 25km north of Khovd.

A small **statue** in the central square honours Aldanjavyn Ayush (1859–1939), a local revolutionary hero who agitated against the Manchus to lower taxation and who was made head of Tsetseg sum after the 1921 revolution.

Information

The Khar Us National Park Office (☎ 2334, fax 1231, **e** kharus@magicnet.mn), opposite the post office, can give information on, and permits, for nearby Khar Us Nuur National Park.

You can get a hot shower for T565 at the public bath house just north of the market. It's open daily from 9 am to 9 pm and sells sachets of shampoo.

You can change US dollars, Chinese yuan or Russian roubles with a couple of money-changers who hang around the market.

Museum

The museum in Khovd city has the usual collection of stuffed wildlife, some excellent ethnic costumes, Buddhist and Kazakh art, and a snow leopard pelt tacked up on the wall. One of the more interesting exhibits is the re-creation of cave paintings at Tsenkheriin Agui (see that section later in this chapter). There are also several examples of the many deer stones scattered around the aimag.

According to the sign above the door, the museum is open weekdays from 8 to noon and 1 to 5 pm, and maybe on Saturday morning; entry costs T1000. It is on a corner, near the police station.

Sangiin Kherem (Manchu Ruins)

Сангийн Хэрэм

At the northern end of the city are some rapidly disappearing walls built around 1762 by the Manchu (Qing dynasty) warlords who once conquered, and brutally governed, Mongolia. The 40,000 sq metre walled-compound once contained several temples, a Chinese graveyard and the homes of the Manchu rulers, though there's little left to see. Three enormous gates provided access. At one time, there was a moat (2m deep and 3m wide) around the 4m-high walls, but this has been completely filled in. The 1500-man Chinese garrison was destroyed after a 10-day siege and two-day battle in August 1912.

The one legacy of Manchurian rule which has remained are the magnificent 200-year-old trees which line the streets of Khovd city.

Tureemel Amarjuulagai Khiid

Турээмэл Амаржуулагай Хийд

The original Shar Süm (Yellow Temple) was built outside of Khovd in the 1770s but was completely destroyed during the Stalinist purge of 1937. The monastery was recently relocated into the centre of the city but it's not all that active.

Hiking

The dry, rugged hills north of the Manchu ruins offer some good opportunities for hiking. Try Yamart Ulaan Uul (Red Goat

Dambijantsan

Also known as Ja Lama, Dambijanstan was the self-proclaimed leader of western Mongolia from 1912-1914. A Kalmuk lama from the Russian Volga, historical records describe Ja Lama as an 'insane and cruel genius', who would beat to death anyone who disobeyed him, even gouging out the eyes of live men. Many locals held him in awe, believing him to be the bullet-proof reincarnation of the Oirad warrior leader.

He was finally arrested by the Russians while trying to set up his own kingdom at Münjig in southern Khovd, and was exiled to Yakutsk in Siberia. In 1918 he somehow managed to make it back to western Mongolia. His first task was to build himself a stone palace, which he financed through a series of highway robberies.

Eventually the central government ran out of patience with the renegade, pretended to offer him a government post and then had him shot. When no-one believed that he had actually been killed, his head was displayed in Uliastai and then Urga (Ulaan Baatar), before it was smuggled to St Petersburg and bizarrely found its way into the private collection of Peter the Great.

Mountain) to the north-east of town, it's a difficult six- to seven-hour round-hike to the peak. An easier option is the small mountain just south of the airport with the *soyombo* national symbol carved on it.

The views are naturally great from these peaks but be careful – if you slip, there's no-one around to help you.

The Buyant Gol is a swift river on the west side of town. The locals go swimming here, and it's a great place to hike around, either upstream or downstream.

Places to Stay

Camping Some of the best camping in western Mongolia is along the Buyant Gol. Just walk south from the town for about 10 minutes (or take a jeep) to the interesting, Islamic-influenced Naadam Stadium. The area is fairly crowded with cows and gers, but you will be left alone. From around mid-September until the cold weather sets in, clouds of mosquitoes descend on the area, so make sure you plenty of insect repellent handy. You may be tempted to drink from the river, but the large numbers of livestock means you should definitely all your drinking water.

If you have your own vehicle, try further along the Buyant, on the road to either Ulaangom or Ölgii.

Hotels The *Buyant Hotel* charges a hefty foreigners' price of US$10/15 for a semideluxe single/double, or US$15/20 for a deluxe, neither of which have hot water. Foreigners are apparently not allowed to stay in the ordinary dormitory rooms for T3000 per bed.

Luckily, the *Khovd Hotel* is a much better deal, and there are no foreigner prices. The simple rooms are OK for T2000, and the second class rooms are also not bad for T3000, especially the rooms with a balcony. If there's more than one of you, the 1st class suite is the real bargain for T4000, as it comes with two bedrooms and a dining room – a palace. There is a clean toilet and cold water washroom down the hall. Halfdeluxe and deluxe rooms come with a toilet and sink (the deluxe has a shower) for T5000/7000 per person.

Both hotels are near the attractive Drama Theatre.

Places to Eat

If the staff can be bothered to open them, the *Buyant Hotel* and *Khovd Hotel* both have restaurants, though you'll have to give them fair warning if you want to eat there.

The main north-south road has several *guanz*, one of which might have some food. Try just south of the museum; diagonally opposite, on both sides of the police station; or next to the monastery.

Entertainment

The *Magsarjaw Theatre*, on the way to the Naadam Stadium, and the *Drama Theatre* both show badly dubbed action films but not much else these days.

Things to Buy

The daily market, south of the town centre, is large, lively and well stocked. It is the best place in western Mongolia for Western goods and stocks a wide range of noodles, rice, tea, meat and bread, as well as other necessities like chocolate bars and soft drinks. Khovd aimag is justifiably famous for its watermelons (normally best in late summer), which are also available at the market.

One or two shops in the town sell some pricey imported foods at prices about 50% higher than in Ulaan Baatar. The best shops are currently the Altan Luu shop and the 'mini delguur' (mini-shop). Both shops are along the road between the market and the central square.

Getting There & Away

Air The four-hour MIAT flight between Ulaan Baatar and Khovd city (via Tosontsengel) leaves on Tuesday, Thursday, Friday (via Bulgan city) and Saturday and costs US$146/256. You may be able to just get a ticket for the Khovd-Tosontsengel leg but only if the flight isn't full.

The airport is 5km south of the city. There may be a bus there when you arrive, but otherwise you will have to get a ride on a jeep for T500 per person or T2000 per jeep. Jeeps leave for the airport from outside the Magsarjaw Theatre.

Khovd-Ulaan Baatar flights (and vice versa) are popular, so it is vital to buy tickets well in advance. If you have a return ticket from Ulaan Baatar then reconfirm it as soon as you arrive. You need to get to the airport at around 8.30 am on the morning of your flight (which normally leaves at 2 pm!) in order to get your numbered boarding card. Then you can wait the remaining four hours until boarding, or return to the city for lunch. There is a *guanz* on the upper floor of the airport.

Our flight had over 70 people booked on the 42-seater flight. At one point a fist fight broke out and the pilot pulled up the ladder as people started climbing onto the plane to get a seat. Really! Be warned – get there very, very early!

Minivan Furgons (Russian-made minivans) wait at the market. If you want a ride try to get a Mongolian speaker to help and ask them to broadcast a message on the loudspeaker. You should be able to get a ride somewhere within a day, or maybe two. Approximate fares at the time of research were T8000 to T10,000 to Altai, T15,000 to Bayankhongor and between T25,000 and T30,000 to Ulaan Bataar.

There's less traffic headed to Bayan-Ölgii (T8000), and less still to Ulaangom but again something should come up. The same applies to hitching.

Jeep There are several jeeps for hire in Khovd city, which makes it the best place to start a trip around western Mongolia. Jeeps cost around T300 per km, including petrol, but you'll have to negotiate hard. Ask around at the market.

The road from Khovd city to Ölgii (211km) is pretty good; to Altai (424km) it is rough and boring in patches; and to Ulaangom (238km) the road is often marred by broken bridges and flooded rivers after heavy rain.

KHAR US NUUR NATIONAL PARK
ХАР УС НУУР

About 40km to the east of Khovd city is Khar Us Nuur (Black Water Lake), the second-largest freshwater lake (15,800 sq km) in Mongolia – but with an average depth of only 4m. Khovd Gol flows into this lake, creating a giant marsh delta. Khar Us Nuur is the perfect habitat for wild ducks, geese, wood grouse, partridges and seagulls, including the rare relict gull and herring gull – and by late summer, a billion or two of everyone's friend, the common mosquito. Be prepared for the blighters, otherwise your life will be a misery. The best time to see the birdlife is in May and late August.

As at Uvs Nuur, birdwatchers may be a little disappointed: the lake is huge, difficult to reach because of the marshes, and locals know very little, if anything, about the birdlife. The best idea would be to go with one of the national park workers and to

head for the delta where the Khovd Gol enters the lake. You'll need several litres of drinking water and mosquito repellent.

The easiest place to see the lake is from the main Khovd-Altai road at the southern tip of the lake, where reed islands also make for good birding. The park plans to encourage ecotourism by setting up observation huts and maybe even ger accommodation in this area. Check with the park office in Khovd.

The outflow from Khar Us Nuur goes into a short river called Chono Kharaikh, which flows into another freshwater lake, **Khar Nuur** (Black Lake), home to some migratory pelicans. There is a dispute about which lake is the deepest in Mongolia: it is either Khar Nuur or Khövsgöl Nuur. The southern end of Khar Nuur flows into **Dorgon Nuur**, which is a large salty pond. The east side of Dorgon Nuur is an area of bone-dry desert and extensive sand dunes.

Just to the south, and between, the Khar and Khar Us lakes, are the twin peaks of **Jargalant Khairkhan Uul** (3796m) and **Yargaitin Ekh Uul** (3464m). You can see the massif as you drive to Ölgii from Altai in Gov-Altai aimag.

TSENKHERIIN AGUI
ЦУНХУРИЙН АГУЙ

The Tsenkheriin Agui (also known as Khoid Tsenkher) caves are reasonably attractive but the drawcard is the cave paintings inside, which are approximately 15,000 years old (some sources say 40,000). There is also about 15,000 years worth of bird dung in the caves, so watch where you step. There are numerous passages to explore, with the largest cavern being about 15m high, with the floor measuring around 12m by 18m. Unfortunately, some recent graffiti has marred the cave paintings. Controversy has erupted among experts about the interpretation of the paintings. It is interesting to note that both mammoths and ostriches are depicted on the walls, proving that both lived in Mongolia up to approximately 15,000 years ago.

The caves are in an attractive setting next to a stream, in Mankhan sum, about 90km south-east of Khovd city. You could hitch a ride to Mankhan centre, just south of the

Khovd city-Altai road, but you'd still have a 25km walk to the caves. With your own jeep you could combine the cave with a visit to Khar Us to make a long day-trip or good overnighter. Bring a strong torch (flashlight), lots of warm clothes and high, dung-proof boots.

If you can't make it to the caves, the museum in Khovd city and the Zanabazar Museum in Ulaan Baatar both have interesting re-creations of the cave paintings.

MÖNKH KHAIRKHAN UUL
МӨНХ ХАЙРХАН УУЛ

At 4362m, Mönkh Khairkhan Uul is the second highest mountain in Mongolia. You can walk up the peak if you approach from the north side. There is plenty of snow and ice on top, so you'd need crampons, an ice axe and rope but the climb is not technically difficult. A jeep trail runs to the base from Mankhan. The peak is known locally as Tavan Khumit.

TSAMBAGARAV UUL NATIONAL PARK
ЦАМБАГАРАВ УУЛ

Tsambagarav Uul, in the far north-west sum of Bayannuur, is one of the most glorious snowcapped peaks in Mongolia. Despite its altitude of 4202m, the summit is relatively accessible and easy to climb compared with Tavanbogd but you'd need crampons and ropes.

One excellent possible jeep route in this region is to travel north-west from the main Khovd-Ölgii road to the **Namarjin Valley**, where there are excellent views of Tsambagarav. From here you can head west and then south to rejoin the main Khovd-Ölgii road, via several **Kazakh settlements** and a beautiful turquoise lake. You'll need to be completely self-sufficient for this trip.

The other main area to visit is the **Bayangol Valley**, to the east of Tsambagarav, 100km and three hours of difficult driving from Khovd. A jeep road leads from Erdeneburen sum centre up the mountainside, following dozens of rocky switchbacks. The valley itself is nothing special but there are fine views south-east to Khar Us Nuur

and you might be able to rent a horse for the hour ride to the Kazakh-populated **Marra Valley**. With help you could do a fine three- or four-day horse trek circling Tsambagarav Uul, or to the Namarjin Valley.

To explore the area, you'll definitely need a driver who knows the area well. Nomads in Ulaan Baatar are a good source of guides and information on this area.

The area became a national park in July 2000, so you can expect standard park entry fees to apply.

Uvs УВС

pop 98,400 • area 69,000 sq km

One of the least visited of Mongolia's aimags, Uvs is dominated by the Ikh Nuuruudin Khotgor – the 39,000 sq km Great Lakes Depression stretching from the enormous Uvs Nuur to the Khovd and Zavkhan aimags. Other geographical features of Uvs aimag, which are definitely worth exploring, are the **Böörög Deliin Els sand dunes**, east of Uvs Nuur; a cluster of other lakes (which are nicer than Uvs Nuur) comprising Achit, Khyargas and Üüreg lakes; the 4037m-high Kharkhiraa Uul; and the gorgeous **Kharkhiraa Valley**.

Uvs aimag was originally named Dorvod after the main ethnic group that inhabited the area. The Dorvod people, who still represent just under half of the population of Uvs, speak their own dialect. Other minority ethnic groups include the Bayad, Khoton and Khalkh.

Uvs is a good place to organise and start a trip around western Mongolia. If you're on a tight budget, it's one of the few places where you could justify renting a jeep to explore the lakes, mountains, valleys and sand dunes – all within a day or so by jeep from Ulaangom.

Be careful if you are headed anywhere near the Tuvan/Russian border. Cattle rustling in this lawless region has turned violent recently, with armed gangs of Mongolians and Tuvans crossing the border at night to steal cattle from each other. You may be stopped by the army if you get too close to the border areas of Tes or Davst sums.

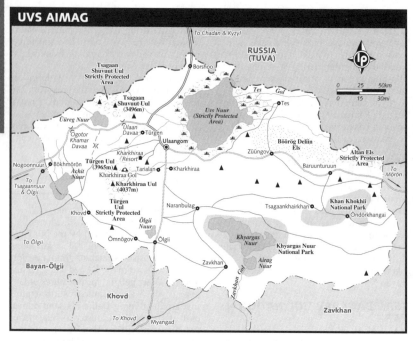

UVS AIMAG

Protected Areas

The Great Lakes Depression is a globally important area of wetland for migratory birds and is a Unesco World Biosphere Reserve. Several other parks have been established in the aimag, which together with parks in Russia, Tuva, China and Kazakstan, form a Central Asian arc of protected areas including:

Uvs Nuur Strictly Protected Area (712,545 hectares) Established in 1994, it consists of four separate areas – Uvs Nuur, Türgen Uul, Tsagaan Shuvuut and Altan Els. Between them, the protected area contains everything from desert sand dunes to snowfields, and marsh to mountain forest. Snow leopards, foxes, wolves, deer and ibex are among the animals protected. The area has been nominated as a World Heritage Site.

Khan Khokhii National Park (220,550 hectares) Established in 2000, it is an important ecological indicator and is home to snow leopard, wolf and musk deer.

Khyargas Nuur National Park (332,800 hectares) Established in 2000.

ULAANGOM
УЛААНГОМ

pop 29,600 • elevation 939m

Ulaangom, which means 'red sand', is a pleasant, tree-lined town. It is a good place to hang around while you explore the countryside, or to plan a trip around western Mongolia: there are good shops, reasonable hotels and a fantastic market.

Like the other western aimag capitals, Ulaangom suffers from power shortages due to unpaid (and unpayable) debts to the nearest power station – across the border in Russia. The situation should improve with the building of the hydroelectric station in Bayan-Ölgii.

The bronze **statue** in front of the city hall is of Yumjaagiyn Tsedenal, who ruled Mongolia for about 40 years until 1983, and was born in Ulaangom. Opposite the town square, another statue honours Givaan, a local hero who was killed in 1948 during clashes with Chinese troops.

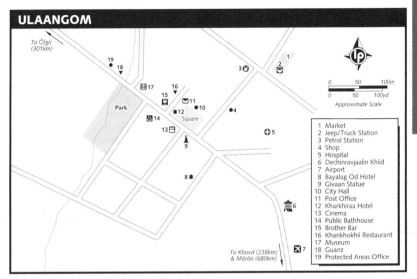

ULAANGOM

To Ölgii
(301km)

Park

Square

Approximate Scale
0   50   100m
0   50   100yd

To Khovd (238km)
& Mörön (680km)

1 Market
2 Jeep/Truck Station
3 Petrol Station
4 Shop
5 Hospital
6 Dechinravjaalin Khiid
7 Airport
8 Bayalag Od Hotel
9 Givaan Statue
10 City Hall
11 Post Office
12 Kharkhiraa Hotel
13 Cinema
14 Public Bathhouse
15 Brother Bar
16 Khankhokhii Restaurant
17 Museum
18 Guanz
19 Protected Areas Office

Information
The Uvs Nuur Strictly Protected Area office (☎ 21243) can provide information on, and permits to, the protected areas in the aimag.

Moneychangers at the market will change US dollars for a rate lower than in Ulaan Baatar.

Museum
This newly renovated museum has good displays on local wildlife and traditional life, with all the standard musical instruments, national costumes and Buddhist art, as well as an excellent shaman headdress, cloak and drum.

The museum is open weekdays from 9 am to 7 pm, Saturday until noon and Sunday from 1 to 6 pm. Entry is T1000.

Dechinravjaalin Khiid
Дэчинравжаалин Хийд
The original monastery was founded in 1757 by Lamaav, whose name means 'monk father'. At the height of its glory, the monastery contained seven small temples, and 2000 monks were in residence but it was pulverised in 1937.

The current monastery is little more than a wall with two gers inside.

Places to Stay
Camping The only place to camp nearby is along Gumbukh Gol, which you cross as you come from Ölgii. Walk about 300m north-west of the town square and find a spot. If you have your own vehicle, camping is far better along the Kharkhiraa Gol or anywhere south of the city on the road to Khovd.

Hotels The monolithic *Kharkhiraa Hotel* has beds in a standard room with a balcony, toilet and cold-water shower for T5000 per person, double the local rate. The deluxe rate of T7000 gets you much the same but more space and maybe a fridge. The hotel has a shop, a sad little *restaurant* and cosy *bar*. The entrance is on the west side, opposite the Khankhokhii Restaurant.

The better option is the private *Bayalag Od Hotel*. Beds in a basic dormitory or four-bed room cost US$5/8; half-deluxe rooms cost US$8 and deluxe rooms cost US$8-12. All prices are per person.

Places to Eat

The restaurant at the **Bayalag Od Hotel** is the best in town. If you are not staying there make a reservation. The food is nothing special, just noodle soups and beef with rice, but the ambience is pleasant.

Another decent place is the **Khankhokhii Restaurant**, just opposite (and upstairs) from the Kharkhiraa Hotel. A surprisingly edible plate of mutton, rice and vegetables costs around T750, and they may have some tasty yoghurt or other surprises if you ask.

If you fancy a warm beer, a nip of vodka or a rowdy conversation with a local, head to the **Brother Bar** next to the Khankhokhii.

Like the other western aimags, a few train wagons around the market serve as cheap **guanz**. The comparative array of fresh bread and vegetables at the market is a good reason to self-cater.

Shopping

Ulaangom has a rapidly expanding market, selling standard goods. There are also lots of clothes and household items from Russia, as well as the odd Mongol hat (T5000) and boots (T70,000). Check out the liquored locals playing bingo at the back corner of the market, looking like they're doing something far more wicked. The market is all but packed away by 5 pm.

The shops scattered around town have a fair selection of pickled vegetables, beer, chocolate and imported goodies.

Getting There & Away

Air MIAT flies between Ulaan Baatar and Ulaangom (with a refuelling stop at Mörön or Tosontsengel) on Monday, Wednesday and Friday. Tickets costs US$144/252. The airport is a dirt field just 1km from the town centre.

Jeep Ulaangom is not overrun by jeeps, but a few do hang around the market. These can be hired for trips around Uvs and western Mongolia for around T250 per km. A few public shared jeeps leave for Ölgii (T9000) and Khovd (T6000) when there are enough people to pack a jeep to bursting point.

The reasonable road between Ölgii and Ulaangom (301km) goes past the delightful lake Üüreg Nuur. Most traffic travels via the south-east corner of Achit Nuur, though some take the older road via the town of Tsagaannuur.

The Khovd city-Ulaangom road (238km) sometimes suffers from flooded rivers and collapsed bridges after heavy rain.

The Russians built a 50km paved road along the western side of the lake, towards the Russian border, but you'll only get to savour part of this if you are headed to Üreg Nuur.

Hitching It shouldn't be difficult to get a lift between Ulaangom and Mörön, but it's not as easy along the road from Ulaangom to Ölgii. From Ulaangom to Khovd, and to the Kharkhiraa Valley, hitching is a lot harder. In Ulaangom, ask around the modern and busy petrol station near the market, and at the market itself.

KHARKHIRAA
ХАРХИРАА

First off, there are several Kharkhiraas. For information on Kharkhiraa Uul and Kharkhiraa Gol see the section below. A more accessible valley, also known as Kharkhiraa, lies further north-east, about 30km east of Ulaangom. Bear in mind that Kharkhiraa is also the name of a sum centre, 23km south of Ulaangom. There's plenty of scope for confusion here so make sure you and your driver know exactly where you are going.

Though smaller than the Kharkhiraa Gol, this valley is surrounded by dense pine forests, has a crystal-clear river (from which it's safe to drink) and is often carpeted with flowers. It is a fine place for some day hikes.

The only hassle with this valley is that the local caretaker has taken it upon himself to charge foreigners national park prices (T1000 per day, plus T3000 for a car), even though the national parks office says there should be no fee to enter the valley. It might be good to have this in writing in case this profiteering continues.

Places to Stay & Eat

The only place to stay in the region is the *Kharkhiraa Resort*, a collection of quaint log cabins and huts hidden among the pine forests. Foreigner prices are T3000 for dormitory accommodation or T6000 for a bed in a rustic cabin. Meals cost T500 to T700 each. The resort is managed by the park office.

Getting There & Away

If you don't have your own vehicle, you could charter a jeep from Ulaangom and arrange for the driver to pick you up later. The cheapest, but most exhausting way is to get a lift to the turn-off at the power station, 11km west on the main road from Ulaangom. From the power station, a gentle, easy-to-follow, 25km trail leads to the gate of the resort. Hitching is not an option; almost no vehicles make it up here.

KHARKHIRAA UUL & TÜRGEN UUL

ХАРХИРАА УУЛ & ТүРГүН УУЛ

The twin peaks of Kharkhiraa Uul (4037m) and Türgen Uul (3965m), which dominate the western part of the aimag, are curiously almost equidistant between Achit, Üüreg and Uvs lakes. As vital sources of the Uvs Nuur, the mountains are part of the Uvs Nuur Strictly Protected Area.

The river valley between the two mountains is the Kharkhiraa Gol, which flows into Uvs Nuur. This valley is the start of some excellent **trekking** routes, which lead up to both mountains, and you could also do some fine day hikes around here with

A 19th century ger camp

your own jeep and camping equipment. The area is mostly populated by Khoton people, famous throughout Mongolia as shamans.

The Kharkhiraa Gol is accessed via the sum centre of Tarialan, 31km south of Ulaangom. To get there, you will have to charter a jeep from Ulaangom or Ölgii, and be prepared for a rough, but scenic, trip. There are remains of some Uighur statues in the region, but you'll need a guide to find them.

UVS NUUR

УВС НУУР

Uvs Nuur is a gigantic inland sea in the middle of the desert. The lake's surface occupies 3423 sq km, making it Mongolia's largest lake, though it's very shallow at an average depth of 12m. (Legend has it that the lake is bottomless.) Many textbooks claim that Khövsgöl Nuur is the largest lake in the country, but that only applies to water volume, not surface area. Uvs Nuur is large enough for you to stand on one shore and not see the other side, creating the impression that you have indeed reached the sea.

Uvs Nuur is five times saltier than the ocean, and devoid of edible fish, but this doesn't mean the lake is dead. The lake's surface is at an altitude of 759m, making it the lowest point in western Mongolia. It has no outlet, so a lot of the shoreline is swampy, making it difficult to reach.

Except for Mongolia's highest peaks, this is the coldest part of the country: in 1974 a temperature of -57°C was recorded. Summer temperatures typically climb to over 40°C, and these extremes are one reason why the lake was chosen as one of ten locations globally to be studied for climate change by the international Geo-Biosphere Program. The lake is part of the Uvs Nuur Strictly Protected Area (see the Protected Areas section under Uvs earlier in this chapter for details).

Despite the superlatives, compared with other lakes in western Mongolia, Uvs Nuur is disappointing: it is extremely large, difficult to reach and contains high levels of saltwater. It is also not great for swimming or camping, though there is a small beach and camping area on the south-western shore, near to Ulaangom. Camping can be hell thanks to the mosquitoes. If you have a jeep, lots of time and a good guide, you will enjoy the scenery and birdlife, otherwise it is best to head for the prettier, smaller and more accessible Üüreg and Achit freshwater lakes.

Birdwatching

Ornithologists have documented over 200 species of birds around Uvs Nuur, including cranes, spoonbills, geese and eagles, as well as gulls that fly thousands of kilometres from the southern coast of China to spend a brief summer in Mongolia.

Birdwatchers, however, could be disappointed: the birdlife is there and *is* impressive, but it is extremely difficult to find. The lake is huge; public transport around it is nonexistent; trails often turn into marsh and sand; only park officials know anything about the birdlife; and you may not be there at the right time anyway. The easiest place to start looking for birdlife is where the rivers enter the lake, but real enthusiasts will have to make it out to the north-eastern delta around Tes. Contact the Uvs Nuur Strictly Protected Area office in Ulaangom for a list of visiting species and ideas on how to spot them.

Getting There & Away

Approaching from the west, the lake (at an elevation of 759m) is an awesome sight from the 2533m Ulaan Davaa pass. You could hitch a ride *to* the lake, and get off along the relatively busy Ulaangom-Mörön road nearby, but you will still need a jeep to get *around* the lake, unless you plan to do a helluva lot of hiking.

Uvs Nuur is only 28km from Ulaangom, but in reality, the trails along the southern and eastern sides skirt around the lake and very few actually lead *to* the lake because of sand dunes, creeks and swamps. The lake is more accessible if you park the jeep or pitch your tent on a trail, and walk about 2km or so to the lake.

ALTAN ELS
АЛТАН УЛС

The road between Ulaangom and Mörön passes the **Böörög Deliin Els** sand dunes, which apparently form the northernmost desert on earth. The sand dunes lead to Altan Els (Golden Sands), part of the Uvs Nuur Strictly Protected Area. Altan Els is another wonderful area for wildlife, if you can find any. You'll need a good jeep and driver, and you must be self-sufficient in everything before exploring this hot and remote region. The Altan Els are on the border of Uvs and Zavkhan aimags, and are an easy detour from the Ulaangom-Mörön road.

KHYARGAS NUUR NATIONAL PARK
ХЯРГАС НУУР

Khyargas Nuur receives a lot less attention than Uvs Nuur, being 'only' half the size and 'only' twice as salty as the ocean. The lake does provide an attractive summer home for birds, but it is not as scenic or as accessible as other lakes in the region. It is still worth a stopover if you are travelling between Uvs Nuur and Khar Us Nuur in Khovd aimag, or driving or hitching towards Tosontsengel in Zavkhan through the mid-eastern part of Uvs aimag.

On the north-western side of Khyargas Nuur, there are some fantastic **hot springs**. Head for the abandoned village where the road leaves the lake, or ask directions at Naranbulag. A national park fee applies around the lake, though you'd be lucky (or unlucky) to find a ranger to pay it to.

South of Khyargas Nuur, but still in the national park is the freshwater lake **Airag Nuur**, at the end of the mighty Zavkhan Gol. Despite the name, the lake is not full of fermented mare's milk, but it does have about 20 breeding pairs of migratory **Dalmation pelicans**. There were about 400 pelicans in the 1960s, but the numbers are tragically decreasing because poachers kill them for their beaks, which are used to make a traditional implement for cleaning horses, called a *khusuur*, or currycomb, which you may see in use at the Naadam Festival.

ÖLGII NUUR
ӨЛГИЙ НУУР

To confuse things a little, another freshwater lake in the region is called Khar Us Nuur, but it is sometimes referred to as Ölgii Nuur. The 20km-long lake is accessible, but is not quite as scenic as Üüreg and Achit lakes. You can swim and fish in Ölgii Nuur, but the camping is not as good – the winds can be horrendous, so pitch your tent securely.

The lake is a welcome place to stop between Ulaangom and Khovd city if you have your own vehicle. Traffic between Ulaangom and Khovd is generally sparse, but you could hitch to and from the lake if you are self-sufficient, have a tent and don't mind waiting.

ÜÜREG NUUR
ҮҮРЭГ НУУР

Large and beautiful Üüreg Nuur (1425m above sea level) is surrounded by stunning 3000m-plus peaks, including Tsagaan Shuvuut Uul (3496m), part of the Uvs Nuur Strictly Protected Area. The freshwater lake has some unidentified minerals and is designated as 'saltwater' on some maps, so it's best to boil or purify all water from the lake. There is a fresh water well on the southeastern corner of the lake near some deserted buildings.

The lake is great for swimming (albeit a little chilly) and locals say there are plenty of fish. The surrounding mountains are just begging to be explored. One added attraction is that we were not attacked by swarms of bloodsucking midges – or perhaps we were just lucky.

Places to Stay
Camping is naturally the only option. The ground is a bit rocky and there is no shade, but you do have access to squillions of gallons of drinking water. There are only a few gers in the area, so you feel like you have the lake to yourself.

Getting There & Away
The definite attraction of the lake is its accessibility: it is just off the main road between Ulaangom and Ölgii. You could hire a jeep from Ulaangom, and maybe arrange for it to pick you up later, or you could hitch a ride there fairly easily.

Along the road south towards Achit Nuur, you can see the permanently snow-capped twin peaks of Kharkhiraa Uul and Türgen Uul.

ACHIT NUUR
АЧИТ НУУР

The largest freshwater lake in Uvs, Achit Nuur is on the border of Uvs and Bayan-Ölgii aimags, and is an easy detour between Ulaangom and Ölgii. It offers stunning sunsets and sunrises and good fishing. If you don't have your own fishing gear, you can probably buy some from the Russian and Tuvan fishermen who work there in the summer.

The lake is home to flocks of geese, eagles and other **birdlife**. One definite drawback is the absolute plethora of mosquitoes during the summer. Some camping spots are better than others for mossies, so look around. Locals claim they are almost bearable by October.

The main settlement on the lake is a Kazakh encampment on the south-east edge.

Getting There & Away
A relatively new bridge just south of the lake has greatly increased the amount of traffic going past the lake between Ulaangom and Ölgii. You can hitch a ride to the lake from either city without too much trouble, or charter a jeep from Ölgii or Ulaangom. The trail from Ölgii is reasonably good and pretty, however the trails from Achit Nuur to Ulaangom and Üüreg Nuur are often tough, but also dramatic.

Zavkhan Завхан

pop 104,000 • area 82,000 sq km

The eastern edge of Zavkhan aimag is the western flank of the Khangai Nuruu, the second-highest mountain range in Mongolia, and a spectacular area of forests and lakes, dotted with snow-clad peaks, whitewater streams and hot and cold springs.

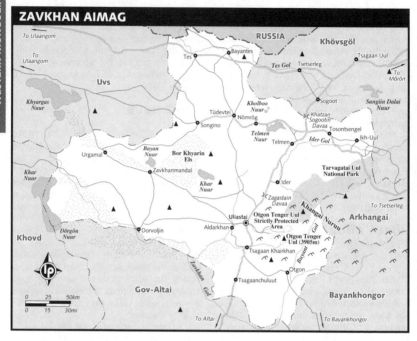

ZAVKHAN AIMAG

The southern and western parts of Zavkhan, usually ignored by visitors and Mongolians because of poor roads and transport, is a sharp contrast – a land of vast deserts, salt lakes and sand dunes where rain falls once or twice a year. Most of the border with Gov-Altai aimag is the Zavkhan Gol, which flows from Khangai Nuruu northwest to Khyargas Nuur in Uvs aimag and drains an area of over 71,000 sq km.

Zavkhan is in an awkward location and very few travellers are likely to pass through much or any of the aimag. This is pity because the scenery is some of the most dramatic and varied in the country; one minute you are travelling through lush valleys and hills and then a few kilometres further, you are in a place reminiscent of a desert from *Lawrence of Arabia*. If going from Khövsgöl to the western provinces, you'll quickly pass through the northern part of Zavkhan, via Tes; travelling from Ulaan Baatar to the west along the better, southern roads, you'll miss the aimag entirely; and if heading from Khövsgöl to the Gobi region, it's far better to go through Arkhangai and Övörkhangai aimags. This is which is unfortunate.

The main ethnic group residing in the aimag are the Khalkh.

ULIASTAI
УЛИАСТАЙ
elevation 1760m
Uliastai is wedged in by mountains on all sides, and has a brisk but dry climate. It is one of the most remote aimag capitals in Mongolia, but is pleasant and quiet, and a logical place to stay while you consider the direction of your plunge into the Mongolian wilderness.

Orientation & Information
The town is divided into two main districts: west of the Chigistei Gol is the central area with the hotels, restaurants and other life-

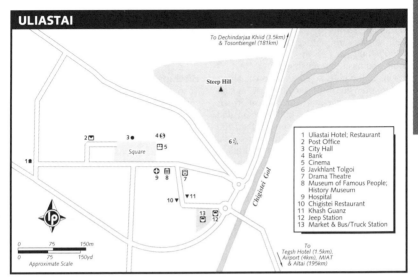

ULIASTAI

To Dechindarjaa Khiid (3.5km)
& Tosontsengel (181km)

Steep Hill

Square

Chigistei Gol

1 Uliastai Hotel; Restaurant
2 Post Office
3 City Hall
4 Bank
5 Cinema
6 Javkhlant Tolgoi
7 Drama Theatre
8 Museum of Famous People;
 History Museum
9 Hospital
10 Chigistei Restaurant
11 Khash Guanz
12 Jeep Station
13 Market & Bus/Truck Station

0   75   150m
0   75   150yd
Approximate Scale

To
Tegsh Hotel (1.5km),
Airport (4km), MIAT
& Altai (195km)

support systems; across the bridge on the eastern bank is the industrial area, which you are unlikely to visit. Like most Mongolian cities, the hillsides are dotted with ger suburbs.

The daily market and surrounding shops have a surprisingly good selection of groceries, so stock up if you're heading into the remote countryside.

The two storey pink-and-white bank, behind the main square, might change US dollars.

Museums

The two museums – the **Museum of Famous People** (ie from Zavkhan aimag) and the **History Museum** – are next to each other on the main street. The former contains a mammoth bone, some fine religious art, and a *tsam* mask, worn during lama dances, made from coral. The 'famous' people from Zavkhan include the writer B Chavukhulan (no, we've never heard of him either) and P Ochirbat, the first democratically elected president of Mongolia.

Both museums are open weekdays from 9 am to 6 pm; entry is T1500 for both.

Dechindarjaa Khiid

Дэчиндаржаа Хийд

This small, well-appointed monastery reopened in 1990 and now has around 50 part-time monks. The monks are very friendly, and you are allowed to watch their ceremonies, which start at about 10 am every day. The monastery is in a ger district, a pleasant 3.5km walk north of the town centre – look out for the silver tin roof as you enter from the north.

Javkhlant Tolgoi

Жавхлант Толгои

This hilltop near the river, and just to the north of the main street, features a pavilion and three concrete animals: an elk, ibex and argali sheep. The views from the top aren't spectacular, but it's worth the short climb to get some notion of how the city is laid out.

Places to Stay

Camping Along the lush valley that hugs the Chigistei Gol for 15km from town, and parallel to the northern road to Tosontsengel, there are some gorgeous (though a little busy) camping spots. Just get off the bus, truck or jeep at somewhere you like.

Hotels The slightly decrepit *Uliastai Hotel* has simple rooms for T1500 per person, as well as OK semi-deluxe/luxury rooms for T3000/4000 per person. All rooms have a toilet and basin but no shower.

On the south-east edge of town, about 1.5km from the bridge over the Chigistei Gol, is the private and better *Tegsh Hotel*. Rooms cost T3000 or T6000 person and there's a public hot shower on site for T500 for 30 minutes, as well as a billiards table and sauna. The hotel is the yellow building, inside a courtyard, past the fire station.

Places to Eat
The *Uliastai Hotel* has a restaurant, but it is often closed. The *Chigistei Restaurant* (also known as Zavkhan Trend) offers the best goulash and salad (T1000) in town. Otherwise, there are several *guanz* around the market, such as the *Khash*.

Getting There & Away
Air MIAT flies between Ulaan Baatar and Uliastai on Monday, Wednesday and Friday for US$124/217. The airport (and MIAT office) is about 4km south-west of town, though you have to drive south-east out of town before swinging west. You'll have to flag down a passing car to get there.

Bus & Minivan There is a weekly bus to Ulaan Baatar (45 hours, T12,000), via Tosontsengel (T5000) every Friday, as well as more frequent minivans (T18,000) and jeeps (T20,000). If you are lucky you might find a minivan or jeep headed north to Mörön, but very little traffic heads south to Altai. Almost all traffic leaves from the market, though the odd jeep leaves from the roundabout north-east of the market.

A bus or minivan leaves Ulaan Baatar every Monday for Uliastai.

Jeep A fair number of jeeps are available in Uliastai. They congregate at the roundabout near the bridge, not far from the market.

Every day, several public shared jeeps leave Uliastai for Tosontsengel (T5000), usually in the morning. The road between Uliastai and Tosontsengel is unpaved, but pretty reasonable and easy to follow – except that the turn-off to Tosontsengel is unmarked: it is 148km north of Uliastai and 33km west of Tosontsengel.

Hitching The road between Uliastai and Tosontsengel is fairly busy, so hitching shouldn't be difficult, but as it rains a fair bit in summer, hanging around for a lift may not be pleasant. Hitching to anywhere else from Uliastai is really hard – Zavkhan's isolated location ensures that few vehicles come this way.

ZAGASTAIN DAVAA
ЗАГАСТАИН ДАВАА
Forty-eight kilometres north-east of Uliastai on the Uliastai-Tosontsengel road is a spectacular mountain pass with the unusual name of Fish Pass. At the top, there are good views, a large ovoo and the largest collection of flies in western Mongolia. Between the pass and Uliastai, the road is paved, indicating that it suffers badly from rain and blizzards, which can start as early as October. This section of road is a great place to pitch your tent and hike around.

OTGON TENGER UUL
ОТГОН ТҮНГҮР УУЛ
Hard-core mountaineers and alpine explorers may want to travel to Otgon Tenger Uul, about 60km east of Uliastai. At 3905m, it is the highest peak in the Khangai Nuruu range and is now part of the 95,510 hectare Otgon Tenger Strictly Protected Area. Normal park fees of T1000 per person per day (plus T3000 per day per vehicle) apply – pay just past the children's camp, about 45km from Uliastai. The road east from Uliastai ends at a run-down holiday *resort*, around 80km from Uliastai, where you could find somewhere to stay.

The pretty alpine lake of **Batur Khunduk Nuur** is said to be in the area and might be worth inquiring about.

TOSONTSENGEL
ТОСОНЦҮНГҮЛ
Tosontsengel is the second-largest city in Zavkhan and perhaps should have been the

aimag capital, as it has more economic justification for its existence than Uliastai: Tosontsengel is the centre of the timber industry in western Mongolia.

Tosontsengel is a poor, dusty '20-horse' town with no market or regular transport. Nevertheless, it is a useful stopover if you are travelling between Khövsgöl and Arkhangai aimags. There is some stunning scenery in the surrounding valleys.

The oriental looking green-roofed building south of the main square is the **Wedding Palace**. There's also a small **monastery** about 500m north of the centre of town.

Places to Stay

Camping Tosontsengel is another reason why you should have a tent with you. From the town square, head south for a few hundred metres to the Ider Gol, on which the town is based, and find a quiet spot.

If you have your own transport there are some lovely valleys, including the beautiful Telmen Khurren Tal, about 10km west of Tosontsengel.

Hotels The white *Rashaant Hotel* on the east side of the square has musty, crumbling rooms for T3000 per person.

You're better off crossing the square to the private *hotel* above the telephone office, where there are two rooms for T2500 per person. The main problem here is the 24-hour shouting from people trying to make telephone calls from the office below.

Places to Eat

The *guanz* at the petrol station, about 800m north-west of the centre, serves some reasonable mutton and noodles. If that doesn't excite you, then it's best to stock up at the *tuut* (kiosks) on the main road, a block north of the main square.

Getting There & Away

Air MIAT flies between Ulaan Baatar and Tosontsengel on Tuesday and Friday for US$100/176. Planes from Ulaan Baatar to Khovd and Ulaangom normally stop in Tosontsengel for refuelling so it might be possible to catch the second leg of the flight westwards.

Jeep The only transport to/from Tosontsengel is the occasional minivan to/from Uliastai (T5000) and the odd vehicle headed between Ulaan Baatar and Uliastai. In Tosontsengel, most transport leaves from the row of kiosks a block north of the main square.

From Tosontsengel, it's 181km southwest to Uliastai (the turn-off to the south is at the 33km point); 273km north-east to Mörön; 533km north-west to Ulaangom and a *long* 803km south-east to Ulaan Baatar.

There are two main roads between Mörön and Tosontsengel: one heads west via Tsagaan-Uul in Khövsgöl aimag, and the other goes via Jargalant in Arkhangai aimag. These two roads are rough, but extremely pretty and worth exploring if you have a good jeep and tent. The Ider Valley between Ikh-Uul and Tosontsengel is particularly pretty.

Hitching If you hang around the petrol station in Tosontsengel, you should be able to get a lift to Uliastai; to anywhere else, you will have to wait a long time.

TELMEN NUUR
ТҮЛМҮН НУУР

This beautiful salt lake is accessible from the town of Telmen, 20km south-east of the lake, on the main Uliastai-Tosontsengel road, or by heading west 25km from the main Mörön/Uliastai crossroads. There is good camping on the east end of the lake (GPS: N48° 48.889', E97° 31.068'), though you'll need your own water.

BAYAN NUUR
БАЯН НУУР

This salt lake, among the **Bor Khyarin Els** sand dunes, is in the remote western part of Zavkhan, and is very difficult to reach. The scenery is fascinating and locals claim there is good fishing.

The Gobi

Along the southern border of Mongolia, five *aimags* (provinces) contain sections of the Gobi Desert: Bayankhongor, Dornogov, Dundgov, Gov-Altai and Ömnögov. The Gobi region is sparsely populated, with little transport and few roads, but it is surprisingly alive with wildlife. You will see thousands of wild and domesticated camels, cranes, hawks and gazelles, and there is no shortage of evidence that dinosaurs once roamed the region.

There are several things to keep in mind when travelling in this unique region. The nights will always be cold, so take a sleeping bag. Dust storms can rock the region at any time but are especially common in April and May. Rabid dogs are not uncommon, so take extra caution around the towns or when approaching a *ger* (traditional felt yurt). Almost every year sees the bubonic plague rear its ugly head in the western parts from about August to October. It is extremely unlikely that you will catch anything nasty, but quarantine restrictions could affect your travel in the region. See Infectious Diseases under Health in the Facts for the Visitor chapter for details.

Very few vehicles travel anywhere except on the main roads, which makes hitching difficult and dangerous. If chartering a jeep, make sure it is reliable. Carry a sleeping bag, tent and sufficient water and food for emergencies if travelling by public bus, minivan, jeep or, especially, if hitching. A plus is that roads in the region are some of the best in Mongolia as the terrain is generally dry and flat.

Carry more water than you might normally need. Except for aimag capitals and ger camps, water supplies are scarce and unreliable. A concrete or wooden structure in the middle of nowhere, with a few gers nearby, is a sure sign of a spring or well (though it may be dry). The water is usually delicious, but you don't know what has pissed in it, so boil or purify it. If the spring or well has a trough, fill it with water; be-

cause by late evening, some parched gazelles and camels will come out of nowhere looking for water to drink – a great sight.

Dundgov Дундговъ

pop 54,800 • area 78,000 sq km

Dundgov (Middle Gobi) consists of flat, dry plains, occasional deserts, rock formations and little else. The northern part of Dundgov is relatively green, but the southern and eastern areas are mostly bone-dry. The main ethic group of this region is the Khalkh.

Dotted around Dundgov (and Arkhangai aimag) are hundreds of ancient graves of

The Gobi Desert

Stretching from the southern Khovd aimag to the Dariganga region in Sükhbataar, and including parts of northern China, the Gobi covers a third of Mongolia. Fossil finds have revealed that the Gobi basin was once part of a large inland sea, though some Mongolians will tell you that the Gobi was formed by the trampling of Chinggis Khaan's army.

Contrary to common preconceptions, most of the Gobi consists of stony, scrubby wasteland: sandy dunes only cover about 3% of the Gobi. The word *gobi* simply means 'desert' in the Mongol language, but Mongolians actually differentiate between 33 types of desert.

The Gobi is a land of extremes: decent rain only falls every two or three years; it can be well over 40°C during the summer, and below -40°C in winter; and storms of dust and sand are fearsome in spring. The very few lakes, such as Orog Nuur and Böön Tsagaan Nuur are starting to dry up, but underground springs continue to provide vital water.

The Gobi is understandably very sparsely populated, but the desolate landscape is home to gazelle, khulan (wild ass), Bactrian two-humped camels, takhi (the Mongolian wild horse), rare saiga antelope, and the world's only desert bear, the Gobi bear, of which there are only 50 left in the wild. The appropriately named desert warbler, and saxaul sparrow, hide in saxaul (zag in Mongolian), a stubby shrub that produces wood so dense that it sinks in water.

revered Mongolian warriors. Little is known about these graves, but they probably pre-date Chinggis Khaan. The graves are about 3m deep, and often contain gold and bronze, but are sacred, and therefore left untouched. They are identifiable by an unnatural collection of large rocks on a small hump.

The advantages of travelling around Dundgov are its proximity to Ulaan Baatar, the good network of jeep trails, and the flat ground that makes it easy to get around. Most visitors, however, ignore Dundgov

and fly or drive straight through to the more developed, and tourist-oriented Ömnögov aimag. If you are travelling overland to Ömnögov, it is worth taking the road via Sangiin Dalai, rather than directly to Dundgov's capital, Mandalgov.

MANDALGOV
МАНДАЛГОВЬ
pop 11,000

Mandalgov came into existence in 1942, when the town consisted of just 40 gers. Today, it's a sleepy town that has had a major population drop, from 19,000 people 15 years ago. The town is very hot in summer. It offers the usual amenities for an aimag capital – an airport, a hotel, a monastery, a museum and a couple of shops. There is more to see around Sangiin Dalai, but Mandalgov is a useful stop-off on the way to Dalanzadgad in Ömnögov.

Museum

The museum is divided into two main sections: a natural history section and a more interesting ethnography and history section. Among the displays is a bronze Buddha made by Zanabazar. There's also a collection of priceless scroll paintings *(thangka)*, old flintlock rifles, bronze arrowheads, silver snuffboxes, pipes, and chess sets carved out of ivory.

The museum is open daily from 9 am to 6 pm, but you may have to find the caretaker to unlock the doors. Entry costs T1000. It is north of the park, next to the Mandalgov Hotel.

Dashgimpeliin Khiid
Дашгимпэлийн Хийд

In 1936 there were 53 temples in Dundgov. A year later, they were reduced to ashes and rubble by the Mongolian KGB. In 1991 Dashgimpeliin Khiid was opened to serve the people of Mandalgov.

The monastery is small, consisting only of a monk's ger and a newly built temple, but it's very active inside. Visitors are welcome, but should show the usual respect. The monastery is 100m north-east of the park.

THE GOBI

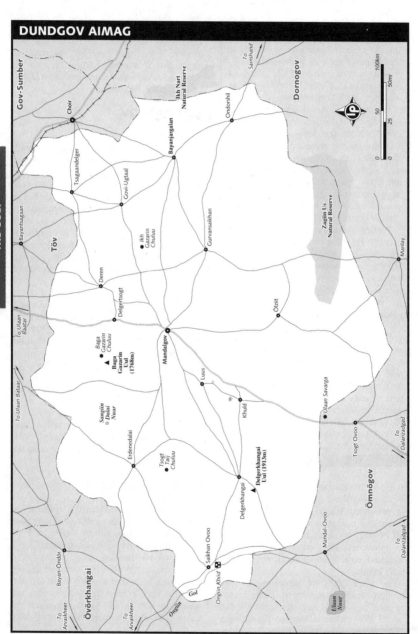

DUNDGOV AIMAG

Mandalin Khar Ovoo

Мандалин Хар Овоо

On top of Mandalin Khar Ovoo, about 150m north-west of the park, is a viewing pavilion. It is worth the short climb for a panorama of all that Mandalgov has to offer (which isn't much). A forlorn **monument** dedicated to the 'everlasting friendship' between Mongolia and the Soviet Union stands nearby.

Places to Stay

Camping Like other Gobi aimag capitals, Mandalgov has no great camping spots; the city has no river, and it's flat and dusty. Your best bet is to walk north of town and find somewhere past Mandalin Khar Ovoo or the monastery.

Hotels The *Mandalgov Hotel* has simple rooms without a bathroom for T3000 or T3700 per person. Deluxe rooms with attached toilet cost T4500 per person. The hotel is on a corner, north of the park.

A better option might be the new private *hotel*, a couple of doors east, that was being built at the time of research.

In the south of town, locals recommend a private hotel known as the *Builder's Hotel*, or Barilgachdin Hotel, run by a local building company. The place looked okay, but was deserted when we dropped by.

Places to Eat

The best place for lunch if you are passing through is the *Delgerkhangai Restaurant*, a canteen-style place, which slops up decent goulash, salad and soup out of huge steel vats. The food at the *Mandalgov Hotel* isn't too bad. There are also several basic *guanz* (cheap restaurants/canteens) at the market, which serve up *khuurshuur* (fried meat pancakes) and *buuz* (steamed meat dumplings). The *Gobiin Chonos Bar* serves up *tsuivan* (fried flat noodles with meat) for T700, but mostly as a chaser for its draught beer.

Getting There & Away

Air MIAT flies between Mandalgov and Ulaan Baatar every Tuesday, en route to Dalanzadgad. Tickets are comparatively

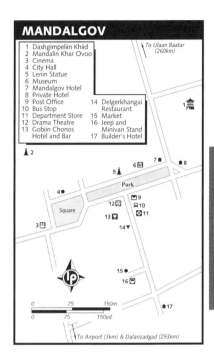

MANDALGOV

1 Dashgimpeliin Khiid
2 Mandalin Khar Ovoo
3 Cinema
4 City Hall
5 Lenin Statue
6 Museum
7 Mandalgov Hotel
8 Private Hotel
9 Post Office
10 Bus Stop
11 Department Store
12 Drama Theatre
13 Gobiin Chonos
   Hotel and Bar
14 Delgerkhangai
   Restaurant
15 Market
16 Jeep and
   Minivan Stand
17 Builder's Hotel

To Ulaan Baatar (260km)

Park

Square

To Airport (3km) & Dalanzadgad (293km)

cheap (US$42), but the flights are a bit unreliable as Mandalgov is only a transit stop, and few people travel here. It might be possible to get on the plane at Mandalgov for the second leg to Dalanzadgad (US$48), though there's a risk that you'll get bumped if there are no seats. The airport at Mandalgov is 3km south of the city.

Bus Crowded buses (T5000) leave Ulaan Baatar for Mandalgov on Monday, Thursday and sometimes Saturday, and buses return to Ulaan Bataar on the same days. In Mandalgov, buses arrive and depart from an impromptu bus stop in front of the post office.

There are no buses to Dalanzadgad, though the Ulaan Bataar service passes through Mandalgov, near the petrol station, and you may be able to get on the bus there.

Jeep Mandalgov is a poor aimag capital and finding a jeep to charter will create a headache – Dalanzadgad is a far better

THE GOBI

place to look. When there is enough demand (which isn't often), public shared jeeps do travel to Ulaan Baatar – but very rarely south to Dalanzadgad. Most locals wait for the bus or hitch a ride on a truck. The best place to look for transport is at the market.

Mandalgov is 260km south of Ulaan Baatar and 293km north of Dalanzadgad.

Hitching As the main road from Ulaan Baatar to Dalanzadgad goes through Mandalgov, hitching is the major form of transport to either place. Getting to Ulaan Baatar or Dalanzadgad on a truck, or another type of vehicle, won't take too long if you are prepared to ask around at the market and wait a while.

BAGA GAZRIN CHULUU
БАГА ГАЗРИН ЧУЛУУ

This is another granite rock formation in the middle of the dusty plains. In the 19th century, two revered monks lived here in gers – remnants of their **rock drawings** can be found in the area. The rocks are worshipped by locals who sometimes make pilgrimages here. Naturally, there is a legend that Chinggis Khaan stayed at the rocks.

Five kilometres away, the highest peak in the area, **Baga Gazrin Uul** (1768m), will take about five hours to climb. The mountain also contains a **cave** with an underground lake. The **mineral water springs** and trees in the region make it a great spot to *camp*, and there are plenty of rocky hills, topped by *ovoo* (sacred pyramid-shaped collections of stone and wood), to explore.

Baga Gazrin Chuluu (GPS: N46° 13.731', E106° 04.472') is in a very remote area, about 60km to the north-west of Mandalgov, and about 80km west of Sangiin Dalai village, not far from Sangiin Dalai Nuur.

SANGIIN DALAI NUUR
САНГИЙН ДАЛАЙ НУУР

Although little more than a large pond, you can see some remarkable birdlife at Sangiin Dalai Nuur. Mongolian larks and various species of eagles, geese and swans come to this spring-fed lake in summer and autumn. The Juulchin travel company runs **birdwatching** trips here and to other nearby lakes.

The temple **Khukh Burd Süm** (GPS: N46° 09.621', E105° 45.590'), which sits on an island in the middle of the tiny lake, was built in the 10th century. Remarkably, the temple was built from rocks that can only be found over 300km away. It was abandoned and in ruins a few centuries after being built.

Three hundred years ago, a **palace** was built here, and 150 years later, the writer Danzanravjaa (see the Sainshand section later in this chapter) built a stage on top of the ruins. Enough of the temple and palace remain to give you some idea of what a magnificent place it once must have been.

There is no shortage of *camping spots* in the area. Another accommodation option might be a sanatorium on the south side of the lake, which has gone bust, been privatised and is now skint. Locals are trying to resurrect the site as a *resort*, with rooms for T1200 to T2000 per person per day, but the dusty site has few charms. One block does have some nice hotel rooms for T3000 or T5000 per person, but it's hard to imagine the place really taking off. Otherwise, you could come on a day trip from the Dundgobi Resort in Erdenedalai, Mandalgov or Sangiin Dalai village if you have a vehicle.

The lake is over halfway between Baga Gazrin Chuluu and Sangiin Dalai village. You will need an experienced driver to find it. There is no hope of getting here on public transport or by hitching.

ERDENEDALAI
УРДЫНУ ДАЛАЙ

This sometime camel-herding community in the middle of nowhere, 114km northwest of Mandalgov, is a good base for visiting nearby attractions if you have your own vehicle. It's also a useful halfway stop between Arvaikheer (in Övörkhangai aimag) and Mandalgov, or an alternative stop to Mandalgov between Ulaan Baatar and Dalanzadgad.

Gimpil Darjaalan Khiid
Гимпил Даржаалан Хийд

This monastery, with its temple **Damba Darjalan Süm**, is a very pleasant surprise after travelling around the dusty and dull countryside. Built in the late 18th century to commemorate the first ever visit to Mongolia by a Dalai Lama, the monastery was once used by about 500 monks. It was the only monastery out of nine in the immediate vicinity to survive the Stalinist purges – by becoming a warehouse and shop.

The monastery was reopened in 1990 and the current Dalai Lama visited in 1992. The small contingent of 20 monks visits three or four times a month. If no-one is there the caretaker, who lives in the ger next door, will open it up for you. The spacious temple has a central statue of Tsongkhapa, some large parasols and some huge drums. Photos are permitted outside the temple but not inside.

Places to Stay & Eat
Erdenedalai is dusty and very small. Walk about 100m in any direction from the monastery and pitch your *tent*. A few inquisitive locals, or a camel or two, may visit.

Like most *sum* (district) capitals, Erdenedalai has a nameless *hotel*. Rooms cost T2000 per person for either a deluxe or ordinary room, so look at more than one room. There is certainly no style or comfort, but you will probably have the place to yourself. Look for the decrepit building with yellow paint and blue windows. There is a decent *guanz* on the ground floor.

The Juulchin-run *Dundgobi Resort* (☎/fax 59 3951), about 30km south of Erdenedalai and 45km north of Tsogt Taij, is the least impressive ger camp in the Gobi region. It's really only worth using if you want to explore the surrounding sites in detail.

Getting There & Away
Every Tuesday and Saturday, a post office truck leaves Ulaan Baatar for Erdenedalai, bypassing Mandalgov. The truck returns on Wednesday and Sunday morning, leaving from Erdenedalai's post office.

Otherwise you will have to hitch a ride. Although the village is small, it is on a

major jeep trail, so a few vehicles come through here every day.

TSOGT TAIJ CHULUU
ЦОГТ ТАИЖ ЧУЛУУ

About 75km south of Sangin Dalai village, there are some inscriptions on rocks written by Mongolian scholars and nationalists, including the last-known descendant of Chinggis Khaan, Tsogt Taij (1561–1637).

Camels

Throughout Mongolia, you will see the two-humped Bactrian camel. They were domesticated thousands of years ago, and are closely related to the rare wild camel known as the *khavtgai*. Of the 355,000 camels in the country, two-thirds can be found in the five aimags that stretch across the Gobi – 93,000 in Ömnögov aimag alone.

One of the five domesticated animals revered by nomads, camels are perfect for long-distance travel in the Gobi (though they are slow, averaging about 5km per hour). They are easy to manage (a camel can last for over a week without water, and a month without food); they can carry a lot of gear (up to 250kg – equal to ten full backpacks); and they provide wool (an average of 5kg per year), and milk (up to 600L a year). They are also a good source of meat, and produce 250kg of dung a year! If the humps are drooping, the camels are in poor health, or need some food or water (if a thirsty camel hasn't drunk for some time it can suck up 200L in a single day).

Normally relaxed, if somewhat aloof, male camels go crazy during the mating season in January-February – definitely a time to avoid approaching one.

The current number of camels is considerably lower than it was just 40 years ago. The decline could be because they are being killed for their meat, and because many nomads are leaving the harsh Gobi and breeding other livestock. In an attempt to stop the decline in numbers, several national parks in the Gobi have been established to protect the 300 or so remaining wild khavtgai.

THE GOBI

Written in 1621, in an ancient Mongolian script, which is hard for locals to understand, the inscriptions are mildly interesting (if a little too well preserved to believe), but hardly warrant a special visit.

ONGIIN KHIID
ОНГИЙН ХИЙД

This small mountainous area along the river, the Ongiin Gol, in the western sum of Saikhan-Ovoo, makes a good resting place to break a trip between the south Gobi and either Ulaan Baatar or Arvaikheer. The bend in the river marks the remains of two ruined monasteries, the **Barlim Khiid** on the north bank, and the **Khutagt Khiid** on the south. Together the complex is known as Ongiin Khiid. There's not much left to see, but there are plenty of interesting ruins to explore.

There are plenty of places to *camp* along the forested riverside.

There are two ger camps in the vicinity. The well-run *Saikhan Ovoo* camp is right on the riverside. Beds in a two- or four-bed ger cost US$10/15, plus around US$5 per meal. It has hot showers and a sauna for US$5 per hour.

A couple of kilometres away in a less interesting location is the *Mongol Khaan*, a German joint venture, which caters mostly to groups. Beds cost around US$10 per person, without meals.

The *Saikhan Gobi* camp is 11km before Ongiin Khiid, on the road from Saikhan-Ovoo. Beds cost US$15 to $20, with three meals and a hot shower included. The owners are open to negotiation if you just want to spend the night in one of the gers.

No public transport runs to Ongiin Khiid.

IKH GAZRIN CHULUU
ИХ ГАЗРИН ЧУЛУУ

This area of unusual rock pinnacles is about 70km north-east of Mandalgov in Gurvansaikhan sum.

ULAAN SUVRAGA
УЛААН СУВРАГА

In the southernmost sum of Ölziit is Ulaan Suvraga, an area that might be described as a 'badlands' or a 'painted desert'. The eerie, eroded landscape was at one time beneath the sea and is rich in marine fossils and clamshells. There are also numerous **ancient rock paintings** in the region.

The museum in Mandalgov has a photograph of Ulaan Suvraga, which you might want to look at to decide if it's worth the effort of getting here. Ulaan Suvraga is a rough 115km south-west of Mandalgov.

Ömnögov Өмнөговъ

pop 46,300 • area 165,000 sq km

Ömnögov (South Gobi) is the largest but least populated aimag in Mongolia, with a population density of only 0.3 people per sq km. The few people who live here are of the Khalkh ethnic group. It's not hard to see why humans prefer to live elsewhere. With an average annual precipitation of only 130mm a year, and summer temperatures reaching an average of up to 38°C, this is the driest, hottest and harshest region in the country.

The Gurvansaikhan Nuruu range in the centre provides the main topographic relief in this pancake-flat region. These mountains reach an altitude of 2825m and support a diverse range of wildlife, including the extremely rare snow leopard (see the boxed text later in this chapter). The mountains also make human habitation marginally possible by capturing snow in winter, which melts and feeds springs on the plains below, providing water for some limited livestock.

Ömnögov supports thousands of black-tailed gazelle, which you may see darting across the open plains. The aimag is also home to one-quarter (93,000) of Mongolia's domesticated camels. The two-million-hectare Gurvansaikhan National Park protects a lot of wildlife and is home to dinosaur fossils, sand dunes and rock formations. The 1,839,176 hectare Small Gobi Strictly Protected Area, in the south-eastern section of the aimag, is the last great bastion of the *khulan*, or wild ass.

THE GOBI

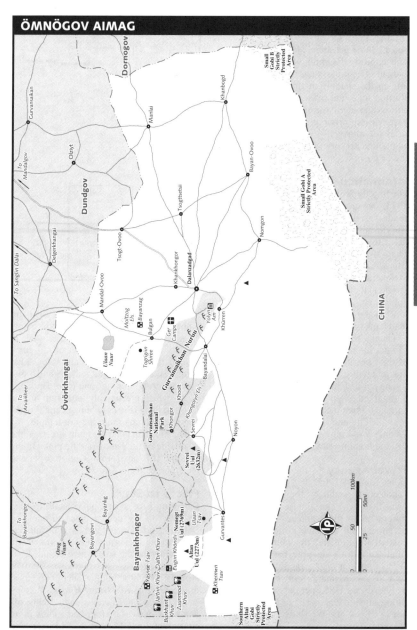

ÖMNÖGOV AIMAG

THE GOBI

DALANZADGAD
ДАЛАНЗАДГАД
pop 12,500 • elevation 1465m
The capital of Ömnögov aimag, Dalanzadgad is a soulless and windy town. Sitting in the shadow of the Gurvansaikhan Nuruu range, the town has reasonable facilities and regular transport, so it's a good base for explorations into the desert. Besides the museum – which is not as good as the one at Yolyn Am – there is little to see or do.

Information
The Strictly Protected Areas office (☎ 3708, 3973, ☒ gtzgobi@magicnet.mn) in the south-west of town has good displays on the Gurvansaikhan National Park and is the place for permits and general information. They also sell the excellent booklet *Gobi Gurvansaikhan National Park* by Bern Steinhauer-Burkhart.

The ITI, or Innovation Bank changes US dollars (cash only) on weekdays from 9 am to 1 pm and 2 to 5 pm, though at rates lower than banks in Ulaan Baatar.

Thanks to a Soros Fund initiative, you can get Internet access on the ground floor of the library for T2000 per hour (though this rate will undoubtedly change).

The public bath house is in a white building marked 'Халуун Ус', in the south-west corner of town, near school No 1. Showers cost T500 and operate daily, except Wednesday, from 10 am to 7 pm. On Sunday the building stays open until 10 pm.

Travel Agency
Gobi Tour (☎ 2995, ☒ enkhtuya_2000@yahoo.com) is run by the same lady that owns the town's guesthouse. It can arrange itineraries to most places in the region, given enough advance notice. Jeep hire costs T360/km and the company has a small supply of sleeping bags and tents. Gobi Tour can also arrange accommodation at a herdsman's *ger* 17km outside Yolyn Am for US$8 per person, and **camel riding** outside Dalanzadgad for T2500 per hour. Check its Web site at www.gobitour.tripod.com.

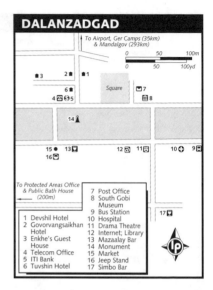

DALANZADGAD

To Airport, Ger Camps (35km) & Mandalgov (293km)

1	Devshil Hotel
2	Govorvangsaikhan Hotel
3	Enkhe's Guest House
4	Telecom Office
5	ITI Bank
6	Tuvshin Hotel
7	Post Office
8	South Gobi Museum
9	Bus Station
10	Hospital
11	Drama Theatre
12	Internet; Library
13	Mazaalay Bar
14	Monument
15	Market
16	Jeep Stand
17	Simbo Bar

To Protected Areas Office & Public Bath House (200m)

South Gobi Museum
Surprisingly, this museum has little on dinosaurs – just a leg, an arm and a few eggs. (All of the best exhibits are in Ulaan Baatar, or in any of a number of museums around the world.) There are a few nice paintings, a huge stuffed vulture, and a display of scroll paintings and other Buddhist items, which presumably makes up for the fact that this is the only aimag capital without a functioning monastery or temple.

The museum is on the main street, on the other side of the park from the pink Drama Theatre. It is open from 9 am to 5 pm and the entrance fee is T1000.

Places to Stay
Camping Like other Gobi capitals, there is no river or any decent place to camp in Dalanzadgad. You will just have to walk one or two kilometres in any direction from town, and pitch your tent somewhere secluded.

Hotels The best budget accommodation in town is *Enkhe's Guest House* (☎ 2995, ☒ enkhtuya_2000@yahoo.com). Enkhe offers beds in two- or four-bed rooms in an apartment for US$5, with a kitchen and

Dinosaurs

In the early 1920s, newspapers brought news of the discovery of dinosaur eggs in the southern Gobi Desert by American adventurer Roy Chapman Andrews. Over a period of two years Andrews' team unearthed over 100 dinosaurs, including Protoceratops Andrewsi, which was named after the explorer. The find included several Velociraptors ('Swift Robber'), subsequently made famous by *Jurassic Park*, and a parrot-beaked Oviraptor ('Egg Stealer'), which had died trying to steal eggs from another dinosaur's nest. Most valuable in Andrews' mind was the discovery of the earliest known mammal skulls, 'possibly the most valuable seven days of work in the whole history of palaeontology to date'.

Subsequent expeditions have returned to the Gobi and added to the picture of life in the late Cretaceous period (70 million years ago), the last phase of dinosaur dominance before the mammals inherited the earth.

One of the most famous fossils so far unearthed is the 'Fighting Dinosaurs', discovered by a joint Polish-Mongolian team in 1971 and listed as a national treasure. The remarkable fossil is of an 80 million-year-old Protoceratops and Velociraptor locked in mortal combat. The raptor's claws remain hooked in the Protoceratops' belly, which is fighting back by clamping the raptor's right arm in its mouth. It is thought that this and other fossilised snapshots were entombed by a violent sand storm or by collapsing sand dunes. One poignant fossil is of a fossilised Oviraptor protecting its nest of eggs from the impending sands.

A picture of the Gobi has emerged as a land of swamps, marshes, rivers and lakes, with areas of sand studded with oases. The land was inhabited by a colourful cast of characters, which included huge duck-billed Hadrosaurs, and also Anklysaurs, which was up to 25 feet tall, armour-plated and had a club-like tail, which acted like a giant mace. Also on the list is the sheep-sized Protoceratops, with a distinctive frilled head. Huge long-necked sauropods like Nemegtosaurus, which may have grown to a weight of 90 tonnes, were hunted by three-toed therapods such as the mighty Tarbosaurus ('Alarming Reptile'), a carbon copy of a Tyrannosaurus Rex, with a 1.2m-long skull packed with razor sharp teeth up to 15cm long.

Other weird and wonderful beasts that once roamed the South Gobi include the bone-headed Pachycephalosaurs, which used their reinforced skulls as battering rams, Ebolotherium, with a periscope-style nose that allowed it to breathe while the rest of it was underwater, and Therizinosaurus, a fierce carnivore, with massive claws over 60cm long. Huge rhinos, over four times the size of an adult elephant and thought to be the largest land mammals ever to have lived, shared the land with tiny rodents, the forerunners of modern day mammalian life.

Less dramatic, but equally important modern fossil finds such as Mononykus, a flightless bird with claw-like limbs instead of wings, have linked the evolution of birds to dinosaurs (Jurassic Park's Velociraptors are now depicted as feathered). The recent discovery of fossilised Gobi marsupials has shown that these animals originate from Asia, not Australia.

With a bit of digging, you may be able to find some dinosaur fossils in the southern Gobi – but please be aware that these fossils are very precious, and far more useful to palaeontologists. Locals may approach you at Bayanzag, the ger camps and even Dalanzadgad to buy some dinosaur bones and eggs. Remember that it is *highly* illegal to export fossils from Mongolia. If you get caught, you'll be in serious trouble.

Apart from the famous sites of Bayanzag and nearby Togrigiin Shiree, the richest sites of Bugiin Tsav, Ulaan Tsav, Nemegt Uul and Khermen Tsav are all in the remote west of Ömnögov aimag and impossible to reach without some serious expedition planning.

Today, the best places to come face-to-face with the dinosaurs of the Gobi are the Museum of Natural History in Ulaan Baatar and the American Museum of Natural History in New York. The latter has a fine Web site at www.amnh.org, which contains a virtual tour of its impressive Gobi dinosaur collection.

THE GOBI

washing machine, but no hot water. She can also provide meals for between T1200 and T1600 a go. Enkhe also has a ger camp opposite the airport, where beds cost US$8. There are clean pit toilets but no shower. To find Enkhe, telephone or email in advance (she will meet your plane) or head for the apartment at No 9, 3rd floor, apartment building 15, a block west of the Devshil Hotel. The guest house can also arrange a ger stay near the Gurvansaikhan National Park entrance.

The *Tuvshin Hotel* is the best hotel but only has two rooms and you'll have to track down the caretaker. Rooms cost US$15 per person. The unsigned entrance is at the corner of the Mongol Bank building.

Otherwise, the *Govorvangsaikhan Hotel* charges from T4000 in a four-bed room to T10,000 for a three-room deluxe suite. There's no hot water.

Opposite, the *Devshil Hotel* (☎ 3786) is a little better, cheaper and easier to pronounce. It has simple but clean double rooms with a balcony for T5000 per person, or T10,000 for a deluxe room with tepid solar-heated water. Dalanzadgad's only real entertainment is the full-size snooker table in the lobby, which costs T2000 for an hour.

Ger Camps About 35km west of Dalanzadgad, three ger camps cater primarily for organised tours. Costs are standard at between US$30 and US$40 per person including meals. You can also rent jeeps, and go on organised tours of the nearby attractions.

The *Juulchin-Gobi Camp* (☎ 2110, fax in Ulaan Baatar 01-312 769, [e] jgobi@magic net.mn) is a huge camp with an airstrip attached. It is popular with organised tours and costs US$20 to US$30 per person including meals, or as low as US$15 for accommodation only. It is about the same standard as the others, but the location isn't as good. Planes fly here direct in summer and sometimes continue on to the Juulchin camp in Khongoryn Els for an extra US$30 or so.

The *Tuvshin Resort* (☎ 350 921, fax 326 419), 7km away, has good hot showers and toilets, and a decent restaurant and bar, but the location is uninteresting and the buildings are ugly.

Closer to Yolyn Am, the *Havtgait Resort* (☎ 311 521, fax 384 097) has the nicest setting, and the facilities are less overrun by groups of tourists. The large dining room serves good food, and the activities are as diverse as karaoke singing in the evening and camel riding during the day. The price of US$40 per person with meals is more negotiable than at the Tuvshin Resort.

Places to Eat

The restaurant attached to the *Govorvangsaikhan Hotel* can rustle up food given some warning, but check the bill carefully. The *Simbo Bar* serves probably the best food in town for about T2000 to T3000 a dish.

The *Mazaalay Bar* serves up simple Mongolian food like khuurshuur and buuz, but the bar is a little rougher than the Simbo. The sign says 'Gobi Beer Bar', which is either a spelling mistake or a clever pun on the word *mazalai*, which is the local word for the Gobi bear.

The shops and market south of the park are reasonably well stocked.

Getting There & Away

Air MIAT flies between Dalanzadgad and Ulaan Baatar on Tuesday and Friday for US$81/142. During the peak season – July to mid-September – MIAT also schedules extra daily flights between Ulaan Baatar and the Juulchin-Gobi ger camp for the same price. Even if you have a ticket to Dalanzadgad, check that you are going to Dalanzadgad city and not just the ger camp.

Khangard Airlines also runs daily flights from mid-July to mid-August between Ulaan Baatar and the Juulchin-Gobi ger camp for the same cost as MIAT.

These flights are popular so book ahead, confirm again and again, and be prepared for some fun and games when checking in and boarding the plane. The airport is a dirt field a few hundred metres north of the town.

Bus Buses leave Ulaan Baatar for Dalanzadgad (via Mandalgov) on Monday and Friday and return to the city from Dalanzadgad on Wednesday and Sunday. Tickets cost T10,000 and the trip takes a gruelling 24 hours. You can book tickets on Wednesday, Thursday, Friday and Saturday.

Jeep The cheapest way to see the attractions in Gurvansaikhan National Park is to take a bus or hitch to Dalanzadgad, where you can hang around for a few days and ask other independent travellers to share a jeep.

Dalanzadgad is the natural starting point for trips into this part of the Gobi, and there are a few (but not many) jeeps for hire. Most jeep drivers hang around the market area. Alternatively, leave a message with the post office or bus station. We were quoted a reasonable price of around T250 per km. The main headaches are the language barrier and finding a driver that is experienced in taking foreigners.

If travelling independently and staying at a ger camp in the national park, most camps rent jeeps for tourist rates of T400 per km, including a driver/guide. This is higher than normal, but in a remote and touristed area this is not too expensive, especially if you are sharing costs.

Public shared jeeps run occasionally to Ulaan Baatar but rarely anywhere else; most people fly or hitch on a truck.

Dalanzadgad is 293km south of Mandalgov and 553km south-west of Ulaan Baatar.

Hitching Hitching around the Gobi Desert, including to the attractions in Gurvansaikhan National Park, is totally impractical and dangerous, and should never be attempted. Hitching between Dalanzadgad and Mandalgov and Sainshand is possible but not easy. Make sure you carry plenty of water, food and a tent and sleeping bag for the inevitable breakdowns.

MANDAL-OVOO
МАНДАЛ-ОВОО
This village, also known as Sharkhulsan, is renowned for the number (about 14,000) and quality of its camels. Just before the start of Tsagaan Sar (Lunar New Year), which takes place in January or February, Sharkhulsan hosts the annual **festival**, the Holiday of the Ten Thousand Camels.

The highlight of this festive, family occasion is the 18km camel race across a nearby region called the Ongiin-Tal steppes. In 1996 nearly 200 camels took part, and the winner took just 45 minutes. And the prize? Another camel!

Nearby is **Ulaan Nuur** (Red Lake), the largest and just about the only lake in Ömnögov. It may not be there when you visit because it often dries out; and it won't quench your thirst either – it is very salty.

BAYANZAG
БАЯНЗАГ
Bayanzag, which means 'rich in saxaul shrubs', is more commonly known as the 'Flaming Cliffs', penned by the palaeontologist, Roy Chapman Andrews. First excavated in 1922, it is renowned worldwide for the number of dinosaur bones and eggs found in the area, which you can see in the Museum of Natural History in Ulaan Baatar or, mostly, in other museums around the world.

Even if you are not a 'dinophile', the eerie beauty of the surrounding landscape is a good reason to visit. It's a classic desert of rock, red sands, scrub, sun and awesome emptiness. There's not much to do once you're here except explore the cliffs.

Local authorities are trying to introduce a fee to the Bayanzag area, making it a 'locally protected area', though no system had been introduced at the time of research.

Bayanzag (GPS: N44° 08.536', E103° 43.206') is 65km north-west of Dalanzadgad and 18km north-east of Bulgan. It can be surprisingly hard to find so you really need to take a driver or guide who's been there before, or ask directions regularly from the few people who live in the area.

A further 22km north-east of Bayanzag is an area of sand dunes called **Moltzog Els**, which might be worth a visit if you aren't planning to visit Khongoryn Els.

GURVANSAIKHAN NATIONAL PARK
Stretching from the border with Bayankhongor almost to Dalanzadgad, the 2.7 million hectare Gurvansaikhan National

THE GOBI

Roy Chapman Andrews

'The romance of the desert will be destroyed. Tourists will sit in heated cars, eating the food of Europe, reading week-old newspapers, and comprehending not at all the glorious history, the tragedy and the romance of the Gobi trails'.

Roy Chapman Andrews

An American palaeontologist from New York, Roy Chapman Andrews (1884–1960), explored the Gobi in the 1920s, and found the first dinosaur eggs, jaws and skulls in Central Asia. Andrews' most famous expeditions were based at Bayanzag, which he famously renamed the 'Flaming Cliffs'.

Andrews had actually come to Mongolia to find the missing link between apes and man and to prove his boss Henry Osborn's theory that Central Asia was the dispersal point for mammalian life. He never found evidence of this, though he did uncover traces of a 20,000-year-old people, which he dubbed the Dune Dwellers. As Chinese bandits and Soviet secret police placed unbearable strains on field work, he abandoned his incomplete excavations after about five expeditions.

From his books and biographies, he was a real-life adventurer, who took the expedition's ambushes, raids, bandits, rebellions and vipers in his stride (the camp killed 47 vipers in their tents one night). He was never one for understatement; as one expedition member said, 'the water that was up to our ankles was always up to Roy's neck'. In reality, the only time an expedition member was injured was when Andrews accidentally shot himself in the leg with his own revolver.

Andrews worked for US intelligence during WWI and also explored Alaska, Borneo, Burma and China. He wrote such Boys' Own classics as *Whale Hunting with Gun and Camera* (1916), *Across Mongolian Plains* (1921), *On the Trail of Ancient Man* and *The New Conquest of Central Asia*. Always kitted out in a felt hat, khakis and a gun by his side, Andrews is widely regarded as the model on which the Hollywood screen character Indiana Jones was based.

On his return to the US Andrews took the directorship of the American Museum of Natural History but was asked to resign in 1941. His death in California in 1960, at the age of 76, went almost unnoticed.

Park is the highlight of the aimag, and the overwhelming reason why any tourist comes here. Unlike other national parks in the Gobi, the Gurvansaikhan does contain a few attractions, and its facilities – ger camps and roads – are reasonably good.

Gurvansaikhan, which means the 'three beauties' and refers to its three ridges (though there are four), contains mountains, dinosaur fossils, sand dunes, rock formations and a valley which, incredibly, has ice for most of the year.

The park also contains over 200 species of birds, including the Mongolian desert finch, cinereous vulture, desert warbler and houbara bustard. Spring brings further waves of migratory birds.

The park also has maybe 600 or more types of plants (a lot of which only bloom after very infrequent heavy rain). The sparse vegetation does manage to support numerous types of animals, such as the black-tailed gazelle, Kozlov's pygmy jerboa and wild ass, and endangered species of wild camel, snow leopard, ibex and argali sheep. In 2000, the park was expanded by over half a million hectares, stretching into Bayankhongor aimag.

Entry Fees

There is a national park entry fee of T1000 per day per person, plus T3000 per day for your vehicle. You can pay the fee and get a permit at the park office in Dalanzadgad, at the entrance to Yolyn Am or from the ranger at Khongoryn Els. In theory, this permit covers the entire park, so if you pay to enter Yolyn Am in the morning and then drive to Khongoryn Els that same day your permit covers you for both sites. Unfortunately local rangers keep a proportion of the park fees and so are keen to charge you as many times as possible. Try to get all the places you want to visit written on your park permit, as this will minimise confusion. Keep your permit receipt as you may need to show it to rangers later in your trip.

Another vagary is the duration of the permit; some park sources say a day's payment lasts for 24 hours, others say just for the day it was purchased. Thus if you arrive at Yolyn Am or Khongoryn Els in the evening you might be charged for that day and the next, unless you camp away from the ranger centre and drive in the next morning.

You can camp in most accessible areas of the park (though not the remote core areas), as long as you stay a fair distance from the ger camps and have your own food and water.

Yolyn Am
Ёолын Ам

Yolyn Am (Vulture's Mouth) was originally established to conserve the birdlife in the region, but it's now more famous for its dramatic and very unusual scenery – it is a valley in the middle of the Gobi Desert, with metres-thick ice almost all year-round.

The small **nature museum** at the gate on the main road to Yolyn Am has a collection of dinosaur eggs and bones, stuffed birds and a snow leopard. There is also an **ethnography museum** in a ger, which is worth a visit.

Look out for the remarkable petrified wood lying by the roadside. The ranger office and museum sell some good souvenirs, including landscape paintings and, amazingly, one of the best collections of Mongolian stamps in the country. Entrance to both museums is T500 and you will have to pay for park entrance here, unless you already paid in Dalanzadgad.

From the museum, the road continues for another 10km to a car park. From there, a pleasant 25-minute walk, following the stream, leads to a gorge full of ice. In winter, the ice is up to 10m high, and continues down the gorge for another 10km. It remains frozen for most of the year, except for about a month starting in late August.

You can walk on the ice – but be careful, especially in late summer.

The surrounding hills offer plenty of opportunities for some fine, if somewhat strenuous, day **hikes**. If you are lucky you might spot ibex or argali sheep along the steep valley ridges.

Yolyn Am (GPS: N43° 29.324', E104° 03.916') is in the Zuun Saikhan Uul range, 46km west of Dalanzadgad. The turn off to the entrance is sign posted, about 40km from Dalanzadgad.

If you are headed from Yolyn Am to Khongoryn Els, an adventurous and rough alternative route takes you through the **Dungenee Am**, a spectacular and narrow gorge. The gorge is blocked with ice until July and can be impassible even after the ice has melted, so check road conditions with the park ranger's office at the park entrance. It is 165km from Yolyn Am to Khongoryn Els.

Places to Stay There are a couple of ger camps near the park. The **Ikhat** camp, east of the turn-off to Yolyn Am, has beds in a ger for around US$10.

The park management has plans to set up ger stays near the park entrance, for US$10 to $15 without meals; inquire at the entrance to Yolyn Am or the park office in Dalanzadgad.

Enkhe's Guest House in Dalanzadgad can arrange a ger stay near the park entrance.

Khongoryn Els
Хонгорйн Улс

The Khongoryn Els are some of the largest and most spectacular sand dunes in Mongolia. Also known as the *duut mankhan* (singing dunes), they are up to 800m high, 12km wide and about 100km long. The largest dunes are at the northwest corner of the range. You can climb to the top of the dunes with a lot of effort and then slide back down if you have a garbage bag handy. The views of the desert from the top are wonderful. There is an information ger near the parking area at the base of the dunes.

The dunes are about 180km from Dalanzadgad and the ger camps. There is no way to get there unless you charter a jeep or are part of a tour.

To properly explore the area, you will need to stay the night in the desert before returning to Dalanzadgad. Otherwise, you can stay at the *Juulchin Gobi 2* ger camp, in the nearby settlement of Khongor, a couple of kilometres from the dunes, which costs about US$25 per person, including meals.

From Khongoryn Els it is possible to follow desert tracks 130km north to Bogd in Övörkhangai. This is a remote and unforgiving area and you shouldn't undertake the trip without an experienced driver and full stocks of food, water and fuel.

Dornogov
Дорноговь

pop 50,500 • area 111,000 sq km
Dornogov (East Gobi) is classic Gobi country – flat, arid and with a sparse population. In a good year, the aimag sprouts short grass, which sustains a limited number of sheep, goats and camels for their ethnic Khalkh owners. In a bad year, the wells go dry, the grass turns brown and the animals die. Unless there is a sudden demand for sand, Dornogov's economic future will continue to be based on the international rail line to China – though recent US interest in local oil reserves may improve things.

If travelling on the train to or from Beijing or Hohhot, you will see a lot of the desolate landscape from the window. If travelling around the Gobi independently, there is little need to come to Dornogov: there are very few interesting attractions, the roads are bad or nonexistent, water is scarce and the facilities are poor.

SAINSHAND
САЙНШАНД
pop 20,000 • elevation 938m
One of Mongolia's most dusty and dry aimag capitals, Sainshand (Good Pond) is important primarily because of its location. The city was founded in 1931 and was called Tushet Khan aimag during Manchu

rule. It is on the main rail line to China, and not far from the Chinese border.

If you are travelling around by jeep, Sainshand makes a useful place to refuel and to stock up with supplies before heading out into the Gobi. There are a few jeeps for hire for trips to the desert, but more are available in Dalanzadgad in Ömnögov aimag. Sainshand is handy because it is the only aimag capital in the Gobi to be linked by train to Ulaan Baatar.

Orientation & Information
Most things needed by the traveller are located around the central park, though the best views are from the tank monument located behind the monastery. The train station is 2km to the north. At the time of research, the telecom office was due for an Internet hook-up.

City Museum
This recently renovated museum houses some interesting items. There are plenty of stuffed Gobi animals, a collection of sea shells and marine fossils (Dornogov was

A musician plays the *morin khuur*

Gers camped by a lake, Tavanbogd National Park

A Sunni Muslim mosque, Bayan-Ölgii

Kazakh man in traditional fox-fur hat

Eagle-hunting is a Kazakh tradition dating back at least 2000 years.

CATHLEEN NAUNDORF

Milking is normally a female chore in nomad culture.

OLIVIER CIRENDINI

A young Mongolian

CATHLEEN NAUNDORF

The wooden roof poles of a *ger*, known as *uni*, are orange in colour, symbolising the sun.

CATHLEEN NAUNDORF

An honoured elder

CATHLEEN NAUNDORF

Felt carpets *(koshma)* of the Kazakhs, with their stylised motifs

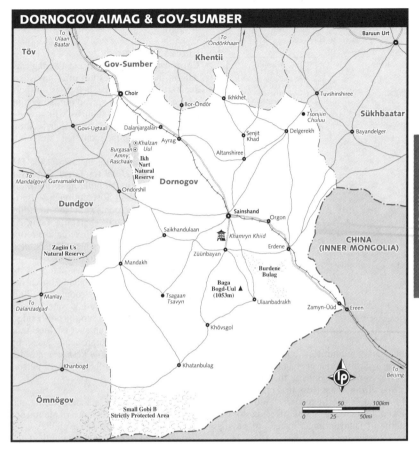

DORNOGOV AIMAG & GOV-SUMBER

To Ulaan Baatar
Baruun Urt
Töv
To Öndörkhaan
Gov-Sumber
Khentii
Choir
Ikhkhet
Tuvshinshiree
Bor-Öndör
Tsonjiin Chuluu
Sükhbaatar
Govi-Ugtaal
Dalanjargalan
Ayrag
Senjit Khad
Delgerekh
Bayandelger
Khalzan Uul
Burgasan Amny Raschaan
Ikh Nart Natural Reserve
Altanshiree
To Mandalgovi
Gurvansaikhan
Ondorshil
Dornogov
Dundgov
Sainshand
Orgon
CHINA (INNER MONGOLIA)
Saikhandulaan
Khamryn Khiid
Zagiin Us Natural Reserve
Züünbayan
Erdene
Mandakh
Burdene Bulag
Baga Bogd-Uul ▲ (1053m)
To Dalanzadgad
Manlay
Tsagaan Tsavyn
Ulaanbadrakh
Zamyn-Üüd
Ereen
Khövsgol
Khanbogd
Khatanbulag
To Beijing
Ömnögov
Small Gobi B Strictly Protected Area
0   50   100km
0   25   50mi

THE GOBI

once beneath the sea) and some dinosaur fossils. The history section includes some eulogies to Manzav, the local *baatar* (hero) who distinguished himself fighting for Mongolian independence during the 1921 revolution. Look out also for the 13th century wooden breastplate worn by a Mongol soldier in Korea and the *morin khuur* (horsehead fiddle), from 1940, decorated with carved images of Lenin and Sükhbaatar.

The museum is open from 9 am to 1 pm and 2 to 6 pm weekdays; entry is T1000. The museum is in the centre of town, a little west of the post office.

Museum of Danzanravjaa

Noyon Khutagt Danzanravjaa (1803–56), a well-known Mongolian writer, composer, painter and medic, was born about 100km south-west of Sainshand. The museum has a collection of gifts presented to Danzanravjaa by Chinese and Tibetan leaders, costumes used in his plays, Buddhist statues presented to him by the 10th Dalai Lama, and some of his paintings. He was also very interested in traditional medicine, so the museum has a collection of herbs.

Look out for the jar in front of his statue, which contains the Danzanravjaa's bones;

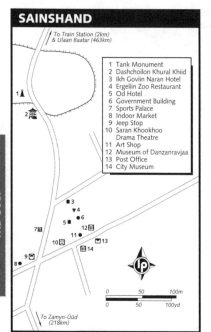

SAINSHAND

To Train Station (2km)
& Ulaan Baatar (463km)

1 Tank Monument
2 Dashchoilon Khural Khiid
3 Ikh Goviin Naran Hotel
4 Ergeliin Zoo Restaurant
5 Od Hotel
6 Government Building
7 Sports Palace
8 Indoor Market
9 Jeep Stop
10 Saran Khookhoo
   Drama Theatre
11 Art Shop
12 Museum of Danzanravjaa
13 Post Office
14 City Museum

To Zamyn-Üüd
(218km)

the poet's mummified body was burned along with his monastery in the 1930s.

The museum, opposite the post office, is open from about 9 am to 5 pm on weekdays and is worth a visit. You may be asked to make a T500 offering to the statue of Danzanravjaa instead of paying an entrance fee.

Dashchoilon Khural Khiid

Дашчойлон Хурал Хийд

This monastery, opened in 1991, is in a large walled-compound at the northern end of the central district. There is an active temple, and though visitors are welcome, photographs are not allowed inside. The 25 monks are very friendly.

Khar Uul

Хар Уул

If you have time on your hands, locals recommend the two- to three-hour hike out to Khar Uul (Black Mountains), south-west of

town. Take lots of water – this is the Gobi, after all.

Places to Stay

Camping Sainshand, like most aimag capitals in the Gobi, does not offer anywhere decent to pitch a tent. The city is not built near a river, and it's spread out, so getting away from the ger suburbs will involve some walking. The best place to head for is the cliffs north of the monastery.

Hotels The best hotel in town is the *Ikh Goviin Naran Hotel* (or Great Gobi Sun Hotel), located in the building of the Mongolian People's Revolutionary Party (MPRP). Simple rooms with bath and toilet start at T3390 per person, rising to T5085/5560 for a half-deluxe/deluxe room. Don't expect any hot water. The hotel is just north of the city hall.

The *Od Hotel* (Od means 'star'), in the west wing of the Government House, has passably clean dormitory rooms for T2000 per person, and there's a hot-water shower room. Enter the hotel from the north side.

Both hotels can fill up after the local train arrives at night. If you are really stuck, try asking at the *Ergeliin Zoo Restaurant*, which has some basic rooms for T2500 per person.

Places to Eat

The two hotels have standard restaurants serving various combinations of mutton and potatoes. Better meals are available at the *Ergeliin Zoo Restaurant*, behind the Government House.

The indoor *market* near the Sports Palace is the best place to stock up on supplies.

Entertainment

The *Saran Khookhoo Drama Theatre* is named after the famous play by the local hero Danzanravjaa, who would be proud that the Sainshand theatre group is considered the best outside of Ulaan Baatar. Unfortunately, performances are sporadic.

Getting There & Away

Because at least one train links Sainshand with Ulaan Baatar every day, there are no flights or scheduled bus services to or from Sainshand.

Train The local train from Ulaan Baatar, which goes through Choir and continues on to Zamyn-Üüd, leaves every day at 4 pm and arrives in Sainshand at the inconvenient time of about 1.45 am – not a great time to find a hotel. There may also be a 10.20 am departure – so check when you book your ticket. Tickets from Ulaan Baatar cost T3060 for a hard seat and T7400 for a soft seat.

The train returns from Zamyn-Üüd to Ulaan Baatar, stopping at Sainshand at 11.20 pm and arriving in Ulaan Baatar at 9.40 am the next morning. This service is not as busy as the northern line (which goes to the large cities of Darkhan and Erdenet), so travelling in hard-seat class to/from Sainshand is often not unbearable.

The Trans-Mongolian Railway and the trains between Ulaan Baatar and Hohhot (in Inner Mongolia) and Ereen (just over the Chinese border) stop at Sainshand, but you cannot use these services just to get to Sainshand, unless you buy a ticket all the way to China. You must take the local daily train.

Getting *on* the Trans-Mongolian at Sainshand for China is fraught with complications unless you have bought your Ulaan Baatar-Beijing/Hohhot ticket beforehand in Ulaan Baatar, and have arranged for someone to tell the train steward at Ulaan Baatar station not to sell your seat. In Beijing, you can only buy a Beijing-Ulaan Baatar ticket, but you can get off at Sainshand.

Jeep It's possible, but not all that easy, to find a jeep in Sainshand. Try the jeep stop south of the Sports Palace. There is little demand for long distance shared jeeps as most locals travel to places connected by train, and almost no tourists come here.

Sainshand is 463km south-east of Ulaan Baatar, and 218km north-west of Zamyn-Üüd.

Hitching For the same reasons that jeeps are scarce, hitching is also hard. You will get a lift to Zamyn-Üüd or to Ulaan Baatar, but the train is quicker, more comfortable and not expensive.

Danzanravjaa

Danzanravjaa was a hot-headed, rebellious monk, a writer, king and popular leader of Mongolia's Red Hat Buddhists. He was recognised as a child prodigy by local people (he began composing and singing his own songs at the age of four) and was proclaimed the Fifth Gobi King in 1809. The Manchu had executed the Fourth Gobi King and forbade another and it was only the 10th Dalai Lama who persuaded the Manchu court to let the young Gobi king live.

Danzanravjaa's fame as a writer, artist and social critic spread far and wide. He received foreign students at his monastery and travelled to foreign countries, bringing his acting troupe with him to study drama.

He was also an expert at martial arts, Tantric studies, yoga, and traditional medicine. He spent months in solitude in caves or in his ger writing. It is said that he so hated being disturbed that he built himself a ger with no door. Some sources allege that the gifted poet and playwright was also a drunken womaniser with severe mental problems, who enjoyed painting pornographic scenes.

Danzanravjaa was supposedly assassinated by the rival Yellow Hat Buddhist sect, the Gelugpa. The people of Dornogov still know many tall tales about his supernatural powers and heroic feats, and locals dream of rebuilding his theatre (see the Khamaryn Khiid section later in this chapter) to again perform his famous play, *Life Story of the Moon Cuckoo*.

THE GOBI

KHAMARYN KHIID
ХАМАРЫН ХИЙД

This new monastery, an hour's drive south of Sainshand, has grown up around the cult of Danzanravjaa, whom many local people believe to have been a living god. His image is sewn into a carpet that hangs in the main hall. The original monastery and three-story theatre, built by Danzanravjaa in 1821, was destroyed in the 1930s. The surroundings hold meditation caves and retreats used by Danzanravjaa and his students.

Altyn Gerel, the curator of the Museum of Danzanravjaa in Sainshand (and the fifth generation in the hereditary line of Danzan-ravjaa's personal protectors, which extends from Danzanravjaa's assistant Balchinchoi-joo) operates a guest *ger* nearby. Contact him at the museum in Sainshand if you are thinking of heading to Khamaryn Khiid.

AROUND SAINSHAND

Probably the best sight in Dornogov, **Senjit Khad** is a natural rock formation in the shape of an arch. It is about 95km north-east of Sainshand in Altanshiree sum.

The volcanic rock formation of **Tsonjiin Chuluu** looks rather like a set of hexagonal organ pipes. It's in the extreme north-east corner of Dornogov, in Delgerekh sum, about 160km along the north-east road from Sainshand.

Some of the largest and most accessible sand dunes in the Gobi are at **Burdene Bulag**. There are also cold water springs in the area, but you will need a guide to find them. The dunes and springs are 30km south-west of Erdene, which is about halfway along the main road between Sainshand and Zamyn-Üüd.

The region around **Khatanbulag** (also known as Ergel) is noted for its cliffs, ancient archaeological artefacts and rare Gobi animals. The ruined **Demchigiin Khiid** is nearby. The sum is 240km south-west of Sainshand, linked by a trail which only an experienced driver could find.

The region around **Tsagaan Tsavyn** (also known as Suikhent) has numerous petrified trees, some on the desert surface and many more buried beneath the sands. Tsagaan Tsavyn is in the remote sum of Mandakh, about 200km south-west of Sainshand, and not far from the main road between Sainshand and Dalanzadgad.

CHOIR
ЧОЙР

Choir, about halfway between Sainshand and Ulaan Baatar, is a town with one foot in the past and the other in the future. Unfortunately the present is pretty grim. The only reason to visit Choir is to explore the nearby springs at Khalzan Uul, or to refuel between Ulaan Baatar and Sainshand.

Around 15km north of the town is the village of Lun Bag, the site of the largest **Soviet air base** in Mongolia. The Russians departed in 1992, leaving behind an eerie ghost town of concrete buildings and statues of MiG fighters. Some of the flats, which formerly housed military personnel, are now occupied by Mongolian families, but many sit empty, the windows broken, the plumbing ripped out and the walls scrawled with graffiti. The Russians left behind something else: the best paved runway in Mongolia.

To promote rapid economic growth, Choir formally seceded from Dornogov – it is now an autonomous municipality called Gov-Sümber, with a population of 13,300 – and was declared a Free Trade Zone. Nothing much was done to promote the area; development was postponed after the change of government in 1996 and is unlikely to take place in the near future.

There are a couple of hotels near the train station. The ***Ortooni (Station) Hotel***, right next to the station, costs T3500 for a bed. The ***Oron Tsootsnii Hotel***, 400m east of the station, costs T3800 in a dormitory style room with a shower.

To Choir, trains leave Ulaan Baatar daily at 4 pm and arrive at 8.45 pm. Tickets cost T1900/5000 for a hard/soft seat. The train returns to Ulaan Baatar on Tuesday and Friday at the unspeakable time of 4.20 am. You may be better off inquiring about the twice-weekly direct train in this direction. The Trans-Mongolian Railway briefly stops in Choir but you won't be able to buy a ticket to get off here (see Getting There & Away under Sainshand earlier).

KHALZAN UUL
ХАЛЗАН УУЛ

Khalzan Uul is an area of natural springs about 50km south of Choir. Locals are crazy about its mineral water, claiming it can cure everything from hangovers to HIV. Local entrepreneurs plan to bottle the water and sell it.

Burgasan Amny Rashaan is another mineral spring just a few kilometres south.

ZAMYN-ÜÜD
ЗАМЫН-ҮҮД

This town has only two claims to fame: it's right on Mongolia's southern border and it is the hottest place in the country. The only reasons to come here are to save money by travelling from Ulaan Baatar to China on local trains, rather than on the dearer international Trans-Mongolian Railway; or if you are planning to visit obscure villages by train in Inner Mongolia. Desertification is a real problem here and sand dunes are starting to pile up between buildings.

Orientation & Information
There is a branch of the Trade & Development Bank on the second floor of the train station and money changers hang outside the station. If you exit Mongolia by minivan or jeep there is an exit tax of T6000, which is worked into the price of the ticket (T8000).

Make sure that your passport and Mongolian and Chinese visas are all in order. One Nigerian man crossing the border here on a dodgy passport was detained in 1999 and two years later was still here – with the authorities running out of ideas as to what to do with him!

Places to Stay & Eat
Right now the town is booming thanks to cross-border trade and there are now three main places to stay.

The *Jintin Hotel*, just next to the train station, has clean rooms with private bathroom for US$30 and US$35, and there are four-bed dorm rooms downstairs for T4500 per bed. There's a good *restaurant* here.

The *Tsagaan Shonkhor*, or White Falcon Hotel, to the right of the train station, isn't half as good. Basic rooms in a dormitory cost T3500 and deluxe rooms cost T10,000 per person.

The *Bayangol Hotel*, opposite the taxi stand, has dorm beds for T2000, and T12,000 for a deluxe room. The food here is said to be very good.

There is also a hotel in Ereen (Érliàn in Pinyin), on the Chinese side of the border.

Getting There & Away
The daily train (No 276) to Zamyn-Üüd, via Choir and Sainshand, leaves Ulaan Baatar every day at 4 pm, arriving around 7.30 am. Tickets cost T3900/9300 for hard/soft seat. The train returns to Ulaan Baatar, leaving at 5.30 pm, arriving the next morning at 9.20 am. Tickets cost T1800/4700 to Sainshand and T3000/7300 to Choir.

From Zamyn-Üüd to Ereen (Érliàn; the Chinese town on the other side of the border) most people take the frequent minivans (T8000) that run the 7km between the train stations of Zamyn-Üüd and Ereen. The minivans are generally quicker than the train.

If you are on the Trans-Mongolian train, or the service between Ulaan Baatar and Hohhot or Ereen, you will stop at Zamyn-Üüd for an hour or two while Mongolian customs and immigration officials do their stuff – usually in the middle of the night. See the Trans-Mongolian Railway entry unde Land in the Getting Around chapter for details.

Bayankhongor
Баянхонгор

pop 92,300 • area 116,000 sq km

This strangely shaped aimag is dominated by the mighty Khangai Nuruu range to the north. Its southern part passes through the Gobi to the Chinese border and includes part of the Mongol Altai Nuruu range. Although somewhat higher than the Khangai Nuruu, the Mongol Altai is a bleak desert range where life is hard even for the durable argali sheep and ibex.

By contrast, the Khangai is lush, providing sufficient snowmelt to make livestock raising and human existence a viable proposition. Bayankhongor, which means 'rich tan' (named after the colour of the horses – or your skin after a couple of hours in the sun) is home to wild camels and asses and the extremely rare Gobi bear.

Most travellers bypass the aimag while travelling along the major southern Ulaan Baatar-Khovd road, but Bayankhongor

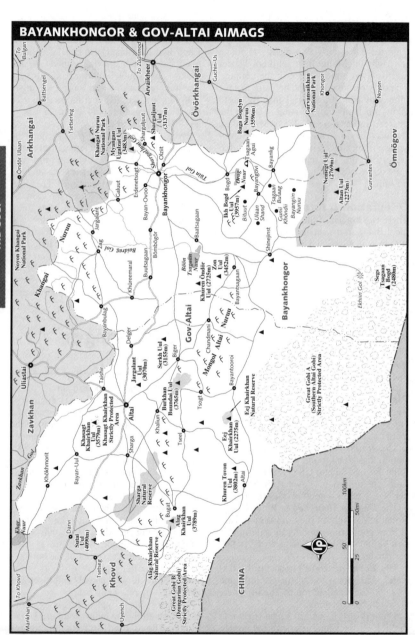

BAYANKHONGOR & GOV-ALTAI AIMAGS

does have some interesting, albeit remote, attractions. Some adventurous travellers have ridden horses from Bayankhongor over the Khangai Nuruu to Tsetserleg in Arkhangai. Getting to these remote places is as much expedition as common travel, but if you are well prepared the area offers some magical trips off the beaten track.

BAYANKHONGOR
БАЯНХОНГОР
pop 23,000 • elevation 1859m

This sprawling capital was established in 1942. Located close to the border with Övörkhangai and Arkhangai aimags, Bayankhongor city is where the Khangai Nuruu, with several peaks of 3000m or more, meets the northern Gobi. It's a good place to stop during the long haul to or from the west, to start explorations to more remote regions to the south, or to go on a day trip to the nearby springs at Shargaljuut.

Lamyn Gegeenii Dedlen Khiid
Ламын Гэгээний Дэдлэн Хийд

There was no ancient monastery on this particular site, but 20km to the east of Bayankhongor city, a monastery existed with the same name. This monastery complex once housed up to 10,000 monks, making it one of the largest in the country. As elsewhere in Mongolia, the communist police descended on the place in 1937 and carted off the monks, who were never seen again. The temple was levelled and today nothing remains. Sadly, the present-day monks seem to have little knowledge of the old temple's history.

The current monastery, built in 1991, is home to only 40 monks. The main temple is built in the shape of a ger, although it's actually made of brick. The main hall features a statue of Sakyamuni flanked by a green and white Tara. The monastery is on the main street, 200m north of the square.

The skyline of Bayankhongor city is dominated by a **stupa** on a hill to the west of the square. If you are staying for a while, take a walk up there for views of the town and nearby countryside.

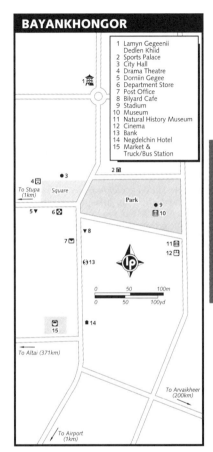

BAYANKHONGOR

1 Lamyn Gegeenii Dedlen Khiid
2 Sports Palace
3 City Hall
4 Drama Theatre
5 Dorniin Gegee
6 Department Store
7 Post Office
8 Bilyard Cafe
9 Stadium
10 Museum
11 Natural History Museum
12 Cinema
13 Bank
14 Negdelchin Hotel
15 Market & Truck/Bus Station

THE GOBI

Museums

The **Aimag Museum**, located inside the sports stadium in the park, is well laid-out and worth a visit, though there are no English captions as yet. There is a good display on Buddhist art, featuring two lovely statues of Tara, some fine old scroll paintings, *tsam* (lama dance) masks and costumes. Other exhibits fall into the standard mould of communist history and model gers.

The museum is open weekdays from 9 am to 5 pm and costs T1000 to enter. Photography is pricey at T2500 per picture.

Disappointed by the lack of badly taxidermal creatures? Head across the street to the **Natural History Museum**. The highlights here are some dinosaur fossils and a replica Tarbosaurus skeleton. Entry is T500 and it has the same opening hours as the Aimag Museum.

Places to Stay
Camping Bayankhongor city is not one of the better aimag capitals for camping. The best place is probably by the Tüin Gol, a few hundred metres east of the city.

Hotels The *Negdelchin Hotel*, at the southern end of the main street, is the only place in town. Three-bed rooms with attached toilet, but no shower, cost T6400 per person. Deluxe rooms with toilet and shower cost T9000.

Places to Eat
The dining room at the *Negdelchin Hotel* serves goulash, rice and salad for T880. The *Dorniin Gegee* shop and guanz next to the department store serves up a similar goulash (T700) or steak and eggs (T900). Alternatively you could try the *Bilyard Cafe*, on the south-west corner of the park or the several *guanz* at the market.

Getting There & Away
Air On Monday, Thursday and Saturday, MIAT flies between Ulaan Baatar and Bayankhongor for US$82/143. The Monday flight is scheduled to stop in Arvaikheer; the others are non-stop. The airport is a dirt field about 1km south of the city.

Bus & Minivan As a central point in southern Mongolia, Bayankhongor is well connected by bus, or better still by minivan to Ulaan Baatar, making this an interesting and cheap, if somewhat uncomfortable, way to reach the western Gobi. Minivans leave Ulaan Baatar every day except Sunday (12 hours, T11,500), and go via Arvaikheer. They stop at the market in Bayankhongor, about 300m south of the square.

If you ask around the market you should be able to find a minivan or jeep headed to

Altai (10 hours, T8000) or even Khovd (24 hours, T15,000).

Jeep It is safe to assume that you will not be able to charter a jeep in Bayankhongor; the city is poor and not developed for tourism – or for anything else, for that matter.

For some reason (certainly nothing to do with the amount of traffic), an excellent paved road starts about 20km east of Bayankhongor city, part of an ambitious plan to complete a decent Ulaan Baatar-Khovd road. The 400km road to Altai is okay; just a little boring in parts.

Hitching Bayankhongor is on the main southern road between Ulaan Baatar and Khovd. A lot of vehicles going in either direction stop here, so getting a ride to Altai or Arvaikheer shouldn't be difficult. South of Bayankhongor, or to Shargaljuut, you will have far less success. Ask around at the market, which doubles as a bus and truck station.

SHARGALJUUT
ШАРГАЛЖУУТ
The major attraction in Bayankhongor aimag is the 300 or so hot- and cold-water **springs** at Shargaljuut. About 60km northeast of Bayankhongor city, the springs are one of the few natural attractions in the Gobi region that are easily accessible from an aimag capital.

The springs and bath houses cover the banks of the river between the peaks of Myangan Ugalzat Uul (3483m) and Shargaljuut Uul (3137m). The hot water, which can reach 50°C, is supposed to cure a wide range of complaints and many Mongolians come for treatment at the neighbouring sanatorium. At the time of research officials were proposing a US$5 foreigner's entry fee to the springs, so check at the entrance gate.

Foreign guests can stay at the *ger camp* and *hotel* at the sanatorium for US$10, including food, but you should try to reserve in advance by calling the manager Mr Yadmaa (not easily done as there is no phone number available, so you will have to get a Mongolian speaker to connect you via the phone operator in Bayankhongor).

Alternatively, you can *camp* farther down from the springs along the valley.

Occasional shared jeeps or minivans leave Bayankhongor's market for Shargaljuut. Chartering a minivan costs around T30,000 return. Alternatively, try the airport at 11 am on Saturday, Monday and Thursday, when a microbus bound for the springs meets incoming passengers from Ulaan Baatar.

GALUUT
ФИВГАЛУУТ

The 25m-deep Galuut canyon is worth a visit if, for some bizarre reason, you are in the region. The **canyon** is only about 1m wide in places. It is 20km south-west of Galuut sum centre, which is about 85km north-west of Bayankhongor town. **Mandal Khiid** is said to be nearby.

BÖÖN TSAGAAN NUUR
БӨӨН ЦАГААН НУУР

This large saltwater lake, at the end of Baidrag Gol, is popular with birdlife, especially the relic gull, whooper swan and geese. The region also boasts extraordinary **volcanic formations**, canyons of cascading streams and **ancient cave paintings**. The lake is about 90km south-west of Bayankhongor city, in Buutsagaan sum.

OROG NUUR
ОГОР НУУР

The saltwater Orog Nuur is at the end of the Tüin Gol, which passes through Bayankhongor city. Also referred to as Shar Burd Nuur, the lake is a good place to watch birdlife. It is nestled in the foothills of Ikh Bogd Uul (3957m) in Bogd sum, a four hour, 110km drive south of Bayankhongor city. With a jeep and local guide it is possible to drive to the top of Ikh Bogd for stupendous views. You can use the lake as a base to visit sights further south.

The *Orog* ger camp, run by the Guchtkhan travel agency, on the south-west corner of the lake (GPS: N45° 02.692', E100° 36.314') costs US$35 with all meals included, or US$10 for accommodation only. You can hire jeeps here for T300 to T400

per km, depending on the length of the trip, and local guides for US$10 per day. For bookings contact Guchtkhan (see Travel Agencies under Information in the Ulaan Baatar chapter).

On the north-east side of the lake is the *Mongol Gobi Resort*, a standard ger camp, costing around US$40 per person, including meals.

BAYANGOVI
БАЯНГОВЬ

The small town of Bayangovi is about 100 km south of Orog Nuur in a beautiful valley dominated by the Ikh Bogd range. While there is nothing of special interest in Bayangovi itself, the surrounding countryside offers a number of intriguing desert sites, which can be visited on a one-day or two-day excursion with the aid of a jeep and a local guide.

Places to Stay & Eat
Gobi Camels (✆/fax 69-2089) ger camp, 6km north-west of town, offers a bed in one of its seven gers for US$30 with all meals included, or US$10 for accommodation only. Facilities include hot showers and satellite TV.

The other alternative is the unmarked *hotel* within a compound on the southern edge of town. Look for the brightly painted guanz and shop at the entrance to the compound. The hotel has 7 beds within an apartment for US$4 per person. The *guanz* offers goulash, soup and khuurshuur for T600.

Getting There & Away
The best way to get to Bayangovi and its surrounding attractions is in your own rented transport, either from Bayankhongor or as part of a longer trip.

Failing this, shared minivans or jeeps occasionally run to Bayangovi from outside the central market at Bayankhongor. There is also a postal truck (T7000) that leaves for Bayangovi from Bayankhongor on Wednesday. Inquire at the post office in Bayankhongor. Once you get to Bayangovi your only option to see the surrounding sites is to hire a jeep from the Gobi Camels camp.

Around Bayangovi

About 90km east of Bayangovi lies **Tsagaan Agui** (GPS: N44° 42.604', E101° 10.187'). Situated in a narrow gorge, the cave once housed Stone Age human beings 700,000 years ago. It features a crystal-lined inner chamber. Entrance to the cave costs T1000 (including a local guide), which is paid at the nearby ger.

Also near Bayangovi are several intriguing rock inscription sites. At **Tsagaan Bulag** (GPS: N44° 35.156', E100° 20.733'), 18km south, a white rock outcrop has the faint imprint of a strange helmeted figure, which locals believe was created by aliens. The area is also home to many herds of camel, attracted to the springs at the base of the outcrop.

Those interested in fossils should visit the petrified forest at **Ulaan Shand**, an area littered with stone logs and stumps, 66km south-west of Bayangovi.

Other noteworthy sites which you could add on to make a full day-trip include the vertical walls of the 4km-long **Gunii Khöndii** gorge, south-east of Ulaan Shand, and the beautiful **Bituut rock**, north of Bayangovi on the southern flank of Ikh Bogd, formed after an earthquake in 1957.

Further afield at **Bayangiin Nuruu** (GPS: N44° 17.218', E100° 31.329'), 90km south of Bayangovi, is a canyon with well-preserved rock engravings and petroglyphs, dating from 3000 BC. The engravings depict hunting and agricultural scenes in a surprisingly futuristic style.

Travelling further south the landscape slowly descends into the Gobi Desert proper, along the border with Ömnögov aimag. In this area are numerous **oases**, amongst them **Jartiin Khuv**, **Daltin Khuv**, **Burkhant** and **Zuunmod**. Look out for the wild horses and camels, black tailed gazelle, antelope and *zam* lizards, which inhabit the area.

This region is rich in fossil sites. **Bugiin Khöndii** (Devil's Valley; GPS N43° 52.869', E100° 01.639') is a large series of rift valleys running parallel to the Altan Uul mountain range. A number of dinosaur fossils have been found here, which are now housed in the Museum of Natural History in Ulaan Baatar. The other fossil site is at **Yasnee Tsav**, an eroded hilly region with some impressive buttes. Local guides claim they can point out authentic fossils at this site.

Continuing south will lead to the other famous fossil site of **Khermen Tsav**. From here one could continue east into the Gobi towards Gurvantes, Noyon and Bayandalai, but be warned that this section of road is notoriously treacherous. Don't go without plenty of water and well-equipped four-wheel drive vehicles.

Getting Around All of the sites mentioned above are very difficult to find without a good local guide. Bodio, the friendly manager of the Gobi Camels ger camp (see the Bayangovi section earlier), can organise local guides for US$15 per day (though few of these speak English so you really still need your own translator). He also hires out jeeps for T300 per km, which includes driver, petrol and local guide and can arrange horse and camel tours for US$5 per person per day, plus US$5 per day for a guide.

Otherwise, contact the Guchtkhan ger camp and travel agency (see the Orog Nuur section).

Gov-Altai
Говъ-Алтай

pop 74,100 • area 142,000 sq km

Mongolia's second-largest aimag is named after the Gobi Desert and the Mongol Altai Nuruu range, which virtually bisects the aimag to create a stark, rocky landscape. There is a certain beauty in this combination, but there is considerable heartbreak too. Gov-Altai is one of the least suitable areas for raising livestock, and therefore one of the most hostile to human habitation. It is hoped that an ambitious Kuwaiti-funded hydro-electric power project and dam on the Zavkhan Gol (near Taishir) will bring an economic upturn to the region.

Somehow a few Gobi bears, wild camels, ibexes and even snow leopards survive, often protected in the several national parks in the aimag. Most of the population live in the north-east corner, where melting snow from the Khangai Nuruu feeds small rivers, creating vital water supplies.

Gov-Altai is famous for its oases, and contains some remote sections of several national parks, but most travellers head further west to the more beautiful and interesting aimags in western Mongolia.

Mountaineers and adventurous hikers with a lot of time on their hands might want to bag an Altai peak. Opportunities include Khuren Tovon Uul (3802m), in Altai sum, Burkhan Buuddai Uul (3765m) in Biger sum, or the permanently snowcapped peak of Sutai Uul (4090m), the highest peak in Gov-Altai. Most climbers approach Sutai Uul from the Khovd side.

National Parks

The beauty of Gov-Altai's diverse and sparsely populated mountain and desert environment has led to the allocation of a large portion of the aimag as national parks:

Alag Khairkhan Natural Reserve (36,400 hectares) Protects Altai habitat, rare plants, snow leopard, argali and ibex.

Great Gobi Strictly Protected Area Divided into 'Gobi A', or Southern Altai Gobi, and 'Gobi B', or Dzungarian Gobi. 'Gobi A' is over 4.4 million hectares in the southern part of the aimag. 'Gobi B' is 881,000 hectares in the south-west of Gov-Altai and in neighbouring Khovd. Together, the undisturbed area is the fourth largest biosphere reserve in the world and protects wild ass, Gobi bears, the wild Bactrian camel and jerboa, among other endangered animals.

Eej Khairkhan Natural Reserve (22,475 hectares) About 150km directly south of Altai, the reserve was created to protect the general environment.

Khasagt Khairkhan Strictly Protected Area (27,448 hectare) The area protects endangered argali sheep and the Mongol Altai mountain environment.

Sharga Natural Reserve Like the Mankhan Natural Reserve in Khovd aimag, it helps to preserve highly endangered species of antelope.

Takhiin Tal On the border of the northern section of Dzungarian National Park. Eight *takhi* (the

Mongolian wild horse) were re-introduced into the wild here in 1996. Experts hope they will survive and flourish in this remote area of the Gobi.

ALTAI
АЛТАЙ
pop 17,500 • elevation 2181m
Nestled between the mountains of Khasagt Khairkhan Uul (3579m) and Jargalant Uul (3070m), the aimag capital is a pleasant tree-lined place, with friendly people. With an interesting museum and a well-stocked market, Altai is a good place to stop on the way to somewhere else – either to or from Khovd, or the national parks to the south.

Information

The bank, opposite the Altai Hotel, will probably change US dollars. It is open on weekdays from 9 am to 1 pm and 2 to 5 pm.

The well-stocked market, 150m south of the Altai Hotel, has a good range of foodstuffs, as well as the odd *del* (traditional long robe) or pair of traditional Mongol boots.

The recently renovated *drama theatre* holds the occasional folk performance.

Dashpeljeelen Khiid
Дашпэлжээлэн Хийд
This small, attractive monastery was built in 1990 and is home to 30 monks. Unlike most others, there was no previous structure on this site. On most days from 10 am, you can witness a ceremony. The monastery is a short walk north-west of the town square.

Museum

Highlights here include some excellent bronze statues, scroll paintings, some genuine Mongol army chain mail, and an interesting shaman costume and drum. Unfortunately there is very little English text.

The museum is open weekdays from 9 am to 1 pm, and 2 pm to 6pm. Entry is T1500, plus T2500 if you want to take photographs.

Places to Stay
Camping The road from Altai to Khovd goes through a surprisingly lush valley for about 10km. So, if you have a tent and

THE GOBI

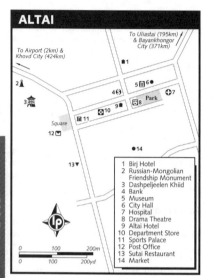

ALTAI

To Uliastai (195km) & Bayankhongor City (371km)

To Airport (2km) & Khovd City (424km)

Park

Square

1 Birj Hotel
2 Russian-Mongolian Friendship Monument
3 Dashpeljeelen Khiid
4 Bank
5 Museum
6 City Hall
7 Hospital
8 Drama Theatre
9 Altai Hotel
10 Department Store
11 Sports Palace
12 Post Office
13 Sutai Restaurant
14 Market

your own vehicle, head out there. A great patch of ground, which you will have to share with a few cows, is only a 20-minute walk north-west of town.

Hotels Except for the basic plumbing, the *Altai Hotel* on the main street is quite luxurious. As a nice touch, many of the rooms even have telephones – though these seldom work. Foreigners are charged about T6000 per person for a simple room with a toilet and basin. Half-deluxe rooms cost T7280 with a toilet but no shower, and deluxe rooms cost T12,240, which gets you a cold shower.

The *Birj Hotel* has simple but clean and bright rooms for T5000. There are no showers and the pit toilet is outside.

Places to Eat

The *Altai Hotel* manages to feed guests with a decent selection of buuz, tsuivan and goulash for around T800. The *Sutai Restaurant*, upstairs in a white building south of the main square, serves up more goulash and soup. Try the *Birj Hotel* for yet more soup or goulash, though the opening times are erratic.

Getting There & Away

Air MIAT flies from Ulaan Baatar to Altai and back on Tuesday, Thursday and Saturday for US$120/210. The airport is 2km north-west of the centre.

Bus & Minivan Altai is as far as minivans from Ulaan Baatar go – any further west and you will have to rely on hitching or take your own jeep. Buses to Altai leave from Ulaan Baatar when full on most days (T18,000), and go through Arvaikheer and Bayankhongor city.

Jeep Altai is not somewhere you should expect to find any reliable jeeps for hire. You are more likely to have success in Uliastai and Khovd city. Shared jeeps are just as uncommon; most people hitch on trucks or anything else that is going their way.

The road from Altai to Khovd city (424km) starts off through a lush valley, then becomes flat and boring. The condition of the road fluctuates wildly and you shouldn't count on an average of more than 25km per hour along this stretch. Altai is also 371km west of Bayankhongor city and 195km south of Uliastai.

Hitching There is some traffic along the main road towards Khovd and Bayankhongor, but you may have to wait a few hours for something suitable. Very few vehicles travel between Altai and Uliastai; you will probably have to wait for something to arrive from Uliastai first. Almost no vehicles venture into the south of Gov-Altai.

The best place to ask around for a shared jeep is at the southern entrance to the market. Expect to pay around T8000 to T10,000 for a ride to Khovd or Bayankhongor.

SOUTHERN ALTAI GOBI STRICTLY PROTECTED AREA

The majority of this 4.4 million hectare national park, also known as 'Gobi A', lies in the south-east corner of Gov-Altai. Established over 20 years ago, the area has been nominated as an International Biosphere Reserve by the United Nations.

Saving the Snow Leopard

The mountain regions of Gov-Altai are home to the beautiful and elusive snow leopard, or *irbis* in Mongolian. Up to 50kg in weight, and about 1m long (the tail is an extra 70cm), snow leopards can easily kill an ibex three times its size. They remain solitary except during the brief mating season.

An estimated 7500 snow leopards live in an area of 1.5 million sq km across China, Pakistan, Afghanistan, India, Nepal and Mongolia (where 1000 to 1500 live). The principal threats are poaching, habitat loss and wild prey loss. Declining numbers of Argali sheep and ibex have forced snow leopards to kill livestock and brought them into conflict with local herders.

It is hoped that the establishment of several national parks, education programs and local income generation projects can help save the snow leopard. Otherwise, the few pelts on display in local museums and even the odd ger camp will be all that is left of this beautiful creature.

Irbis is a local organisation which protects snow leopards in Mongolia by providing alternative sources of income to herders in snow leopard habitat. The company sells and markets locally made handicrafts, such as felt mats and camel and cashmere goods, with proceeds going jointly to producers and a conservation fund. To find out more about this project check out the Web site at www.irbis-enterprises.com.

If you would like more information about the protection of the snow leopard, contact the International Snow Leopard Trust (☎ 206-632 2421, fax 632 3967), 4649 Sunnyside Ave N, Seattle, Washington, 98103 USA.

The park is remote and very difficult to reach, which is bad news for visitors but excellent news for the fragile flora and fauna. Almost completely uninhabited by humans, the park helps to protect about 50 Gobi bears and some wild camels, as well as the desert environment and scarce water sources for the animals.

There are a few mountains over 1200m, and several springs and oases, which only an experienced guide will find. To explore the park, start at Biger, turn south-west on the trail to Tsogt, and head south on any jeep trail you can find.

You will need a very reliable vehicle and an experienced driver, and you must be completely self-sufficient with supplies of food, water and camping gear.

EEJ KHAIRKHAN UUL
ҮҮЖ ХАЙРХАН УУЛ

Near the base of the Eej Khairkhan Uul (2275m), just north of 'Gobi A' National Park, you could camp at some delightful **rock pools** and explore the nearby **caves**. You will need a guide to show you around. Almost no suitable drinking water is available, so take your own into the area.

An A-frame *hut* is sometimes available for rent near the pools, but you should always have your own camping equipment.

About 30 minutes walk west of the hut are some spectacular, ancient **rock paintings** of ibex, horsemen and archers.

The mountain is about 150km south of Altai, and is part of the Eej Khairkhan Natural Reserve.

Language

Mongolian is a member of the Ural-Altaic family of languages, which includes Finnish, Hungarian, Turkish, Kazakh, Usbek and Korean. The traditional Mongolian script looks like Arabic turned 45 degrees, and is still used by the Mongolians living in China (Inner Mongolia, parts of Xinjiang, Qinhai, Liaoning and Jilin). In 1944, the Russian Cyrillic alphabet was adopted, with the two additional characters, Ө and ү. It remains in use today in Mongolia and also in two autonomous republics of Russia – Buryatia and Kalmykia.

Mongolian can also be written in Romanised form, though the 35 Cyrillic characters give a better representation of Mongolian sounds than the paltry 26 of the Roman alphabet. Partly a result of Russian influence, different Romanisation schemes have been used, and this has caused widespread confusion. A loose standard was adopted in 1987, so the capital city previously written as 'Ulan Bator' (transliterated Russian spelling), is now Ulaan Baatar.

Mongolian pronunciation is not easy. In the words of travel writer Tim Severin, the Mongol language is 'like two cats coughing and spitting at each other until one finally throws up'. One particular word, which conveys agreement or encouragement (rather like nodding one's head) is little more than a sharp, guttural intake of breath, as if you were having difficulty breathing.

It's important to give double vowels a lengthened pronunciation, as getting it wrong can affect meaning. Bolded letters in the following words and phrases represent word stress. If all vowels in a word are short, the first will take the stress and the rest will become 'neutral' (as the 'e' in 'open'). In words with one long vowel, stress will fall on that vowel and any short vowels in the word will become neutral. If there's more than one long vowel the stress will generally fall on the penultimate syllable.

If you'd like a more comprehensive guide to the language, pick up a copy of Lonely Planet's *Mongolian phrasebook*.

Mongolian Cyrillic Alphabet

А а	a	as the 'u' in 'but'
Г г	g	as in 'get'
Ё ё	yo	as in 'yonder'
И и	i	as in 'tin'
Л л	l	as in 'lamp'
О о	o	as the 'o' in British 'hot'
Р р	r	as in 'rub'
У у	u	as the 'ou' in 'source'
Х х	kh	as the 'ch' in Scottish *loch*
Ш ш	sh	as in 'shoe'
Ы ы	y	as the 'i' in 'ill'
Ю ю	yu	as the 'yo' in 'yoyo'
	yü	long, as the word 'you'
Б б	b	as in 'but'
Д д	d	as in 'dog'
Ж ж	j	as in 'jewel'
Й й	i	as in 'tin'
М м	m	as in 'mat'
Ө ө	ö	long, as the 'u' in 'fur'
С с	s	as in 'sun'
Ү ү	ü	long, as the 'o' in 'who'
Ц ц	ts	as in 'cats'
Щ щ	shch	as the 'shch' in 'fresh chips
ь		* 'soft sign' (see below)
Я я	ya	as in 'yard'
В в	v	as in 'van'
Е е	ye	as in 'yes'
	yö	as the 'yea' in 'yearn'
З з	z	as the 'dz' sound in 'suds'
К к	k	as in 'kit'
Н н	n	as in 'neat'
П п	p	as in 'pat'
Т т	t	as in 'tin'
Ф ф	f	as in 'five'
Ч ч	ch	as in 'chat'
Ъ ъ		* 'hard sign' (see below)
Э э	e	as in 'den'

* The letters ь and ъ never occur alone, but simply affect the pronunciation of the previous letter – ь makes the preceding sound soft, ie, the consonant before it is pronounced as if there's a very short 'y' after it, while ъ makes the previous sound hard, ie, prevents it being pronounced as if there's a 'y' after it.

Greetings & Civilities

Hello.
*sain baina **uu**?*
Сайн байна уу?
(literally, 'how are you?')
Fine. How are you?
*sain ta sain baina **uu**?*
Сайн. Та сайн байна уу?
Fine.
sain
Сайн.
What's new?
*sonin **saikhan** yu baina?*
Сонин сайхан юу байна?
Nothing really.
*taivan **saikhan***
Тайван сайхан.
(literally, 'It's peaceful.')
Goodbye.
*bayar**tai***
Баяртай.

If you're visiting a family, especially in the country, having agreed that everybody's fine, you should proceed to asking about family members and livestock and only then to more general matters:

How is your family?
*tan**ai** ger bül**iin**hen sain **uu**?*
Танай гэр бүлийнхэн сайн уу?
I hope your animals are fattening up nicely?
*mal **süreg targan tavtai** yü?*
Мал сүрэг тарган тавтай юү?
Are you very busy?
*ta ajil ikhtei baina **uu**?*
Та ажил ихтэй байна уу?
I'm very busy.
*bi tun za**vgüi** baina*
Би тун завгүй байна.

Essentials

Yes.
tiim
Тийм.
No.
ügüi
Үгүй.

Six Essential Phrases

Cynics say that the six most widely heard phrases in Mongolia are *medehgui* (don't know), *baikhgui* (don't have), *chadakhui*, (can't do) *magadgui* (maybe), *margaash* (tomorrow) and *za*, which roughly translates to, well, 'za'. *Za* is a catch-all phrase, said at the conclusion of a statement, meaning something akin to 'well ...', 'so then ...' or 'ok', and is a fiendishly addictive word.

Thanks.
*bayarla**laa***
Баярлалаа.
I'm sorry/Excuse me.
*uuchl**aarai***
Уучлаарай.
I'm sorry, what did you say?
*uuchl**aarai**, ta yu gej khelsen, **be**?*
Уучлаарай, та юу гэж хэлсэн, бэ?

Small Talk

What's your name?
*tan**y** neriig khen gedeg ve?*
Таны нэрийг хэн гэдэг вэ?
My name is ...
*min**ii** neriig ... gedeg*
Миний нэрийг ... гэдэг.
What country are you from?
ta ali ulsaas irsen be?
Та аль улсаас ирсэн бэ?
I'm from ...
bi ... ulsaas irsen
Би ... улсаас ирсэн.
How old are you?
ta kheden nastai ve?
Та хэдэн настай вэ?
I'm ... years old.
bi ... nastai
Би ... настай.
Are you married?
ta ger bültei yü?
Та гэр бүлтэй юү?
No, I'm not.
ügüi, bi ger bulgüi
Үгүй, би гэр бүлгүй.
Yes, I'm married.
tiim, bi ger bültei
Тийм, би гэр бүлтэй.

Do you have any children?
ta khüühedtei yü?
Та хүүхэдтэй юу?

Language Difficulties

Do you speak English?
ta angliar yairdag uu?
Та англиар ярьдаг уу?
Could you speak more slowly?
ta arai aajuukhan yarina uu?
Та арай аажуухан ярина уу?
Please point to the phrase in the book.
ta ene khellegiig nomon deer zaaj ögnö uu?
Та энэ хэллэгийг номон дээр зааж өгнө уу?
I understand.
bi oilgoloo
Би ойлголоо.
I don't understand.
bi oilgokhgüi baina
Би ойлгохгүй байна.

Getting Around

How can I get to ...?
... ruu bi yaj ochikh ve?
... руу би яаж очих вэ?
How much is it to go to ...?
... hurehed yamar ünetei ve?
... хүрэхэд ямар үнэтэй вэ?

Where is the ... ?
... khaana baidag ve?
... хаана байдаг вэ?
train station
galt teregenii buudal
галт тэрэгний буудал
bus station/stop
avtobusny buudal
автобусны буудал
trolley-bus stop
trolleibusny buudal
троллейбусны буудал
ticket office
tasalbag tugeegüür
тасалбаг түгээгүүр

Is it far?
khir khol ve?
Хир хол вэ?

Can I walk there?
tiishee yavgan ochij bolokh uu?
Тийшээ явган очиж болох уу?

What times does ... leave/arrive?
... kheden tsagt yavdag/irdeg ve?
... хэдэн цагт явдаг/ирдэг вэ?
the bus
avtobus   автобус
the trolley-bus
trolleibus   троллейбус
the train
galt tereg   галт тэрэг
the plane
niseh ongots   нисэх онгоц

Does this bus go to ...?
ene avtobus ... ruu yavdag uu?
Энэ автобус ... руу явдаг уу?
Which bus goes to ...?
... ruu yamar avtobus yavdag ve?
... руу ямар автобус явдаг вэ?
Can you tell me when we get to ...?
bid khezee ... khurehiig helj ögnö uu?
Бид хэзээ ... хүрэхийг хэлж өгнө үү?
I want to get off!
bi buumaar baina!
Би буумаар байна!
Is this seat taken?
ene suudal khüntei yüü?
Энэ суудал хүнтэй юу?
What is this station called?
ene yamar nertei buudal ve?
Энэ ямар нэртэй буудал вэ?
What is the next station?
daraagiin buudal yamar nertei buudal ve?
Дараагийн буудал ямар нэртэй буудал вэ?

Directions

What ... is this?
ene yamar ... ve?
Энэ ямар ... вэ?
square
talbai   талбай
street
gudamj   гудамж
suburb
düüreg   дүүрэг

municipality
  khotyn zakhirgaa хотын захиргаа
north
  khoid/umard хойд/умард
south
  urd/ömnö урд/өмнө
east
  züün/dorno зүүн/дорно
west
  baruun/örnö баруун/өрнөд

behind/after
  khoino/ard хойно/ард
in front/before
  ömnö/urd өмнө/урд
to the left
  züün tiish зүүн тийш
to the right
  baruun tiish баруун тийш
straight ahead
  chigeeree чигээрээ урагшаа
  uragshaa

Accommodation

Can you recommend a good hotel?
  ta sain zochid buudal zaaj ögnö üü?
  Та сайн зочид буудал зааж өгнө үү?

Signs	
Орох Хаалга	**Entrance**
Гарах Хаалга	**Exit**
Орж Болохгүй	**No Entry**
Гарч Болохгүй	**No Exit**
Эмэгтэйчүүдийн	**Ladies**
Эрэгтэйчүүдийн	**Gentlemen**
Хүнгүй	**Vacant**
Захиалгатай	**Reserved**
Касс	**Cashier**
Лавлах	**Information**
Шуудан	**Post**
Такси	**Taxi**
Хаалттай	**Closed**
Анхаар	**Caution**
Засвартай	**Under Repair**
Тамхи Татахыг Хориглоно	**No Smoking**
Зураг Авахыг Хориглоно	**No Photography**

Can you show me on the map?
  ta gazryn zurag deer zaaj ögnö üü?
  Та газрын зураг дээр зааж өгнө үү?
Do you have any rooms available?
  tanaid sul öröö baina uu?
  Танайд сул өрөө байна уу?
I'd like a single room.
  bi neg khünii öröö avmaar baina
  Би нэг хүний өрөө авмаар байна.
I'd like a double room.
  bi khoyor khünii öröö avmaar baina
  Би хоёр хүний өрөө авмаар байна.
What's the price per night/week?
  ene öröö khonogt/doloo khonogt yamar üntei ve?
  Энэ өрөө хоногт/долоо хоногт ямар үнэтэй вэ?
Can I see the room?
  bi ene öröög üzej bolokh uu?
  Би энэ өрөөг үзэж болох уу?
Are there any others?
  öör öröö baina uu?
  Өөр өрөө байна уу?

Around Town

Where's the nearest ...?
  oirkhon ... khaana baidag ve?
  Ойрхон ... хаана байнаг вэ?
bank
  bank банк
department store
  ikh delgüür их дэлгүүр
hotel
  zochid buudal зочид буудал
market
  zakh зах
post office
  shuudan шуудан
public bath house
  niitiin khaluun нийтийн халуун
  usny gazar усны газар

When will it open?
  khezee ongoikh ve?
  Хэзээ онгойх вэ?
When will it close?
  khezee khuukh ve?
  Хэзээ хаах вэ?
I'd like to change some money.
  bi mönggo solikh gesen yum
  Би мөнгө солих гэсэн юм.

I'd like to change some travellers cheques.
bi chek solikh gesen yum
Би чек солих гэсэн юм.

What's the exchange rate?
solikh khansh hed baina ve?
Солих ханш хэд байна вэ?

Do you have a (town) map?
tanaid (khotyn) zurag baina uu?
Танайд (хотын) зураг байна уу?

Can I take photographs?
zurag avch bolokh uu?
Зураг авч болох уу?

Can I take your photograph?
bi tany zurgiig avch bolokh uu?
Би таны зургийг авч болох уу?

The Herder's Domain

We'd like to see inside a herder's ger.
(a felt tent)
bid malchny gert orj üzekh gesen yum
Бид малчны гэрт орж үзэх гэсэн юм.

How long will it take to get there?
tend khürekhed khir udakh ve?
Тэнд хүрэхэд хир удах вэ?

Can we walk there?
bid yavgan yavj bolokh uu?
Бид явган явж болох уу?

Please hold the dogs!
nokhoi khorio!
Нохой хогио!

We'd like to drink some kumiss.
bid airag uukh gesen yum
Бид айраг уух гэсэн юм.

cooking pot
togoo   тогоо
cowdung box
arag   араг
door
khaalga   хаалга
felt material
esgii   эсгий
felt roof cover
esgii deever   эсгий дээвэр
ger
ger   гэр
kumiss bag
khökhüür   хөхүүр
smoke-hole cover in a ger
örkh   өрх

Emergencies

Help!
  tuslaarai!   Туслаарай!
Stop!
  zogs!   Зогс!

Call ...!
  ... duudaarai!   ... дуудаарай!
an ambulance
  türgen tuslamj   түргэн тусламж
a doctor
  emch   эмч
the police
  tsagdaa   цагдаа

I'm ill.
  minii biye övdöj baina
  Миний бие өвдөж байна.
Please take me to hospital.
  namaig emnelegt khürgej ögnö üü?
  Намайг эмнэлэгт хүргэж өгнө үү?
Could you help me please?
  ta nadad tsuslana uu?
  Та надад туслана уу?
I've lost my way.
  bi töörchikhlöö
  Би төөрчихлөө.
I wish to contact my embassy.
  bi elchin saidiin yaamtaigaa kholboo
  barimaar baina
  Би элчин сайдын яамтайгаа холбоо
  баримаар байна.
Where is the toilet?
  biye zasakh gazar khaana baidag ve?
  Бие засах газар хаана байдаг вэ?

stove
zuukh   зуух
support post
bagana   багана
wooden frame for flue in a ger
toono   тооно
wooden lattice of a ger
khana   хана

camel
temee   тэмээ
chicken
takhia   тахиа
cow
ünee   үнээ

Menu Decoder

шөл (shöl) – soup
хуйцай (khuitsai) – vegetable & meatball soup
банштай шөл (banshtai shöl) – dumpling soup
бантан (bantan) – cream soup
гурилтай шөл (guriltai shöl) – handmade noodle soup
гоймонтай шөл (goimontoii shöl) – noodle soup

ногоон зууш (nogoon zuush) – vegetable salad
байцаан зууш (baitsaani zuush) – cabbage salad
луувангийн зууш (luuvangiin zuush) – carrot salad
нийслэл зууш (niislel zuush) – potato salad

хуушуур (khuushuur) – fried meat pancake
бууз (buuz) – steamed mutton dumplings
цуйван (tsuivan) – fried noodles with meat
бифштекс (bifshteks) – patty
мах (makh) – meat
хонины мах (khoniny makh) – mutton
шницель (shnitsel) – schnitzel
хуурга (khuurga) – meat in sauce

шарсан өндөг (sharsan öndög) – fried egg
талх (talkh) – bread
шарсан тахиа (sharsan takhia) – fried chicken
загас (zagas) – fish
будаатай (budaatai) – with rice
ногоотой (nogootoi) – with vegetables
зайдас/сосиск (zaidas/sosisk) – sausage
төмстэй (temstei) – with potato
цөцгий (tsötsgii) – sour cream

цай (tsai) – tea
банштай цай (banshtai tsai) – dumplings in tea
сүүтэй цай (süütei tsai) – Mongolian milk tea
рашаан ус (rashaan us) – mineral water
шар айраг (shar airag) – beer

donkey
    iljig   илжиг
enclosure
    malyn khashaa   малын хашаа
goat
    yamaa   ямаа
herding (literally: 'cattle breeding')
    mal aj akhui   мал аж ахуй
horse
    mori   морь

pig
    gakhai   гахай
reindeer
    tsaa buga   цаа буга
sheep
    khoni   хонь
summer camp
    zuslan   зуслан
yak
    sarlag   сарлаг

Numbers

0	*teg*	тэг
1	*neg*	нэг
2	*khoyor*	хоёр
3	*gurav*	гурав
4	*döröv*	дөрөв
5	*tav*	тав
6	*zurgaa*	зургаа
7	*doloo*	долоо
8	*naim*	найм
9	*yös*	ес
10	*arav*	арав
11	*arvan neg*	арван нэг
12	*arvan khoyor*	арван хоёр
13	*arvan gurav*	арван гурав
14	*arvan döröv*	арван дөрөв
15	*arvan tav*	арван тав
16	*arvan zurgaa*	арван зургаа
17	*arvan doloo*	арван долоо
18	*arvan naim*	арван найм
19	*arvan yös*	арван ес
20	*khori*	хорь
21	*khorin neg*	хорин нэг
22	*khorin khoyor*	хорин хоёр
30	*guch*	гуч
40	*döch*	дөч
50	*taiv*	тавч
60	*jar*	жар
70	*dal*	дал
80	*naya*	ная
90	*yör*	ер
100	*zuu*	зуу
101	*zuun neg*	зуун нэг
111	*zuun arvan neg*	зуун арван нэг
1000	*myangga*	мянга
2000	*khoyor myangga*	хоёр мянга

one million
    saya   сая

Glossary

agui – cave
aimag – a province/state within Mongolia
airag – fermented mare's milk
arat – herdsman
arkhi – the common word to describe home-made vodka
ashkhana – restaurant (Kazakh)

babal – stone figures believed to be Turkic grave markers; known as *khunni chuluu* (man stones) in Mongolian
bag – village, a subdivision of a *sum*
baga – little
bayan – rich
bodhisattva – Tibetan-Buddhist term; applies to a being that has voluntarily chosen not to take the step to nirvana in order to save the souls of those on earth
Bogd Gegen – hereditary line of reincarnated Buddhist leaders of Mongolia, which started with Zanabazar; the third holiest leader in the Tibetan Buddhist hierarchy
Bogd Khaan (Holy King) – title given to the Eighth Bogd Gegen (1869–1924)
bulag – spring
buuz – steamed meat dumplings

chuluu – rock; rock formation

davaa – a mountain pass
deer stones – upright grave markers from the Bronze and Iron ages on which are carved stylised images of deer; known as *bugan chuluu*
del – the all-purpose, traditional coat or dress worn by men and women
delger – richness, plenty
delgüür – a shop
dombra – two-stringed lute (Kazakh)
dorje – thunderbolt symbol, used in Tibetan Buddhist ritual
dorno – east
dov – hill
dund – middle

els – sand; sand dunes
erdene – precious

Furgon – Russian-made 11-seater minivan

gegen – saint; saintlike person
ger – traditional circular felt yurt
gol – river
guanz – canteen or cheap restaurant
gudamj – street

hard seat – the common word to describe the standard of the 2nd-class train carriage
hashaa – fenced-in ger, often found in suburbs
hutagt – reincarnation

ikh – big
Inner Mongolia – separate province within China

Jebtzun Damba – also known as Bogd Gegen, a hereditary line of reincarnated spiritual leaders of Mongolia. The first was Zanabazar and the eighth was the Bogd Khaan

Kazakh – an ethnic group of people from Central Asia, mostly living in western Mongolia; people from Kazakhstan
khaan – king or chief
khagan – great khaan
khaganate – Pre-Mongol empire
Khalkh – the major ethnic group living in Mongolia
khar – black
khiid – a Buddhist monastery
khot – city
khulan – wild ass
khüree – originally used to describe a 'camp', it is now also in usage as 'monastery'
khuriltai – nomadic congress during the Mongol era
khürkhree – waterfall
khutugtu – reincarnated lama, or living god
khuurshuur – fried, flat meat pancake
kino – cinema
kumiss – the Russian word for *airag*

lama – Tibetan Buddhist monk or priest
Lamaism – properly known as Vajramana, or Tibetan Buddhism
Living Buddha – common term for reincarnations of Buddhas; Buddhist spiritual leader in Mongolia

maral – Asiatic red deer
morin khuur – horse-head fiddle
mörön – another word for river
MPRP – Mongolian People's Revolutionary Party

Naadam – a game; the Naadam Festival
nuruu – mountain range
nuur – lake

ömnö – south
ordon – palace
örgön chölöö – avenue
Outer Mongolia – northern Mongolia during Manchurian rule (the term is not currently used to describe Mongolia)
ovoo – a shamanistic collection of stones, wood or other offerings to the gods, usually found in high places

rashaant – mineral springs

shay – tea (Kazakh)
shaykhana – tea house (Kazakh)
soft seat – the common word to describe the standard of the 1st-class train carriage
soyombo – the national symbol
SPA – Strictly Protected Area
stupa – a Buddhist religious monument composed of a solid hemisphere topped by a spire, containing relics of the Buddha; also known as a pagoda, or *suburgan* in Mongolian
sum – a district; the administrative unit below an *aimag*
süm – a Buddhist temple

takhi – the Mongolian wild horse; also known as Przewalski's horse
tal – steppe
thangka – scroll painting; a rectangular Tibetan Buddhist painting on cloth, often seen in monasteries
tögrög – the unit of currency in Mongolia
töv – central
Tsagaan Sar – 'white moon' or 'white month'; a festival to celebrate the start of the lunar year
tsam – lama dances; performed by monks wearing masks during religious ceremonies
tsast – snow
tsuivan – noodles
tsuivan gazar – noodle stall
tuut – kiosk selling imported foodstuffs

ulaan – red
urtyn-duu – traditional singing style
us – water
uul – mountain
uurga – traditional wooden lasso used by nomads

yurt – the Russian word for *ger*

zakh – a market
zud – a particularly bad winter

LONELY PLANET

Guides by Region

Lonely Planet is known worldwide for publishing practical, reliable and no-nonsense travel information in our guides and on our Web site. The Lonely Planet list covers just about every accessible part of the world. Currently there are 16 series: Travel guides, Shoestring guides, Condensed guides, Phrasebooks, Read This First, Healthy Travel, Walking guides, Cycling guides, Watching Wildlife guides, Pisces Diving & Snorkeling guides, City Maps, Road Atlases, Out to Eat, World Food, Journeys travel literature and Pictorials.

AFRICA Africa on a shoestring • Cairo • Cairo City Map • Cape Town • Cape Town City Map • East Africa • Egypt • Egyptian Arabic phrasebook • Ethiopia, Eritrea & Djibouti • Ethiopian (Amharic) phrasebook • The Gambia & Senegal • Healthy Travel Africa • Kenya • Malawi • Morocco • Moroccan Arabic phrasebook • Mozambique • Read This First: Africa • South Africa, Lesotho & Swaziland • Southern Africa • Southern Africa Road Atlas • Swahili phrasebook • Tanzania, Zanzibar & Pemba • Trekking in East Africa • Tunisia • Watching Wildlife East Africa •   Watching Wildlife Southern Africa • West Africa • World Food Morocco • Zimbabwe, Botswana & Namibia
Travel Literature: Mali Blues: Traveling to an African Beat • The Rainbird: A Central African Journey • Songs to an African Sunset: A Zimbabwean Story

AUSTRALIA & THE PACIFIC Auckland • Australia • Australian phrasebook • Australia Road Atlas • Cycling Australia • Cycling New Zealand • Fiji • Fijian phrasebook • Healthy Travel Australia, NZ and the Pacific • Islands of Australia's Great Barrier Reef • Melbourne • Melbourne City Map • Micronesia • New Caledonia • New South Wales • New Zealand • Northern Territory • Outback Australia • Out to Eat – Melbourne • Out to Eat – Sydney • Papua New Guinea • Pidgin phrasebook • Queensland • Rarotonga & the Cook Islands • Samoa • Solomon Islands • South Australia • South Pacific • South Pacific phrasebook • Sydney • Sydney City Map • Sydney Condensed • Tahiti & French Polynesia • Tasmania • Tonga • Tramping in New Zealand • Vanuatu • Victoria • Walking in Australia • Watching Wildlife Australia • Western Australia
Travel Literature: Islands in the Clouds: Travels in the Highlands of New Guinea • Kiwi Tracks: A New Zealand Journey • Sean & David's Long Drive

CENTRAL AMERICA & THE CARIBBEAN Bahamas, Turks & Caicos • Baja California • Bermuda • Central America on a shoestring • Costa Rica • Costa Rica Spanish phrasebook • Cuba • Dominican Republic & Haiti • Eastern Caribbean • Guatemala • Guatemala, Belize & Yucatán: La Ruta Maya • Healthy Travel Central & South America • Jamaica • Mexico • Mexico City • Panama • Puerto Rico • Read This First: Central & South America • World Food Mexico • Yucatán
Travel Literature: Green Dreams: Travels in Central America

EUROPE Amsterdam • Amsterdam City Map • Amsterdam Condensed • Andalucía • Austria • Baltic States phrasebook • Barcelona • Barcelona City Map • Berlin • Berlin City Map • Britain • British phrasebook • Brussels, Bruges & Antwerp • Brussels City Map • Budapest • Budapest City Map • Canary Islands • Central Europe • Central Europe phrasebook • Corfu & the Ionians • Corsica • Crete • Crete Condensed • Croatia • Cycling Britain • Cycling France • Cyprus • Czech & Slovak Republics • Denmark • Dublin • Dublin City Map • Eastern Europe • Eastern Europe phrasebook • Edinburgh • Estonia, Latvia & Lithuania • Europe on a shoestring • Europe phrasebook • Finland • Florence • France • Frankfurt Condensed • French phrasebook • Georgia, Armenia & Azerbaijan • Germany • German phrasebook • Greece • Greek Islands • Greek phrasebook • Hungary • Iceland, Greenland & the Faroe Islands • Ireland • Italian phrasebook • Italy • Krakow • Lisbon • The Loire • London • London City Map • London Condensed • Madrid • Malta • Mediterranean Europe • Mediterranean Europe phrasebook • Moscow • Mozambique • Munich • Netherlands • Norway • Out to Eat – London • Out to Eat – Paris • Paris • Paris City Map • Paris Condensed • Poland • Portugal • Portuguese phrasebook • Prague • Prague City Map • Provence & the Côte d'Azur • Read This First: Europe • Romania & Moldova • Rome • Rome City Map • Russia, Ukraine & Belarus • Russian phrasebook • Scandinavian & Baltic Europe • Scandinavian phrasebook • Scotland • Sicily • Slovenia • South-West France • Spain • Spanish phrasebook • St Petersburg • St Petersburg City Map • Sweden • Switzerland • Tuscany • Ukrainian phrasebook • Venice • Vienna • Walking in Britain • Walking in France • Walking in Ireland • Walking in Italy • Walking in Spain • Walking in Switzerland • Western Europe • World Food France • World Food Ireland • World Food Italy • World Food Spain
Travel Literature: Love and War in the Apennines • The Olive Grove: Travels in Greece • On the Shores of the Mediterranean • Round Ireland in Low Gear • A Small Place in Italy • After Yugoslavia

INDIAN SUBCONTINENT Bangladesh • Bengali phrasebook • Bhutan • Delhi • Goa • Healthy Travel Asia & India • Hindi & Urdu phrasebook • India • Indian Himalaya • Karakoram Highway • Kerala • Mumbai (Bombay) • Nepal • Nepali phrasebook • Pakistan • Rajasthan • Read This First: Asia & India • South India • Sri Lanka • Sri Lanka phrasebook • Tibet • Tibetan phrasebook • Trekking in the Indian Himalaya • Trekking in the Karakoram & Hindukush • Trekking in the Nepal Himalaya
Travel Literature: The Age of Kali: Indian Travels and Encounters • Hello Goodnight: A Life of Goa • In Rajasthan • A Season in Heaven: True Tales from the Road to Kathmandu • Shopping for Buddhas • A Short Walk in the Hindu Kush • Slowly Down the Ganges

ISLANDS OF THE INDIAN OCEAN Madagascar & Comoros • Maldives • Mauritius, Réunion & Seychelles

MIDDLE EAST & CENTRAL ASIA Bahrain, Kuwait & Qatar • Central Asia • Central Asia phrasebook • Dubai • Farsi (Persian) phrasebook • Hebrew phrasebook • Iran • Israel & the Palestinian Territories • Istanbul • Istanbul City Map • Istanbul to Cairo on a shoestring • Jerusalem • Jerusalem City Map • Jordan • Lebanon • Middle East • Oman & the United Arab Emirates • Syria • Turkey • Turkish phrasebook • World Food Turkey • Yemen
Travel Literature: Black on Black: Iran Revisited • The Gates of Damascus • Kingdom of the Film Stars: Journey into Jordan

NORTH AMERICA Alaska • Boston • Boston City Map • California & Nevada • California Condensed • Canada • Chicago • Chicago City Map • Deep South • Florida • Great Lakes • Hawaii • Hiking in Alaska • Hiking in the USA • Las Vegas • Los Angeles • Los Angeles City Map • Miami • Miami City Map • New England • New Orleans • New York City • New York City City Map • New York City Condensed • New York, New Jersey & Pennsylvania • Oahu • Out to Eat – San Francisco • Pacific Northwest • Rocky Mountains • San Francisco • San Francisco City Map • Seattle • Southwest • Texas • USA • USA phrasebook • Vancouver • Virginia & the Capital Region • Washington, DC • Washington, DC City Map • World Food Deep South, USA
Travel Literature: Caught Inside: A Surfer's Year on the California Coast • Drive Thru America

NORTH-EAST ASIA Beijing • Beijing City Map • Cantonese phrasebook • China • Hiking in Japan • Hong Kong • Hong Kong City Map • Hong Kong Condensed • Hong Kong, Macau & Guangzhou • Japan • Japanese phrasebook • Korea • Korean phrasebook • Kyoto • Mandarin phrasebook • Mongolia • Mongolian phrasebook • Seoul • Shanghai • South-West China • Taiwan • Tokyo
Travel Literature: In Xanadu: A Quest • Lost Japan

SOUTH AMERICA Argentina, Uruguay & Paraguay • Bolivia • Brazil • Brazilian phrasebook • Buenos Aires • Chile & Easter Island • Colombia • Ecuador & the Galapagos Islands • Healthy Travel Central & South America • Latin American Spanish phrasebook • Peru • Quechua phrasebook • Read This First: Central & South America • Rio de Janeiro • Rio de Janeiro City Map • South America on a shoestring • Trekking in the Patagonian Andes • Venezuela
Travel Literature: Full Circle: A South American Journey

SOUTH-EAST ASIA Bali & Lombok • Bangkok • Bangkok City Map • Burmese phrasebook • Cambodia • Hanoi • Healthy Travel Asia & India • Hill Tribes phrasebook • Ho Chi Minh City • Indonesia • Indonesian phrasebook • Indonesia's Eastern Islands • Java • Lao phrasebook • Laos • Malay phrasebook • Malaysia, Singapore & Brunei • Myanmar (Burma) • Philippines • Pilipino (Tagalog) phrasebook • Read This First: Asia & India • Singapore • Singapore City Map • South-East Asia on a shoestring • South-East Asia phrasebook • Thailand • Thailand's Islands & Beaches • Thailand, Vietnam, Laos & Cambodia Road Atlas • Thai phrasebook • Vietnam • Vietnamese phrasebook • World Food Thailand • World Food Vietnam

ALSO AVAILABLE: Antarctica • The Arctic • The Blue Man: Tales of Travel, Love and Coffee • Brief Encounters: Stories of Love, Sex & Travel • Chasing Rickshaws • The Last Grain Race • Lonely Planet Unpacked • Not the Only Planet: Science Fiction Travel Stories • On the Edge: Extreme Travel • Sacred India • Travel with Children • Travel Photography: A Guide to Taking Better Pictures

LONELY PLANET

You already know that Lonely Planet produces more than this one guidebook, but you might not be aware of the other products we have on this region. Here is a selection of titles that you may want to check out as well:

Read This First: Asia & India
ISBN 1 86450 049 2
US$14.95 • UK£8.99

Mongolian phrasebook
ISBN 0 86442 308 X
US$5.95 • UK£3.50

Healthy Travel Asia & India
ISBN 1 86450 051 4
US$5.95 • UK£3.99

Available wherever books are sold

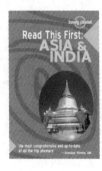

Index

Abbreviations

Text

Bold indicates maps.

Bold indicates maps.

Bold indicates maps.

Boxed Text

MAP LEGEND

CITY ROUTES

.... Freeway
.... Primary Road
.... Secondary Road
.... Street
.... Lane

= = = = ... Unsealed Road
.... One Way Street
.... Pedestrian Street
.... Stepped Street
.... Tunnel

COUNTRY ROUTES

.... Major Road (sealed)
.... Major Road
.... Minor Road
.... Minor Road (Unsealed)

BOUNDARIES

.... International
.... State
.... Disputed
.... Fortified Wall

HYDROGRAPHY

.... River, Creek
.... Canal
.... Lake

.... Dry Lake; Salt Lake
.... Rapids
.... Waterfalls

TRANSPORT ROUTES & STATIONS

.... Train
.... Underground Train
.... Metro

.... Walking Trail
.... Walking Tour
.... Path

AREA FEATURES

.... Building
.... National Park

.... Market
.... Protected Areas

.... Town Square
.... Sand Dunes, Desert

.... Cliff
.... Swamp Area

POPULATION SYMBOLS

○ **CAPITAL** .... National Capital
◉ **CAPITAL** .... State Capital

● **CITY** .... City
● **Town** .... Town

● Village .... Village
.... Urban Area

MAP SYMBOLS

■ .... Place to Stay

▼ .... Place to Eat

● .... Point of Interest

⊞ ☒ ...... Airfield, Airport	⬠ .... Hut	)(........... Pass	⊚ .... Spring
⑤ .... Bank	⬠ .... Internet Cafe	⊙ .... Petrol Station	⑭ .... Sports Palace
🏛 .... Buddhist Temple	※ .... Lookout	⊞ .... Police Station	⬠ .... Taxi Stand
⬠ ⬠ ... Bus Stop/Terminal	🗼 .... Monument	▭ .... Post Office	☎ .... Telephone
⌂ .... Cave	▲ ⌃ ... Mountain, Range	⬠ .... Pub or Bar	⬠ .... Temple
⊟ .... Cinema	⬠ .... Museum	⬠ ...Public Bath House	☗ .... Theatre
⬠ .... Embassy	⬠ .... National Park	⬠ .... Ruins	❶ .. Tourist Information
✛ .... Hospital	⬠ .... Oasis	⊗ .... Shopping Centre	▭ .... Transport

Note: not all symbols displayed above appear in this book

LONELY PLANET OFFICES

Australia
Locked Bag 1, Footscray, Victoria 3011
☎ 03 8379 8000 fax 03 8379 8111
email: talk2us@lonelyplanet.com.au

UK
10a Spring Place, London NW5 3BH
☎ 020 7428 4800 fax 020 7428 4828
email: go@lonelyplanet.co.uk

USA
150 Linden St, Oakland, CA 94607
☎ 510 893 8555 TOLL FREE: 800 275 8555
fax 510 893 8572
email: info@lonelyplanet.com

France
1 rue du Dahomey, 75011 Paris
☎ 01 55 25 33 00 fax 01 55 25 33 01
email: bip@lonelyplanet.fr
www.lonelyplanet.fr

World Wide Web: www.lonelyplanet.com *or* AOL keyword: lp
Lonely Planet Images: lpi@lonelyplanet.com.au